BPP

UNIVERSITY

D1492716

Performance Management

The Professional Practice Series

The Professional Practice Series is sponsored by The Society for Industrial and Organizational Psychology, Inc. (SIOP). The series was launched in 1988 to provide industrial and organizational psychologists, organizational scientists and practitioners, human resources professionals, managers, executives and those interested in organizational behavior and performance with volumes that are insightful, current, informative and relevant to *organizational practice*. The volumes in the Professional Practice Series are guided by five tenets designed to enhance future organizational practice:

1. Focus on practice, but grounded in science
2. Translate organizational science into practice by generating guidelines, principles, and lessons learned that can shape and guide practice
3. Showcase the application of industrial and organizational psychology to solve problems
4. Document and demonstrate best industrial and organizational-based practices
5. Stimulate research needed to guide future organizational practice

The volumes seek to inform those interested in practice with guidance, insights, and advice on how to apply the concepts, findings, methods, and tools derived from industrial and organizational psychology to solve human-related organizational problems.

Previous Professional Practice Series volumes include:

Published by Jossey-Bass

Evolving Practices in Human Resource Management
Allen I. Kraut, Abraham K. Korman, Editors

Individual Psychological Assessment
Richard Jeanneret, Rob Silzer, Editors

Performance Appraisal
James W. Smither, Editor

Organizational Surveys
Allen I. Kraut, Editor

Employees, Careers, and Job Creating
Manuel London, Editor

Published by Guilford Press

Diagnosis for Organizational Change
Ann Howard and Associates

Human Dilemmas in Work Organizations
Abraham K. Korman and Associates

Diversity in the Workplace
Susan E. Jackson and Associates

Working with Organizations and Their People
Douglas W. Bray and Associates

Performance Management

Performance Management

Putting Research into Action

James W. Smither and

Manuel London, Editors

JOSSEY-BASS
A Wiley Imprint
www.josseybass.com

Published by Jossey-Bass
A Wiley Imprint
989 Market Street, San Francisco, CA 94103-1741—www.josseybass.com

Jossey-Bass books and products are available through most bookstores. To contact Jossey-Bass directly call our Customer Care Department within the U.S. at 800-956-7739, outside the U.S. at 317-572-3986, or fax 317-572-4002.

Jossey-Bass also publishes its books in a variety of electronic formats. Some content that appears in print may not be available in electronic books.

Library of Congress Cataloging-in-Publication Data
　　Performance management : putting research into action / James W. Smither and Manuel London, editors.
　　　　p.　cm.—(The professional practice series)
　　Includes index.
　　ISBN 978-0-470-19232-0 (cloth)
　　　1. Career development.　2. Employee motivation.　I. Smither, James W.　II. London, Manuel.
　　HF5549.5.C35P45 2009
　　658.3'128—dc22
　　　　　　　　　　　　　　　　　　　　　　　　　　　　2009013926

Printed in the United States of America
FIRST EDITION
HB Printing　　　　10 9 8 7 6 5 4 3 2

The Professional Practice Series

To Robin, Amy, Sean, and my parents
—JWS

To Marilyn, David, Jared
—ML

Contents

Foreword

Performance management is one of the cornerstones of Human Resource practice in organizations. No matter where you work, how big or small your organization or how simple or complex the business model, effective performance management is a key requirement if you have any number of employees. It all begins with performance management. Specifically, what are the jobs we need our employees to do, how do we measure their performance in these jobs, and how do we design and implement systems to reinforce performance standards that have been set?

So, before an organization can even begin to think about the more lofty practice areas like individual assessment, talent management, or succession planning it must be able to nail the basics of measuring day-to-day performance. Organizations who set their sights on hiring the best and the brightest and building a diverse work force must first have a crystal clear understanding of what they are hiring people to do and how the will be deemed successful or not. Companies desiring to offer the very best training and development or organization development programs must first be able to assess the requirements of the jobs for which they are training and developing their leaders and managers.

That is why this topic and this volume are so critical to HR, I/O and OD practitioners alike. It is also one of the reasons why Janine and I reached out to Jim and Manny to commission this edition for the SIOP Professional Practice series. Both are excellent researchers, professionals, authors, and editors. Moreover, Jim's prior SIOP Professional Practice edition on performance appraisal from 1998 was very popular and we wanted them to take the discussion to the next level. With this volume we feel that they certainly have accomplished this mission. Whether it's very current issues such as the Sarbanes-Oxley Act (SOX), CEO performance management and the role of the Board of Directors in that process, to the potential benefits and costs of instituting a forced ranking system, the content here should be of great benefit to practitioners and managers alike. In addition, Jim and Manny have approached this edition with a very balanced scientist-practitioner perspective, so not only do the chapters cover the current state of the art of performance management, but there is also insight for academics into where future research might be most beneficially directed.

Having evolved from performance appraisal to performance management over the last 10 years the field has indeed shifted in its orientation. This volume displays the very latest thinking from an I/O psychology perspective regarding how you quantify, measure and track performance in organizations. We hope that both practitioners and academics alike find it useful in their work. Our sincerest thanks to Jim and Manny for taking the field to the next level.

May 2009
Allan H. Church
Janine Waclawski
Series Editors

Introduction

Over the past decade or so, the term "performance management" has come to replace the phrase "performance appraisal" in many organizations. Whereas performance appraisal emphasized the (usually annual) evaluation of an employee's performance, performance management refers to an ongoing process that includes setting (and aligning) goals, coaching and developing employees, providing informal feedback, formally evaluating performance, and linking performance to recognition and rewards. The goal of this ongoing process is to enhance the employee's performance (as well as job satisfaction and commitment to the organization) and the performance of the organization.

This book contains seventeen chapters. Each offers useful guidelines for practitioners to enhance the quality of performance management systems and processes. The authors offer dozens of real-world examples to illustrate how performance management systems can be effectively designed and implemented. Unlike many "pop" management books, which are often filled merely with personal opinion, the chapters in this book draw on years of empirical research in industrial and organizational psychology. Doing so allows the authors to present evidence-based "best practices" in performance management.

Some of the authors in this book are full-time practitioners who work for leading consulting firms that have collectively provided performance management support to hundreds of organizations. In addition to their strong hands-on experience, our "practitioner" authors are especially valued because they have all published their work in leading peer-refereed journals. Other authors in this book are located at universities where they have spent years conducting and publishing research related to performance management. But nearly all of our "academic" authors bring years of consulting or corporate experience to their writing.

In sum, this is a book written by scientist-practitioners and we hope it exemplifies the scientist-practitioner model at its best.

The central goal of this book is to distill lessons from research that are of value to practitioners (including human resource managers, consultants, and line managers who are at the heart of the performance management process). The authors have tried to provide the reader with a brief and non-technical understanding of what research studies have learned about performance management and the implications of this research for practitioners. The result includes what we believe are evidence-based suggestions that can guide the reader's efforts to design and implement performance management systems and processes.

Overview of Chapters

Herman Aguinis ("An Expanded View of Performance Management") provides a broad overview of performance management. He describes the many purposes that can be served by performance management systems, presents a six-stage performance management process, and identifies fourteen features associated with effective performance management systems.

William Schiemann ("Aligning Performance Management with Organizational Strategy, Values, and Goals") describes the importance of alignment for large and small companies (including the relationship between alignment and financial performance). He reviews seven drivers of alignment while emphasizing the pivotal role played by a company's culture. He also provides a detailed case study that illustrates the process of linking organizational vision, strategy, and goals to behaviors. He concludes by describing four core elements that distinguish organizations with effective performance management systems from other organizations.

Peter Heslin, Jay Carson, and Don VandeWalle ("Practical Applications of Goal-Setting Theory to Performance Management") note that the results from goal setting depend on five factors: goal commitment, task complexity, goal framing, team goals, and feedback. They describe recent research developments and present straightforward guidelines to help practitioners manage each of these five factors to enhance performance management.

David Peterson ("Coaching and Performance Management: How Can Organizations Get the Greatest Value?") begins by presenting a continuum of organizational approaches to coaching that evolves from completely unstructured and ad hoc to relatively strategic and systemic. He then describes the "Development Pipeline," a model of the five necessary and sufficient conditions for any type of systematic development, and its application to coaching. He then illustrates the differences in conversations when coaching is primarily forward-looking and developmental in nature from those in which the person being coached is underperforming or not meeting important expectations. He also reviews the pros and cons of using internal versus external coaches and offers an eleven-step approach to maximize the value of external coaches.

Paul Squires ("The Role of On-the-Job and Informal Development in Performance Management") begins by defining informal learning (where on-the-job training is considered a specific instance of informal learning). He then describes characteristics of the workplace and the worker that lead to more effective informal learning. He concludes with practical recommendations (and two real-world examples) to facilitate informal learning.

Eduardo Salas, Sallie Weaver, Michael Rosen, and Kimberly Smith-Jentsch ("Managing Team Performance in Complex Settings: Research-Based Best Practices") describe four capacities (*adaptive capacity, leadership capacity, management capacity,* and *technical capacity*) required for team effectiveness and use these capacities as a framework that can guide the performance management process in team settings. They present a set of best practices drawn from their practical experience as well as the team, performance management, project management, and human resources literature.

Edward Mone ("CEO Performance Management") reviews events of the last ten to fifteen years that have shaped the business landscape, executive compensation, and the evaluation of CEOs. He uses a detailed, real-world example to describe the CEO performance management process (including goal setting, feedback, CEO appraisal, and compensation) and then compares this process to best practices in this area. He also offers guidelines to increase the effectiveness of the board of directors (including the composition of the board and compensation of its members).

David Day and Gary Greguras ("Performance Management in Multi-National Companies") address the challenge faced by multi-national companies in dealing with national culture as they design and implement performance management processes. Using Project GLOBE as a framework, they briefly review and describe the performance management implications of eight dimensions (performance orientation, future orientation, gender egalitarianism, assertiveness, individualism and collectivism, power distance, humane orientation, and uncertainty avoidance) that can be used to describe national culture. They note the danger of taking generalizations based on cultural dimensions too far and discuss the role of organizational culture versus national culture in shaping performance management practices. They conclude with eleven recommendations for practice.

Richard Reilly and Zvi Aronson ("Managing Contextual Performance") begin by defining contextual performance (distinguishing it from task performance) and then review the antecedents and outcomes of contextual performance. Next, they describe issues associated with managing contextual performance, including appraising contextual performance, recognizing and rewarding contextual performance, the effect of the feedback environment on contextual performance, whether contextual performance does (or should) influence career development and advancement, and legal considerations.

Valerie Sessa, Christopher Pingor, and Jennifer Bragger ("Using Performance Management As a learning Tool") present a case that illustrates how performance management can be used to transform an organization's culture to a performance *and* learning culture in which adaptive, generative, and transformative employee learning occurs. They describe how a self-learning component can be added to a performance management system.

Leanne Atwater and Teri Elkins ("Diagnosing, Understanding, and Dealing with Counterproductive Work Behavior") begin by describing the nature, prevalence, and consequences of counterproductive work behavior (CWB), including abuse against others (such as incivility, workplace violence, and sexual harassment) and production deviance (including poor performance, sabotage, theft, and withdrawal behaviors). Next they address the issue of diagnosing the causes of CWB (including a variety of individual and job-context factors). They also review a variety of approaches to dealing with CWB and offer recommendations for best practice.

Peter Dominick ("Forced Rankings: Pros, Cons, and Practices") describes in detail the potential advantages and risks associated with forced ranking systems. For organizations that elect to implement such a system, he presents important questions and issues related to their design and implementation.

Autumn Krauss and Lori Anderson Snyder ("Technology and Performance Management: What Role Does Technology Play in Performance Management?") describe the role that technology can play when developing and using a performance management system. They begin by reviewing electronic performance monitoring and performance management of telecommuting workers. They then illustrate how technology can support various purposes of performance management, including strategic, administrative, informational, developmental, organizational maintenance, and documentation. Next they describe how technology can help communicate the organization's mission and priorities and ensure that priorities are in alignment across the organization, as well as facilitate performance planning, execution, and assessment. They address issues and complications (such as information overload, overexposure, time requirements, overreliance on automation, miscommunication, technology literacy) that can accompany the use of technology and conclude with recommendations for implementing a technology-based performance management system.

Thomas Diamante ("Authentic Performance: The Valuation of Behavior as a Negotiated Business Outcome") describes performance negotiation as the ongoing process by which a supervisor and employee arrive at an agreement about the value of an employee's contribution to business. He first presents a systemic model of the components of performance negotiation. Next, he describes a five-step approach to valuing employee performance and concludes with a case study that illustrates the process.

Stanley Silverman and Wendy Muller ("Assessing Performance Management Programs and Policies") present a model of six assessment points that can be embedded in a comprehensive performance management system, and they illustrate the application of their assessment model using the case of a hypothetical manufacturing company. Throughout the chapter, they provide detailed guidance for organizations that seek to assess the impact of their performance management system.

Nancy Tippins and Susan Coverdale ("Performance Management of the Future") review current worker and workplace trends that are likely to have an effect on performance management programs of the future and describe sixteen ways that performance management programs will need to be adapted to remain effective.

We (Jim Smither and Manny London, "Best Practices in Performance Management") conclude by drawing on the insights and recommendations of the authors who contributed chapters to this book, as well as other research, to develop a sketch of best practices in performance management.

Acknowledgments

This book reflects the efforts and talents of many people. We thank Allan H. Church and Janine Waclawski, editors of the Professional Practice Series, for giving us the opportunity to edit this volume. We are also grateful to the Society for Industrial and Organizational Psychology for sponsoring this series and volume. Most importantly, we are deeply indebted to the thirty-one authors who contributed to this book. Each contributed an enormous amount of time, energy, and expertise. This is really their book, not ours. Finally, we thank our families, friends, and colleagues for their patience and support.

Jim Smither and Manny London

The Authors

Herman Aguinis is a professor of organizational behavior and human resources and dean's research professor at Indiana University's Kelley School of Business. His research is interdisciplinary and addresses organizational behavior, human resource management, and research methods and analysis. He is the author of *Performance Management* (2nd ed.), *Applied Psychology in Human Resource Management* (6th ed.) with W. F. Cascio, and *Regression Analysis for Categorical Moderators*. He has edited two additional books: *Opening the Black Box of Editorship* (with Y. Baruch, A. M. Konrad, and W. H. Starbuck) and *Test-Score Banding in Human Resource Selection*. In addition, he has written about seventy refereed journal articles in JAP, PPsych, AMR, AMJ, OBHDP, and elsewhere. He is a Fellow of the American Psychological Association, the Association for Psychological Science, and the Society for Industrial and Organizational Psychology and is past editor-in-chief of *Organizational Research Methods*.

Zvi H. Aronson is a senior lecturer at Stevens Institute of Technology, where he teaches courses in applied psychology. He has two main research interests: the role of personality in project leader and team performance and the role that culture plays in project success. His work has appeared in the *International Journal of Selection and Assessment,* the *Journal of Engineering and Technology Management,* and in several book chapters. Zvi serves as a reviewer for the *Journal of Engineering and Technology Management.* Earlier work experiences in applied psychology at Bakara Ltd., Israel, included training and selection. He also serves as the head of the Institute Review Board at Stevens Institute of Technology. Dr. Aronson earned his B.A. in behavioral sciences from Ben-Gurion University in Israel and his Ph.D. in applied psychology from Stevens Institute of Technology.

Leanne Atwater is professor of management and chair of the management department in the C.T. Bauer College of Business at the University of Houston. She received her Ph.D. from Claremont Graduate School. Her areas of research include leadership, feedback processes, and employee discipline. She has published over fifty scholarly articles in journals such as *Journal of Applied Psychology, Personnel Psychology, Journal of Management, Leadership Quarterly, Journal of Organizational Behavior, Human Resource Management Journal,* and *Journal of Organizational and Occupational Psychology.* She has co-authored two scholarly books entitled *The Power of 360 Degree Feedback* and *Leadership, Feedback, and the Open Communication Gap,* as well as many book chapters. Dr. Atwater serves on the editorial boards of *Leadership Quarterly, Military Psychology,* and *Group and Organization Management.* Dr. Atwater is a Fellow in the Society for Industrial and Organizational Psychology and a member of the Academy of Management.

Jennifer Bragger is an associate professor of industrial and organizational psychology at Montclair State University. She received her Ph.D. in social and organizational psychology from Temple University. She has also taught at The College of New Jersey and worked at the Institute for Survey Research at Temple University. Dr. Bragger has done consulting in the areas of statistical analysis, personnel selection and validation, assessment center rating, and organizational health and safety for Cigna, Prudential, MetLife, and Schering Plough. Her research activities include bias in selection and performance appraisal, the job interview, stereotype threat in organizational settings, work-family conflict, and escalation of commitment. Her recent publications have appeared in the *Journal of Applied Psychology, Journal of Applied Social Psychology, Journal of Organizational Behavior, Journal of Business and Psychology, Public Personnel Management,* and the *Academy of Management Review.*

Jay B. Carson (jcarson@cox.smu.edu) is an assistant professor of management and organizations at the Edwin L. Cox School of Business, Southern Methodist University. He received his Ph.D. in organizational behavior with a minor in human resource management and strategy from the Robert H. Smith School of Business, University of Maryland. He teaches courses in organizational behavior, management, and teams to undergraduates, MBAs, and executives. His research has been published in the *Academy of Management Journal* and in book chapters. His primary research interests are in teams, leadership, and cross-cultural issues, with a current focus on shared leadership, internal team leadership, ethical leadership, and team goal alignment.

Susan H. Coverdale is a principal in the Selection Practice Group at Valtera. Her primary responsibilities include development and validation of employee selection systems as well as managerial and executive level assessment. Before joining Valtera, she worked as an independent consultant providing human resources consulting services in the areas of employee selection, performance evaluation, training program development and facilitation, employee surveys, executive assessment and coaching, succession planning, and management development. Prior to establishing her own consulting business, Dr. Coverdale provided a wide range of consulting services through her association with HReasy and Lopez and Associates, Inc. She began her career as the coordinator of career development for Conoco, Inc. Dr. Coverdale received her Ph.D. in industrial and organizational psychology from the University of Houston. She is a member of the American Psychological Association and the Society for Industrial and Organizational Psychology.

David V. Day is the Woodside Professor of Leadership and Management in the School of Business at the University of Western Australia. Since 1999 he has also held the position of adjunct research scientist with the Center for Creative Leadership. Dr. Day serves as an associate editor of the *Journal of Applied Psychology, Leadership Quarterly,* and *Human Resource Management Review* and is a consulting editor for several other journals in the fields of management and industrial-organizational psychology. Dr. Day is a member of the Academy of Management, American Psychological Society, International Leadership Association, International Association of Applied Psychology, Society of Organizational Behavior, and Fellow of the American Psychological Association and the Society for Industrial and Organizational Psychology. He received his Ph.D. in industrial-organizational psychology in 1989 from the University of Akron.

Thomas Diamante is senior vice president at Corporate Counseling Associates, a human capital consulting firm. His practice is focused on executive development, talent management, selection and advancement planning, performance management, and organizational change management. He is formerly of Merrill Lynch, where he was vice president, corporate strategy and development, in Global Securities Research and Economics. Prior to Merrill Lynch, Dr. Diamante was a senior manager and lead change consultant for KPMG Consulting. Earlier in his career he was national manager, human resources and professional development, at Philip Morris Companies (Altria). Dr. Diamante holds a Ph.D. in industrial and organizational psychology from The Graduate Center, City University of New York, as well as the M. Phil. from the same institution. His B.A. in psychology is from Stony Brook University. He is a New York State licensed psychologist and complemented his industrial degree with post-doctoral training in clinical psychology at the Institute for Behavior Therapy in New York. He is a member of the Associate's Council, Children's Aid Society, and serves on the board of directors for ENACT, Inc., a non-profit focused on social, emotional, and intellectual development of at-risk New York City schoolchildren.

Peter G. Dominick is a faculty member at Stevens Institute of Technology, where he is coordinator of leadership development education within the W.J. Howe School's Executive MBA, Project Management, and Undergraduate Business and Technology programs. His consulting work includes executive coaching, team building, and process consultation. He has also developed selection, assessment, and skill-building programs for a variety of civil, corporate, and educational organizations. Leadership and behavioral skills development are major themes in his writing and research. Other research interests include project leadership and virtual team effectiveness. Dr. Dominick received his Ph.D. in applied psychology from Stevens, earned his M.A. in organizational psychology from Columbia University, and completed his undergraduate studies in industrial and labor relations at Cornell University. In 2005, he received the Howe School's Outstanding Teacher Award and in 2007 was the recipient of the Harvey N. Davis Award for Distinguished Teaching.

Teri Elkins is an associate professor of management and the faculty and staff ombudsperson at the University of Houston, where she joined the faculty in 1997. Dr. Elkins received her undergraduate degree from Baylor University and a Ph.D. and J.D. from the C.T. Bauer College of Business, University of Houston. She teaches in the areas of business law, employment law, managerial communication, human resource management, conflict management, and organizational behavior and coordinates an internship program with the Equal Employment Opportunity Commission. Dr. Elkins has published scholarly articles on the topics of employment discrimination, sexual harassment, employee selection practices, affirmative action plans, leadership, and academic internship programs. Her articles have appeared in the *Journal of Applied Psychology, Journal of Applied Social Psychology, Leadership Quarterly, Sex Roles, SAM Advanced Management Journal, International Journal of Innovation and Technology Management, Journal of Managerial Issues,* and the *Journal of Occupational Health Psychology.* Dr. Elkins is a member of the Academy of Management, International Ombudsman Association, and the Association, for Conflict Resolution.

Gary J. Greguras is an associate professor of organizational behavior and human resources in the Lee Kong Chian School of Business at Singapore Management University. He received his Ph.D. in industrial-organizational psychology in 1998 from Bowling Green State University. His research interests include performance measurement and development, personality, and job attitudes. He currently serves on the editorial boards of the *Journal of Applied Psychology, Journal of Management,* and *Human Performance.*

Peter A. Heslin is an assistant professor of management at the Cox School of Business, Southern Methodist University, Dallas, Texas. He has two main research interests: the nature of career success in different contexts and how managers' implicit assumptions affect their performance appraisals, coaching, and justice. He teaches graduate courses in organization behavior, leading organizational change, and managing across cultures. Dr. Heslin has consulted in these areas to corporations, including

Citibank, IBM, Zurich Insurance, KPMG, and Procter & Gamble. He has authored or co-authored over a dozen articles in journals such as the *Journal of Applied Psychology, Journal of Organizational Behavior,* and *Personnel Psychology.* He serves on five editorial boards, including *Applied Psychology: An International Review, Journal of Occupational and Organizational Behavior, and the Journal of Organizational Behavior.* Dr. Heslin received his Ph.D. in organizational behavior and human resource management from the Rotman School of Management, University of Toronto.

Autumn D. Krauss is a senior scientist at Kronos Talent Management, responsible for the development of technology-enabled talent management solutions. One of her research and practice focuses is the identification of relevant behavioral competencies that can support talent management practices (for example, selection, performance appraisal) and how these competency-based processes can be supported through technology. She has served as the principal investigator and co-principal investigator on grant projects funded by the Centers for Disease Control and Prevention and the National Institute for Occupational Safety and Health. Dr. Krauss earned her master's and doctorate degrees in industrial/organizational psychology from Colorado State University, and a bachelor of arts degree in psychology and business administration from La Salle University in Philadelphia.

Edward M. Mone has more than twenty-five years of experience in career, leadership, and organization change and development. He is currently vice president for organization development at CA, Inc., where he is responsible for such functions as management and leadership training and development, succession planning, the company-wide employee opinion survey and employee research, and performance management and career development systems. He was previously vice president for organization development at Cablevision and director of people processes and systems at Booz Allen Hamilton, Inc. He was HR division manager for strategic planning and development at AT&T. Before that, he was a partner in an outplacement and career management firm. He is an adjunct faculty member at the College of Business, State University of New York at Stony Brook. He holds an M.A. in counseling psychology and has completed doctoral coursework at Teachers College, Columbia University. He has co-authored and co-edited books, book chapters, and articles in the areas of human resources and organization development, including *HR to the Rescue: Case Studies of HR Solutions to Business Challenges* and *Fundamentals of Performance Management.* He is president of Edward M. Mone & Associates, a firm specializing in organization and leadership development.

Wendy M. Muller is currently a doctoral candidate in industrial/ organizational psychology at The University of Akron. Her research interests include performance management, emotional labor, and motivation.

David B. Peterson, senior vice president and practice leader for Personnel Decisions International's worldwide coaching services, is an internationally recognized expert on coaching and executive development. His expertise is particularly helpful to organizations in creating strategic advantage through learning and development. He is the author of groundbreaking research showing that coaching produces significant and lasting changes—as rated by the individuals themselves and their bosses—at a magnitude three times greater than conventional training programs. Dr. Peterson joined PDI in 1985 and became practice leader for coaching services in 1990. With colleague Mary Dee Hicks, he has authored two best-selling books: *Development FIRST: Strategies for Self-Development* and *Leader As Coach: Strategies for Coaching and Developing Others.* In demand as a speaker, Dr. Peterson has been quoted in publications, including *The Wall Street Journal, Fortune, Time, Harvard Business School Newsletter, Investor's Business Daily, CFO, Training, The Washington Post,* and *USA Today.* He received his Ph.D. in industrial/organizational and counseling psychology from the University of Minnesota.

Christopher Pingor is a student at Montclair State University and is currently working on his thesis in the area of readiness to learn. His current areas of interest include employee motivation and life stages, organizational learning, job interviews, performance management, grounding and communication among couples, and the psychology of magic. He currently works as an account executive at The Essex Companies in New York City. He completed his B.A.

in psychology from Montclair State University and is currently completing a master's degree in psychology with a concentration in industrial and organizational psychology.

Richard R. Reilly is emeritus professor of technology management at Stevens Institute of Technology, where he headed Ph.D. programs in applied psychology and technology management. He has been a research psychologist for Bell Laboratories, AT&T, and Educational Testing Service, as well as a consultant to government and industry in areas such as assessment, innovation, and organizational performance. He has published over seventy articles in journals and has authored several books, including *Blockbusters: The Five Keys to Developing Great New Products* with Gary Lynn and *Uniting the Virtual Workforce: Transforming Leadership and Innovation in the Globally Integrated Enterprise* with Karen Sobel Lojeski. He is on the advisory board of the Institute of Innovation and Information Productivity and is an advisor to the National Board of Medical Examiners on physician behavior. Dr. Reilly is certified with the American Board of Professional Psychology and is on the editorial board of *Personnel Psychology* and the *International Journal of E-Collaboration*. He is a Fellow of the American Psychological Association and the American Psychological Society. Dr. Reilly earned his bachelor of science from Fordham University and his Ph.D. in organizational psychology from the University of Tennessee.

Michael A. Rosen is a doctoral candidate in the Applied Experimental and Human Factors Psychology Program at the University of Central Florida and has been a senior graduate research associate at the Institute for Simulation and Training since the fall of 2004, where he won the student researcher of the year in 2006. He is currently a MURI-SUMMIT graduate research fellow and focuses on developing theory, methods, and tools for understanding and measuring cognitive and social processes in team problem solving. His research interests include individual and team decision making and problem solving, human-computer interaction, performance measurement, and simulation-based training in high-stress, high-stakes domains such as healthcare and the military. He has co-authored over twenty peer-reviewed journal articles and book chapters related to these interests, as well as numerous proceedings papers and presentations at national and international conferences.

Eduardo Salas is a trustee chair and Pegasus Professor of Psychology at the University of Central Florida. He has co-authored more than three hundred journal articles and book chapters, has edited eighteen books, has served or is on fifteen editorial boards, is past editor of *Human Factors* journal and current associate editor of the *Journal of Applied Psychology*. His expertise includes assisting organizations in fostering teamwork, designing and implementing team training strategies, facilitating training effectiveness, managing decision making under stress, and developing performance measurement tools.

William A. Schiemann is founder and CEO of Metrus Group, an organizational and research advisory firm headquartered in Somerville, New Jersey. Metrus Group specializes in strategy development, performance measurement, and employee alignment. For the past twenty-five years, Dr. Schiemann and his colleagues have consulted extensively on the development and implementation of business strategies and balanced scorecards, employee and customer surveys, performance management and measurement, productivity and quality improvement, and mergers and acquisitions. Dr. Schiemann speaks internationally before a wide number of public and private audiences and is author of *Reinventing Talent Management: How to Maximize Performance in the New Marketplace* and co-author of *Bullseye! Hitting Your Strategic Targets Through High-Impact Measurement.* He has also written extensively for many management and professional publications. Dr. Schiemann received a Ph.D. in organizational psychology from the University of Illinois and is the recipient of the prestigious Distinguished Alumnus Award from the University of Illinois.

Valerie I. Sessa is an associate professor of industrial and organizational psychology at Montclair State University in New Jersey. Previously, she was a research scientist and director at the Center for Creative Leadership in Greensboro, North Carolina. Dr. Sessa has also worked as a consultant in a variety of areas, most recently assessing middle and high-potential managers using instruments, behavioral assessment centers, and feedback. Consulting activities include Bellevue Medical Center, Ciba-Geigy Pharmaceuticals, Citibank, New York Hospital System, and Xerox. Her research interests include continuous learning at the individual, group, and organizational levels, managing team effectiveness, and executive assessment and selection. Dr. Sessa is the author of *Executive Selection: Strategies for Success* (with Jodi Taylor), *Continuous Learning in Organizations: Individual, Group, and Organizational Perspectives,* and *Work Group Learning: Understanding, Improving, and Assessing How Groups Learn in Organizations* (both with Manny London). Her research publications have appeared in *Consulting Psychology Journal, Industrial and Commercial Training, Human Resource Development Review, Journal of Applied Behavioral Science, Journal of Applied Psychology, Journal of Management Development,* and *The Psychologist Manager Journal.* Her work has also appeared in such periodicals as *BusinessWeek, Fast Company,* and *The Harvard Business Review.* Dr. Sessa received her B.A. in psychology from the University of Pennsylvania and her master's and doctoral degrees in industrial and organizational psychology from New York University.

Stanley B. Silverman is currently dean of Summit College and professor of social science at The University of Akron. He has advised some of the largest organizations in the world and is co-author of the book, *Working Scared: Achieving Success in Trying Times.* His work has been published in major journals and he has been a guest on the *Today Show* discussing workplace issues. In addition to performance management, his current research focuses on arrogance in the workplace.

Kimberly Smith-Jentsch is an assistant professor in the Department of Psychology at the University of Central Florida and the director of the Team and Workforce Development Laboratory. She has authored numerous articles in the *Journal of Applied Psychology, Personnel Psychology,* and the *Journal of Organizational Behavior,* as well as in ten book chapters and over fifty conference presentations. Additionally, her research has produced a number of applied products and numerous performance and shared cognition metrics that have been used by Navy, law enforcement, and FAA air traffic control personnel. Dr. Smith-Jentsch has been honored as a NAVAIR Senior Scientist, awarded the Dr. Arthur E. Bisson award for Naval Technology Achievement, and the M. Scott Meyers award for applied research in the workplace by the Society for Industrial and Organizational Psychology.

Lori Anderson Snyder is an assistant professor in the Department of Psychology at the University of Oklahoma. Dr. Snyder received her master's and doctorate degrees in industrial/organizational psychology from Colorado State University. Her research interests include occupational health, diversity and discrimination, and developmental performance feedback. She has recently published research on these topics in *Research in Personnel and Human Resource Management, Journal of Applied Social Psychology,* and *Research in Organizational Stress and Well-Being.* She is part of a research team that was awarded the Douglas W. Bray and Ann Howard Award from the Society for Industrial and Organizational Psychology in 2005 for assessment center research focused on leadership development and is currently funded by the National Science Foundation to promote recruitment, retention, and leadership of women at the University of Oklahoma.

Paul Squires is president of Applied Skills & Knowledge, Inc. He is an industrial psychologist with twenty-five years of experience with organizational assessment and design, process improvement, training development, performance management, assessment development and validation, computer-based training, and project management. Prior to starting AS&K in 1999, he was vice president and practice manager for Assessment Solutions Inc. Training and Development Services. Dr. Squires' client list includes PricewaterhouseCoopers, KPMG, Merrill Lynch, Bristol-Myers-Squibb, IRS, Siemens, the U.S. Department of Labor, Motorola, Hewlett-Packard, Avon, and Novartis, to name a few. Prior to his consulting career, Dr. Squires held senior positions at AT&T Corporate Human Resources, with primary responsibility for selection, testing, employment and staffing, internal staffing systems, and employee development. He was director of Lucent Technologies' Microelectronics International University, responsible for developing a single world-wide training organization providing support to eighteen thousand employees. He holds a Ph.D. in educational psychology from Fordham University.

Nancy T. Tippins is a senior vice president and managing principal of Valtera Corporation, where she is responsible for the development and execution of firm strategies related to employee selection and assessment. She has extensive experience in the development and validation of selection tests and other forms of assessment, including performance appraisals for all levels of management and hourly employees as well as in designing performance management programs and leadership development programs. Prior to joining Valtera, Dr. Tippins worked as an internal consultant in large Fortune 100 companies (Exxon, Bell Atlantic, GTE) developing and validating selection and assessment tools. Dr. Tippins is active in professional affairs and is a past president of SIOP. She is a Fellow of the Society for Industrial and Organizational Psychology (SIOP), the American Psychological Association (APA), and the American Psychological Society (APS). Dr. Tippins received M.S. and Ph.D. degrees in industrial and organizational psychology from the Georgia Institute of Technology.

Don VandeWalle (dvande@cox.smu.edu) is the chair of the Management and Organizations Department at the Cox School of Business at Southern Methodist University. His research interests include goal orientation, feedback-seeking behavior, self-regulation, and the influence of implicit theory beliefs on leadership behavior. Dr. VandeWalle's published research includes articles in the *Journal of Applied Psychology,* the *Journal of Management, Personnel Psychology,* and the *Journal of Organizational Behavior.* He currently serves on the editorial boards of the *Journal of Applied Psychology* and *Organizational Behavior and Human Decision Processes.* Dr. VandeWalle earned his Ph.D. in organizational behavior and strategic management from the Carlson School of Management at the University of Minnesota.

Sallie J. Weaver is a doctoral student in the industrial/organizational psychology program at the University of Central Florida (UCF). She earned her B.S. from Florida State University with a concentration in performance management and her M.S. from UCF. As a graduate research associate at the Institute for Simulation and Training, she is a lead student on multiple applied organizational training and evaluation projects. Her research interests include individual and team training, simulation, organizational culture, aging in the workforce, and metric development.

CHAPTER 1

AN EXPANDED VIEW OF PERFORMANCE MANAGEMENT*

Herman Aguinis

An Expanded View of Performance Management

The purpose of this chapter is to provide an expanded view of the performance management process that subsumes the traditional I/O psychology performance appraisal literature. It is an expanded view in relation to the traditional I/O psychology treatment of the topic in five different ways. First, it goes beyond an almost exclusive emphasis, some would say almost an obsession, on the measurement of performance and includes a consideration of what happens before and after performance is measured (that is, the role of time and context). Second, although the I/O

*This research was conducted in part while Herman Aguinis held the Mehalchin Term Professorship in Management at the University of Colorado Denver and visiting appointments at the University of Salamanca (Spain) and University of Puerto Rico. I thank Charles A. Pierce, Manuel London, and Jim W. Smither for comments on previous drafts. This chapter includes material from and is based on the following book: Aguinis, H. (2009). *Performance management* (2nd ed.). Upper Saddle River, NJ: Pearson Prentice Hall.

Address correspondence to Herman Aguinis, Professor of Organizational Behavior and Human Resources and Dean's Research Professor, Kelley School of Business, Indiana University (email: haguinis@indiana.edu).

psychology literature treats the topic as being almost exclusively in the industrial psychology domain, this chapter places performance management equally in the industrial psychology and organizational psychology domains (cf. Aguinis & Pierce, 2008). Third, the chapter goes beyond an almost exclusive emphasis on the individual level of analysis by considering unit- and organizational-level strategic goals and team performance. Fourth, it goes beyond the traditional performance appraisal literature and considers the explicit link between performance assessment and administrative decisions (for example, allocation of rewards, promotions). Fifth, it is an expanded view because it relies on research produced by other fields such as communication, education, information systems, international business, marketing, organizational behavior, public administration, social psychology, sociology, and business strategy. My hope is that this chapter's expanded view of the performance management process will make a contribution toward the closing of the science-practice gap in the area of performance management.

The Science-Practice Divide and Performance Management

There is a documented gap between research conducted by human resource management (HRM) and industrial and organizational (I/O) psychology academics and the practice of HRM and I/O psychology in organizations. For the most part, academics conduct research on topics only tangentially relevant to practitioners and, on the other side of the divide, practitioners implement practices that do not seem to be based on rigorous research (Cascio & Aguinis, 2008a; Rynes, Colbert, & Brown, 2002; Rynes, Giluk, & Brown, 2007). Muchinsky (2004) noted that, unfortunately, researchers, in general, are not necessarily concerned about how their theories, principles, and methods are put into practice outside of academic study. In fact, Latham (2007) recently issued a severe warning that "We, as applied scientists, exist largely for the purpose of communicating knowledge to one another. One might shudder if this were also true of another applied science, medicine" (p. 1,031). On the other hand, Muchinsky (2004) noted that practitioners, in general, are deeply concerned with matters of implementation. This increasing science-practice schism is particularly puzzling in the case of I/O psychology because the field was created and seems to be predicated fundamentally on the principles of the scientist-practitioner model (Bass, 1974; Dunnette, 1990; McHenry, 2007; Murphy & Saal, 1990; Rupp & Beal, 2007).

The general science-practice gap is particularly evident in the area of performance management. Practitioners are interested in several issues directly related to performance management, including talent management, leadership development, intensification of work as employers try to increase productivity with fewer employees, and managing change (Fay, 2006; Schramm, 2006; Schwind, 2007). On the other hand, a review by Cascio and Aguinis (2008a) showed that the five most popular topics published in the *Journal of Applied Psychology* (JAP) from 2003 to 2007 are (1) job satisfaction/attitudes/involvement/commitment; (2) work groups/teams; (3) performance appraisal/feedback; (4) organizational cultures, climates, policies, citizenship; and (5) behavior, prediction of processes, and outcomes. That same review found that the five most popular topics published in *Personnel Psychology* (PPsych) also between 2003 and 2007 are (1) behavior, prediction of processes and outcomes; (2) performance appraisal/feedback; (3) psychometrics/testing issues; (4) test validity/validation issues; and (5) work groups/teams (Cascio & Aguinis, 2008a).

Three conclusions can be drawn from this information. First, given that Cascio and Aguinis (2008a) coded the articles published in JAP and PPsych using fifty different categories, the congruence between the two lists of the top five most popular topics is remarkable and suggests that these publication trends are sound indicators of common, underlying trends in the research produced in the field of I/O psychology. Second, a comparison of the topics in which practitioners are interested with those in which academics are interested shows tangential overlap only. While the topic "performance appraisal/feedback" is included on the lists for both journals, the majority of articles address topics that are not sufficiently broad to address practitioner concerns about talent management and leadership development, to mention just two. The third conclusion is that practitioners interested in implementing sound research-based performance management practices can rely on the research produced by HRM and I/O psychology (for example, performance appraisal). However, given the tangential overlap between practitioner interests and publication trends in I/O psychology, there is a need to go beyond HRM and I/O psychology into additional fields of study.

The organization of the chapter is as follows. The first section defines performance management and describes six key purposes served by performance management systems. The second section describes the performance management process. The third and final section describes performance management best practices. For a more detailed discussion of each of the issues discussed in this chapter, see Aguinis (2009).

What Is Performance Management?

Consider the following situation (Aguinis, 2009, p. 2):

> Sally is a sales manager at a large pharmaceutical company. The fiscal year will end in one week. She is overwhelmed with end-of-the-year tasks, including reviewing the budget she is likely to be allocated for the following year, responding to customers' phone calls, and supervising a group of ten salespeople. It's a very hectic time, probably the most hectic time of the year. She receives a phone call from the human resources (HR) department: "Sally, we have not received your performance reviews for your ten employees; they are due by the end of the fiscal year." Sally thinks, "Oh, those performance reviews. . . . What a waste of my time!" From Sally's point of view, there is no value in filling out those seemingly meaningless forms. She does not see her subordinates in action because they are in the field visiting customers most of the time. All that she knows about their performance is based on sales figures, which depend more on the products offered and geographic territory covered than the individual effort and motivation of each salesperson. And nothing happens in terms of rewards, regardless of her ratings. These are lean times in her organization, and salary adjustments are based on seniority rather than on merit. She has less than three days to turn in her forms. What will she do? She decides to follow the path of least resistance: to please her employees and give everyone the maximum possible rating. In this way, Sally believes the employees will be happy with their ratings and she will not have to deal with complaints

or follow-up meetings. Sally fills out the forms in less than twenty minutes and gets back to her "real job."

As is illustrated by this vignette, which describes a situation that is painfully familiar to many readers, performance management systems are often under-utilized and also misused. In fact, in many organizations, poorly implemented performance management systems can do more harm than good, as was demonstrated by a legal case in the construction industry (FMI Corporation, 2000). A female employee was promoted several times and succeeded until she started working under the supervision of a new manager. She stated in her lawsuit that, once she was promoted and reported to the new manager, that boss ignored her and did not give her the same support or opportunities for training that her male colleagues received. After eight months of receiving no feedback from her manager, she was called into his office, where the manager told her that she was failing, resulting in a demotion and a $20,000 reduction in her annual salary. When she won her sex-discrimination lawsuit, a jury awarded her $1.2 million in emotional distress and economic damages.

In addition to an increased risk of litigation, there are several other detrimental outcomes of poorly implemented systems, including employee burnout and job dissatisfaction, damaged relationships, and increased turnover (Brown & Benson, 2005; Gabris & Ihrke, 2001). In addition, there is a large opportunity cost because poorly implemented systems waste time and resources, including time and money.

Before designing a performance management system, there needs to be a clear definition of performance management. Performance management is a "continuous process of identifying, measuring, and developing the performance of individuals and teams and aligning performance with the strategic goals of the organization" (Aguinis, 2009, p. 3). Note that the key components of this definition are that this is a continuous process and that there is an alignment with strategic goals. If a manager fills out a form once a year because this is a requirement of the "HR cops," then this is certainly not a continuous process. Also, evaluating employee performance (that is, performance appraisal) without clear considerations of the extent to which an individual is contributing to unit and organizational performance and about how performance will improve in the future is also not consistent with this definition of performance management.

Why Implement a Performance Management System?

Performance management systems can serve six important purposes (cf. Cleveland & Murphy, 1989) (see Exhibit 1.1 for a summary).

Exhibit 1.1 Summary of Six Purposes of a Performance Management System.

Strategic: It links the organization's goals with individual goals, thereby reinforcing behaviors consistent with the attainment of organizational goals.

Administrative: It is a source of valid and useful information for making decisions about employees, including salary adjustments, promotions, employee retention or termination, recognition of superior performance, identification of poor performers, layoffs, and merit increases.

Communication: It allows employees to be informed about how well they are doing, to receive information on specific areas that may need improvement, and to learn about the organization's and the supervisor's expectations and what aspects of work the supervisor believes are most important.

Developmental: It includes feedback, which allows managers to coach employees and help them improve performance on an ongoing basis.

Organizational maintenance: It yields information about skills, abilities, promotional potential, and assignment histories of current employees to be used in workforce planning as well as assessing future training needs, evaluating performance achievements at the organizational level, and evaluating the effectiveness of human resource interventions (for example, whether employees perform at higher levels after participating in a training program).

Documentation: It yields data that can be used to assess the predictive accuracy of newly proposed selection instruments as well as important administrative decisions. This information can be especially useful in the case of litigation.

1. *Strategic purpose.* By linking the organization's goals with individual goals, the performance management system reinforces behaviors consistent with the attainment of organizational goals. Moreover, even if for some reason individual goals are not achieved, linking individual goals with organizational goals serves as a way to communicate what are the most crucial business strategic initiatives. As an illustration of how performance management can serve a strategic purpose, consider the case of Sears Holdings Corporation, the third largest broad-line retailer in the United States ($55 billion in annual revenues, about 3,900 retail stores in the United States and Canada) and the leading home appliance retailer as well as a leader in tools, lawn and garden products, home electronics, and automotive repair and maintenance (Berner, 2005). Following the merger of Kmart Corp. and Sears, Roebuck & Company, Aylwin B. Lewis was promoted to chief executive and tasked with a strategic culture change initiative in hopes of reinvigorating the struggling retail company. A strategic objective is to move from an inward focus to a customer service approach. A second key objective is to bring about an entrepreneurial spirit whereby store managers strive for financial literacy and are challenged to identify opportunities for greater profits. Several aspects of the performance management system are now being used to achieve these strategic objectives. For example, employee duties and objectives are being revised so that employees will spend less time in back rooms and more time interacting with customers to facilitate purchases and understand customer needs. In addition, leadership communication with employees and face-to-face interaction are being encouraged. Lewis spends three days per week in stores with employees and frequently quizzes managers on their knowledge, such as asking about profit margins for a given department. The greatest compliment employees

receive is to be referred to as "commercial" or someone who can identify opportunities for profits. All Sears headquarters employees are also required to spend a day working in a store, which many had never done before. Executive management has identified five hundred employees, considered potential leaders, who are given training and development opportunities specifically aimed at cultural and strategic changes. In sum, the performance management system at Sears is used as a strategic tool to change Sears' culture because senior management views encouraging key desired behaviors as critical to the company's success in the marketplace.

2. *Administrative purpose.* Performance management systems are a source of valid and useful information for making administrative decisions about employees. Such administrative decisions include salary adjustments, promotions, employee retention or termination, recognition of superior individual performance, identification of poor performers, layoffs, and merit increases. In other words, the implementation of reward systems based on information provided by the performance management system falls within the administrative purpose. If an organization does not have a good performance management system in place, administrative decisions are more likely to be based on personal preferences, politics, and otherwise biased decisions. Having a good system in place is particularly relevant for the implementation of contingent pay (CP) plans, also called *pay-for-performance.* CP means that individuals are rewarded based on how well they perform on the job. Thus, employees receive increases in pay based wholly or partly on job performance. Originally, CP plans were used only for top management. Gradually, the use of CP plans has extended to sales jobs. Currently, CP plans are pervasive, and more than 70 percent of workers in the United States and the United Kingdom (Baty, 2006) are employed by organizations implementing some type of variable play plan. Many of these organizations tie variable pay (for example, bonus, commission, cash award, lump sum) directly to performance. CP plans are becoming popular worldwide (Milliman, Nason, Zhu, & De Cieri, 2002), which highlights the important administrative purpose of performance management systems.

3. *Communication purpose.* A performance management system can be an excellent communication device. Employees are informed about how well they are doing and receive information on specific areas that may need to be improved. Also, related to the strategic purpose described above, performance management systems are a conduit to communicate the organization's and the supervisor's expectations and what aspects of work the supervisor believes are most important.

4. *Developmental purpose.* Feedback is an important component of a well-implemented performance management system. Managers can use feedback to coach employees and improve performance on an ongoing basis. This feedback allows for the identification of strengths and weaknesses as well as the causes for performance deficiencies (which could be due to individual, group, or contextual factors). Of course, feedback is useful only to the extent that remedial action is taken and concrete steps are implemented to remedy any deficiencies (Aguinis & Kraiger, 2009). Another aspect of the developmental purpose is that employees receive information about themselves that can help them individualize their career paths. Thus, the developmental purpose refers to both short-term and long-term aspects of development.

5. *Organizational maintenance purpose.* An important component of any workforce planning effort is the talent inventory, which is information on current resources (for example, skills, abilities, promotional potential, and assignment histories of current employees). Performance management systems are the primary means through which accurate talent inventories can be assembled. Other organizational maintenance purposes served by performance management systems include assessing future training needs, evaluating performance achievements at the organizational level, and evaluating the effectiveness of HRM interventions (for example, whether employees perform at higher levels after participating in a training program). None of these activities can be conducted effectively in the absence of a good performance management system.

6. *Documentation purpose.* Performance data can be used to assess the predictive accuracy of newly proposed selection instruments

(Cascio & Aguinis, 2008b). For example, a newly developed test of computer literacy can be administered to all administrative personnel. Scores on the test can then be paired with scores collected through the performance management system. If scores on the test and on the performance measure are correlated, then the test can be used with future applicants for the administrative positions. Second, performance management systems allow for the documentation of important administrative decisions. This information can be especially useful in the case of litigation.

As noted earlier, many performance management systems are under-utilized and, hence, do not serve all of these six purposes. For example, results of a survey of industrial and organizational psychologists working in human resources departments in more than one hundred different organizations indicated that the two most frequent purposes are administrative (salary decisions) and developmental (to identify employees' weaknesses and strengths) (Cleveland & Murphy, 1989). There is much to gain if organizations are able to use their performance management systems for all six purposes. This would have an important impact on organizations as well as possibly entire countries, given the pervasiveness of performance management systems worldwide. For example, a recent survey of almost 1,000 HRM professionals revealed that 96 percent of Australian companies currently implement some type of performance management system (Nankervis & Compton, 2006). Similarly, results of a survey of 278 organizations, about two-thirds of which are multinational corporations, from fifteen different countries, indicated that about 91 percent of organizations implement a formal performance management system (Cascio, 2006). Moreover, organizations with formal and systematic performance management systems are 51 percent more likely to perform better than the other organizations in the sample regarding financial outcomes and 41 percent more likely to perform better than the other organizations in the sample regarding other outcomes, including customer satisfaction, employee retention, and other important metrics.

Maximizing the Purposes Served by Performance Management: Illustration

There are numerous examples of organizations that implement performance management systems that allow them to accomplish the multiple objectives described above. Consider the case of SELCO Credit Union in Eugene, Oregon, a not-for-profit consumer cooperative that was established in 1936 (Fandray, 2001). SELCO's eight branches serve nearly eighty thousand members. SELCO offers many of the same services offered by other banks, including personal checking and savings accounts, loans, and credit cards. Recently, SELCO scrapped an old performance appraisal system and replaced it with a new multipurpose and more effective performance management system. First, the timing of the new system is now aligned with the business cycle, instead of the employee's date of hire, to ensure that business needs are aligned with individual goals. This alignment serves both strategic and informational purposes. Second, managers are given a pool of money that they can work with to award bonuses and raises as needed, which is more effective than the complex set of matrices that had been in place to calculate bonuses. This improved the way in which the system is used for allocating rewards and therefore serves an administrative purpose. Third, managers are required to have regular conversations with their employees about their performance and make note of any problems that arise. This gives the employees a clear sense of areas in which they need improvement and also provides documentation if disciplinary action is needed. This component serves both informational and documentation purposes. Finally, the time that was previously spent filling out complicated matrices and forms is now spent talking with the employees about how they can improve their performance, allowing for progress on an ongoing basis. This serves a developmental purpose.

Many organizations may have a so-called performance management system, but this may be a performance appraisal at best and an administrative hurdle imposed by the HR department at worst. So it is not sufficient to have any type of performance management system, but one should have one that serves as many of the six purposes described above as possible. The next section addresses a performance management process that allows organizations to maximize the benefits of their system.

Performance Management Process

As noted earlier, performance management is a continuous process. However, when a system is first implemented, the process follows the following stages (Aguinis, 2009; Grote, 1996): (1) pre-requisites, (2) performance planning, (3) performance execution, (4) performance assessment, (5) performance review, and (6) performance renewal and recontracting. Each of these stages is described next. The flow of the performance management process is depicted graphically in Figure 1.1.

Stage 1: Prerequisites

There are two important prerequisites that are needed before a performance management system is implemented: (1) knowledge of the organization's mission and strategic goals and (2) knowledge of the job in question. If there is a lack of clarity regarding where the organization wants to go, or the relationship between the organization's mission and strategies and each of its unit's mission and strategies is not clear, there will be a lack of clarity regarding what each employee needs to do and achieve to help the organization get there. An organization's mission and strategic goals are a result of strategic planning, which allows an organization to clearly define its purpose or reason for existing, where it wants to be in the future, the goals it wants to achieve, and the strategies it will use to attain these goals. Once the goals for the entire organization have been established, similar goals cascade downward, with departments setting objectives to support

Figure 1.1 Flow of the Performance Management Process.

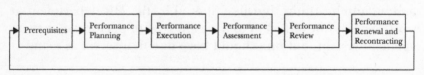

the organization's overall mission and objectives. The cascading continues downward until each employee has a set of goals compatible with those of his or her unit and the organization.

As an example, Exhibit 1.2 shows how the Key Bank of Utah successfully developed a performance management system that

Exhibit 1.2 Cascading of Goals from the Organizational to the Departmental and Individual Level at Key Bank of Utah.

Organizational Level

- *Mission statement:* The mission of the corporation is to operate as a high-performing financial institution providing a wide range of profitable, competitive, and superior financial services in our market.
- *Goals:* To attract and retain an outstanding staff who are highly motivated and productive and who vigorously pursue revenue-generating and cost-reduction strategies.
- *Strategy:* Critically review our existing branches and departments to ensure that all branches are consistent in their goals, strategies, and profit objectives.

Departmental Level

- *Mission (department level)*: We will increase the knowledge, management skills, and decision-making abilities of our branch managers so that we will minimize losses and other operating expenses while maximizing the profitability of our branching systems.

Individual (Supervisor) Level

- *Position description for HR manager*: Administers a comprehensive human resources program in the division to ensure the expertise, effectiveness, motivation, and depth (including providing appropriate management succession) to the division's staff members.

Individual (Employee) Level

- *Individual performance:* Information on various responsibilities, standards expected, goals to be reached, and actions to be taken to improve performance in the future.

is aligned with the strategic plan of the organization (Addams & Embley, 1988). To do this, the bank first involved managers at all hierarchical levels to develop an organization mission statement. Next, they developed goals and strategies that would help achieve Key Bank's mission. The mission statement, goals, and strategies at the organizational level served as the foundation for developing the strategies for individual departments and units. To develop these, senior managers met with each department manager to discuss the organization's goals and strategies and to explain the importance of having similar items in place in each department. Subsequently, each of the departmental managers met with his or her employees to develop a department mission statement and goals. One important premise in this exercise was that each department's mission statement and objectives had to be aligned with the corporate mission statement, goals, and strategies. After organizational and departmental goals and strategies were aligned, managers and employees reviewed individual job descriptions. Each job description was tailored so that individual job responsibilities were clear and contributed to meeting the department's and the organization's objectives. Involving employees in this process helped them to gain a clear understanding of how their performance affected the department and, in turn, the organization.

The second important prerequisite before a performance management system is implemented is to understand the job in question. This is done through job analysis. Job analysis is a process of determining the key components of a particular job, including activities, tasks, products, services, and processes. There are numerous types of job analytic tools, including some that focus on specific personality traits needed for various positions (Aguinis, Mazurkiewicz, & Heggestad, 2009). A job analysis is a fundamental prerequisite of any performance management system. Without a job analysis, it is difficult to understand what constitutes the required duties for a particular job. If we don't know what an employee is supposed to do on the job, we won't know what needs to be evaluated and how to do so.

Stage 2: Performance Planning

The performance planning stage has the goal for employees to have a thorough knowledge of the performance management system.

In fact, at the beginning of each performance cycle, the supervisor and the employee meet to discuss, and agree on, what needs to be done and how it should be done. This performance planning discussion includes a consideration of (1) results, (2), behaviors, and (3) development plan.

Results. Results refer to what needs to be done or the outcomes an employee must produce. A consideration of results needs to include the key accountabilities, or broad areas of a job for which the employee is responsible for producing results. A discussion of results also includes specific objectives that the employee will achieve as part of each accountability. Objectives are statements of important and measurable outcomes. Finally, discussing results also means discussing performance standards. A performance standard is a yardstick used to evaluate how well employees have achieved each objective. Performance standards provide information about acceptable and unacceptable performance (for example, quality, quantity, cost, and time). Consider the job of university professor. Two key accountabilities are (1) teaching (preparation and delivery of instructional materials to students) and (2) research (creation and dissemination of new knowledge). An objective for teaching could be "to obtain a student evaluation of teaching performance of 3 on a 4-point scale." An objective for research could be "to publish two articles in scholarly refereed journals per year." Performance standards could be "to obtain a student evaluation of teaching performance of at least 2 on a 4-point scale" and "to publish at least one article in scholarly refereed journals per year." Thus, the objective is the desired level of performance, whereas the standard is usually a minimum acceptable level of performance.

Behaviors. Although it is important to measure results, an exclusive emphasis on results can give an incomplete picture of employee performance. This is particularly true today because, in contrast to the hierarchical organization chart of the 20th-century organization, the 21st-century organization is far more likely to look like a web: a flat, intricately woven form that links partners, employees, external contractors, suppliers, and customers in various collaborations (Cascio & Aguinis, 2008b). Accordingly, for some jobs it may be difficult to establish precise objectives and standards. For other jobs, employees may have control over how they do their jobs, but not over the results of their behaviors. For example, the sales figures of a salesperson could be affected more by the assigned sales territory than by the salesperson's ability and performance. Behaviors, or how a job is done, thus constitute an important component of the planning phase. This is probably why, in addition to sales figures, salespeople like to be appraised on such behavioral criteria as communications skills and product knowledge (Pettijohn, Parker, Pettijohn, & Kent, 2001).

A consideration of behaviors includes discussing competencies, which are measurable clusters of knowledge, skills, and attitudes (KSAs) that are critical in determining how results will be achieved (cf. Shippmann et al., 2000). Examples of competencies are customer service, written or oral communication, creative thinking, and dependability. Returning to the example of the professor, assume that teaching is done online and that numerous technology-related problems exist, so that the resulting teaching evaluations are deficient (that is, lower than the standard of 2). This is an example of a situation in which behaviors should be given more importance than results. In this situation, the evaluation could include competencies such as online communication skills (for example, in the chat room).

Development plan. An important step before the review cycle begins is for the supervisor and employee to agree on a development plan. At a minimum, this plan should include identifying areas that need improvement and setting goals to be achieved in each area. Development plans usually include both results and behaviors. Achieving the goals stated in the development plan allows employees to keep abreast of changes in their field or profession. Such plans highlight an employee's strengths and the areas in need of development, and they provide an action plan to improve in areas of weaknesses and further develop areas of strength (Reyna & Sims, 1995). In a nutshell, personal development plans allow employees to answer the following questions:

- How can I continually learn and grow in the next year?
- How can I do better in the future?
- How can I avoid performance problems faced in the past?

Information to be used in designing development plans comes from the appraisal form. Specifically, a development plan can be designed based on each of the performance dimensions evaluated. For example, if the performance dimension "communication" is rated as substandard, this area would be targeted by the development plan. In addition, however, development plans focus on the knowledge and skills needed for more long-term career aspirations. In addition to improved performance, the inclusion of development plans and, in more general terms, the identification of employee strengths and weaknesses as part of the performance management system have another important benefit: employees are more likely to be satisfied with the system (Boswell & Boudreau, 2000).

The direct supervisor or line manager has an important role in the creation and completion of the employee's development plan. This active role will help the supervisor understand the process from the employee's perspective, anticipate potential roadblocks and defensive attitudes, and create a plan in a collaborative fashion (Dunning, 2004). First, the supervisor needs to explain what would be required for the employee to achieve the desired performance level, including the steps that an employee must take to improve performance. This information needs to be provided together with information on the probability of success if the employee completes the suggested steps. Second, the supervisor has a primary role in referring the employee to appropriate development activities that can assist the employee in achieving her goals. This includes helping the employee select a mentor, appropriate reading resources, courses, and so forth. Third, the supervisor reviews and makes suggestions about the development objectives. Specifically, the supervisor helps assure the goals are achievable, specific, and doable. Fourth, the supervisor has primary responsibility for checking on the employee's progress toward achieving the development goals. For example, the supervisor can remind the employee of due dates and revise goals if needed. Finally, the supervisor needs to provide reinforcements so the employee will be motivated to achieve the development goals. Reinforcements can be extrinsic and include rewards such as bonuses and additional benefits, but reinforcements can also include the assignment of more challenging and interesting work that takes advantage of the new skills learned.

Supervisors themselves need to be motivated to perform functions that will support the employees' completion of their development objectives. For this to happen, supervisors must be rewarded for doing a good job in helping their employees develop. Consider how this is done at KLA-Tencor Corporation, one of the world's top ten manufacturers of semiconductor equipment (Ellis, 2003). At KLA-Tencor, between 10 and 30 percent of supervisors' bonus pay is directly tied to employee development. Employee development is measured in terms of employee training and certification levels. Managers are given at least quarterly updates on the status of their staff development. In addition, employees themselves are rewarded for engaging in development activities. In fact, only employees with up-to-date training and certification levels are eligible for bonuses. Thus, employee development is successful at KLA-Tencor because both employees and managers are directly rewarded for employee development. After several years of implementing these practices, employee development has become the norm and is part of KLA-Tencor's culture.

As an example of the implementation of development plans, consider the case of General Mills (Ellis, 2004), where individual development plans (IDPs) are promoted strongly throughout the company. The Minneapolis, Minnesota-based General Mills is an international foods company. Some of the best-known brands include Pillsbury, Cheerios, Green Giant, and Yoplait. The formally written IDPs are completed annually, but the expectation is for ongoing conversations between managers and employees, focusing not only on competencies that are well developed and those that are in need of improvement, but also on employees' career aspirations. The company's IDP season promotes the process for employees by hosting speakers, offering web-based learning tools, and holding workshops for employees and managers to get the most out of the process. Some of these sessions are specifically tailored to different kinds of positions within the company with different needs in the development process. Also, the IDP is kept separate from the annual performance appraisal, as the belief is that development planning cannot be sufficiently addressed in the context of appraisal.

Finally, a tool that has become popular in helping employees, particularly those in supervisory roles, improve performance by gathering information from different groups is the 360-degree feedback system (Morgeson, Mumford, & Campion, 2005). These systems are called 360-degree systems because information is gathered from individuals all around the employee. Specifically, information on what performance dimensions could be improved is gathered from superiors, peers, customers, and subordinates. This information is usually collected anonymously to minimize rating inflation. Employees also rate themselves on the various performance dimensions and compare self-perceptions with the information provided by others. A gap analysis is conducted to examine the areas for which there are large discrepancies between self-perceptions and the perceptions of others. A 360-degree feedback system report usually includes information on dimensions for which there is agreement that further development is needed. This information is used to create a development plan. Implementing a 360-degree feedback system should not be a one-time-only event. The system should be in place and data collected over time on an ongoing basis. The implementation of ongoing 360-degree feedback systems is sometimes labeled a 720-degree feedback system, referring to the fact that the collection of 360-degree data takes place at least twice. In short, administering the system only once will not be as beneficial as administering the system repeatedly.

Once the prerequisites are met and the planning phase has been completed, we are ready to begin the implementation of the performance management system. This includes performance execution, assessment, review, and renewal and recontracting.

Stage 3: Performance Execution

Once the review cycle begins, the employee strives to produce the results and display the behaviors agreed on earlier as well as to work on development needs. The employee has primary responsibility and ownership of this process. Employee participation does not begin at the performance execution stage, however. As noted earlier, employees need to have active input in the development of the job descriptions, performance standards, and the creation of the rating form. In addition, at later stages, employees are active participants in the evaluation process in that they provide a self-assessment and the performance review interview is a two-way communication process.

Although the employee has primary responsibilities for performance execution, the supervisor also needs to do his or her share of the work. Supervisors have primary responsibility over the following issues:

- *Observation and documentation.* Supervisors must observe and document performance on a daily basis. It is important to keep track of examples of both good and poor performance.
- *Updates.* As the organization's goals may change, it is important to update and revise initial objectives, standards, and key accountabilities (in the case of results) and competency areas (in the case of behaviors).
- *Feedback.* Feedback on progression toward goals and coaching to improve performance should be provided on a regular basis, and certainly before the review cycle is over.
- *Resources.* Supervisors should provide employees with resources and opportunities to participate in development activities. Thus, they should encourage (and sponsor) participation in training, classes, and special assignments. Overall, supervisors have a responsibility to ensure that the employee has the necessary supplies and funding to perform the job properly.
- *Reinforcement.* Supervisors must let employees know that their outstanding performance is noticed by reinforcing effective behaviors and progress toward goals. Also, supervisors should provide feedback regarding negative performance and how to remedy the observed problem. Observation and communication are not sufficient. Performance problems must be diagnosed early, and appropriate steps must be taken as soon as the problem is discovered.

As an example of this shared responsibility in an actual organization, consider the case of Lockheed Martin Corporation, an advanced technology company that was formed in March 1995 with the merger of two of the world's premier technology companies: Lockheed Corporation and Martin Marietta Corporation. Lockheed Martin has approximately 140,000 employees worldwide

(*The Baltimore Sun*, 2003). They are engaged in the research, design, development, manufacture, and integration of advanced technology systems, products, and services. Lockheed Martin's performance management system includes the active participation of both employees and their supervisors. Specifically, employees write their own performance management objectives based on organization and unit objectives. Then, managers approve the objectives and are encouraged to give ongoing feedback about the progress toward meeting the objectives. The actual performance appraisal form is an electronic, one-page computer screen. The program was designed to "involve employees in setting their own goals, to make those goals clear, and to provide regular feedback on their progress toward achieving those goals."

What determines whether an employee is performing well or not? A combination of three factors allows some people to perform at higher levels than others: (1) declarative knowledge, (2) procedural knowledge, and (3) motivation. Declarative knowledge is information about facts and things, including information regarding a given task's requirements, labels, principles, and goals. Procedural knowledge is a combination of knowing what to do and how to do it and includes cognitive, physical, perceptual, motor, and interpersonal skills. Motivation involves three types of choice behaviors: (1) choice to expend effort (for example, "I will go to work today"), (2) choice of level of effort (for example, "I will put in my best effort at work" versus "I will not try very hard"), and (3) choice to persist in the expenditure of that level of effort (for example, "I will give up after a little while" versus "I will persist no matter what").

Because performance is affected by the combined effect of three different factors, managers must find information that will allow them to understand whether the source of the problem is declarative knowledge, procedural knowledge, motivation, or some combination of these three factors. If an employee lacks motivation but the manager believes the source of the problem is declarative knowledge, the manager may send the employee to a company-sponsored training program so that he can acquire the knowledge that is presumably lacking. On the other hand, if motivation is the problem, then the implementation of some type of CP plan may be a good intervention. This is why performance management systems need not only to measure performance but also to provide information about the source of any performance deficiencies, which is done in the performance assessment stage.

Stage 4: Performance Assessment

In the assessment phase, both the employee and the manager are responsible for evaluating the extent to which the desired behaviors have been displayed, and whether the desired results have been achieved. Although many sources can be used to collect performance information (for example, peers or subordinates), in most cases the direct supervisor provides the information. This also includes an evaluation of the extent to which the goals stated in the development plan have been achieved. This is the stage of the performance management process that has received the greatest attention from I/O psychology researchers (Aguinis & Pierce, 2008; Bennett, Lance, & Woehr, 2006).

It is important that both the employee and the manager take ownership of the assessment process. The manager fills out his or her appraisal form, and the employee should also fill out his or her form. The fact that both parties are involved in the assessment provides good information to be used in the review phase. When both the employee and the supervisor are active participants in the evaluation process, there is a greater likelihood that the information will be used productively in the future. Specifically, the inclusion of self-ratings helps emphasize possible discrepancies between self-views and the views that important others (that is, supervisors) have. It is the discrepancy between these two views that is most likely to trigger development efforts, particularly when feedback from the supervisor is more negative than are employee self-evaluations.

The inclusion of self-appraisals is also beneficial regarding important additional factors. Self-appraisals can reduce an employee's defensiveness during an appraisal meeting and increase the employee's satisfaction with the performance management system, as well as enhance perceptions of accuracy and fairness and therefore acceptance of the system (Shore, Adams, & Tashchian, 1998).

As an illustration, consider the case of ENSR, a full-service global provider of environmental and energy development services to industry and government (LaChance, 2006). ENSR's two thousand professionals provide clients with consulting, engineering, remediation, and related services from more than seventy worldwide locations, including forty-five in the United States. ENSR has created and utilizes a scorecard with six categories that are directly linked to its five-year vision: health and safety, employee engagement, client loyalty, cost management, profitability, and revenue growth. This information is used in the company's evaluation of current performance for individuals and groups with a scorecard that shows current performance against "average" internal performance and "top 25 percent performance." Managers are expected to utilize the scorecard in discussions about performance and to discuss the relationship between the metrics and the directives and initiatives from senior management. The scorecard is a tool used to motivate employees to achieve top performance and to provide a clear link between each individual and team activity to the strategic objectives of the organization. In summary, ENSR utilizes a balanced scorecard tool to assist managers in assessing and reviewing performance and ensuring a close link to the objectives of the organization.

Stage 5: Performance Review

The performance review stage involves the meeting between the employee and the manager to review their assessments. This meeting is usually called the appraisal meeting or discussion. The appraisal meeting is important because it provides a formal setting in which the employee receives feedback on his or her performance. In spite of its importance in performance management, the appraisal meeting is often regarded as the "Achilles' heel of the entire process" (Kikoski, 1999). This is because many managers are uncomfortable providing performance feedback, particularly when performance is deficient (Ghorpade & Chen, 1995). This high level of discomfort, which often translates into anxiety and the avoidance of the appraisal interview, can be mitigated through training those responsible for providing feedback. Providing feedback in an effective manner is extremely important because it leads not only to performance improvement but also to employee satisfaction with the system. For example, a study involving more than two hundred teachers in Malaysia, including individuals with distinct Chinese, Malay, and Indian cultural backgrounds, found that when they received effective feedback, they reported greater satisfaction with the system, even when they received low performance ratings (Rahman, 2006). At this point, however, let's emphasize that people are apprehensive about both receiving and giving performance information, and this apprehension reinforces the importance of a formal performance review as part of any performance management system. For example, Jack Welch, former CEO of GE, has addressed this issue in many of his public appearances since he retired. At an appearance in front of an audience of about two thousand managers, he asked them if their organizations had integrity (Rogers, 2006). As was expected, a vast majority of managers, about 95 percent, raised their hands. Then he asked the same audience if their organization's leaders provide subordinates with honest and straightforward performance feedback. Only about 5 percent of the people raised their hands. Avoiding giving negative feedback is very dangerous because it conveys the message that mediocrity is acceptable and damages the morale of the top performers.

In most cases, the appraisal meeting is regarded as a review of the past, that is, what was done (results) and how it was done (behaviors). For example, a survey including more than 150 organizations in Scotland showed that performance management systems in more than 80 percent of organizations emphasize the past (Soltani, 2003). However, the appraisal meeting should also include a discussion of the employee's development progress as well as plans for the future. The conversation should include a discussion of goals and development plans that the employee will be expected to achieve over the period before the next review session. In addition, a good appraisal meeting includes information on what new compensation, if any, the employee may be receiving as a result of his or her performance. In short, the appraisal discussion focuses on the past (what has been done and how), the present (what compensation is received or denied as a result), and the future (goals to be attained before the upcoming review session).

In general, Grossman and Parkinson (2002) offer the following six recommendations for conducting effective performance reviews:

1. Identify what the employee has done well and poorly by citing specific positive and negative behaviors.
2. Solicit feedback from your employee about these behaviors. Listen for reactions and explanations.
3. Discuss the implications of changing, or not changing, the behaviors. Positive feedback is best, but an employee must be made aware of what will happen if any poor performance continues.
4. Explain to the employee how skills used in past achievements can help him or her overcome any current performance problems.
5. Agree on an action plan. Encourage the employee to invest in improving his or her performance by asking questions such as "What ideas do you have for ____?" and "What suggestions do you have for ____?"
6. Set up a meeting to follow up and agree on the behaviors, actions, and attitudes to be evaluated.

Stage 6: Performance Renewal and Recontracting

The final stage in the performance process is renewal and recontracting. Essentially, this is identical to the performance planning component. The main difference is that the renewal and recontracting stage uses the insights and information gained from the other phases. For example, some of the goals may have been set unrealistically high given an unexpected economic downturn. This would lead to setting less ambitious goals for the upcoming review period.

The performance management process includes a cycle that starts with prerequisites and ends with performance renewal and recontracting. The cycle is not over after the renewal and recontracting stage. In fact, the process starts all over again: there needs to be a discussion of prerequisites, including the organization's mission and strategic goals and the job's KSAs. Because markets change, customers' preferences and needs change, and products change, there is a need to continuously monitor the prerequisites so that performance planning, and all the subsequent stages, are consistent with the organization's strategic objectives. Recall that, in the end, one of the main goals of any performance management system is to promote the achievement of organization-wide goals. Obviously, if managers and employees are not aware of these strategic goals, it is unlikely that the performance management system will be instrumental in accomplishing the strategic goals.

Additional Issues to Consider Regarding Team Performance

A team is in place when two or more people interact dynamically and interdependently and share a common and valued goal, objective, or mission (Reilly & McGourty, 1998). Examples of teams range from a group of top managers working together face-to-face on an ongoing basis with the goal of achieving corporate goals to a group of programmers in India and the United States writing programming code that eventually will be put together as one software program. Teams do not have to be permanent, and team members do not have to be in the same geographical location. In fact, team members do not need to have ever met in person to be members of the same team. As long as they work together, need each other, and share common goals, they are considered to be members of the same team. Numerous organizations are structured around teams, including teams called autonomous work groups, process teams, and self-managing work teams (Scott & Einstein, 2001).

Organizations that choose to include a team component in their performance management system must provide answers to the following questions:

1. How do we assess relative individual contribution? How do we know the extent to which particular individuals have contributed to team results? How much has one member contributed in relation to the other members? Are there any slackers or free-riders on the team? Is everyone contributing to the same

extent, or are some members covering up for the lack of contribution of others?

2. How do we balance individual and team performance? How can we motivate team members so that they support a collective mission and collective goals? In addition, how do we motivate team members to be accountable and responsible individually? In other words, how do we achieve a good balance between measuring and rewarding individuals in relation to team performance?

3. How do we identify individual and team measures of performance? How can we identify measures of performance that indicate individual performance versus measures of performance that indicate team performance? Where does individual performance end and team performance begin? Finally, based on these measures, how do we allocate rewards to individuals versus teams?

We can use the same six stages described earlier and include team performance by following these six basic principles (Salas, Burke, & Fowlkes, 2006):

1. *Make sure your team is really a team.* As noted above, there are different types of teams. Before a team component is introduced in the performance management system, we need to make sure the organization has actual teams.

2. *Make the investment to measure.* Measuring team performance, as is the case with measuring individual performance, takes time and effort. The organization must be ready to make this investment for the measures to yield useful data.

3. *Define measurement goals clearly.* Defining how the data will be used (for example, administrative versus developmental purposes, or both) is a decision that must be taken before measures of team performance are designed. As is the case with individual-level data and discussed throughout the book, there are different variables that must be taken into account in relationship to the measures' purpose (for example, what will be the sources of data, how data will be collected, and so forth).

4. *Use a multi-method approach to measurement.* The measurement of team performance is complex. Thus, multiple methods and sources of data are often necessary.
5. *Focus on process as well as outcomes.* Behavioral/process-oriented measures as well as results are as useful for individual as for team performance management systems. Thus, serious consideration must be given to how both types of measures will be used within the context of managing team performance.
6. *Measure long-term changes.* Although short-term processes and results are easier to measure, it is important to also consider long-term measures of performance. Team performance must be sampled over a variety of contexts and also over time.

Consider each of the stages of the performance management process shown in Figure 1.1 and how they can be modified to accommodate a team component. First, regarding prerequisites, in addition to considering the team as a whole, we need to identify KSAs that will allow individuals to make a positive contribution to the team. These include not only KSAs related directly to the task at hand, such as a programmer who needs to have knowledge of the programming language. These are KSAs that are especially conducive to team performance, such as communication, decision making, collaboration, team leadership, and self-control (Cheng, Dainty, & Moore, 2005; Reilly & McGourty, 1998; Rousseau, Aubé, & Savoie, 2006). Regarding performance planning, this stage must include team-level considerations. Specifically, results expected of the team, behaviors expected of team members, and developmental objectives to be achieved by the team and its members. Regarding performance execution, team members need to be committed to goal achievement and should take a proactive role in seeking feedback from one another as well as from the supervisor (if there is one). In terms of performance assessment, all team members must evaluate one another's performance as well as the performance of the team overall. In addition, the supervisor evaluates the performance of each team member as well as that of the team as a whole. Finally, members from other teams also evaluate the performance of the team. This would apply only if members of other teams have first-hand experience with the performance of the team in question.

It is important to emphasize that three types of performance need to be assessed: (1) individual performance regarding task performance, which refers to the specific activities required by one's individual job, such as a programmer's ability write quality code; (2) individual performance regarding contextual performance, which refers to specific activities that contribute to team performance, such as team members cooperating with each other; and (3) team performance as a whole. Regarding the performance review, at least two meetings are needed. First, the supervisor meets with all members of the team together. The focus of this meeting is to discuss overall team performance, including results achieved by the team as a whole. Information for this meeting comes from team members evaluating their collective performance, other teams evaluating the team in question, and the supervisor's evaluation. Second, the supervisor meets with each team member individually. The focus of this meeting is to discuss how the individual's behaviors contributed to team performance. Information for this meeting comes from individuals evaluating their own performance, peer ratings of the individual's performance, and the supervisor's evaluation. Finally, the performance renewal and recontracting stage is identical to the performance planning stage; however, performance renewal and recontracting uses information gathered during the review period to make adjustments as needed. For example, some new key accountabilities and competencies may be included. Conversely, some goals may have to be adjusted either upward or downward.

In short, including team performance as part of the performance management system involves the same basic components that are included in individual performance. An important difference is that, in addition to individual performance, the system includes individual performance as it affects the functioning of the team, as well as the performance of the team as a whole.

Performance Management Best Practices

What do we know about performance management best practices? What are the features of a performance management system that are likely to produce good results in terms of individual, team, and organizational performance? The following characteristics are likely to allow a performance management system to be successful, and several of the chapters in this book describe these features in detail. Note that practical constraints may not allow for the implementation of all these features. The reality is that performance management systems are seldom implemented in an ideal way (McAdam, Hazlett, & Casey, 2005). For example, there may not be sufficient funds to deliver training to all people involved, supervisors may have biases in how they provide performance ratings, or people may be just too busy to pay attention to a new organizational initiative that requires their time and attention. However, as scientist-practitioners, we should strive to place a check mark next to each of these characteristics: the more features that are checked, the more likely it will be that the system will live up to its promise.

- *Strategic congruence.* The system should be congruent with the unit and organization's strategy. In other words, individual goals must be aligned with unit and organizational goals.
- *Thoroughness.* The system should be thorough regarding four dimensions. First, all employees should be evaluated (including managers). Second, all major job responsibilities should be evaluated (including behaviors and results). Third, the evaluation should include performance spanning the entire review period, not just the few weeks or months before the review. Finally, feedback should be given on positive performance aspects as well as those that are in need of improvement.
- *Practicality.* Systems that are too expensive, time-consuming, and convoluted will obviously not be effective. Good, easy-to-use systems (for example, performance data are entered via user-friendly software) are available for managers to help them make decisions. Finally, the benefits of using the system (for example, increased performance and job satisfaction) must be seen as outweighing the costs (for example, time, effort, expense).
- *Meaningfulness.* The system must be meaningful in several ways. First, the standards and evaluations conducted for each job function must be considered important and relevant. Second, performance assessment must emphasize only those

functions that are under the control of the employee. For example, there is no point in letting an employee know he or she needs to increase the speed of service delivery when the supplier does not get the product to him or her on time. Third, evaluations must take place at regular intervals and at appropriate moments. Because one formal evaluation per year is usually not sufficient, informal quarterly reviews are recommended. Fourth, the system should provide for the continuing skill development of evaluators. Finally, the results should be used for important administrative decisions. People will not pay attention to a system that has no consequences in terms of outcomes that they value.

- *Specificity.* A good system should be specific: it should provide detailed and concrete guidance to employees about what is expected of them and how they can meet these expectations.
- *Identification of effective and ineffective performance.* The performance management system should provide information that allows for the identification of effective and ineffective performance. That is, the system should allow for distinguishing between effective and ineffective behaviors and results, thereby also allowing for the identification of employees displaying various levels of performance effectiveness. In terms of decision making, a system that classifies or ranks all levels of performance, and all employees, similarly is useless.
- *Reliability.* A good system should include measures of performance that are consistent and free of error. For example, if two supervisors provided ratings of the same employee and performance dimensions, ratings should be similar.
- *Validity.* The measures of performance should also be valid. In this context, validity refers to the fact that the measures include all relevant performance facets and do not include irrelevant performance facets. In other words, measures are relevant (include all critical performance facets), not deficient (do not leave any important aspects out), and are not contaminated (do not include factors outside of the control of the employee or factors unrelated to performance). In short, measures include what is important and do not assess what is not important and outside of the control of the employee. For example, the gondolieri in the City of Venice (Italy) have had a performance

management system for about one thousand years (Johnston, 2005). Among other relevant performance dimensions, older versions of the performance management system required gondolieri to demonstrate their level of rowing skills and their ability to transport people and goods safely. These are clearly relevant dimensions. However, the system was contaminated because it included the following requirement: "Every brother shall be obliged to confess twice a year, or at least once and if after a warning, he remains impenitent, he shall be expelled . . . [from the gondolieri guild]."

- *Acceptability and fairness.* A good system is acceptable and is perceived as fair by all participants. Perceptions of fairness are subjective, and the only way to know whether a system is seen as fair is to ask the participants. We can ask about distributive justice, which includes perceptions of the performance evaluation received relative to the work performed, and perceptions of the rewards received relative to the evaluation received, particularly when the system is implemented across countries. For example, differences in perceptions may be found in comparing employees from more individualistic (for example, the United States) to more collectivistic (for example, Korea) cultures (Chang & Hahn, 2006). If a discrepancy is perceived between work and evaluation or between evaluation and rewards, then the system is likely to be seen as unfair. In addition, we can ask about procedural justice, which includes perceptions of the procedures used to determine the ratings as well as the procedures used to link ratings with rewards. Because a good system is inherently discriminatory, some employees will receive ratings that are lower than those received by other employees. However, we should strive to develop systems that are regarded as fair from both distributive and procedural perspectives because each type of justice perception leads to different outcomes. For example, a perception that the system is not fair from a distributive point of view is likely to lead to a poor relationship between employee and supervisor and lowered satisfaction of the employee with the supervisor. On the other hand, a perception that the system is unfair from a procedural point of view is likely to lead to decreased employee commitment toward the organization and increased intentions to leave (Erdorgan, 2002). One way to improve both distributive and procedural justice is to set clear rules that are applied consistently by all supervisors.

- *Inclusiveness.* Good systems include input from multiple sources on an ongoing basis. First, the evaluation process must represent the concerns of all the people who will be affected by the outcome. Consequently, employees must participate in the process of creating the system by providing input regarding what behaviors or results will be measured and how. Second, input about employee performance should be gathered from the employees themselves before the appraisal meeting (Cawley, Keeping, & Levy, 1998). In short, all participants must be given a voice in the process of designing and implementing the system. Such inclusive systems are likely to lead to more successful systems, including less employee resistance, improved performance, and fewer legal challenges (Elicker, Levy, & Hall, 2006).

- *Openness.* Good systems have no secrets. First, performance is evaluated frequently and performance feedback is provided on an ongoing basis. Therefore, employees are continually informed of the quality of their performance. Second, the appraisal meeting consists of a two-way communication process during which information is exchanged, not delivered from the supervisor to the employee without his or her input. Third, standards should be clear and communicated on an ongoing basis. Finally, communications are factual, open, and honest.

- *Correctability.* The process of assigning ratings should minimize subjective aspects; however, it is virtually impossible to create a system that is completely objective because human judgment is an important component of the evaluation process. When employees perceive an error has been made, there should be a mechanism through which this error can be corrected. Establishing an appeals process, through which employees can challenge what may be unjust decisions, is an important aspect of a good performance management system.

- *Standardization.* Good systems are standardized. This means that performance is evaluated consistently across people and time. To achieve this goal, the ongoing training of the individuals in charge of appraisals, usually managers, is a must.

- *Ethicality.* Good systems comply with ethical standards. Operationally, this means that the supervisor suppresses his or her personal self-interest in providing evaluations. In addition, the supervisor evaluates only performance dimensions for which she has sufficient information, and the privacy of the employee is respected (cf. Eddy, Stone, & Stone-Romero, 1999).

How do we know whether the performance management system is working? First, before implementing the system organization-wide, it is a good idea to pilot-test it because we can identify potential problems and glitches and we can take corrective action before the system is put in place. Pilot-testing consists of implementing the entire system, including all of its components, but only with a select group of people. Results are not recorded in employees' records. Instead, the goal is that the people participating in the pilot-test provide feedback on any possible problems and on how to improve the system.

For example, the pilot-test may reveal that the system was not as inclusive as originally intended and that only employees at or above a certain hierarchical position had participated in the process of designing the performance measurement instruments. Consequently, some employees felt that the system was not fair and that important performance dimensions were left out. So the system was not considered adequate regarding the inclusiveness, acceptability and fairness, and validity criteria. In short, the pilot-test provides useful information that allows for a fine-tuning of the system before it is implemented organization-wide. In this particular example, the instruments would be revised giving a voice to all employees.

When the testing period is over and the performance management system has been implemented organization-wide, it is important to use clear measurements to monitor and evaluate the system. In a nutshell, a decision needs to be made about how to evaluate the system's effectiveness, how to evaluate the extent to which the system is being implemented as planned, and how to evaluate the extent to which it is producing the intended results. As an example, the United States federal government takes the evaluation of performance management systems very seriously (Mulvaney, Zwahr, & Baranowski, 2006). Since the early 1990s, several laws have been passed that mandate federal agencies to develop a strategic plan, a performance plan, and a performance report. Although these initiatives concern agencies and not individuals, ultimately the performance of any agency depends on the performance of the individuals working in that unit. The net result of such laws as the Government Performance and Results Act is an increase in accountability and funding allocation based on performance. Thus, federal agencies are required to evaluate the relative efficiency of their various management techniques, including performance management systems.

Evaluation data should include reactions to the system and assessments of the system's operational and technical requirements. For example, a confidential survey could be administered to all employees asking about perceptions and attitudes about the system. This survey can be administered during the initial stages of implementation and then at the end of the first review cycle to find out whether there have been any changes. In addition, regarding the system's results, one can assess performance ratings over time to see what positive effects the implementation of the system is having. Finally, interviews can be conducted with key stakeholders, including managers and employees who have been involved in developing and implementing the performance management system (Harper & Vilkinas, 2005).

Several additional measures can be used on a regular basis to monitor and evaluate the system:

- *Number of individuals evaluated.* One of the most basic measures is to assess the number of employees who are actually participating in the system. If performance evaluations have not been completed for some employees, we need to find out who they are and why a performance review has not been completed.
- *Distribution of performance ratings.* An indicator of quality of the performance assessments is whether all or most scores are too high, too low, or clumped around the center of the distribution. This may indicate intentional errors such as leniency, severity, and central tendency. Distributions of performance ratings can be broken down by unit and supervisor to determine whether any trends exist regarding rating distortion and whether these

distortions are localized in particular units. Note that there may be exceptional units in which most employees are outstanding performers and units in which most employees are poor performers. This is the exception to the rule, however, and such distributions usually indicate intentional errors on the part of raters.

- *Quality of information.* Another indicator of quality of the performance assessments is the quality of the information provided in the open-ended sections of the forms. For example, how much did the rater write? What is the relevance of the examples provided?
- *Quality of performance discussion meeting.* A confidential survey can be distributed to all employees on a regular basis to gather information about how the supervisor is managing the performance discussion meetings. For example, is the feedback useful? Has the supervisor made resources available so the employee can accomplish the development plan objectives? How relevant was the performance review discussion to one's job? To what degree have development objectives and plans been discussed?
- *System satisfaction.* A confidential survey could also be distributed to assess the perceptions of the system's users, both raters and ratees. This survey can include questions about satisfaction with equity, usefulness, and accuracy.
- *Overall cost/benefit ratio.* A fairly simple way to address the perceived overall impact of the system is to ask participants to rate the overall cost/benefit ratio for the performance management system. This is a type of bottom-line question that can provide convincing evidence for the overall worth of the system. This perceived cost/benefit ratio question can be asked in reference to an individual (employee or manager), her job, and her organizational unit. Note that the perceived cost/benefit ratio may not be the same as the actual cost/ benefit ratio. However, as is the case with most organizational interventions involving people (Farmer & Aguinis, 2005), perceptions are crucial because they will determine the amount of support and resources to be allocated to the intervention.
- *Unit-level and organization-level performance.* Another indicator that the system is working well is provided by the measurement

of unit- and organization-level performance. Such performance indicators might be customer satisfaction with specific units and indicators of the financial performance of the various units or the organization as a whole. We need to be aware that it may take some time for changes in individual and group performance level to be translated into unit- and organization-level results. We should not expect results as soon as the system is implemented; however, we should start to see some tangible results at the unit level a few months after the system is in place.

Conclusion

In today's globalized, fast-paced, and interconnected world, it is relatively easy to gain access to the competition's technology and products. Thanks to the Internet and the accompanying high speed of communications, technological and product differentiation is no longer a key competitive advantage in most industries. For example, most banks offer the same types of products (for example, different types of savings accounts and investment opportunities). If a particular bank decides to offer a new product or service (for example, online banking), it will not be long until the competitors offer precisely the same product. As noted by James Kelley, performance management project leader at Idaho Power, "Technology is a facilitator, but not a guarantor, of effectiveness of efficiency of a company's workforce" (Generating buzz, 2006).

Organizations with motivated and talented employees offering outstanding service to customers are likely to pull ahead of the competition, even if the products offered are similar to those offered by the competitors. Customers want to get the right answer at the right time and they want to receive their products and services promptly and accurately. Only people can make these things happen and produce a sustainable competitive advantage. Performance management systems are key tools that can be used to transform people's talent and motivation into a strategic business advantage. Unfortunately, although 96 percent of HRM professionals report that performance management is their number one concern, fewer than 12 percent of HR executives and technology managers believe that their organizations have aligned strategic organizational priorities with employee performance (Workforce performance is top HR priority, 2005). Researchers in the fields of HRM and I/O psychology have the tools and skills to produce knowledge that will help improve the implementation of performance management systems (Aguinis & Pierce, 2008). To do so, however, we first need to expand our view of performance management so we go beyond performance appraisal and place PM within the broader organizational context. Also, we need to integrate PM with other HRM functions (for example, staffing, training, compensation, and succession planning) and conduct research on issues of concern to practitioners (Aguinis & Pierce, 2008). Such research has great potential in terms of closing the much discussed science-practice gap (Cascio & Aguinis, 2008a).

References

Addams, H. L., & Embley, K. (1988). Performance management systems: From strategic planning to employee productivity. *Personnel, 65,* 55–60.

Aguinis, H. (2009). *Performance management* (2nd ed.). Upper Saddle River, NJ: Pearson Prentice Hall.

Aguinis, H., & Kraiger, K. (2009). Benefits of training and development for individuals and teams, organizations, and society. *Annual Review of Psychology, 60,* 451–474.

Aguinis, H., Mazurkiewicz, M. D., & Heggestad, E. D. (2009). *Using web-based frame-of-reference training to decrease biases in personality-based job analysis: An experimental field study. Personnel Psychology, 62,* 405–438.

Aguinis, H., & Pierce, C. A. (2008). Enhancing the relevance of organizational behavior by embracing performance management research. *Journal of Organizational Behavior, 29,* 139–145.

Bass, B. M. (1974). The substance and the shadow. *American Psychologist, 29,* 870–886.

Baty, P. (2006, October 13). Bonus culture sweeps sector. *Times Higher Education Supplement.* Retrieval date: February 8, 2007, from LexisNexis™ Academic.

Bennett, W., Lance, C. E., & Woehr, D. J. (Eds.) (2006). *Performance measurement: Current perspectives and future challenges.* Mahwah, NJ: Lawrence Erlbaum Associates.

Berner, R. (2005, October 31). At Sears, a great communicator. *Business Week*. Available online at http://www.businessweek.com/magazine/content/05_44/b3957103.htm. Retrieval date: November 7, 2007.

Boswell, W. R., & Boudreau, J. W. (2000). Employee satisfaction with performance appraisals and appraisers: The role of perceived appraisal use. *Human Resource Development Quarterly, 11*, 283–299.

Brown, M., & Benson, J. (2005). Managing to overload? Work overload and performance appraisal processes. *Group & Organization Management, 30*, 99–124.

Cascio, W. F. (2006). Global performance management systems. In I. Bjorkman & G. Stahl (Eds.), *Handbook of research in international human resources management* (pp. 176–196). London, UK: Edward Elgar Ltd.

Cascio, W. F., & Aguinis, H. (2008a). Research in industrial and organizational psychology from 1963 to 2007: Changes, choices, and trends. *Journal of Applied Psychology, 93*, 1062–1081.

Cascio, W. F., & Aguinis, H. (2008b). Staffing 21st-century organizations. *Academy of Management Annals, 2*, 133–165.

Cawley, B. D., Keeping, L. M., & Levy, P. E. (1998). Participation in the performance appraisal process and employee reactions: A meta-analytic review of field investigations. *Journal of Applied Psychology, 83*, 615–633.

Chang, E., & Hahn, J. (2006). Does pay-for-performance enhance perceived distributive justice for collectivistic employees? *Personnel Review, 35*, 397–412.

Cheng, M., Dainty, A. R. J., & Moore, D. R. (2005). Towards a multidimensional competency-based managerial performance framework: A hybrid approach. *Journal of Managerial Psychology, 20*, 380–396.

Cleveland, J. N, & Murphy, R. E. (1989). Multiple uses of performance appraisal: Prevalence and correlates. *Journal of Applied Psychology, 74*, 130–135.

Dunnette, M. D. (1990). Blending the science and practice of industrial and organizational psychology: Where are we and where are we going? In M. D. Dunnette & L. M. Hough (Eds.), *Handbook of industrial and organizational psychology* (2nd ed., Vol. 1, pp. 1–27). Palo Alto, CA: Consulting Psychologists Press.

Dunning, D. (2004). *TLC at work: Training, leading, coaching all types for star performance*. Palo Alto, CA: Davies-Black.

Eddy, E. R., Stone, D. L., & Stone-Romero, E. F. (1999). The effects of information management policies on reactions to human resource information systems: An integration of privacy and procedural justice perspectives. *Personnel Psychology, 52,* 335–358.

Elicker, J. D., Levy, P. E., & Hall, R. J. (2006). The role of leader-member exchange in the performance appraisal process. *Journal of Management, 32,* 531–551.

Ellis, K. (2003). Developing for dollars. *Training, 40*(5), 34–38.

Ellis, K. (2004). Individual development plans: The building blocks of development. *Training, 41*(6), 20–25.

Erdogan, B. (2002). Antecedents and consequences of justice perceptions in performance appraisals. *Human Resource Management Review, 12,* 555–578.

Fandray, D. (2001, May). The new thinking in performance appraisals. Workforce Online. http://www.workforce.com/archive/feature/22/28/68/index.php?ht=selco%20selco. Retrieval date: November 7, 2007.

Farmer, S., & Aguinis, H. (2005). Accounting for subordinate perceptions of supervisor power: An identity-dependence model. *Journal of Applied Psychology, 90,* 1069–1083.

Fay, C. H. (coordinator) (2006, August). *Human resource vice presidents' concerns, human resource researchers' opportunities.* Professional Development Workshop delivered at the meeting of the Academy of Management, Atlanta, Georgia.

FMI Corporation. (2000, November 15). *Using performance reviews to improve employee retention: Contractor's business management report, 2,* Denver, Colorado.

Gabris, G. T., & Ihrke, D. M. (2001). Does performance appraisal contribute to heightened levels of employee burnout? The results of one study. *Public Personnel Management, 30,* 157–172.

Generating buzz: Idaho Power takes on performance management to prepare for workforce aging. (2006, June). *Power Engineering.* Retrieved February 14, 2007 from http://pepei.pennnet.com/articles/article_Display.cfm?Section=ARCHI&ARTICLE_ID=258477&VERSION_NUM=2&p=6.

Ghorpade, J., & Chen, M. M. (1995). Creating quality-driven performance appraisal systems. *Academy of Management Executive, 9,* 32–39.

Grossman, J. H., & Parkinson, J. R. (2002). *Becoming a successful manager: How to make a smooth transition from managing yourself to managing others* (pp. 142–145). Chicago: McGraw-Hill Professional.

Grote, D. (1996). *The complete guide to performance appraisal.* New York: American Management Association.

Hammonds, K. H. (2005, August). Why we hate HR. *Fast Company, 97.* http://www.fastcompany.com/magazine/97/open_hr.html. Retrieval date: November 7, 2007.

Harper, S., & Vilkinas, T. (2005). Determining the impact of an organisation's performance management system. *Asia Pacific Journal of Human Resources, 43,* 76–97.

Johnston, J. (2005). Performance measurement uncertainty on the Grand Canal: Ethical and productivity conflicts between social and economic agency? *International Journal of Productivity and Performance Management, 54,* 595–612.

Kikoski, J. F. (1999). Effective communication in the performance appraisal interview: Face-to-face communication for public managers in the culturally diverse workplace. *Public Personnel Management, 28,* 301–322.

LaChance, S. (2006). Applying the balanced scorecard. *Strategic HR Review, 5*(2), 5.

Latham, G. P. (2007). A speculative perspective on the transfer of behavior science findings to the workplace: "The times they are a-changin." *Academy of Management Journal, 50,* 1027–1032.

McAdam, R., Hazlett, S., & Casey, C. (2005). Performance management in the UK public sector: Addressing multiple stakeholder complexity. *International Journal of Public Sector Management, 18,* 256–273.

McHenry, J. (2007, April). *We are the very model.* Presidential address delivered at the meeting of the Society for Industrial and Organizational Psychology, New York.

Milliman, J., Nason, S., Zhu, C., & De Cieri, H. (2002). An exploratory assessment of the purposes of performance appraisals in North and Central America and the Pacific Rim. *Human Resource Management, 41,* 87–102.

Morgeson, F. P., Mumford, T. V., & Campion, M. A. (2005). Coming full circle: Using research and practice to address 27 questions about 360-degree feedback programs. *Consulting Psychology Journal: Practice and Research, 57,* 196–209.

Muchinsky, P. M. (2004). When the psychometrics of test development meets organizational realities: A conceptual framework for organizational change, examples, and recommendations. *Personnel Psychology, 57,* 175–209.

Mulvaney, R. R. H., Zwahr, M., & Baranowski, L. (2006). The trend toward accountability: What does it mean for HR managers? *Human Resource Management Review, 16,* 431–442.

Murphy, K. R., & Saal, F. E. (Eds.) (1990). *Psychology in organizations: Integrating science and practice.* Mahwah, NJ: Lawrence Erlbaum Associates.

Nankervis, A. R., & Compton, R. (2006). Performance management: Theory in practice? *Asia Pacific Journal of Human Resources, 44,* 83–101.

Pettijohn, L. S., Parker, R. S., Pettijohn, C. E., & Kent, J. L. (2001). Performance appraisals: Usage, criteria and observations. *Journal of Management Development, 20,* 754–781.

Rahman, S. A. (2006). Attitudes of Malaysian teachers toward a performance-appraisal system. *Journal of Applied Social Psychology, 36,* 3031–3042.

Reilly, R. R., & McGourty, J. (1998). Performance appraisal in team settings. In J. W. Smither (Ed.), *Performance appraisal: State of the art in practice* (pp. 245–277). San Francisco: Jossey-Bass.

Reyna, M., & Sims, R. R. (1995). A framework for individual management development in the public sector. *Public Personnel Management, 24,* 53–65.

Rogers, B. (2006). High performance is more than a dream—It's a culture. *T+D, 60*(1), 12.

Rousseau, V., Aubé, C., & Savoie, A. (2006). Teamwork behaviors: A review and an integration of frameworks. *Small Group Research, 37,* 540–570.

Rupp, D. E., & Beal, D. (2007). Checking in with the scientist-practitioner model: How are we doing? *The Industrial-Organizational Psychologist, 45*(1), 35–40.

Rynes, S. L., Colbert, A. E., & Brown, K. G. (2002). HR professionals' beliefs about effective human resource practices: Correspondence between research and practice. *Human Resource Management, 41,* 149–174.

Rynes, S. L., Giluk, T. L., & Brown, K. G. (2007). The very separate worlds of academic and practitioner periodicals in human resource management: Implications for evidence-based management. *Academy of Management Journal, 50,* 987–1008.

Salas, E., Burke, C. S., & Fowlkes, J. E. (2006). Measuring team performance "in the wild:" Challenges and tips. In W. Bennett, C. E. Lance, and D. J. Woehr (Eds.), *Performance measurement: Current perspectives and future challenges* (pp. 245–272). Mahwah, NJ: Lawrence Erlbaum Associates.

Schramm, J. (2006, June). *SHRM workplace forecast.* Alexandria, VA: Society for Human Resource Management.

Schwind, K. M. (2007). *The future of human resource management: Emerging HRM needs and tools.* Alexandria, VA: Society for Human Resource Management Foundation.

Scott, S. G., & Einstein, W. O. (2001). Strategic performance appraisal in team-based organizations: One size does not fit all. *Academy of Management Executive, 15,* 107–116.

Shippmann, J. S., Ash, R. A., Battista, M., Carr, L., Eyde, L. D., Hesketh, B., Kehoe, J., Pearlman, K., Prien, E. P., & Sanchez, J. I. (2000). The practice of competency modeling. *Personnel Psychology, 53,* 703–740.

Shore, T. H., Adams, J. S., & Tashchian, A. (1998). Effects of self-appraisal information, appraisal purpose, and feedback target on performance appraisal ratings. *Journal of Business and Psychology, 12,* 283–298.

Soltani, E. (2003). Towards a TQM-driven HR performance evaluation: An empirical study. *Employee Relations, 25,* 347–370.

The Baltimore Sun (2003, December 14). The best appraisals of workers can be simple; objectivity, feedback are important features, p. D6.

Thomas, S. L., & Bretz, R. D. (1994). Research and practice in performance appraisal: Evaluating employee performance in America's largest companies. *SAM Advanced Management Journal, 59*(2), 28–34.

Workforce performance is top HR priority. (2005). *T+D, 59*(7), 16.

CHAPTER 2

ALIGNING PERFORMANCE MANAGEMENT WITH ORGANIZATIONAL STRATEGY, VALUES, AND GOALS*

William A. Schiemann

In the 1970s, alignment was a major concern for me and thousands of drivers escaping for a weekend in Tijuana, Mexico. The road to Tijuana was pocked by hundreds of potholes that could swallow whole tires, leaving only two strategies: drive excruciatingly slowly while maneuvering circuitously around this moonscape, or step on the gas and hope to "hydroplane" over the impediments. Neither really worked, as evidenced by a plethora of auto alignment and body shops that dotted the entrance to Tijuana.

In the past two decades, the concept of "alignment" has taken off with fits and starts, much of the initial rally propelled by the quality movement of the 1980s and 1990s. Organizations like Volvo,

*I am much indebted to my entire research team, in particular Emily Smith, who provided stellar research assistance for this chapter. Other important support was provided by Cristina Matos, Bret Weinshank, Colette Tarsan, and Peter Tobia, without whose input, challenges, and editing this chapter would not have been possible.

American Express, Federal Express, WD-40 Company (WD-40), UPS, CIT, Caterpillar, and others have devoted considerable energy to ensure that there is alignment between their organizational visions on one hand, and important organizational outcomes such as employee productivity, retention and customer satisfaction on the other. And to ensure this, the leaders focus on a host of factors—organizational communications, balanced scorecards, employee goal setting and feedback, managing the right competencies and rewards, and achieving employee behaviors that give them an edge in strategy execution.

What is this phenomenon of alignment that seems to be so important to these and hundreds of other major organizations across the globe? And how does it help propel them to successful results? These questions will be the focus of this chapter, which addresses the strategic connection of performance management systems to organizational strategy and goals.

Alignment and Performance Management

So what is "alignment," and how is it related to performance? There have been many different definitions of alignment. Nadler and Tushman (1997) and their colleagues were among early proponents of what they called organizational congruence, extending some of the early work by Katz and Kahn (1966) showing the theoretical importance of the connections of organizational inputs, through-puts, and outputs into a cohesive framework for managing over-all organizational performance. Nadler and Tushman say, "Other things being equal, the greater the total degree of congruence, or fit, among various components, the more effective the organization will be," or essentially "the degree to which strategy, work, people, structure, and culture are smoothly aligned will determine the organization's ability to compete and succeed." Harold Leavitt at Stanford (Leavitt, 1965) and Jay Galbraith at MIT (Galbraith, 1977) were pursuing similar models of organizations that suggested there must be a good fit of various organizational components for the organization to be successful.

This early foundational thinking spawned other work such as that of Beer and his colleagues on organizational fit (1999), Kaplan and Norton on the balanced scorecard (1996), and Schiemann and Lingle on strategic alignment and performance measurement (1999). For example, Kaplan and Norton (1996) introduced the concept of the balanced scorecard in the 1990s to help show the importance and need to balance four different organizational elements: financial, external (for example, customers), internal learning, and operations. Schiemann and Lingle (1999) extended that thinking further by adding two additional scorecard elements (people and environment) and a way to connect the elements of the model in a cause-effect value chain (or value map). This was followed similarly by Kaplan and Norton with a related mapping model (2004). An example of the value mapping model will be illustrated later in the chapter. While holistic, many organizational applications of these models have focused on using the strategic scorecard (and/or strategy map) as a focal point for connecting business or functional goals to unit, team, or individual goals.

Another important use of the concept of alignment is with respect to the connectedness of interdependent business processes and work groups, often referred to as "horizontal alignment." Much of this work sprang out of the quality movement and process re-engineering. It frequently addresses the extent to which work units are effectively connected with each other to deliver high-value products or services to customers. Just as with the automobile, high alignment means less organizational wobble or drag.

For purposes of this chapter, alignment is defined as *the extent to which employees are similarly connected to or have a consistent line of sight to the vision and direction of the organization and its customers, often encapsulated within its current strategy.* This would include three elements (see Figure 2.1): (1) the line of sight of employees' behaviors and results with unit, department, and overall organizational goals; (2) the line of sight to customers' needs and expectations; and (3) behaviors that are in sync with the organization's brand.

Figure 2.1 Alignment.

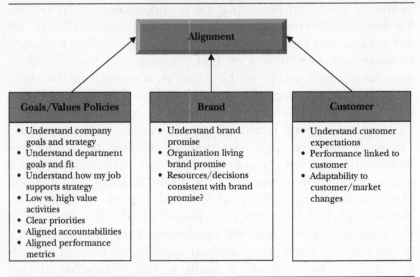

Goals/Values Policies	Brand	Customer
• Understand company goals and strategy • Understand department goals and fit • Understand how my job supports strategy • Low vs. high value activities • Clear priorities • Aligned accountabilities • Aligned performance metrics	• Understand brand promise • Organization living brand promise • Resources/decisions consistent with brand promise?	• Understand customer expectations • Performance linked to customer • Adaptability to customer/market changes

How Important Is Alignment?

In order to understand alignment most broadly, I examined published and unpublished research, the practices of some purportedly stellar organizations, and published accounts of alignment in action. To better understand the practitioner viewpoint, I also interviewed over forty executives from a variety of industries, geographies, and senior roles (for example, CEOs, COOs, CHROs, and VPs of learning) to obtain their viewpoints on alignment, ranging from the critical success factors to what works and doesn't work in practice.

While none of the senior executives I interviewed and researched regarding alignment thought it was easy, they all described its importance in various ways. GE assumes alignment as a prerequisite for success. Robert Nardelli, in speaking to the Executive Club of Chicago while he was CEO of Home Depot, said that alignment was his core responsibility, and he went on to explain that this responsibility extended to the alignment of strategy, values, customers, employees, and communities. Valerie Norton, the former first vice president of talent management for New York Life, said that it is hard to set a learning agenda if you don't have clear goals and an understanding of the competencies required to support them. At FedEx, alignment is viewed as critical to attracting the best employees at all levels of the company. "We find that we've got to treat our employees as customers," said Bill Margaritis, senior vice president of global communications at FedEx (Pellet, 2008).

Alignment is not just an issue for large corporations. For example, in the fewer than four hundred employee company WD-40, CEO Garry Ridge, says "Having people aligned with your vision and strategy is imperative." Henry S. Givray, chairman and CEO of SmithBucklin Corporation, the world's largest association management and professional services firm, stated that the most important alignment involves cultural values: "If people share the same values, their organization can pursue any strategy successfully." Connie Rank-Smith, VP of HR for Jewelers Mutual Insurance Company, told me that "Alignment is crucial regardless of firm size." At the time, they had about 185 employees.

Are these wishful views from the top? Do they have any research support? In our search for sound research in this area, we did not find many controlled studies. However, the research and case examples that we did find strongly supported the connection of alignment to important business and personal outcomes.

For example, in a climate study conducted by Six Seconds Institute for Organizational Performance, Pomeroy (2005) reports that research scientist Fiedeldey-Van Dijk found that 47 percent of the difference between low and high customer service scores is predicted by alignment, accountability, and collaboration. For retention, 43 percent of the difference in low versus high retention is predicted by alignment, leadership, and collaboration (Pomeroy, 2005).

A study of an Australian apparel firm (Kantabutra, 2007) found that organizational alignment was a clear factor in driving customer and employee satisfaction. Communication of the vision, coupled with employee empowerment, were important factors in creating employee satisfaction and a direct correlate of customer satisfaction.

Jack in the Box, the 40,000+ employee quick-serve restaurant group, found that alignment was significantly correlated (.38) with people's intention to leave (a good predictor of actual turnover), and that, in turn, was significantly correlated (.33 and .38, respectively) with sales and profit. Even more impressive were the connections of alignment with employees' discretionary effort (.75). And discretionary effort, despite other intervening variables, such as market differences, was significantly correlated (.36 and .44, respectively) with sales and profit.

In a study the Metrus Group conducted among fifty-six hospitals, alignment was significantly correlated (.23) with EBITDA (earning before interest, taxes, depreciation, and amortization). And in another study conducted by Metrus (Kostman & Schiemann, 2005) with the American Society of Quality that included approximately two thousand organizations, the authors found that, of the firms that were in the top quartile on alignment, 64 percent were in the top third in financial performance, compared to the bottom alignment quartile, of which only 41 percent were in the top one-third in financial performance.

Another way to look at alignment is in terms of the negative consequences of being misaligned. The list below summarizes a range of consequences of low alignment from theory, practice, research, and interviews with senior leaders.

The Business Impact of Low Alignment

- Confusing brand promise
- Many urgent but not important activities
- Non-competitive costs due to low productivity resulting from misdirected activities or talent
- Burnout—working hard, but not smart
- Overstaffing, to compensate for time lost on low-value activities
- Slow strategy execution
- Low teamwork; high conflict across interdependent units
- Talent loss
- Low customer satisfaction/loyalty

When alignment is low, there are many cited effects on employees, employers, and customers. One of the most insidious outcomes of low alignment is wasted time and energy. When individuals (or teams or units) are not well aligned with the vision, organizational goals, or what customers need and want, extra energy is required to reach the goals because time is often diverted to low- or no-value-added activities. This not only reduces the impact on results, but is also frustrating to the individuals (or teams) involved because they may feel that their efforts are not creating success—either a lack of accomplishment or that they are struggling to hit key goals after expending considerable effort. This often creates stress (related to work-life balance; perceptions of time wasted) and other dysfunctional outcomes, ranging from poor performance to turnover.

In fact, LifeCare Inc. found that the single biggest barrier to on-the-job productivity last year was being "overloaded" with work, according to a majority of workers polled by them (Leading productivity killers . . . , 2008): 39 percent of all workers said they simply did not have enough time to accomplish all of their assigned tasks. This overload is certainly a misalignment of goal expectations with employees' perceived ability to accomplish those objectives and/or a lack of clarity about job expectations, which 12 percent of their polled workers reported.

Furthermore, a survey by Watson Wyatt found that 48 percent of U.S. employers say stress caused by working long hours is affecting business performance. It can also harm retention rates. According to Watson Wyatt (2007/2008a), stress is the most frequently cited reason U.S. workers give for why they would leave a company; 40 percent cite it as one of their top reasons, but employers don't list stress among the five most common reasons they think workers leave (Watson Wyatt, 2007/2008b).

Hence, there is strong evidence that alignment can drive good or bad performance, and to listen to most of the leaders interviewed, it is a key factor for success, which raises the question: What drives high alignment?

What Drives Alignment?

Based on the literature review, case studies, and interviews with senior practitioners, we have identified seven important success factors that distinguish effectively aligned organizations. For each success factor, I will share what was learned from a combination of published research, practitioner experience, identified best practices, and available survey research data. Because of the proprietary nature of many survey research practices, I will draw on a large database from the Metrus Group, which contains questions related to alignment and performance management. The seven drivers of high alignment include:

1. A clear, agreed-on vision and strategy
2. Translation of the vision and strategy into clear, understandable goals and measures
3. Acceptance, or passion for, the vision, strategy, goals among those who are implementing them
4. Clarity regarding individual roles and requirements in supporting the strategic goals—and the extent to which these have been effectively cascaded and interlinked across the organization
5. Sufficient capabilities (talent, information, and resources) to deliver the behaviors needed to reach the goals
6. Clear, timely feedback on goal attainment and the drivers of those goals
7. Meaningful incentives to encourage employees to develop or deploy sufficient capabilities to achieve the goals

Furthermore, there was considerable evidence from a variety of sources that culture is also an important overall ingredient in the alignment recipe. Because of its more general influence, I will address culture after addressing the seven more specific drivers.

One interesting discovery is that these elements do not appear to be compensatory, although I did not find any strong research studies that focused on all of these elements. But from a logical standpoint, it is hard to imagine that excelling on feedback alone, for example, yet not understanding the strategy, will help drive performance (except perhaps in the wrong direction). In an informal study we conducted over a series of Conference Board audiences (mostly VPs and directors) regarding the above elements, we found that each of the individual success factors was not very predictive of managers' ratings of how well their employees understood their business strategies (see Figure 2.2).

**Figure 2.2 Why Strategies and Behavior Disconnect:
Percentage of Rater Agreement.***

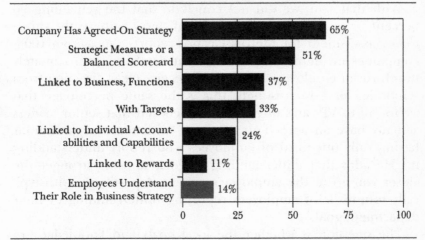

*The percentages represent the cumulative agreement of raters for each element and for the ones above that element.

But interestingly, when we look at the *cumulative* agreements that their organizations did a good job of each of the above elements, we could accurately account for their ratings of employees' understanding of their business strategy. For example, while many of the success factors (for example, agreed-on strategy and rewards linked to performance) were present in one-quarter to two-thirds of the respondents, only 14 percent of organizations reported that their employees had a good understanding of their strategy and direction. So we looked at the cumulative knockout effect, and it helped to explain this finding. For example, if only two-thirds of VPs and directors said their senior leadership teams agreed on the business strategy, we took that as an upper limit for how many organizations could have employees who then understand the strategy. Of those organizations with senior agreement, which of those had done a good job of translating it to measurable objectives, of cascading it, of setting clear goals, of rewarding employees and so forth? When you look at it that way, only 11 percent of the organizations have all of the above factors working for them to create a clear line of sight from employees to the strategy. This number is quite close to the 14 percent who reported that their employees really understand the strategy and its implications for them.

With that said, we did not conclude that the remaining 90 percent or so were flying totally blind. Jerry Seibert, the director of assessment for Metrus Group, reports that across 100+ companies in Metrus Group's current database, approximately two-thirds of employees believe they receive clear direction from senior leaders—interestingly, this is the same percentage that we found of VPs and directors who believed that senior leaders actually have an agreed-on strategy—"with some organizations having only one-third of employees who report understanding it." He adds that understanding of goals appears stronger the closer you go to the employee's unit or department, with typically four-fifths of employees reporting understanding of their department goals.

The question is whether the local goals and knowledge are highly aligned with senior leadership or not. In many cases, goals are set based on past performance expectations, reactions to market and management demands, or a "best try" basis. But that is a far cry from truly understanding and engaging in the organization's future mission. In our interviews, we have heard too many managers lament that their people are "working hard but not smart," sadly in a context of concerns about sufficient future talent.

We concluded from this and other cases that these seven drivers must be part of an integrative package, as cases such as WD-40, GE and SmithBucklin (to be discussed later) have demonstrated.

Let's take a look at each of these success factors:

1. A Clear, Agreed-On Vision and Strategy

While this may seem self-evident, reality suggests that it isn't. Despite its discussed importance, there is often little agreement on what vision is and how it should be formulated. Vision is frequently confused with or combined with mission, goals, strategy, values, and organizational philosophy (Kantabutra, 2007). Our research with over five hundred VPs and directors from Conference Board audiences suggests that nearly one-third of organizations (reported by VPs and above) do not have a clearly agreed-on strategy.[1] How can this be the case?

The reality, based on our interview results, is that many organizations have multiple strategies lodged in the minds of different executives. For example, a number of years ago I was asked by the CEO of a major media giant to assess how well his executives were executing their new strategy. Sadly, I had to report back that I had heard eleven different strategies articulated—and there were only fourteen members on the senior leadership team!

While some organizations do not have a strategy, the more insidious problem is that strategy often means different things, depending on which seat you occupy at the executive table. As one interviewed leader said, "If they are not on the same page, the ripple effect throughout the organization is enormous." If top management is not in agreement on the strategy and goals, then alignment throughout the organization is not possible.

How does this happen? In addition to the problem of competing strategies, our interviews and case histories also reveal that part of the confusion stems from the way in which strategy is addressed at the top level. One retired financial services executive put it succinctly, "The leadership team agrees on broad strategic principles at the 50,000-foot level, but often fails to drill down to the level at which real tradeoffs need to be made."

In our strategic advisory work, for example, we have seen many leadership groups endorsing statements such as "We will be the most admired brand" or "We will be the most customer intimate," but then fail to drill down to the level at which resource tradeoffs and tactical priorities occur. Does customer intimacy mean that the company will forego some less customer-intimate, but more cost-effective, processes? Does "most admired" mean by customers, employees, communities, Wall Street, or all of the above? And how will that be operationalized? The failure to effectively drill down far enough results in functional silos defining their own strategies that are aligned in name but not necessarily in meaning.

2. Translation of the Vision and Strategy into Clear, Understandable Goals and Measures

While agreement is a necessary first step, a great vision or strategy that is locked in the CEO's drawer is not likely to have much impact on behaviors or impact on customers or competitors.

That is exactly what we found when we interviewed leaders for a global cement company. Members of the leadership team described a clandestine meeting in the Pocono Mountains at which the strategy was revealed by the CEO. Despite having little input to the strategy, team members were expected to go out and execute it. Only one small problem. They needed great memories because after the get-away meeting, the strategy was literally locked in the CEO's drawer. When we confronted the CEO about this, he pulled out the key, opened the drawer, and held up the strategy, proudly refuting our challenge that his company might not have one. He bellowed, "We have a great strategy, but we cannot let anyone see it." We asked why, and he spouted, "If employees know, the unions will know it, and then our competitors will know it." When we asked him how it would be effectively executed if people—especially his top team—did not understand it, he replied, "I have divided elements of it on a 'need to know' basis." This approach hardly ensures that the entire team is rowing in the same direction.

The employees of this company are not alone. According to Ventana Research (Smith, 2008), only about half (52 percent) of companies do a good job of aligning departmental plans with overarching corporate goals. The "keep them in the dark" approach also flies in the face of increasing cultural expectations of transparency and candor. Henry S. Givray, the chairman and CEO of SmithBucklin, the world's largest association management and professional services firm, said it best. "Transparent communication and decision making with employees and with client organizations inspire engagement and trust—which are the building blocks for achieving sustainable growth and success in any service business." While the "secret strategy" approach of the cement mogul prevented his employees from divulging the strategy to competitors, it also prevented them from playing a meaningful role in implementation.

When examined from the viewpoint of the average employee, a look at the Metrus Group database revealed that, on average, only 66 percent of employees in 119 firms give management favorable ratings on clearly communicating the vision, direction, or strategy of the organization. And these numbers are probably more favorable than the total population of firms, given that these 119 organizations represent those that conduct regular surveys of their people—arguably a more enlightened cohort than the average company.

Some companies have made considerable progress in communicating the overall strategy. For example, Volvo with its 92,000 global employees has grown from a baseline level of 67 percent to 84 percent of employees understanding their overall strategy and direction (Nordblom, 2008). Much of this was attributed to a concerted effort to increase the capabilities of their middle managers through more effective communications tools. Despite these strengths, they state that their "key challenge is clearly the ability of supervisors to translate and break down overall strategic objectives into goals and targets that are meaningful to each individual."

3. Acceptance, or Passion for, the Vision, Strategy, Goals Among Those Who Are Implementing

While understanding an agreed-on strategy is a foundation, people must also embrace it. We recently completed an employee survey for a New York headquartered global financial services organization. We tested for exactly this. Employees in North America, Europe, and Asia all demonstrated increased understanding of the business strategy—a key problem noted on the prior year's survey. And while North America largely accepted and supported the vision, employees in Europe did not. Essentially, they got it, but didn't embrace it. From the performance results of Europe, it was clear that this organization had the minds but not the hearts of its European employees.

Henry S. Givray, chairman and CEO of SmithBucklin, put it succinctly: "We could not have achieved the incredible results that we have without securing both the hearts and the minds of our employees." When we were doing work for Wal-Mart a few years ago, a woman came up to me seeking a private meeting. When she cornered me in the hall, she described how she had worked at Nordstrom in the past and how "they really understand service." She went on to describe how she was building a covert operation of "service trekkies" who would help employees of Wal-Mart eventually "get it." While she was obviously passionate about her mission, it was not the strategy of Wal-Mart. Their strategy is built on operational excellence leading to low prices; in contrast, Nordstrom's has been built on outstanding service leading to customer intimacy. In Mr. Givray's view of mind and heart, she would be labeled as "right person—wrong fit."

4. Clarity Regarding Individual Roles and Requirements in Supporting the Strategic Goals—And the Extent to Which They Have Effectively Cascaded and Interlinked Goals Across the Organization

This is an area that has been well researched, with some outstanding early work done by Locke and Latham (1990) that demonstrated some critical components that drive performance. One of those factors was goal clarity. Early experiments concluded that those with clearer and more difficult (but attainable) goals had better performance results.

But clear goals alone are not enough. In order to deliver high organizational performance, human resource management practices have to be aligned to corporate strategy (Nel et al., 2004; Thomson, 1999). In setting goals, "The most effective practice is to establish a hierarchy of goals where each level supports goals directly relevant to the next level, ultimately working toward the organization's strategic direction and critical priorities" (Pulakos, 2004).

Research also reveals that two other factors are important: employee acceptance of goals and the number of goals. Pulakos (2004), for example, states that "Goals should be set in no more than three areas" based on her review of goal-setting research. Too many goals at once impede success.

It is also important to periodically (for example, quarterly) reexamine and update goals when changing circumstances demand. Flexibility is a key ingredient of successful goal setting. Goal setting also includes the development of an action plan to accomplish goals. This holds the employees accountable for both accomplishing goals and how they go about doing so.

The trend is away from a more directive mode—"Here are your goals"—to a more collaborative goal-setting process. What is evolving is the management of performance through value contribution—the amount of value the subordinate's performance adds to the overall organizational performance. The traditional way of managing performance by measuring whether the employee has achieved prescribed objectives seems no longer adequate.

In reviews of employee survey databases at Metrus Group for the past twenty years, goal setting is more effectively implemented than feedback. In 104 organizations that we studied recently, 76 percent of employees agreed that their performance goals are clear. In reviews of a number of variations in how this question is worded, an average of 70 to 78 percent of employees believe that they have clear goals. However, there are a number of organizations in which fewer than 50 percent of employees say they have goals, or goals that are linked to the department or company goals.

In contrast, when they were asked about feedback and coaching, the favorable responses are lower. For example, for the question "I receive regular feedback from my supervisor," 67 percent of employees in sixty-nine database organizations agree; however, when employees are asked if they received feedback that helps them improve performance, the percent who agree drops to 64 percent, with organizations scoring as low as 38 percent.

A contrasting viewpoint (Clutterbuck, 2008), not yet sufficiently tested, argues that too much emphasis is placed on early, rigid goal setting and that, in reality, business (and life planning) is too complex for those goals to remain fixed. Instead, they advocate a more evolutionary approach to goal setting, that allows goals to "jell" over time while also incubating more commitment from the goal owner. The challenge with this approach might be the duration of the time in which the organization is adrift and unaligned. This approach might be most effective for organizations requiring frequent changes in goals or for units in which innovation is a dominant requirement, and early structure might hinder innovative outcomes.

5. Sufficient Capabilities (Talent, Information, and Resources) to Deliver the Behaviors Needed to Reach the Goals

While alignment captures the notion of focus, it will be difficult to deliver on those goals (and their measurable targets) without developing the right talent (for example, knowledge, skills, and abilities), information, and resources. This is the fuel in the alignment engine that enables the most effective priorities—behaviors, actions, initiatives—to be successfully carried out. General Electric provides compelling evidence that such investment in human capital pays off (McNamara, 1999).

A great example of the importance of sufficient capabilities was driven home to me during an engagement with a regional U.S. bank.

> The bank that I worked with had developed an exciting new strategy to gain an increased share of its customers' wallets—the percentage of their customers' total financial services spend across the bank's range of financial services. The approach was to consolidate customer contacts to one loan officer in each branch, so he or she could become more customer intimate, truly understanding the breadth and depth of individual customers' needs. This would enable the bank to customize their offerings for each customer, which would make this bank more valuable to those it served. For the bank, it offered opportunities to cross-sell products with minimal additional expense. Focus groups with loan officers and customers said it was a great idea.
>
> After extensive training of loan officers and much hoopla, the initial rollout fizzled. Customers actually threatened to leave, as did "red in the face" loan officers. While an important part of capabilities is talent, it was information that sank the ship. When customers came into a branch, the IT system would not allow loan officers access to information on bank relationships that were initiated at other branches. Customers wanting to discuss small business loans, equity lines, mortgages, or other business with an officer could not do so without taking a time-wasting detour both to the past and to multiple locations.

Having high capabilities requires having not only the right talent or skills—the "usual suspects" when things go awry—but also the right information and resources at the moment of truth for the customer.

6. Clear, Timely Feedback on Goal Attainment and on the Drivers of Those Goals

As discussed above under goal setting, clear goals are not enough to achieve the best performance. Research has shown that those who receive more frequent and specific performance feedback and coaching are better performers than those who do not (Locke

& Latham, 1990; London, 2002). These researchers have shown that feedback that is closer to the performance itself is most effective. Some organizations that are quite good at setting goals are often weak on performance feedback or coaching. This is often a function of the formality of the goal-setting process versus the informality of the feedback process. While roles such as sales representative often have structured feedback (often monthly or weekly with attendant rewards), other roles have feedback that falls short of the principles of good feedback. Such feedback:

• Comes late in the performance cycle, well after people are invested in their performance or at a stage when changes will not have much effect on results
• Is diffuse and subjective
• Is primarily a judgment, dependent on the views of different stakeholders
• Is provided in a context of other motivators (such as financial rewards)
• Conflicts with the perception of the person whose performance is being evaluated

DeNisi and Kluger (2000) elaborate on some of the reasons why feedback is not as effective as often assumed. And, according to Du Plessis, Beaver, and Nel (2006), providing feedback and coaching at quarterly reviews during the year is better than surprising employees with shocking performance ratings at the end of the year when it is too late for any corrective action. Nearly all of the research and customary wisdom suggest that the appraisal and reviews should be conducted in a non-threatening manner and that continuous discussion rather than an infrequent formal review is more effective. While historical wisdom suggested that the conversation should focus on gaps and developmental activities to close the gaps, others such as Buckingham and Coffman (1999) suggest that the conversation instead should be focused on leveraging strengths. Their position is that individuals rarely are willing or able to close talent gaps.[2]

DeNisi and Griffin (2001) report that most managers are unhappy with various facets of performance appraisals and therefore performance management; nevertheless, they still agree that such appraisals are very important. They provide a benchmark for organizations to better assess the quality of their recruiting and selection processes to recruit only the most appropriate employees. They also play an important role in training and development to help employees to improve their performance.

7. Meaningful Incentives to Encourage Employees to Develop or Deploy Sufficient Capabilities to Achieve the Goals

There has been considerable research conducted on reward and incentive systems, from basic operant conditioning experiments with piece rate payouts to more holistic reward systems like Scanlon plans that reward the collective accomplishments of groups of employees, originally developed to increase productivity in manufacturing plants. While there has been considerable focus on individual incentive and rewards systems, others argue that linking compensation to a company's performance is beginning to make sense for more and more businesses (Gibson, 1995). A compensation system based on enterprise success allows everyone to share the organizational success and see how their performance contributes to the whole (Fitzgerald, 1995).

Rewards in various forms—bonus plans, recognition, the job itself, and incentive systems—have all been shown to be more or less effective in different circumstances. Much of their effectiveness has been contingent on the ability to link individual or team performance to meaningful rewards and to provide those rewards in a timely fashion.

Rewards have been shown to be more effective when administered close to performance. Sales positions are notorious for tightly linking pay to performance. It should also be said, however, that sales individuals may value pay and incentive systems more than some other groups of employees, such as research and development.

When employees believe in the performance measures and accept the reward systems, then their performance can be enhanced. However, critics say that merit plans often have many defects and that employees are often skeptical that pay is really linked to performance (De Cieri et al., 2003; DeNisi & Griffin

2001; McGinty & Hanke, 1989; Meehan, 1992). And to make matters worse, Longenecker, Sims, and Gioia (1987) provide evidence of deliberate distortion or manipulation for political or other purposes.

Much of the work of Hackman and Oldham (1980) focused on the job itself as a reward, and appropriately they set out to research the critical factors that drive more rewarding jobs, such as task variety or complexity. While there has been much research in this area, often conflicting, it is fair to say that the job itself can be highly rewarding for some groups of employees and certainly more so for certain individuals. This means that organizations that are able to offer more flexible, tailored-to-the-individual reward packages are more likely to reap the benefits of the reinforcing effect of rewards on performance.

Another issue of debate is the level of specificity of the goals and rewards. While Locke and others argue that the more specific one is in identifying the specific behaviors and results desired, the better the chances are of seeing those results; still it begs the question of whether the organization really understands all of the specific behaviors that are needed to achieve broader, more strategic results, such as better cost of goods sold, profitability, and other broader organizational outcomes.

A few years ago, in working with a global medical diagnostics firm, we observed a phenomenon of sales plummeting in December, causing this firm to miss forecasts repeatedly. When we conducted focus groups with sales reps, the phenomenon was easy to understand. The reward system only paid handsomely for target results; there were minimal incentives for extra achievements. This resulted in salespeople holding back their closes until the beginning of the next year, thus getting a head start on their next payout cycle. The company got what it rewarded, not what it wanted at the broader financial level.

Recognition was another frequently mentioned component of the entire reward structure. In looking at employee survey results from both the Metrus and publicly available databases over the past thirty years, I found that recognition is often rated as important to employees, but appears to be underutilized in many organizations. The average organization in the Metrus database obtains only 46 percent endorsement of the question: "I am regularly thanked or recognized when I do a good job." A number of organizations scored lower than 30 percent on this item, while some firms show scores as high as 79 percent favorable. This form of reward scores lower than financial rewards (typically 50 to 60 percent favorable) and the job itself (typically 70 to 80 percent favorable). Hillgren and Cheatham (2000) identify important steps required to effectively link rewards to objectives.

Impact of Culture

In launching the discussion of these seven key success factors, I previously noted that culture has been identified as a more general or foundational driver of alignment and performance by a number of leaders interviewed, in particular among a few of the most successful firms. Henry S. Givray, chairman & CEO of SmithBucklin, was perhaps the most vocal about the criticality of the "right" culture. When he thinks about alignment, he thinks first about the alignment of people with values. "While the mission and goals may be the 'brains' or rational side of alignment, a company's cultural values are the 'heart' of its long-term success and endurance." He was quick to point out that people who are not aligned on values will have difficulty working together on any mission. But "even executives who have different operating styles can overcome those differences if they share the same vision and values."

Garry Ridge, the CEO of WD-40, is also passionate about culture. He speaks and lives by the values he espouses. He answers his own phone, returns e-mails in twenty-four hours (usually much faster from my experience), offers a daily e-mail thought to all employees (always upbeat and inspirational), provides an update on the business weekly, and is ready to address any violations of cultural norms quickly. According to others in the organization, he sets the standard and does not expect employees to do anything that he would not hold himself accountable for. The company's performance management system is solidly based on values of shared accountability for results, teamwork, open communication, and action. Managers also share accountability for bringing up new employees to top performance levels. WD-40's incentive systems and high revenue-to-employee ratio (low overhead) require that each employee pull his or her weight.

WD-40's corporate values (see below) were employee-generated through a process that engaged many employees. The senior team also generated a set of overarching principles that govern how employees should behave, reducing the need for many detailed and narrow rules and policies. When difficult situations occur, or decisions are made, the leadership team uses the principles as a template to ensure that action is consistent with values.

WD-40 Company Corporate Values

- We value doing the right thing.
- We value creating positive lasting memories in all of our relationships.
- We value making it better than it is today.
- We value succeeding as a team while excelling as individuals.
- We value owning it and passionately acting on it.
- We value sustaining the WD-40 economy.

The success factors that have been discussed here represent the biggest issues that this author has seen from research and practice, but there are many others covered in a variety of reviews (DeNisi & Kluger, 2000; Smither, 1998), as well as in articles conveying the how-to steps of creating and using a performance management system (Beatty, Baird, Schneier, & Shaw, 1995; Cardy, 2003; Fisher, 1997; Grote, 1996; Mohrman, Resnick-West, & Lawler, 1989; Weatherly, 2004), although many focus most specifically on the performance appraisal process.

Let us now take a look at the entire process of linking organizational vision, strategy, and goals to behaviors.

Outreach Airlines: From Strategy to Results

I have selected a combination of two U.S. airlines, Southwest and Continental, to illustrate how these seven elements, as well as culture, come together.[3]

Clear, Agreed-On Strategy

When Southwest decided to challenge the historical airline business model, it identified several strategic assumptions or pillars (see Figure 2.3) that, if executed well, would allow the company to outmaneuver long established rivals, resulting in greater profitability. Three of those pillars included:

- Leveraging of aircraft—a major cost in the airline business— more effectively than their competitors by creating faster turnaround of planes, operating from less congested airports, and standardizing repair and management of aircraft by utilizing all Boeing 737s
- Creating a lean, productive, and flexible workforce, partly through high ownership programs and flexible union contracts
- Reducing ticket costs by avoiding the travel agents usage and on-line vendors

These pillars represent the unique value proposition of the business. The test, of course, is in the execution. The pillars needed to be understood and supported by employees (and suppliers) at all levels.

Figure 2.3 Airline Strategy Pillars.

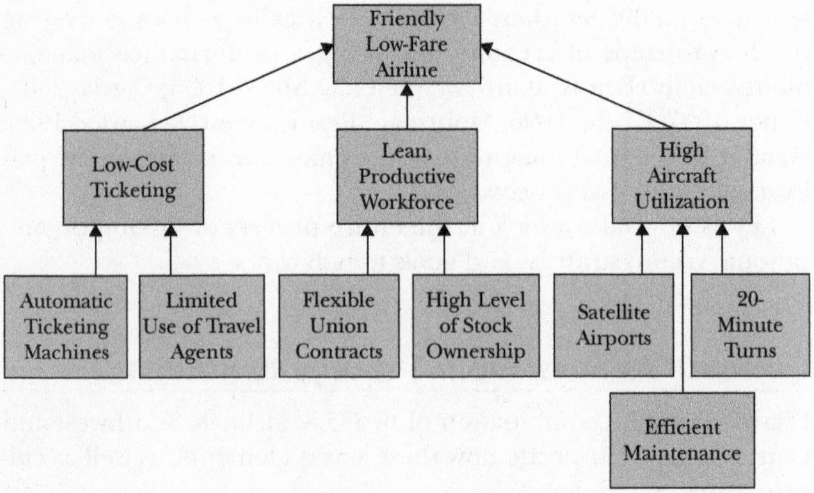

Translating Strategy to Measures

Whether it is the strategy of Southwest, Continental, or Singapore Airlines, successful organizations translate their strategies into a critical few areas that must be managed well. Kaplan and Norton (1996) and Schiemann and Lingle (1999) have demonstrated the importance of using balanced or strategic scorecards that capture the critical strategic results and drivers (for example, market share, on-time performance, high productivity) that reflect the value proposition—the strategic pillars—of the business, as well as the measures of those concepts. Measures provide a quantitative way to determine how much of a particular concept (for example, on-time flights) is occurring; targets provide a desired amount of that concept (for example, 85 percent on time). While measures in general can be motivating in the short term, targets provide more focus and sustainable energy, especially if they are stretch targets over more than a single budget cycle (Schiemann & Lingle, 1999).

In the airline example, pillars such as those shown in Figure 2.3 can be more fully developed into scorecard maps (see Figure 2.4) that capture the value proposition of the business. Typically, these scorecards (and maps) contain the critical financial, customer, operational, employee, community, and environmental (for example, regulatory safety) factors that are essential to implement the pillars. Schiemann and Lingle (1999) discuss the process and roles of consultants and leadership teams in creating such maps in their book *Bulls-eye, Hitting Your Strategic Targets Through High-Impact Measurement.* Says John Lingle: "The process is not very time-consuming; but it requires strategic thinking and a good cause-effect mindset." He has honed his process to convert a good strategy into a scorecard and map in about one to two days of time with the leadership team. "Of course," says Lingle, "this assumes that the leadership team has a clearly defined strategy. Otherwise, we have to back up and cover basics."

The benefits shown by Schiemann and Lingle (1999) and Kaplan and Norton (2004) of such maps are that they display the relationships of the strategic concepts, including both strategic results and drivers of those results (often referred to as critical success factors). For example, "high return on capital invested"

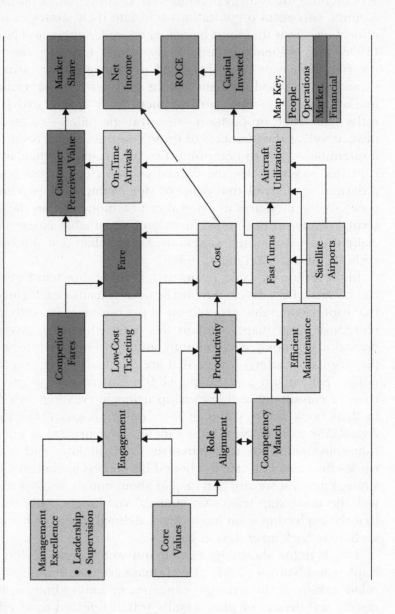

Figure 2.4 Strategic Value Map.

(ROCI) in Figure 2.4 represents a desired result, while faster turnaround of aircraft, on-time performance, and maintenance that allows the planes to stay in the air more are drivers of ROCI. In Figure 2.4 you can see the cause-effect link, with downstream results displayed on the right and upstream drivers displayed to the left, and the expected cause-effect connections shown by the arrows connecting the different elements.

Each of the elements in the model has a corresponding measure. For example, on-time performance could be measured by the time the plane leaves the gate against the published departure time, by the "wheels down" time or the gate arrival time against the published arrival time, or other possibilities. The important thing is that everyone understands what "on time" means, and when defined clearly, measures provide the specificity needed to describe what "on time" means, how it will be assessed, what current performance (baseline) looks like, what future success should look like (targets), and who is accountable for making that happen.

The advantage of identifying these scorecard elements is that this model provides a blueprint and rallying point for performance. In Gordon Bethune's case, one reason Continental Airlines went *From Worst to First* was the strong commitment to on-time performance. He and his leadership team believed that almost all employees could rally around the on-time goal because so many different roles had an impact on it: logistics, pilots, flight attendants, gate agents, maintenance, and baggage handlers, among others. This measure served to unify for the different functional groups that were essential to good performance.[4]

Cascading the Goals

The next step is making these goals relevant (understandable and meaningful) to functional roles, such as gate agents. Lingle again cautions, "Regardless of the function, the internal team that guides the cascade process must have good strategic thinking and measurement skills, as well as a level of influence in the organization." This helps middle managers and functional people to quickly understand what the scorecard means to the organization and to them. Few organizations can afford to have employees engaged in protracted debates over measures.

Figure 2.5 shows the current (baseline) and target performance for on-time performance that represented success for the airline. It also shows some of the roles that can influence that performance. Gate agents, for example, have four roles in Figure 2.5 that might influence on-time performance, such as check-in timeliness or boarding.

Boarding is one of the most important tasks of a gate agent. Figure 2.5 shows the impact of potential improvements in boarding speed (in this case from 37 to 25 minutes) on important outcomes such as customer satisfaction and retention and operational costs. To accomplish this, the gate agents might need to negotiate effectively with customers with connection problems or manage an overbooking situation. It is almost always possible to use a Pareto analysis[5] to identify the critical few roles or tasks that will have the largest impact on on-time performance. This enables gate agents to focus on the factors that, if improved, would have the greatest impact on a key role in achieving higher on-time performance.

Figure 2.5 Linking Strategic Scorecard to Accountabilities.

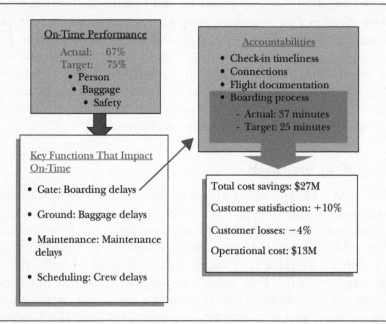

Competencies to Support the Strategy

Even if gate agents do play a critical role in on-time performance, they must have certain competencies that are related to those roles, especially the most important tasks in those roles. For example, negotiating skills are one of the most important skills because weak negotiators (and communicators) can waste a lot of time with a few customers who can detract from the boarding process. Planning skills are another competency that can play a big role. Gate agents who are better able to prepare for the flight (special requests, handicap needs, incoming flight delays) will be better able to expedite boarding when the opportunity avails itself. As you can see in Table 2.1, Agent 004 has better competency matches (either meeting or exceeding the levels desired for this role) to the Target Profile than does Agent 008.

Table 2.1 also shows how the effective prioritization of those competencies can be used in the selection of high-potential performers. For example, the flight attendant applying for a gate agent role might be a better prospect than the logistics specialist because the competency profile is better matched (for example, negotiating, communications) to the target profile than that of the logistics specialist.

Finally, Rewards Are Critical

While the figures in the table above show the linkage of the overall goals with key roles (gate agent) and competencies, they do not show the behind-the-scenes challenge of securing understanding and motivation required to support those goals. Gordon Bethune addressed the importance of establishing urgency and credibility during his turnaround at Continental Airlines. He met with union leaders, employees and managers, and banks, among others, to convince them of the importance of changes being made, such as the criticality of on-time performance. He had to convince them that it made sense economically (to banks and employees alike), and that they would be rewarded for achieving better on-time performance.

Gordon Bethune closed the loop on his Continental turnaround by offering incentives to all employees for each month

Table 2.1 Competency Evaluation Worksheet.

Gate Agent Competencies	Communication	Planning	Organization	Negotiations	Detail Orientations	Strategic Thinking	Teamwork
Target Profile	H	M	M	H	M	L	M
Agent 004	H	H	H	H	H	L	M
Agent 008	M	H	H	L	H	L	L
Flight Attendant 148	H	M	M	M	L	L	H
Logistics Specialist 329	L	H	M	L	H	H	L

H = high; M = medium; L = low

that the airline finished in the top three (originally top five) in on-time performance against their competitors. This reward went to all employees under the belief that this was a team effort to accomplish that goal. Suddenly, pilots, flight attendants, gate agents, logistics and maintenance employees were all in the game together. If they exceeded their own departmental goals, but hindered other functions from hitting their targets, they would all lose. This helped to break down silos.

It was an impressive example that supports Locke and other behavioral researchers by demonstrating that clear goals (on-time performance) and frequent (monthly), specific (on-time performance records) feedback connected with rewards drive change. Continental Airlines went from bottom of the pack to a top-five performer in only a few months, propelling to a top-three performer for much of the next year. It was such a good idea that U.S. Airways has borrowed the idea to propel their on-time performance from dismal, back-of-the-pack performance for many years to number one in mid-2008. Parallel to Continental, U.S. Airways has offered similar incentives for reaching best on-time performance (McCartney, 2008).

Performance Management Systems: Why Do They Fail?

While we have discussed the importance of the strategy-performance management link, and considerable research and history of organizations implementing performance management, why are so many performance management systems failing to achieve the desired impact? And why are so many employees, managers, and even a good percentage of HR professionals questioning the value of performance management? For example, in a recent Human Resource Planning Society (HRPS) workshop, a vice president of HR, who has served in key human resource roles for numerous Fortune 500 firms, echoed the sentiments of many others. "Does performance management really work? It often fails to achieve its desired objectives and often creates dysfunctional outcomes." She is not alone. I have heard similar views increasingly expressed by many other professionals. Is performance management fundamentally flawed?

Interviews with organizational leaders, performance management users, HR professionals, as well as an examination of case studies and research, reveal that there are a number of reasons for both the failures and the frustrations, as well as the handful of successes. Let us take a look at a few of the most salient factors.

1. *Performance Management Versus Performance Appraisal.* Our HR VP's "emperor wears no clothes" observation was challenged by at least one other professional in the HRPS seminar, who said, "Be careful not to confuse performance management and performance appraisal," noting that performance management should be viewed broadly as a collection of the values, systems, initiatives, and behaviors that help to create peak performance. In contrast, the performance appraisal process—often the annual setting of goals and yearly performance review—is more frequently the target of criticisms in philosophy, execution, or both. This distinction is an important one in that there are a number of broader factors beyond talent that play a role in the overall performance management process, such as the performance philosophy, organizational structure, technology enablers, or supply chain resources, that may also affect overall performance. So in looking for shortfalls, it is important to focus on elements of that overall performance process that are not working.

2. *Discipline Gap.* One of the striking features of many of the interviews, cases, and research notes relates to an apparent lack of effective implementation. Like so much else in organizational life, performance management and appraisal system failures may be a result of poor execution or a lack of authentic management commitment (Rodgers & Hunter, 1991; Rodgers, Hunter, & Rogers, 1993). Books by Bossidy and Charan (2002), and Welch and Byrne (2001), and many popular articles have focused on potentially embarrassing execution questions. Do managers know what the performance management processes are? Are they actually setting goals in the manner intended? Do people have the resources, tools, and ability to achieve the goals? Do they regularly provide feedback and coaching? Are rewards being distributed consistent with the performance philosophy?

3. *Accountability.* Accountability and execution often are intertwined and confused. While execution typically refers to implementing a well-designed performance management process effectively, accountability typically focuses more on individual or team goal attainment (or the process of getting there) and its consequences. Are there consequences for low performers who step up to achieve objectives?

Leaders such as Jack Welch at General Electric, Larry Bossidy at Allied Signal and then Honeywell, and leaders at PepsiCo have been noted for holding people accountable for results. Says Welch, "The problem isn't about one individual—it has a negative influence on the morale and productivity of co-workers, who aren't blind to the individual's poor performance and who may also begin to accept and deliver mediocrity" (Rogers, 2006).

The view that people who excel tend to resent working with others who aren't held to the same standard is supported by other researchers (Zachary & Fischler, 2007), who conclude that recruitment and retention of top performers is the ultimate payoff.

At the individual level, GE has been known for expecting the "what" (goal attained) and also holding people responsible for the "how" (the methods used to obtain the results). Those who failed both tests were destined for reassignment. And those who obtained short-term results but perhaps sacrificed values, people, or sanctioned methods in the process were deficient as long-term leadership prospects. Those missing results but doing all the "right" things would be given additional chances.

Microsoft requires employees to set ambitious goals or "commitments" that are created in consultation with their peers and supervisors and later made public. Peer pressure, or even just peer awareness, is a powerful motivating factor (Heath, 2008). This form of "horizontal accountability" asks team members to assume high levels of responsibility for goals and performance, without the intervention by a supervisor or coach (Ray, 2007).

And here, philosophies differ widely. Some, like the comments of our wary HR VP quoted earlier, suggest that, no matter how well things are designed, the appraisal process is flawed—perhaps even going against the human grain. The critiques related to accountability are numerous:

- Many systems—forced ranking, for example—pit people against people, which damages teamwork and the achievement of broader group goals
- Systems mix monetary and other rewards with development or improvement goals, therefore creating conflicting objectives—do I want to get the highest rating or acknowledge skill gaps that I could improve in the future?
- Appraisal systems are threatening to self-esteem and self-worth by performance labeling as a "winner" or "loser"
- Many appraisal systems cause people to do what is pre-programmed or "expected" versus what is "right." For example: "Hit the target," even if conditions have changed or the target creates dysfunctional outcomes
- Managers are never skilled enough to truly conduct a complex psychological process, such as setting realistic goals, giving and receiving feedback, and coaching

4. *Measurement Scarcity or Overload.* One of the frequently debated issues is how "measured" the performance management process should be. Some organizations with high trust levels might be able to hold candid conversations without the negative baggage just described. In our research, we have found very few top-performing organizations without effective measures in place to drive overall performance. The variance seems to be more in the degree of measurement as you move down the organization and in the priority of those measures.

For example, Continental Airlines put an emphasis on on-time performance over many tactical measures, making priorities very clear. Jack Welch gave his leaders a choice: Either their businesses become the top three in their industry in financial performance or they would be sold. And WD-40 is certainly focused on bottom-line performance. It has achieved an enviable $1.25M of revenue per employee.

At the individual level, research has shown that too many simultaneous goals (and measures) can reduce performance, but most studies show that multiple goals pursued with enough lead time can actually enhance performance (Locke & Latham, 1990). But clearly there is an upper limit, which is not well established by research because the attainment of goals is dependent on many factors, such as complexity of tasks, goal difficulty, skill of performer, and interdependence of the goals. Experienced practitioners have often suggested that three to five primary goals are most effective. Seven is often mentioned as an upper limit. However, creating seven categories of sub-goals under seven major goals is simply violating that principle and is likely to disperse focus.

5. *Lack of Balance (for example, short- versus long-term; single versus multiple stakeholders)*. One of the biggest issues is how to balance the needs of many different constituencies. At the top of the organization, Kaplan and Norton (1996) suggested a balanced scorecard of four buckets to capture the major areas that every business must manage. The issue here is not simply the volume of goals as we just discussed, but the tradeoffs across those areas of focus to ensure that the organization is not optimizing one area (such as profit) at the expense of another (such as customer satisfaction).

The same principles hold at the team or function level. My colleagues at Metrus often conduct surveys of employees, internal customers, and top management (essentially a department or functional 360). The value is that functional leaders and teams often discover that they are managing one stakeholder well and another poorly, due to different needs, priorities, resources, or skills. Or they are strong in one area (such as technical) and weaker in another (such as communication).

At the individual level, the same holds true. The area of work-life balance is based on this multidimensional view. If one is focused on work to the exclusion of other life-balancing activities, often relationships deteriorate, hobbies disintegrate, and, for many, life satisfaction declines. For example, the accounting industry has found that to compete for and keep the best talent, they have needed to become far more flexible (Gold, 2008). In fact, RSM McGladrey has taken a rarely observed step: actually discussing life goals with employees as part of future planning and work-life balance.

A great deal of work over the past several decades has reinforced the view that this "balance" principle helps organizations and individuals maintain the health of their overall system (for example, overall corporate growth or life satisfaction), whether at the enterprise, functional, or individual level.

6. *Failure to Assess Impact.* A final area of challenge is assessing the impact of the performance management system in helping an organization to execute its strategy. Do better performance management practices help the organization achieve superior performance: profitability, revenue growth, customer loyalty and retention, retention of top performers? When we asked the leaders of the superior performing organizations from my interviews, there was no doubt in their belief that a strong performance management system drives results.

We could find few examples of organizations that formally measure the impact of their performance management systems. One approach that this author has seen work is through the use of a balanced scorecard or strategic measures at the organization or unit level. In effect, these strategic measures define ROI; they are the strategic gauges of success. For example, when the organization invests in better goal setting, it should see increased clarity regarding the critical financial, customer, operational, and employee outcomes and drivers of organizational success. When such a system is in place, it is much easier to assess how well cascaded goals (and their achievement) are having an impact on key business outcomes.

Putting It All Together

Despite all the criticism leveled at performance management systems, there are organizations such as WD-40, SmithBucklin, and GE that make it work. Why? Four core elements set them apart:

- *Holism.* The performance management systems of WD-40, SmithBucklin, and GE are not isolated systems but rather highly integrated into the philosophy, values, and systems of the organization. Garry Ridge, the CEO of WD-40, says that this is part of the important values of the organization and "each part must complement the rest." For example, "You cannot have values such as 'Making it better than it is today,' and then not measure, manage, and reward to that goal."

In the organizations that were the most effective, performance management elements were tied closely to values, management style and philosophy, customers, and other systems (for example, hiring, development, and rewards).

- *Role Modeling.* The performance management (and appraisal) process is driven by the top team's example. When I asked Bill Conaty, the recently retired top HR leader for GE under Jack Welch and then Jeff Immelt, about his reflections on the performance management differences of Welch and Immelt, he said it was style—not expectations. Both modeled and expected top performance from their respective teams. When James Kilts became CEO of Gillette, he instituted quarterly performance reviews at every level of the company, including the executive level. The business began to flourish as a result, outperforming its competitors, which Kilts attributes to Gillette's "driven" culture (Rogers, 2006).

- *Cultures That Evoke Self-Accountability.* As evidenced in the Gillette example, organizations with superior performance management systems also have high expectations of their managers and manage those systems in a disciplined way. They have annual goals, quarterly reviews, feedback from key stakeholders (customers, employees, peers), quantitative information, and frequent discussions. These various public sources of feedback make it nearly impossible for performers to be unclear about where they stand.

Nancy Ely, the VP of human resources for WD-40, said that Garry Ridge, the CEO, spends enormous amounts of his time ensuring that people "don't have excuses." Leaders are expected to "help employees at all levels get an 'A'," by spending the time needed to ensure that the right goals are set and then becoming a resource to ensure that people are "getting A's." Says Nancy Ely, "This means immediately working with people who are getting B's or C's to get them back on track." They spend a lot of time keeping the performance bar high and quickly addressing gaps—they don't wait for annual reviews.

Another refreshing view of accountability turns the traditional formula around and focuses on creating self-accountability—the kind that individuals or teams often create for themselves in volunteer organizations, hobbies, and other personally motivating ambitions. Marathon runners routinely set higher and higher standards of achievement. Other sports participants and fans look for new records of performance. Adults often take night courses to maximize their learning and excel at a hobby. A number of the successful leaders talked indirectly about creating this type of culture—one in which employees set stretch targets on their own and are motivated to reach new heights. For example, when Mike Burgett, the former head of U.S. operations for QIAGEN Sciences, Inc., developed a new biotech operation in Maryland, he created a culture that supported self-managed work teams. These teams achieved a 20 percent lower rate in the cost of goods sold, compared to other operations within the company.

- *Don't Over-Complicate.* While their processes are not simple, these organizations avoid unnecessary complexity. While a disciplined process is time-consuming and requires constant vigilance, these organizations do not make the evaluation process and steps so complicated that they break down under their own weight. For example, WD-40 says simply that they want every employee to get an "A." Goals are set as agreements between coaches and employees about what an "A" means. They agree on the measures, and then employees largely manage their routes to "A" performance. When they veer off-target, managers are ready to jump in to help them with resources, information, and skills enhancements to get them back on the path to an "A." Over time, they have developed a strong culture that almost self-regulates. Longer-term employees at first work with new employees to help them get to "A" performance. If this fails to happen, then peers are ready to ask management to take corrective action.

Conclusions

The field of performance management, and its connection to strategy, has evolved greatly over the past several decades, although research has been slow to catch up. There is a plethora of research at the individual level and a paucity of research at the unit or organizational level. While there has been an increasing amount of theory at the strategic and organizational level—balanced scorecard, organizational fit, and people equity come to mind—much more research is needed to understand what is working and why.

On the practical side, performance management remains a major challenge. In preparing this chapter, I found few organizations that truly demonstrated wholesale success in their attempts to link strategy to performance management. Organizations such as GE, WD-40, and SmithBucklin are still the exceptions to the rule. Several major gaps stand out across most of the less than stellar organizations. Lack of disciplined execution and accountability are two interrelated gaps; while organizations increasingly talk about their great systems, many still lack the organizational discipline to drive performance management holistically. Their practices too often find managers scrambling to complete goals well into the performance period and frantically trying to complete reviews necessary to get pay increases out by the deadline, rather than building an integrated performance management system, and all that it implies.

The second big gap is tied to the skills of performance "managers." Short of training them as psychologists, many struggle with the challenges of setting proper goals with their people, providing timely and meaningful feedback in a constructive fashion, and coaching people to bring out the best in them. With the increasing growth of service industries coupled with the likely shortage of talent in the next several decades, this will continue to be a major stumbling block. Organizations such as GE, Procter & Gamble, and Starbucks recognize how important, yet difficult, the roles of performance managers are, and have invested significant resources to ensure that developing leaders master these skills; they quickly weed out those who cannot truly groom top performers.

A final challenge perhaps is the efficacy of performance appraisal, which heretofore is most often a confrontational experience with evaluators frequently scoring those evaluated more critically than the ratees score themselves—creating a constant expectations gap. The most promising practices to overcome this dilemma include:

- Clear goals and measures that are mutually agreeable and quantifiable.
- Self-managed work teams that have group goals. While this begs the question of the measurement of group goals, it does solve some individual issues. For example, as long as individuals are willing to live with the team results, there is less focus on micromanaging individual activities, milestones, and contributions, allowing teams more flexibility to make adjustments to tasks as needed to help the team achieve the broader goal. Others have argued, however, that unless the stakes are sufficiently high, peers will not apply the necessary incentives on weaker performers to improve their effectiveness.
- Holistic reward plans, such as Scanlon plans that reward an entire organizational group. The rewards for on-time performance used by Bethune during the Continental turnaround is a good example of a holistic approach. Jack Stack, the CEO of Springfield Remanufacturing, used this type of approach to achieve great success after the buyout of the company in the 1980s. The company was featured on the CBS television show *60 Minutes* for the level of success it had achieved (Stack & Burlington, 1992). These systems tend to have few disputes over the measures, once they are established and clarify what employees must do to hit the important targets. Since often there is less measurement of individuals, it may be uninspiring for those used to (or needing) high individual recognition; and it may take more time to identify those not pulling their weight, although some argue that there is more peer pressure on non-performers in these environments.
- Placing more of the responsibility for goal setting and monitoring in the laps of employees and teams. While leaders need to sign off on employee or team objectives, individuals are placed more in the position of value managers, having to demonstrate that their volunteered objectives help the organization achieve its key goals and values. This means they have an incentive to understand the business better and how they contribute to it. Furthermore, the responsibility rides

with them to track and demonstrate to management that they are hitting the targets and adding value. This shifts the role of managers to one of negotiating goals that make a difference and then to closely monitoring and coaching performance. Since the burden rests with the individual performers to "sell" their goals and performance, it is more akin to selling a product or service to a customer, removing some of the "entitlement" aspects to traditional systems.

While no system will be perfect, it is clear that organizations will need some process to ensure that their performance is sufficient to execute their strategies better than their competitors. It seems clear from both research and practitioners that there are both a set of principles, many of which are long known but not necessarily well executed, that are essential for strong performance, as well as unique characteristics of an organization—its culture, leadership style, and strategy, for example—that require those principles to be tailored to the particular context. Copying one's performance management neighbor does not seem to work well. Instead, the leading firms interviewed appear to uniquely tailor the performance management system to their strategy, culture, and management style, but do so holistically. That is, they manage to ensure that their values, management style, and human resource systems are aligned and part of a cohesive framework. Within that, they apply many of the proven principles of performance management; for example, clear direction; well-articulated specific goals; rapid, effective feedback and coaching; and good incentives. While not perfect, they provide tested and researched practices that will help the organization fulfill its mission.

References

Beatty, R. W., Baird, L. S., Schneier, E. C., & Shaw, D. G. (1995). *Performance, measurement, management, and appraisal sourcebook.* Amherst, MA: Human Resource Development Press.

Beer, M. (1999, September). Organizational fitness: The context for successful balanced scorecard programs. *Harvard Business Review.*

Bethune, G. (1999). *From worst to first: Behind the scenes of Continental's remarkable comeback.* Hoboken, NJ: John Wiley & Sons.

Bossidy, L., & Charan, R. (2002). *Execution: The discipline of getting things done.* New York: Crown Business.

Buckingham, M., & Coffman, C. (1999). *First, break all the rules.* New York: Simon & Schuster.

Cardy, R. L. (2003). *Performance management: Concepts, skills, and exercises,* Armonk, NY: M. E. Sharpe, Inc.

Clutterbuck, D. (2008, May). Are you a goal junkie? *Training Journal,* pp. 43–46.

De Cieri, H., Kramar, R., Noe, A. R., Hollenbeck, J. R., Gerhart, B., & Wright, P. M. (2003). *Human resource in Australia; Strategy people performance.* Sydney: McGraw-Hill, Australia.

DeNisi, A. S., & Griffin, R. W. (2001). *Human resource management.* Boston: Houghton Mifflin.

DeNisi, A. S., & Kluger, A. N. (2000). Feedback effectiveness: Can 360-degree appraisals be improved? *Academy of Management Executive, 14*(1), 129–139.

Du Plessis, A. J., Beaver, B., & Nel, P. S. (2006, Spring). Closing the gap between current capabilities and future requirements in HRM in New Zealand: Some empirical evidence. *Journal of Global Business and Technology,* pp. 33–47.

Fisher, S. G. (1997). *The manager's pocket guide to performance management.* Amherst, MA: HRD Press.

Fitzgerald, W. (1995). Forget the form in performance appraisals. *HR Magazine, 40*(12), 36–38.

Galbraith, J. (1977). *Organization design.* Reading, MA: Addison-Wesley.

Gibson, V. M. (1995, February). The new employee reward system. *Management Review,* pp. 13–18.

Gold, L. (2008, March 31). Other paths: Firms find flexible work programs boost retention, productivity. *Accounting Technology,* pp. 3–5.

Grote, D. (1996). *The complete guide to performance appraisal.* New York: American Management Association.

Hackman, J. R., & Oldham, G. R. (1980). *Work redesign.* Upper Saddle River, NJ: Prentice Hall.

Heath, D. (2008, February). Make goals, not resolutions. *Fast Company,* (122), pp. 58–59.

Hillgren, J. S., & Cheatham, D. W. (2000). *Understanding performance measures: An approach to linking rewards to the achievement of organizational objectives.* Scottsdale, AZ: WorldatWork.

Kantabutra, S. (2007, Fall). Identifying vision realization factors in apparel stores: Empirical evidence from Australia. *International Journal of Business, 12*(4), 445–460.

Kaplan, R. S., & Norton, D. P. (1996). *The balanced scorecard: Translating strategy into action.* Boston: Harvard Business School Press.

Kaplan, R. S., & Norton, D. P. (2004). *Strategy maps: Converting intangible assets into tangible outcomes.* Boston: Harvard Business School Press.

Katz, D., & Kahn, R. (1966). *Social psychology of organizations.* Hoboken, NJ: John Wiley & Sons.

Kostman, J. T., & Schiemann, W. (2005, May). People equity: The hidden driver of quality. *Quality Progress,* pp. 37–42.

Leading productivity killers in today's market: Overwork, stress. (2008, April). *HR Focus, 85*(4), 8.

Leavitt, H. (1965). Applied organization change in industry. In J. March (Ed.), *Handbook of organizations.* Chicago: Rand McNally.

Locke, E. A., & Latham, G. P. (1990). *A theory of goal setting and task performance.* Upper Saddle River, NJ: Prentice-Hall.

London, M. (2002). *Job feedback* (2nd ed.). Mahwah, NJ: Lawrence Erlbaum Associates.

Longenecker, C. O., Sims, H. P., Jr., & Gioia, D. A. (1987). Behind the mask: The politics of employee appraisals. *Academy of Management Executive, 1,* 183–193.

McCartney, S. (2008, July 22). How US Airways vaulted to first place. *The Wall Street Journal,* p. D3.

McGinty, R. L., & Hanke, J. (1989). Compensation management in practice—Merit pay plans: Are they truly tied to performance? *Compensation and Benefits Review, 12*(5), 12–16.

McNamara, C. P. (1999, October/December). Making human capital productive. *Business and Economic Review,* pp. 10–13.

Meehan, R. H. (1992). Why merit increase programmes fail. *Compensation and Benefits Management, 8*(4), 46–50.

Mohrman, A. M., Jr., Resnick-West, S. M., & Lawler, E. E. III (1989). *Designing performance appraisal systems: Aligning appraisals and organizational realities.* San Francisco: Jossey-Bass.

Nadler, D. A., & Tushman, M. L. (1997). *Competing by design: The power of organizational architecture.* New York: Oxford University Press.

Nadler, D. A., Gerstein, M. S., Shaw, R. B., & Associates (1992). *Organizational architecture: Designs for changing organizations.* San Francisco: Jossey-Bass.

Nel, P. S., van Dyk, P. S., Haasbroek, G. D., Schultz, H. B., Sono, T., & Werner, A. (2004). *Human resource management.* Cape Town: Oxford University Press, Southern Africa.

Nordblom, C. (2008, February/March). Taking measurement a step further at Volvo group. *Strategic Communication Management, 12*(2), 20–23.

Pellet, J. (2008, January/February). The reputation questions. *Chief Executive*, (231), 45–46.

Pomeroy, A. (2005, May). Climate control. *HRMagazine, 50*(5), 18.

Pulakos, E. D. (2004). Performance management. *SHRM Foundation Effective Practices Guidelines.*

Ray, D. (2007). Managing horizontal accountability. *The Journal for Quality and Participation, 30*(4), 24–28.

Rodgers, R., & Hunter, J. E. (1991). Impact of management by objectives on organizational productivity. *Journal of Applied Psychology, 76*, 322–336.

Rodgers, R., Hunter, J. E., & Rogers, D. L. (1993). Influence of top management commitment on management program success. *Journal of Applied Psychology, 78*, 151–155.

Rogers, B. (2006, January). High performance is more than a dream—It's a culture. *T&D, 60*(1), 12.

Rummler, G. A., & Brache, A. P. (1995). *Improving performance: How to manage the white space on the organization chart.* San Francisco: Jossey-Bass.

Schiemann, W., & Lingle, J. (1999). *Bulls-eye—Hitting your strategic targets through high-impact measurement.* New York: The Free Press.

Smith, M. (2008, March). Sales and operations planning: Making BPM work. *Business Performance Management, 6*(1), 4–8.

Smither, J. W. (Ed.). (1998). *Performance appraisal: State of the art in practice.* San Francisco: Jossey-Bass.

Stack, J., & Burlington, B. (1992). *The great game of business.* New York: Currency Doubleday.

Thomson, A. (1999, December 1). Human resources: Demonstrating the human touch. *European Venture Capital Journal,* pp. 16–20.

Watson Wyatt. (2007/2008a). *Building an effective health & productivity framework.* New York: Watson Wyatt's 2007/2008 Staying @ Work Research Report.

Watson Wyatt. (2007/2008b). *Playing to win in a global economy.* New York: Watson Wyatt's 2007/2008 Global Strategic Rewards Research Report and United States Findings.

Weatherly, L. A. (2004). Performance management: Getting it right from the start. *SHRM Research Quarterly, 2*, 1–10.

Welch, J., & Byrne, J. A. (2001). *Jack: Straight from the gut.* New York: Warner Books.

Zachary, L. J., & Fischler, L.A. (2007, December). The FACT model. *Leadership Excellence, 24*(12), 20.

Notes

1. We had actually administered a survey with this same question beginning in the early 1990s to executives and upper-middle managers (directors or senior managers) at Conference Board and other leadership conferences. When we repeated these surveys to a variety of audiences (conference attendees, national samples, client organizations), we found results that varied little from the 1990s through the recent periods. Agreement on strategy does not seem to be getting noticeably better.

2. Although it has been argued by Buckingham and his colleagues that it is not possible, or perhaps worth it, to try to address skills gaps; rather, they argue that it is more important to focus instead on developing people's strengths. Clearly, this approach would change the nature of the feedback and development component of performance reviews, but does not easily explain what organizations are to do with all of the "misfit skills," short of reassigning many employees to different roles. And, would that be effective (or cost-effective) for the many players in roles in which only a few skill gaps exist?

3. Continental Airlines had recently merged with the failing Eastern Airlines, whereas Southwest Airlines started with a non-traditional approach to airline management from its inception.

4. Since those halcyon days, Bethune has retired and Continental has slipped somewhat in on-time performance as of this writing.

5. Pareto analysis is a method to identify the contribution that different drivers, or causes, have on particular outcomes. This has led to the common 80–20 rule that suggests that 20 percent of the causes create 80 percent of the impact.

CHAPTER 3

PRACTICAL APPLICATIONS OF GOAL-SETTING THEORY TO PERFORMANCE MANAGEMENT

Peter A. Heslin, Jay B. Carson, and
Don VandeWalle

Performance management involves all the initiatives managers undertake to guide and motivate high performance. Such initiatives have traditionally focused on providing formal performance appraisals, rewards, and recognition for high performance, as well as taking remedial action to address performance deficiencies. Performance management can also facilitate adaptability and continually improving performance in rapidly changing contemporary workplaces. To do so, however, traditional periodic performance appraisal initiatives need to be supplemented by ongoing performance coaching (London, 2003).

A key ingredient for effectively coaching employees is the prudent use of goal setting. The prime axiom of goal setting theory is that specific, difficult goals lead to higher performance than when people strive to simply "do their best" (Locke, 1966; Locke & Latham, 1990). The performance benefits of challenging, specific goals have been demonstrated in hundreds of laboratory and field studies (Locke & Latham, 1990, 2002). Such goals positively affect the performance of individuals (Baum & Locke, 2004), groups (O'Leary-Kelly, Martocchio, & Frink, 1994), organizational units (Rogers & Hunter, 1991), as well as entire organizations (Baum,

Locke, & Smith, 2001)—and over periods as long as twenty-five years (Howard & Bray, 1988; Locke & Latham, 2002).

By providing direction and a standard against which progress can be monitored, challenging goals can enable people to guide and refine their performance. It is well documented in the scholarly (Locke & Latham, 2002) and practitioner (Latham, 2004) literature that specific goals can boost motivation and performance by leading people to *focus* their attention on specific objectives (Locke & Bryan, 1969), increase their *effort* to achieve these objectives (Bandura & Cervone, 1983), *persist* in the face of setbacks (Latham & Locke, 1975), and develop *new strategies* to better deal with complex challenges to goal attainment (Wood & Locke, 1990).

Through such motivational processes, challenging goals often lead to valuable rewards such as recognition, promotions, and/or increases in income from one's work (Latham & Locke, 2006). Working to attain valued goals relieves boredom by imbuing work with a greater sense of purpose. Even though setting high goals sets the bar higher to obtain self-satisfaction, attaining goals creates a heightened sense of efficacy (personal effectiveness), self-satisfaction, positive affect, and sense of well-being—especially when the goals conquered were considered challenging (Wiese & Freund, 2005). By providing self-satisfaction, achieving goals often also increases organizational commitment (Tziner & Latham, 1989), which in turn positively affects organizational citizenship behavior (Organ, Podsakoff, & Mackenzie, 2006), negatively affects turnover (Wagner, 2007), and increases the strength of the relationship between difficult goals and performance (Locke & Latham, 1990, 2002).

Specific challenging goals do not, however, necessarily lead to such desirable personal and organizational outcomes. Rather, the results from goal setting depend critically on issues pertaining to goal commitment, task complexity, goal framing, team goals, and feedback. The purpose of this chapter is to discuss recent developments regarding how these five factors can be managed to enable effective performance management.

Goal Commitment

A statistical review of eighty-three studies revealed that goal commitment is a critical ingredient for goals to lead to high performance, especially when goals are difficult (Klein, Wesson, Hollenbeck, &

Exhibit 3.1 Goal Commitment Scale.*

1. It's hard to take this goal seriously. (R)
2. Quite frankly, I don't care if I achieve this goal or not. (R)
3. I am strongly committed to pursuing this goal.
4. It wouldn't take much to make me abandon this goal. (R)
5. I think this is a good goal to shoot for.

Note: Items followed by "(R)" indicate that the item should be reverse-scored before analysis.

Developed by Klein, Wesson, Hollenbeck, Wright, and DeShon (2001)

Alge, 1999). A study with rehabilitation counselors at a state agency found that feedback had a positive relationship with work performance only for those individuals with high goal commitment; it had a negative relationship with performance for those with lower goal commitment (Renn, 2003). Thus, the well-validated five-item scale for assessing goal commitment developed by Klein, Wesson, Hollenbeck, Wright, and DeShon (2001), as outlined in Exhibit 3.1, is of practical value to organizational researchers and practitioners alike. Responses are provided on a five-point Likert scale using strongly disagree to strongly agree anchors.

Locke and Latham (2002) suggest that two key categories of approaches for building goal commitment are to increase goal importance, including the desirability of the outcomes people expect from working to attain their goals, and also to foster self-efficacy, that is, people's belief that they can attain the goal.

Goal Importance

There are at least five ways to convince people that goal attainment is worthwhile. These include (a) eliciting a public commitment to goals, (b) communicating an inspiring vision, (c) using an empathy box analysis (Latham, 2001) to understand and alter the perceived consequences of goal commitment, (d) providing financial incentives for goal attainment, and (e) expressing confidence that the goal will be achieved.

First, having people make a *public commitment* to a goal enhances their commitment to it, presumably because acting contrary to their public pronouncement would induce the personally and socially undesirable impression of hypocrisy (Cialdini, 2001; Festinger, 1957). In the late 1990s when PepsiCo spun off of its Restaurant Division (Pizza Hut, Taco Bell, and KFC) to create YUM! Brands, the YUM! leadership sought to elicit commitment to the promulgated "Founding Truths" regarding the intended more decentralized and restaurant-centered culture of the newly formed organization. While exiting the official launch celebration of YUM!, restaurant general managers (RGMs) were invited to sign their names on a poster of the Founding Truths and to become a "founder," but only if they agreed with the principles of the new company. Although it was emphasized that signing was strictly voluntary and there would be no implicit penalty for not signing, over 80 percent of the attending RGMs left their signatures, thereby making a public commitment to the new company's espoused cultural values. "Founder's Day," as it is now called, has become a yearly event celebrating the culture of YUM! . . . and often features signatories being photographed in front of the poster they have just publicly signed (Mike & Slocum, 2003).

Second, goal commitment can be built by leaders *communicating an inspiring vision* or a superordinate goal for followers to rally around. An effective vision creates excitement and energy in employees; is consistent with the values, objectives, and strategic advantages of the organization; and facilitates unified action consistent with the vision. A classic example of such a vision is Winston Churchill's (1940) proclamation that, despite Britain being under grave threat from a more powerful advancing Nazi military:

> I have, myself, full confidence that if all do their duty, if nothing is neglected . . . we shall outlive the menace of tyranny, if necessary for years, if necessary alone . . . Whatever the cost may be, we shall fight on the beaches, we shall fight on the landing grounds, we shall fight in the fields and in the streets, we shall fight in the hills; we shall never surrender . . .

Other examples of compelling visions that have built strong commitment to macro-level goals include Martin Luther King's "I have a dream" speech; John F. Kennedy's inaugural address in which he urged Americans to: "Ask not what your country can do for you, but what you can do for your country" and his 1961 vision to put a man on the moon before the end of the decade; Walt Disney's motto of fostering "learning through entertainment"; and Jack Welch's decree that General Electric was to become a "boundaryless organization" and to be either number one or number two in any industry where they compete (Latham, 2003). Barack Obama's vision of a more united and egalitarian United States, encapsulated in statements such as: "What binds us together is greater than what drives us apart" (Obama, 2006, p. 2), and "There is not a black America and a white America and Latino America and Asian America—there's the United States of America" (Obama, 2004), attracted a record-breaking number of donations in support of his goal to become the Democratic nominee for the 2008 U.S. presidential election. Inspiring visions and superordinate goals are not limited to nations or even organizations, but may also be useful to managers at the department or team levels. For instance, a group of demoralized hospital janitors became invigorated by their team's vision of making *their* hospital a safe and pleasant environment for all hospital patients, staff, and visitors.

Third, an *empathy box analysis* (Latham, 2001, 2003) is based on two underlying premises: (a) understand the anticipated consequences and you will understand people's behavior and (b) change the anticipated consequences and you will change people's behavior. As underscored by reinforcement theory (Luthans & Stajkovic, 1999), employees are only likely to commit to a goal when they perceive that doing so is in some way in their best interests. For instance, senior management at Weyerhaeuser Forest Products was having trouble obtaining employee commitment to a company goal to reduce shrinkage (theft by employees) from approximately $1 million per year to less than $1,000 per year. To help managers identify the outcomes that employees expected as a result of committing to or rejecting the goal of honest behavior, Latham (2001, 2003) developed and applied the concept of an empathy box analysis. Based on the first premise (a) outlined above, the procedure involved first asking a random sample of employees, which presumably included some of the thieves, variants of the following four questions:

1. What are the upsides for you of being honest?
2. How might you suffer from being honest?

3. What positive outcomes could you personally expect from stealing?
4. What negative outcomes might you expect from engaging in theft?

A sample of an empathy box is shown in Table 3.1.[1]

In response to Question 1, Latham discovered that, aside from personal pride in one's integrity, no positive consequences were perceived for honest behavior (DB). Regarding Question 2, employees (and supervisors) had experienced substantial peer pressure and harassment to not "rock the boat" by reporting theft (DB). Pertaining to Question 3 about the perceived benefits of stealing, the thieves did not seem to be selling the stolen goods or seeking revenge against the company. However, some employees relished the "challenge," "thrill," and "excitement" of stealing, as well as taking pride in their proficiency at doing so (UB). Finally, owing to a relatively tight labor market, powerful union, and firm export contracts with Japan, there was little concern about being fired if caught stealing (UB). The biggest problem created by the theft was wives complaining about cluttered garages! In summary, the most potent anticipated consequences were negative for the DB of being honest . . . and positive for the UB of stealing.

In contrast to the usual focus on rewarding DBs and punishing UBs, a systematic empathy box analysis often reveals creative alternatives for answering Question 5: *How can the incentive structure be changed to increase commitment to the DB?* At Weyerhaeuser, an amnesty day was declared during which anyone could return any

Table 3.1 Empathy Box Analysis Protocol.*

	Positive	Negative
Desired Behavior (**DB**)	Cell 1	Cell 2
Undesired Behavior (**UB**)	Cell 3	Cell 4

*Note: Adapted from Latham (2001, 2003)

stolen equipment under the presumption that they were "just doing so for a friend." This removed the negative consequence for being honest. In addition, a library system was implemented whereby any employee could borrow company equipment, as long as he or she checked it out and signed a waiver indemnifying the company against any injuries resulting from use of the borrowed equipment. This defused the thrill of stealing. The overall result of these virtually costless initiatives to change the incentive structure pertaining to honest behavior, as perceived by employees, was the return of massive amounts of valuable equipment and a substantial decrease in subsequent theft (Latham, 2001, 2003).

Fourth, *monetary incentives* can increase the importance people attach to goals. However, this approach to building goal commitment can be problematic, by potentially discouraging risk-taking and creativity, rupturing relationships, and encouraging short-termism (Kohn, 1993). Fortunately, Locke (2004) provides a highly useful discussion regarding the nature, pros, and cons of five different methods of making financial incentives contingent upon levels of performance and goal attainment. This discussion can be used to make conscious trade-offs about the most suitable incentive system to use—if any (Kohn, 1993)—in a given work context.

Fifth, managers can build the perceived value of goal attainment by supportively *expressing confidence* that "the goal can and will be achieved" (Latham, 2004, p. 127). This approach probably fosters goal commitment by increasing employees' self-efficacy, as discussed next.

Self-Efficacy

It is well established that goal commitment is predicted by a person's level of self-efficacy (Wofford, Goodwin, & Premack, 1992), that is, level of belief in his or her capability to successfully perform a particular task (Bandura, 1986). There are three key sources of self-efficacy. The most potent is *enactive self-mastery*, followed by *role modeling*, and then *verbal persuasion*.

Enactive self-mastery occurs when people experience success at performing at least portions of a task. By implication, failures can lower self-efficacy. Mastery experiences are facilitated by breaking down difficult tasks into small, relatively easy steps that progressively become more difficult. Together with adequate feedback and resources (for example, equipment and information) to perform effectively, such a process tends to enable the high rate of initial successes that forms a firm basis for high self-efficacy. Remembering to acknowledge and value even minor performance improvements and intermediary achievements is also important for building self-efficacy through enactive self-mastery (Bandura, 1986, 1997).

Role modeling happens when a person wanting to learn a task observes and identifies with another person's proficient performance of that task. Role models can inspire confidence that those observing them can act in a similarly successful manner. Models are most effective at raising self-efficacy when they are personally liked and are perceived as having attributes (such as age, gender, talent, and ethnicity) similar to those of the individuals who observe them. An important implication is that managers should think carefully before assigning mentors, especially without the input of those being mentored (Ragins, Cotton, & Miller, 2000). Individuals may learn and become more confident from observing both the successes and failures of others, as long as they feel confident that they can avoid repeating the errors they observe (Bandura, 1986, 1997).

Verbal persuasion increases self-efficacy when individuals are encouraged, by people they respect, regarding their capacity to learn and perform effectively (Bandura, 1986). Positive self-talk can also raise self-efficacy (Latham & Budworth, 2006). Efficacy-raising feedback highlights how consistent efforts have enabled substantial improvements, as well as the progress made, rather than involving peer comparisons or making reference to how far individuals have to go until their ultimate objective is achieved. Effective verbal persuasion is reinforced with corresponding actions. For example, telling individuals that they are capable but not assigning them any challenging tasks tends to erode both employees' self-efficacy and a manager's credibility. In contrast, having individuals draw up a progress chart before complimenting them on their genuine progress, where applicable, is a potent way of raising employees' sense of what they can achieve (Bandura, 1986, 1997). For concrete guidance on how to apply these three principles for developing self-efficacy, Heslin and Klehe (2006) provide a twenty-item behavioral self-assessment of the extent to which managers increase the self-efficacy of their employees by providing effective mastery experiences, role modeling, and verbal persuasion.

Insulating Self-Efficacy

As mentioned earlier, when performing challenging tasks, setbacks are inevitable. However, such experiences are less likely to weaken self-efficacy when people hold the implicit belief that their abilities are (a) relatively *malleable* and able to be developed incrementally through persistent effort and strategy development, rather than (b) essentially *fixed* and unlikely to change much over time, as implied by the traditional notion of a person's IQ (Wood & Bandura, 1989). The self-efficacy-protecting assumption that abilities can be developed—originally labeled an "incremental implicit theory of intelligence" (Dweck, 1986, p. 1045) and more recently a "growth mindset" (Dweck, 2006)—can be developed through several means. These include (a) informing people that their skills are "developed through practice," rather than "reflect their basic cognitive capabilities" (Wood & Bandura, 1989, p. 410); (b) having people read a compelling scientific testimonial regarding how, with effort and practice, abilities can be cultivated throughout most of the life span (Chiu, Hong, & Dweck, 1997); and (c) attributing successful performance to a person having "worked hard," rather than "being smart" (Mueller & Dweck, 1998).

Heslin, Latham, and VandeWalle (2005) developed an intervention that enables managers to create a sustained growth mindset among working adults. They randomly assigned managers to participate in either an "incremental intervention"/ growth mindset workshop based on principles of self-persuasion (Aronson, 1999) or a placebo control workshop. One of the five activities in the growth workshop involves participants recalling an area in which they once had low ability, though can now perform quite well (for example, playing golf), before pondering (a) how they developed their skills in this area (for example, through sustained effort and coaching) and (b) why undertaking similar developmental initiatives could not enable them to also cultivate a skill they would like to develop (such as playing the piano) but assume they have no inherent talent to develop. Six weeks later, compared to those in the placebo control, participants who received the incremental intervention had a significantly greater growth mindset and also acted in theoretically predicted ways (see also Heslin, VandeWalle, & Latham, 2006).

In summary, goal commitment can be increased through public commitments, inspiring visions, using an empathy box analysis to understand and change the consequences that employees anticipate, financial incentives, and expressing confidence that the goal will be achieved. Goal commitment can also be built by cultivating self-efficacy through application of the principles of enactive self-mastery, role modeling, and verbal persuasion (Bandura, 1986, 1997), as concretely illustrated by Heslin and Klehe's (2006) self-assessment measure. Self-efficacy is insulated from the potentially efficacy-lowering effects of setbacks by cultivating a growth mindset (Wood & Bandura, 1989) using a range of techniques reviewed by Dweck (1999, 2006; see also Heslin & VandeWalle, 2008).

Task Complexity

Complex tasks are those on which the path to goal achievement is not immediately apparent or easily understood. Wood (1986) defined task complexity as involving three aspects: *component complexity* (signified by the number of acts and information cues involved in completing a task), *coordinative complexity* (indicated by the type and number of relationships among the acts and information cues), and *dynamic complexity* (reflecting the degree of changes in acts and information cues over time, as well as the relationships among them). Granted the need to devote time and mental effort to understanding complex tasks and mastering skills in order to competently complete them, Wood, Mento, and Locke (1987) investigated whether task complexity reduces the positive effect of difficult, specific outcome goals on task performance. Consistent with their hypotheses, Wood, Mento, and Locke's meta-analysis revealed that difficult goal effects on performance were strongest ($d = .76$) for easy tasks (those involving reaction time and brainstorming tasks) and weakest ($d = .42$) for more complex tasks (business decision making, scientific and engineering work, and faculty research).

A prototypically complex task is performed by air traffic controllers. At any given point in time, there are often many planes flying in an airport's vicinity (component complexity), their trajectories need to be considered in relationship to each other (coordinative complexity), and the relationships between planes' trajectories constantly change (dynamic complexity). Kanfer and Ackerman (1989) reasoned that owing to the considerable cognitive demands involved in air traffic control (ATC), striving for performance goals when first learning such a task might create cognitive overload and thereby slow learning and lower initial performance. In an experimental study involving 568 U.S. Air Force recruits learning an ATC task, Kanfer and Ackerman observed that participants given a goal felt more "pressured," became more distracted, and exhibited lower ATC performance than participants instructed to just "do their best." This research illustrates that a goal to attain a specific outcome can "impede task learning when presented prior to an understanding of what the task is about" (Kanfer & Ackerman, 1989, p. 687).

Subsequent research has established that goals actually *can* be helpful even during the early stages of complex skill acquisition, as long as they are the right kinds of goals. Two viable alternatives are *proximal* goals and *learning* goals, as described next.

First, using a modestly complex business game, Latham and Seijts (1999) replicated Kanfer and Ackerman's (1989) observation that participants performed better with a vague "do-your-best" goal than with a specific *distal* (ultimate outcome) goal. However, when *proximal* (short-term, intermediate) goals were set in addition to the distal goal, self-efficacy and profits were significantly higher than in the do-your-best condition or in the condition where only a distal goal had been set. Feedback on performance relative to proximal goals seems to facilitate the development of effective strategies needed to perform well on complex tasks.

Second, people first learning a complex task can be given a *learning goal* to focus their effort on discovering strategies or procedures necessary to effectively perform a task (Dweck, 1986). Consistent with Kanfer and Ackerman's (1989) cognitive resource allocation theory, a person's limited attention is explicitly directed to learning and mastering the task rather than worrying about his or her performance outcome. Winters and Latham (1996) found that, when performing a relatively simple task, there were no significant differences in performance between those with a learning goal relative to those instructed to "do your best." People with a specific high performance goal had the highest performance. Only when the task was complex did a learning goal lead to higher performance than a do-your-best or a high performance goal.

Similarly, using a complex simulation that examined entrepreneurial behavior in starting up and maintaining a business, Noel and Latham (2006) found that those who used a learning goal were able to keep their simulated firms running longer than those with a performance outcome goal. Together these findings suggest that learning goals are valuable when complex skills need to be acquired. After proficiency has been developed, high specific performance goals should be set (Seijts & Latham, 2005).

To summarize, novices at complex tasks should not be given specific, challenging goals. Rather, they ought to be given either proximal goals (such as "sell ten units this month," rather than "sell 120 units this year") or specific learning goals (such as "discover five new strategies for responding constructively to potential customers who do not initially react positively to your sales initiatives").

Goal Framing

Goals can be framed in several different types of ways that affect how well people learn and perform. Goals can be framed either negatively ("During the following year, try not to lose more than five out of your forty current customers") or positively ("During the following year, try to keep at least thirty-five out of your forty current customers"). Negatively framed goals lead to more anxiety, as well as lower persistence and performance, compared to goals that are framed positively (Roney, Higgins, & Shah, 1995).

Under Jack Welch's leadership, General Electric (GE) was well known for its encouragement of "stretch goals" that challenge employees to achieve objectives that they do not yet know how to reach (Kerr & Landauer, 2004). GE was also renowned for the threatening policy of firing the bottom 10 percent of employees on annual performance ratings. Given the high task complexity, stress, and work overload that increasingly characterize modern workplaces, Drach-Zahavy and Erez (2002) investigated performance differences depending on whether difficult tasks are framed as a *challenge*, providing an opportunity for self-growth, or as a *threat*, regarding which effective strategies to deal with it are not readily available. As hypothesized, challenge appraisals yielded consistently better performance than threat appraisals. However, those who viewed the task as a threat performed better when they had learning goals rather than performance outcome goals. Finally, difficult performance goals induced high adaptation to change when the work context was perceived as challenging, but poor adaptation and performance when the work context was perceived as threatening.

Regardless of whether people adopt a difficult learning or performance goal, errors are bound to occur during the process of goal pursuit. Workplace errors can be extremely costly to careers, organizations, and even human health, as illustrated by the Exxon Valdez and Space Shuttle *Challenger* disasters, as well as the Enron and Chernobyl financial and nuclear meltdowns, respectively. Not surprisingly, most traditional training programs focus on teaching participants how to avoid errors. However, from a psychological perspective, errors also provide important information that can enable learning and potentially reduce or eliminate future errors.

Michael Frese and colleagues (Frese et al., 1991) thus developed the concept of *error management*, whereby errors encountered during the learning process are construed as opportunities to learn what does not work. In contrast to error prevention training in which errors are punished with low grades, error management training is designed to reduce the negative emotional effects of errors. People are taught to frame errors positively by pairing negative feedback with statements such as "Errors are a natural part of the learning process!" or "The more errors you make, the more you learn!" Such training facilitates learning from computer software training, as measured both immediately and one week after training (Heimbeck, Frese, Sonnentag, & Keith, 2003), apparently as a function of reducing anxiety and increasing systematic planning, monitoring, and learning from one's progress during task completion (Keith & Frese, 2005). Given the dynamic nature of the tasks performed by many modern-day knowledge workers, it is noteworthy that the superiority of error management training over traditional error-avoidant methods is especially pronounced for promoting transfer-of-training to novel tasks (Keith & Frese, 2008).

In summary, goals are generally best framed positively rather than negatively. Especially when goals are challenging, it is important to help people to frame them as a challenge from which they may learn, rather than a threat in which failure is foreseeable. Finally, it is prudent for managers to emphasize that errors along the path to goal attainment are a natural part of the learning process. This can reduce emotional distraction and promote the deep learning employees need to effectively tackle novel challenges as they arise.

Team Goals

The rise of teamwork and team-based organizational forms has created a shift in how managers understand and practice goal setting. Many of the basic fundamentals of individual goal setting can be translated to groups of people. Team goals that are specific and difficult have consistently positive effects on team performance (O'Leary-Kelly, Martocchio, & Frink, 1994). These difficult team goals also improve performance through the same mechanisms of increased focus, effort, persistence, and developing new strategies for complex tasks (Weingart, 1992). While team goals function in similar ways to individual goals, there are also several unique issues that make goal setting more complex in team settings.

When specific difficult goals are set by a team, each team member does not necessarily personally adopt the team goal. Even if they do, conflicts can occur between personal and team goals. In order for individuals' efforts to be directed toward team performance, the team goal must be adopted as their own. Mitchell and Silver (1990) found that team performance can suffer on simple tasks when team members' personal goals compete with those of other team members. Cohen and colleagues (1999) examined how organizations set and communicate direction for knowledge work teams, including alignment of goals among individuals, teams, and the organization, as well as how specific and measurable the goals were. They found that goal alignment around organizational priorities led to higher team performance.

Goal alignment is akin to the effects of a yoke on harnessing the efforts of a team of animals in the same direction, or the effect of rails on aligning the direction of train cars. If members of a team have goals that are "pulling" in a different direction than the goals of other team members, this will result in diminished effort and performance by the team, as well as possible "friction" or "sparks." In order to achieve better goal alignment, electronic *performance dashboards* are being used in organizations to facilitate team goal setting and monitoring of team performance relative to both team and organizational goals. These software programs enable users to set team goals that are consistent with the organization's vision, and to track—in real time—key performance indicators relative to goals, all the way down to the team or individual level. Dashboards can help provide feedback to teams leading to a focus on team goals and performance (DeShon, Kozlowski, Schmidt, Milner, & Wiechmann, 2004).

A primary way for managers to align individual goals with team goals is to seek commitment to a superordinate goal. When people perceive that the attainment of other people's goals might decrease the probability of attaining their own goal, they tend to withhold information and ideas, as well as sometimes even acting to obstruct others' goal pursuit (Stanne, Johnson, & Johnson, 1999). In order for managers to get buy-in for team goals, they can use many of the same techniques discussed previously in regard to establishing the importance of a specific goal. These include public commitments to the team and/or others, an inspiring vision related to team goals, incentives, or consideration of perceived consequences. Two additional initiatives are developing team efficacy and enabling participation in setting team goals.

Team Efficacy

Team efficacy refers to a team's belief that it can successfully perform a specific task (Lindsley, Brass, & Thomas, 1995). Teams that have high efficacy choose more difficult goals, persist in their efforts, and seek to improve their task strategies. In an experiment involving undergraduate students participating in a computerized tank battle simulation, team efficacy explained 58 percent of the variance in team-set goal difficulty, and it had an indirect effect on performance via goal difficulty (Durham, Knight, & Locke, 1997). Difficult team goals can increase team efficacy, as well as subsequent strategic risk-taking and team performance (Knight, Durham, & Locke, 2000). Team efficacy also works together with goal alignment to increase team performance. In a meta-analysis of studies on team efficacy, Gully and colleagues (2002) found that teams that had high levels of team efficacy and high levels of goal alignment, along with group rewards, demonstrated the best performance.

Participation in Setting Team Goals

People are more likely to commit to difficult goals that are important to them personally. Participation in the setting of goals improves team performance by enhancing the importance of goals to each team member and thereby increasing goal commitment (O'Leary-Kelly, Martocchio, & Frink, 1994). However, participation in team goal setting may not always be an option for managers. Latham, Erez, and Locke (1988) found that participation in goal setting does increase goal commitment, but that assigned goals are also effective so long as a compelling purpose or rationale for the goal is given. *Telling and selling,* rather than just *telling* people what their goals are, helps them to understand why the goal is important and therefore enhances goal commitment.

Team goals can induce productive cooperation *and* competition. At Whole Foods Market, the largest natural-foods grocer in the United States, the culture is based almost entirely on teamwork. Each store has eight to ten teams with designated leaders and clear performance goals. How they reach those goals is up to each team. Teams are given the responsibility for all decisions about labor spending, ordering, pricing, as well as hiring new team members. They are rewarded as a team with gainsharing bonuses based on team performance (profitability in their area). These high levels of shared responsibility for team processes and outcomes produce high levels of cooperation within teams. They also produce competition between teams, stores, and even regions in the areas of quality, service, sales, growth, productivity, and profitability. This competition increases team identity and loyalty, although its intensity needs to be kept in check so as not to undermine organizational identity and cooperation (Fishman, 1996).

Finally, providing information and feedback related to both team goals and organizational goals enables teams to stay aligned with a shared vision and fosters higher levels of cooperation. For instance, in a study of the relationship between Chinese companies and their suppliers, Wong, Tjosvold, and Yu (2005) reported that the relationship between a high level of a shared vision among employees and low levels of opportunistically taking unfair advantage of others was mediated partially by cooperative goal setting. Whole Foods makes performance information and feedback readily available to all employees. They post a fax of regional sales reports by team on a weekly basis and make detailed store-level information on profitability available to all employees on a monthly basis. They even make a book available on an annual basis that includes salary details for all employees all the way up to the CEO (Fishman, 1996). When organizations are able to foster a culture of cooperation and trust, this increases the level of feedback and knowledge-sharing available to their teams. This information works together with self-set team goals to produce higher team performance (Quigley, Tesluk, Locke, & Bartol, 2007).

In summary, team goals work in a similar manner to individual goals, but involve some unique and complex considerations. Managers wanting to improve team performance using goals should be sure to seek goal alignment within the team and the organization by developing a shared vision of specific and challenging superordinate goals. They should particularly attend to the development of team efficacy and should either involve the team in setting goals or provide a clear and compelling rationale for assigned goals. The tension between cooperative and competitive goals should be managed carefully, and managers should seek to maximize the information and feedback available to teams.

Feedback

For challenging goals to lead to high performance, they need to be accompanied by adequate feedback (Erez, 1977). However, not all feedback is helpful. Indeed a meta-analysis (statistical review) of 607 feedback interventions revealed that, in 38 percent of cases, feedback actually had a *negative* impact on performance (Kluger & DeNisi, 1996). Feedback can also be viewed as not accurate or useful, potentially leading to feelings of discouragement and anger (Brett & Atwater, 2001). It is thus important for managers to be aware of how to provide feedback in a manner most likely to bring about a positive change in behavior. Five principles suggested by DeNisi and Kluger (2000) for providing effective feedback are as follows:

First, focus on the specific behavior and/or performance in question, rather than on what you think the feedback indicates about the person (for example, his character, professionalism, integrity, and so forth). The latter type of feedback is likely to yield resentment, defensiveness, and distraction from what the person can do to act/perform more effectively in the future.

Second, provide information relating to needed personal or team performance improvements and minimize information relative to the performance of others (for example, you did better than 85 percent of the other team members, departments, and so on). Even if social comparative feedback is apparently positive, as in the example just provided, research (Kluger & DeNisi, 1996) clearly shows that such feedback elicits an ego focus (Butler, 1987), usually making it less productive than feedback that frames a person's performance relative to his or her goals, past performance, or rate of improvement.

Third, be explicit about the precise nature of the desired behavior and how/when to exhibit it. For instance, "during staff meetings, I encourage you to strive to take no more than your fair share of air time by talking either too long or too often."

Fourth, strive to ensure that your feedback provides a basis for setting specific, relevant goals. An example is: "Why not try to limit yourself to no more than three to five comments and/or questions per meeting, each no longer than about one minute each?"

Fifth, the amount of data presented ought to be minimized so as not to overwhelm the person or elicit an unhelpfully distracting ego focus. While people often seek data on how well they are performing relative to others, this is likely to render feedback less effective by focusing their attention on themselves rather than on how they can perform (more) effectively.

Besides the guidance provided by DeNisi and Kluger (2000), there are at least two other empirically based recommendations for providing effective feedback. First, deliver feedback in an informational rather than a controlling way, as doing so makes a person's subsequent performance more likely to improve. The positive impact on performance of using a supportive style is particularly pronounced when the feedback presented is negative (Zhou, 1998).

Second, realize that greater feedback specificity is not always preferable. Although increasing the specificity of feedback facilitates initial performance, it also discourages exploration and undermines the learning needed for later, more independent performance (Goodman, Wood, & Hendrickx, 2004). Even though highly specific feedback may be better for helping resolve a specific issue and reducing errors of exactly the same type, less specific feedback can facilitate learning which behaviors are associated with negative outcomes and how to fix unanticipated problems (Goodman & Wood, 2004).

To summarize, feedback is most likely to foster positive changes in behavior when it is presented in a supportive manner and is specific about the behavioral and performance improvements needed, thereby providing a foundation for goal setting. However, caution is warranted to avoid being overly specific, so as not to limit the extent to which any lessons learned from the feedback generalize to other novel work predicaments.

Conclusion

Given the key role of coaching and goal setting in performance management (London, 2003), we have outlined five key issues to keep in mind when coaching employees to improve their performance. After discussing recent research developments related to these issues, we have provided concrete recommendations for the effective application of goal setting to performance management. Latham and Locke (2006), as well as Latham and Mann (2006), discuss additional issues and insights relevant to the shrewd use of goal setting in the context of performance management.

References

Aronson, E. (1999). The power of self-persuasion. *American Psychologist, 54*, 873–890.

Bandura, A. (1986). *Social foundations of thought and action.* Englewood Cliffs, NJ: Prentice Hall.

Bandura, A. (1997). *Self-efficacy: The exercise of control.* New York: Freeman.

Bandura, A., & Cervone, D. (1983). Self-evaluative and self-efficacy mechanisms governing the motivational effects of goal systems. *Journal of Personality and Social Psychology, 45*, 1017–1028.

Baum, J. R., & Locke, E. A. (2004). The relationship of entrepreneurial traits, skill, and motivation to subsequent venture. *Journal of Applied Psychology, 89*, 587–598.

Baum, J. R., Locke, E., & Smith, K. (2001). A multi-dimensional model of venture growth. *Academy of Management Journal, 44*, 292–303.

Brett, J. F., & Atwater, L. E. (2001). 360 feedback: Accuracy, reactions, and perceptions of usefulness. *Journal of Applied Psychology, 86*, 930–942.

Butler, R. (1987). Task-involving and ego-involving properties of evaluation: Effects of different feedback conditions on motivational perceptions, interest, and performance. *Journal of Educational Psychology, 79*, 474–482.

Chiu, C., Hong, Y., & Dweck, C. S. (1997). Lay dispositionism and implicit theories of personality. *Journal of Personality and Social Psychology, 73*, 19–30.

Churchill, W. (1940). *We'll fight them on the beaches.* Broadcast on BBC radio on June 4, 1940.

Cialdini, R. B. (2001). *Influence: Science and practice.* Needham Heights, MA: Allyn & Bacon.

Cohen, S. G., Mohrman, S. A., & Mohrman, A. M., Jr. (1999). We can't get there unless we know where we are going: Direction setting for knowledge work teams. In R. Wageman (Ed.), *Research on managing groups and teams: Groups in context, Vol. 2* (pp. 1–31). Stamford, CT: JAI Press.

DeNisi, A. S., & Kluger, A. N. (2000). Feedback effectiveness: Can 360-degree appraisals be improved? *Academy of Management Executive, 14,* 129–139.

DeShon, R. P., Kozlowski, W. J., Schmidt, A. M., Milner, K. R., & Wiechmann, D. (2004). Multiple-goal, multilevel model of feedback effects on the regulation of individual and team performance. *Journal of Applied Psychology, 89,* 1035–1056.

Drach-Zahavy, A., & Erez, M. (2002). Challenge versus threat effects on the goal-performance relationship. *Organizational Behavior and Human Decision Processes, 88,* 667–682.

Durham, C. C., Knight, D., & Locke, E. A. (1997). Effects of leader role, team-set goal difficulty, efficacy, and tactics on team effectiveness. *Organizational Behavior and Human Decision Processes, 72*(2), 203–231.

Dweck, C. S. (1986). Motivational processes affecting learning. *American Psychologist, 41,* 1040–1048.

Dweck, C. S. (1999). *Self-theories: Their role in motivation, personality, and development.* Philadelphia: Psychology Press.

Dweck, C. S. (2006). *Mindset: The new psychology of success.* New York: Random House.

Erez, M. (1977). Feedback: A necessary condition for the goal setting-performance relationship. *Journal of Applied Psychology, 62,* 624–627.

Fishman, C. (1996). Whole Foods is all teams. *Fast Company, 2,* 1–7.

Festinger, L. (1957). *A theory of cognitive dissonance.* Evanston, IL: Row, Peterson.

Frese, M., Brodbeck, F. C., Heinbokel, T., Mooser, C., Schleiffenbaum, E., & Thiemann, P. (1991). Errors in training computer skills: On the positive function of errors. *Human–Computer Interaction, 6,* 77–93.

Goodman, J. S., & Wood, R. E. (2004). Feedback specificity, learning opportunities, and learning. *Journal of Applied Psychology, 89,* 809–821.

Goodman, J. S., Wood, R. E., & Hendrickx, M. (2004). Feedback specificity, exploration, and learning. *Journal of Applied Psychology, 89,* 248–262.

Gully, S. M., Incalcaterra, K. A., Joshi, A. & Beaubien, J. M. (2002). A meta-analysis of team efficacy, potency, and performance: Interdependence and level of analysis as moderators of observed relationships. *Journal of Applied Psychology, 87*(5): 819–832.

Heimbeck, D., Frese, M., Sonnentag, S., & Keith, N. (2003). Integrating errors into the training process: The function of error management instructions and the role of goal orientation. *Personnel Psychology,* *56,* 333–361.

Heslin, P. A., & Klehe, U. C. (2006). Self-efficacy. In S. G. Rogelberg (Ed.), *Encyclopedia of industrial/organizational psychology* (Vol. 2, pp. 705–708). Thousand Oaks, CA: Sage.

Heslin, P. A., Latham, G. P., & VandeWalle, D. M. (2005). The effect of implicit person theory on performance appraisals. *Journal of Applied Psychology, 90,* 842–856.

Heslin, P. A., & VandeWalle, D. (2008). Managers' implicit assumptions about personnel. *Current Directions in Psychological Science, 17,* 219–223.

Heslin, P. A., VandeWalle, D., & Latham, G. P. (2006). Engagement in employee coaching: The role of managers' implicit person theory. *Personnel Psychology, 59,* 871–902.

Howard, A., & Bray, D. (1988). *Managerial lives in transition.* New York: Guilford Press.

Kanfer, R., & Ackerman, P. L. (1989). Motivation and cognitive abilities: An integrative/aptitude-treatment interaction approach to skill acquisition. *Journal of Applied Psychology, 74,* 657–690.

Keith, N., & Frese, M. (2005). Self-regulation in error management training: Emotion control and metacognition as mediators of performance effects. *Journal of Applied Psychology, 90,* 677–691.

Keith, N., & Frese, M. (2008). Effectiveness of error management training: A meta-analysis. *Journal of Applied Psychology, 93,* 59–69.

Kerr, S., & Landauer, S. (2004). Using stretch goals to promote organizational effectiveness and personal growth: General Electric and Goldman Sachs. *Academy of Management Executive, 18,* 134–138.

Klein, H. J., Wesson, M. J., Hollenbeck, J. R., & Alge, B. J. (1999). Goal commitment and the goal-setting process: Conceptual clarification and empirical synthesis. *Journal of Applied Psychology, 84,* 885–896.

Klein, H. J., Wesson, M. J., Hollenbeck, J. R., Wright, P. M., & DeShon, R. D. (2001). The assessment of goal commitment: A measurement model meta-analysis. *Organizational Behavior and Human Decision Processes, 85,* 32–55.

Kluger, A. N., & DeNisi, A. (1996). The effects of feedback interventions on performance: A historical review, a meta-analysis, and a preliminary feedback intervention theory. *Psychological Bulletin, 119,* 254–284.

Knight, D., Durham, C. C., & Locke, E. A. (2001). The relationship of team goals, incentives, and efficacy to strategic risk, tactical implementation, and performance. *Academy of Management Journal, 44,* 326–338.

Kohn, A. (2003). Why incentive plans cannot work. *Harvard Business Review, 71,* 54–63.

Latham, G. P. (2001). The importance of understanding and changing employee outcome expectancies for gaining commitment to an organizational goal. *Personnel Psychology, 54,* 707–716.

Latham, G. P. (2003). Goal setting: A five-step approach to behavior change. *Organizational Dynamics, 32,* 309–318.

Latham, G. P. (2004). The motivation benefits of goal setting. *Academy of Management Executive, 18,* 126–129.

Latham, G. P., & Budworth, M. H. (2006). The effect of training in verbal self-guidance on the self-efficacy and performance of Native North Americans in the selection interview. *Journal of Vocational Behavior, 68,* 516–523.

Latham, G. P., Erez, M., & Locke, E. A. (1988). Resolving scientific disputes by the joint design of crucial experiments by the antagonists: Application to the Erez-Latham dispute regarding participation in goal setting. *Journal of Applied Psychology, 73,* 753–772.

Latham, G. P., & Locke, E. A. (1975). Increasing productivity with decreasing time limits: A field replication of Parkinson's law. *Journal of Applied Psychology, 60,* 524–526.

Latham, G. P., & Locke, E. A. (2006). Enhancing the benefits and overcoming the pitfalls of goal setting. *Organizational Dynamics, 35,* 332–340.

Latham, G. P., & Mann, S. (2006). Advances in the science of performance appraisal: Implications for practice. In G. P. Hodgkinson & J. K. Ford (Eds.), *International review of industrial and organizational psychology* (Vol. 21, pp. 295–337). Hoboken, NJ: John Wiley & Sons.

Latham, G. P., & Seijts, G. H. (1999). The effects of proximal and distal goals on performance on a moderately complex task. *Journal of Organizational Behavior, 20,* 421–429.

Lindsley, D. H., Brass, D. J., & Thomas, J. B. (1995). Efficacy-performance spirals: A multilevel perspective. *Academy of Management Review, 20,* 645–678.

Locke, E. A. (1966). The relationship of intentions to level of performance. *Journal of Applied Psychology, 50,* 60–66.

Locke, E. A. (2004). Linking goals to monetary incentives. *Academy of Management Executive, 18,* 130–133.

Locke, E., & Bryan, J. (1967). Performance goals as determinants of level of performance and boredom. *Journal of Applied Psychology, 51,* 120–130.

Locke, E. A., & Bryan, J. (1969). The directing function of goals in task performance. *Organizational Behavior and Human Performance, 4,* 35–42.

Locke, E. A., & Latham, G. P. (1990). *A theory of goal setting and task performance.* Englewood Cliffs, NJ: Prentice Hall.

Locke, E. A., & Latham, G. P. (2002). Building a practically useful theory of goal setting and task motivation: A 35-year odyssey. *American Psychologist, 57,* 705–717.

London, M. (2003). *Giving, seeking, and using feedback for performance improvement.* Mahwah, NJ: Lawrence Erlbaum Associates.

Luthans, F., & Stajkovic, A. D. (1999). Reinforce for performance: The need to go beyond pay and even rewards. *Academy of Management Executive, 13,* 49–57.

Mike, B., & Slocum, J. W. (2003). Slice of reality: Changing culture at Pizza Hut and YUM! Brands, Inc. *Organizational Dynamics, 32,* 319–331.

Mitchell, T. R., & Silver, W. S. (1990). Individual and group goals when workers are interdependent: Effects on task strategies and performance. *Journal of Applied Psychology, 75,* 185–193.

Mueller, C. M., & Dweck, C. S. (1998). Praise for intelligence can undermine children's motivation and performance. *Journal of Personality & Social Psychology, 75,* 33–52.

Noel, T., & Latham, G. P. (2006). The importance of learning goals versus outcome goals for entrepreneurs. *International Journal of Entrepreneurship and Innovation, 7,* 213–220.

Obama, B. (2004). *The audacity of hope.* Keynote address delivered on 27 July 2004 to the Democratic National Convention. Boston, Massachusetts.

Obama, B. (2006). *The audacity of hope: Thoughts on reclaiming the American dream.* New York: Crown.

O'Leary-Kelly, A. M., Martocchio, J. J., & Frink, D. D. (1994). A review of the influence of group goals on group performance. *Academy of Management Journal, 37*(5), 1285–1301.

Organ, D. W., Podsakoff, P. M., & Mackenzie, S. B. (2006). *Organizational citizenship behavior: Its nature, antecedents and consequences.* Thousand Oaks, CA: Sage.

Quigley, N. R., Tesluk, P. E., Locke, E. A., & Bartol, K. M. (2007). A multilevel investigation of the motivational mechanisms underlying knowledge sharing and performance. *Organization Science, 18,* 71–88.

Ragins, B. R., Cotton, J. L., & Miller, J. S. (2000). Marginal mentoring: The effects of type of mentor, quality of relationship, and program design on work and career attitudes. *Academy of Management Journal, 43,* 1177–1194.

Renn, R. W. (2003). Moderation by goal commitment of the feedback-performance relationship: Theoretical explanation and preliminary study. *Human Resource Management Review, 13,* 561–580.

Rogers, R., & Hunter, J. (1991). Impact of management by objectives on organizational productivity. *Journal of Applied Psychology, 76,* 322–336.

Roney, C. J. R., Higgins, E. T., & Shah, J. (1995). Goals and framing: How outcome focus influences motivation and emotion. *Personality and Social Psychology Bulletin, 21,* 1151–1160.

Seijts, G. H., & Latham, G. P. (2000). The effects of goal setting and group size on performance in a social dilemma. *Canadian Journal of Behavioral Science, 32,* 104–116.

Seijts, G. H., & Latham, G. P. (2005). Learning versus performance goals: When should each be used? *Academy of Management Executive, 19,* 124–131.

Stanne, M. B., Johnson, D. W., & Johnson, R. T. (1999). Does competition enhance or inhibit motor performance: A meta-analysis. *Psychological Bulletin, 125,* 133–154.

Tziner, A., & Latham, G. P. (1989). The effects of appraisal instrument, feedback and goal-setting on worker satisfaction and commitment. *Journal of Organizational Behavior, 10,* 145–153.

Wagner, C. M. (2007). Organizational commitment as a predictor variable in nursing turnover research: Literature review. *Journal of Advanced Nursing, 60,* 235–247.

Wegge, J., & Haslam, S. A. (2005). Improving work motivation and performance in brainstorming groups: The effects of three group goal-setting strategies. *European Journal of Work and Organizational Psychology, 14,* 400–430.

Weingart, L. R. (1992). The impact of group goals, task component complexity, effort, and planning on group performance. *Journal of Applied Psychology, 77,* 682–693.

Wiese, B. S., & Freund, A. M. (2005). Goal progress makes one happy, or does it? Longitudinal findings from the work domain. *Journal of Occupational and Organizational Psychology, 78,* 287–304.

Winters, D., & Latham, G. (1996). The effect of learning versus outcome goals on a simple versus a complex task. *Group and Organization Management, 21,* 236–250.

Wofford, J. C., Goodwin, V. L., & Premack, S. (1992). Meta-analysis and the antecedents of personal goal level and of the antecedents and consequences of goal commitment. *Journal of Management, 18,* 595–615.

Wong, A., Tjosvold, D., & Yu, Z. (2005). Organizational partnerships in China: Self-interest, goal interdependence and opportunism. *Journal of Applied Psychology, 90*, 782–791.

Wood, R. E. (1986). Task complexity: Definition of the construct. *Organizational Behavior and Human Decision Processes, 37*, 60–82.

Wood, R. E., & Bandura, A. (1989). Impact of conceptions of ability on self-regulatory mechanisms and complex decision making. *Journal of Personality and Social Psychology, 56*, 407–415.

Wood, R. E., & Locke, E. A. (1990). Goal setting and strategy effects on complex tasks. In B. Staw & L. L. Cummings (Eds.), *Research in organizational behavior* (Vol. 12, pp. 73–109). Greenwich, CT: JAI Press.

Wood, R. E., Mento, A. J., & Locke, E. A. (1987). Task complexity as a moderator of goal effects: A meta-analysis. *Journal of Applied Psychology, 72*, 416–425.

Zhou, J. (1998). Feedback valence, feedback style, task autonomy, and achievement orientation: Interactive effects on creative performance. *Journal of Applied Psychology, 83*, 261–276.

Note

1. Granted that in this scenario, *honesty* was the desired behavior (DB) and theft/stealing was the undesired behavior (UB), the questions represent a specific application of the first four steps in the general empathy box protocol presented in Table 3.1.

CHAPTER 4

COACHING AND PERFORMANCE MANAGEMENT

How Can Organizations Get the Greatest Value?

David B. Peterson

Informal coaching has long been a part of leadership development and performance management in organizations. Since the mid-1990s, however, coaching has taken on a new importance as organizations have increasingly come to see leadership talent as one of their key competitive advantages. Organizations have responded by training managers in coaching skills, hiring external coaches, and setting up structured coaching programs and processes. This chapter explores how organizations can get the greatest value from coaching by examining the variety of roles played by managers, human resource professionals, and executive coaches.

The chapter begins with an overview of two coaching frameworks that serve as the organizing structure for the remainder of this chapter. The first framework outlines four stages of how organizations typically evolve in their approach to coaching. The second outlines seven important considerations in the process of coaching.

Organizational Approaches to Coaching: Four Stages

To set the stage for what is happening in many organizations today, consider a continuum of organizational approaches to coaching that evolves from completely unstructured and ad hoc to relatively strategic and systemic (Peterson & Little, 2008; see also Clutterbuck & Megginson, 2005; Hunt & Weintraub, 2007; Underhill, McAnally, & Koriath, 2007; Valerio & Lee, 2005).

Stage 1: Ad Hoc Coaching—Driven by Individuals

At first, coaching in most organizations is driven almost exclusively by individuals, typically when a boss, HR professional, or potential coaching client decides he or she would like to find a coach. Although individual participants are likely to obtain significant value from coaching, the lack of coordination across the organization means that it is difficult to evaluate how much coaching is taking place, who is delivering it, who is receiving it, and how much value it is providing to the organization overall. Coaching at this stage is reactive rather than proactive, typically in response to a specific problem (for example, an abrasive manager) or sudden need (for example, on-boarding a key executive in a challenging role). This stage exemplifies the situation depicted by Sherman and Freas (2004) in their article on "The Wild West of Executive Coaching."

Stage 2: Managed Coaching—Driven by a Champion or Sponsor

Organizations typically enter the second stage when one of two things happens. Either someone questions the value of all the random coaching that is occurring and seeks to rein in costs and prevent inappropriate uses of coaching, or someone decides that coaching is such a powerful tool that its use must be harnessed in a more organized and methodical fashion to gain the full value. The first step in either case is to appoint someone as manager of coaching, whose task is to manage all the external coaches running around the organization, including establishing selection criteria, defining coaching processes, and measuring participant satisfaction. As organizations set up processes to manage their external coaching resources, many at this stage also begin to provide clearer expectations and basic training in coaching skills to their managers. Rarely, however, do organizations at this point establish formal criteria for who receives coaching, nor do they measure the overall organizational benefits of coaching.

Stage 3: Proactive Coaching—Driven by a Business Need

Organizations at the third stage of the continuum typically use coaching in an organized, planful fashion to address a specific business issue or need, such as accelerating high potential development, on-boarding new leaders, driving a change in culture, or facilitating integration following a merger or acquisition. The benefit to the organization as a whole, as well as to individual participants, is now a key factor. Organizations typically define criteria for who delivers coaching, for who receives coaching, and for the coaching process itself. Some organizations at this level set up internal coaching roles or formalize the coaching expectations for their HR and leadership development professionals. Some of the more sophisticated organizations at this stage may define different tiers of coaching, such as providing internal coaches for new hires from outside the organization and providing external coaches for promotions from within, or providing internal coaches for most middle managers and external coaches for most executives (Holstein, 2005; McDermott, Levenson, & Newton, 2007).

Stage 4: Strategic Coaching—Driven by Organizational Talent Strategy

Currently there are very few organizations at the fourth stage of the continuum, where coaching is integrated into the organization's overall talent management strategy and is used as a key tool in developing high priority or pivotal talent pools (Boudreau & Ramstad, 2007). At this stage, organizations use coaching to maximize the value for individual participants, specific talent pools, and the broader organization by making sure that investments in coaching are clearly aligned with business strategy and organizational needs, *and* that coaching is the most appropriate and cost-effective method for the purpose. Organizations at the fourth stage are explicit about what is expected of managers as coaches, as well as what coaching needs are served by managers, internal professionals, and external coaches.

A Framework for Coaching and Performance Management

There is a wide variety of definitions, models, and approaches to coaching, as represented in the collections edited by Kilburg and Diedrich (2007), Palmer and Whybrow (2007), and Stober and Grant (2006), just as a sample. This chapter presents a seven-part framework of important aspects of coaching and performance management, suitable for comparing and incorporating many diverse approaches, which will be used to examine how organizations at each stage of the organizational continuum can optimize their coaching efforts.

At the center of this framework is the Development Pipeline (Hicks & Peterson, 1999; Peterson, 2006), a model of the five necessary and sufficient conditions for any type of systematic development. The pipeline metaphor highlights that this is a constraint model (Goldratt & Cox, 1992), such that the amount of change a person can make is constrained by which aspect of the pipeline is most narrow. The other elements of particular importance to coaching are the coaching relationship itself and the organizational context (Peterson & Hicks, 1996). These seven elements are defined as:

1. **The coaching relationship.** The extent to which the working relationship between the coach and person is characterized by trust, acceptance, understanding, and other relationship factors that support learning and development. Coaches can build and enhance the coaching partnership by being respectful and listening attentively, focusing on the people's agendas and helping them accomplish their own goals, being supportive and encouraging, and being accepting and non-judgmental (Kouzes & Posner, 2005; O'Broin & Palmer, 2007; Peterson & Hicks, 1996; J. Rogers, 2004; Smither & Reilly, 2001).

2. **Insight.** The extent to which the person understands what areas need to be developed or changed in order to be more effective. In many coaching models, there is a strong, sometimes almost exclusive, emphasis on feedback as the primary tool for insight, yet full insight requires an understanding

of four elements (Peterson & Hicks, 1996): (a) knowledge of the person's own goals, values, and motivations, (b) how the person perceives his or her own abilities and style, (c) how others perceive the person (that is, feedback from others), and (d) the success factors and what is expected in a given role. These four elements are summarized into what Peterson (2006) calls the GAPS Grid: Goals and Values, Abilities, Perceptions, and Success Factors. Coaches can increase participants' insight by helping them gain a clearer understanding of those four elements and how they relate to each other (Ellinger & Bostrom, 1999; Elliott et al.,1994; Kluger & DeNisi, 1996; Prochaska, DiClemente, & Norcross, 1992; Prochaska, Norcross, & DiClemente, 1994).

3. **Motivation.** The degree to which the person is willing to invest the time and energy it takes to develop oneself. Coaches can work with people to build motivation by clarifying both personal and organizational reasons for change, focusing on small, easy steps to initiate the process; identifying personal and organizational barriers that make change difficult; and discussing specific steps for addressing barriers and challenges (Dweck, 1986, 2000; Miller & Rollnick, 2002).

4. **Capabilities.** The extent to which the person has the skills and knowledge that are needed. Coaches can enhance capabilities by sharing new ideas and best practices, helping people find appropriate resources and opportunities to learn, exploring alternative ways to handle difficult situations, and practicing new skills and behaviors in realistic situations (Druckman & Bjork, 1991; Peterson & Hicks, 1996).

5. **Real-world practice.** The extent to which the person has opportunities to try new skills at work. Coaches can facilitate transfer and generalization to the real world by identifying specific situations where change is appropriate, helping people determine how they will put small changes into practice every day, working with people to create personal strategies for assessing in real-time what is working well and what they need to do differently (Druckman & Bjork, 1991; Holton & Baldwin, 2003; Peterson, 2002; Peterson & Muros, 2008).

6. **Accountability.** The extent to which there are internal and external mechanisms for paying attention to change and providing

meaningful consequences. Coaches can enhance accountability by encouraging people to make specific commitments for action, following up on commitments in a timely way, and encouraging people to enlist others to give them feedback and discuss progress (Cameron & Pierce, 1994; Holton & Baldwin, 2003; Prochaska, DiClemente, & Norcross, 1992; Prochaska, Norcross, & DiClemente, 1994; R. W. Rogers, 2004; Peterson & Muros, 2008).

7. **Organizational context.** The extent to which the organizational context, including boss and HR support, organizational systems, culture, norms, and social relationships, support the coaching process. Coaches can enhance the organizational context by teaching the person to anticipate and address barriers, enlisting other people in the process, and consulting with HR and senior leaders about creating a conducive climate for development (Hunt & Weintraub, 2002, 2007; Peterson & Hicks, 1996; Underhill, McAnally, & Koriath, 2007).

The Manager's Role

Managerial coaching has been recognized as a powerful tool for developing employees, enhancing job satisfaction and improving job performance (Hamlin, Ellinger, & Beattie, 2006; Jarvis, Lane, & Fillery-Travis, 2006). Goleman (2000; Goleman, Boyatzis, & McKee, 2002) outlines how effective a leader can be in using a coaching style to get results across a wide range of business situations, yet also observes that it is the least used of the six leadership styles they studied. On a similar note, Lombardo and Eichinger (2002) observe that, whereas coaching is one of the leadership behaviors most desired by direct reports, it is unfortunately one of the least practiced. That contrast is exacerbated by the fact that the coaching most people want is facilitative, supportive, and aimed at their own goals and needs, whereas the type of coaching they are more likely to receive is directive and aimed at accomplishing the manager's or organization's goals (Keep & Rainbird, 2000; Peterson, Uranowitz, & Hicks, 1996). This tendency is greatest in organizations that are toward the ad hoc end of the organizational coaching continuum, where little guidance or training on coaching is provided. In fact, in Stage 1, ad hoc organizations rarely use the word "coaching," and the typical approach to coaching is viewed as similar to good performance management: setting performance expectations, providing feedback and advice, and holding people accountable for performance. What organizations can do, therefore, to get the greatest value at Stage 1 is to ensure that managers take those three elements seriously (for example, include these behaviors in performance evaluations) and perform them well (for example, provide relevant tools and training that support the process). Setting clear performance expectations, for example, might involve discussions of goal setting (Smither & Reilly, 2001), job and role descriptions, competency models, team and business unit objectives, organizational norms and values, as well as specific expectations of the manager. Providing feedback and advice at this stage is often best accomplished by teaching fairly simple, concrete models, such as DESC: Describe the behavior, Express your feeling about it, Specify the desired change, and state the Consequences if the desired change does not occur (Bower & Bower, 2004). Holding people accountable may be as simple as ensuring periodic discussions of performance and effective annual performance reviews.

In terms of the coaching framework, managers in Stage 1 organizations tend to focus on Insight ("Here's what we need from you and how I see you performing currently") and Accountability ("Here's my evaluation of how you did this year"). Done well, even such an elementary approach can have a very positive impact on performance.

At Stage 2, Managed Coaching, organizations realize that coaching is an important skill for managers and begin to incorporate coaching into competency models and performance reviews and also provide training on coaching, although it is usually optional. They often describe coaching as a regular part of a manager's job, although this typically remains an expectation rather than a reality. They tend to focus on four aspects of the coaching framework, building on the Insight and Accountability elements common to Stage 1 organizations and incorporating a focus on Capabilities and Real-World Practice.

- *Insight.* Rather than the one-way process described earlier (communicate expectations and give feedback), managers may now be expected to help employees clarify their personal goals and values, career plans, and development priorities, and put together development plans that focus on building skills for current performance as well as for future performance. The insight conversation thus becomes a more collaborative, shared process.

- *Capabilities and Real-World Practice.* Managers become more responsible for ensuring that people are learning and applying new skills. A common practice is to find ways to facilitate on-the-job learning (hence these two elements are combined here) through new responsibilities, special projects, and stretch assignments.
- *Accountability.* At this stage, the accountability often shifts from purely on performance ("How well did you perform?") to incorporate accountability for development itself ("What did you learn?"). Examples include requiring development plans from people and measuring progress against them as part of the performance review cycle.

To optimize value here, organizations can provide management training in the required skills, formalize the organizational processes and tools that support these behaviors, communicate the importance and value of coaching to the organization, and provide role models of effective coaching and development. Many organizations at this stage have also launched 360-degree feedback processes, so it is helpful to find ways to link the 360 results into the development planning and coaching process.

Because one of the biggest barriers to coaching at every stage is lack of time, it is important that organizations find simple tools and ways to support managers. One useful, easily learned tool is the GROW model (Alexander, 2007; Passmore, 2007; Whitmore, 2002), a basic framework for coaching conversations:

Goal setting for the session as well as short term and long term

Reality checking to explore the current situation

Options and alternative strategies or courses of action

What is to be done, When, by Whom, and the Will to do it (sometimes labeled as Will, Wrap-Up, or Way forward).

Whitmore (2002) points out that coaching based on the GROW conversation is designed to increase the person's awareness (insight)

and responsibility (accountability), which are, as noted above, the two aspects of the coaching framework typically emphasized in Stage 1 and 2 organizations.

Research conducted by Longenecker and colleagues (Longenecker & Ariss, 2002; Longenecker & Fink, 2001; Longenecker & Neubert, 2003, 2005) captures the state of coaching in Stage 1 and 2 organizations very well. They find that:

1 Most managers receive little or no formal on-the-job coaching after training programs.
2. Most managers receive little structured or ongoing performance feedback.
3. When feedback does occur, it tends to be reactive rather than proactive in nature.
4. The higher people rise in an organization, the less likely they are to receive effective and meaningful performance feedback (Longenecker & Neubert, 2005).

Longenecker and Neubert (2005) surveyed forty-five focus groups of managers to find out what they valued in a manager-coach. They list ten behaviors in order of frequency of mention.

1. Clarify what results/performance outcomes are needed/desired (82 percent).
2. Provide honest, ongoing, balanced performance feedback (78 percent).
3. Impart feedback based on an accurate assessment of performance (71 percent).
4. Know the junior manager's strengths and weaknesses (69 percent).
5. Offer expert advice on performance improvement (64 percent).
6. Develop a working relationship based on mutual benefit and trust (60 percent).
7. Understand the context, pressure, and demands of the junior manager's job (58 percent).
8. Support the junior manager in solving work problems (53 percent).
9. Help the junior manager prioritize and stay focused (47 percent).
10. Create accountability for performance improvement (44 percent).

Note that the first four all relate to Insight: "What is expected of me and where do I stand?" Without that information as a starting point, little can be done through coaching or through any means to improve performance. Four other items connect clearly to the coaching framework: Item 5 speaks to Capabilities, Item 6 to the Coaching Relationship, Item 7 to the Organizational Context, and Item 10 to Accountability. The other two items may relate to multiple aspects of the framework, but not as clearly, for example. Item 8 has aspects related to the Relationship and to Real-World Practice, while Item 9 might be related to Insight, Motivation, and/or Real-World Practice.

Research by the Gallup Organization (Buckingham & Clifton, 2001; Buckingham & Coffman, 1999), based on surveys of over a million employees and detailed interviews with eighty thousand managers, also emphasizes the essential nature of insight for development and performance. Buckingham and Coffman identified twelve questions that differentiate highly effective managers from less effective managers. Question 1, which they regard as fundamental to all the rest, is, "Do I know what is expected of me at work?" Even though their purpose was not to examine coaching, and the majority of the questions have to do with employee satisfaction and a positive working environment, several other questions speak directly to the manager's role as coach. Question 5, for example ("Does my supervisor or someone at work seem to care about me as a person?"), is directly related to the coaching relationship, and Question 6 ("Is there someone at work who encourages my development?") is linked to the Relationship, Motivation, and Accountability.

Another study also found insight to be at the top of the list. In-depth interviews with fifty-eight executives from Fortune 250 organizations found that managers reported that in their coaching with others they were most likely to provide feedback and advice, work on development plans, and focus on specific skills (Peterson, Uranowitz, & Hicks, 1996). When asked what they most valued in the coaching they received, the same executives again listed feedback and advice as most important, but then the lists diverged significantly. Their second and third most-wanted items were to have trusting relationships and information on organization strategy and how that relates to their development.

These three sets of research, along with others (for example, Ellinger & Bostrom, 1999), reinforce the essential role of insight in managerial coaching. The coaching relationship also is mentioned, but at a lower level of importance. Nonetheless, it can be a critical element in the overall effectiveness of coaching (Hamlin, Ellinger, & Beattie, 2006; O'Broin & Palmer, 2007; Peterson & Hicks, 1996) and it may matter even more in certain cultures outside the United States (for example, Noer, Leupold, & Valle, 2007). Hoppe (1998) points out that leaders in individualistic cultures, such as in the United States, tend to be less comfortable depending on others for support, whereas managers in collectivist cultures such as China, Mexico, Japan, Indonesia, and Singapore consider it their duty to guide and counsel their employees, and employees look to them for support.

Organizations at Stages 1 and 2 tend to be reactive in terms of how they and their managers approach coaching and performance development. In Stage 3, Proactive Coaching, the focus shifts in two key ways—to using coaching proactively as a solution and to directing its use at broader organizational priorities and talent pool needs as well as individual needs. Stage 3 organizations build on the foundation established previously (clear Insight and Accountability) and add a stronger emphasis on Motivation and the Organizational Context. In terms of Motivation, organizations are often beginning to talk about coaching as an important leadership development technique for accomplishing business results, and finding ways to encourage groups of key people (pivotal talent pools; Boudreau & Ramstad, 2007) to participate. The Organizational Context is addressed as organizations launch coaching programs specifically designed to support and align with business priorities and other internal initiatives (Hunt & Weintraub, 2007; Peterson & Little, 2008).

Perhaps the most critical shift in coaching at Stage 3 is increasing differentiation and clarification of the specific coaching roles of managers, HR, and external coaches. One organization, for example, that was trying to drive decision making down the organizational hierarchy in an effort to be faster moving and more customer focused provided the following guidelines. These guidelines were originally prompted by discussions about how to use coaching as part of the culture change process, and led to a more clearly delineated approach to coaching roles in general.

- Managers are expected to address all basic coaching situations on their teams, defined as issues of underperformance and marginal performance; helping new members of their team get up-to-speed quickly; coaching for solid performers to keep them motivated, engaged, and growing; and support development for top performers and high-potentials to help them advance.
- HR generalists are expected to provide coaching in three areas. First, to coach managers on their coaching skills and, in particular, help them coach people and performance problems they were otherwise reluctant to deal with. In the past, HR professionals in this organization had often been viewed as the primary coaches when poor performers needed feedback or counsel. Now, they were explicitly directed not to become involved except as coaches to the manager. Second, to coach managers who have recently participated in the company-wide training on driving decision making downward in the organization in order to help them make appropriate changes in their management style. Third, to coach managers who were recently promoted.
- External coaches were only to be used in rare situations after a summary of the business rationale was approved, such as coaching new hires at the vice presidential level or higher, or coaching critical leaders in extremely complex or challenging situations.

To support these changes, managers in this organization were required to attend a half-day of web-based training, and HR coaches were provided a three-day workshop on coaching skills. Senior executives also were engaged to share examples of how coaching had helped them become more effective leaders.

Organizations at Stage 4, Strategic Coaching, typically view coaching as an integral part of a manager's job and often talk about building a learning culture or a culture of coaching and development (Clutterbuck & Megginson, 2005). One of the distinguishing features of this stage is that coaching is integrated into overall talent management strategy, so managers are typically expected to incorporate coaching and learning into their regular activities. Organizations at this level generally have a clear sense of where they are focusing their leadership development activities— for example, high-potentials, high performers, leaders moving into new roles, and those in the most critical positions—and they expect manager-coaches to align their coaching with those priorities. Some organizations with a clear talent strategy are even being explicit about where they do not want managers to spend their time coaching, such as those that prefer to eliminate rather than coach the bottom 5 percent of workers as identified in their forced ranking process.

Performance Management vs. Developmental Coaching

Although the fundamentals of coaching are similar regardless of purpose, it may help to highlight the differences in conversations where coaching is primarily forward-looking and developmental in nature from those in which the person being coached is underperforming or not meeting important expectations. The GAPS Grid (see Table 4.1; Peterson, 2006), a framework for coaching conversations that addresses Insight and Motivation, can be used to illustrate some of the key differences:

Goals and Values refers to what motivates the person's behavior at work, which is essential to understanding their efforts to perform and to develop themselves. Each person's most powerful motivations are unique, although most people share a number of values to some extent, including money, recognition, affiliation and a sense of belonging, security, sense of purpose, opportunities to learn, and feeling valued.

Abilities refers to the person's view of his or her own skills, abilities, and style.

Perceptions refers to how others (for example, boss, colleagues, direct reports, coach, family) see the person.

Success Factors refers to the expectations of others regarding what it takes to be successful in a given role. Success Factors on the job may be found in job descriptions, annual goal setting and

Table 4.1 GAPS Grid with Representative Questions.

	Where the person is	What matters
The person's view	**Abilities:** How the person sees him- or herself • How does this person see his or her own major strengths? • Where does he or she see weaknesses or areas he or she would like to get better at? • What abilities does he or she feel will serve best at accomplishing what matters? • What aspects of his or her skills or style get in the way of accomplishing what matters? • What skills does the person think have contributed most to success so far? • What additional skills does he or she think would be helpful?	**Goals and Values:** What matters to the person • What are the person's most important goals, values, and interests? • What motivates the person at work? • What is most demotivating to him or her? • What does he or she find most rewarding? • What inspires the person to do his or her best? • What work activities does he or she enjoy? • What would make work more fulfilling for the person? • What does the person care most about in life? • What gives the person the greatest sense of satisfaction?
Views from other perspectives (boss, coach, peers, colleagues, senior management, family, friends, social networks, and others)	**Perceptions:** How others see the person • How do others perceive the person? • What do other people say about him or her? • How do others view the person's strengths, weaknesses, style, and impact? • To what do other people attribute this person's successes and failures?	**Success Factors:** What matters to others • What is necessary for this person to be successful in his or her current role? How are those factors changing? • What does this person's boss value and expect? • What types of people and what skills are most valued in this organization? Why? • What does the boss (and other senior managers) expect of someone in this role? • What do relevant competency models, job descriptions, and performance metrics say about success in this role? • What social norms and organizational values are people expected to follow?

objectives, competency models, organizational and cultural values, and informal analysis of who is and is not successful, as well as in the implicit assumptions and unspoken social norms for behavior.

The primary purpose of performance management conversations is to drive immediate changes in current behavior to meet expectations. Therefore, the most appropriate starting point in the conversation is Success Factors, followed by Perceptions, to indicate exactly what is expected of the person and where the person is falling short. After the external input is discussed, it makes sense to examine the person's Goals and Motivations, to gauge his or her level of commitment to making the desired changes. Although genuine dialogue and mutual understanding are still desired in this type of conversation, it is essential that the person clearly understand the manager's views.

Developmental coaching conversations have a wider range of purposes (enhance current job performance, build capabilities for future success, increase job satisfaction, fulfill one's potential, and so forth), and it is generally most appropriate to begin with a discussion of the person's Goals and Values. Beginning there builds the coaching relationship by showing an interest in the person and clarifies the person's motivations to perform and to develop, which is necessary to sustain any development effort. The second part of the conversation explores the relevant Success Factors (for the current role or a desired future role), followed by a discussion of Abilities and Perceptions to determine where development will have the greatest ROI in helping the person achieve what matters.

A common mistake in both conversations is starting with feedback (Perceptions data). It is much more effective to specify the objectives first (accomplishing more of what matters to one or both parties—Goals and Values or Success Factors) and then discuss how each party views the person relative to those objectives (Abilities and Perceptions).

Other differences in the two types of conversations are displayed in Table 4.2.

Finally, it is worth noting that each type of conversation has at least one significant barrier that often gets in the way of managers

Table 4.2 Key Differences Between Performance Management and Development Coaching Conversations.

	Developmental Coaching	Performance Management
Purpose	• Varied, including building capabilities for current or future roles, enhancing job satisfaction, preparing for change, increasing agility and versatility, etc.	• Drive immediate changes in current behavior to meet expectations
Insight and Motivation: GAPS conversation	• Start with Goals and Values, then Success Factors	• Focus on Success Factors, then Perceptions
Ongoing feedback	• Periodic, primarily driven by the learner	• Regular feedback and evaluation of progress against expectations
Accountability	• Primary accountability placed on learning and developmental progress over time	• Strong focus on accountability for performance against specific objectives, with specific consequences clearly identified
Time frame	• Typically six months to a year	• Typically three months or less

making the time for them. For developmental coaching, managers are often under a great deal of pressure to deliver immediate results and thus are unlikely to spend time coaching where the payoff is not relatively quick and tangible. For performance management, the conversations may be difficult, surfacing defensive, argumentative, and even emotionally volatile responses from people. Thus, many managers tend to defer discussion or approach it in vague generalities that are less likely to offend but equally unlikely to accomplish desired changes.

One way to encourage managers to take coaching seriously is to incorporate coaching-related items into 360-degree feedback and organizational surveys, such as, "My manager spends time coaching me," "My manager makes coaching a priority," "My manager is an effective coach" (Peterson, 2002; Peterson & Kraiger, 2004, Underhill, McAnally, & Koriath, 2007). Some best manager-coach practices are shown in Table 4.3.

Table 4.3 Best Practices for Manager-Coaches.

1. Coaching relationship	• Take time to explore what is important to the person you are coaching—his or her goals, values, and motivations.
	• Communicate your desire to help the person develop and ask what kind of coaching he or she would like from you.
	• Communicate the positive expectation that you believe in the person and his or her ability to learn and make significant progress on objectives.
2. Insight	• Clearly communicate expectations and success factors.
	• Provide feedback and discuss performance relative to those expectations.
	• Ask questions that help people reflect on their own behaviors, performance, and impact.
3. Motivation	• Help people clarify their goals and motivations related to work and to their own development.
	• Identify specific personal and organizational benefits for development.
4. Capabilities	• Provide specific advice and guidance on how to improve performance and behavior.
	• Encourage them to prepare development plans.
	• Support training, stretch assignments, and provide opportunities for on-the-job learning.

(Continued)

Table 4.3 (*Continued*)

5. Real-world practice	• Ask people what exactly they will to do to make progress on their development objectives, and where and when they plan to do it.
	• Help them find or create opportunities that stretch their capabilities.
6. Accountability	• Hold regular (for example, monthly) conversations to gauge progress against development objectives.
	• Ask people what they have learned recently and what they will do in the next month to continue learning.
7. Organizational context	• Ask people what organizational barriers are getting in their way and brainstorm ways they can work around them.
	• Be a role model of learning by seeking feedback and coaching from others, sharing development priorities and progress openly, and talking about why development is important to you personally.

The Role of Human Resources and Internal Coaches

Human resource professionals are often at the nexus of coaching in organizations, given their role in supporting managers in handling performance issues, coaching leaders directly, sourcing and managing external coaches, and supporting the external coaching process. Although there is a growing emphasis on having HR generalists provide coaching internally (Hunt & Weintraub, 2007; Jarvis, Lane, & Fillery-Travis, 2006), there is a wide range of roles that they may be expected to fill, including any or all of the following:

- Provide counsel and perspective to key leaders as a trusted adviser.
- Coach and advise managers on their people issues.
- Facilitate broad-based feedback to employees.

- Support development planning efforts.
- Provide career coaching, planning, and exploration.
- Handle sensitive and challenging people issues.
- Coach people when managers lack the time, skills, or courage.

There is also a wide range regarding the centrality of the coaching duties to the person's role, from a simple addition to the existing responsibilities all the way to serving exclusively as a dedicated internal coach. In any case, the trend toward a greater emphasis on internal coaching seems likely to continue, driven as it is by organizations' desires to manage costs and build internal capabilities (Jarvis, Lane, & Fillery-Travis, 2006). Internal coaches may have several advantages over external coaches as well. For example, they are likely to understand the organization's business, culture, and politics; have greater opportunities to observe the person in action and provide immediate, real-time feedback; and be able to take advantage of coachable moments to leverage both formal and informal coaching. However, it is essential that internal coaches have a clear charter. Internal coaching has been much more successful in organizations where the purpose is clear, whether that is to provide support during and after a leadership development program, facilitate organizational change, assist in leadership transitions, or support organizational mergers (Frisch, 2001, 2005; Hunt & Weintraub, 2007).

Internal coaches also face several key challenges, especially compared to external coaches. First, they often have dual roles and potential conflicts of interest, such as when they are expected to reduce headcount in their organizational role and encourage people to talk openly about their development needs and career goals in their coaching role. The dual roles can also make prioritizing and finding time for their coaching difficult when they are pulled in other directions. Second, building trust and managing confidentiality is a challenge when the people they are coaching wonder whose side the person is on and what will happen with any information they share. Third, internal coaches, especially in organizations where HR does not have a strong reputation, often have a harder time establishing credibility than external coaches might, unless they can quickly demonstrate business savvy and offer useful advice and insights. There are several ways to address these issues, starting with making sure that internal coaches are screened, trained, managed, and evaluated as carefully as are external coaches. Giving them a clear mission, having them coach individuals outside their working group, and making sure they have sufficient time to allocate to coaching are also critical (Frisch, 2001; 2005; Hunt & Weintraub, 2007).

Finally, it is useful to compare where external or internal coaches are most useful. For example, one organization chose to use internal coaches—who know the organization well—for on-boarding newly hired executives from outside the organization while using external coaches—who are experts in leadership competencies and helping people get up-to-speed quickly—to facilitate leadership transitions for current employees who are promoted or moving into new roles.

In general, external coaches are most appropriate in working with top executives, with highly confidential or sensitive issues where the person does not want an internal person involved, and when internal coaches don't have the time, specific expertise, or credibility (Holstein, 2005; McDermott, Levenson, & Newton, 2007). Internal coaches are most appropriate when on-the-job observation and real-time coaching are critical and when deep knowledge of the politics, personalities, or relationships is important. In addition, it is recommended that organizations begin to think more about how to partner internal and external coaches, so that external coaches might have shorter, higher-impact engagements with the internal coaches, serving to reinforce desired changes over time through regular feedback and support.

The Role of External Coaches

When organizations begin to use external coaches, they most frequently do so in an ad hoc fashion, pursuing separate searches for an appropriate coach for each individual who needs coaching. As coaching grows in frequency, they tend to start lists of coaches with informal notes on which coaches are best suited for various needs and audiences. These lists tend to get more formalized until organizations set up processes to screen, select, and manage their pool of coaches, thus entering Stage 2, Managed Coaching. At that point, some organizations begin to set parameters for what a typical engagement might look like, often driven by constraints around how much money they will allocate or the amount of time they allow for the coaching. Rarely, however, do organizations set out to strategically design a comprehensive process for managing the coaching conducted by external coaches, such as is outlined here. The following recommendations address five key aspects— who is coached, who delivers the coaching, what the coaching process looks like, what organizational supports are involved, and how coaching is measured, evaluated, and enhanced. As in earlier sections of this chapter, the recommendations are tailored to the maturity level of the organization as reflected in the four stages of organizational approaches to coaching.

Note that the eleven steps as listed follow a logical sequence designed to optimize the value of coaching for the amount of effort invested. However, all the steps are likely to be useful regardless of the order in which organizations choose to implement them.

At Stage 1, Ad Hoc Coaching, where the process is driven by individuals (for example, a participant, boss, or HR person), the primary goal is to ensure highly effective coaching to help individual participants achieve their learning objectives.

Step 1. Select the Right Coach for the Need

There are so many different types of coaches, with different backgrounds and approaches, that it is often difficult for individuals to identify the most suitable type of coach. Unfortunately, the focus of this search is often on finding "the right coach" without adequate consideration of "the need." Given that the need is typically around enhancing effectiveness in business settings, some organizations have determined that they will only hire coaches with real business experience. However, there are three fundamental questions to be addressed in determining suitability of coaches for a given need:

1. How familiar are they with this type of person and the world they live in? The coach needs to understand the vocabulary, issues, and challenges of the person in order to establish credibility and to find solutions that will actually work in their world.

2. What is the coach's track record in working with people on this type of issue? Obviously, if a leader is working on strategic thinking, it is helpful if the coach is familiar with a variety of approaches and tools that can be used and has successfully helped others enhance this capability.
3. What is the coach's approach to helping people learn across the entire Development Pipeline? This is essential because there is a significant difference between helping someone who is motivated to learn about strategic thinking but simply doesn't have the tools and someone who isn't sure exactly what he or she needs to get better at and is even somewhat defensive about the need to change.

For the first two questions, it is relatively easy to assess both the need and the coach's level of experience and expertise in working with similar people on similar issues. For the third question, the following questions can be useful for screening coaches.

Insight: What is your process for identifying the topics and issues to work on? What do you do when the person is already clear on the need versus when he's not sure? What do you do when the person's view is different from the boss's or HR's view?

Motivation: How do you enhance the person's motivation to work on development? How do you work with defensiveness or resistance?

Capabilities: How do you help people acquire the skills and knowledge they need?

Real-World Practice: How do you help people put into action what they know? What steps do you take to make sure the people are comfortable taking risks and trying new things?

Accountability: How do you measure and evaluate progress? How do you make sure people feel a sense of accountability to get good? How do you ensure people stick with their development plans when it is difficult or when distractions come up?

Based on the different needs reflected in the Development Pipeline, there are four fundamentally different types of coaches:

1. Feedback coaches, such as those who routinely administer and interpret 360-degree feedback surveys and/or other personality surveys, interview the person's peers and colleagues, and help put together development plans and action steps.

Whether this involves a simple 360 survey and a one- or two-hour session all the way to intensive assessment and interviews with dozens of colleagues, the major goal is to gather and interpret feedback and launch the development process with a development plan.

2. Insight and Accountability coaches, such as many personal and life coaches, trusted advisors, program follow-up coaches (coaches who meet for an hour a month for a period after the individual attends some other development program). This type of coach tends to clarify the person's goals, values, and specific action steps and then follows up to see how well the person is progressing on accomplishing what matters to him or her.

3. Content coaches, such as former business leaders, mentors, content experts and gurus, academics, and authors tend to focus on building capabilities, giving advice, and/or teaching relevant models, skills, and knowledge.

4. Development experts or learning partners, such as many highly experienced coaches, often with a background in psychology or the behavioral sciences, who focus on the process of helping people develop regardless of where they are constrained in the Development Pipeline.

All of these coaches have value and can be extremely effective when matched with the right need. However, feedback and content coaches may not be as effective when motivation is the issue, and the first two types are not as useful when the person knows what he or she needs to work on but simply needs the right tools and capabilities. The first two types of coaches tend to charge less than the latter two, because of the level of expertise involved, so it is wise not to hire a coach who has more (or different) expertise than needed.

Step 2. Engage the Right Team to Support the Development Process

Even with the ideal coach, development works best as a coordinated team effort, where each person plays a role to support learning and transfer. Bosses and/or other organizational sponsors should provide input on the goals of the coaching, review and sign off on the development objectives, provide encouragement and support to the learner, provide ongoing feedback, evaluate progress, help remove obstacles, and identify opportunities for applying the new skills. They may also play an important role in communicating to others to manage perceptions and facilitate recognition of the progress being made. Human resources plays a role in ensuring appropriate feedback is brought in to the picture, measuring progress, evaluating the coach's work, overseeing the overall process, and gauging suitability of the coach for other possible work in the organization. Even the participant may need to be educated on his or her role, including being receptive to the feedback, making coaching sessions a priority, devoting sufficient time and attention to working on objectives, seeking feedback from a range of others, and keeping the sponsor and HR up-to-date on what he or she is learning, how things are progressing, and what assistance might be needed. The coach may be the team leader, clarifying expectations and ensuring that roles are clearly understood, but each person needs to play a part to optimize the development process.

At Stage 2, Managed Coaching, the use of coaching is typically driven by a champion or sponsor, with the primary goal being to set up a structured program or process to manage individual coaching engagements across the organization. The first two steps from Stage 1 are important building blocks for continuing to get the greatest value.

Step 3. Manage the Pool of Coaches

Best practices in Stage 2 begin with establishing a suitable line-up of coaches and making sure they understand how to work effectively in a given organization. A useful approach may include the following:

- Define appropriate criteria for coaches who match the needs of the coaching participants, recognizing that the criteria might vary for different purposes.
- Screen coaches carefully against those criteria, even those coaches who are already established inside the organization.
- Select a relatively small pool (so the group is easier to manage) who meet the criteria, commit to learn about the organization, make themselves available, and agree to work within specified guidelines.

- Orient coaches to the organization—key players, culture, values, strategy, business dynamics—as well as the coaching process you would like them to follow. Educate them about the HR systems, especially existing development tools, models, language, and processes that they can leverage and reinforce.
- Meet with them periodically to learn what they are seeing and to keep them up-to-date with what is happening inside the organization.
- Evaluate their performance by talking with participants about what the coaches did and how well they did it.

Step 4. Design a Clear Coaching Process

To ensure quality and consistency, each organization should set specific expectations for the type of coaching process (or processes, depending on the variety of needs they have) that they would like their coaches to follow. One of the challenges is finding the right balance between consistency and flexibility (Peterson, 2002). Unfortunately, many organizations over-engineer the process, to the extent that they set up a one-size-fits-all program that eliminates one of the greatest values of coaching—its flexibility as an individually tailored solution. For example, some organizations have mandated 360-degree surveys for everyone at the outset and no more than eight one-hour sessions. The mandatory feedback survey can be a waste of time when people already have a clear sense of what they need to work on or, as occasionally happens, have just completed a separate 360 survey as part of another process. The schedule and duration also needs to be flexible, to accommodate different needs, different contexts, and often very different starting points. One organization set up three processes to address the most common needs they saw:

- Coach-facilitated 360-degree feedback and development planning, including thirty-minute interviews with the person's boss and two or three others.
- Focused coaching, of up to ten hours, scheduled as desired by the coach and participant. Some people opted for monthly one-hour conversations, whereas others had fewer but much longer, more intensive working sessions.

- In-depth coaching, typically twenty to thirty hours of coaching over a six- to nine-month period, for people with significant development needs or who were moving into much larger roles or who faced significant challenges in their business.

Participants in each of these options were afforded considerable flexibility. However, to ensure consistency, there were several requirements: each coaching participant needed the support of his or her boss and the HR person; had to submit a written development plan with specific learning objectives and a clear link to business results; had to submit a written summary of progress and the value to the business; and had to participate in an evaluation interview with HR at the end of the coaching.

Key considerations in setting up a logical, flexible process include identifying:

- Who is eligible to receive coaching and for what purposes (including specifying when coaching is not appropriate and what alternatives might be appropriate)
- Who may authorize/approve coaching
- Who pays for the coaching and how much can be spent
- Who has input into the coaching objectives, how formal they are
- How progress is to be tracked and evaluated
- How coaches will be sourced and matched to participants
- The role of boss and HR, and any other players who are involved
- How confidentiality and communication will be handled
- What the timeframe is expected to be
- How the engagement will end and what kind of ongoing support is available for continued development
- How outcomes will be evaluated
- Who will see outcome data and how information will be used to improve the process

Step 5. Market and Promote Coaching

It is surprising how many organizations will invest considerable effort in designing coaching programs and guidelines and then not market them internally to promote their use and educate consumers on the best practices for using external coaches. On the one hand, organizations interested in managing the use of external coaches should let people know how to find an approved coach, what the expectations are for the coaching process, and how to participate in the evaluation process so that they can continue to receive input and improve their system. On the other hand, organizations that are interested in getting the greatest value from coaching should be promoting coaching to the people they would most like to participate, those for whom they think coaching can really make a difference. Communicating the value to participants and to the organization, making it easy to sign up and participate, and making the funding readily available for specified audiences are important to ensuring that coaching is utilized optimally.

Step 6. Measure the Impact

There is strong research and case-study evidence that coaching is an effective leadership development tool (Jarvis, Lane, & Fillery-Travis, 2006; Peterson & Kraiger, 2004). However, because of the time and money it requires and the huge variability in coaches and approaches, it is still important that organizations evaluate their own processes to make sure they are getting the level of results they seek. In addition, they can use satisfaction and outcome data to improve their own processes, including which coaches they use for what purposes, who receives coaching, how they match coaches to need, and where they can simplify the process and take costs out. The evaluation might be as simple as a few brief questions (To what extent was this coaching worthwhile? How effective was your coach? What recommendations do you have for improving the coaching process in the future?) to a detailed analysis of each component of the process (coach, administrative procedures, communication, organizational supports, the participant's own effort and commitment, what exactly was learned, the business impact, and so on). Peterson and Kraiger (2004) outline a step-by-step process for identifying the purposes of the evaluation (for example, improvement, marketing, evaluation), the audience, the questions, the data-collection process, analysis, and communication of the results, as well as providing a complete sample survey.

At Stage 3, Proactive Coaching, where coaching is driven by a business need and the focus shifts to developing pivotal talent pools as well as individuals, the primary goal is to establish structured coaching programs to enable and accelerate organizational change or response to external or internal needs. Two more specific steps supplement and build on the six preceding steps.

Step 7. Tailor Coaching to Your Organization's Development Culture and Values

Lawrence (1998) illustrates this principle extremely well in her discussion of how difficult systematic group development was at her financial investment company and why coaching was such an ideal fit with their culture. Among other reasons, she stated that it was a very individualistic culture, so individual coaching could be tailored to each person. It was private, so people did not have to reveal their anxieties and weaknesses to others. The scheduling was totally flexible, so they never had to be away from the stock markets for more than a short period of time and they could easily interrupt the coaching as needed. The organization is strongly relationship-based, which fits well with the ongoing relationship established in coaching. Finally, their culture is very results-oriented, and coaching could be focused quickly on the areas that would have clear payoff.

Another way to think about tailoring coaching to the company culture begins with assessing five organizational values related to the Development Pipeline and how they may facilitate or impede development.

- *Candor* (related to Insight): Do people talk openly about expectations, work performance, and development needs? When candor is high, people tend to have higher levels of insight and are typically more receptive to feedback and discussing their developmental priorities.
- *Trust* (related to Motivation): Do leaders walk their talk and show concern for other people's interests? When people trust their leaders, they are more motivated to work on their

development, believe the feedback they are hearing, try new things, take risks, and work toward longer-term goals.

- *Curiosity* (related to Capabilities): Do people value learning? Do they explore new ideas and discuss alternative ways to do things? In general, organizations that value and emphasize curiosity are more receptive to learning and to sharing knowledge with each other.
- *Flexibility* (related to Real-World Practice): Do people take reasonable risks and try new things? Are they able to move across boundaries to take on stretch assignments or find challenging new tasks? Development is much easier in settings that tolerate or even encourage risk taking and trying new things.
- *Accountability* (related to Accountability): Are people accountable for meeting their objectives and delivering on commitments? To the extent that the culture values and encourages personal accountability, the coach may not have to take as much responsibility to ensure follow-through, whereas in low accountability cultures, the coach may have to systematically monitor and build in accountability at every step.

When these values are present in an organization, development tends to be much easier in that area. For example, when an organization is high on candor, people tend to have higher levels of insight to begin with, and coaches tend to find it easier to facilitate insight with the people they coach. When candor is low, coaching participants may not have heard much direct, honest feedback, they may not have as clear a picture of exactly what is expected of them, and they may be more skeptical of information and perspectives that they have not heard before. Attempts to increase insight in low candor cultures, whether through coaching or any other development process, need to be more structured, systematic, and thorough in order for the message to be received and accepted. The same is true for the other values—when they are high, coaching efforts in that area can be relatively straightforward, and when they are low, it is important that the coaching process emphasize and structure the methods to address them.

Some other common organizational values that influence development include:

- *Results orientation,* which tends to drive short-term performance-related feedback and advice, but short-circuits longer-term developmental coaching efforts. In a results-oriented culture, coaches need to make sure they are emphasizing practical, tangible skills that are directly connected to business results.
- *Respect for people,* which, depending on how it is manifested, can either enhance coaching through its focus on helping people fulfill their potential or make honest feedback and coaching quite difficult due to the emphasis on being nice and maintaining harmony at any cost. Coaches working in this type of culture typically need to emphasize relationship-building and will be more effective when they can show how their work enhances results in a people-positive way.
- *Diversity,* which again may enhance or impede coaching, depending on whether it is reflected in creating an environment in which everyone is encouraged to perform as well as possible or in which everyone is allowed to express personal flaws and foibles out of respect for individual differences.
- *Competitiveness,* where people tend to coach and aid those on their team to optimize short-term results, but not take a longer-term, broader perspective on development.

Step 8. Differentiate Internal and External Coaching Roles and Equip Internal Coaches

There are six distinct coaching roles that people may play, although few organizations use all of them: the manager, a peer coach, a mentor, an HR/OD professional, a dedicated internal coach, and an external executive coach. Expectations for each of these roles can be narrow or broad, and formal or informal. Organizations are encouraged to carefully think through how they would like to use each role, if at all, and how they will equip people to fulfill those expectations. The purpose of this principle is to identify the person best suited, in terms of time, skills, and availability, to meet a given set of needs, starting with what type of coaching is the responsibility of the manager (and what kind of training and organizational supports required to do so effectively) and when an external coach might be involved. Most of these roles, such as the manager-coach and external coach, are addressed elsewhere in this chapter, so here are a few notes on the others.

Peer coaches are often used as part of broader development programs, to coach and hold each other accountable for learning over a defined period of time. Mentors are typically senior-level executives, often from a different function or business unit, whose role is to share their expertise and experience with more junior leaders. Both roles have the advantages of building relationships and teamwork in the organization, requiring little additional investment (although the opportunity cost of taking managers' time away from their regular jobs is rarely acknowledged) and having face validity as relevant, credible resources. The disadvantages are often lack of time and commitment (many might ask what the incentive is for them to spend time coaching someone in a different business unit), lack of skills, and lack of a clear process. Many mentoring and peer coaching programs launch successfully and then fall by the wayside, as the pairs often have positive initial meetings and then lose focus as they try to figure out what exactly they are supposed to do next. Organizations that want to implement peer coaching and mentoring are encouraged to define clear objectives and timetables; provide a useful structure to all the meetings (not just the first one or two); provide appropriate training, support, and tools; find ways to make scheduling and follow-through easy and automatic (not simply leaving it up to the participants to schedule time on their own); and track progress.

At Stage 4, Strategic Coaching, where coaching is driven by talent strategy, the primary goal is to integrate coaching into the organization's talent management systems to develop key talent pools and create greater competitive advantage for both the organization and the individual participants.

Step 9. Align Coaching with Business Needs and Talent Strategy

By this point, most organizations have taken steps to ensure that there is a business rationale for coaching. What is new at Stage 4 is that organizations focus proactively on groups of people, rather than just on individuals, based on their overall business needs and talent strategy. One organization, for example, identified business unit leaders as their most critical talent pool and launched three coaching programs aimed at accelerating development for identified high-potential candidates for such roles, facilitating the transition into the role to get new business unit leaders up-to-speed as quickly as possible, and updating and expanding the capabilities of managers who had been in the role for a while or who were not performing at the top of their game. Another organization identified four pivotal talent groups and designed coaching programs to match their development needs—new executives hired from outside the organization, newly promoted senior managers, high-potential mid-level leaders (often intended to fill the roles of the recently promoted), and leaders in mission-critical roles such as those entering or expanding into new markets (Peterson & Little, 2008). Both organizations systematically sought out and encouraged leaders in the targeted groups to participate in coaching and concomitantly reduced funding for other coaching needs as a means to keep total spending on coaching reasonable but maximize the ROI.

Talent strategy and any associated coaching programs must adjust to the times, of course. To ensure that coaching continues to provide optimal value, organizations must periodically ask themselves who the most critical talent pools are and to what extent coaching is an appropriate solution for their development.

Step 10. Integrate Coaching into Your Talent Management System

Coaching is such a flexible process that it can support virtually any learning and development need. Organizations with a systemic view of coaching ask themselves where coaching fits into the total talent management system, for example, selection (transition coaching, on-boarding for new hires), performance and rewards (performance coaching), leadership development (coaching for high-potentials, executive teams, or as a follow-on to other development programs), and succession management (preparing for new roles, career development, retention). However, just because coaching might be helpful does not mean that it is best-suited or cost-effective for any of those needs, and organizations must find the best-fit solution from an array of options: 360-degree feedback, web-based learning, classroom training, action learning, executive education, job rotation, coaching, and various blended designs of these and other methods. Organizations that truly get the greatest value from coaching are those that know as much about when *not* to use coaching as they do about when to use it.

Step 11. Measure the Organizational Impact and Use the Input to Improve Coaching Processes

This builds on Step 6 (measure the individual impact) to evaluate how well coaching is building talent that contributes directly to organizational outcomes, including team and organizational performance, leadership effectiveness, morale and motivation, retention of critical talent, talent readiness on the succession plan, and so forth. One of the keys to measuring the broader impact of coaching is to identify and define criteria for organization-level talent issues. There are two simple and yet often-overlooked issues here. First, find a talent problem that senior executives are concerned about that coaching can help address—this should be part of the analysis in Steps 10 and 11. Second, use whatever measures you have available to immediately establish a baseline so that you can measure and demonstrate progress (if any) due to coaching. If there are no existing measures, simply survey executives and ask them to rate how severe the problem is. For example, if they say there is a lack of qualified candidates for general manager positions, and you are using coaching to prepare high-potential candidates for that role, consider using a three-or-four-item survey on that topic that you can repeat annually. Keeping the survey quick, simple, and immediately directed at the coaching issue can provide useful data on whether or not coaching is providing the desired results.

Asking several open-ended questions of coaching participants and their managers can also be useful to target the optimal participants, improve the coaching process, and upgrade the quality of your coaches in the future (Peterson & Kraiger, 2004). For example: "What did you [the participant] learn from this coaching?" "What was the business impact?" "What can we do to improve the value our organization receives from coaching?" "What would have helped you make a greater contribution to the business?"

At least annually, those responsible for coaching and talent management should review the data and ask questions such as,

"How well are we addressing business needs and organizational objectives through coaching?" "What has changed in our organization and what do we need to do differently to gain optimal value from our coaching?" "Where is the most pivotal talent pool today and in what ways might coaching be appropriate for them?"

Building a Culture of Coaching and Development

Recently there has been an increase in the number of organizations seeking to create a culture of coaching. On the one hand, this appears a worthy goal in light of so many organizations striving to be agile and adaptable and employees crying out for more coaching and development opportunities. On the other hand, focusing exclusively on coaching to meet those needs seems idealistic and unduly emphasizes the solution over the need. For organizations, being able to perform well under a variety of changing conditions seems to be the goal, and coaching is just one way to do so. For individuals, career advancement, better opportunities, and greater rewards are likely goals, and continual learning and access to better opportunities are key. Teaching people how to learn for themselves is perhaps even more important than coaching, and yet rarely discussed (Peterson & Hicks, 1995).

Although it may partly be semantics, building a *performance-oriented culture* where coaching and self-guided development are valued might be a better way to describe what organizations are seeking. Talking about a coaching culture and then not fully delivering on that is likely to create false expectations and ultimately greater cynicism when it becomes clear that organizations still care more about performance than development (Lindbom, 2007). See Table 4.4 for some best practices.

Many of the keys to building a culture of coaching are already described above. In addition, the following are recommended (Clutterbuck & Megginson, 2005; Hunt & Weintraub, 2007; Lindbom, 2007; Underhill, McAnally, & Koriath, 2007; Whybrow & Henderson, 2007):

- Start at the top, with senior executives as sponsors and role models for coaching. In parallel to Kanter's assessment that

Table 4.4 Best Practices for Building a Culture of Coaching, Learning, and Development.

1. Coaching relationship	• Ensure senior leaders demonstrate high levels of candor, trust, openness.
	• Ensure leaders act as role models by communicating how they have coached others and how they have personally benefited from being coached.
	• Encourage managers and employees to discuss what they would like from each other to support their development, for example, feedback, support, encouragement, questions rather than criticism.
2. Insight	• Clearly communicate the importance of coaching and learning.
	• Clearly communicate the expectation that people be active learners and coaches.
	• Clearly communicate what kinds of things you expect people to be learning, that is, link specific development priorities to business strategy and organizational objectives.
	• Encourage people to seek feedback from others.
3. Motivation	• Cultivate credible and visible role models for learning, starting with yourself.
	• Recognize, reward, and reinforce learning.
	• Create heroes.
	• Tell stories about people who are developing.
4. Capabilities	• Teach people skills and strategies for self-development.
	• Teach managers core skills and strategies for coaching and developing others.
	• Provide tools for seeking feedback and preparing actionable development plans.

(Continued)

Table 4.4 (*Continued*)

5. Real-world practice	• Tolerate mistakes. Encourage people to talk about them and what they learned from them.
	• Encourage stretch assignments.
	• Build in opportunities for reflection at the end of projects and assignments: What did we learn? What would we do differently next time?
6. Accountability	• Metrics—survey employees on quality and frequency of coaching from their managers.
	• Metrics—survey people on their progress against development priorities.
	• Reward managers for developing and sharing talent.
7. Organizational context	• Survey employees on organizational barriers to learning and development and take action against relevant items.
	• Leaders as role models.
	• Build coaching and self-development into existing systems: competency models, performance appraisal, promotions, hiring
	• Provide a common language and experience for everyone.
	• Offer a varied menu of developmental tools and programs.

leaders "are more powerful role models when they learn than when they teach" (1997, p. 56), senior executives are powerful role models for a coaching culture when they talk about the coaching they have received and how they have benefited from coaching, as well as when they talk about how they make coaching others a priority.

• Provide incentives and rewards for coaching.
• Make coaching and developing others a criterion for selection, promotion, and advancement in managerial ranks.

Conclusion

In sum, coaching—whether delivered by managers, HR, internal expert coaches, or executive coaches—is a powerful tool for performance management and for developing individual and organizational capabilities. Yet it is relatively expensive in terms of time and money, so it needs to be focused where it will make the greatest difference. Five key considerations are essential:

1. How do we make sure we coach the right people to make the biggest difference?
2. How do we make sure we use the right coaches equipped with the right skills for the need?
3. How do we design the right process?
4. How do we provide the right organizational supports?
5. How will we evaluate and continually improve what we are doing?

It is probably impossible to design the ideal coaching system. Yet that is no reason to delay starting now, working wherever you are with whatever resources you have, to take steps to get greater value from the coaching that is being done in your organization today.

References

Alexander, G. (2007). Behavioral coaching—The GROW model. In J. Passmore (Ed.), *Excellence in coaching: The industry guide.* Philadelphia: Kogan Page.

Boudreau, J. W., & Ramstad, P. M. (2007). *Beyond HR: The new science of human capital.* Cambridge, MA: Harvard Business School Press.

Bower, S. A., & Bower, G. H. (2004). *Asserting yourself: A practical guide for positive change* (2nd ed.). Cambridge, MA: Da Capo.

Buckingham, M., & Clifton, D. O. (2001). *Now, discover your strengths.* New York: Free Press.

Buckingham, M., & Coffman, C. (1999). *First, break all the rules: What the world's greatest managers do differently.* New York: Simon & Schuster.

Cameron, J., & Pierce, W. D. (1994). Reinforcement, reward, and intrinsic motivation: A meta-analysis. *Review of Educational Research, 64*(3), 363–423.

Clutterbuck, D., & Megginson, D. (2005). *Making coaching work: Creating a coaching culture.* London: Chartered Institute of Personnel and Development.

Druckman, D., & Bjork, R. A. (1991). *In the mind's eye: Enhancing human performance.* Washington, DC: National Academy Press.

Dweck, C. S. (1986). Motivational processes affecting learning. *American Psychologist, 41,* 1040–1048.

Dweck, C. S. (2000). *Self-theories: Their role in motivation, personality, and development.* Philadelphia: Psychology Press.

Ellinger, A. D., & Bostrom, R. P. (1999). Managerial coaching behaviors in learning organizations. *Journal of Management Development, 18*(9), 752–771.

Elliott, R., Shapiro, D. A., Firth-Cozens, J., Stiles, W. B., Hardy, G. E., Llewelyn, S. P., & Margison, F. R. (1994). Comprehensive process analysis of insight events in cognitive-behavioral and psychodynamic-interpersonal psychotherapies. *Journal of Counseling Psychology, 41,* 449–463.

Frisch, M. H. (2001). The emerging role of the internal coach. *Consulting Psychology Journal, 53*(4), 240–250.

Frisch, M. H. (2005). Extending the reach of executive coaching: The internal coach. *Human Resource Planning, 28*(1), 23.

Goldratt, E. M., & Cox, J. (1992). *The goal: A process of ongoing improvement* (2nd rev. ed.). Great Barrington, MA: North River Press.

Goleman, D. (2000, March/April). Leadership that gets results. *Harvard Business Review, 78*(2), 78–90.

Goleman, D., Boyatzis, R., & McKee, A. (2002). *Primal leadership: Realizing the power of emotional intelligence.* Boston: Harvard Business School Press.

Hamlin, R. G., Ellinger, A. D., & Beattie, R. S. (2006). Coaching at the heart of managerial effectiveness: A cross-cultural study of managerial behaviors. *Human Resource Development International, 9*(3), 305–331.

Hicks, M. D., & Peterson, D. B. (1999). The development pipeline: How people really learn. *Knowledge Management Review, 9,* 30–33.

Holstein, W. J. (2005, November). Best companies for leaders. *Chief Executive, 213,* 24–30.

Holton, E. F., & Baldwin, T. T. (Eds.). (2003). *Improving learning transfer in organizations.* San Francisco: Jossey-Bass.

Hoppe, M. H. (1998). Cross-cultural issues in leadership development. In C. D. McCauley, R. S. Moxley, & E. Van Velsor (Eds.), *The center for creative leadership handbook of leadership development* (pp. 336–378). San Francisco: Jossey-Bass.

Hunt, J. M., & Weintraub, J. R. (2002). *The coaching manager: Developing top talent in business.* Thousand Oaks, CA: Sage.

Hunt, J. M., & Weintraub, J. R. (2007). *The coaching organization: A strategy for developing leaders.* Thousand Oaks, CA: Sage.

Jarvis, J., Lane, D. A., & Fillery-Travis, M. (2006). *The case for coaching: Making evidence-based decisions on coaching.* London: Chartered Institute of Personnel and Development.

Kanter, R. M. (1997). *On the frontiers of management.* Cambridge, MA: Harvard Business School Press.

Keep, E., & Rainbird, H. (2000). Towards the learning organization. In S. Bach & K. Sisson (Eds.), *Personnel management: A comprehensive guide.* Oxford: Blackwell.

Kilburg, R. R., & Diedrich, R. C. (Eds.). (2007). *The wisdom of coaching: Essential papers in consulting psychology for a world of change.* Washington, DC: American Psychological Association.

Kluger, A., & DeNisi, A. (1996). The effects of feedback interventions on performance: A historical review, meta-analysis and preliminary feedback theory. *Psychological Bulletin, 119,* 254–285.

Kouzes, J., & Posner, B. (2005). When leaders are coaches. In M. Goldsmith & L. Lyons (Eds.), *Coaching for leadership: The practice of leadership coaching from the world's greatest coaches* (pp. 136–143). San Francisco: Pfeiffer.

Lawrence, K. (1998, March). Using executive coaching to accelerate just-in-time learning at Fidelity Investments. Presentation at the Fast Development for Fast Companies conference, San Francisco.

Lindbom, D. (2007). A culture of coaching: The challenge of managing performance for long-term results. *Organization Development Journal, 25*(2), 101–106.

Lombardo, M. M., & Eichinger, R. W. (2002). *The leadership machine.* Minneapolis, MN: Lominger Ltd.

Longenecker, C. O., & Ariss, S. S. (2002). Creating competitive advantage through effective management education. *Journal of Management Development, 21*(9), 640–654.

Longenecker, C. O., & Fink, L. S. (2001). Improving management performance in rapidly changing organizations. *Journal of Management Development, 20*(1), 336–346.

Longenecker, C. O., & Neubert, M. J. (2003). The management development needs of front-line managers: Voices from the field. *Career Development International, 8*(4), 210–218.

Longenecker, C. O., & Neubert, M. J. (2005). The practices of effective managerial coaches. *Business Horizons, 48,* 493–500.

McDermott, M., Levenson, A., & Newton, S. (2007). What coaching can and cannot do for your organization. *Human Resource Planning, 30*(2), 30–37.

Miller, W. R., & Rollnick, S. (2002). *Motivational interviewing: Preparing people for change.* New York: Guilford Press.

Noer, D. M., Leupold, C. R., & Valle, M. (2007). An analysis of Saudi Arabian and U.S. managerial coaching behaviors. *Journal of Managerial Issues, 19*(2), 271–287.

O'Broin, A., & Palmer, S. (2007). Reappraising the coach-client relationship: The unassuming change agent in coaching. In S. Palmer & A. Whybrow (Eds.), *Handbook of coaching psychology* (pp. 295–324). New York: Routledge.

Palmer, S., & Whybrow, A. (Eds.). (2007). *Handbook of coaching psychology.* New York: Routledge.

Passmore, J. (2007). Behavioural coaching. In S. Palmer & A. Whybrow (Eds.), *The handbook of coaching psychology* (pp. 73–85). London: Brunner-Routledge.

Peterson, D. B. (2002). Management development: Coaching and mentoring programs. In K. Kraiger (Ed.), *Creating, implementing, and managing effective training and development.* San Francisco: Jossey-Bass.

Peterson, D. B. (2006). People are complex and the world is messy: A behavior-based approach to executive coaching. In D. R. Stober & A. M. Grant (Eds.), *Evidence-based coaching handbook* (pp. 51–76). Hoboken, NJ: John Wiley & Sons.

Peterson, D. B., & Hicks, M. D. (1995). *Development FIRST: Strategies for self-development.* Minneapolis, MN: Personnel Decisions.

Peterson, D. B., & Hicks, M. D. (1996). *Leader as coach: Strategies for coaching and developing others.* Minneapolis, MN: Personnel Decisions.

Peterson, D. B., & Kraiger, K. (2004). A practical guide to evaluating coaching: Translating state-of-the-art techniques to the real world. In J. E. Edwards, J. C. Scott, & N. S. Raju (Eds.), *The human resources program evaluation handbook* (pp. 262–282). Thousand Oaks, CA: SAGE Publications.

Peterson, D. B., & Little, B. (2008, Jan–Feb). Growth market: The rise of systemic coaching. *Coaching at Work, 3*(1), 44–47.

Peterson, D. B., & Muros, J. (2008, August). Accountability and transfer of learning in executive coaching. Invited address, American Psychological Association, Boston.

Peterson, D. B., Uranowitz, S. W., & Hicks, M. D. (1996, August). Management coaching at work: Survey of current practices in Fortune 250 organizations. Presented at the annual conference of the American Psychological Association, Toronto, Ontario.

Prochaska, J. O., DiClemente, C. C., & Norcross, J. C. (1992). In search of how people change: Applications to addictive behaviors. *American Psychologist, 47,* 1102–1114.

Prochaska, J. O., Norcross, J. C., & DiClemente, C. C. (1994). *Changing for good.* New York: William Morrow.

Rogers, J. (2004). *Coaching skills: A handbook.* New York: Open University Press.

Rogers, R. W. (2004). *Realizing the promise of performance management.* Bridgeville, PA: DDI Press.

Sherman, S., & Freas, A. (2004). The wild west of executive coaching. *Harvard Business Review, 82*(11), 82–89.

Smither, J. W., & Reilly, S. P. (2001). Coaching in organizations: A social psychological perspective. In M. London (Ed.), *How people evaluate others in organizations: Person perception and interpersonal judgment in I/O psychology.* Mahwah, NJ: Lawrence Erlbaum Associates.

Stober, D. R., & Grant, A. M. (Eds.). (2006). *Evidence based coaching handbook.* Hoboken, NJ: John Wiley & Sons.

Underhill, B. O., McAnally, K., & Koriath, J. J. (2007). Executive coaching for results. San Francisco: Berrett-Koehler.

Valerio, A. M., & Lee, R. J. (2005). *Executive coaching: A guide for the HR professional.* San Francisco: Pfeiffer.

Whitmore, J. (2002). *Coaching for performance* (3rd ed.). London: Nicholas Brealey.

Whybrow, A., & Henderson, V. (2007). Concepts to support the integration and sustainability of coaching initiatives within organizations. In S. Palmer & A. Whybrow (Eds.), *Handbook of coaching psychology* (pp. 407–430). New York: Routledge.

CHAPTER 5

THE ROLE OF ON-THE-JOB AND INFORMAL DEVELOPMENT IN PERFORMANCE MANAGEMENT

Paul Squires

Awareness of the importance of informal learning to the effectiveness of performance management and to the success of an organization has occurred over the past ten years. A search of the literature reveals very few articles about on-the-job training and informal development until the 1990s and then an increase thereafter. The increase in literature about informal learning may in large part be attributable to two events. One was Peter Senge's publication in 1990 of *The Fifth Discipline*, which describes the author's vision of a learning organization. The second was the public appearance of the Internet in 1994 and the terrific growth in the number of Internet users and Internet traffic since that time. Perhaps as a result of easy access to information and the increased interest in learning organizations, articles about informal learning and the qualities of an organization that promote informal learning began to appear more frequently (Birdi, Allan, & Warr, 1997; Lievens, Harris, VanKeer, & Bisqueret, 2003; Loewenstein & Spletzer, 1994). Psychologists (and managers) have known for a long time that, regardless of the extent of access to information, and even in the most supportive learning environment, there are individual differences in those who learn on the job or transfer formal learning to improved performance on the job (Gully, Payne, Koles, & Whiteman, 2002; Snow, 1986).

A critical component of effective performance management is the point in the process where the manager and employee, having agreed on targets for development, create the employee's development plan. The development plan may include formal learning, such as classroom training, or informal learning, such as on-the-job training, or both. As will be argued shortly, the vast majority of learning that occurs in an organization is informal learning, including learning that comprises development plans. For this reason, informal learning is a critical component of effective performance management. And, as will be described below, when practiced correctly, performance management includes informing the learner of the learning objective, providing learning guidance, giving informative feedback, and assessing performance.

A thorough understanding of the role of on-the-job training and informal learning in performance management includes knowledge of a very wide range of disciplines, including industrial psychology, labor economics, learning theory, and organizational theory. It is not the purpose of this chapter to present a thorough vetting of these disciplines and theories and their impact on designing and implementing performance management. Rather the purpose of this chapter is twofold. One is to present the reader with specific information and principles from these disciplines that will broaden the reader's understanding of on-the-job training and informal learning. This information and principles can improve the design and implementation of performance management programs. The second purpose of this chapter is to provide practical recommendations, based on the information and principles, for building and managing performance management programs.

The chapter begins with ideas from labor economics that provide a broader context for on-the-job training and informal learning and are valuable to a manager who wants to address the ever-present issue of the value proposition for informal learning. Next, the definition of informal learning will be discussed because there is no consensus in the literature. Throughout the chapter, on-the-job training is considered a specific instance of informal learning. The incidence of informal learning and the methodological challenges to measuring informal learning will be reviewed. The characteristics of the workplace and the characteristics of the worker that result in more frequent and more effective informal learning will be presented. These findings are most important to a manager who is designing or implementing a performance management program. Finally, the chapter concludes with practical recommendations to facilitate informal learning and two examples of projects completed by the author in which informal learning played a prominent role in performance management.

Informal Learning and Human Capital

An interesting perspective on the importance of informal learning to an organization and the economy in general is provided by labor economists. Their view is that informal learning contributes importantly to the growth of human capital. Becker (1993, p. 12), explaining the expanding interest in human capital,[1] stated, "The main motivating factor has probably been a realization that the growth of physical capital, at least as conventionally measured, explains a relatively small part of the growth of income in most countries. The search for better explanations has led to improved measures of physical capital and to an interest in less tangible entities such as technological change and human capital." The importance of human capital to the wealth of a society is substantial, especially in advanced countries. The wealth of a nation can be divided into human and nonhuman capital, where the latter includes a nation's natural resources, buildings, equipment, and other tangible objects. In 1994, the per capita wealth—human and nonhuman—in North America was $405,000. Most of that wealth (76 percent) was attributable to human capital (Ehrenberg & Smith, 2006, p. 276). In less developed countries, the portion due to human capital is smaller (60 percent), but still substantial.

According to labor economists, human capital comprises the skills and knowledge a worker possesses and "rents out" to an employer for a period of time (Ehrenberg & Smith, 2006, p. 276). Workers and employers both invest in human capital. The worker invests through efforts at formal and informal learning. The employer invests through formal and informal learning (on-the-job training). The employer benefits from human capital investments through increases in productivity, and the worker benefits from investments in his or her own human capital, although not right away, by increases in earnings. For both workers and employers, the benefits of formal and informal learning are delayed, just like any investment. Workers are willing to forego higher current earnings while they acquire additional skills and knowledge. Employers are willing to sacrifice productivity and incur costs while the worker is gaining skills and knowledge while on the job.

Labor economists have reported for a long time the contribution of formal education to gains in worker lifetime earnings. Table 5.1 provides an example. The table illustrates the earnings differential between those with a college education compared to those with a high school education, separately for males and females. On the left side of the table are the rates of high school graduation and on the right are the ratios of earnings that indicate, for example, that in 2001 female college graduates aged twenty-five to thirty-four earned 1.70 times as much as their age cohorts who graduated from high school. In all years for males and females, the ratios are greater than 1.0, indicating that in all

Table 5.1 Earnings Differential by Education Level.

Year	College Enrollment Rates (%) of New High School Graduates		Ratios of Mean Earnings of College to High School Graduates, Ages 25 to 34, Prior Year	
	Male	Female	Male	Female
1970	55.2	48.5	1.38	1.42
1980	46.7	51.8	1.19	1.29
1990	57.8	62.0	1.48	1.59
2001	59.7	63.6	1.77	1.70

cases college graduates earn more than high school graduates. This relationship between level of education and earnings holds for all levels of formal education, including comparisons of those who graduated from high school and those who did not and those with graduate school training compared to those who completed college only.

Labor economists have noted that differences in earnings are attributable to many factors, including education, socio-economic status, and skills and abilities. Labor economists have also noted that the differences in earnings for different levels of education increase over time. They have also observed that the most rapid increase in the earnings for men and women occurs in the first ten years of their careers and then it flattens out. Labor economists attribute the cause of both of these phenomena to informal learning. First, the increase over time in the wage differentials for different levels of education is caused, according to human capital theory, by the fact that those with greater levels of formal education learn on the job more rapidly and more willingly than those with lower levels of education. Therefore, those with greater amounts of formal education seek out and are offered by their employers more opportunities for informal learning. Consequently, in later years, the earnings differentials are due to greater amounts and more rapid informal learning among the better educated. Regarding the second phenomenon, the rapid increase in earnings during the first ten years of a career is attributable to the fact that workers are less willing to invest in formal or informal learning as they grow older because, like any investment, the payoff period is shorter (fewer earning years to retirement as they age) and therefore the benefit of the investment is less. Most formal and informal learning occurs in the first ten years of a worker's career. A third interesting phenomenon noted by labor economists and explained by informal learning is the fact that the correlation between formal education and earnings is greatest at about the ten-year point in a worker's career. Before and after that period, the correlation is lower. This is explained by combining the first two phenomena. If those with greater amounts of formal education participate in more informal learning, especially during the early stages of their careers, they will reap the benefits of the investment in the succeeding years. This creates a wage differential that is greatest at about ten years into a worker's career. At this point, the variance between earnings levels reaches its peak. Thereafter, workers with more formal education invest less time in informal learning, and eventually the rate of increase in their earnings slows, and the variance between themselves and those who participated in informal learning to a lesser degree is reduced.

Perhaps the economist who has spoken most trenchantly about informal learning and its importance to an organization and the economy is Gary Becker (1993) in his book *Human Capital.* In his discussion about on-the-job training, Becker points out, "Many workers increase their productivity by learning new skills and perfecting old ones while on the job." Becker also states, "Theories of firm behavior, no matter how they differ in other respects, almost invariably ignore the effect of the productive process itself on worker productivity. This is not to say that no one recognizes that productivity is affected by the job itself; but the recognition has not been formalized, incorporated into economic analysis, and its implications worked out." Becker then goes on to address this gap. He developed equations that explain the value of informal learning. In those formulations, he distinguishes between general training and specific training. General training is training that provides a worker with the skills and knowledge to be more productive, not only with the current organization, but with others as well. As a result, workers pay the cost of general training and reap its rewards in the form of greater earnings in whatever organization they are employed. Specific training (primarily on-the-job training), on the other hand, is training that is useful and productive only in the organization that provides it. The organization and the worker pay the costs of specific training and they both reap its benefits. Becker included separate estimates of general and specific training in his formulations.

In the context of human capital, the developmental discussions and informal feedback provided by supervisors in the course of managing the performance of their staffs take on a different light. From the human capital perspective, performance management plays a crucial role in the development of an organization's human capital.

What Is Informal Learning?

At one level the difference between informal and formal learning is easy to define. If the learner is in a classroom or participating in a structured computer-based training program, the learning is formal; otherwise it is informal. However, a few examples of different types of learning activities quickly demonstrate the inadequacy of this simple definition. For example, is the use of a job aid considered formal or informal learning? Is coaching or mentoring considered formal or informal learning? Is a lunchtime discussion with a classmate about a concept just covered in a classroom considered formal or informal learning? Is using a knowledge base or searching the internet for needed information considered formal or informal learning? Researchers answer these questions differently because they define informal learning in different ways (Lievens, Harris, Van Keer, & Bisqueret, 2003; Loewenstein & Spletzer, 1994; Skule, 2004).

Examples of informal learning described by researchers include mentoring, ad-hoc training sessions by co-workers, reading internal publications, attending webinars, browsing a website, reading a book or article, observing an expert perform job tasks, and receiving constructive feedback from a supervisor. Some (Loewenstein & Spletzer, 1994, p. 2) define informal learning as learning that "is produced jointly with the primary output of the worker. . . . " Others (Berings, Doornbos, & Simons, 2006) define informal learning as "implicit or explicit mental and/or overt activities and processes, embedded in working and work-related performance, leading to relatively permanent change in knowledge, attitude, or skills." These researchers seem to emphasize the setting in which the learning occurs as an important factor that defines informal learning. There appears to be an assumption among these researchers that if the learning is in a work setting, it is unstructured and therefore informal. However, in a study about informal learning (Versloot, de Jong, & Thijssen, 2001), the researchers examined the informal learning that takes place in the work setting but the learning was structured. They studied informal learning, which they described as "a form of job-oriented training which is located in the workplace. The trainee performs practical assignments according to a training plan and is instructed by an experienced colleague or supervisor." But when one considers all the ways in which workers learn in the work setting—many of them quite structured such as mentoring and web-based self-paced learning—defining informal learning by the setting in which it occurs is unsatisfactory. Perhaps it is helpful to define informal learning by considering both the structure and setting simultaneously. This approach creates the need to define structure and setting. Defining the settings as on-the-job, web-based, or classroom is simple and unambiguous. However, what are the characteristics of structured and unstructured learning? If there was a list of characteristics, then some learning would contain all of these characteristics, some would include none, and some would contain a few. A simple dichotomy—structured versus unstructured—is insufficient.

There are different perspectives on the characteristics of structured learning, stages of learning (Bloom, 1956; Kanfer & Ackerman, 1989), and principles of instructional design (Mager, 1997). For example, Gagne identifies events of instruction (Gagne & Medsker, 1995) that are critical to well-structured training, including gaining attention, informing the learner of the objective, stimulating recall of prior learning, presenting the stimulus, providing learning guidance, eliciting the performance, giving informative feedback, assessing performance, and enhancing retention and transfer. Structured learning, then, may be defined as learning that is planned, designed, and delivered using principles of instructional design.[2] The more principles of instructional design that are present in the learning, the more structured the learning is, and when there are few or none, it is unstructured.

Table 5.2 presents a categorization of modes of learning that may prove useful to classify different types of learning, including informal learning. The columns represent the different settings in which learning occurs and the rows indicate the degree of structure contained in the learning situation.

Consider one of the categories in Table 5.2, for example, the category formed by the intersection of "moderately structured learning" and "work setting." If a worker is reading a methods and procedure manual in the work setting, the learning may be considered informal. The manual's content may be based on

Table 5.2 Modes of Learning.

	Work Setting	Web-Based	Classroom
Unstructured Learning	Self-paced: Observe how a co-worker performs complex job duties. Group: Share a short-cut or safety tip with a colleague.	Self-paced: Look up information about six sigma methods on the Internet. Group: Send a text or instant message to a colleague to obtain needed information.	Group: Brainstorm and problem solve in a meeting.
Moderately Structured Learning	Self-paced: Read a methods and procedure manual. Group: Receive feedback from the supervisor about work performance.	Self-paced: Listen to a pod-cast. Group: Participate in a blog that is part of a community of practice.	Group: Attend presentations at a professional organization conference.
Structured Learning	Self-paced: Use a performance support tool at a work station. Group: Participate in formal coaching sessions with the master performer on the production line.	Self-paced: Participate in a self-paced training program. Group: Attend a course available through the company's learning management system.	Group: Attend a finance course delivered by an instructor.

job-related learning objectives and the content may be approved by subject matter experts. In this sense the learning is structured. However, the timing of the learning and the fit between the stage of the learner's mastery and the difficulty of the materials may not be a good one. In this sense, the learning is unstructured.

Further, the learner is reading the manual in the work setting so, for that reason, the learning may be considered informal.

In contrast, consider the category formed by the intersection of "unstructured learning" and "work setting." Because unstructured learning lacks most of the features of moderately or well structured learning, there is no control of the quality of the learning. This does not mean that unstructured learning cannot be good quality learning. Observing a master performer work through a difficult problem can be an excellent way to learn. Psychologists have known for a long time that observation learning is very powerful (Bandura, 1986). Receiving a tip from an experienced and expert worker is certainly valuable. An important limitation of unstructured learning is that it runs the risk of passing on bad habits, inefficient methods, and conventional ways of doing things. The learner may misunderstand and misapply what was observed, and the tip from the experienced colleague might be a bad one.

Learning, whether formal or informal, can be self-paced or performed with others. In the work setting and web-based columns in Table 5.2, there are two examples of learning: one is self-paced and the other is group-based. Classroom learning is, by its very nature, with a group. An example of a web-based, moderately structured learning activity that is performed with others is participating in a blog that is part of a community of practice. More specifically, a radio frequency engineer who participates in a blog with other radio frequency engineers to share opinions, news, and facts about recent Federal Communication Commission regulatory changes is using the web and learning in a moderately structured manner.

Incidence of Informal Training

While intuitively it would appear self-evident that the majority of learning that a worker experiences is informal, few studies have attempted to measure it. One challenge to measuring the amount of informal learning that occurs in the workplace is the difficulty in defining it. Nevertheless, researchers who do attempt to study it estimate that between 75 and 96 percent of all learning in organizations occurs informally. But estimates vary widely. In a BLS report (Loewenstein & Spletzer, 1994), the results from the Current Population Survey indicated that 44 percent of workers receive formal training and 16 percent reported "yes" when asked if they had participated in informal training. In the same report, the authors describe the results from a survey of 2,625 employers that asked them to provide information about formal and informal training practices. Referring to the first three months on the job, formal training was provided by 13 percent of the employers and informal training was provided by 96 percent of employers. The informal training was unstructured and in the work setting and included activities such as assistance from co-workers, extra guidance provided by supervisors, and opportunities to work with or observe more experienced workers. The authors conclude that this latter finding—96 percent of workers receive informal learning—is probably a more accurate reflection of employer practices.

In a study of 1,500 Canadian adults, Mitchell and Livingstone (2002) reported that over 90 percent of the respondents participated in informal learning activities during the past year, with an average of fifteen hours per week compared to three hours per week of formal training. While fifteen hours per week seems to be a large portion of a work week, it is important to keep in mind that much informal learning occurs at the same time as productive work activities are carried out, during work breaks, and after work hours. The most common purpose for informal learning was to gain knowledge to keep up with the current job or careers. Two-thirds of respondents indicated that the informal learning was directed at learning computer skills required to perform their jobs. In a survey administered to 147 employers in Singapore (Osman-Gani & Jacobs, 2005), the most frequently used method of training among ten different methods was on-the-job training. This finding was consistent for all six industry sectors surveyed, including manufacturing, construction, financial and business services, transportation and communication, commerce, and other. Considering these findings and the wide range of learning activities covered by the unstructured and moderately structured categories in Table 5.2, the best estimate of the portion of workers who engage in informal learning is approximately 90 percent.

Methodological Issues Associated with Informal Learning

Conducting research about informal learning is not only challenging when attempting to determine the frequency of its occurrence, but in many other regards as well. There are many methodological issues that arise when designing or conducting studies of informal learning. Chief among them, as previously discussed, is the fact that the definition of informal learning differs among researchers. Advances in the understanding of informal learning and its impact on the individual, on the organization, and on organizational processes such as performance management cannot be achieved until there are agreed-upon operational definitions.

Most studies of informal learning are field studies that use surveys to gather data retrospectively about what employees do when learning informally (Berings, Doornbos, & Simons, 2006). Because they are field studies, isolation of the informal learning techniques and their effectiveness is more challenging than if the techniques were studied in a laboratory setting. Because the survey ratings of informal learning activities are retrospective, they are subject to forgetting and misperception. Informal learning research is further challenged because the learning techniques and activities studied are predetermined, and the list in the survey may not provide the opportunity to identify other and different techniques and activities that the informal learner may have used. Some researchers use interviews to collect data about informal learners. This provides the opportunity to gather richer and more varied information about how informal learning occurs. Interviews are more effective than surveys in gaining insights into the acquisition of tacit knowledge and unobservable skills and knowledge. The same is true of learning logs, personal narratives, and the creation of learning maps. However, these studies tend to be qualitative and often lack desired rigor (Berings, Doornbos, & Simons, 2006). Observation is used to gather information about informal learning. Observation can provide information about learning behaviors and the time spent on these behaviors. Observation can also identify the network of contacts an informal learner uses to learn.

Perhaps the best approach is to combine these methods to achieve a level of convergent validity. Qualitative methods such as learning logs and interviews might be used to build hypotheses about the techniques and tacit knowledge used for effective informal learning. Cognitive psychology researchers (Davison, Vogel, & Coffman, 1997) have successfully used think-aloud methods and comparisons of expert and novice think-aloud protocols to "observe" the cognitive process and thinking used by problem solvers. These hypotheses can then be studied in laboratory settings and in surveys to gather more rigorous empirical evidence of their importance to informal learning. For example, in the laboratory setting, those who have successfully transferred newly acquired skills to the work setting might be interviewed to identify the tacit skills and knowledge they used when applying the newly acquired skills in the work setting. Role plays that simulate work settings that facilitate or inhibit transfer and that include use of work samples provide the opportunity to study interventions, mediator variables, and workplace factors that influence transfer of learning.

A difficult challenge for informal learning researchers is the complexity of informal learning. Due to the lack of structure and the wide range of work settings in which it occurs, isolating key variables that facilitate or inhibit informal learning will be challenging. The rapid advances in information technology add complexity. Researchers must understand how tools such as blogs, pod-casts, chat rooms, text messaging, and instant messaging are used and can be used for informal learning.

Work context variables are important for informal and formal learning. Regarding the latter, when a worker completes classroom training and returns to the work setting, the extent to which learning gained in the classroom transfers to the work setting and results in improved performance has been the focus of much research (Baldwin & Ford, 1988). Since the transfer of training requires the worker to learn informally how to apply the knowledge, skills, and abilities gained in the classroom to the particular situation of his or her work setting, transfer of training may be considered a special type of informal learning. It is logical to assume then that the work context factors that influence transfer of training will largely be the same as those that support informal learning. Factors that influence training transfer include the transfer climate of the work setting (for example, access to experts and opportunities to practice new gained skills and knowledge) as well as individual difference (for example, openness and extraversion) variables. Researchers must design more complex studies that can account for individual differences and work context variables and their interaction that are present in informal learning settings.

Characteristics of the Workplace That Enhance Informal Learning

If organizations wish to achieve Senge's vision and become learning organizations, then they need to take actions to create a work environment that facilitates informal learning. If managers want to provide successful developmental opportunities following completion of a performance management process, then they must provide a work environment that supports informal learning and training transfer. Researchers have examined the characteristics of organizations that facilitate informal learning. Studies of informal learning in the workplace indicate that it is enhanced when there is sufficient task variation, workers have the opportunity to participate in temporary work teams, they have the opportunity to consult with experts inside and outside of the organization, and they have the opportunity to change their work duties and roles periodically (Eraut, 2000). In other studies, jobs that enabled workers to participate in communities of practice in which the communications and interactions are informal, but there are opportunities for problem solving and innovation, facilitate informal learning (Skule, 2004). Programs and incentives for sharing knowledge, job mobility, and autonomy on the job were found to facilitate informal learning as well (Marsick, 2003).

In a study of factors that assist or inhibit learning of new job assignments among 604 naval officers, the researchers (Morrison & Brantner, 1992) examined job characteristics, work context, and work environment factors that influenced informal job learning. Researchers found that job characteristics that influenced learning were role complexity, job significance, and job challenge. Work factors that influenced informal learning of the job were the organization's climate (for example, cooperation of leaders and competence of peers and subordinates) and pace of work.

Skule (2004) hypothesizes that some jobs are more learning intensive than others. Learning-intense jobs are characterized by three factors. These are jobs that require extensive learning for newly hired workers. These jobs have a long learning curve even when the worker has the requisite educational background. Learning-intense jobs require skills and knowledge that must be continually practiced or updated. In other words, workers who leave these jobs will quickly lose their competence to perform the job successfully. Skule also posited that there are seven work environment conditions that facilitate informal learning. These conditions include a work context that possesses a high degree of exposure to change, a high degree of exposure to demands from customers and managers, frequent communication with colleagues, managerial responsibilities such as decision making, project management, extensive professional contacts through trade associations and conferences, receiving feedback such as seeing the direct results of one's efforts, management support for learning, and the presence of rewards (for example, higher salaries and advancement opportunities) for proficiency.

In a telephone survey of thirteen hundred workers from eleven different industries and a wide range of jobs, the survey results indicated that jobs can be accurately measured as learning intense or learning deprived. Some evidence for this finding was the presence of a significant correlation between the highest level of education for a worker and the learning intensive score for the worker's job (r = .25). More interestingly, Skule found industry differences in the distribution of learning-intense jobs. For example, the oil industry at 40 percent and the banking, insurance, and commercial services industries at 35 percent each had the largest portion of learning-intensive jobs. The wholesale industry at 38 percent and the retail, hotel, and restaurant industries at 20 percent each had the most learning-deprived jobs.

As stated above, transfer of learning is related to informal learning because the instructional assumption is that the learning that occurs in the classroom will be applied in the work setting. The learner has the responsibility to translate the skills and knowledge gained in formal instruction to the work setting.

This assumes that the learner continues to learn on his or her own by learning where, when, and how to apply the newly gained skills and knowledge in the work setting. This description fits into the unstructured, work-setting learning category in Table 5.1 and therefore is informal learning. Baldwin and Ford (1988) put forth a model of training transfer in which characteristics of the trainee, the work environment, and the training design influenced how well the trainee learned and how well the learning transferred to the work setting. Their research supported their view that social support in the work setting and opportunities to use the newly acquired skills and knowledge on the job are important work environment factors that influence the transfer of learning. The importance of trainee and work environment characteristics to successful transfer of learning was demonstrated in a study of eighty pilots learning assertiveness skills, specifically independence and directness, to improve flight team performance (Smith-Jentsch, Salas, & Brannick, 2001). The best predictor of the transference of independence and directness skills was team leader support, a work environment characteristic. Trainee perception of transfer climate support and a trainee's predisposition to act assertively were the best predictors of transfer of learning among the trainee characteristics studied. Interestingly, the contribution of trainee perception of transfer climate support to the prediction of learning transfer was greater for those trainees with an external locus of control. Rouillier and Goldstein (1993) identified four situational factors (goal cues, social cues, task cues, and self-control cues) and four consequences (positive feedback, negative feedback, punishment, and no feedback) that create a transfer of learning climate that can facilitate or inhibit the informal learning required to support the use of newly acquired skills and knowledge on the job. Tracey, Tannenbaum, and Kavanagh (1995) distinguished between a transfer of training climate and a continuous learning culture and, using structural equation models, demonstrated that each predicted post-training behavior. Transfer of training climate focuses on observable characteristics of the work setting such as when a supervisor meets with the trainee to discuss how the training can be applied to the job. Continuous learning culture refers to the norms and values of an organization and occurs when a manager encourages independent and innovative thinking at work. In a meta-analysis of factors that influence training motivation, the researchers concluded that transfer climate, job involvement, and emphasizing the job and career benefits of training increased the motivation to learn which, in turn, led to greater job performance.

In a different approach to training transfer, Williams and Rosenbaum (2004) recommend an approach to accelerate learning when the worker returns to the job after formal training. In their book, *Learning Paths*, the authors focus on the time between the end of formal training until the time when the worker is fully competent. They labeled this "the time to proficiency." This time to proficiency is when informal learning occurs, and the authors propose a strategy called the 30/30 plan to reduce the time to proficiency for workers. Their plan enhances informal learning in order to reduce the time to proficiency by 30 percent in the first thirty days after formal training is completed.

Characteristics of the Worker That Influence Informal Learning

Characteristics of the worker have been shown to be important to formal learning. For example, individual differences in cognitive ability have been shown to be strong predictors of job and training performance (Hunter & Schmidt, 1996; Jensen, 1980). In the Baldwin and Ford (1988) model of training transfer, they state that cognitive ability, personality, and motivation are important worker characteristics that influence transfer of learning. These same characteristics are very likely to have a strong effect on informal learning, though there are few studies, other than formal training and transfer of learning studies, that demonstrate the relationship.

In a meta-analysis of the "big five" personality dimensions, the researchers found that individual differences in openness to experience and extraversion were significantly correlated with learning proficiency (Barrick & Mount, 1991). A separate meta-analysis showed that locus of control, conscientiousness, anxiety, age, cognitive ability, self-efficacy, valence, and job involvement influenced training motivation (Colquitt, LePine, & Noe, 2000).

Self-efficacy is a critical construct in social cognition and has been shown to play a key role in the transfer of learning (Birdi & Warr, 1997; Frayne & Geringer, 2000), and learning and behavior change generally (Bandura, 1986, Cervone, 2004).

Assessment centers, which measure a range of personality and leadership dimensions, have been shown to predict training performance (Gaugler, Rosenthal, Thornton, & Bentson, 1987). In a study of learning proficiency and language acquisition for European managers preparing for job assignments in Japan, a large number of cognitive, leadership, and personality variables were measured (Lievens, Harris, Van Keer, & Bisqueret, 2003) using interviews, written assessments, and assessment center exercises. The results indicated that learning proficiency was predicted by assessment center exercise scores for teamwork, communication, adaptability, and organizational and commercial awareness. Openness to experience was the only personality measure that positively correlated with learning proficiency. Some influences on informal learning are shown in Table 5.3.

Pulakos, Arad, Donovan, and Plamondon (2000) provided evidence of the importance of worker adaptability in the work setting. The researchers developed a taxonomy of work situations that require workers to demonstrate adaptability. Over nine thousand critical incidents developed by managers were evaluated by five industrial psychologists who determined that thirteen hundred of them required a worker to demonstrate adaptability. From these they created an eight-dimension model of adaptability. In a subsequent study they tested the reliability and validity of a Job Adaptability Inventory (JAI). The JAI diagnoses a job's adaptive performance requirements along eight dimensions: handling emergencies, handling work stress, solving problems creatively, dealing with uncertain situations, learning, interpersonal adaptability, cultural adaptability, and physically oriented adaptability. Exploratory and confirmatory factor analyses supported the validity of the JAI. Knowing the adaptive requirements of a job, a manager can make better selection decisions about who is most suited for a position, provide required training to support a worker's adaptive skills, and give more valuable guidance in performance management situations.

Table 5.3 Influences on Informal Learning.

Individual Factors	Work Context Factors
Openness to experience	Task variation
Cognitive ability	Feedback
Extraversion	Job mobility
Locus of control	Role autonomy
Conscientiousness	Role complexity, challenges
Anxiety	Participation in temporary teams
Age	Access to experts in and outside
Self-efficacy	of the organization
Valence	Opportunity to use new skills and
Job involvement	knowledge
Teamwork	Social support in work setting
Communication	Incentives in sharing knowledge
Adaptability	Pace of work
Organizational awareness	Competence of peers
Commercial awareness	Exposure to customer and manager demands
	Frequency of communication with colleagues

Unlike formal learning research, there is a dearth of information in the informal learning literature regarding a set of worker characteristics, including metacognition, goals, and self-efficacy, and how they influence informal learning. This chapter is not intended to provide a review of all of these characteristics, but there is every reason to believe that they play important roles. Arguably most important among these factors is metacognition. Metacognition is the thinking and monitoring a person does about one's own cognitive activities. Research has demonstrated the importance of metacognition to learning (Flavell, 1979; Sternberg, 1988). When a person considers different approaches to learning, that person is engaging in metacognitive activities. When a person recognizes apparent contradictions in instructional information and, further, recognizes the need to resolve the contradiction in order to master the information, that person is engaging in metacognitive activities. The unstructured conditions of informal learning would require the learner to exercise more metacognitive skills than are required in a formal learning situation. In an informal learning situation, there is no instructor to guide the learner through the learning process. The monitoring, assessing, sequencing, and prioritizing of learning must all be provided by the learner.

Goal orientation also influences learning (Dweck & Leggett, 1988; Schmidt & Ford, 2003). Goal orientation is the tendency among some learners to compare their learning progress to their prior levels of mastery. This orientation has been called mastery goal orientation (Baldwin & Ford, 1988; Salas & Cannon-Bowers, 2001). By contrast, other learners compare their mastery to others or assess their skill levels as a measure of self-worth. This orientation has been called performance orientation (Dweck & Leggett, 1988). Those with a mastery orientation are more successful learners and they experience less stress in their learning experience. In an informal learning setting, it is reasonable to expect that the mastery-oriented learner would be more open to the suggestions and learning opportunities offered by colleagues and the supervisor compared to a learner with a performance orientation.

Self-efficacy is another worker characteristic that plays an important role in learning (Bandura, 1986; Schmidt & Ford, 2003). Self-efficacy is the belief one holds about one's chances of performing an activity successfully. Self-efficacy tends to be situationally specific, that is, one may have high self-efficacy for calculating the cost of completing a project, but low self-efficacy when required to make a formal presentation to others about the project's costs. Self-efficacy is related to outcome expectancies and perseverance. One's self-efficacy is related to one's expectations of success or failure. Additionally, those with greater self-efficacy are more likely to persevere in the face of failure. They will continue to make an effort to learn, despite the uncertainty and confusion that accompanies learning. The success achieved by perseverance, in turn, improves outcome expectancies and enhances self-efficacy. In an informal learning situation, self-efficacy would be critical to success. In a formal learning situation, the instructor may provide encouragement and point to areas of success that increase positive outcome expectancies and self-efficacy. However, in an informal learning setting, the learner must possess these characteristics in order to succeed.

There is an important interplay among metacognition, goal orientation, and self-efficacy. Learners who engage in greater amounts of metacognitive activity learn more, and this increases self-efficacy. This relationship is greater for those with a mastery orientation than those with a performance orientation. In a study of adults attempting to learn how to create web pages, researchers (Schmidt & Ford, 2003) demonstrated this interplay. Learners who engaged in greater amounts of metacognition achieved greater levels of mastery of declarative knowledge, did better on the training assessment, and reported higher levels of self-efficacy. These effects were found even after adjusting for prior ability and experience with web pages. In addition, learners with a mastery orientation reported more metacognitive activity during the web training than learners with a performance orientation. Regarding informal learning settings, the researchers concluded, "The results have implications for many learning contexts in which there is a great deal of learner control and limited feedback."

Performance Management, Work and Worker Characteristics

Considering the studies of work environment and worker characteristics as a whole, what conclusions might be reached and what implications are there for the design and administration of a successful performance management program? First, some conclusions can be reached about the work environment and worker characteristics. Work environments matter—greater informal learning occurs when managers and supervisors support learning in the work setting. This includes more systemic actions such as setting policies that support informal learning and implementing reward systems that encourage independent thinking and innovation. Managers should ensure that more local and concrete actions occur, such as providing workers with time to practice their newly acquired skills when they return to the work setting, demonstrating how the new learning is applied to the job, providing access to experts, and providing opportunities for job changes. Jobs that are challenging, provide feedback, and whose tasks are varied facilitate the occurrence of informal learning.

The research on worker characteristics that facilitate either the transfer of learning or structured learning provides guidance for actions to facilitate informal learning. It is certainly no surprise that cognitive ability is important to learning of any kind. Personality dimensions that were consistently found to be important to learning were openness to experience and extraversion. Considering the lack of structure present in informal learning, these qualities may be even more important to the success of informal learning. The same may be said of metacognition, goal orientation, and self-efficacy. The social cognition literature consistently identifies the importance of these worker characteristics and others to behavior change. The presence of these cognitive skills and personal characteristics is likely to be even more important in an informal learning setting than in a structured one.

In light of these findings, some recommendations for performance management can be made. While some of these recommendations may benefit from greater empirical support, these are suggestions that can be made while making only modest inferential leaps from the current literature on formal and informal learning.

1. Transfer climate is an important element of a culture for continuous learning. If managers and supervisors take steps to enhance the transfer climate for learning, then a culture of continuous learning will, more likely, arise. Performance management will be enhanced when the development needs that are identified in a performance feedback session are implemented in an environment that supports formal and informal learning at the policy and local levels.

2. Ensure policies, norms, and systems exist that support informal learning. For example, new technologies that support communication and access to information should be routinely implemented; workers should be expected to learn and use these technologies; workers should be encouraged to try different approaches to problem solving; and workers should be expected to attend a fixed number of hours of training per year (for example, forty) from which informal learning will flow once back on the job.

3. Ensure job assignments are challenging, tasks are varied, and workers have the opportunity to change jobs. The performance management process offers opportunities to address these issues openly and to take corrective action as necessary.

4. When workers are placed in new jobs or given new job duties, the need for informal learning arises immediately. The need for performance feedback is greater when a person takes a new job or takes on important new responsibilities. Facilitating informal learning at these times is important and can be directly addressed.

5. If structured training is included in a development plan, the supervisor or a competent peer should be available to demonstrate how to apply the newly acquired skills when the worker returns to the work setting.

6. In addition to more cognitive ability, those workers who are high in openness to experience, extraversion, or self-efficacy are more likely to benefit from formal or informal learning. Workers who do not possess these qualities are less likely to benefit from informal learning. Consequently, these worker characteristics should be taken into account when creating a development plan.

7. Recognize that workers who demonstrate a performance goal orientation are less likely to learn informally. These workers should receive more structured learning opportunities than informal learning opportunities. The supervisor should make the worker aware of the importance of approaching learning situations with a mastery goal orientation.

8. The supervisor should avoid making comparisons to others but rather provide ipsative feedback, that is, feedback that

compares the worker's performance and present skill levels against previous performance and skill levels.

9. Provide access to experts, inside and outside the organization, and the time to learn from them. There are a wide range of methods to accomplish this recommendation, including low-tech approaches such as lunch hour meetings with experts and high-tech approaches such as using social networking technology to build contacts. Participating in communities of practice and brainstorming solutions are facilitated by these networking technologies.

10. Recognize work situations that create the need for informal learning and take steps to facilitate it. For example, when uncertain organizational situations arise such as an organizational restructure, a manager can proactively meet with workers to identify impacts, learning gaps, and solutions to minimize impacts and close learning gaps.

Best Practices in Performance Management and Informal Learning

The following sections provide two best practice examples of informal learning integrated into a performance management system. The two examples are descriptions of projects the author led for U.S.-based, global Fortune 500 corporations. One project focused on managers and the second project focused on union-represented, front-line workers. Referring to Table 5.2 in which modes of learning were categorized according to the setting and the amount of structure in the instructional design, these examples reflect the moderately and less-structured learning in the work setting. The manager project is web-based and the front-line worker is not. In both cases, the best practice examples include, in a very important role, information obtained from a job analysis. Task, skill, and knowledge information from a job analysis was used to ensure that performance assessments, feedback sessions, and developmental activities were tied closely to job requirements. This was true when the search for developmental activities was initiated by the worker or by the supervisor providing the performance feedback.

Managers

The organization wanted to provide a better way for its performance management system to support the development of the leadership skills among its managers. The organization has several business units that produce and sell widely different products and services. The solution had to support the development of leadership skills among all managers in all parts of the business.

The first step was to conduct a job analysis that identified the critical work activities managers must perform in order to be successful. Therefore, the job analysis focused on the core work activities that are performed by all managers. This can be a difficult challenge due to the great variety of work performed by managers. For example, human resource managers and marketing strategists are likely to have few work activities in common. The solution to this challenge existed in recognizing that there is no requirement in the performance management system for all managers to perform all of the work activities. Managers could pick those that were most important to them. The work activities, however, needed to cover the full range of core work performed at different levels of management. Also, the organization had a leadership model that had to be included in the solution. Consequently, the goal of the job analysis was to identify the work activities that were associated with the organization's leadership model at different levels of management. There needed to be enough overlap between key work activities and the dimensions of the leadership model to enable managers to receive some guidance about their pursuit of informal learning. The leadership model included six dimensions: strategic thinking, business acumen, communication, sense of urgency, customer focus, and change management. Four groups of work activities were identified in the job analysis (Table 5.4).[3]

The job analysis included the identification of the knowledge requirements for each group of work activities. There were sixteen categories of knowledge, each of which contained six to twelve more specific knowledge statements. For example, the work activities for "Manage metrics and scorecards" included requirements to possess knowledge of accounting, performance

Table 5.4 Four Groups of Work Activities.

Work Functions	Tasks
Provide input to the creation of the strategic plan.	1. Review each department's contribution to the strategic plans to identify opportunities for alignment.
	2. Identify new and emerging trends in the market conditions, financial markets, technology, regulatory changes, and competitive landscape of the business to inform strategic decisions.
	3. Present the strategic plan and highlights to management for approval.
	4. Create performance metrics to measure the success of the strategic plan.
	5. Create HR, IT, sales, and logistics plans that are required to support the strategic plan.
	6. Align roles, responsibilities, and accountabilities with the goals of the strategic plan.
Set performance expectations in collaboration with employees.	1. Review the strategic plan to determine what performance results will be required from employees.
	2. Review and revise employees' goals and objectives that deliver results aligned with the strategic plan requirements.
	3. Review and revise employees' metrics, benchmarks, and criteria that will be used to evaluate attainment of goals and objectives.
	4. Build employee acceptance and buy-in by communicating a shared understanding of goals, objectives, and expected results.

Manage metrics and scorecards.	1. Assess the performance level and variance of a business process to determine the need for a metric.
	2. Review existing metrics to avoid creating a redundant metric.
	3. Create benchmarks for new metrics to ensure the standard is set appropriately.
	4. Determine person(s) responsible for producing the metric, reporting frequency, and target audience for the metric.
Communicate senior leadership's vision, goals, and desired results to the organization.	1. Understand vision, messages, goals, and desired results.
	2. Determine group's actions and results that can influence the achievement of vision, goals, and desired results.
	3. Communicate to team members so that each individual understands how his or her actions, performance, and results can impact achievement of vision, goals, and desired results.
	4. Gather feedback from team members and others to ensure they understand the message and the actions they can take to contribute to achievement of vision, goals, and desired results.

metrics, and financial analysis, to name a few. These knowledge categories included more detailed information. The accounting and financial analysis knowledge categories included more detailed information (Table 5.5).

A job analysis survey was conducted to determine the importance and difficulty of the work activities to managers' jobs. A representative sample of four hundred managers rated the importance of the work activities. In this way, evidence that these work activities were core to all managers was obtained, and the rating results were used to scale the work activities from less difficult to most difficult. Less difficult work activities were more often performed at lower levels of management, and more difficult work activities were performed at higher levels of management.

The alignment of these groups of work activities with the leadership dimensions provided the performance framework within which managers' formal and informal developmental activities were identified. The alignment is presented in Table 5.6.

Next, for each group of work activities and for each leadership dimension, learning resources were identified. Learning resources were identified for novice, intermediate, and advanced levels of performance on the work activities. A team of subject-matter

Table 5.5 Additional Categories.

Accounting	Financial Analysis
Balance sheet	Break-even and tradeoff analysis
Cash flow	Financial planning
Cost accounting	Simple and compound interest, net present value
Income statement	
DOH: days on hand	Capital appropriation request process
DSO: days sales outstanding	Ratio analysis (e.g., asset, operating cost, profitability, current ration, ROS, gross margin)
Net revenues	
Cost of goods sold (COGS)	
	Risk analysis techniques
	ROI analysis, pay-back analysis

Table 5.6 Performance Framework.

Groups of Work Activities	Leadership Dimensions					
	Strategic Thinking	Business Acumen	Communication	Sense of Urgency	Customer Focus	Change Management
Communicate senior leadership's vision, goals, and desired results to the organization.						
Provide input to the creation of the strategic plan.						
Set performance expectations in collaboration with employees.						
Manage metrics and scorecards.						

experts mapped existing courses available in the training organization to the performance framework. In this way, the formal training available in the organization was evaluated with regard to its fit to the leadership needs of managers. While this step aligned the formal training to the performance framework, the subject-matter experts then identified gaps in the formal curricula that had to be closed with the development of new courses or filled with informal training. The subject-matter experts then embarked on an effort to identify informal training to fill the gaps. This included the identification of webinars, blogs, experts' email addresses, knowledge bases, methods and procedure guidelines, pod-casts, books, CDs, websites, and so forth. The knowledge categories proved to be very helpful to the subject-matter experts who identified learning resources for the work activities. Next, the performance framework was put online so that it could be used for assessing development needs. The assessment can be performed by the managers, by team members, or it can be used as a multi-source feedback tool. Regardless, the results of the assessment identify skill gaps in the managers' leadership skills. Because learning resources are mapped to work activities, the assessment results also provide a learning prescription. Many of these learning resources are informal because they will be engaged at the behest of the manager, in the work setting, when the manager determines it is needed. The performance framework is used to support the performance management process in the following way:

1. During the planning phase of the performance management process, the manager and the supervisor identify which of the work activities in the performance framework are critical to the accomplishment of the manager's annual objectives, which are aligned with the strategic plans and goals of the organization.
2. Next, the manager's performance on the work activities selected in Step 1 is rated. This can be completed by the manager, the manager's supervisor, or both. Separate ratings are made for each leadership dimension for each work activity.
3. Finally, the manager and the supervisor decide which developmental activities to include in the manager's developmental plan. Completion of these activities can be tracked online by the supervisor.

4. During subsequent feedback sessions, the work activities can be re-assessed or new ones assessed and different learning resources can be identified. Managers can assess themselves on any work activities, at any time, and identify appropriate learning resources. In the case of formal learning resources (such as classroom training), managers must receive the approval of their supervisors to participate in the training.

The critical success factors for this best practice are the presence of a well-executed job analysis, the careful and comprehensive alignment of learning resources to work activities, and the use of information systems to support the functionality provided to managers and their supervisors.

Front-Line Workers

The project was conducted at one of the U.S. plants of this global manufacturing company. The plant employed approximately five hundred people, of whom about 350 were front-line workers. The manufacturing process in this plant included five major processes (storage of raw materials, initial processing of raw materials, operation of the production line, product quality testing, and shipping). Each of these processes was critically dependent on the effectiveness and efficiency of the prior process to maintain high levels of productivity. The objective of the project was to enhance the overall skill level of the workers, enable them to perform multiple work assignments, and implement a skill-based advancement and pay system. The management of the plant provided the project leader with a team of five front-line workers, one from each of the business processes, to assist in the project. These front-line workers were subject-matter experts for the business processes they represented.

The first step was to conduct a job analysis that identified the critical work activities performed by the front-line workers in each of the five business processes. Front-line workers and supervisors participated in focus groups and interviews in order to identify the job tasks and knowledge requirements for the jobs. After the supervisors and managers approved the initial job analysis results for each business process, the job analysis information was used to create paper-based surveys. The surveys gathered importance ratings for each of the job tasks and knowledge to identify those that were most critical to success on the job. An example of the tasks and associated knowledge included in a utility job in the initial processing of the raw materials is provided in Table 5.7.

The job analysis achieved two collateral benefits during the completion of that work. First, the plant was implementing a new quality control program that affected the task and knowledge requirements of the jobs in all five processes. The job analysis included these new tasks and knowledge requirements, thereby facilitating the integration of the new quality process into workers' jobs. Second, there was a high rate of customer complaints related to shipping errors. The job analysis focus groups and interviews uncovered deficiencies in knowledge requirements and the need to perform additional tasks. The deficiencies were immediately addressed and the work was redesigned. Subsequently, the rate of customer complaints dropped by 70 percent.

Table 5.7 Sample Tasks.

Tasks

- Take white and black liquid sample for testing, using sample gathering procedure.
- Take pulp samples, using sample gathering procedure, for testing.
- Perform test procedures on pulp samples, using applicable testing equipment, for comparison to target values.
- Perform test procedures on the white and black liquid samples, using applicable testing equipment, for comparison to target values.
- Enter test results, using DCS computer system, to update production process information.

Knowledge

- Personal protective equipment requirements
- Liquid testing tools
- Washer test procedures
- DCS interface

After the job analysis was completed, the performance management program at the plant was redesigned. The positions within a business process were hierarchically arranged. Workers progressed from the lower to the higher level, and higher-paying positions based on the availability of a job opening, seniority, and judgments by their supervisor that they were capable of mastering the job duties of the higher level job. Previously, newly hired or newly promoted front-line workers learned the position through informal learning on their own or from on-the-job training by their co-workers for a single position in one of the work processes. Performance appraisals were conducted informally with little or no attention given to employee development. In order to improve the performance management program, the project leader proceeded in the following manner. First, subject-matter experts rated the level of mastery that front-line workers needed to achieve in order to perform successfully the critical job tasks identified in the job analysis. Second, the front-line workers in each business process were evaluated using the critical job tasks from the job analysis. Prior to the evaluation, the trainer for each business process met with the supervisors in each business process to gain the support, and in many cases the assistance, of the supervisors in performing the evaluation. Third, the results of these evaluations were compared to the mastery standards created by the subject-matter experts. Skill gaps for each worker were identified and, finally, individual development plans were created for each front-line worker. The implementation of the individual development plans was the responsibility of the trainer for that business process.

In order to support and complement the new performance management process and to enable the development of a pay-for-skill compensation system, two additional initiatives were undertaken. The first initiative was the development of more objective methods to determine if a front-line worker had mastered the skills and knowledge needed to receive additional pay. The objective methods developed were job knowledge and work sample tests. Test blueprints were created from the job analysis results, and multiple-choice tests of the job knowledge required to perform critical tasks successfully were developed. Front-line workers were required to pass the job knowledge tests in order to demonstrate their mastery of a position. In addition to the job knowledge test, work sample tests for each position in each business process were developed. These work sample tests required front-line workers to demonstrate their proficiency in performing critical job tasks while being observed and evaluated by trained evaluators. The trained evaluators were the trainers, supervisors, or front-line workers who were considered to be master performers in the business process. Front-line workers were required to pass the job knowledge test and the work sample test for the duties in a position in order to receive additional pay. Front-line workers who did not qualify on the assessments were provided with remedial training—formal and informal. The second initiative that proceeded in parallel with the development of the assessments was to revamp the training. It was important to revamp the training in parallel with the assessment development because for those who did not qualify on the assessments, out of a sense of fairness and efficiency, the availability of quality, job-related training was considered of paramount importance. The availability of training that enabled front-line workers to build the skills needed to obtain higher pay was critical to their acceptance of the pay-for-skills program. The first step in revamping the training was to identify the skills and knowledge taught by the formal courses. The list of skills and knowledge from the courses was compared to the job analysis results to identify gaps, redundancies, and obsolete training content. Course content that aligned with the job analysis results was maintained, content that didn't was redesigned or discarded. In this process, the trainers determined that some of the training was best taught in a formal classroom setting and some was best taught through on-the-job training. The work sample tests identified many of the skills that were best taught through on-the-job training. When new course content was developed by the trainers or external vendors, the job analysis results were used to establish learning objectives. The course content of vendors who wanted to sell training programs to the organization was screened using the job analysis results.

When the project was completed, the plant had a performance management program that was tightly integrated with training and employee development. The job knowledge and work sample tests became the new approach to performance appraisal. Front-line workers were motivated to obtain formal and on-the-job training for critical job skills in order to obtain higher pay. Formal training was available for them to close knowledge and skill gaps identified by the assessments, and trainers were available to provide on-the-job training as needed.

Informal Learning and Development Planning

A critical part of successful performance management is good development planning, and a substantial portion of development planning includes informal learning activities. While there is little guidance from the empirical literature about the characteristic of good development planning, it seems reasonable to assume that, if most development planning activities are informal, then that literature applies to creating effective development plans. Development activities that involve informal learning should use principles from informal learning as a guide. For example, a sales manager might include "make a sales presentation to a client with the sales manager in attendance after participating in three sales planning sessions and sales calls with a top salesperson in the district" in a subordinate's development plan to enhance skills in preparing a sales presentation. This example of a development activity complies with empirical findings in informal learning because it includes a specific and challenging goal of increasing sales presentation skills, offers the opportunity to have contact with experts to improve those skills, ensures the skills will be practiced on the job and be observed by the sales manager, who can reinforce the learning. Finding examples of good informal learning activities presents a challenge to many managers. Two sources of ideas and examples of development activities are e-Advisor[4] and a Center for Creative Leadership publication that provides guidance for selecting development activities and examples of nearly one hundred assignments for development in one's current job (Lombardo & Eichinger, 1989).

Summary

This chapter addressed informal learning and its relation to performance management. A definition of informal learning was offered as a means to clarify what it is and what it is not.

Greater consistency and agreement among practitioners of informal learning are needed to enable them to build effective performance management programs. Greater consistency and agreement among researchers of informal learning are needed to enable them to understand, measure, and build models for optimizing informal learning in performance management programs and in organizations generally. Considering the pervasiveness and importance of informal learning to organizations that seek to improve their performance management programs and be high-performing learning organizations, it is somewhat surprising that there is not more good quality research about informal learning. However, there are many good quality studies that provide practical guidance about the work environment and trainee characteristics that facilitate the transfer of learning to the work setting. This research serves as a sort of surrogate for research on informal learning. This chapter attempted to present those findings and their advice. Finally, in order to enhance the informal learning experience for the reader of this chapter, the author provided two real-world examples and ten recommendations for enhancing informal learning in organizations.

References

Baldwin, T. T., & Ford, J. K. (1988). Transfer of training: A review and direction for future research. *Personnel Psychology, 41*, 63–105.

Bandura, A. (1986). *Social foundations of thought and action: A social cognitive theory.* Englewood Cliffs, NJ: Prentice Hall.

Barrick, M. R., & Mount, M. K. (1991). The big five personality dimensions and job performance: A meta-analysis. *Personnel Psychology, 44*, 1–26.

Becker, G. S. (1993). *Human capital* (3rd ed.). Chicago: University of Chicago Press.

Berings, M., Doornbos, A. J., & Simons, P. (2006). Methodological practices in on-the-job learning research. *Human Resource Development Journal, 9*(3), 333–363.

Birdi, K., Allan, C., & Warr, P. (1997). Correlates and perceived outcome of four types of employee development activity. *Journal of Applied Psychology, 82*(6), 845–857.

Bloom, B. S. (1956). *Taxonomy of educational objectives.* New York: David McKay.

Cervone, D. (2004). The architecture of personality. *Psychological Review*, *111*(1), 183–204.

Colquitt, J. A., LePine, J. A., & Noe, R. A. (2000). Toward an integrative theory of training motivation: A meta-analytic path analysis of 20 years of research. *Journal of Applied Psychology*, *85*(5), 678–707.

Davison, G. C., Vogel, R. S., & Coffman, S. G. (1997). Think-aloud approaches to cognitive assessment and the articulated thoughts in simulated situations paradigm. *Journal of Consulting and Clinical Psychology*, *65*(6), 950–958.

Dweck, C. S., & Leggett, E. L. (1988). A social-cognitive approach to motivation and personality. *Psychological Review*, *95*, 256–273.

Lombardo, M. M., & Eichinger, R. W. (1989). *Eighty-eight assignments for development in place*. Greensboro, NC: Center for Creative Leadership.

Ehrenberg, R. G., & Smith, R. S. (2006). *Modern labor economics: Theory and public policy*. New York: Pearson Addison-Wesley.

Eraut, M. (2000). Non-formal learning and tacit knowledge in professional work. *British Journal of Educational Psychology*, *70*, 113–136.

Ericsson, K. A., Krampe, R. T., & Tesch-Romer, C. (1993). The role of deliberate practice in the acquisition of expert performance. *Psychological Review*, *100*, 363–406.

Flavell, J. H. (1979). Metacognition and cognitive monitoring: A new area of cognitive-developmental inquiry. *American Psychologist*, *34*, 906–911.

Frayne, C. A., & Geringer, J. M. (2000). Self-management training for improving job performance: A field experiment involving salespeople. *Journal of Applied Psychology*, *85*(3), 361–372.

Gagne, R. M., & Medsker, K. L. (1995). *The conditions of learning and theory of instruction* (4th ed.). New York: Wadsworth.

Gaugler, B. B., Rosenthal, D. B., Thornton, G. C., & Bentson, C. (1987). Meta-analysis of assessment center validity. *Journal of Applied Psychology*, *72*, 493–511.

Gully, S. M., Payne, S. C., Koles, K. L. K., & Whiteman, J. A. K. (2002). The impact of error training and individual differences on training outcomes: An attribute-treatment interaction perspective. *Journal of Applied Psychology*, *87*(1), 143–155.

Holladay, C. L., & Quinones, M. A. (2003). Practice variability and transfer of training: The role of self-efficacy generality. *Journal of Applied Psychology*, *88*(6) 1094–1103.

Hunter, J. E., & Schmidt, F. L. (1996). Intelligence and job performance: Economic and social implications. *Psychology, Public Policy, and Law*, *2*, 447–472.

Jensen, A. R. (1980). *Bias in mental testing.* New York: The Free Press.

Kanfer, R., & Ackerman, P. L. (1989). Motivation and cognitive abilities: An integrative/aptitude-treatment interaction approach to skill acquisition. *Journal of Applied Psychology, 74,* 657–690.

Lievens, F., Harris, M. M., Van Keer, E., & Bisqueret, C. (2003). Predicting cross-cultural training performance: The validity of personality, cognitive ability, and dimensions measured by an assessment center and a behavioral description interview. *Journal of Applied Psychology, 88*(3), 476–489.

Loewenstein, M. A., & Spletzer, J. R. (1994). *Informal training: A review of existing data and some new evidence.* Washington, DC: U.S. Department of Labor, Bureau of Labor Statistics, BLS Working Papers, Working Paper 254.

Mager, R. F. (1997). *Preparing instructional objectives* (3rd ed.). Atlanta, GA: CEP Press.

Marsick, V. J. (2003). Invited reaction: Informal learning and the transfer of learning, how managers develop proficiency. *Human Resource Development Quarterly, 14,* 389–395.

Mitchell, L., & Livingstone, D. W. (2002). Informal learning practices of bank branch workers. New Approaches to Lifelong Learning (NALL), Working Paper 64.

Morrison, R. F., & Brantner, T. M. (1992). What enhances or inhibits learning a new job? A basic career issue. *Journal of Applied Psychology, 77*(6), 926–940.

Osman-Gani, A. M., & Jacobs, R. L. (2005) Technological change and human resource development practices in Asia: A study of Singapore-based companies. *International Journal of Training and Development, 9*(4), 271–280.

Peterson, C., Maier, S. F., & Seligman, M. E. P. (1993). *Learned helplessness: A theory for the age of personal control.* New York: Oxford University Press.

Pulakos, E. D., Arad, S., Donovan, M. A., & Plamondon, K. E. (2000). Adaptability in the workplace: Development of a taxonomy of adaptive performance. *Journal of Applied Psychology, 85*(4), 612–624.

Rouillier, J. Z., & Goldstein, I. L. (1993). The relationship between organizational transfer climate and positive transfer of training. *Human Resources Development Quarterly, 4,* 377–390.

Salas, E., & Cannon-Bowers, J. A. (2001). The science of training: A decade of progress. *Annual Review of Psychology, 52,* 471–499.

Schmidt, A. M., & Ford, J. K. (2003). Learning within a learner control training environment: The interactive effects of goal orientation and metacognitive instruction on learning outcomes. *Personnel Psychology, 56*(2), 405–430.

Senge, P. (1990). *The fifth discipline.* New York: Currency Doubleday.

Skule, S. (2004). Learning conditions at work: A framework to understand and assess informal learning in the workplace. *International Journal of Training and Development, 8*(1), 8–21.

Smith-Jentsch, K. A., Salas, E., & Brannick, M. T. (2001). To transfer or not to transfer? Investigating the combined effects of trainee characteristics, team leader support, and team climate. *Journal of Applied Psychology, 86*(2), 279–292.

Snow, R. E. (1986). Individual differences and the design of educational programs. *American Psychologist, 41,* 1029–1039.

Sternberg, R. J. (1988). *The triarchic mind: A new theory of human intelligence.* New York: Viking Penguin.

Sternberg, R. J., & Kolligian, J. Jr. (1990). *Competence considered.* New Haven, CT: Yale University Press.

Summers, B., Williamson, T., & Read, D. (2004). Does method of acquisition affect the quality of expert judgment? A comparison of education with on-the-job learning. *Journal of Occupational and Organizational Psychology, 77,* 237–258.

Tracey, J. B., Tannenbaum, S. I., & Kavanagh, M. J. (1995). Applying trained skills on the job: The importance of the work environment. *Journal of Applied Psychology, 80*(2), 239–252.

Versloot, B. M., de Jong, J. A., & Thijssen, J. G. (2001). Organizational context of structured on-the-job training. *International Journal of Training and Development, 5*(1), 2–22.

Wagner, R. K. (1997). Intelligence, training, and employment. *American Psychologist, 52*(10), 1059–1069.

Williams, J., & Rosenbaum, S. (2004). *Learning paths.* San Francisco, CA: Pfeiffer.

Notes

1. Becker won the Nobel Prize in economics in 1992 for his work on human capital.
2. To this an industrial psychologist familiar with the principles of content validity might add that subject-matter experts confirm the accuracy and job-relatedness of the training content.
3. For the purpose of this example, only four groups of work activities will be described. In this project, there were eighteen of these groups of work activities.
4. e-Advisor is available from Personnel Decisions, Inc.

CHAPTER 6

MANAGING TEAM PERFORMANCE IN COMPLEX SETTINGS

Research-Based Best Practices

Eduardo Salas, Sallie J. Weaver, and Michael A. Rosen

Department of Psychology, Institute for Simulation and Training, University of Central Florida

AND

Kimberly A. Smith-Jentsch

Department of Psychology, University of Central Florida

Within the last decade, the face of work has greatly changed—teams are integral to the majority of business practices, the complexity of work has greatly evolved, and the time to complete work seems to continually shrink (Devine, Clayton, Phillips, Dunford, & Melner, 1999; Goldstein & Gilliam, 1990). To practitioners this is clear in our daily work with clients. The modern economy demands that our clients continually anticipate the changing needs and desires of their customers in what often feels like nano-seconds.

They must do this with the utmost effectiveness and efficiency in order to maintain a competitive advantage. Consequently, organizations have turned to team-based work arrangements in order to maximize the use of employee expertise, to juggle multiple projects and deadlines, to reduce errors, and to streamline operations (Baker, Gustafson, Beaubien, Salas, & Barach, 2005). The most recent large-scale random sample of U.S. organizations indicates that 48 percent of organizations utilize some type of team (Devine, Clayton, Phillips, Dunford, & Melner, 1999). Furthermore, this survey indicates that the most common type of team reported was "project teams"—those formed in order to remedy a defined, specialized project or goal and tend to be cross-functional (Sundstrom, McIntyre, Halfhill, & Richards, 2000).

The trend toward team-based work is also reflected in reports indicating organizations are adopting team-based systems in order to cope with the changing nature of work—characterized by increased cognitive and technological complexity (Ilgen, 1994). From teams responsible for managing complex problems and adapting to a changing economy (project teams) to teams responsible for efficiently executing production in the organization (production teams), team performance plays a critical role in organizational outcomes. Managing the performance of these different types of teams is therefore a critical element of organizational effectiveness and competitive advantage.

The central aim of this chapter is to provide scientifically rooted guidance for managing team performance in organizations. To this end, we begin with a set of definitions to clarify our conceptualization of teams and team performance management. Second, we discuss the performance management process in relation to teams. Third, we outline five key organizational capacities and discuss how team performance is linked to each. Fourth, we present a set of research-based best practices for managing team performance to support each of the five key organizational capacities.

What Constitutes a Team?

By definition a team is a distinguishable set of two or more people interacting toward a common goal with specific roles and boundaries on tasks that are interdependent and that are completed within a larger organizational context (Kozlowski & Bell, 2003; Salas, Dickinson, Converse, & Tannenbaum, 1992). The tasks which teams work on tend to require dynamic exchange of team member resources (including information), coordination of activities, adaptability to task demands, and an organizational structure that organizes members (Swezey, Meltzer, & Salas, 1994). Both task interdependence and outcome interdependence characterize team-based work (Wageman, 2001). Task interdependence refers to the inherent nature of the work itself that requires cooperation for completion, while outcome interdependence refers to the degree to which shared outcomes (rewards) are contingent on collective performance. Compared to individual-level performance management processes, team-level performance management processes must be designed to measure the outputs of combined effort, but also retain individual accountability. You get what you measure and reinforce at both levels; therefore there must be a way to balance performance management strategies at multiple levels while also accounting for membership on multiple teams.

There are also legal implications for multi-level performance measurement. U.S. federal regulations require, in most cases, that at least one critical element of team-level performance assessment is based on individual performance (U.S. Office of Personnel Management, n.d.). By building in individual accountability, the regulation provides for the ability to demote or terminate employees on the basis of unacceptable performance. One stipulation, though, regards manager or supervisor performance. Legally, it is permissible to develop a critical element that holds managers/supervisors accountable for the performance of their team so long as it considers their level of leadership responsibilities for the team.

Teams and Performance Management

Performance management (PM) offers an evidence-based methodology to guide performance measurement, strategic planning, feedback, and reinforcement in order to maximize effectiveness and efficiency at both the team and individual level without being mutually exclusive. Although PM is frequently used synonymously with terms such as performance appraisal and performance review, PM is a process that includes more than simply assessment. It also includes facets of motivation, situational and environmental influences, measure design, feedback, and employee development. According to Armstrong (2000), PM is comprehensive in terms of organizational culture; it does not rely on the cultural assumption that managers are solely responsible for the performance of their teams. Instead, managers and team members share responsibility and are jointly accountable for results.

The term "performance management" refers to the process of measuring, monitoring, and maximizing on-the-job performance (Armstrong, 2000; Dransfield, 2000). PM focuses on outputs, results, and meeting goals and objectives efficiently and effectively. In team settings, PM is founded upon the notion of aligning the goals of the team with the overall goals and preferred results of the organization. Teams present a special case of PM, however, in that there are basically two management systems operating simultaneously, one at the individual level and one at the team level. Effective team PM seamlessly interweaves these systems, while maintaining indicators of both individual and team-level effectiveness. This theme runs throughout the best practices presented in this paper.

The Facets of Team Performance Management (TPM)

Letts, Ryan, and Grossman (1998) suggest four key capacities for organizational effectiveness that easily translate into a guide for performance management for team effectiveness.

Adaptive capacity refers to the ability of the team to maintain focus on the "external" environment. In this sense the external environment includes "clients" who are within the same organization, but outside of the team itself, and influences completely external to the organization that impact the team's ability to meet its goals. In particular, this capacity focuses on maximizing performance, while continually adjusting and aligning the team itself to respond to those needs and influences. Adaptive capacity is cultivated through attention to assessments, collaborating and networking, and planning.

Leadership capacity refers to the ability of both the team leader and the individual members of the team to set direction for the team and its resources and also guide activities to follow that direction. Leadership capacity is cultivated through attention to visioning, establishing goals, directing, motivating, making decisions, and solving problems.

Management capacity is the ability of the team to ensure effective and efficient use of its resources. Management capacity is accomplished through careful development and coordination of resources, including people (their time and expertise), money, and facilities.

Technical capacity is the ability to design and operate products and services to effectively and efficiently deliver services to customers. The nature of that technical capacity depends on the particular type of products and services provided by the team and greater organization.

These four facets provide a framework to guide the performance management process in teams. Using this framework as a foundation, we present a set of best practices in the following section synthesized and accumulated from practical experience and the relevant team, performance management, project management, and human resources literature. These practices are illustrated by examples from encounters with clients, and we provide some tips for execution and implementation.

Best Practices for Addressing the Facets of TPM

Within each of the capacities outlined above, we outline relevant best practices and illustrative examples from the field. Table 6.1 contains a list of the practices we suggest, as well as implementation tips and relevant citations.

Adaptive Capacity

Adaptive team performance is an iterative process whereby team members engage in individual and team-level performance and alter their performance processes in order to more effectively respond to a changing context of work (Burke, Stagl, Klein, Goodwin, Salas, & Halpin, 2006). In order to build and manage

Table 6.1 Best practices for performance management of teams.

Best Practice	Tips	Selected References
	Adaptive Capacity	
1. Build flexible and adaptable team players.	• Build mutual performance monitoring and back-up behavior skills in team members using cross training and other methods. • Build mutual trust among team members.	• Salas, Sims, & Burke, 2005; Porter et al., 2003; Burke, Fiore, & Salas, 2003
2. Build a big play book: Encourage a large team task strategy repertoire.	• Provide a safe environment to practice new performance strategies (for example, use simulation-based training).	• Orasanu, 1990; Salas, Priest, Wilson, & Burke, 2006
3. Create teams that know themselves and their work environment.	• Team cue recognition training. • Perceptual contrast training. • Build team communication skills (information exchange, closed-loop communication).	• Salas, Cannon-Bowers, Fiore, & Stout, 2001; Wilson, Burke, Priest, & Salas, 2005

4. Build teams that can tell when the usual answer isn't the right answer.

- Develop team planning skills.
- Use guided error training to promote an understanding of when the routine solution is not the appropriate solution.

- Lorentez, Salas, & Tannenbaum, 2005

5. Develop self-learning teams: Train teams to help themselves.

- Team self-correction training; team leader debrief skills.
- Foster a team learning orientation, psychological safety.

- Smith-Jentsch, Zeisig, Acton, & McPherson, 1998; Bunderson & Sutcliffe, 2003; Edmondson, 1999

6. Don't let the weakest link have the strongest voice: Build teams that take advantage of their resources.

- Develop a strong team orientation in team members.
- Promote assertiveness.
- Build diversity of expertise and transactive memory.

- Eby & Dobbins, 1997; Hollenbeck, Ilgen, Sego, Hudlund, Major, & Phillips, 1995

Leadership Capacity

7. Articulate and cultivate a shared vision that incorporates both internal and external clients.

- Ask how the team will make a difference for internal and external clients.
- Establish measurable indicators of team success.
- Determine what the team hopes to accomplish in its wildest dreams.

- Christenson & Walker, 2004; Williams & Laugani, 1999; Briner, Hastings, & Geddes, 1996

(Continued)

Table 6.1 *(Continued)*

Best Practice	Tips	Selected References
8. Create goals the team can grow with: Build hierarchically aligned goals with malleability and flexibility at both the individual and team levels.	• Include all team members in goal generation. • Set team and individual level goals that are aligned with upper-level goals. • Allow overall goals to have wiggle room and build flexibility into subgoals. • Ensure that there are multiple strategies to reach the goal.	• Locke & Bryan, 1967; Getz & Rainey, 2001
9. Build motivation into the performance management process: Make clear connections between actions, evaluations, and outcomes.	• Team members should be encouraged and rewarded for praising colleague accomplishments and being supportive during setbacks. • Only utilize group-level incentives and rewards for work performance. • Create opportunities for taking major responsibility for some elements of the task for each member. • Make the connections between actions, results, evaluations, and outcomes clear.	• Pritchard & Ashwood, 2008; Swezey & Salas, 1992; Oser, McCallum, Salas, & Morgan, 1989

10. Team leaders must champion coordination, communication, and cooperation.

- Build the team to reflect the various forms of expertise required by the tasks at hand.
- Foster the use of external sources (temporary members, consultant team members) if the expertise is not inherent in the team.
- Divide tasks to suit individual expertise, but do allow opportunities for growth.
- Remember that leader does not equal expert, defer to those with the expertise (see Best Practice Number 5).

- Dyer, 1984; Zalesney, Salas, & Prince, 1995; Salas, Wilson, Murphy, King, & Salisbury, in press

11. Understand the "why": Examine both failures and successes during debriefings.

- Review instances of both effective and ineffective behavior during feedback sessions.
- Recognize failures as learning opportunities.

- Zakay, Ellis, & Shevalsky, 2004; Ellis & Davidi, 2005

(Continued)

Table 6.1 *(Continued)*

Best Practice	Tips	Selected References
Management Capacity		
12. Clearly define what to measure: Develop and maintain a systematic and organized representation of performance.	• Develop a document or set of documents explicitly linking KSAs to performance metrics, feedback, and outcomes (for example, reinforcement, promotion, pay). • The purpose of measurement should drive measure development.	• Kurtz & Bartram, 2002; Bartram, 2005; Stevens & Campion, 1994
13. Uncover the "why" of performance: Develop measures that are diagnostic of performance.	• Foster an understanding of why performance was effective or ineffective. • Incorporate measures which include outcomes and processes. • The purpose of measurement should drive measure development.	• Cannon-Bowers & Salas, 1997

- Avoid "easy" measures that miss large amounts of performance-related information.
- Measure performance from multiple perspectives. Solicit input from team members, for example, using 360-degree feedback.
- Develop a discipline of pre-brief→performance→debrief.

14. Measure typical performance continuously.
- Measure performance over time.
- Choose to measure what employees "will do."
- Automate as much of the performance monitoring process as possible.
- Provide ongoing, diagnostic feedback that identifies and removes roadblocks to effective performance.

- Sackett, Zedeck, & Fogli, 1988; Klehe & Anderson, 2007

(Continued)

Table 6.1 *(Continued)*

Best Practice	Tips	Selected References
	Technical Capacity	
15. Include teamwork competencies in formal performance evaluations.	• Offer both team and individual level reinforcement (both formal and informal).	• Salas, Kosarzycki, & Tannenbaum, 2005; Murphy & Cleveland, 1995
16. Have a plan for integrating new team members, and execute it.	• Clearly define teamwork and taskwork competencies needed for effective performance and ensure new team members possess these KSAs.	• Levine & Choi, 2004; Cannon-Bowers & Salas, 1997
17. Assess and foster shared mental models.	• Measure and provide feedback (cue-strategy associations). • Cross-training, interpositional knowledge training. • Encourage a culture of learning. • Develop a strong sense of "collective" trust, teamness, and confidence.	• Cannon-Bowers, Salas, & Converse, 1993; Cooke et al., 2007; Mohammed & Dumville, 2001; Blickensderfer, Cannon-Bowers, & Salas, 1998

Multi-Team Membership

18. Develop or select for individual personal discipline and organizational skills.
- Include these skills in KSA and competency definition.
- Ensure modes of distributed communication, information systems, and access to necessary organizational materials remotely.
- Ancona & Caldwell, 2007

19. Communicate the "big picture": Facilitate a global awareness of competing goals and deadlines of all teams.
- Coordinate meetings of team leaders to discuss multiple deadlines.
- Create global Gantt chart with real-time updates if possible.
- Mortensen, Woolley, & O'Leary, 2007

20. Maturity counts: Recognize that a multi-team framework works best for mature projects.
- Apply MTM to mature teams or projects.
- Have at least one member 100 percent dedicated to a single team during the kickoff period to ensure continuity.
- Mortensen, Woolley, & O'Leary, 2007

21. Foster trust: Cultivate a culture of information sharing.
- Foster information sharing.
- Cultivate a culture of error reporting and feedback that focuses on learning from mistakes, not punishment.
- Salas, Sims, & Burke, 2005; Bandow, 2001; Webber, 2002

effective adaptive capacity on the team level, a performance management process should attend to the following:

Best Practice #1: Build Flexible and Adaptable Team Players

Team performance is multi-level, and a major source of adaptive capacity in a team resides in the ability of team members to shift their task responsibilities on the fly. Underlying this capacity is the team members' skill at understanding when they need to adjust performance (that is, mutual performance monitoring) and how to assist their fellow team members when necessary (back-up behavior). To implement this best practice, a performance management process should train mutual performance monitoring and back-up behavior skills. Additionally, for mutual performance monitoring and back-up behavior to be effective, team members must have mutual trust (Porter, Hollenbeck, Ilgen, Ellis, West, & Moon, 2003; Salas, Sims, & Burke, 2005). If team members do not trust one another, mutual performance monitoring and back-up behavior will be interpreted negatively and be detrimental to team performance.

Best Practice #2: Build a Big Play Book: Encourage a Large Team Task Strategy Repertoire

Effective teams recognize when a plan is not working and are able to switch to a new plan or task performance strategy when necessary. A large repertoire of possible task strategies ensures the ability to switch to a more effective strategy based on either different environmental or situational demands. For example, it has been found that effective airline crews are those that use downtime during long flights to engage in practice for unanticipated emergencies (Orasanu, 1990). Essentially, these teams are engaging in "what if" scenarios and expanding the potential performance strategies available to a team. To achieve this, a performance management process should provide safe opportunities for a team to experiment with new types of performance. Simulation-based training (SBT) is a powerful tool to this end because it allows teams to practice performance strategies in environments replicating the real world environment, but without the risks associated with failure (see Salas, Priest, Wilson, & Burke, 2006).

Best Practice #3: Create Teams That Know Themselves and Their Work Environment

Adaptation requires an understanding or awareness of (1) changes in the environment that impact current team performance, (2) an understanding of how the team currently meets its task demands, and (3) how it is capable of adjusting to new demands (that is, what is happening in the environment, how the team is responding currently, and what alternative courses of action are available to the team). This requires team members to balance an external and internal focus, to have an awareness of the broader task environment/organization and the internal workings of the team. This can be facilitated in two ways. First, team members with a more robust understanding of the task environment and what changes mean to the team will be more responsive to critical external events. Techniques for facilitating this include team cue recognition training, a method designed to enhance employees' situational awareness by teaching them to focus on relevant cues (Salas, Cannon-Bowers, Fiore, & Stout, 2001), and perceptual contrast training, a technique that involves presenting trainees with contrasting examples of a scenario, teaching them to recognize the differences between the scenarios, and facilitating their interpretations of the positives and negatives associated with each (Wilson, Burke, Priest, & Salas, 2005), Second, team communication skills are critical for distributing the detection of important changes made by one team member to the rest of the team. Training in team communication skills ensures that critical changes detected by one team member are quickly and effectively spread to the rest of the team (Smith-Jentsch, Zeisig, Acton, & McPherson, 1998).

Best Practice #4: Build Teams That Can Tell When the Usual Answer Isn't the Right Answer

Like individuals, teams develop routines or standard responses, a "business as usual" pattern of performance. These routines can result in efficiency in relatively static environments, but when the environment changes the routine response may no longer be an effective response. Therefore, to build adaptive capacity, a performance management process should develop teams capable of recognizing the complexity of their environment (and the significance of changes in that environment) as well as a capacity to plan in an adaptive and flexible manner. To this end, guided error training can be used to build an understanding in teams of when the routine response is not the correct response. This type of training is purposefully designed to guide trainees toward making errors, giving them the opportunity to experience the actions that lead to problems. Facilitators provide corrective support during training once errors have been made and trainees are able to apply these new strategies in follow-up practice sessions. Guided error training allows teams to see the consequences of using the wrong performance strategy when the environment changes and to develop a better understanding of how to deal with novel situations (Wilson, Burke, Priest, & Salas, 2005).

Best Practice #5: Develop Self-Learning Teams: Train Teams to Help Themselves

To adapt effectively, a team must learn from its past performance. This means a performance management strategy should develop the culture and tools for team learning within each team such as performance diagnosis and debriefing/feedback skills. Developing debriefing, feedback, and coaching skills, particularly in the leader, are approaches to doing this. For example, as part of a team training program evaluated by the authors, surgical teams learned how to conduct briefings and to debrief before and after each case, during which they utilized peer coaching techniques to discuss ways to improve in future cases. Additionally, team self-correction training can give team members the skills to assess the effectiveness of their own behavior as well as others, and to give constructive feedback (Smith-Jentsch, Zeisig, Acton, & McPherson, 1998). Because team learning is dependent to a large degree on aspects of the team culture and team affects, a team performance management process should foster a team learning orientation (Bunderson & Sutcliffe, 2003) and psychological safety (Edmondson, 1999).

Best Practice #6: Don't Let the Weakest Link Have the Strongest Voice: Build Teams That Take Advantage of Their Resources

Adaptive teams need to take advantage of the full range of knowledge and experience available to them, both internally and through available external resources. To do this, the team performance management process should focus on three critical areas. First, teams must have a sense of collective orientation wherein all members are free to contribute and the weight of each member's input is determined by his or her relevant functional expertise, not status or rank (Eby & Dobbins, 1997). Building a team composed of individuals focused on the team goals and not their own personal goals is critical. This can be accomplished through selection, training, or structuring of the reward system to reinforce the primacy of team goals. Second, assertiveness of individual team members should be developed. Collective orientation sets the stage for contributions from all, but team members must be willing and able to be assertive and offer input. Third, teams should have an accurate and robust transactive memory, that is, an understanding of who knows what on a team and in the broader organization (Austin, 2003). By knowing the extent and type of expertise possessed by team members, the team can better evaluate the input of different members (Hollenbeck, Ilgen, Sego, Hudlund, Major, & Phillips, 1995). The more diverse the expertise within this transactive memory, the more knowledge resources the team has available.

Leadership Capacity

Leadership entails the capability to set the team's direction and to guide the activities of the team toward its goals (Kozlowski, Gully, McHugh, Salas, & Cannon-Bowers, 1996; Letts, Ryan, & Grossman, 1998). Specifically, leadership involves visioning, goal setting, motivation, decision making, and problem solving (Kozlowski, Gully, McHugh, Salas, & Cannon-Bowers, 1996). The importance of effective leadership to team performance cannot be understated and involves "social problem solving that promotes coordinated, adaptive team performance by facilitating goal definition and attainment" (Burke, Stagl, Klein, Goodwin, Salas, & Halpin, 2006; Salas, Burke, & Stagl, 2004, p. 343). A performance management process that maximizes leadership capacity should promote the following.

Best Practice #7: Articulate and Cultivate a Shared Vision That Incorporates Both Internal and External Clients

The vision of the team must be aligned with the vision and mission of the organization. Vision gives meaning to team goals and is an important component of team culture (Christenson & Walker, 2004). It helps members to focus and direct their efforts. The vision statement must be clear, achievable, negotiable, and understood by all members of the team (Williams & Laugani, 1999). Furthermore, the vision should be defined in terms that allow it to be measured. By defining the team's vision in measurable terms, it can underlie the entire performance management process. Some of the key questions used to develop a team vision have been adapted from work by Briner, Hastings, and Geddes (1996). During vision development, be sure to ask: (1) How will this team make a difference to the organization? (2) How will this team make a difference to their external clients? (3) How will we know when the team has been successful? and (3) What in our wildest dreams would you like this team to achieve? It is also vital to conduct "reality checks" to see whether the vision is truly reflective of both the current and future needs of both internal and external clients throughout the vision development process (Christenson & Walker, 2004).

As noted earlier, teams must consider the needs of others within the organization (that is, other teams or individuals) and of those outside the organization (clients) (Ancona, 1990). Teams that actively manage these external demands become more effective and efficient (Pfeffer, 1972; Pfeffer & Salancik, 1978). The new buzzword "X-teams" was developed to describe teams that emphasize an external focus. They are defined as teams in which members and leaders have high levels of external activity (that is, ambassadorship, task coordination, and scouting, feedback seeking), extreme execution (maximize internal dynamics), and flexible phases (leaders set explicit phases with clear milestones) (Ancona & Bresman, 2007). Incorporating this broadened focus into the process of defining a team's vision can help drive the development of a clear vision statement that is understood, motivational, and credible, as well as demanding and challenging (Christenson & Walker, 2004).

Best Practice #8: Create Goals the Team Can Grow with: Build Hierarchically Aligned Goals with Malleability and Flexibility at Both the Individual and Team Levels

The complexity of modern work tasks and the volatile nature of the current work environment demand malleability. Malleable goals are those that can be revised or are flexible enough in their original definition in order to reflect the real-time context, pressures, and available resources teams have access to. Comparatively, rigid goals are those that are not reactive to changes in the contextual environment and the degree to which unforeseen changes impact employee ability to meet subgoals. Even if they are short-term, certain types of goals may be so rigid as to limit optimal performance (Locke & Bryan, 1967). For example, employees may give up trying to accomplish a rigid goal if they feel they have fallen irrevocably behind should they fail to meet a subgoal (Getz & Rainey, 2001). Malleable goals are related to team adaptability; the team must be prepared to act in the presence of unforeseen barriers, yet still feel that they are accomplishing their goals and objectives. Overly rigid goals can stifle motivation and perpetuate team member frustration.

Goals should be arranged in an alignment hierarchy in order to achieve flexibility; individual goals should be aligned with team goals, and team goals should be aligned with the greater organizational goals. An innovative method for ensuring goal alignment and flexibility was encountered by one of the editors while working with a global pharmaceutical and consumer healthcare company. Part of the organization was structured in cross-functional teams wherein each team was responsible for a consumer product line (for example, an over-the-counter pain reliever). Each team had two vice-presidential-level co-leaders: one from marketing and one from R&D. These co-leaders had a few direct reports, but most of the people on the team were functional specialists (for example, advertising, regulatory affairs, medical) who reported to functional VPs (not the team's co-leaders). The senior VPs (one from marketing and one from R&D) who were responsible for all product lines first created a strategy for the entire consumer product organization that was visually represented using a "fishbone." This was cascaded to team (product-line) co-leaders, who then created a strategy (their own fishbone) for their product line. A meeting was then held which included product-line team members (who, by the way, worked together in a common workspace no matter who they report to). During this meeting, the co-leaders, first described the high-level strategy/ fishbone and then described the team's (that is, the product line's) strategy/fishbone. During the latter part of the meeting, each team member identified parts of the team's (product line's) fishbone where they were expected to make a contribution and proceeded to set individual goals that were explicitly linked to specific parts of the team's fishbone. The net result was that the team's strategy/fishbone was strongly linked to the higher-level organizational fishbone, and each person on the team had goals explicitly linked to specific parts of the team's (product line's) fishbone. Aligning and managing team performance in such a highly matrixed organization is enormously challenging, but can be done when goals are generated hierarchically.

Best Practice #9: Build Motivation into the Performance Management Process: Make Clear Connections Among Actions, Evaluations, and Outcomes

Motivation can only be high when employees see clear connections among: (a) their actions and the results they produce, (b) the actual level of results they produce and the evaluation of these results, (c) the outcomes they receive based on these evaluations, and (d) the degree that these outcomes satisfy their needs (Pritchard & Ashwood, 2008). A large component of building in motivation is contained in the measurement process used to assess performance and how outcomes are allocated as a result of these performance assessments. These outcomes may be formal (such as promotions or raises) or informal (such as social praise or recognition). Effective teams tend to comprise of members who provide positive reinforcement for the accomplishments of teammates and support for the team overall (Oser, McCallum, Salas, & Morgan, 1989; Swezey & Salas, 1992). Conversely, these team members are also supportive when mistakes are made. Effective teams should institute some form of reward for members who display such supportive behaviors (Swezey & Salas, 1992). Such individualized incentives are not recommended, however, for individual level performance. When tasks are interdependent, as in team-based work, such individual incentives or rewards can undermine cohesiveness, cooperation, and increase undesirable intra-team competition (Pritchard & Ashwood, 2008).

Team members who feel central to the success of the team, those who see strong connections among their actions, results, evaluations, and outcomes, tend to feel more motivated and satisfied with their team experience. One way to foster this feeling suggested by Swezey and Salas (1992) is to "provide opportunities for each team member to take lead responsibility for designing and directing a major task-related activity which affects the entire team" (p. 230). Allowing each team member to act in an overtly central role (even if only for a portion of the project) gives them the chance to experience dealing with the barriers, anxiety, and responsibility inherent in such endeavors.

Best Practice #10: Team Leaders Must Champion Coordination, Communication, and Cooperation

The leader must recognize and make use of the full range of expertise of the team members in order to solve problems. Differentiation of expertise across team members is a key characteristic of teams (Dyer, 1984), especially teams dealing with complex problems; however, leaders must coordinate and help direct this mix of expertise, especially in times of uncertainty and conflict. Facilitating coordinated responses between multiple individuals with different types and levels of expertise is a key element of team effectiveness (Zalesny, Salas, & Prince, 1995). For instance, Shin & Zhou (2007) found that heterogeneity among teammates in terms of their educational backgrounds led to increased creativity for teams led by transformational leaders (for example, charismatic, high levels of consideration, and so on), but not for teams with leaders who did not adopt this style. It was suggested that transformational leaders enabled these educationally diverse teams to capitalize on their pooled cognitive resources effectively to maximize creativity.

Team leaders play a vital role in the development and facilitation of the teamwork enabling skills (for example, shared mental models, communication) that foster effective team performance (Kozlowski, Gully, McHugh, Salas, & Cannon-Bowers, 1996). Although formal training of these skills is possible and suggested, constraints such as time and resources often mean that team members must learn these skills on the job, while working in team environments. The leader must facilitate both individual skills (such as active listening) and team-level skills (such as closed-loop communication) in order to make sure that (1) all individuals have the capacity to perform and (2) the synergy of these skills occurs to create effective team performance.

Best Practice #11: Understand the "Why": Examine Both Failures and Successes During Debriefings

One way leaders may be able to do this is via the feedback that they provide to their team members. During these sessions, a key question is "why" the level of performance occurred. The surgical teams participating in the team training evaluated by the authors noted earlier used this technique during their briefings, specifically focusing on three main questions: What did we do well? What did we not do so well? and What can we improve in the next case? A common assumption is that providing feedback and review of negative instances of performance enhances employee motivation more than review of successful performance (Sitkin, 1992). The notion is that unexpected outcomes, such as a failure, are more motivationally salient than instances in which things work according to plan and that these unexpected outcomes also have stronger affective impact as well (Feldman, 1989; Shepperd & McNulty, 2002). Rarely do we plan to fail—What would be the point of exerting any effort toward an outcome we know is fruitless? Therefore, these instances are considerably more unexpected than success. Evidence indicates that managers in the field tend to agree with this assumption. For example, managers are more likely to implement learn-from-experience processes, such as event reviews, after a negative event occurs, as opposed to after a successful event (Zakay, Ellis, & Shevalsky, 2004). But can we learn nothing from our successes? Recent empirical evidence suggests that previous assumptions prematurely discounted the effects of including reviews of successful performance in feedback sessions. Feedback that included reviews of both positive and negative aspects of performance has been shown to generate richer mental models of performance and to actually facilitate performance improvement (Ellis & Davidi, 2005).

Management Capacity

Team management entails monitoring performance in order to ensure the effective use of both human and material capital. It means creating an environment in which "people can perform as individuals and yet cooperate toward attainment of group goals" (Koontz, 1961, p. 186). Performance measurement and assessment form the foundation of team management, driving optimal performance, as well as performance improvement interventions. In order to maximize performance, practitioners should develop a comprehensive management plan that includes:

Best Practice #12: Clearly Define What to Measure: Develop and Maintain a Systematic and Organized Representation of Performance

Job performance is clearly multidimensional (Batram, 2005; Borman, 1991). It is vital to have a clear representation of overall team performance in order to develop measures that tap all relevant performance dimensions effectively. For example, the Great Eight Competency Framework is utilized by many practitioners and researchers in developing individual-level competencies and performance measures because it provides a clear delineation of the major competency areas comprising job performance and has been validated in a large number of samples (Batram, 2005). The "great eight" include: leading and deciding, supporting and cooperating, interacting and presenting, analyzing and interpreting, creating and conceptualizing, organizing and executing, adapting and coping, and enterprising and performing. See Batram (2005) for a detailed review of all eight competencies. Supporting and cooperating includes the degree to which the individual fosters team and peer performance; therefore the framework builds accountability into the representation of individual performance. A clear representation of team performance must be developed that is organized and systematic, with a similar representation of individual performance delineating individual accountability for team performance. That is, PM for team involves evaluating the team as a whole in addition to individual team members. An organization-specific job analysis helps identify the behavioral and performance indicators of relevant teamwork knowledge, skills, and abilities (KSAs) (Stevens & Campion, 1994). In order to obtain a valid picture of performance, though, job analysis data must include both front-line employees, managers, supervisors, and other relevant stakeholders. Furthermore, different measurement approaches may be better suited for capturing different aspects of performance (Shadish, Cook, & Campbell, 2002).

Best Practice #13: Uncover the "Why" of Performance: Develop Measures That Are Diagnostic of Performance

The goal of the PM process is to optimize performance. This can only be done if we understand the "why" of performance. We must know what level of performance occurred and what contributed to this overall performance level. The ability to systematically understand the underpinnings of performance drives feedback and improvement. In order to understand performance, it is important to view it from multiple perspectives. Different sources of performance data (for example, supervisors, teammates, self-evaluation) tap different aspects of performance.

Measurement often serves multiple purposes (such as performance appraisal, training). Therefore, it is likely that multiple approaches to measurement are necessary to capture adequate performance information (Cannon-Bowers & Salas, 1997). The key to valid performance measurement is to avoid "easy" measures that miss large amounts of performance-related information. For example, it may be easy to measure the hit rate of a military fighter flight crew; however, if your purpose is to maximize performance, then diagnostic measurement is most desirable. The hit rate does not indicate the type of communication, coordination, or other interactions of the team members that contribute to whether or not the correct friend/foe decision was made. One way to incorporate diagnosticity into performance measures is to consider their level of controllability, that is, the degree to which changes in actual employee effort correspond with changes in the measure (Pritchard, Bedwell, Weaver, Fullick, & Wright, 2008). Highly controllable measures such as number of client phone calls made are directly related to the effort put forth by employees and provide indicators of what employees are actually doing with their time. Diagnostic measures capture why performance happens.

Best Practice #14: Measure Typical Team Performance Continuously

Inherently, variations in performance occur over time (Borman, 1991). By measuring performance continuously, a more comprehensive picture emerges. Technology revolutionized organizational ability to monitor performance continuously, with many companies turning toward online dashboards and other similar methodologies to maintain real-time performance monitoring (Anonymous, 2006; Broda & Culgave, 2006). This real-time picture of performance can be used to generate real-time feedback (corrective or positive). The closer that feedback occurs to when the actual behavior occurred, the greater the impact of such feedback (Pritchard & Ashwood, 2008). Additionally, continuous monitoring allows employee performance under typical performance conditions to be captured. Compared to maximal performance conditions, typical performance conditions lessen the salience that performance is being monitored and evaluated, employees are not explicitly told to do their best, and their performance is represented as a mean over an extended period of time (Sackett, Zedeck, & Fogli, 1988). Conversely, under maximal performance conditions, employees are explicitly made aware of performance monitoring and evaluation, are explicitly told to perform their best, and are only measured for a short period of time. Whereas maximal conditions are good for measuring what teams "can" do, typical conditions are necessary to understand what teams "will" do. For example, only being evaluated on performance during a monthly branch visit from the general region manager would provide a picture of maximal performance on that day, but an incomplete representation of performance overall. Measures of typical performance are desirable because they represent both an employee's ability and his or her motivation (Klehe & Anderson, 2007).

Best Practice #15: Include Teamwork Competencies in Formal Performance Evaluations

The adage is that you "get what you measure"; therefore, if you want teams to demonstrate effective teamwork behaviors (such as communication or collaboration), then measurement dimensions that reflect these competencies must be included in the performance evaluation system (Salas, Kosarzycki, & Tannenbaum, 2005). Including teamwork competencies in performance appraisal instruments underscores their importance to team success and makes the exact competencies of importance more salient to team members (Murphy & Cleveland, 1995). In practice, we tend to find that, if teamwork is formally assessed at all, it is listed as a single generic category, whereas more task-work-oriented competencies are specified in greater and more concrete detail. Teamwork is multi-faceted and can be defined in terms of specific observable behaviors. When it is, team members are more likely to consider it an important aspect of their jobs—one worth focusing their attention on. Supervisors responsible for assessing team performance will be better able to provide meaningful data regarding teamwork performance if they have clear definitions to work with and receive frame-of-reference training that illustrates positive and negative examples of various teamwork dimensions.

Technical Capacity

In the context of teams, technical capacity involves two equally important domains. First, individual team members must be competent at their individual tasks (that is, task work). Second, they must be competent at managing the interdependencies between their own work and that of their fellow team members (that is, teamwork). Teams cannot excel without both components. Frameworks of teamwork competencies have been developed (Cannon-Bowers & Salas, 1997) and revised (Salas, Rosen, Burke, & Goodwin, in press) and represent the KSAs underlying effective team performance. Additionally, much is known about how these competencies are manifested in expert teams (Salas, Priest, Wilson, & Burke, 2006).

Best Practice #16: Have a Plan for Integrating New Team Members, and Execute It

Seamless coordination of inputs from individual team members is a hallmark of expert teams. For this to occur, team members must have a shared understanding of the team's task, their own work, their team members' roles and responsibilities, and the team goals. When there is turnover in team membership, the team is at risk for losing this shared understanding. The team should have a plan for integrating new team members, for familiarizing the new members with the team, and vice versa. This involves identifying the teamwork and task work requirements necessary for performance in the team and ensuring that team members have the right mix of competencies (individual expertise as well as teamwork competencies). In order for teams to capitalize on their mix of expertise, it is critical that they share an accurate understanding of who knows what. Researchers refer to this as "transactive memory" (Wegner, 1986). Research on transactive memory (for example, Austin, 2003) suggests that this shared knowledge about one another enables teams to determine which member is most appropriate for which tasks (specialization). For instance, we found that air traffic controllers who believed their team to be highly competent but did not share knowledge about the specific distribution of expertise were nonetheless resistant to asking for or accepting backup from one another (Smith-Jentsch, Kraiger, Salas, & Cannon-Bowers, in press).

Best Practice #17: Assess and Foster Shared Mental Models

Shared mental models enable many aspects of effective team performance (Cannon-Bowers, Salas, & Converse, 1993). Therefore, a team performance management process must assess shared mental models within a team and provide feedback to team members. Although several techniques exist for capturing and analyzing shared mental models (for example, Mohammed & Dumville, 2001), cue-strategy associations (a technique that involves directly linking cues in the environment with appropriate coordination strategies) afford diagnosticity and the development of learning points (Cannon-Bowers, Tannenbaum, Salas, & Volpe, 1995). Additionally, cross-training (Blickensderfer, Cannon-Bowers, & Salas, 1998; Volpe, Cannon-Bowers, Salas, & Spector, 1995) can be used to build shared mental models within teams.

Multi-Team Membership

In addition to the six capacities defined by Letts, Ryan, and Grossman (1998), we also consider the implications of multi-team membership (MTM). The wide use of project-based teams in the workplace (for example, Devine, Clayton, Phillips, Dunford, & Melner, 1999) suggests that it is becoming a more common possibility to be a member of multiple teams that comprise the same organization. These teams, as defined by Sundstrom, McIntyre, Halfhill, and Richards (2000), carry out highly defined, specialized, time-limited projects and often disband upon project completion. These teams are highly cross-functional and differentiated. They have a high degree of specialization, independence, and autonomy and a low degree of integration with other work units. For example, an employee may serve as a team lead for an R&D team, but may also be a non-lead member of the marketing team. MTM is concerned with the capacity to split individual time and resources across multiple teams. A study of 401 MBA professionals indicated that 67 percent worked on more than one team at a time (Mortensen, Woolley, & O'Leary, 2007). The literature regarding MTM is currently sparse; however, combining what is currently suggested with well-evidenced support from the general team literature, we suggest the following.

Best Practice #18: Develop or Select for Individual Personal Discipline and Organizational Skills

In addition to the necessary expertise to complete the tasks at hand, team members working in multiple teams must also have highly developed organizational and time management skills. Autonomy is usually maximized in these situations (Ancona & Caldwell, 2007); therefore it is imperative to select individuals with high levels of personal discipline and organizational skills or to help selected individuals develop these skills through training.

Best Practice #19: Communicate the "Big Picture": Facilitate a Global Awareness of Competing Goals and Deadlines of All Teams

In MTM environments, it is vital to plan for global ripple effects—deadlines or slippage on projects for one team can impact work on other teams. Inter-team coordination and planning can help to mitigate this problem, although a contingency plan must be in place such that certain members can pick up slack when others must dedicate a significant amount of their resources to another team for a brief period of time. Global awareness is key. Team leadership can play a key role in this aspect. Meetings of team leaders can help to foster global awareness of deadlines and planning.

Best Practice #20: Maturity Counts: Recognize That a Multi-Team Framework Works Best for Mature Projects

MTM frameworks tend to work best for more mature projects. Those in their early stages may need several people dedicated full time in the initial stages. Also apply MTM frameworks to "modular" projects in which work can be done by separate individuals in assigned pieces and then recombined. Furthermore, this individual progress must include regular meetings to keep everyone aligned (Mortensen, Woolley, & O'Leary, 2007). Expectations and deadlines must be crystal clear, yet malleable.

Best Practice #21: Foster Trust: Cultivate a Culture of Information Sharing

Because MTM work occurs asynchronously, members must be able to trust that it is being done. The juggling of multiple projects does not offer team members the opportunity to pick up the slack of other members who don't pull their weight. Mutual trust is a supporting and coordination mechanism necessary for effective teamwork, as noted earlier (Salas, Sims, & Burke, 2005). It is a shared belief that team members will perform their roles, while protecting the interests of the team, cultivated through information sharing, and a willingness to admit errors and receive feedback (Bandow, 2001; Webber, 2002). This capability becomes even more vital when employees are members of multiple teams and face-to-face communication and coordination is reduced.

Conclusions

From front-line action and performance teams focused on behavioral coordination to top-level project development and planning teams responsible for building the knowledge of the organization, teams are an integral component of how organizations do work. An individual's performance can be considered in isolation from others with decreasing frequency, and this trend shows no signs of relenting or reversing. This necessitates the consideration of teamwork in performance management systems. Team-based work adds a layer of complexity to the performance management process; however, it can be effectively executed with strategic, salient cultivation of the adaptive, leadership, management, and technical capacities of the team. In this chapter we have presented a synthesis of the literature in the form of a practical set of best practices for implementing the PM process in team-based work. Furthermore, we have attempted to provide practical guidance for managing performance in environments of multi-team membership. As multi-team membership grows in prevalence, understanding effective processes for managing both individual and team-level performance becomes vital. Overall, understanding the levers that drive performance and the role of performance measurement will help ensure that your performance management processes are helping to cultivate expert teams.

References

Ancona, D. (1990). Outward bound: Strategies for team survival in organizations. *The Academy of Management Journal, 33*(2), 334–365.

Ancona, D., & Bresman, H. (2007, September). Thinking outside the team. *HR Magazine,* 133–136.

Ancona, D. G., & Caldwell, D. (2007). Improving the performance of new product teams: How a team manages its boundaries can affect its performance and, in turn, the duration of the product development cycle. *Research-Technology Management, 50*(5), 37–43.

Anonymous (2006). Winners: Best practices awards 2006. *Business Intelligence Journal, 11*(4), 58–63.

Armstrong, M. (2000). *Performance management: Key strategies and practical guidelines.* Denver, NH: Kogan Page.

Austin, J. R. (2003). Transactive memory in organizational groups: The effects of content, consensus, specialization, and accuracy on group performance. *Journal of Applied Psychology, 88*(5), 866–878.

Baker, D. P., Gustafson, S., Beaubien, J. M., Salas, E., & Barach, P. (2005). Medical team training programs in health care. *Advances in Patient Safety: From Research to Implementation* (Vol. 4, pp. 253–267). Rockville, MD: Agency for Healthcare Research and Quality.

Baker, D. P., Salas, E., King, H., Battles, J., & Barach, P. (2005). The role of teamwork in professional education of physicians: Current status and assessment recommendations. *Journal on Quality and Patient Safety, 31*(4), 185–202.

Bandow, D. (2001). Time to create sound teamwork. *The Journal for Quality and Participation, 24,* 41–47.

Batram, D. (2005). The great eight competencies: A criterion-centric approach to validation. *Journal of Applied Psychology, 90*(6), 1185–1203.

Blickensderfer, E., Cannon-Bowers, J. A., & Salas, E. (1998). Cross-training and team performance. In J. A. Cannon-Bowers & E. Salas

(Eds.), *Making decisions under stress: Implications for individual and team training* (pp. 299–311). Washington, DC: APA.

Borman, W. C. (1991). Job behavior, performance, and effectiveness. In M. D. Dunnette & L. M. Hough (Eds.), *Handbook of industrial and organizational psychology* (2nd ed., Vol. 2). Palo Alto, CA: Consulting Psychologists Press.

Briner, W., Hastings, C., & Geddes, M. (1996). *Project leadership.* Hampshire, UK: Gower.

Broda, T., & Culgage, K. (2006, July/August). Improving business operations with real-time information: How to successfully implement a BAM solution. *Business Integration Journal,* Retrieved January 14, 2008, from: http://www.bijonline.com/index.cfm?section=article&aid=353#.

Bunderson, J. S., & Sutcliffe, K. M. (2003). Management team learning orientation and business unit performance. *Journal of Applied Psychology, 88*(3), 552–560.

Burke, C. S., Fiore, S. M., & Salas, E. (2003). The role of shared cognition in enabling shared leadership and team adaptability. In J. Conger & C. Pearce (Eds.), *Shared leadership: Reframing the hows and whys of leadership* (pp. 103–122). London: Sage.

Burke, C. S., Stagl, K. C., Klein, C., Goodwin, G. F., Salas, E., & Halpin, S. M. (2006). What type of leadership behaviors are functional in teams? A meta-analysis. *The Leadership Quarterly, 17,* 288–307.

Cannon-Bowers, J. A., & Salas, E. (1997). Teamwork competencies: The interaction of team member knowledge, skills, and attitudes. In H. F. O'Neil, Jr. (Ed.), *Workforce readiness: Competencies and assessment* (pp. 151–174). Mahwah, NJ: Lawrence Erlbaum Associates.

Cannon-Bowers, J. A., Salas, E., & Converse, S. (1993). Shared mental models in expert team decision making. In N. J. J. Castellan (Ed.), *Individual and group decision making* (pp. 221–246). Mahwah, NJ: Lawrence Erlbaum Associates.

Cannon-Bowers, J. A., Tannenbaum, S. I., Salas, E., & Volpe, C. E. (1995). Defining team competencies and establishing team training requirements. In R. Guzzo, E. Salas, & Associates (Eds.), *Team effectiveness and decision making in organizations* (pp. 333–380). San Francisco: Jossey-Bass.

Christenson, D., & Walker, D. H. T. (2004). Understanding the role of "vision" in project success. *Project Management Journal, 35*(3), 39–52.

Cooke, N. J., Cannon-Bowers, J. A., Kiekel, P. A., Rivera, K., Stout, R. J., & Salas, E. (2007). Improving teams' interpositional knowledge through cross training. *Human Factors and Ergonomics Society Annual Meeting Proceedings, 2,* 390–393.

Devine, D. J., Clayton, L. D., Phillips, J. L., Dunford, B. B., & Melner, S. B. (1999). Teams in organizations: Prevalence, characteristics, and effectiveness. *Small Group Research, 30,* 678–711.

Dransfield, R. (Ed.). (2000). *Human resource management.* Oxford, UK: Heinemann.

Dyer, J. L. (1984). Team research and team training: A state-of-the-art review. In F. A. Muckler (Ed.), *Human factors review* (pp. 285–323). Santa Monica, CA: Human Factors Society.

Eby, L. T., & Dobbins, G. H. (1997). Collectivistic orientation in teams: An individual and group-level analysis. *Journal of Organizational Behavior, 18,* 275–295.

Edmondson, A. C. (1999). Psychological safety and learning behavior in work teams. *Administrative Science Quarterly, 44,* 350–383.

Ellis, S., & Davidi, I. (2005). After-event reviews: Drawing lessons from successful and failed experiences. *Journal of Applied Psychology, 90*(5), 857–871.

Feldman, D. C. (1989). Careers in organizations: Recent trends and future directions. *Journal of Management, 15,* 135–156.

Getz, G. E., & Rainey, D. W. (2001). Flexible short term goals and basketball shooting performance. *Journal of Sports Behavior, 24,* 31–41.

Goldstein, I. L., & Gilliam, P. (1990). Training system issues in the year 2000. *American Psychologist, 45*(2), 134–143.

Hollenbeck, J. R., Ilgen, D. R., Sego, D. J., Hudlund, J., Major, D. A., & Phillips, J. (1995). Multilevel theory of team decision making: Decision performance in teams incorporating distributed expertise. *Journal of Applied Psychology, 80,* 292–316.

Ilgen, D. R. (1994). Jobs and roles: Accepting and coping with the changing structure of organizations. In M. G. Rumsey & C. B. Walker (Eds.), *Personnel selection and classification* (pp. 13–32). Mahwah, NJ: Lawrence Erlbaum Associates.

Klehe, U., & Anderson, N. (2007). Working hard and working smart: Motivation and ability during typical and maximal performance. *Journal of Applied Psychology, 92*(1), 978–992.

Koontz, H. (1961). The management theory jungle. *The Journal of the Academy of Management, 4*(3), 174–188.

Kozlowski, S. W. J., & Bell, B. S. (2003). Work groups and teams in organizations. In W. C. Borman, D. R. Ilgen, & R. J. Klimoski (Eds.), *Handbook of psychology: Industrial and organizational psychology* (Vol. 12, pp. 333–375). Hoboken, NJ: John Wiley & Sons.

Kozlowski, S. W. J., Gully, S. M., McHugh, P. P., Salas, E., & Cannon-Bowers, J. A. (1996). A dynamic theory of leadership and team effectiveness: Developmental and task contingent leader roles. *Research in Personnel and Human Resource Management, 14*, 253–285.

Kurtz, R., & Bartram, D. (2002). Competency and individual performance: Modeling the world of work. In I. T. Robertson, M. Callinan, & D. Bartram (Eds.), *Organizational effectiveness: The role of psychology* (pp. 227–255). Chichester, UK: John Wiley & Sons.

Letts, C. W., Ryan, W. P., & Grossman, A. (1998). *High performance nonprofit organizations: Managing upstream for greater impact.* San Francisco: Jossey-Bass.

Levine, J. M., & Choi, H. (2004). Impact of personnel turnover on team performance and cognition. In E. Salas & S. M. Fiore (Eds.), *Team cognition: Understanding the factors that drive process and performance* (pp. 153–176). Washington, DC: American Psychological Association.

Locke, E. A., & Bryan, J. F. (1967). Performance goals as determinants of levels of performance and boredom. *Journal of Applied Psychology, 51*, 120–130.

Lorentez, S. J., Salas, E., & Tannenbaum, S. I. (2005). Benefiting from mistakes: The impact of guided errors on learning, performance, and self-efficacy. *Human Resource Development Quarterly, 16*(3), 301–322.

Mohammed, S., & Dumville, B. C. (2001). Team mental models in a team knowledge framework: Expanding theory and measure across disciplinary boundaries. *Journal of Organizational Behavior, 22*(2), 89–103.

Mortensen, M., Woolley, A. W., & O'Leary, M. B. (2007). Conditions enabling effective multiple team membership: Virtuality and virtualization. *Proceedings of the International Federation of Information Processing Working Groups 8.2 on Information Systems and Organizations and 9.5 on Virtuality and Society,* July 29–31, Portland, Oregon.

Murphy, K. R., & Cleveland, J. N. (1995). *Understanding performance appraisal: Social, organizational, and goal-based perspectives.* Thousand Oaks, CA: Sage.

Orasanu, J. (1990, October). *Shared mental models and crew performance* (Tech. Report 46). Princeton, NJ: Princeton University, Cognitive Sciences Laboratories.

Oser, R., McCallum, G. A., Salas, E., & Morgan, B. B., Jr. (1989). *Toward a definition of teamwork: An analysis of critical team behaviors* (Tech. Rep. No. 89604). Orlando, FL: Naval Training Systems Center.

Pfeffer, J. (1972). Merger as a response to organizational interdependence. *Administrative Science Quarterly, 17*(3), 382–394.

Pfeffer, J., & Salanick, G. R. (1978). *The external control of organizations.* New York: Harper & Row.

Porter, C. O., Hollenbeck, J. R., Ilgen, D. R., Ellis, A. P., West, B. J., & Moon, H. (2003). Backing up behaviors in teams: The role of personality and legitimacy of need. *Journal of Applied Psychology, 88*(3), 391–403.

Pritchard, R. D., & Ashwood, E. L. (2008). *Manager's guide to diagnosing and improving motivation.* New York: Psychology Press.

Pritchard, R. D., Bedwell, W. L., Weaver, S. J., Fullick, J. M., & Wright, N. (2008). Maximizing controllability in performance measures. Unpublished manuscript, University of Central Florida, Orlando.

Sackett, P. R., Zedeck, S., & Fogli, L. (1988). Relations between measures of typical and maximum job performance. *Journal of Applied Psychology, 73,* 482–486.

Salas, E., Burke, C. S., & Stagl, K. C. (2004). Developing teams and team leaders: Strategies and principles. In D. Day, S. J. Zaccaro, & S. M. Halpin (Eds.), *Leader development for transforming organizations: Growing leaders for tomorrow* (pp. 325–355). Mahwah, NJ: Lawrence Erlbaum Associates.

Salas, E., Cannon-Bowers, J. A., Fiore, S. M., & Stout, R. J. (2001). Cue-recognition training to enhance team situation awareness. In M. McNeese, E. Salas, & M. Endsley (Eds.), *New trends in collaborative activities: Understanding system dynamics in complex environments* (pp. 169–190). Santa Monica, CA: Human Factors and Ergonomics Society.

Salas, E., Dickinson, T. L., Converse, S. A., & Tannenbaum, S. I. (1992). Toward an understanding of team performance and training. In R. J. Swezey & E. Salas (Eds.), *Teams: Their training and performance* (pp. 3–29). Norwood, NJ: Ablex.

Salas, E., Kosarzycki, M. P., & Tannenbaum, S. I. (2005). Aligning work teams and HR practices. In R. J. Burke and C. L. Cooper (Eds.), *Reinventing HRM: Challenges and new directions* (pp. 133–149). New York: Routledge.

Salas, E., Priest, H. A., Wilson, K. A., & Burke, C. S. (2006). Scenario-based training: Improving military mission performance and adaptability. In A. B. Adler, C. A. Castro, & T. W. Britt (Eds.), *Military life: The psychology of serving in peace and combat* (Vol. 2: Operational Stress, pp. 32–53). Westport, CT: Praeger Security International.

Salas, E., Rosen, M. A., Burke, C. S., & Goodwin, G. F. (2008). The wisdom of collectives in organizations: An update of the teamwork competencies. In E. Salas, G. F. Goodwin, & C. S. Burke (Eds.), *Team effectiveness in complex organizations: Cross-disciplinary perspectives and approaches.* Mahwah, NJ: Lawrence Erlbaum Associates.

Salas, E., Rosen, M. A., Weaver, S. J., Held, J. D., & Weissmuller, J. J. (under review). Practical guidelines for performance measurement in simulation-based training. *Ergonomics in Design.*

Salas, E., Sims, D. E., & Burke, C. S. (2005). Is there a big five in teamwork? *Small Group Research, 36*(5), 555–599.

Shadish, W., Cook, T., Campbell, D. (2002). *Experimental & quasi-experimental designs for generalized causal inference.* Boston: Houghton Mifflin.

Shepperd, J. A., & McNulty, J. K. (2002). The affective consequences of unexpected outcomes. *Psychological Science, 13*, 85–88.

Shin, S. J., & Zhou, J. (2007). When is educational specialization heterogeneity related to creativity in research and development teams? Transformational leadership as a moderator. *Journal of Applied Psychology, 92*(6), 1709–1721.

Sitkin, S. B. (1992). Learning through failure: The strategy of small losses. In B. M. Staw & L. L. Cummings (Eds.), *Research in organizational behavior* (Vol. 14). Greenwich, CT: JAI Press.

Smith-Jentsch, K. A., Kraiger, K., Salas, E., & Cannon-Bowers, J. A. (in press). Can familiarity breed backup? Interactive effects of perceived team efficacy and shared teammate knowledge. *Human Factors.*

Smith-Jentsch, K. A., Zeisig, R. L., Acton, B., & McPherson, J. A. (1998). Team dimensional training: A strategy for guided team self-correction. In J. A. Cannon-Bowers & E. Salas (Eds.), *Making decisions under stress: Implications for individual and team training* (pp. 271–297). Washington, DC: American Psychological Association.

Stevens, M. J., & Campion, M. A. (1994). The knowledge, skill, and ability requirements for teamwork: Implications for human resource management. *Journal of Management, 20*(2), 503–530.

Sundstrom, E., McIntyre, M., Halfhill, T., & Richards, H. (2000). Work groups: From the Hawthorne studies to work teams of the 1990s and beyond. *Group Dynamics: Theory, Research, and Practice, 4*(1), 44–67.

Swezey, R. W., Meltzer, A. L., & Salas, E. (1994). Some issues involved in motivating teams. In H. F. O'Neil, Jr., & M. Drillings (Eds.), *Motivation: Theory and research* (pp. 141–169). Mahwah, NJ: Lawrence Erlbaum Associates.

Swezey, R. J., & Salas, E. (1992). Guidelines for use in team-training development. In R. J. Swezey & E. Salas (Eds.), *Teams: Their training and performance.* Norwood, NJ: Ablex.

U.S. Office of Personnel Management. (n.d.). *Managing team performance FAQs.* Retrieved 12 March 2008 from: https://www.opm.gov/perform/faqs/team.asp#Q1.

Volpe, C. E., Cannon-Bowers, J. A., Salas, E., & Spector, P. (1995). The impact of cross-training on team functioning. *Human Factors, 38*, 87–100.

Wageman, R. (2001). How leaders foster self-managing team effectiveness: Design choices versus hands-on coaching. *Organization Science, 12,* 559–577.

Webber, S. S. (2002). Leadership and trust facilitating cross-functional team success. *Journal of Management Development, 21,* 201–214.

Wegner, D. M. (1986). Transactive memory: A contemporary analysis of the group mind. In B. Mullen & G. R. Goethals (Eds.), *Theories of group behavior* (pp. 185–205). New York: Springer-Verlag.

Williams, G., & Laugani, P. (1999). Analysis of teamwork in an NHS community trust: An empirical study. *Journal of Interprofessional Care, 13*(1), 19–28.

Wilson, K. A., Burke, C. S., Priest, H. A., & Salas, E. (2005). Promoting health care safety through training high reliability teams. *Quality and Safety in Health Care, 14,* 303–309.

Zakay, D., Ellis, S., & Shevalsky, M. (2004). Outcome value and early warning indications as determinants of willingness to learn from experience. *Experimental Psychology, 51*(2), 150–157.

Zalesny, M. D., Salas, E., & Prince, C. (1995). Conceptual and measurement issues in coordination: Implications for team behavior and performance. In G. R. Ferris (Ed.), *Research in personnel and human resources management* (Vol. 13, pp. 81–115). Greenwich, CT: JAI Press.

CHAPTER 7

CEO PERFORMANCE MANAGEMENT*

Edward M. Mone

Introduction

Overview

This chapter will focus on the process of CEO performance management, which includes goal setting, feedback, and appraisal, as well as tying the outcome of the performance management process to CEO compensation. Much has happened in the general business landscape that has affected CEO performance management and compensation since the Graddick and Lane (1998) chapter appeared. These events will be discussed below, but at the heart of it all, corporate greed and scandal have led to numerous legislative reforms targeted at significant improvement in corporate governance. As a result, today's boards of directors are being held to new standards of performance, particularly in one of their primary roles: CEO performance management. In fact, the focus on board effectiveness in the practice of organization consulting is fairly recent and driven largely by these same events, as noted by Nadler, Behan, & Nadler (2006), and as evidenced by a

---

*Note: Special thanks to Lisa Bernardi and Carolyn Stine, organization development analysts at CA, Inc., for their research support.

234 PERFORMANCE MANAGEMENT

complement of recent books (Brown, 2006; Carver, 2006; Charan, 2005; Nadler, Behan, & Nadler, 2006) aimed at improving board functioning and effectiveness.

Since the process of CEO performance evaluation or management is still somewhat private and inaccessible to most academics and practitioners, this chapter includes a detailed focus on this process at FORTX, a pseudonym for a Fortune 1000 company. As the FORTX CEO performance management process is discussed, it will be examined and compared to what may be considered best practices that are driven by research, legislation, and regulation.

Overall, this chapter includes a brief review of Graddick and Lane (1998); a look at the key events and reforms that have shaped CEO performance management, compensation, and corporate governance since the late 1990s; a detailed discussion of FORTX's CEO performance management process and its tie to CEO compensation; a review of literature particularly relevant to CEO performance management, compensation, and board effectiveness; and a closing summary and final words, with recommendations for further action and research.

Where We Have Been

In their chapter on evaluating executive performance, not just CEO performance, some of what Graddick and Lane (1998) highlighted included the need to satisfy constituencies—customers, shareholders, and employees—and to establish goals for these constituencies, and to do so before determining measures of executive performance. They also stated that this linkage to executive performance planning is not as strong as desired. In addition, they discussed the importance of executive competencies and how behavioral and leadership competency objectives were becoming more frequently used as supplements to key measurement systems when establishing executive performance goals. The weighting of these goals and competencies, however, as measures of performance varied and were not always clearly defined. There was also significant variation in how goals and measures influenced compensation decisions.

Graddick and Lane (1998) concluded with the following messages:

- Evaluating executive performance is somewhat mysterious, given the lack of published literature, with approaches being best described as informal and inconsistent;
- Executives want and need clear goals and objectives, ongoing candid feedback, and a system that tightly links pay and performance;
- Appropriate non-financial measures, such as employee satisfaction, particularly in leading to customer satisfaction and business results, as well as executive competencies that are linked to driving business outcomes, should be used to improve the evaluation process;
- The stability of the executive appraisal process is influenced by practices and processes brought from one company to another by the CEO (for example, 360-degree feedback), the dynamic nature of the marketplace, and frequent organization changes;
- Executives need to remain in an assignment long enough to evaluate their impact;
- HR needs to sell the value of performance management to executives, as well as highlight the cost of neglecting effective performance evaluations, as executives often do not have a formal process, and that HR should keep the process simple to minimize paperwork and time; and
- "There is still important work to be done to strengthen our approaches for evaluating executive performance." (p. 400)

Their advice is still relevant, and there is still some mystery to the process. However, the overall landscape has significantly changed since the late 1990s, and those changes have had enormous influence on CEO evaluation, compensation, and corporate governance, increasing the transparency of the CEO performance management process to a greater extent. A serious process for assessing CEO performance is no longer an option; it clearly is a "must have" (Oliver Wyman, 2003). Today formal CEO appraisals are a requirement for publicly traded U.S. companies, although the mandate focuses exclusively on evaluating past performance to determine compensation (Nadler, Behan, & Nadler, 2006). However, boards seem to be improving at the task of CEO evaluation, according to a recent survey (Mercer Delta Consulting, 2005) of directors of Fortune 1000 companies: 80 percent of respondents rated their CEO evaluation process as effective or very effective.

Key Events and Reforms

Bainbridge (2007) and Schminke, Arnaud, and Kuenzi (2007) offer a history of events since the 1990s that have shaped the business landscape, executive compensation, and CEO evaluation, and these include:

- The 1994 change to tax laws, attempting to control excesses in compensation, limited the expense deduction for executive compensation to $1 million, but exempted incentive-based compensation (such as stock options) from this cap.
- The stock market bubble of the late 1990s further emphasized the focus on stock options, as rising stock prices made options look quite attractive, but this was followed by the less jubilant years of 2000 to 2002.
- The lack of strong governance by corporate management and boards of directors that led, by and large in this environment, to accounting scandals—caused by the desire to meet financial targets ("make the numbers") and to bring value to stock options—at Enron, WorldCom, Tyco, and Global Crossings, which surfaced during the period of October 2001 to early 2002.
- The passage of the Public Company Accounting Reform and Investor Protection Act of 2002, known as the Sarbanes-Oxley Act (SOX), aimed at improving internal controls, requiring the certification of financial statements by the CEO and CFO, ensuring independent auditors and board audit committees composed of only independent directors, establishing rules to increase the transparency of financial reporting as well as providing protection for whistle blowers and more severe penalties for corporate misconduct.
- The implementation of more stringent listing requirements by the NYSE and NASDAQ, including shareholder approval of all equity-based compensation plans.

Furthermore, legislation was recently passed that now requires disclosure of all aspects of CEO compensation, including severance agreements, pensions, bonuses, perks, and the calculations for short- and long-term compensation.

Clearly, the major goal or thrust of the above legislative and regulatory changes is to improve corporate governance, and these changes can be considered a broad and continuing response to a number of accounting scandals that had as their primary cause the incentive to be dishonest to add value to stock options. Problems in corporate governance can now significantly affect CEOs, as Title III of SOX provides for severe penalties if a corporation is obliged to restate its financials due to misconduct, including a return by the CEO and CFO of any bonus, incentive, or equity-based compensation, as well as any profits received from the sale of stock, during the twelve-month period following the original issuance of the financials.

FORTX's CEO Performance Management Process

FORTX Context

Before presenting FORTX's current CEO performance management process, it is important to note that, like many other companies over the past several years, FORTX has had its share of challenges and publicity, involving shareholder concerns, board member changes, and turnover in senior leadership. FORTX's current CEO faces the challenges of building a more ethical workforce and changing the company's culture to one of empowerment, with greater accountability and reward for performance.

Factors Shaping FORTX's CEO Performance Management Process

FORTX's process has been shaped by a number of factors, including: FORTX's history; Sarbanes-Oxley, and other legislation and rules (such as IRS regulation 162m, which provides guidance for the tax treatment of long-term compensation and the type of performance measures that can be used in the calculation of compensation); and best practices, brought forward by board members with expertise in corporate governance, a leading consulting firm with expertise in executive compensation and appraisal that serves as an advisor to FORTX, and FORTX's chief human resources officer.

Given the above factors, a major goal was to establish the FORTX CEO performance management process, which includes the awarding of compensation, as a transparent process free from any ostensible manipulation relative to evaluating and reporting organizational performance, as well as to awarding executive and CEO compensation.

By the close of FORTX's most recent fiscal year, the CEO would have had several years of experience in the role, including, of course, working through the CEO evaluation process with FORTX's board.

Goal Setting

The goal-setting phase of the performance management process is initiated by the CEO with FORTX's overall business plan serving as the context. Since the beginning of the CEO's tenure, the CEO has written a narrative, documenting the progress to be made against each of FORTX's main goals or objectives. Today these objectives still remain the focus, but there is a greater emphasis on identifying specific financial targets and other quantitative measures. This emphasis is now possible because the CEO and the senior leadership team (the team of FORTX's most senior functional leaders), over the past few years, developed a clearer understanding of how FORTX operates and of the most critical and important measures of success and indicators of business growth.

As a result, at the beginning of FORTX's most recent fiscal year (the year that will be highlighted here to illustrate the process at FORTX), the CEO introduced the FORTX "Company Scorecard." Not unlike other scorecard methodologies (for example, Kaplan & Norton, 1996), measures and metrics were created in four major areas, including: corporate and financial; products and services; customers; and employees. Samples of these measures are presented in Exhibit 7.1.

Exhibit 7.1 FORTX's Organization Scorecard Categories and Sample Measures.

- Corporate financial: revenue, earnings per share, cash flow from operations, and operating margin; and costs as a percent of revenue, including selling and general and administrative costs
- Products and services: product penetration and contract renewals
- Customers: customer perception and customer satisfaction
- Employees: employee engagement and employee satisfaction

Although these measures and metrics will be detailed in the CEO's narrative, those upon which the CEO is evaluated *and* compensated include operating income, cash flow from operations, revenue growth, earnings per share, and customer satisfaction. The rationale for the selection of these measures will be discussed later. The narrative, as well, may include the personal actions the CEO intends to take; however, the CEO does include a behavioral self-assessment as part of the year-end evaluation (see *CEO Appraisal,* below).

Once the narrative is complete, the CEO will initially verify targets (such as a *cash flow from operations* target in the billions of dollars, within a range, for example, of plus or minus $45 million) with the CFO and then work together with the board compensation committee to finalize them, with the next step in the process being a full board review and, ultimately, approval. This would conclude the goal-setting phase.

Feedback

Contrary to what might be expected, the regularly scheduled meetings of the board of directors are not the usual forum for providing performance feedback to the CEO at FORTX. Typically, board meetings focus on general updates and changes to strategy, leadership, mergers and acquisition activity, and the ongoing performance of FORTX. However, at the conclusion of each board meeting, the board meets without the CEO; this type of meeting is referred to as an *executive session*. During each executive session, CEO performance is discussed. Following these sessions, and on a rotating basis, a director will provide specific feedback to the CEO, on a one-to-one basis.

Providing performance feedback is also accomplished more informally, and may, for example, come from an individual board member regarding company strategy, or from a board committee, such as the audit committee, on operational issues. The primary vehicle for this more informal and regular feedback, however, can be characterized as the constant communication flow, with a regular focus on CEO performance, between the board chairman and the CEO. This feedback focuses on what the chairman or board has observed or may be driven on an exception basis. For example, to further improve CEO and senior leadership team effectiveness, the chairman recommended engaging an external consultant to administer 360-degree feedback and a variety of personality and leadership style assessments to all of the senior leadership team members, including the CEO, and subsequently to conduct a series of two-day team-building sessions. It would be fair to say that the chairman acts like a supervisor in this respect, providing feedback and counsel to the CEO. In fact, an emphasis on development for a relatively new CEO is an important focus for a board of directors and should be part of the overall evaluation process (Nadler, Behan, & Nadler, 2006).

CEO Appraisal

CEO appraisal at FORTX is an annual process, and the first major step in the evaluation of performance is taken by the CEO. The CEO writes a self-appraisal in narrative form—actually a letter to the board—which is predominantly a discussion of company performance, referencing the extent to which targets for the measures detailed in the goal-setting narrative and outlined in the company scorecard have been met, measures situated within the context of FORTX's major objectives. As a result, the appraisal of the CEO largely reflects an appraisal of FORTX's performance. The progress against each one of the major objectives is also rated on a four-point scale (ineffective, somewhat effective,

effective, and very effective). This part of the narrative (edited for publication) might read as follows:

> *Objective 2: Building an ethically-driven culture of empowerment and accountability—Effective.* "Given past leadership and FORTX's history, we are making significant progress in creating an ethically driven culture in which empowerment, strong performance and accountability are rewarded. We have implemented a number of programs, including company-wide ethics and compliance training and leadership training for middle- and senior-level managers. . . . Although we continue to make progress, we are still, in essence, rebuilding FORTX's culture. . . . "

The CEO's self-appraisal or letter is initially sent to the corporate governance and compensation committees for their joint review, evaluation, and recommendation to the full board. Accompanying this letter is the CEO's self-assessment using the behavioral component of "The CEO Evaluation," which is available from Boardroom Metrics (2005) and is shown, in brief, in Exhibit 7.2. The full board then evaluates the CEO's performance. Of course, during this executive session, the CEO is absent. At the conclusion of the session, the chairman provides feedback to the CEO.

Compensation

When reviewing the CEO's self-appraisal, the compensation committee will also consider the extent to which results were achieved and how that determines the level of compensation awarded, metrics for which were set during goal setting. The CEO's targeted total compensation includes a 20 percent base pay component and an 80 percent variable component, with the latter determined by the extent to which the metrics were achieved. The variable pay component, however, can range from 0 to 200 percent of target, depending on company performance.

The CEO's variable compensation has both short-term and long-term components. The short-term component, a cash bonus, is awarded on an annual basis, ranging from 0 to 200 percent of target. This component is based on measures that make the most sense in the short run, including operating income, revenue growth, and

Exhibit 7.2 The CEO Evaluation.*

- Leadership: The CEO . . .
  - Has clearly defined the basic purpose and mission of the organization
  - Communicates effectively with internal and external stakeholders to build support for the mission, vision, goals, and direction of the organization
- Management: The CEO . . .
  - Delegates effectively to members of the senior management team and other staff
  - Clearly articulates priorities and ensures management focus and accountability around addressing priorities
- Working with the board: The CEO . . .
  - Has a strong working relationship with the board chair
  - Helps educate the board on the organization
- Financial management: The CEO . . .
  - Has a solid, up-to-date understanding of the organization's income statement, balance sheet, cash flow, and other financial measures relevant to its business and financial situation
  - Ensures that the organization's financial records are accurate and up-to-date

---

*Note: This is only a partial list of the factors in each category. At FORTX, each is rated on a four-point scale.

Source: Adapted from Boardroom Metrics, 2007.

---

customer satisfaction. The long-term component, also with a target range of 0 to 200 percent, is a restricted stock award that vests immediately after a three-year period, and it has two components. The first component of long-term compensation, accounting for 60 percent of the overall award, is based on annual targets for operating income and revenue growth. The second component is based on three-year targets for cash flow from operations and earnings per share. This second component accounts for the remaining 40 percent of long-term compensation. Overall, the long-term component is structured to promote both executive retention and a focus on long-term company performance; the final determination of value and, of course, payout, are both made at the end of a three-year period.

It is important to re-emphasize that the CEO's cash bonus and restricted stock award are quantitatively driven—compensation levels are determined in advance, based on measures and targets set during the goal-setting phase. The compensation committee only has negative discretion: the committee cannot authorize any compensation greater than the payouts indicated by the targets achieved, but it does have the power to reduce those payouts based on CEO performance or other factors directly influencing the success of FORTX.

Finally, the primary rationale for the measures chosen that have an effect on compensation is simply that these are the critical measures for FORTX's success, and they are utilized in compensation in such a way as to reward and drive behavior that focuses on long-term success, with each year building toward success in subsequent years—or over the long run.

The FORTX Process and the State of Practice

Compensation Committee

We begin this section with a discussion of the compensation committee, given its role in setting, approving, and evaluating goals and the attainment of the CEO's metrics and targets and in recommending the level of compensation to be paid for the extent to which those performance metrics and targets were achieved.

Certainly FORTX is in compliance with the New York Stock Exchange (NYSE) Listed Company Manual section 303A.05 (2004), which requires all listed companies to have a compensation committee, and that the committee must consist solely of independent directors. In general, the role of a compensation committee (Bainbridge, 2007) is to review and approve, or recommend to the full board, compensation for the CEO, as well as to have oversight for the corporation's compensation policies and practices. This role is articulated in corporate governance guidelines (readily found, for example, on corporate websites, including those for companies such as Consolidated Edison, McDonald's Corporation, Kraft Foods Inc., Southwestern Energy Company, State Street Corporation, and The Charles Schwab Corporation). The stated purpose of FORTX's compensation committee is as follows:

> The Committee's general purpose is to enable the Board to fulfill its responsibilities with respect to executive compensation, including: (a) reviewing and approving all goals and objectives impacting CEO compensation; analyzing and evaluating CEO performance with respect to those goal and objectives; and (b) based on this evaluation, determining and approving the CEO's compensation, as well as incentive and equity-based compensation for other senior-level executives.

Furthermore, the NYSE also requires the committee to have a written charter declaring its power to set CEO performance goals and evaluate performance, and to establish the CEO compensation plan. The committee should also have the power to hire an external consultant for advice. The Securities and Exchange Commission (SEC), besides requiring extensive disclosure of compensation in the company's annual proxy statement, instituted a new requirement in July of 2006, called the Compensation and Discussion Analysis (CD&A), necessitating a discussion and analysis of all aspects of the company's stock option plan (Bainbridge, 2007). FORTX is in compliance with these NYSE and SEC requirements.

Compensation for CEOs

For at least the last ten to fifteen years, CEO pay has been the subject of much press, mostly critical, focusing on whether CEOs are worth the compensation they receive (Epstein & Roy, 2005; O'Reilly & Main, 2007; Silva & Tosi, 2004). Today compensation committees are under more intense public scrutiny as some excessive severance packages have made the headlines of tabloids and business publications alike—Michael Ovitz receiving $140 million and Richard Grasso, $187.5 million (Brountas, 2004; Charan, 2005).

The principal-agent model (Laffront & Mortimer, 2002) underlies the theory and practice of executive compensation (Conyon,

2006; O'Reilly & Main, 2007). This model involves shareholders (the principals) creating the most economical compensation plan possible that will motivate CEO (agent) performance to maximize firm value. Usually the board of directors (and more specifically, the compensation committee) acts on behalf of the shareholders (or principals) to maximize firm value, but excesses in CEO pay and scandals have still found their way into the public's eye, including those occurring at Walt Disney Company, Adelphia Communications Corporation, and Tyco International (O'Reilly & Main, 2007). Conyon (2006) reports that the main driver of CEO pay gains in recent years (1993–2003) has been grants for stock options; and he also discusses that there is a positive correlation between companies that have been the target of fraud allegations and option incentives. Quite recently, what has come to light is the number of firms that have engaged in options "back dating" (instead of using the closing price on the date the grant is made as the option strike price, going back in time and picking a date when the stock closed at a lower price) and "spring loading" (issuing a grant just before news is announced that is guaranteed to drive up the share price). Finally, a major influence on the CEO's cash compensation, according to O'Reilly and Main (2007), may be the degree of reciprocity and social influence that exists between the board and the CEO, with higher levels of reciprocity and social influence leading to higher levels of cash compensation.

Long-term compensation, when based on more than just financial metrics and driven by a broader view (that is, a corporate social responsibility view) of satisfying stakeholders (customers, employees, local communities, government, and others), can have a positive effect on corporate financial performance (Deckop, Merriman, & Gupta, 2006). In this study, six dimensions of corporate social responsibility (CSR) were measured, which included "taking positive action in the areas of community relations, human rights, the safety of the firm's product or service, the environment, diversity in fairness and hiring, and other aspects of employee relations" (p. 333). So, for example, a possible measure in the area of diversity and fair hiring might be to increase the number of diverse hires at the senior management levels, with the metric being a year-over-year increase. In terms of the effect of corporate social performance (CSP) on compensation, what Deckop, Merriman, and Gupta (2006) found is that CSP is positively correlated with a long-term compensation focus, it is seen as a contributor to corporate financial performance, and, although some firms have direct CEO incentives to improve CSP, it appears that a long-term compensation focus in and of itself also promotes CSP. Much of the attention on CSP, the authors note, has been caused by the recent scandals involving senior corporate executives.

More broadly, this approach, to consider more than just stockholders and financial measures in the evaluation and rewarding of CEO performance, is consistent with the view expressed by a number of authors (see Exhibit 7.3 for a summary of key considerations when determining CEO compensation). Charan (2005), for example, argues for the need to move away from the single financial measure, such as stock price increases or EPS (earnings per share) growth. To do so, he suggests the following key tasks for boards to consider as they develop an effective CEO compensation package:

- Define a philosophy of compensation that reflects the board's intentions for the company.
- Within the framework of that philosophy, define multiple objectives.
- Match the objectives with both cash and equity awards, as appropriate.
- Design a compensation framework that depicts the relationship between total compensation and the objectives to be achieved.
- Conduct a meaningful quantitative and qualitative evaluation of the CEO's performance.
- Consider severance pay, input from HR, and external consultancy.

Unfortunately, perhaps, Epstein and Roy (2005) report that CEO performance continues to be defined mostly in terms of financial results and that this focus neglects the inputs, processes, and outputs leading to those results. Their review of the proxy statements in August of 2004 of fifty-nine of *Fortune* magazine's America's Most

Exhibit 7.3 Determining CEO Compensation—Considerations.

- Ensure the board develops and articulates an appropriate philosophy of compensation for the CEO, considering strategic objectives, industry best practices, and legal and regulatory requirements.
- The compensation committee, in conjunction with the full board, should determine which objectives will drive short- and long-term compensation, the nature of the compensation, such as cash, restricted stock, or other methods, and how compensation levels will be calculated based on targeted measures and metrics.
- To take advantage of tax regulations, consider that the measures and metrics that drive compensation must be findable, quantifiable, and able to be calculated by a third party.
- Utilize, for example, operating income, revenue growth, and customer satisfaction as the basis for determining short-term compensation.
- As the basis for long-term compensation, consider, for example, cash flow from operations and earnings per share; also consider multiple-year targets for operating income and revenue growth.
- Consistent with the corporate social responsibility perspective, set compensation-driven measures and metrics, where possible.
- Discretion in evaluating performance for awarding year-end compensation should be limited to negative discretion and not allow for any compensation beyond the levels and targets set during goal setting.

Admired Companies showed that 100 percent of the sample used financial performance indicators, and that of a list drawn from the literature of eleven other categories of non-financial performance indicators (for example, strategic planning—strategy formulation, reengineering, management of acquisitions; succession planning—management succession planning; management style—leadership, teamwork, personal excellence; controls and risk management—regulatory compliance and risk management; management of customer relations and growth—customer satisfaction, market share, sales), measures were used from little more than two categories. Twenty-six companies used just one category, fourteen used two categories, and only three companies used measures from six categories. As might be expected, the category "management of customer relations and growth" was the second-most-used category (measures from this category were chosen by 42 percent of companies).

The continued focus on financial performance, particularly in turbulent business and economic times, is further supported by a *BusinessWeek* (Thornton, 2007) cover story, with the following headline: "Perform or perish: For CEOs of private-equity-owned companies, the pressure to deliver is getting unbearably intense." Private equity firms are expecting their CEOs to deliver quick financial results and improvements and to ensure that the changes they make become the new way of doing business. Finally, a series of CEOs, including Stan O'Neal of Merrill Lynch and Chuck Prince of Citibank ("Cracks in," 2007), have recently been dismissed as a result of the subprime mortgage fiasco brought to light in late 2007; both O'Neal and Prince were at the helm when their firms lost billions of dollars due to their holding of large positions in CDOs (collaterized-debt obligations, which pool mortgage-backed and other credit instruments). In spite of their performance, both of these CEOs walked away with hefty, multi-million-dollar severance packages.

It appears that financial performance is the major reason for CEO dismissal. For example, a recent study (Kaplan & Minton, 2006) indicates an average CEO tenure of approximately six years and shows that board-driven turnover is significantly related to firm performance relative to industry, industry performance relative to the overall market, and the performance of the overall stock market. Jenter and Kanaan (2006) find, as well, that boards are more likely to dismiss a CEO who underperforms his or her industry peer group during times of low industry and market returns, in other words, when financial performance becomes more prominent and important. Oddly enough, the CEO's job used to be about stewardship of the corporation's assets for stakeholders, but today it is all about the bottom line for investors (Lucier, Kocourek, & Habbel, 2006).

For FORTX's CEO, 80 percent of total targeted compensation is variable, as discussed earlier. Because of changes to the tax status of options, FORTX's past history of excessive CEO compensation, and an improved focus on pay-for-performance, FORTX has ceased using stock options. The CEO's long-term compensation is now completely in the form of restricted stock awards. Although FORTX does use more than just financial results to track and evaluate its own and its CEO's overall performance, as discussed earlier, the CEO's compensation is primarily affected by two stakeholder groups: the firm's customers and business partners. Although employees are also included as a stakeholder group in the company scorecard, the associated measures and metrics are not directly pay influencing. This approach is largely due to IRS regulation 162m, which requires that the metrics used to determine compensation (to ensure its tax deductibility) are findable, quantifiable, and can be calculated by a third party—which is readily true of the typical financial measures reported and used. Finally, FORTX has no direct or single metric for corporate social performance.

Performance Management, Goal Setting, Feedback, and Appraisal

In general, the study of performance appraisals or evaluations for CEOs is lacking in the literature, due primarily to the reluctance of boards of directors to divulge details about how they make decisions (Silva, 2005; Silva & Tosi, 2004), and the fact that the majority of what is available is speculative and prescriptive.

Rivero (2004; see also Tyler & Biggs, 2001, for a comparable approach to the yearly initiation of the process) recommends answering the following questions as a first step in creating or revising a CEO evaluation or performance management process: what is the purpose of the evaluation (for example, compensation for performance, CEO development); what will be measured (for example, bottom-line financial metrics, operational leadership, personal impact); who will be involved in the evaluation (the compensation committee, full board, customers, employees, etc.); and how and when will the evaluation be implemented (What are the steps in the process? When and how frequently will feedback be given?). The answers to these questions should also be clear, from a practical perspective, even if the process is in a steady state and not undergoing revision. For FORTX, the *purpose* of the process is primarily compensation for performance, with a focus on development; the *measures* are largely quantitative, with a major emphasis on financial and operational measures (see Exhibit 7.1); and *involved* in the evaluation are both the compensation committee and the full board. The *steps* in the process have been described earlier in the chapter.

Conger, Finegold, and Lawler (1998) highlight three forces driving interest in CEO performance evaluations, that still operate today and include: (1) the general awareness of the critical roles played by CEOs; (2) shareholder activism, pressuring boards to take more responsibility and action for CEO performance evaluation; and (3) the evolution and enhancement of performance management systems and processes, including the use of 360-degree feedback. It should be clear that these forces, as well as the more recent legislative reforms and regulations, have certainly shaped the CEO performance management process at FORTX, with the greatest impact coming from shareholder activism and the broader scope of legislation and reforms affecting most large organizations.

Conger, Finegold, and Lawler (1998) also note four major outcomes of CEO or performance management: (1) raising the accountability for performance and defining the link between performance and compensation; (2) clarifying strategic direction; (3) promoting better CEO-board relations; and (4) fostering the development of the CEO. For FORTX, the CEO evaluation process has increased the focus on accountability, including the use of better measures of organization performance, and it has more clearly linked these measures to CEO compensation. This has led to a sharpening of business strategy—better and more quantitative measures have helped FORTX to focus most appropriately on each of its major objectives, and the ongoing nature of the feedback process has helped to keep CEO and firm performance on track, strengthen the relationship with the board, and in particular, with the board chairman, which has allowed for, as discussed earlier, a greater focus on development for both the CEO and the senior leadership team.

Conger, Finegold, and Lawler (1998; see also: Boren & Heidrick, 2004; Johnson & Bancroft, 2005; Nadler, Behan, & Nadler, 2006; Oliver Wyman, 2003; Rivero, 2004) describe the three typical steps

**Exhibit 7.4 CEO Overall Performance Management (PM)
Process—Considerations.**

- Ensure the PM process is driven by the organization's strategic plan.
- Detail and document all aspects of the PM process—roles, responsibilities, timelines, process flow, and so forth.
- Align the PM process calendar and timelines with the corporate calendar.
- Involve the CEO, the compensation committee, and the full board in goal setting.
- Provide performance feedback on a regular basis to the CEO, both informally and formally.
- Base the CEO's overall PM evaluation on the extent to which agreed-to targets were achieved, and include input from the CEO via a self-appraisal, the compensation committee, and the board chairman, as well as all other board members.
- Award compensation based on agreed-to levels of goal attainment.

---

in an effective CEO evaluation or performance management process. From the discussion of FORTX's process, you will note that FORTX's steps are similar, but at FORTX, there is no formal mid-course review; feedback is more informal, primarily in discussions between the CEO and the chairman. The three typical steps are listed below. You will also find a summary of considerations for the overall CEO performance management process in Exhibit 7.4 (detailed considerations for goal-setting, feedback, and appraisal appear in subsequent tables).

1. Establishing evaluation targets at the start of the fiscal year
   - CEO and board develop an annual strategic plan, setting short- and long-term objectives
   - CEO sets personal performance targets and measures, and should include development goals
   - Presentation to board committee (compensation and/or governance), and then to final board, along with financial rewards for performance

2. Reviewing performance mid-course
   - CEO use of board meetings to highlight achievements
   - Individual meetings with board members for performance feedback
3. Assessing final results at year-end
   - CEO writes self-evaluation
   - Board members assess performance, using narratives and rating scales
   - Compensation committee and board make compensation decisions

Conger, Finegold, and Lawler (1998) make additional recommendations, including the need to take into consideration those actions that the CEO can control directly, that objectives should go beyond just the financial, and that input from customers and employees and benchmarking within and outside the industry of the CEO's performance should be considered when evaluating overall performance. Nadler, Behan, and Nadler (2006), Oliver Wyman (2003), and Rivero (2004) suggest three broad areas of focus for CEO performance dimensions or goals: bottom-line impact (for example, financial success, as measured by net operating revenue, operating cash flow, net income earning per share, among others); operational impact (for example, improvements in organizational functioning, products, and strategy implementation, as well as morale, customer satisfaction, research and development, and others); and leadership effectiveness (for example, the CEO's actions and personal impact, including meeting and addressing the needs of key customers, identifying a successor, and building relationships with external stakeholders).

Regarding the preceding set of recommendations, it is fair to say that the measures and targets established at FORTX are not largely in "direct control" of the CEO; his actions, for example, cannot directly increase cash flow. The objectives do go beyond the financial (see Exhibit 7.1), and the CEO's performance is benchmarked against similar companies. Although the CEO does submit the Boardroom Metrics (2005) CEO self-assessment along with the narrative evaluating overall performance, and the self-assessment does focus on CEO actions and behaviors, it does not play a major role in the overall evaluation but it may influence decisions regarding the CEO's overall success, tenure, discretion related to compensation, and other items.

Charan (1998) recommends that CEO evaluations have both a look back and a look forward and that boards consider the following questions:

- Is the CEO building for the future?
- Does the company's strategic direction reflect reality, considering opportunities and challenges?
- Does the CEO have a firm understanding and grasp on company operations?
- Is the CEO creating the management team of the future?
- Is the CEO building positive relationships with external stakeholders?
- Is the CEO delivering results?

Rivero (2004) also suggests clarifying the extent to which the overall process is "backward facing," in that it focuses on past performance, and "forward facing," in that it focuses on future objectives and whether the CEO has the competencies and vision to achieve those objectives. According to Oliver Wyman (2003), backward-facing evaluations focus on organization performance and CEO compensation, as measured by goal accomplishment and other quantitative measures; forward-facing evaluations focus on CEO capability and CEO development, measured through the quality of the CEO's vision and strategy and other qualitative indicators. Both objectives are important. Charan (1998) suggests creating two processes, with the board using the look back to determine annual compensation and the look forward to evaluate the CEO's total leadership and to provide feedback. Although best practice would suggest separating discussions of both process objectives, for example, as it is done at Honeywell, due to a number of practical considerations, the discussions can be combined if done well, for example, as done at Target Corporation (Oliver Wyman, 2003). See Exhibit 7.5 for an overview of considerations for CEO goal setting.

FORTX's process tends to combine both looks, but it does not explicitly call for separate conversations. For example, its quantitative

Exhibit 7.5 CEO Goal Setting—Considerations.

- Set both short- and long-term goals and objectives in the context of the strategic plan.
- Establish measures and metrics for each objective.
- Utilize both quantitative and qualitative objectives.
- Go beyond financial objectives alone and consider the needs of stakeholders such as employees, customers, the community.
- Identify CEO key competencies and behaviors and set appropriate measures and metrics.
- Set backward-facing objectives for the year-end evaluation to determine firm and CEO performance.
- Set forward-facing objectives (development focused) to emphasize CEO development.
- From a process perspective:
  - The CEO, using the context of strategy, drafts the goals and objectives and reviews key financial and operational metrics with the CFO and development objectives with the chief human resources officer.
  - The CEO reviews the goals, objectives, measures, and metrics with the compensation committee with the purpose of coming to initial agreement and determining how the goals and objectives link to compensation.
  - The CEO and compensation committee review with the full board the goals, objectives, measures, and metrics and how they will drive compensation and work toward agreement and final approval.

measures, such as earnings per share, not only assist in evaluating past performance, but also provide a look to the future and help to answer the question of whether the CEO is positioning FORTX for further growth. Measures such as customer satisfaction and employee satisfaction also operate similarly. In contrast, a measure such as an increase in stock price (not a measure used at FORTX) could only be backward-facing. As mentioned earlier, the CEO's self-assessment contains an evaluation of leadership behaviors (see Exhibit 7.2), and this assessment, which can be considered more forward-facing, does focus on the questions and recommendations raised above by Charan (1998), Oliver Wyman (2003), and Rivero (2004).

Most authors (Conger, Finegold, & Lawler, 1998; Nadler, Behan, & Nadler, 2006; Parmenter, 2003; Rivero, 2004; Silva & Tosi, 2004; Tyler & Biggs, 2001) argue for the use of 360-degree feedback for evaluating more subjective goals, obtaining anonymous input from a broader and wider audience, and to provide feedback for development to help the CEO understand what actions help or hinder his or her effectiveness. In fact, research by Silva & Tosi (2004) suggests that guaranteeing board members anonymity when it comes to evaluating the CEO will increase the likelihood of more reliable and valid ratings of CEO performance. Among the above group of authors, however, there is some disagreement as to whether 360-degree feedback should be used for administrative purposes or only for development. In either event, Sala (2003) shows that senior executives had greater discrepancy between self- and other-ratings than lower-level managers and individual contributors—further supporting the use of 360-degree feedback for CEOs—and suggests that this may be due to the lack of others above them in the hierarchy who have the opportunity to provide feedback and that managers and leaders at lower levels in the organization may be less inclined to give constructive feedback to those at higher levels. You will recall that FORTX's chairman has engaged a consultant to provide 360-degree feedback for the CEO and the senior leadership team. In terms of raters, specific guidelines were given, and they included, at least for the CEO, that a minimum number of board members and direct reports must be invited to participate in the process. At this time, 360-degree feedback is being used solely for development purposes, and no decision has been made as to whether or not this feedback will be incorporated in the CEO performance management process on a more formal and regular basis. Considerations for CEO feedback are listed in Exhibit 7.6.

Charan (1998) provides several process options for capturing feedback on the CEO's performance for the year-end evaluation or appraisal. The first involves a single board member, perhaps the chairman of the compensation or governance committee, soliciting and then synthesizing the feedback he or she gathers from each director independently. Another involves governance or compensation committee members dividing the task of obtaining feedback in one-on-one sessions, synthesizing the feedback together. A third approach is to use a questionnaire, with both

Exhibit 7.6 CEO Feedback—Considerations.

- Articulate the framework for providing feedback, including, for example, who delivers the feedback and when it is delivered, as part of the overall performance management process.
- Provide the CEO feedback in both formal and informal ways.
- Ensure the board chairman and committee chairs have informal and formal opportunities to provide feedback.
- Feedback can be delivered informally, on event, via telephone, email, or in person.
- Informal feedback can also be delivered after executive sessions held by either the full board or a board committee.
- Focus feedback primarily on progress toward objectives, CEO development, and, as they arise, any critical business or operational issues.
- Utilize a mid-year review, which can be more or less informal, as an opportunity for an extended and focused performance and development conversation.
- Formal feedback, in the context of performance management, at least take place during the year-end appraisal conversation.
- Feedback can be collected in a number of ways, for example, via a 360-degree feedback survey or through interviews with board members.

---

structured and open-ended questions, to collect feedback from each board member, and then to have the committee chairman analyze and synthesize the feedback.

Nadler, Behan, and Nadler (2006) discuss a number of ways of delivering feedback, including one-on-one sessions by the board leader or the chair of the appropriate committee (for example, the governance or compensation committee); they also state that the person delivering the feedback should have both the trust and the respect of the board and the CEO. One recent study (What directors think, 2005), reporting on who provided the feedback to the CEO after the year-end evaluation was completed, showed that 54 percent of the time it was the compensation committee chair and 18 percent of the time it was the board chair.

Finally, Charan (1998) suggests delivering the feedback in two steps. In the first step, two board members present the feedback to the CEO in private. Using two board members helps to make delivering the feedback less dependent on the personality of a single board member. In step two, at a board meeting, the full board and the CEO discuss the feedback and the CEO's response to it. This step helps to verify and ensure that the feedback was delivered accurately and understood.

Reviewing FORTX's year-end feedback process in light of the literature, we find that the compensation committee plays the key role in reviewing the CEO's performance, analyzing the self-assessment, and making a recommendation to the board. The board then reviews the recommendation and comes to a final agreement regarding CEO performance and compensation. The chairman is responsible for providing the board's overall evaluation feedback to the CEO. Obviously, the feedback is delivered in a one-on-one session. It is also a one-step process; it does not include Charan's second step, a follow-up discussion with the CEO and the full board. In Exhibit 7.7, you will find a summary view of considerations for the CEO's overall year-end evaluation or appraisal.

Barriers to Effective Implementation of the CEO Evaluation or Performance Management Process

Oliver Wyman (2003) cites four main barriers to the effective implementation of a CEO evaluation or performance management process:

- *Uncertainty concerning board member roles and responsibilities,* primarily caused by the number of stakeholders involved in the process and its unfamiliarity to most board members. To address this, the board should have a clear charter describing roles and responsibilities in connection with the overall CEO performance management process, using, perhaps, the three typical steps discussed earlier in the chapter as the framework for outlining who does what and when they do it.
- *The lack of time and energy given the board's overall responsibilities—* as will be discussed shortly—directors spend only sixteen to twenty-two hours a month on board-related work, which is typically time spent on strategy, monitoring performance, and

Exhibit 7.7   CEO Appraisal—Consideration.

- The year-end appraisal is the prime opportunity for formal feedback.
- Encourage the CEO to prepare a self-appraisal, providing context, background, and rationale that can help to explain the extent to which the goals and objectives were achieved.
- Encourage the CEO to complete an assessment of his or her development goals and behaviors, either via a narrative, a survey checklist, or as part of a 360-degree feedback process.
- Collect feedback on CEO performance from board members and others, for example, the CEO's direct reports.
- Use a 360-degree feedback process to evaluate and support development efforts; use judiciously if it is intended to affect the evaluation of overall performance.
- Base the CEO's overall evaluation on both those goals and objectives that are tied to compensation and those that are not, as not all goals and objectives link to compensation directly.
- The compensation committee should initially assess and evaluate the CEO's performance, as well as review the CEO's self-appraisal, and then present its findings to the full board for review and final determination of overall performance and compensation.
- The board chairman and the chair of the compensation committee should jointly deliver the year-end performance evaluation to the CEO, with a focus on corporate performance or more back-facing objectives. A second, separate discussion, more forward-facing, should focus on the CEO's progress against development goals and consider the CEO's capability to lead the organization into the future.
- As a final step, the full board should meet with the CEO to discuss the CEO's overall performance evaluation and the CEO's response.

---

so forth. Boards need a well-designed process, integrated with their overall work efforts both in and out of formal commit-tee and board sessions, to help them to accept accountability for and efficiently and effectively engage in the performance management of the CEO.

- *Disagreement over the criteria for the evaluation,* which can occur among board members, as well as between board members and the CEO, based on their own views of what is important. Therefore, it is critical to spend ample time at the beginning of the process coming to agreement on goals, measures, and metrics and to be sure that they are the best possible for effectively evaluating business and CEO performance and success.
- *A lack of information about qualitative performance,* because, in general, most boards spend their time gathering and evaluating quantitative or "hard" data, and they find it difficult to define, collect, and measure qualitative performance in valid and reliable ways. This can be remedied by engaging the chief human resources officer to identify a professional resource that can help the board put in place a sound and appropriate measure, such as a 360-degree feedback survey.

Nadler, Behan, and Nadler (2006) add director intimidation or fear of delivering a difficult appraisal to the list. Underlying this fear is the anticipated reaction of the CEO, who more than likely will have a difficult time accepting any constructive feedback. Finally, Tyler and Biggs (2001) add the failure to explicitly define the totality of the CEO's responsibility and authority, which of course would make any subsequent evaluation quite arbitrary, and the concern that the special nature of the board-CEO relationship will be disturbed, making board-CEO relations more difficult, at least in the short run.

From FORTX's perspective, these barriers did not affect the creation of the CEO evaluation process. At FORTX, given its history, as well the continuing legislative reforms, the board's sense of accountability, responsibility, and empowerment is extremely strong: the board needs to ensure all aspects of governance are of the highest standards.

High-Level Assessment of the CEO Performance Management Process

Oliver Wyman (2003) suggests a number of questions to use to assess the quality and comprehensiveness of a CEO evaluation or performance management process. These questions reflect, to some extent, the recommendations for an effective process suggested by Charan (1998), Oliver Wyman (2003), as well as Rivero (2004). However, the questions also encourage a step back and a higher-level view of the process. These questions include:

- Is there an explicit description of the overall process?
- Is there an explicit process calendar with deadlines and milestones?
- Is the process calendar aligned with the corporate calendar?
- Does the process include a mid-year check-in?
- Does the process include a focus on CEO development and opportunities for development feedback?
- Is the process consistent with the company's values and culture?
- Can the process be revised as needed to ensure overall quality?

In the context of FORTX's overall process, most of the above questions have already been addressed and answered favorably, by and large. The key question that seems to remain unanswered is the last. Evidence does suggest that FORTX's CEO performance management process can be revised. Consider, for example, the recent introduction of 360-degree feedback for the CEO and the continuous improvement in the quality and relevance of measures and metrics, which resulted in the recent launch of the FORTX company scorecard.

Increasing the Effectiveness of the Board of Directors

Composition and Effectiveness of the Board

Given the board's critical role in the CEO performance management process, it is important to ensure that each board member, board committee, and the full board can function, in general, as effectively as possible. To that end, what follows is a discussion of how to increase board member effectiveness and improve the composition of the board, as well as findings related to board and board member evaluations and the influence of board member compensation on the monitoring of CEO performance. You will find in Exhibit 7.8, however, considerations for improving board member effectiveness, specifically in the context of performance management.

Although board member independence (being a board member, but not a company insider) has been touted as desirable, Kocourek, Burger, and Brichard (2003) state that research to support whether board independence correlates with company financial performance (quantitative) is inconclusive. The authors go on to discuss the need for qualitative reform, indicating the importance of:

- Selecting the right board members—with the right competencies, expertise, and personalities
- Training the board members regularly—helping them to acquire a thorough understanding of the business
- Giving the board members the right information—providing both credible and comprehensive information, both quantitative and qualitative
- Balancing the board and the CEO's power—letting independent directors select new directors, hold executive sessions, and control committee chairmanships

Exhibit 7.8 Increasing Board Member Effectiveness at Performance Management—Considerations.

- Include experience with CEO evaluation and executive compensation as selection criteria for any new board member.
- Train board members on the principles of effective performance management and the key aspects, especially the rules and regulations that influence executive compensation.
- Coach board members on how to deliver feedback effectively and constructively.
- Provide board members with regular and frequent updates on the CEO's performance against goals.
- Evaluate board members on their ability to effectively execute their roles in the performance management process.
- Compensate board members with equity, to the extent possible, to drive motivation and a long-term perspective.

- Nurturing a culture of collegial questioning—creating an atmosphere of mutual confidence and trust
- Gaining an adequate commitment of time—establishing benchmarks for expected participation
- Measuring and improving performance—establishing board performance metrics and evaluations

Recent surveys give a picture of progress of the extent to which boards are growing more effective. For example, from a 2005 survey (Mercer Delta Consulting), we find that directors felt their boards were primarily independent of management, they voiced opinions that conflict with the CEO's, they were provided sufficient information and adequately informed, and they worked well with senior management. Another survey (What directors think, 2005) reveals that corporate directors say they are not satisfied with their succession planning efforts, although they are effective in overseeing CEO compensation, and that the CEO is still primarily responsible for setting the board meeting agenda. This survey also reveals that directors are receiving enough financial and business information, but not enough information on employee and customer satisfaction.

Both of the above surveys report that director training, although improving, is still a need and that, from a time perspective, directors are spending anywhere from sixteen to twenty-two hours a month on board-related work.

Finally, a number of authors (Brountas, 2004; Charan, 2005; Nadler, Behan, & Nadler, 2006) provide recommendations for how to conduct full-board and committee-level evaluations (a listing requirement of the NYSE), as well as recommendations for evaluations of individual directors. Brountas (2004) and Charan (2004) remark that the assessment of individual directors is gaining acceptance, even though the process has not been favored historically because directors prefer not to be in the position of evaluating their colleagues. While the "What directors think" (2005) study reports that 84 percent of those surveyed say that the entire board's performance is evaluated on a regular basis and that 67 percent say those evaluations are effective, only 37 percent responded that individual board members are evaluated on a regular basis, but 70 percent say these evaluation are effective.

From the Mercer Delta Consulting (2005) survey, we find that 71 percent and 70 percent of respondents say, respectively, that the board evaluation and committee evaluations are effective.

What about FORTX? Given its history, it has gone to great lengths to select board members who can bring the needed talent, expertise, and experience to FORTX. There are regulatory changes that drive board member training, and the FORTX board is advised of those changes and avenues for training, as well as other recommended training, by its legal counsel. FORTX also provides board members, on a regular basis, with informal training on matters of company operations, strategy, business unit operations, and so forth, and board members also receive necessary updates at board meetings to help them understand changes in the business. Board members, as well, do receive credible and comprehensive information, both quantitative, for example, provided by FORTX's enterprise-wide reporting system, as well as more qualitative information, provided, for example, by FORTX's annual employee opinion survey. Although the CEO may participate and can have input, processes such as conducting searches for new board members, determining committee chairmanships, and others are under the board's control. The board culture, as well as the board-CEO relationship, can be characterized as more cooperative than not, and mutual confidence and trust continue to grow as FORTX has been enjoying a relative turnaround in its performance. FORTX clearly articulates and communicates the expected commitment of time required for board and committee membership, as well as the time needed for work in preparing for board sessions, work in between sessions, training, and other measures. Finally, evaluations are done in executive session by each committee and the board overall. There is no process in place for individual board member evaluation.

Compensation of Board Members

It appears that how board members are rewarded influences how they monitor and evaluate CEO performance. Silva (2005) found that board members who receive stock as compensation for their membership use more quantitative (for example, financial) information in their evaluations, maximizing the interests of shareholders, consistent with agency theory. The use of stock as compensation was negatively correlated to the use of qualitative information, but board members who tended to receive higher salaries as compensation tended to use quantitative criteria to a lesser extent. Finally, board member motivation was positively correlated with the use of quantitative information and negatively correlated with the use of qualitative information.

Compensation for FORTX's board members, consistent with a long-term focus, is in the form of equity, although members have the discretion of choosing up to 50 percent of their compensation in cash.

Summary and Recommendations

The CEO performance management process continues to evolve, with corporate scandals, shareholder activism, legislation, and regulatory reforms providing significant impetus for the introduction of greater rigor and transparency to the overall process. Boards of directors, as a result, have received a wake-up call and are growing ever more accountable for ensuring effective corporate governance, including CEO performance management and compensation. Boards are also growing more satisfied with their progress and effectiveness, overall, as evidenced by recent surveys (Mercer Delta Consulting, 2005; What directors think, 2005). Finally, as Nadler, Behan, and Nadler (2006) report, if not for the recent requirements, countless CEOs would continue to go on as they did before, without a formal performance review.

Where does this leave us? For as much research as there is behind performance appraisal and performance management (focused mostly, however, at lower levels in organizations), there is room for improvement in its application in organizations. For example, recent employee opinion survey results show that only slightly more than the majority of FORTX employees believe that performance management is a valued process at FORTX. FORTX does have a strong, if not a best-in-class, web-based performance management system and process, supported by extensive instructor-led and online training, as well as other related support tools and process guidelines. However, 2008 employee opinion survey results for four key performance management questions, when compared to Towers Perrin-ISR's (2007) proprietary employee opinion survey norms based on a group of thirty-five "high performing" organizations, show FORTX scoring somewhat lower on two of four questions. The four survey questions are

- My manager provides me with ongoing feedback that helps me improve my performance (FORTX scored lower, 64 percent versus 72 percent favorable response)
- I have a clear understanding of how my performance is evaluated (FORTX scored lower, 66 percent versus 78 percent favorable response)
- My most recent year-end performance appraisal was fair (FORTX scored equal, 73 percent favorable response)
- I am satisfied with the amount of recognition I receive from my manager (FORTX scored higher, 65 percent versus 57 percent favorable response)

Although survey results show there is still some need to enhance the typical performance management process even across high-performing organizations, the process can still provide a framework and basis for CEO evaluation. In fact, the three steps discussed earlier for an effective CEO evaluation are similar to what might be called a more generic fundamental performance management process (see, for example, Mone & London, 2002). Slowly, it seems, boards and CEOs are building processes that have, to some extent:

- Goal setting (which, frankly, has been more organizational than personal and more quantitative than qualitative)
- Ongoing feedback (either formal or informal, at board meetings or in one-on-one sessions with directors)
- A year-end evaluation (usually with metrics and a set of targets)
- The capability to better match performance and compensation (compensation ranges are usually set in connection with quantitative targets, limiting the discretion of the compensation committee or board to behave in more arbitrary ways)
- A CEO self-assessment component

Where do we go next? There is still more to learn about the effectiveness of the current practice of CEO performance management. To date, the prime focus has been just putting a

CEO evaluation process in place. What follows is the need to ensure that the efforts of boards and CEOs are not just about compliance, but also about full engagement and commitment to the process. This will involve a number of factors. The first is the need for boards and CEOs to genuinely accept and grow more comfortable with the idea of a rigorous CEO performance evaluation, and, by and large, recent surveys are indicating just that. Second, board members need to continue to improve their ability to work with CEOs to set meaningful goals and targets, monitor performance and provide constructive coaching and feedback, and to rigorously evaluate CEO performance. Part of the difficulty, however, lies in the fact that board members themselves are often other CEOs or senior executives, who may not even have effective evaluation processes in their own organizations. Third, CEOs will need to grow more comfortable with the performance management process and continue to improve their ability to partner with their boards throughout the process. Fourth, training for board members was discussed earlier in this chapter, but that was in the context of learning about the company, its strategy, challenges, and so on, as well as the need to meet any regulatory requirements. Training board members in the practice and skill of delivering feedback and in executing on all other phases of the evaluation process would not only increase their comfort, but also make them and the process more effective.

Continuing research with respect to the above four factors will be important. In addition, those counseling and advising today's boards and CEOs have an opportunity to shape the process more immediately. There is less mystery surrounding boards today than ever before, and as the mystery continues to unfold, it becomes clear that a board is a group, if not a team, targeted with a mission and set of responsibilities. Senior HR executives working within their organizations can provide counsel to their CEOs regarding group and team dynamics to help improve overall board functioning and, perhaps, may be positioned to advise the board chairman; they can also, as necessary, work to gain the ear of the chairman or compensation committee leader to guide and influence CEO behavior. Senior HR executives can also work with and engage a variety of consultants to help them shape overall board behavior and the interaction between the board and the CEO. A number of authors (LaFasto &

Larson, 2001; Larson & LaFasto, 1989; London & London, 2007; Nadler, Spencer, & Associates, 1998; Sessa & London, 2006) provide useful insights and practical approaches for improving team effectiveness. HR executives can also use their expertise, from a selection perspective, and perhaps working closely with the board chairman, to identify the skills and requirements necessary to be an effective board member and to help the board to select new board members (see, for example, Nadler, Behan, & Nadler, 2006).

The pressures facing today's corporations, boards, and CEOs are certainly challenging. It is unlikely that these pressures and challenges will subside in the near future, and it is also unlikely that stockholder and shareholder activism will decline. In addition, there may still be room for further legislation and reforms. As we consider what may be ahead, our opportunity is to take advantage of the current and probable future climates to further drive rigor and effectiveness in today's and tomorrow's CEO performance management process.

References

Bainbridge, S. M. (2007). *The complete guide to Sarbanes-Oxley: Understanding how Sarbanes-Oxley affects your business.* Avon, MA: Adams Business.

Boardroom Metrics. (2005). *The CEO evaluation.* Retrieved March 12, 2008, from http://www.boardroommetrics.com/ceo-evaluation-form.html.

Boren, S. S., & Heidrick, R. L. (2004). Get serious to make CEO evaluations work. *Directors and Boards, 28*(3), 54–56.

Brountas, P. B. (2004). *Boardroom excellence.* San Francisco: Jossey-Bass.

Brown, J. (2006). *The imperfect board member.* San Francisco: Jossey-Bass.

Carver, J. (2006). *Boards that make a difference* (3rd ed.). San Francisco: Jossey-Bass.

Charan, R. (1998). *Boards at work.* San Francisco: Jossey-Bass.

Charan, R. (2005). *Boards that deliver: Advancing corporate governance from compliance to competitive advantage.* San Francisco: Jossey-Bass.

Conger, J., Finegold, D., & Lawler, E. E. (1998). CEO appraisals: Holding corporate leadership accountable. *Organizational Dynamics, 27*(1), 7–20.

Conyon, M. J. (2006). Executive compensation and incentives. *Academy of Management Perspectives, 20*(1), 25–44.

Cracks in the edifice. (2007, November). *The Economist.* Retrieved August 15, 2007, from http://www.economist.com/finance/displaystory .cfm?story_id=10111659.

Deckop, J. R., Merriman, K. K., & Gupta, S. (2006). The effects of CEO pay structure on corporate social performance. *Journal of Management, 32*(3), 329–342.

Epstein, M. J., & Roy, M. (2005). Evaluating and monitoring CEO performance: Evidence from U.S. compensation committee reports. *Corporate Governance, 5*(4), 75–87.

Graddick, M. M., & Lane, P. (1998). Evaluating executive performance. In J. W. Smither (Ed.), *Performance appraisal: The state of the art in practice* (pp. 370–403). San Francisco: Jossey-Bass.

Jenter, D. C., & Kanaan, F. (2006). *CEO turnover and relative performance evaluation.* MIT Sloan Research Paper No. 4594-06.

Johnson, C. W., & Bancroft, E. (2005). *CEO measurement and evaluation: The three p's.* Retrieved August 15, 2008, from http://www.trusteemag.com/trusteemag_app/jsp/articledisplay.jsp?dcrpath=TRUSTEEMAG/PubsNewsArticleGen/data/2005/0505TRU_DEPT_AboveBoard.

Kaplan, R. S., & Norton, D. P. (1996). *The balanced scorecard: Translating strategy into action.* Boston: Harvard Business School Press.

Kaplan, S. N., & Minton, B. A. (2006). How has CEO turnover changed? Increasingly performance sensitive boards and increasingly uneasy CEOs. NBER Working Paper No. W12465.

Kocourek, P. F., Burger, C., & Brichard, B. (2003). Corporate governance: Hard facts about soft behaviors. *Strategy+Business.* Retrieved August 15, 2008, from http://www.strategy-business.com/press/article/8322?pg=0.

Laffront, J., & Mortimer, D. (2002). *The principal-agent model.* Princeton, NJ: Princeton University Press.

LaFasto, F., & Larson, C. (2001). *When teams work best.* Thousand Oaks, CA: Sage.

Larson, C., & LaFasto, F. (1989). *Teamwork: What must go right, what can go wrong.* Thousand Oaks, CA: Sage.

London, M., & London, M. (2007). *First-time leaders of small groups.* San Francisco: Jossey-Bass.

Lorsch, J. W., & Nadler, D. A. (2004). *Report of the National Association of Corporate Directors Blue Ribbon Commission on Board Leadership.* Washington, DC: National Association of Corporate Directors.

Lucier, C., Kocourek, P., & Habbel, R. (2006). CEO succession 2005: The crest of the wave. *Strategy+Business, 43,* 100–113.

Mercer Delta Consulting. (2005). *USC/Mercer Delta Corporate Board Survey.* New York: 2005. Retrieved April 8, 2008, from http://www.oliverwyman.com/ow/pdf_files/un_Board_Survey_2005.pdf.

Mone, E., & London M. (2002). *Fundamentals of performance management.* London: Spiro Press.

Nadler, D. A., Behan, B. A., & Nadler, M. B. (2006). *Building better boards: A blueprint for effective governance.* San Francisco: Jossey-Bass.

Nadler, D. A., & Spencer, J. L. (1998). *Executive teams.* San Francisco: Jossey-Bass.

New York Stock Exchange. (2004, November). *NYSE Listed Company Manual.* Retrieved August 15, 2008, from http://www.nyse.com/Frameset.html?nyseref+http%3A//www.nyse.com/regulation/listed/1182508124422.html&displayPage=/lcm/lcm_section.html.

O'Reilly, C. A., & Main, B. G. M. (2007). Setting the CEO's pay: It's more than simple economics. *Organizational Dynamics, 36*(1), 1–12.

Oliver Wyman. (2003). *CEO evaluation: Navigating a new relationship with the board.* Retrieved February 13, 2008, from http://www.oliverwyman.com/ow/pdf_files/CEO_Evaluation_Insight.pdf.

Parmenter, D. (2003, April). Measuring the boss: Just how good (or bad) is your CEO? *NZ Management Magazine.* Retrieved August 15, 2008, from http://www.rapidsurvey.com/360_Survey_article_measure_boss.html?webid=MGT&articleid=9838.

Rivero, J. C. (2004, September/October). CEO evaluation: Navigating a new relationship. *The Corporate Board,* pp. 22–26.

Sala, F. (2003). Executive blind spots: Discrepancies between self-other ratings. *Journal of Consulting Psychology: Research and Practice, 54*(4), 222–229.

Schminke, M., Arnaud, A., & Kuenzi, M. (2007). The power of ethical work climates. *Organizational Dynamics, 36*(2), 171–186.

Sessa, V., & London, M. (2006). *Continuous learning in organizations: Individual, group and organizational perspectives.* Mahwah, NJ: Lawrence Erlbaum Associates.

Silva, P. (2005). Do motivation and equity ownership matter in board of directors' evaluation of CEO performance? *Journal of Managerial Issues, 17*(3), 346–360.

Silva, P., & Tosi, H. L. (2004). Determinants of the anonymity of the CEO evaluation process. *Journal of Managerial Issues, 16*(1), 87–102.

Thornton, E. (2007, November 5). Perform or perish [Electronic version]. *BusinessWeek.* Retrieved February 15, 2008, from http://www.businessweek.com/magazine/content/07_45/b4057001.htm.

Towers Perrin-ISR. (2007).

Tyler, J. L., & Biggs, E. L. (2001, May). Practical governance: CEO performance appraisal. *Trustee, 54*(5), 18–21.

What directors think. (2005). *Corporate Board Member, 8*(6).

CHAPTER 8

PERFORMANCE MANAGEMENT IN MULTI-NATIONAL COMPANIES

David V. Day and Gary J. Greguras

Because Indonesians believe it is impolite to openly disagree with someone, they rarely say "no." The listener is expected to be perceptive enough to discern a polite "yes (but I really mean no)" from the actual "yes." This is rarely a problem when speaking in Bahasa Indonesia because the language has at least twelve ways to say "no" and many ways to say "I'm saying yes, but I mean no." This subtlety is lost when translated into many foreign languages, including English.
MORRISON AND CONAWAY (2006, P. 234)

Effective performance management is a complex and difficult process to manage even under the best of circumstances. So imagine trying to discern whether an Indonesian employee is saying "yes, I agree with you" or is actually saying "yes (but I really mean no)." Just think of the possibilities for miscommunication! Couple this with the tendency for Indonesians to show great deference to superiors and to tell superiors only what they want to hear. Performance management becomes a tricky process in such a scenario, especially if the boss is not Indonesian. But this chapter is not about managing in Indonesia; rather, it is about challenges facing multi-national companies, where culture and language differences can contribute to misunderstandings and impede effective performance management processes.

As other chapters in this book attest, performance management consists of a number of processes dealing with communicating expectations about individual performance, assessing performance through quantitative ratings or qualitative narratives, and providing feedback for administrative or developmental purposes, among other things. An effective performance management system—regardless of culture—requires a manager to do three things: (a) *define performance* including setting goals, deciding how to measure accomplishments, and providing regular feedback about progress toward accomplishments; (b) *facilitate performance* by eliminating roadblocks to successful performance, providing adequate resources, and staffing effectively; and (c) *encourage performance* by providing the right type and amount of rewards in a timely manner, and doing so fairly (Cascio, 2006). But what is fair? What is considered to be fair in the United States could be considered to be grossly unfair in Qatar.

A primary challenge facing multi-national companies (MNCs) in terms of successfully managing human resource management practices—and performance management in particular—is to understand and deal with the role of national culture. The purpose of this chapter is to more fully explore the challenges facing MNCs in the performance management process and to address in detail the challenges that cultural differences may pose.

Before examining the general challenges facing MNCs and the more specific ones associated with performance management, it makes sense to first define an MNC. Also sometimes referred to as a "transnational" company, an MNC can be defined as a company or enterprise that manages offices, has production facilities, or delivers services in more than one country. MNCs usually have a centralized head office where they coordinate global activities. Budgets of very large MNCs rival those of many small countries.

Some authors draw a distinction between MNCs that are conglomerates, *global companies* with centralized decision making and largely standardized products (such as Unilever and Ford Motor Company), and *international companies* that focus on project or product development across nations and world-wide sharing of knowledge (such as IBM) (Bartlett & Ghoshal, 1998). Given that the focus of this book is on professional practice, we do not draw a strong distinction between these different types of transnational companies but rather treat them all as variants of MNCs. Each may have slightly different cultural challenges; however, what unites them is the important role that cultural differences play in the success or failure of the performance management process.

Challenges of MNCs

MNCs face considerable challenges in doing business. This includes but is not limited to challenges associated with introducing products or services across multiple cultural contexts, complying with different national legal requirements and systems, facing global competitors with access to cheaper manpower or raw materials, and competing globally for talent. There are also challenges related to human resource management practices in MNCs that can impede company success. Because of the influences of culture and language, performance management may be one area of human resource management that is most difficult to implement successfully.

Language frames the way that people make sense of objects, issues, and others in their social and physical environment. Language also shapes the messages that are communicated between parties. Failing to consider the importance of language differences in the workplace opens up the possibility that messages will be "lost in translation" somewhere in the communication process. But culture also is an important consideration because it influences the expectations that people have about what is and is not appropriate and acceptable behavior.

There are many different definitions of culture; however, there is some agreement that culture is shared among members of the community, it is adaptive or has been adaptive in the past, and it is passed on across time and generations (Gelfand, Erez, & Aycan, 2007). Culture can operate at multiple levels, including that of a business unit, an entire organization, or a nation or geographic region. One of the important underlying issues that we will consider in terms of understanding the role of culture on performance management is the relative strength of organizational culture versus national culture.

In a previous publication, Eggebeen (2002) examined a number of issues to consider in the cross-cultural implementation of organizational interventions, including performance management. Most of these issues concerned differences in language or culture (or both). Some of the culture-related issues outlined by Eggebeen with regard to performance management included:

- The effect of subtle differences in meaning and interpretation of performance competencies or the dimensions on which individual performance is evaluated;
- The culturally based willingness of raters and employees to talk openly and deliver difficult messages (think of Indonesia);
- The use of multiple rating sources resulting in overt or covert resistance when subordinates are asked to rate their superiors;
- Feelings of insult and disrespect on the part of superiors if critical feedback comes from subordinates;
- Different comfort levels with regard to personal disclosure that includes ratings or discussions of the job performance of others; and
- Culturally variable aspirations for personal growth and development, as well as the importance of ambition and career advancement.

Taken as a hodge-podge of cultural tendencies, trying to design and implement a culturally sensitive MNC-based performance management system would be quite a daunting task. It is fortunate that recent research has helped to forge taxonomies of cultural dimensions on which various nations have been compared. We will next review these dimensions and the respective implications of each dimension for performance management in MNCs (see Table 8.1 for a summary).

Cultural Dimensions and Implications

Project Global Leadership and Organizational Behavior Effectiveness Research Program (GLOBE) was a ten-year research program headed by Bob House and colleagues (House, Hanges, Javidan, Dorfman, & Gupta, 2004). The overall goal of the project was to increase the understanding of different cultures and

Table 8.1 Cultural Dimensions, Descriptions, and Performance Management Implications.

Cultural Dimension	Description	Performance Management (PM) Implications
Performance Orientation (PO)	Beliefs regarding the nature of work performance, the appropriate level of performance standards, and the orientation around innovation and performance improvement.	Preferences for PM systems emphasizing achievement and rewarding individual merit (high PO) over those that emphasize loyalty and cooperation and reward members based primarily on age and seniority (low PO).
Future Orientation (FO)	The relative importance placed on the future as compared to the past or the present.	Long-term performance goals are set with an emphasis on intrinsic job motivation (high FO). Expectations of immediate rewards and a focus on setting short-term goals (low FO).
Gender Egalitarianism (GE)	Societal beliefs regarding what is appropriate for men and women, and specifically whether biological sex should influence the roles assigned in business organizations.	Access to professional development opportunities might be limited for women, and there could be resistance or resentment to feedback from female superiors (low GE). Male managers need to be aware of and minimize possible condescension of female subordinates (high GE).

(Continued)

Table 8.1 (*Continued*)

Cultural Dimension	Description	Performance Management (PM) Implications
Assertiveness (A)	Values oriented around tough, assertive, and dominant behavior as compared to tenderness and modesty.	Employees who are rewarded tend to be aggressive, competitive, and dominant; feedback tends to be blunt and direct (high A). At the other end of the continuum (low A), employees are rewarded for getting along and building relationships. Confrontational styles would be considered unacceptable.
Individualism (I) and Collectivism (C)	Based on a person's relationship to other people and whether individual competition is valued over collective group welfare.	Individual achievement is rewarded and feedback tends to focus on task performance (I). Team-based achievement is rewarded and relationship-based feedback is preferred (C).
Power Distance (PD)	Degree to which societal members accept that power is distributed unequally in organizations.	Performance feedback is one-way from superior to subordinate and assigned goals more likely (high PD). Greater participation in the PM process, higher comfort level in disagreeing with superiors, and more mutually set goals (low PD).

Humane Orientation (HO)	Degree to which societal members encourage and reward fairness, friendliness, generosity, and support.	There is a great deal of supervisory concern and support in assisting an employee reach personal and professional goals, as well as greater tolerance for mistakes (high HO). Little interest in helping an employee grow or develop with a low threshold of tolerance for mistakes (low HO).
Uncertainty Avoidance (UA)	The extent that societal members seek orderliness, structure, and formalized procedures to govern their daily lives.	The PM process would include extensive documentation and adhere to formal procedures (high UA). Informal feedback and a lack of formal protocol would be the PM norm (low UA).

Note: Adapted from House, Hanges, Javidan, Dorfman, and Gupta (2004) thereby improve cross-cultural interactions. Data were gathered across sixty-two societies reflecting the responses of over seventeen thousand managers from more than 950 different organizations around the world. Although much of the GLOBE project was focused on issues of cross-cultural leadership, there was also a comparison of different societies on a standard set of cultural attributes. Each of these dimensions is briefly reviewed, followed by an overview of the performance management implications of each respective dimension. We chose to focus on cultural practices rather than cultural values in our comparisons. Practices pertain to "what is," whereas values address "what should be." As such, practices appear to be the more relevant manifestation of culture for our purposes.

Performance Orientation

Of obvious relevance to performance management are the cultural beliefs regarding the nature of work performance, the level of performance standards to which employees are held, as well as the orientation around innovation and performance improvement. Countries with a high performance orientation (for example, Switzerland, Singapore, Hong Kong, New Zealand, South Africa) value training and development programs, emphasize results and reward good performance, value taking initiative, and view feedback as necessary for improvement. Countries with a low performance orientation (for example, Greece, Venezuela, Russia, Hungary, Qatar) value loyalty and belongingness, emphasize seniority and experience over individual performance, view merit pay as potentially destructive and economic motivation in general as inappropriate, and consider feedback and individual appraisal as personally judgmental.

Given the preceding description, it would be expected that members of high performance orientation societies would prefer performance management systems that emphasize achieving and rewarding results. Members of countries with low performance orientations would choose a performance management system that emphasizes loyalty and cooperation and that primarily rewards age and seniority. Overall, the level of goal setting (challenging/unchallenging) and the role of feedback (appropriate/inappropriate) would be critical concerns in managing performance across countries with very different performance orientations.

Future Orientation

Cultures vary in terms of the relative importance placed on the past, present, and future. Cultures with a high future orientation, and thus a low present orientation (for example, Singapore, Switzerland, South Africa, Netherlands, Malaysia), tend to value long-term success over short-term wins, delay gratification over longer time periods, have organizations with longer strategic orientations, and have individuals who are intrinsically motivated. Those societies with a low future orientation and high present orientation (for example, Russia, Argentina, Poland, Hungary, Guatemala) place higher priorities on immediate rewards, maintain a shorter strategic orientation, and have individuals who tend to be more instrumentally and less intrinsically motivated.

In terms of performance management, higher future orientation would likely translate into longer-term performance goals and an emphasis on intrinsic motivation, as well as more attention given to employee training and succession planning. Cultures with a lower future orientation would be more likely to expect relatively immediate rewards, set short-term goals, and attend less to the succession planning of employees.

Gender Egalitarianism

This dimension reflects societal beliefs about whether biological sex should influence the roles that members play in business organizations. Those cultures with high gender egalitarianism (for example, Hungary, Russia, Poland, Denmark, Sweden) rely less on biological sex in determining societal roles, whereas those cultures low on gender egalitarianism (for example, South Korea, Kuwait, Egypt, India, Switzerland) tend to emphasize greater male domination in roles with power.

Gender egalitarianism could manifest itself in performance management mainly through issues associated with evaluation, feedback, and opportunities for professional development and promotion. When the level of gender egalitarianism is low, it would be expected that female bosses could experience a great deal of resistance and possibly even resentment when trying to convey performance feedback, especially if that feedback is critical of performance. Male managers might experience difficulties in cultures with high levels of gender egalitarianism if they are perceived as patronizing or condescending to female subordinates. In terms of professional development opportunities, cultures high on gender egalitarianism would be more likely to favor equal opportunity for women with regard to access to relevant professional development programs and experiences relative to low gender egalitarianism cultures. Gender egalitarianism might also be expected to affect reward allocation such that cultures with low gender egalitarianism may perceive males as a family's primary income earners and therefore might compensate them more than their female counterparts, whereas cultures with high gender egalitarianism would be expected to value equal compensation for males and females.

Assertiveness

The cultural dimension of assertiveness is based on whether members of a society should be assertive and tough-minded or unassertive and tender in their social relationships. Nations that are high on assertiveness (for example, Albania, Nigeria, Hungary, Germany, Hong Kong) tend to value tough, assertive, and dominant behavior from everyone, see competition as a good thing, emphasize direct and unambiguous communication, and emphasize results over relationships. Nations low on assertiveness (for example, Sweden, New Zealand, French-speaking Switzerland, Japan) value modesty and tenderness, see assertiveness as socially inappropriate, disapprove of merit pay as potentially destructive to harmony and cooperation, and value people and warm relationships over win-lose competition.

Cultural differences in assertiveness could affect underlying performance expectations in an organization (for example, competition versus cooperation) as well as the communication style of the appraisal, and the manner in which individual feedback is handled. Specifically, in high assertiveness cultures, employees who are aggressive, dominant, and tough will be more likely to be rewarded and promoted, and feedback will be presented in a direct if not confrontational manner. In cultures that are low on assertiveness, getting along would likely be valued over trying to get ahead—especially at the expense of others. Individual merit will be downplayed in favor of tradition, seniority, and loyalty. Because ambiguity and subtlety in communication tend to be preferred, feedback would likely be indirect with an emphasis on opportunities for face saving to occur.

Individualism and Collectivism

This cultural dimension refers to a person's relationship with other people, whereby individualistic societies value individual competition and welfare over collective group welfare. This cultural dimension would be expected to influence the level or type of achievement that will be evaluated as part of the performance management process. Individualistic cultures (for example, Greece, Hungary, Germany, Argentina, Italy) have members whose orientation toward the organization emphasizes their unique skills and abilities as employees, where mainly short-term relationships are formed, employees change companies at their own discretion, and individual goals take precedence over group goals. Collectivist cultures (for example, Sweden, Japan, Singapore, Denmark, China) have organizations whose members assume they are highly interdependent with the organization, stress the importance of making personal sacrifices in meeting their professional obligations, have a more long-term relationship with the organization, and value group goals over individual goals.

Both the nature of the performance goals as well as the approach to feedback are expected to vary across individualist and collectivist cultures. Specifically, individualistic cultures are more likely to emphasize personal achievement, whereas collectivist cultures are more likely to emphasize team-based achievement in appraisals. In terms of how the appraisal review is conducted, it can be expected that supervisors in individualistic cultures provide feedback more directly and that focus is on task-related issues, whereas in collectivist cultures a more personal manner will be adopted in providing mainly relationship-oriented feedback (Milliman, Nason, Gallagher, Huo, Von Glinow, & Lowe, 1998). Another likely difference is that employees from individualistic societies will be more likely to provide higher self-ratings and more differentiated ratings of others, whereas employees from collectivistic societies are more likely to provide modest self-ratings and less differentiated ratings of others in their attempts to maintain harmony, facilitate teamwork, and reach consensus. As another example, employees in individualistic cultures likely prefer economic rewards, whereas employees from collectivistic cultures may prefer non-economic rewards because they may serve to increase affiliation and recognition (Aycan, 2000).

Power Distance

This dimension refers to the degree to which individuals in a culture accept that power is distributed unequally in organizations. In high power distance cultures (for example, Morocco, Nigeria, El Salvador, Zimbabwe, Argentina), individuals readily accept the unequal distribution of power and show great respect and deference to superiors. The rank or position of an individual is important as is obeying leaders. In low power distance cultures (for example, Denmark, South Africa, Netherlands, Bolivia, Israel), individuals tend to view themselves as being equal or similar to their superiors. Information and power are more widely shared in low power distance countries.

It would be expected that employees would have more input into the performance management process in low power distance cultures and that employees would feel more comfortable disagreeing with supervisors about performance feedback. In high power distance cultures, communication would likely be expected to be one-way from the superior to the subordinate and that overt disagreements on the part of the subordinate would be considered inappropriate. The nature of performance goals would also likely differ. In low power distance cultures, performance goals would likely be mutually set between a superior and subordinate but assigned by the superior in high power distance cultures. The degree or type of feedback-seeking behaviors would also likely differ based on the power distance of the culture, with employee monitoring perhaps being more prevalent in high power distance cultures and directly asking for feedback being more prevalent in low power distance cultures. Also, in low power distance cultures, the subordinate is responsible for performance improvement, whereas for high power distance cultures, superiors are held responsible for developing the subordinate (Milliman, Nason, Gallagher, Huo, Von Glinow, & Lowe, 1998). Recent research also noted a significant negative correlation between power distance and the use of 360-degree feedback systems across twenty-one countries (Peretz & Fried, 2008), with companies in high power distance cultures less likely to use 360-degree feedback than those companies in low power distance cultures.

Humane Orientation

This dimension is defined as the degree to which societal members encourage and reward fairness, friendliness, generosity, and support. Members of high humane orientation societies (for example, Zambia, Philippines, Ireland, Malaysia, Thailand) consider others in the community to be important, take responsibility for promoting the well-being of others, and place a high priority on values such as benevolence, kindness, love, and generosity. Low humane orientation societies (for example, Germany, Spain, Greece, Hungary, France, Singapore) have members who emphasize self-interest and self-enhancement, show little concern or support for others, believe that power and material possessions motivate people, and place a high priority on values such as pleasure, comfort, and self-enjoyment.

Humane orientation would manifest itself in the performance management process primarily in terms of the relative level of concern, support, and sensitivity that a supervisor would show toward an employee. In high humane orientation cultures, supervisors would be more likely to be sensitive to and support the personal and professional goals of an employee than in a low humane orientation culture. There also would be differences in their respective levels of tolerance for mistakes, with supervisors from high humane orientation cultures showing greater tolerance than those from low humane orientation cultures. Although it is somewhat speculative in nature, it might also be expected that employees from high humane orientation cultures would value or exhibit more altruistic organizational citizenship behaviors as compared to employees from low humane orientation cultures.

Uncertainty Avoidance

This cultural dimension refers to the extent that societal members prefer orderliness, consistency, structure, and formalized procedures and laws to govern their daily lives. Cultures high on uncertainty avoidance (for example, Switzerland, Sweden, Singapore, Denmark, Germany) have members who tend to formalize interactions with others, document agreements and keep meticulous records, show stronger resistance to change, and express little tolerance for breaking rules. Cultures low on uncertainty avoidance (for example, Russia, Hungary, Guatemala, Bolivia, Greece) have members who tend to be relatively more informal in their interactions with others, rely on the word of others they trust rather than a formal written agreement, show greater openness to change, and have greater tolerance for breaking rules.

It is expected that members of high uncertainty avoidance cultures would emphasize documenting and following formal procedures in the performance management process. Those from low uncertainty avoidance cultures would be more likely to provide informal performance feedback and to rely less on formal procedures or extensive paperwork. Conversely, there is evidence of a positive correlation between uncertainty avoidance and the existence of formal performance appraisal programs across MNCs (Peretz & Fried, 2008). Research has also suggested that individuals who are less tolerant of ambiguity are more likely to seek feedback more frequently as a way to manage their daily uncertainties. By extension, employees from high uncertainty avoidance cultures might be expected to engage in feedback seeking more often than those from low uncertainty avoidance cultures.

Limitations with Comparisons of Cultural Value Differences

The Project GLOBE research (House, Hanges, Javidan, Dorfman, & Gupta, 2004), as well as earlier cross-cultural work by Geert Hofstede (2001), Shalom Schwartz (1994), and Harry Triandis (1994), in particular, demonstrate the importance of cultural differences in influencing the thinking and behavior of members of different societies. There are two additional issues regarding culture that are worth noting. The first issue is that there is a risk of taking these generalizations too far. Consider again the example of Indonesia. In describing the behavioral tendencies of Indonesians, it is easy to lose sight of the fact that Indonesia is a far-reaching archipelago comprising 17,508 separate islands with an overall population of over 234 million people, making it the world's fourth largest nation in terms of population. Indonesia is also the most populous Muslim-majority country in the world, although it is also comprised of significant numbers of Hindus, Buddhists, and Christians. Consider that more than 90 percent of the residents of the Indonesian island of Bali follow the practices of Balinese Hinduism. Because of this religious influence, local Bali culture is different than that of Java (where Jakarta is located), which is different in many ways from Sumatra, which is different from Lombok, and on and on. So to claim that "Indonesians do this" or "Indonesians think like that" is likely to be a gross over-simplification, which can lead to stereotyping and other dysfunctional categorizations. The situation becomes even more complex when the possible combination of interactions between cultural dimensions is considered.

The second issue to consider is that, although cultures may be differentiated in terms of their values (as discussed above), other factors also differentiate cultures. For example, the strength (the clarity and pervasiveness) of social norms and the degree of tolerance for violations of those norms reflect a society's "tightness" or "looseness" (Gelfand, Nishii, & Raver, 2006). Cultural tightness-looseness differentiates cultures beyond the differences observed when only considering cultural values. The concept of cultural tightness-looseness is conceptually related to the concept of strong versus weak cultures. Next we address the importance of organizational culture and whether organizational culture is stronger than national or societal culture. Despite the importance of this issue, it has attracted virtually no research attention.

The Role of Organizational Culture

Hofstede's (2001) research on "culture's consequences" with regard to organizational functioning is considered to be a landmark in the field of cross-cultural organizational studies. Nonetheless, critics have argued that even though the research was ambitious in terms of incorporating respondents from more than seventy countries, they were all IBM employees. Questions have been raised as to whether we can generalize his findings to other organizations operating in the same countries. This question still begs an answer, although the next phase of GLOBE research findings (still unpublished) might be able to partially address this issue.

Not only do nations and societies have cultures, but so do organizations. For many years, IBM managers were known for their regimented dress code (dark blue suit, white shirt, conservative tie). Did that reflect a certain IBM culture? In an interview with former IBM CEO Louis V. Gerstner, Jr., he lamented finding on his arrival that there was an IBM culture of crisp white shirts, hordes of administrative assistants, and the culture of the individual "with a capital I" that reflected the me-first attitude of employees (Lagace, 2002, p. 1). But these things were not culture per se; rather, they reflected the underlying sense of values and identity that were manifested in these and other practices. Gerstner came to realize eventually that at IBM "culture is everything" in terms of the values and identity of this organization (Lagace, 2002, p. 2).

Organizational cultures are important to consider, but it is perhaps even more important to consider the distinction between strong and weak cultures. One way to think about culture strength is in terms of the level of agreement across employees on the underlying values and norms of the organization, the guiding philosophy for doing business, and the repercussions associated with violating important norms and values. At the other end of the continuum are weak cultures in which there are few if any strong company traditions, few values and beliefs that are widely shared across employees, norm violations are tolerated, no strong sense of company identity exists, and there are many fractured subcultures.

One reason to consider the role of organizational culture in cross-cultural performance management is to figure out whether organizational culture trumps national culture. Or is it the other way around? This is important potentially in deciding whether to implement a single performance management system across multiple cultures—and the likely success of that decision—or to try to manage multiple, culturally specific systems depending on location. Unfortunately, there is little or no published research on the relative effectiveness of alternative performance management practices in MNCs (Cascio, 2006). For that reason, we chose to interview HR managers from several MNCs to better understand the performance management practices and strategies used by their respective organizations and to generate several recommendations for performance management in MNCs.

Recommendations for Practice

We interviewed four HR practitioners who currently work or have worked with MNCs in Singapore (Bristol-Myers Squibb, American Express, Safeway, Seagate) to get their perspectives regarding cross-cultural performance management. Their respective position titles were either human resources director or regional HR director. We conducted approximately thirty- to forty-five-minute semi-structured interviews with each of the participants. Exhibit 8.1 provides the questions we used for our interview protocol. Although the sample size is quite small, the interviewees' answers were essentially identical on all of the major issues (for example, the role of national culture versus organizational culture; implementing one performance management system or various systems depending on the culture). Based on the limited cross-cultural performance management research, combined with findings from related streams of research (basic social-psychological research), and our interviews with HR professionals, we offer the following recommendations for practice.

1. Impart a Strong Organizational Performance Management Culture

For organizations to effectively manage employee performance across cultures, the performance management system should be directly tied to the organization's vision, objectives, and goals. To effectively do so, it is critically important that the performance management system has the support and involvement of top management. Top management should be involved in its development and implementation, and organizational resources

Exhibit 8.1 MNC Performance Management Interview Protocol.

1. What challenges or obstacles does your organization face when attempting to manage performance across cultures?
2. What "best practices" would you recommend to effectively manage performance across cultures? Any "do's" and "don'ts" that you could highlight?
3. Do you recommend one performance management system across different cultures? Or do you recommend different systems for different cultures? If you recommend different systems, on what attributes should the systems differ (for example, should the reward systems, training systems, or evaluation and feedback processes differ)?
4. Do you think that national or organizational culture plays a larger role in your organization's performance management system?
5. Does your performance management system (for example, training) explicitly address cultural differences? If so, how?
6. Can you provide a critical incident or two illustrating when culture influenced some aspect of your organization's performance management system (for example, when feedback, goals, or rewards did not operate as intended because of cultural difference)?

should be available to support every aspect of the performance management system (such as training, providing rewards). To strengthen the performance management culture of an organization, managers could be evaluated or rewarded based on their effectiveness of managing the performance of their subordinates. The importance of top management's explicit support for the performance management system may be especially important in some cultures (for example, high power distance cultures). For example, as one respondent noted:

> In many Eastern cultures, the CEO is the role model. If the CEO smokes, everyone smokes. If the CEO flirts, everyone flirts. If the CEO is serious, everyone is serious. So for Western companies going into the East, make sure you find a CEO who truly represents the

values of your organization and not just someone who is willing to take the risk of moving to China. Always get a person who is your best.

Another HR practitioner noted:

Organizational culture is often a bigger factor than national/geographic cultures. For example, the degree to which managers address conflict, hold individuals accountable, and promote risk taking is very driven by the organizational culture, and these values strongly influence how the performance management system actually gets used.

Top management members who impart the company's values and link these values to its performance management systems are critically important to the system's effectiveness. A strong corporate culture can attenuate the influence of national culture.

2. Develop an Organizational Theory of Performance

In addition to having an organizational culture that supports its performance management system, organizations should develop a shared theory of performance across the organization. Specifically, there should be a shared understanding of the type of behaviors, processes, and outcomes that are important and valued by the organization. Our respondents noted that developing an organizational theory of performance is considerably more difficult (and important) when its development is across cultures. As noted by one of our respondents, the very meaning of performance itself often differs across cultures. For example, he noted:

From a Western perspective, employee performance focuses on achievement and outputs, whereas from an Eastern perspective, often performance reflects the amount of effort the employee exerted. It is important to understand culturally why these differences exist. When you cut across cultures you have to understand why working hard should get a good rating instead of achievement. Coming from the Western world, in most organizations, the ground rules are laid and the infrastructure is there so that you can say your job is this, and therefore, I measure you on achievement because all the backup is there. You want a PC, it is there, you plug it in, and it works. You want access to

Internet information and it is there. Now, in certain companies in China, for example, effort counts because to get a computer on your table you have to go through so many red tapes, and to have it connected to the Internet, which is censored anyway, you also have to cut through the red tape, so for a very simple target for achievement you have to consider effort.

3. Do Your Homework

Prior to implementing a performance management system in different cultures, practitioners should be intimately aware of the cultural differences and sensitivities that may influence its effectiveness. Becoming aware of cultural sensitivities should involve spending time with, and preferably hiring, locals who will be more familiar with the local culture. Spend time "on the ground" to begin to understand the complexities of the local culture.

4. Translate Meaning, Not Just Words

A common theme across all discussions involving cross-cultural issues that is worth repeating is that the *meaning* of behaviors, beliefs, or words should be translated to facilitate understanding. The translation of meaning often is seen as one of the major obstacles to successfully implementing performance management systems across cultures. Two examples illustrate this point. As one HR practitioner noted:

> One of our core behaviors is "energizing others." Even though we developed the definition and the behavioral anchors (used for selection, assessment, and development) were developed with international employees' input, we found that in Latin America the word "energizes" is translated as "stimulates" and we had to make some local adjustments to the definition.

As another example, the word influence can mean very different things in a Western context compared to an Eastern context. As one respondent noted:

> In a Western context, influence can be interpreted as being political, but in China if you don't have guanxi, you don't have influence, then you might as well not be there.

This raises another important point that our practitioners noted—do not hire local people only because they are fluent in the local language and the language of the parent company. Rather, try to hire individuals who have an understanding of the subtle nuances of the different languages *and* cultures. In addition to translating meaning and not just words, several of our interviewees noted that the performance management tools (the electronic system) should be in each country's local language to facilitate the effectiveness of the systems and to "make the systems their own."

5. Hire Local HR Personnel

Initially it probably is important for organizations to staff the HR function with expatriate employees so that the organization's culture can be communicated and instilled and so that the performance management processes can be implemented. After all, locals unfamiliar with the organization cannot create the type of organizational culture you want because they will not be familiar with it. However, several of the HR experts we interviewed felt strongly that, after a period of time, the HR functions should be primarily staffed by local employees who will likely better understand the local culture, may be viewed as being more approachable by local employees, and therefore will be able to help your organization deal with cultural differences.

6. Use the Same System—But Allow Flexibility

All of the HR experts we interviewed suggested that a single, organization-wide performance management system should be used. After all, the system should be linked to the organization's culture, objectives, and goals, which are likely invariant across cultures. Importantly, given that employees frequently are moved from one location to another, the consistency of expectations and processes is important. One of our interviewees noted the potentially widespread implications of not using the same core performance management system across different cultures:

> Organizations need to have the same core principles and philosophies around the world. They also need to have the same standards for what high performance looks like. If you have too many differences, you cannot easily move talent around the world,

which has longer-term implications for the company. It also leads to losing great talent in the local countries because their career paths end at the country level.

Uniformity of the system should also enhance perceptions that employees are treated fairly across different cultures, although fairness itself may be culturally defined as mentioned above. Although a single system was advocated by our respondents, each of them noted that the system should allow for local flexibility. One of our respondents recalled an incident in China when a Western manager insisted that a local Chinese employee who was caught stealing be prosecuted in order to set an example that stealing would not be tolerated by the organization. The other Western managers agreed, the employee went to trial, was convicted, and was executed for the crime. This clearly illustrates an earlier point, that cultural differences in legal systems need to be considered with regard to how performance is managed across cultures. Another vivid example of when organizations may need to allow flexibility in how they manage performance is the case of Wal-Mart in China. Wal-Mart in the United States has a long history of resisting unionization; however, in China within a short period of time Wal-Mart was unionized.

7. Train All Users

Training users of performance management systems is important regardless of whether the system is used cross-culturally or not, but takes on added importance when implemented across cultures. Training users can help communicate and reinforce the organization's shared theory of performance, and, in doing so, clarify expectations. Training should include all users (raters and ratees) and should be used to clarify roles and responsibilities, to improve managers' ability to give feedback, to facilitate the completion of forms, and so forth. An important aspect of training is to demonstrate how the performance management system is aligned with other HR systems and the business needs and objectives of the organization. Another important aspect of training is teaching your managers how to manage the communication session—role play, rehearse, and provide feedback. If they are foreign, make sure they understand the nuances; if local, make sure they understand how to appropriately deliver the message. As one of our respondents noted:

> Some locals will water things down or sugar coat things. . . . Often managers in Eastern cultures find it difficult to give the tough message . . . and sometimes they have difficulty differentiating rough from tough because they believe if you are not rough you are not tough.

With respect to training, our respondents suggested two additional recommendations. First, the content of the training should be the same across geographical locations, but trainers may need to allow for differences in how the training is delivered (for example, in high power distance countries, managers and subordinates may need to be trained separately, whereas in low power distance countries, managers and subordinates may be able to be trained during the same session). Second, it was suggested that, when training in a particular region, employees from the same country/region be allowed to sit together so that they can communicate in their own languages and think about how to apply the learning back home.

8. Use Extensive Realistic Job Previews When Hiring

Many of our HR experts noted the especially important role that personnel selection plays in a cross-cultural context and the implications that hiring has for the subsequent performance management of employees. In particular, they noted that the use of extensive realistic job previews (RJPs) was critically important. They suggested using RJPs that explicitly address the organizational culture and its performance management system so that applicants can assess whether the potential cultural differences are something to which they can adapt.

9. Use International Representation of Leaders

Above we noted the importance of top management for imparting a strong organizational performance management culture. Similarly, our HR practitioners thought it was important to have company or HR leaders from various geographical offices involved in the planning, development, and implementation of the performance management systems. Involving an international representation of leaders ensures that global perspectives are considered and addressed and that a consistent organizational theory of performance is developed and integrated into the company's performance management system.

10. Consider Culture's Influences on Performance Management Activities

For the majority of this chapter, we highlighted how various dimensions of cultural values may influence the performance management systems of organizations (for example, goal-setting, feedback seeking). Our list of recommendations would be severely deficient if we did not recommend that these other issues be considered.

11. Don't Blame Everything on Culture

It is easy to blame everything that does not work as intended on culture when, in fact, the problems that arise may have nothing to do with culture. It is easy to misattribute daily misunderstandings, obstacles, or frustrations to culture, when in fact your boss may just be a jerk.

Summary and Conclusions

In many ways it is difficult to overestimate the role that culture plays in performance management in MNCs. At the core of performance management is communication, which can be a highly nuanced tool. As also discussed in this chapter, values are often culturally based. The values that individuals adopt with regard to what work performance means, how to provide appropriate feedback, and the proper forms of social interactions in organizations (among other things) are important and can vary as a function of national culture.

Having recognized the importance of culture in managing performance in organizations, we also need to note that sound performance management practices can help to alleviate the HR challenges caused by culture. Although more research is needed to examine this proposition, we believe that a strong organizational culture will override national culture in most cases. Nonetheless, understanding the potential influences of culture—both national and organizational—on performance and performance management provides a solid foundation on which to build the practices and processes for managing performance effectively in MNCs.

References

Aycan, Z. (2000). Cross-cultural industrial and organizational psychology: Contributions, past developments, and future directions. *Journal of Cross-Cultural Psychology, 31*, 110–128.

Bartlett, C. A., & Ghoshal, S. (1998). *Managing across borders: The transnational solution* (2nd ed.). Boston: Harvard Business School.

Cascio, W. F. (2006). Global performance management systems. In G. K. Stahl & I. Björkman (Eds.), *Handbook of research in international human resource management* (pp. 176–196). Cheltenham, UK: Edward Elgar.

Eggebeen, S. L. (2002). Going global: Additional considerations inherent in cross-cultural implementation. In J. W. Hedge & E. D. Pulakos (Eds.), *Implementing organizational interventions: Steps, processes, and best practices* (pp. 270–296). San Francisco: Jossey-Bass.

Gelfand, M. J., Erez, M., & Aycan, Z. (2007). Cross-cultural organizational behavior. *Annual Review of Psychology, 58*, 479–514.

Gelfand, M. J., Nishii, L. H., & Raver, J. L. (2006). On the nature and importance of cultural tightness-looseness. *Journal of Applied Psychology, 91*, 1225–1244.

Hofstede, G. (2001). *Culture's consequences: Comparing values, behaviors, institutions, and organizations across nations* (2nd ed.). Thousand Oaks, CA: Sage.

House, R. J., Hanges, P. J., Javidan, M., Dorfman, P. W., & Gupta, V. (Eds.). (2004). *Culture, leadership, and organizations: The GLOBE study of 62 societies.* Thousand Oaks, CA: Sage.

Lagace, M. (2002, December 9). Gerstner: Changing culture at IBM. Lou Gerstner discusses changing the culture at IBM. *HBS Working Knowledge,* http://hbswk.hbs.edu/archive/3209.html.

Milliman, J., Nason, S., Gallagher, E., Huo, P., Von Glinow, M. A., & Lowe, K. B. (1998). The impact of national culture on human resource management practices: The case of performance appraisal. *Advances in International Comparative Management, 12*, 157–183.

Morrison, T., & Conaway, W. A. (2006). *Kiss, bow, or shake hands: The bestselling guide to doing business in more than 60 countries* (2nd ed.). Avon, MA: Adams Media.

Peretz, H., & Fried, Y. (2008, August). *National values, performance appraisal and organizational performance: A study across 21 countries.* Paper presented at the Annual Meeting of the Academy of Management, Anaheim, California.

Schwartz, S. H. (1994). Beyond individualism-collectivism: New cultural dimensions of values. In N. N. Ashkanasy, C. Wilderon, & M. F. Peterson (Eds.), *The handbook of organizational culture and climate* (pp. 417–436). Thousand Oaks, CA: Sage.

Triandis, H. C. (1994). *Culture and social behavior.* New York: McGraw-Hill.

CHAPTER 9

MANAGING CONTEXTUAL PERFORMANCE

Richard R. Reilly and Zvi H. Aronson

The pace of organizational change in the 21st century is accelerating. Fueled by technology and globalization, networked structures are replacing traditional hierarchical models, and teams are becoming the primary organizational unit. Although the way that we work today is very different from the way we worked twenty years ago, effective management of employee performance is still a key to organizational success. Our rewards and recognition systems still focus primarily on task completion and goal achievement. But there is another side to employee performance that is equally important but often unrecognized and unrewarded. Contextual performance refers to activities that are not task- or goal-specific but that make individuals, teams, and organizations more effective and successful. Contextual performance includes cooperating and helping others, voluntarily performing *extra-role* activities, persevering with enthusiasm and extra determination to complete assignments successfully, defending the organization's goals, and adhering to organizational policies, even when this is inconvenient. These non-traditional contextual performance behaviors have become even more important with the advent of virtual teams and project-based work. Indeed, the notion of teamwork itself incorporates contextual behaviors.

A chemical engineer at Schering-Plough performing drug development/process engineering work explains:

> Contextual performance plays a huge role in multicultural teams. I'm currently participating on a multi-disciplinary, multicultural team spanning NJ–Puerto Rico–Singapore. Without contextual performance behaviors, the project would simply grind to a halt. We have to be open with each other, be able to share information/ resources, communicating/touching base frequently, and be active and prepared for meetings. We have to be willing to pick up the slack when needed—there is no room for "well, that's not my job." We are working for a common cause and that needs to come first. Without the citizenship behaviors, the team's activities would not be completed efficiently.

The literature we review for this chapter on contextual performance is guided by the model depicted in Figure 9.1. We first consider several important antecedents of contextual performance including dispositional variables, national and organizational culture, and leader behavior. After that, we describe the organizational, group, and individual level outcomes of contextual performance followed by affective outcomes. Subsequently,

Figure 9.1 Contextual Performance and Organizational Citizenship.

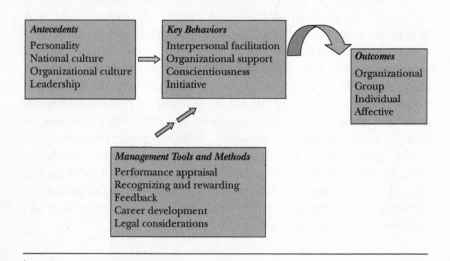

we focus on aspects fundamental to managing contextual performance including appraisal, recognition, rewards, feedback, career development, and legal considerations, and conclude with a related set of recommendations.

Contextual performance can be distinguished from task performance in several ways. First, task-related behaviors contribute directly or indirectly to the technical core, that is, the mechanisms by which the organization produces its goods and services (Borman & Motowidlo, 1993). Contextual performance, on the other hand, influences and supports the social and psychological environment of the organization, the environment in which the technical core operates. A second way to draw the distinction is to consider behaviors that are prescribed versus those that are not prescribed. Unlike behaviors typically delineated in a job or role description, contextual performance behaviors are discretionary behaviors that are less likely to be prescribed (Borman & Motowidlo, 1993; Motowidlo & Van Scotter, 1994). A final way to distinguish contextual behavior is in terms of the knowledge, skill, ability, or other attributes needed to perform those behaviors. Job-specific behaviors are more likely to be a function of knowledge, skills, and abilities (KSAs) and the KSAs should vary depending on the job. Contextual behaviors, on the other hand, are more likely to be a function of other attributes related to personality and motivation and are common across many jobs. As job descriptions become less meaningful and team-based work becomes the norm, the helpful, voluntary, and loyal behaviors involved in contextual performance should become even more crucial for organizational performance.

In an early paper, Organ (1988) introduced the concept of organizational citizenship behavior (OCB) as "individual behavior that in the aggregate aids organizational effectiveness, but is neither a requirement of the individual's job nor directly rewarded by the formal system." Organ and others initially viewed OCB as including five dimensions, but later work (for example, Podsakoff & Mackenzie, 1994) distilled the five dimensions into three categories: helping behaviors, civic virtue, and sportsmanship. Later, Borman and his colleagues (Borman, Buck, Hanson, Motowidlo, Stark, & Drasgow, 2001) proposed a three-factor model that included three categories of contextual performance: interpersonal support, organizational support, and conscientiousness initiative. Although the Borman et al. model is somewhat broader, the two models are closely aligned, as shown in Table 9.1.

Other researchers have also proposed models that include contextual performance (Brief & Motowidlo, 1986; Campbell, 1990) but all of the models describe patterns of behavior that are similar. Motowidlo (2000) suggested that the labeling issue is less important than careful definition and measurement of the behavioral dimensions that these behaviors capture.

As we have noted, contextual performance is particularly important in team settings. The interpersonal helping, job dedication, and initiative reflective of contextual performance help to make teams function effectively. The task interdependence characteristic of most teams requires cooperation. Sharing information and acts of helpfulness could be viewed as essential competencies for effective team performance (LePine, Hanson, Borman, & Motowidlo, 2000). Thus, cooperation and helping behaviors in a team setting are more likely to be viewed as task behaviors and be formally recognized as a part of the job. Stevens and Campion (1994) developed a model that suggested there is a set of interpersonal (conflict resolution, collaborative problem solving, and communication) and self-management (including goal setting/ performance management and planning/task coordination) competencies essential for effective team performance. These capabilities become important in team settings because of the increased importance of social and interpersonal requirements. Where job knowledge is paramount for successful task performance, teamwork knowledge should be important for successful contextual performance (Morgeson, Reider, & Campion, 2005). Thus, a job analysis conducted to identify the basic KSAOs needed for performance in a team setting should include both task activities and elements of contextual performance.

Antecedents of Contextual Performance

Contextual performance behaviors have several important antecedents, including dispositional variables, national and organizational culture, and leader behavior.

Table 9.1 Contextual Performance and Organizational Citizenship.

Contextual Performance Behaviors	OCB Behaviors
Interpersonal support includes helping others by offering suggestions, teaching them useful knowledge or skills, directly performing some of their tasks, and providing emotional support for some of their problems. Also, cooperating with others by accepting suggestions, informing them of events they should know about, and putting team objectives ahead of personal interests. Showing consideration, courtesy, and tact in relations with others, as well as motivating, and showing confidence in them.	*Helping behaviors* include helping others with or preventing the occurrence of work-related problems. Helping is the broadest category and includes behaviors related to altruism, peacekeeping, and cheerleading.
Organizational support includes favorably representing the organization by defending and promoting it, as well as expressing satisfaction and showing loyalty by staying with the organization despite hardships. Also, supporting the organization mission and objectives, complying with organizational rules and procedures, and suggesting improvements.	*Civic virtue* include behaviors demonstrating that an employee responsibly participates in, and is concerned about, the life of the company.
Conscientiousness initiative includes persisting with extra effort despite difficult conditions, taking initiative to do all that is necessary to accomplish objectives, even if they are not normally part of one's duties, and finding additional productive work to perform when one's duties are completed. Also, developing knowledge and skills by taking advantage of opportunities within the organization and outside the organization through the use of one's own time and resources.	*Sportsmanship* includes a willingness on the part of the employee to tolerate less than ideal circumstances without complaining.

Personality and Contextual Performance

Because contextual performance involves voluntary, discretional behaviors, some researchers have argued that personality and other dispositional variables will be more accurate predictors of contextual performance than cognitive ability (Motowidlo, Borman, & Schmitt, 1997). A meta-analysis by Hurtz and Donovan (2000) showed that conscientiousness, agreeableness, and emotional stability predicted contextual performance. The validities for conscientiousness and emotional stability were similar for task and contextual performance, but agreeableness had higher validities with the interpersonal support dimension of contextual performance. Research on team performance, which emphasizes contextual behaviors, has also explored the role of personality. Bell (2007) found strong meta-analytic validities for conscientiousness and agreeableness with team performance and somewhat lower but significant validity for extraversion.

National Culture

Hofstede (1984) defined several dimensions that describe national cultures, two of which have particular relevance to contextual performance behavior. *Power distance* is a cultural characteristic assessed by the influence that leaders have over subordinates. In high *power distance* cultures, leaders' influence is asymmetrical— leaders have much greater influence over subordinates. When power distance is low, influence is more symmetrical and both leaders and followers can influence one another. Paine and Organ (2000) note that in cultures characterized by low power distance, employees should view OCB civic virtue, helping behavior, initiative, and self-development as expected because authority and leadership are shared. In high power distance cultures, other contextual behaviors such as OCB sportsmanship—continuing to work without complaining and compliance—might be more common.

A second cultural dimension, *individualism-collectivism*, reflects an emphasis on one's own personal values and interests versus the interests and values of one's larger group. A collectivist culture should encourage contextual performance behaviors that benefit the group and view these behaviors as expected, normative, and part of the prescribed duties of the job. Lam, Hui, and Law (1999) found that OCB sportsmanship and courtesy were more likely to be perceived as required in collectivist cultures such as Japan and Hong Kong than in individualistic cultures such as Australia and the United States. Organizational commitment, another antecedent of OCB, should be high in collectivist cultures because of the importance of the "in" group in shaping perceptions of self-identity (Paine & Organ, 2000). Lower levels of OCB should be evident in individualistic cultures, which are characterized by loosely knit social structures in which individuals are responsible for taking care of themselves. In sum, in collectivist cultures, contextual performance appears to be part of what employees are generally expected to do—regardless of job description or prospects for rewards, other than honor within the group.

Organizational Culture

Organizational cultures can also influence contextual performance. Organizational cultures include behavioral norms that can be defined as expectations regarding appropriate and inappropriate behaviors (McGrath, 1984). Behavioral norms arise for several reasons: first, because of certain values shared by organizational members (O'Reilly, Chatman, & Caldwell, 1991); second, because they make working together easier and more pleasurable; and third, because they have been proven to be effective and efficient in achieving organizational goals. The development of such norms is often encouraged and reinforced by an organization to draw out desirable behaviors from its members (Cabrera & Bonache, 1999). For example, many organizations explicitly publish "corporate values" such as teamwork, integrity, and respect for individuals.

Leadership

The behavior of leaders can have an influence on the contextual performance of followers in a variety of ways.

First, leaders can help to *clarify expectations and goals*. Instrumental leadership (House & Dessler, 1974) stresses the importance of communicating what is expected of followers. Clarifying expectations can help to create behavioral norms that promote contextual performance behaviors. Transformational leaders promote OCB by encouraging the acceptance of group goals and promoting cooperation among followers. These behaviors should enhance employees' sense of shared identity and the likelihood that self-interests will be willingly abandoned for more collectivist endeavors, resulting in contextual performance behaviors.

Second, leaders' *interactions* with followers can shape contextual performance in a variety of ways. Research on Leader-Member-Exchange theory shows that high-quality exchanges tend to be associated with employee behavior that benefits the supervisor and goes beyond the formal job duties (Liden & Graen, 1980). Employees may be motivated to engage in contextual performance behaviors and perform at a high level to reciprocate for rewards and support provided by the leader. In a more recent study, researchers found that high-quality exchange relationships are related to altruism OCB, which corresponds to interpersonal support contextual performance behavior (Uhl-Bein & Maslyn, 2003). Research suggests that supportive leader behavior can increase employee contextual performance, as employees may feel the need to reciprocate for benevolent supervisor behavior (Podsakoff, MacKenzie, & Bommer, 1996; Schnake, Cochran, & Dumler, 1995).

Third, treating employees fairly and equitably can also create conditions for increased contextual performance behaviors. An example would be consistently recognizing or rewarding good employee performance. Fairness increases trust and role clarity, two keys to contextual performance (Konovsky & Pugh, 1994; MacKenzie, Podsakoff, & Rich, 2001; Podsakoff, MacKenzie, Moorman, & Fetter, 1990). Fairness on the part of the leader also motivates employees to demonstrate OCB because it produces a sense of unspecified obligation that is paid with OCB (Pillai, Schruesheum, & Williams, 1999), and it promotes trust and enhances employee confidence that contributions to the organization, perhaps in the form of contextual performance, may be rewarded in the future.

Finally, leaders can empower employees, which should increase contextual performance behaviors. As we noted earlier, decreasing the social distance between manager and employee leads to increases in contextual performance, but empowerment can also take place through shared leadership and servant leadership. Leadership in teams might be the domain of more than just one designated or emergent individual. Leadership in teams may be shared as members interact with one another. Shared leadership is a group process in which leadership is distributed among, and stems from, team members (Pearce & Sims, 2002). Leadership functions such as developing and mentoring other team members and performance management can be accomplished by distributing these functions to the members themselves. Shared leadership can result in an enhanced feeling of responsibility among group members toward the group, which ought to motivate these individuals to do all that is necessary to accomplish objectives, strengthening contextual performance behaviors, such as conscientiousness initiative. Also, because leadership is shared, members understand one another's roles and are more likely to know when help and consideration are needed during work challenges. Shared leadership, because it increases overall knowledge of the team and its goals, should also increase members' self-efficacy. This should translate into greater ability and motivation to generate suggestions for change.

Servant leadership is a different way of thinking about leading. According to Greenleaf (1997), the essence of leadership is recognizing that the leader has a moral responsibility to serve the needs of the followers, customers, and society, in addition to the needs of the organization. Servant leaders nurture and defend, as well as empower employees. They encourage their followers to take responsibility for their actions. Servant leaders establish trust by being honest and open with followers, behaving in a manner consistent with the values they espouse, and demonstrating trust in their followers. Servant leaders attend to the needs of their followers and help to develop their capabilities as well. As a result of these activities, employees should reciprocate by performing contextual performance behaviors. Interestingly, Ehrhart (2004) notes that followers of servant leaders are inspired by the model set by their leaders to become servant leaders themselves, and in consequence ought to display higher levels of OCB.

Outcomes of Contextual Behavior

Contextual performance can enhance productivity in a variety of ways (Podskoff & MacKenzie, 1997). For example:

- Interpersonal support, such as teaching co-workers useful skills or offering suggestions, may enhance co-worker productivity in the immediate situation and over time, as "best practices" are shared throughout work groups and departments.
- Interpersonal facilitation, involving cooperative and courteous treatment of co-workers, might aid in a manager's productivity by reducing time or energy spent on group-maintenance activities.
- Employee compliance with organizational rules and procedures allows managers to focus on tasks that do not involve disciplining or closely monitoring subordinates.
- Suggesting organizational improvements may give managers valuable feedback as to how to improve productivity.
- Individuals who exhibit high levels of conscientiousness may seek out new opportunities for new knowledge and skill development, removing some of the burden for employee development from the manager.
- Contextual performance can also contribute to customer satisfaction (Morrison, 1995). Conscientious employees go beyond customer expectations. Those exhibiting civic virtue would make suggestions to improve quality and customer satisfaction. Sportsmanship and courtesy create a positive climate among employees that spills over to customers. In terms of interpersonal support, altruistic workers would be more likely to help internal and external customers.

Organizational and Group-Level Outcomes

Podsakoff and MacKenzie (1994) found a significant relationship between contextual performance in 116 insurance agency units and objective performance measures, with OCB accounting for 17 percent of the variance in unit performance. In another study, employee citizenship in units of a restaurant chain was significantly related to revenue, customer satisfaction, and quality of service, even after controlling for employees' formally required job performance (Walz & Niehoff, 2000). Another study of a restaurant chain found that unit contextual performance was significantly related to overall profits (Koys, 2001). A study of 306 pharmaceutical sales teams found that teams with higher levels of OCB performance were significantly more likely to reach their sales quotas than teams that exhibited fewer citizenship behaviors (Podsakoff, MacKenzie, Paine, & Bachrach, 2000). Podsakoff, Ahearne, and MacKenzie (1997) found a significant relationship between several dimensions of OCB and productivity in a paper mill. A study of virtual teams (Sobel-Lojeski, Reilly, & Dominick, 2007) found a significant relationship between OCB and innovative behavior at the team level. In sum, the research evidence supports the relationship between contextual performance and important group level organizational outcomes.

Individual Performance

There is some evidence that contextual performance influences overall performance ratings (Motowidlo & Van Scotter, 1994; Podsakoff & Mackenzie, 1994; Van Scotter & Motowidlo, 1996). Moreover, contextual performance appears to contribute unique variance to overall ratings (Motowidlo & Van Scotter, 1994; Van Scotter & Motowidlo, 1996). Borman and Motowidlo (1993) suggest that the influence of contextual performance on overall performance ratings should be more pronounced in managerial jobs, since managerial positions do not contribute directly to the technical core of an organization, and differences between task and contextual performance components are not as straightforward as in other jobs. MacKenzie, Podsakoff, and Fetter (1993) found support for this view among thirty-two national sales managers in an international pharmaceutical firm. Contextual performance accounted for 37 percent in the variance in overall performance ratings, and objective sales performance accounted for only 5 percent. MacKenzie, Podsakoff, and Paine's (1999) study showed that contextual performance accounted for more variance in ratings of 161 insurance managers than for 987 insurance agents at an insurance company.

Taken together, the research suggests that contextual performance accounts for unique variance in supervisor ratings of employee overall performance, beyond that explained by task performance, especially for managerial employees.

Affective Outcomes

Organ and Ryan (1995) provided the most compelling evidence for a relationship between contextual performance and job satisfaction in a meta-analytic review that showed significant correlations between satisfaction and a number of different measures of contextual performance, although they were not clear about the direction of causality. In another paper, Van Scotter (2000) suggested that contextual performance should influence job satisfaction. Van Scotter found that supervisors' contextual performance ratings of Air Force mechanics had a unique influence on job satisfaction as measured several years later. It seems viable that, since contextual performance supports the social and psychological work environment of organizations, it should influence employee satisfaction; however, this idea has largely been ignored.

One explanation of why contextual behaviors might be correlated with satisfaction is reciprocity. Bateman and Organ (1983), for example, claimed that satisfied employees always seek reciprocity with their managers by performing contextual behaviors. Bateman and Organ (1983) offer two different conceptual frameworks for explaining why job satisfaction might influence contextual behavior. First, according to social exchange theory, employees will seek equity with benefactors by seeking to reciprocate. Satisfied employees may choose to perform helping behaviors that are valued by their superiors, but are not prescribed job requirements. The assumption is that, by providing satisfying work conditions, supervisors or employers are giving more to the employee-employer relationship than the employee can return through task performance alone. The converse may also be true, however. Contextual performance can be more readily withheld by employees who perceive that their supervisors or employers are not giving enough to the employee-employer relationship. The second explanation relates to positive mood states. Bateman and Organ note that social psychological experiments have shown that positive mood states lead to more altruistic behavior.

The relationship between contextual behavior and organizational commitment, reflecting the bond between the individual and the organization, has produced mixed results. Tompson and Werner (1997) and Schappe (1998) found a relationship between organizational commitment and contextual performance for samples of MBA students and insurance employees. Research at the team level (Ellemers, de Gilder, & van de Heuvel, 1998; Shenhar, Aronson, & Reilly, 2007) found that commitment was significantly correlated with contextual behavior. Other research (Morman, Niehoff, & Organ, 1993; Tansky, 1993) found no evidence of the organizational commitment-contextual performance relationship. These conflicting results were explained by Organ and Ryan's (1995) meta-analysis, which indicated that there is a low but positive relationship between organizational commitment and contextual performance. In another meta-analytic study, Organ (1997) used estimated population correlation coefficients of satisfaction, affective commitment, fairness, and leader consideration to estimate a latent variable of morale. He found support for the influence of morale on OCB, with an estimated path coefficient of .69.

In sum, the weight of evidence strongly supports a relationship between important affective outcomes such as satisfaction and commitment with contextual performance.

Managing Contextual Performance

As with all employee performance, there are several fundamental aspects to managing contextual performance including appraisal, recognition, rewards, feedback, career development, and legal considerations.

Performance Appraisal

Contextual behaviors can influence performance appraisals in at least two ways. First, based on the norm of reciprocity, supervisors might seek to repay employees for contextual performance by giving more favorable evaluations (MacKenzie, Podsakoff, & Fetter, 1991; 1993). Second, if managers have a schema (a mental representation) of a "good employee" that includes high contextual performance, then employees who demonstrate high levels of contextual performance will be more likely to be rated favorably. Moreover, because appraisal decisions often result in a search for distinctive information, discretionary contextual performance behaviors are more likely to be noticed and considered in the final evaluation (DiNisi, Caffery, & Meglino, 1984).

Organizations and managers should be explicit as to whether and how contextual performance is considered in the appraisal process for two reasons. First, failure to communicate the relative importance of contextual performance might create confusion among employees regarding the relationship between in-role performance, contextual performance, and performance appraisals and could lead to lower levels of performance in both areas. Second, explicitly clarifying how contextual behaviors are valued will have the added benefit of creating perceptions of procedural fairness among employees (Cohen-Charash & Spector, 2001), as the following example demonstrates.

J.P. Morgan (now part of Chase), a leading firm in the financial services industry, evaluates employees in their market risk infrastructure line of business on what are termed "themes." These themes include financial performance, control, partnership, and people. The partnership and people themes clearly reflect a variety of contextual behaviors related to the interpersonal support, organizational support, and conscientiousness initiative categories described earlier. Professionals and associates are rated on contextual behaviors related to teamwork, leadership, firm-wide commitment, and inclusivity, as shown in Table 9.2. The contextual performance behaviors that are appraised are clearly communicated and appear on the firm's intranet website.

A second example of how contextual behaviors are explicitly integrated into the appraisal process is provided by a global pharmaceutical company. An associate director told us that the firm understands the value that contextual performance brings in running an efficient organization. This organization incorporates contextual performance behaviors related to its company values into a 360-degree appraisal process. Each employee's direct manager, peers, and project team members provide specific observations on behaviors related to quality, integrity, respect for people, leadership, and collaboration. These observations are incorporated into the supervisor's overall performance rating of the employee.

Table 9.2 Sample of a Performance Appraisal for Investment Bankers.

Partnership

Professional
- Shares information, knowledge, and ideas that may help others succeed.
- Gives feedback directly to colleagues in an open and supportive manner.
- Demonstrates understanding of how own role impacts team's success.
- Collaborates with colleagues to accomplish team goals.
- Consistently responds to colleagues' requests.
- Shares credit with others.

Teamwork

Associate
- Works well with colleagues across different teams across the globe.
- Proactively improves or enhances relationships/partnerships within the broader team.
- Actively engages other team members to create a more positive environment and improve morale.

People

Professional
- Where appropriate, takes action on own, without waiting for direction from others.
- Speaks up with his/her own ideas or viewpoint.
- Persists and continues to strive for a goal despite obstacles and setbacks.
- Takes ownership of work.

Leadership

Associate
- Considered a role model by peers, colleagues, and managers in terms of pursuit of excellence and positive attitude.
- Actively seeks ways to take on new/additional responsibilities and challenges.

(Continued)

Table 9.2 (*Continued*)

Firm-Wide Commitment		• Seeks opportunities to help set direction or solve key problems where appropriate. • Influences and motivates others to express opinions and share ideas.
	Professional	• Participates in a firm-wide initiative, such as recruiting, training, task forces. • Participates in ongoing forums as appropriate (town halls, panel discussions, focus groups).
	Associate	• Plays an active role in training and developing junior members of the team. • Actively participates in firm-wide initiatives, such as recruiting, training, task forces. • Participates in ongoing forums as appropriate and frequently makes useful contributions (town halls, panel discussions, focus groups).
Inclusivity	**Professional**	• Considers diverse perspectives to get to best outcome. • Consistently treats colleagues with fairness and respect and helps provide opportunities for everyone to contribute and succeed. • Is engaged in recruiting, retention, or other efforts designed to attract and retain a more diverse talent pool. • Addresses non-inclusive behavior directly and constructively, seeking help from management if needed.
	Associate	• Mentors and provides honest and constructive feedback to diverse employees so they can develop.

Recognizing and Rewarding Contextual Performance Behavior

Colgate-Palmolive, a U.S. multinational corporation focused on the production, distribution, and provision of household, health-care, and personal products, such as soaps, detergents, and oral hygiene, has a program called "The Chairman's You Can Make a Difference," or YCMAD. The program seeks to recognize and reward the accomplishments of individuals and teams that have made a difference to the organization through their contributions and personal leadership. YCMAD is aligned with the three business objectives: Drive Growth; Fund Growth; and Make Colgate the Best Place to Work. There are three award levels: period, annual, and global, which are given in Colgate stock. Awarding stock was chosen as a symbol of the link between each employee's contribution and the company's success. YCMAD recognizes employee contextual performance in several areas:

- Actions that make their own or their colleagues' time, effort, and energy more productive, effective, and efficient
- Obtaining acquired knowledge and skills beyond current expertise
- Exhibiting high levels of initiative

The YCMAD programs are organized around a general set of guidelines provided by corporate headquarters. These guidelines apply universally to every local program, every country, and every participating unit, ensuring equal treatment of all employees. An essential requirement for the program's success is the visible support of the senior managers. An intranet site, including an operational manual, provides recommended roles and responsibilities for all program sponsors, notes a Colgate plant manager. The site provides detailed recognition and rewards criteria, capturing many contextual performance behaviors.

Another example of a recognition program was provided by a technical analyst for Verizon, who told us, "We do receive rewards (for OCB), but they are not monetary in any way. We generally receive two types of rewards. One is general overall recognition that the employees pass among each other. It is called the 'dolphin award,' and it is a stuffed dolphin because dolphins swim in teams and look after one another. Each teammate gets to keep the dolphin for two weeks, then passes it to the next team member of his or her choosing based on that team member's participation on the team. There is a bias with this reward because those working in the field are not generally recognized if they do not have much interaction with the team (such as myself)."

This last example raises an interesting issue for managing contextual performance. Not every employee has an equal opportunity to perform visible contextual behaviors. Employees who work collaboratively are much more likely to have such opportunities than employees whose work is by its nature less collaborative. Some workers who do not engage in highly visible contextual performance behavior may be unfairly denied organizational rewards when they are, in fact, highly valuable employees. Moreover, this lack of fairness is likely to be associated with the performance appraisal system being viewed more cynically, which, in turn, is likely to adversely affect workers' job attitudes and increase turnover. Thus, managers should collect information from peers, subordinates, and customers when assessing contextual performance.

Research evidence supports the influence of contextual performance on reward decisions. Kiker and Motowidlo's (1999) results suggest that both task and contextual performance contribute to supervisory reward decisions, with a stronger influence of effective contextual performance for employees with higher levels of task performance. Van Scotter, Motowidlo, and Cross (2000) investigated the relationship between task and contextual performance to both formal (rank) and informal rewards (for example, letters of recommendation, acknowledgements of good performance made in a group meeting, and recommendations to participate in development programs) over a two-year period in a sample of Air Force mechanics. Their results suggest that contextual performance accounts for unique variance in performance rewards and more unique variance than task performance in informal rewards.

Taken together, it seems reasonable that employees be compensated for engaging in contextual performance since these behaviors relate to organizational effectiveness and managers consider them when evaluating an employee's performance.

For example, McKinsey & Company, a global management consulting firm, ties bonuses to performance, including several areas of contextual performance: communication and interaction, teamwork, and attitude/initiative. Contextual performance behaviors include being punctual, good attendance record, flexibility—working past shifts to complete the job, working with enthusiasm, and demonstrating commitment, taking appropriate initiative, and showing great interest in learning new skills—willing to help out whenever need arises, following office etiquette religiously, and accepting feedback in a constructive way. Bonuses are awarded as a percentage of salary depending on whether the employee meets or exceeds expectations.

Rewarding contextual performance involves a couple of key challenges. First, it may be difficult to obtain a complete picture of an employee's contextual behavior. As a manager from a major telecommunications company observes, "In my team, we work in many different locations around the country. In a lot of cases, we primarily work from home. Many of our helping behaviors are limited by this distance variable. Since there is little face-to-face interaction, many on the team have no idea when another member may be struggling or has a heavy workload."

Even in co-located environments, altruistic behaviors might be observed by only one or two co-workers, for example. Other contextual behaviors, such as those related to sportsmanship and civic virtue, might be more observable and more likely to be rewarded. This may lead to an increase of behaviors that are more observable and a decrease in less observable behaviors such as altruism, courtesy, and helping.

One solution is a 360-degree contextual performance rating process, which would incorporate ratings from the supervisor, peers, subordinates, customers, and the employee.

A second challenge involves the impact of rewards on employee motivation. Behaviors that are rewarded become more salient to employees but may also shift the motivation for engaging in contextual behavior from intrinsic to extrinsic. This could lead to more impression management and even a decrease in contextual behavior if rewards are not available. One approach is to structure rewards around the team or unit level, which should encourage employees to engage in actual contextual performance versus impression management. Profit-sharing plans, for example, can encourage interpersonal facilitation and organizational support contextual performance, since remuneration hinges on the aggregate performance of the larger unit. Benefits are allocated equally to members or are based on some other criterion, but are not necessarily based on individual productivity. Such a program would be characterized by a loosely contingent reward system based on a person's total contribution to the group. Wyeth Pharmaceutical's PRIDE (Program Recognizing Initiative, Dedication, and Excellence) program rewards team and individual initiative, dedication, and excellence.

Feedback on Contextual Performance

Feedback is a subset of the available information in the work environment that indicates how well an individual is meeting his or her goals. It conveys which behaviors are desired by the organization and includes an evaluation of the quality of relevant work behaviors (London, 2003; Steelman, Levy, & Snell, 2004). The quality of feedback has been shown to lead to increases in contextual performance behaviors, especially in the area of interpersonal support (Findley, Giles, & Mossholder, 2000). Important aspects of the feedback session include the accuracy of the message that is delivered by the supervisor, the manner in which the message is delivered, the credibility of the individual providing feedback, and the perceived fairness of the message.

More broadly, the feedback environment, as opposed to the formal performance appraisal process, includes the daily interactions between members of an organization (Steelman, Levy, & Snell, 2004). Relationships between the feedback environment and work outcome variables such as contextual performance behavior were examined through the mediating effects of affective commitment (Norris-Watts & Levy, 2004). Results indicate that an employee's perceptions of his or her supervisor feedback environment were found to be related strongly to his or her level of affective commitment, which in turn was found to be related to contextual performance.

If supervisors are aware that the feedback environment in terms of their daily interactions with subordinates affects subordinate contextual performance behaviors, they can be coached to shape these interactions to elicit more desired behaviors (Norris-Watts & Levy, 2004). These individuals can be reminded to deliver: (1) credible feedback, which emphasizes the importance of the supervisor's expertise, fairness, and trustworthiness as a feedback provider—making sure the supervisor is familiar with the employee's entire performance on the job; (2) quality feedback—the consistency and usefulness of feedback. These individuals can also be made aware of (3) feedback delivery—the considerateness and tactfulness with which the feedback message is presented by the supervisor; (4) feedback availability—the amount of contact the recipient has with the supervisor and the effort the recipient needs to expend in order to receive feedback—whether the supervisor is usually available when the report seeks performance information; (5) favorable/unfavorable feedback—generally, letting employees know when they do a good job; making employees aware on those occasions when job performance is below expectations; (6) promoting feedback seeking—supervisors should be reminded that they should be consistently promoting feedback-seeking behaviors in their subordinates for development purposes—encouraging the employee to ask for feedback whenever the employee is uncertain about his or her job performance. Shaping the supervisory feedback environment in this way can benefit various aspects of employee performance. However, interestingly, it seems that creating such a supportive feedback environment is more strongly related to an employee's interpersonal facilitation contextual performance, which benefits other individuals in the organization, than it is to the remaining dimensions of contextual performance (Norris-Watts & Levy, 2004).

Research also suggests that mentoring may lead to increased contextual performance. Donaldson, Ensher, and Grant-Vallone (2000) show that variations in the quality of mentoring influence OCB. The authors note that mentors frequently serve as role models for altruism OCB, which corresponds to interpersonal support contextual performance, by being good mentors and providing support to their protégés. Their longitudinal investigation shows that employees reporting higher-quality mentoring relationships in terms of instrumental and psychological support reported engaging in higher levels of OCB altruism.

Career Development

Given the benefits of contextual performance to organizational effectiveness, it seems reasonable that managers should make promotion decisions not only on the basis of job performance, but also by considering employees' contextual performance. Interestingly, a recent study (Carmeli, Shalom, & Weisberg, 2007) found that employees who were promoted in their organization exhibited low absenteeism and lateness, had a greater tendency to work overtime, and performed their jobs better than those who had not earned a promotion. However, no evidence was found of differences in career mobility between individuals who displayed OCB altruism and compliance, corresponding to interpersonal and organizational support contextual performance, and individuals who were low on these behaviors. This may be explained by the intangibility and interpersonal nature of contextual performance behaviors. Absenteeism, lateness, and overtime are behaviors that are more tangible and measurable. Bergeron (2007) argues that spending too much time on OCB may disadvantage individuals when it comes to career advancement. She suggests that employees and the organization pay attention to the balance between the resources allocated to OCB versus task performance. Of course, this may also lead to some selectivity in the types of OCB that individuals may want to perform. Behaviors that are visible, likely to be reciprocated, and likely to be rewarded are more likely to be performed.

Conscientious, initiative behaviors are more visible and may be more likely to contribute to promotions. A technical analyst said, "To get promoted you are expected to work longer hours without pay, and you are also expected to be on call more often. They (employees in a higher level) are expected to take more ownership in their duties without having to be motivated by management."

Some of the employees we interviewed expressed more positive opinions about the relationship between interpersonal contextual performance and career advancement. One employee expressed it this way, "I personally believe OCB is beneficial in career advancement and have been utilizing it. In my line of work several members of other teams in different departments of the organization will come and ask for my assistance or knowledge on a topic. I gladly halt my tasks and help in the discussion and nine times out of ten work on the tasks they requested. This has provided me with strong working relationships with other departments within the organization. I have also been able to push some of my own projects into these groups and have received valid outputs. I also behave in this manner because I want to broaden my knowledge and experience within the organization. This knowledge and the relationships I am making will help me achieve my goal of career advancement within the company."

This statement shows that, first, when reciprocity is given, contextual behavior can actually contribute to one's own task performance and, second, that contextual performance can help build strong social networks that over time can benefit the employee in a number of ways.

Another employee at J.P. Morgan added that, since the guidelines for evaluating employees related to task and contextual performance appear on the company's intranet site and the behaviors vary by job title, people utilize the behavioral guideline information as a roadmap for development. Individuals utilize this information to see whether it is appropriate for them to request a move to the next job level. They can then use their contextual performance behavior information to their advantage during meetings with their managers. Similar to a behavior description interview, employees can be asked to back up their claims of engaging in contextual performance, by describing the specific situations in which they helped a colleague, for example, and referencing others in the organization who can verify this contention,

The J.P. Morgan example shows the benefits of clearly stating criteria for advancement. Employees understand that contextual behaviors are valued and can be proactive in appraisal and promotions discussions regarding their own contextual performance. Moreover, making the criteria explicit should enhance perceptions of procedural fairness with implications for satisfaction and commitment.

Legal Considerations

Effective management of contextual performance involves consideration of several legal issues. Performance appraisals, promotion decisions, and other decisions impacting employees are subject to scrutiny under a number of different laws including Civil Rights Legislation and the Americans with Disabilities Act.

From a Civil Rights perspective, the influence of contextual performance on adverse impact should be considered. Is a broader performance criterion likely to work against any gender, age, or cultural group? The research suggests little adverse effects of including contextual performance in performance ratings. No gender effects were found in studies reviewed by Organ and Ryan (1995). Graham (1989) reported that females were rated higher on the dimension of interpersonal helping, although the extent to which such differences were based on gender stereotyping was not apparent. Tompson and Werner (1997) found small and generally non-significant results for age and gender on task performance and numerous contextual performance dimensions. Research suggests that including contextual performance as part of job performance criteria will actually reduce adverse impact in selection since the predictors of contextual performance have little adverse impact.

From a logical and legal point of view, job analysis should be the foundation for most human resources management practices. Information from a job analysis is paramount for making decisions concerning selecting, training, compensating, and appraising employees. Decisions by governmental agencies and the courts have strengthened the notion that HRM decisions are required to be based on job-relevant criteria (Werner & Bolino, 1997). If performance is viewed as including both task and contextual performance, then job analysis procedures ought to be expanded as well. In team settings, the job analysis ought to include both task activities and elements of contextual performance. However, job analysis might work best in work environments in which the nature and content of jobs change slowly, as opposed to the dynamic environmental changes many organizations experience.

A critical incident approach to job analysis might be helpful in capturing contextual performance behaviors (Borman & Motowidlo, 1993). Some suggest that perhaps traditional job analysis and position description methods have not identified behaviors that are often important at the extreme high end of job performance, behaviors that are part of excellence in job performance (Schmidt, 1993). Others propose to differentiate between essential task elements of a job, those most likely to appear in a written job description, versus emergent task elements, which develop as individuals try to carry out their jobs in particular work settings (Ilgen & Hollenbeck, 1991). A similar separation explicitly documenting the task-related behaviors versus the contextual-performance elements of the job, at the individual, organization, and team levels, could be implemented by organizations that believe that contextual performance contributes to the effective functioning of the organization. In a parallel attempt, although for a different cause, many organizations documented the essential functions of jobs and separated these clearly from the more secondary job functions. Such a distinction followed the employment provisions of the Americans with Disabilities Act, which has been in effect since 1992. It prohibits discrimination against disabled individuals who can perform the "essential functions" of the job. Although space does not permit a thorough discussion of essential functions, it should be noted that, because many contextual behaviors are discretionary, they may not meet the standard of essential job functions as defined by ADA. Thus, ADA raises the interesting possibility that a person who is adversely affected because of contextual performance might have a case if the cause of poor performance was related to a disability.

Recommendations

Contextual performance behaviors are important for the well-being of organizations and the employees who work in those organizations. Contextual performance should be an integral part of performance management systems. Following are some specific recommendations that we offer based on our review of literature and our interviews.

1. Managers responsible for selecting or choosing employees for work assignments in which contextual performance is especially important should consider using dispositional measures,

such as a five-factor personality test, and selecting employees who score high on agreeableness and conscientiousness. An alternative would be to use an interview that incorporates the measurement of contextual performance through behavioral description questions.

2. For employees in other cultures, an analysis of power distance and individualism-collectivism can help to guide management of contextual performance. In high power distance cultures or individualistic cultures, special attention should be paid to promoting the importance of the group or other interventions that might reduce distance.

3. Contextual behaviors should be made explicit and should be recognized. They should become part of the appraisal discussion, and organizations should include contextual performance as part of feedback, coaching, and mentoring programs. Managers should be trained on assessing and providing feedback on contextual behaviors.

4. Managers should recognize the "context" in considering contextual performance. Some jobs offer little opportunity to demonstrate certain kinds of contextual behaviors, whereas other jobs provide ample opportunity. Appraisal, recognition, rewards, and promotional opportunities should strike an appropriate balance between the task demands and contextual performance opportunities in a job. Contextual performance should not be overemphasized at the expense of productivity or quality.

5. In assessing contextual performance, managers should be sensitive to impression management and should collect information using tools such as 360-degree feedback from peers, subordinates, and customers.

6. Organizations should think carefully about rewarding individual contextual performance. Group- or unit-level rewards should be considered as alternatives to individual compensation or bonuses.

7. Contextual performance should be considered in career advancement. Contextual behaviors are usually linked to explicit organizational values, and leaders who exemplify these values will be those who are high in the relevant areas of contextual performance. Thus, managers should be trained to

avoid ignoring contextual behaviors when considering employees for promotional opportunities or other assignments.

References

Bateman, T. S., & Organ, D. W. (1983). Job satisfaction and the good soldier: The relationship between affect and employee "citizenship." *Academy of Management Journal, 26*(4), 587–595.

Bell, S. T. (2007). Deep level composition variables as predictors of team performance: A meta-analysis. *Journal of Applied Psychology, 92,* 595–615.

Bergeron, D. M. (2007). The potential paradox of organizational citizenship behavior: Good citizens at what cost? *Academy of Management Review, 32,* 1078–1095.

Borman, W., Buck, D. E., Hanson, M. A., Motowidlo, S. J., Stark, S., & Drasgow, F. (2001). An examination of the comparative reliability, validity, and accuracy of performance ratings made using computerized adaptive rating scales. *Journal of Applied Psychology, 86,* 965–973.

Borman, W. C., & Motowidlo, S. J. (1993). Expanding the criterion domain to include elements of contextual performance. In N. Schmitt & W. Borman and Associates (Eds.), *Personnel selections in organizations.* San Francisco: Jossey-Bass.

Brief, A. P., & Motowidlo, S. J. (1986). Prosocial organizational behaviors. *Academy of Management Review, 11*(4), 710–725.

Cabarera, E. F., & Bonache, J. (1999). An expert HR system for aligning organizational culture and strategy. *Human Resource Planning, 22*(1), 51–60.

Campbell, J. P. (1990). Modeling the performance prediction problem in industrial and organizational psychology. In M. D. Dunnette & l. M. Hough (Eds.), *Handbook of industrial and organizational psychology* (Vol. 1, 2nd ed., pp. 687–732). Palo Alto, CA: Consulting Psychologists Press.

Carmeli, A., Shalom, R., & Weisberg, Y. (2007). Considerations in organizational career advancement: What really matters. *Personnel Review, 36*(2), 190–205.

Cohen-Charash, Y., & Spector, P. E. (2001). The role of justice in organizations: A meta-analysis. *Organizational Behavior and Human Decision Processes, 86*(2), 278.

DeNisi, A. T., Caffery, B., & Meglino, M. (1984). A cognitive view on performance appraisal process: A model and research propositions. *Organizational Behavior and Human Performance, 33,* 360–396

Donaldson, S. I., Ensher, E. A., & Grant-Vallone, E. J. (2000). Longitudinal examination of the mentoring relationship on organizational commitment and citizenship behavior. *Journal of Career Development,* *26,* 233–349.

Ehrhart, M. G. (2004). Leadership and procedural justice climate as antecedents of unit-level organizational citizenship behavior. *Personnel Psychology, 57,* 61–94.

Ellemers, N., de Gilder, D., & van den Heuvel, H. (1998). Career-oriented versus team-oriented commitment and behavior at work. *Journal of Applied Psychology, 83*(5), 717–730.

Findley, H. M. , Giles, W. F., & Mossholder, K. W. (2000). Performance appraisal process and systems facets: Relationships with contextual performance. *Journal of Applied Psychology, 85,* 634–640.

Graham, J. W. (1989). Organizational citizenship behavior: Construct redefinition, operationalization and validation. Unpublished manuscript. Loyola University of Chicago.

Greenleaf, R. K. (1997). *Servant leadership. A journey into the nature of legitimate power and greatness.* New York: Paulist Press.

Hurtz, G. M., & Donovan, J. J. (2000). Personality and job performance: The big five revisited. *Journal of Applied Psychology, 85,* 869–879.

Hofstede, G. (1984). *Culture's consequences: International differences in work-related values.* London: Sage.

House, R. J., & Dessler, G. (1974). The path-goal theory of leadership: In J. G. Hunt & L. L. Larson (Eds.), *Contingency approaches to leadership.* Carbondale, IL: Southern Illinois University Press.

Ilgen, D. R., & Hollenbeck, J. R. (1991). The structure of work: Job design and roles. In M. D. Dunnette & L. M. Hough (Eds.), *Handbook of industrial and organizational psychology* (2nd ed.) (pp. 165–207). Palo Alto, CA: Consulting Psychologists Press.

Kiker, D. S, & Motowidlo, S. J. (1999). Main and interaction effects of task and contextual performance of supervisory rewards decisions. *Journal of Applied Psychology, 84*(4), 602–609.

Konovsky, M. A., & Pugh, S. D. (1994). Citizenship behavior and social exchange. *Academy of Management Journal, 37*(3), 656–669.

Koys, D. J. (2001). The effects of employee satisfaction, organizational citizenship behavior, and turnover on organizational effectiveness: A unit-level, longitudinal study. *Personnel Psychology, 54*(1), 101–115.

Lam, S. K, Hui, C., & Law, K. S. (1999). Organizational citizenship behavior: Comparing perspectives of supervisors and subordinates across four international samples. *Journal of Applied Psychology, 84*(4), 594–601.

LePine, J. A., Hanson, M. A., Borman, W. C., & Motowidlo, S. J. (2000). Contextual performance and teamwork. Implications for teamwork. *Research in Personnel and Human Resources Management, 19,* 53–90.

Liden, R. C., & Graen, G. (1980). Generalizability of the vertical dyad linkage model of leadership. *Academy of Management Journal, 23,* 451–465.

London, M. (2003). *Job feedback: Giving, seeking and using feedback for performance improvement* (2nd ed). Mahwah, NJ: Lawrence Erlbaum Associates.

MacKenzie, S. B., Podsakoff, P. M, & Fetter, R. (1991). Organizational citizenship behavior and objective productivity as determinants of managerial evaluations of salespersons' performance. *Organizational Behavior and Human Decision Processes, 50,* 123–150.

MacKenzie, S. B., Podsakoff, P. M., & Fetter, R. (1993). The impact of organizational citizenship behavior on the evaluations of salesperson performance. *Journal of Marketing, 57,* 70–80.

MacKenzie, S. B., Podsakoff, P. M., & Paine, L. B. (1999). Do citizenship behaviors matter more for managers than for salespeople? *Academy of Marketing Science Journal, 27*(4), 396–410.

MacKenzie, S. B, Podsakoff, P. M., & Rich, G. A. (2001). Transformational and transactional leadership and salesman performance. *Journal of the Academy of Marketing Science, 29*(2), 115–134.

McGrath, J. E. (1984). *Groups: Interaction and performance.* Upper Saddle River, NJ: Prentice-Hall.

Morgeson, F. P., Reider, M. H., & Campion, M. A. (2005). Selecting individuals in team settings: The importance of social skills, personality characteristics, and teamwork knowledge. *Personnel Psychology, 58*(3), 583–612.

Morman, R. H., Niehoff, B. P., & Organ, D. W. (1993). Treating employees fairly and organizational citizenship behavior: Sorting the effects of job satisfaction, organizational commitment, and procedural justice. *Employee Responsibilities and Rights Journal, 6*(3), 209–225.

Morrison E. W. (1995). Organizational citizenship behavior as a critical link between HRM practices and service quality. *Human Resource Management, 35,* 493–512.

Motowidlo, S. J. (2000). Some basic issues related to contextual performance and organizational citizenship behavior. *Human Resources Management Review, 71,* 618–629.

Motowidlo, S. J., Borman, W. C., & Schmitt, M. J. (1997). A theory of some basic differences in task and contextual performance. *Human Performance, 10*(2), 71–83.

Motowidlo, S. J., & Van Scotter, J. R. (1994). Evidence that task performance should be distinct from contextual performance. *Journal of Applied Psychology, 79*(4), 475–480.

Napier, B. J., & Ferris, G. R. (1993). Distance in organizations. *Human Resources Management Review, 3,* 321–357.

Norris-Watts, C., & Levy, P. E. (2004). The mediating role of affective commitment on the relation of the feedback environment to work outcomes. *Journal of Vocational Behavior, 65,* 351–365.

O'Reilly, C., Chatman, J., & Caldwell, D. (1991). People and organizational culture: A profile comparison approach to assessing person-organization fit. *Academy of Management Journal, 34,* 487–516.

Organ, D. W. (1988). *Organizational citizenship behavior: The good soldier syndrome.* Lexington, MA: Lexington Books.

Organ, D. W. (1997). Towards an explication of morale: In search of the m factor. In C. I. Cooper & S. E. Jackson (Eds.), *Creating tomorrow's organizations.* London: John Wiley & Sons.

Organ, D. W., & Ryan, K. (1995). A meta-analytic review of attitudinal and dispositional predictors of organizational citizenship behavior. *Personnel Psychology,* pp. 775–780.

Paine, J. B., & Organ, D. W. (2000). The cultural matrix of organizational citizenship behavior: Some preliminary, conceptual and empirical observations. *Human Resources Management Review, 10*(1), 45–59.

Pearce, C. L., & Sims, H. P., Jr. (2002). Vertical versus shared leadership as predictors of the effectiveness of change management teams: An examination of aversive, directive, transactional, transformational, and empowering leader behaviors. *Group Dynamics: Theory, Research, and Practice, 6,* 172–197.

Pillai, R., Schruesheum, C. A., & Williams, E. S. (1999). Fairness perceptions and trust as mediators for transformational and transactional leadership: A two sample study. *Journal of Management, 25*(6), 897–933.

Podsakoff, P. M., Ahearne, M., & MacKenzie, S. B. (1997). Organizational citizenship behavior and the quantity and quality of work group performance. *Journal of Applied Psychology, 82,* 262–270.

Podsakoff, P. M., & MacKenzie, S. B. (1994). Organizational citizenship behavior and sales unit effectiveness. *Journal of Marketing Research, 31,* 351–36.

Podsakoff, P. M., & MacKenzie, S. B. (1997). The impact of organizational citizenship on organizational performance: A review and suggestions for future research. *Human Performance, 10*(2), 133–151.

Podsakoff, P. M., MacKenzie, S. B., & Bommer, W. H. (1996). A meta-analysis on the relationship between Kerr and Jermier's substitute for leadership and employee job attitudes, role perceptions, and performance. *Journal of Applied Psychology, 81,* 380–399.

Podsakoff, P. M., MacKenzie, S. B., & Fetter, R. (1993). Substitute for leadership and management of professionals. *Leadership Quarterly, 4,* 1–44.

Podsakoff, P. M., MacKenzie, S. B., Moorman, R. H., & Fetter, R. (1990). Transformational leader behaviors and their effects on followers' trust in the leader, satisfaction, and organizational citizenship behaviors. *Leadership Quarterly, 1*, 107–142.

Podsakoff, P. M., MacKenzie, S. B., Paine, J. B., & Bachrach, D. G. (2000). Organizational citizenship behaviors: A critical review of the theoretical and empirical literature and suggestions for future research. *Journal of Management, 26*(3), 513–563.

Schappe, S. P. (1998). The influence of job satisfaction, organizational commitment and fairness perceptions on organizational citizenship behavior. *The Journal of Psychology, 132*(3), 277–290.

Schmidt, F. L. (1993). Personnel psychology at the cutting edge. In N. Schmitt & W. C. Borman (Eds.), *Personnel selection in organizations* (pp. 497–515). San Francisco: Jossey-Bass.

Schnake, M., Cochran, D. M., & Dumler, M. P. (1995). Encouraging organizational citizenship behavior: The effects of job satisfaction, perceived equity, and leadership. *Journal of Managerial Issues, 7*, 209–221.

Shenhar, A. J., Aronson, Z. H., & Reilly, R. R (2007). Project spirit and its impact on project success. In R. R. Reilly (Ed.), *The human side of project management.* Newton Square, PA: Project Management Institute.

Sobel-Lojeski, K., Reilly, R. R., & Dominick, P. (2007, January 3–5). Multitasking and innovation in virtual teams. *Proceedings of the 39th Annual Hawaii International Conference on System Sciences.* Honolulu, Hawaii.

Steelman, L. A., Levy, P. E., & Snell, A. F. (2004). The feedback environment scale. Construct definition, measurement and validation. *Educational and Psychological Measurement, 64*, 165–184.

Stevens, M. J., & Campion, M. A. (1994). The knowledge, skill, and ability requirements for teamwork: Implications for human resource management. *Journal of Management, 20*, 503–530.

Tansky, J. W. (1993). Justice and organizational citizenship behaviors: What is the relationship? *Employee Responsibility and Rights Journal, 6*(3), 195–207.

Tompson, H. B., & Werner, J. M. (1997). The impact of role conflict/facilitation on core and discretionary behaviors: Testing a mediated model. *Journal of Management, 23*(4), 583–601.

Uhl-Bein, M., & Maslyn, J. M. (2003). Reciprocity in manager-subordinate relationship: Components, configurations and outcomes. *Journal of Management, 29*(4), 511–532.

Van Scotter, J. R. (2000). Relationship of task performance and contextual performance with turnover, job satisfaction and affective commitment. *Human Resources Management Review, 10*(1), 79–95.

Van Scotter, J. R., & Motowidlo, S. J. (1996). Interpersonal facilitation and job dedication as separate facets of contextual performance. *Journal of Applied Psychology, 81*(5), 525–531.

Van Scotter, J. R., Motowidlo, S. J., & Cross, T. C. (2000). Effects of task and contextual performance on systematic rewards. *Journal of Applied Psychology, 85*(4), 526–535.

Walz, S. M., & Niehoff, B. P. (2000). Organizational citizenship behaviors: Their relationship to organizational effectiveness. *Journal of Hospitality and Tourism Research, 24*(3), 301–319.

Werner, J. M., & Bolino, M. C. (1997). Explaining U.S. Courts of Appeals decisions involving performance appraisal: Accuracy, fairness, and validation. *Personnel Psychology, 50*, 1–24.

CHAPTER 10

USING PERFORMANCE MANAGEMENT AS A LEARNING TOOL*

Valerie I. Sessa, Christopher Pingor, and Jennifer Bragger

This chapter is presented as a case to demonstrate the changing needs of an organization and the role of an executive who is trying to facilitate and indeed lead this change. In this particular case, the organization is coping with changes of such magnitude that past successful business practices are now constraining the organization. To prosper, or even survive, it is becoming evident that the organization and the people within will need to transform. The executives in the case believe that instilling learning at the individual level into the culture is the key to transforming the organization. Although there are many systems within the organization that need to change in order to change a culture and transform an organization, this chapter highlights the role of performance management in making such a change. As the case progresses, we will present relevant literature so that the reader will understand the research and theory that are the foundation

---

*We would like to formally thank Christopher for bringing the three-phase performance management process to life by drawing Figure 10.1.

for how adapting the current performance management system can instill a learning culture into the organization. The goal of this chapter is to show how performance management can be adapted to create or strengthen a learning culture that encourages employees to learn adaptively, generatively, and transformatively. And as the employees learn and change and interact within and with the organization, the organization itself also undergoes learning and change—thus learning and change at each level are interdependent on learning at the other level.

Using a model of learning proposed by Sessa and London (2006) and London and Sessa (2007), we define individual learning as "a deepening and broadening of an individual's capabilities by adapting to meet changing conditions, adding new behaviors, competencies, skills, and knowledge, and developing into a more and more sophisticated thinking and emoting person through reflection on her or his own actions and consequences." Learning can happen in one of three ways. Most often, employees "adapt" to change. Something new happens in an employee's environment that causes the old way of doing things to no longer work. So with little or no conscious effort, they do something new. If it "works," they continue with this new behavior. Often there is little realization on the part of the employee or others that they have "learned." In some instances, employees recognize the change, anticipate the change, and even work to induce the change in their environment and thus "generate" learning. They respond by purposefully acquiring new knowledge, skills, behaviors, and competencies. In this instance, the employee and others recognize that learning has occurred. Finally, in rare instances, the environment changes so drastically that, in order to survive, the employee must undergo a dramatic and fundamental change in order to survive in the new environment, they "transform." During this process, people reconstruct the way they interpret reality. They develop a new understanding of themselves and their relationships.

As you read this chapter, you will note that we have emphasized looking at performance management from a different perspective. Rather than infusing this chapter with brand new ideas about performance management techniques, our goal is transformative learning, to reconstruct your way of thinking about performance management. Our hope is that what you will take away from the chapter are not "answers" but ways of looking at your own performance management system, understanding the learning it is currently calling for in employees, seeing how it is impacting the organization, and finally having ideas for tweaking, modifying, or even overhauling your system to encourage the learning desired.

The Case

Christine leaned back from the document she had been studying and sat back in her chair. She was looking at the report one more time before handing it to the CEO and top management team for them to read in preparation for the presentation that she and the vice president of HR would give on their proposed new performance management system to the top and middle management in the company.

The last few years had been exciting. She had been hired two and a half years ago in the newly created position of chief learning officer at PayRoll Services International, Inc. (PRSII). PRSII is a global organization with locations in North America (including most states in the United States), Europe, Australia, and parts of Asia. They employ over forty thousand associates. The organization was founded in 1956 when the founder noticed a need to provide payroll services to local businesses. The organization had since grown to become one of the largest suppliers of such services to small businesses as well as large corporations throughout the world.

The chief learning officer position had been created and Christine had been selected for the position because of a number of things that had been going on both inside and outside the company that had suggested to the CEO that organizational transformation was needed. Although PRSII was the largest company of this sort in the world at this point, with no large serious competitors, in the last few years they had seen a growth of local competitors—small agile companies that were willing and able to customize, at a lower price, services for companies in their immediate region. None of these companies was a threat at the international level. As PRSII had been focused on international growth, they had paid little attention to local competitors, but there were now enough of them across countries and regions to take serious notice.

The company did have great products, but it didn't have the capabilities of the smaller firms in completely customizing for each customer. The CEO believed that the company's strong performance culture, which had been successful in the past, needed to be changed to a learning culture—which is why he had created the position of chief learning officer.

From the very beginning, PRSII had had a strong performance culture. For example, when developing the performance management system that was in place now, the company had actually spent time defining performance and considering what it should mean for their organization. The definition that they had decided to use was "those outcomes that are produced or behaviors that are exhibited in order to perform certain job activities over a specific period of time" (Bernardin & Beatty, 1984). In developing the company and the systems within it, they focused on organizational goals and had tried to update various systems, such as the performance management system, to stay in step with company start-up, company growth, and, a few years ago, the exponential growth that occurred as they went international. They had also involved many of their employees in the development process of their performance management system, and had ensured that expectations around management and employee performance (outcomes and behaviors) were clear; exceptional performance was rewarded, and performance problems were addressed immediately and fairly (including encouragement, training, mentoring, confrontation, transfer, or removal). And finally, in line with the company, emphasis in the performance management system had been around creating efficient processes to get things done—and here, they had concentrated on effectively and efficiently delivering services and products to the customer (Wriston, 2007). The company was quite proud of the fact that it had a strong performance culture. Managers around the world liked to say, "PRSII is a machine; it has the control, coordination, and consistency to execute its tasks around the world." Management and employees had a strong shared knowledge base, mental models, and common beliefs on "how things worked" in the company. Structures across the organization were highly interdependent, and goals were clear. That is, until recently, when control, coordination, and consistency began to turn into restraint, complication, and uniformity. Shared knowledge systems and mental models felt more like being locked in, interdependent systems felt like being stuck, and goal orientation felt like resource constraints as the company needed to respond to the new environment (Beinhocker, 2006). This was when the CEO had pitched the idea to Christine that he wanted to change the performance culture to a learning culture.

That was where she came in and convinced the CEO and others that there may be a better way to proceed. Christine smiled as she remembered; she had been pretty bold during her interview with her ideas on learning and her vision for how to proceed with the company. Luckily, the CEO and her peers had been impressed with her ideas and had hired her. And the VP of HR had even joined with her to create an integrated learning and management system. But she had spent the last few years now trying to prove herself and her ideas.

Her first idea was that, paradoxically, the performance culture was too strong. A strong culture is great when the environment is stable and change is incremental. The environment had been stable until the company went international. However, a strong culture can get in the way in more volatile environments that require a more transformational change (Sorensen, 2002). Becoming an international company and the rise of so many new competitors at the local level had resulted in an environment that was arguably much more volatile than any the company had experienced until now. The performance culture had to be weakened, at least until the company could transform; then the performance culture could be re-strengthened as needed (until the environment destabilized once again, as it most certainly would in the future).

The second idea that she pitched to the CEO was to switch the "machine" metaphor currently used in the organization to a "living systems" metaphor. In her reading, she had been influenced by the work of Sessa and London (2006; London & Sessa, 2007) on living systems and learning. Living systems, whether individuals, groups, or organizations, exist to do intention bound work (Jacques, 2002). They (living systems) typically do not exist to learn, but they learn naturally as they work; they cannot help learning.

They learn by selecting goals, determining how to achieve them, and overcoming obstacles in the process. They also track their own progress and evaluate the outcomes of their efforts. Systems learn as part of this goal-oriented production process. While engaged in work, systems find themselves in situations in which the old way of doing things does not work—they are triggered to learn (whether and what triggers them is related to the system's readiness to learn), they learn what they need, and then they continue with their work. These systems learn as they work by exploring alternative actions and experimenting with behaviors and activities that produce a variety of outcomes. They learn as they adopt different goals, experiment with new behaviors, seek feedback, and try different ways of interacting.

Systems (whether individuals, groups, or organizations) and the environments in which they live and operate are constantly changing. Most times, systems are adapting to the environment and in some cases changing the environment. From the system's perspective, this is a constant process of maintenance, adaptation, and evolution as work progresses, obstacles are overcome, goals are achieved, outcomes are evaluated, and new goals are established (Capra, 1997; Laszlo, 2002). This evolutionary process may mean *adaptation* such as slight, often unnoticed changes in behaviors and work processes or a *generation* of new, creative behaviors, methods, and/or structures to improve performance. From a "living systems" perspective, however, sometimes the environment calls for a radical *transformation* so that the system takes new forms and produces outcomes that are amazingly different from what the system did before. Systems that fail to change, or that change in ways that don't work (don't recognize changing demands, overcome barriers, or address competitive forces), will fail, perhaps to die forever or to be reborn. In general, systems that thrive in constantly changing environments often re-create themselves, usually incrementally (as with *adaptation)*, but sometimes *transformatively*.

While Christine and the entire top management team agreed that the company did need to transform at this point to stay competitive (and perhaps even survive), what was unclear was the kind of learning that the employees within the company needed to do to help the organization transform. Did the employees need to *adapt?* Did they need to *"generate"* the new knowledge, skills, abilities, and behaviors necessary to thrive? Or in moving to a more regional team-based customer-responsive organization, did the employees also have to undergo *transformation?* Through discussions with the top management team, they finally agreed that they needed to inject a "self-learning" culture into the organization, which would require *adaptive, generative, and transformative* learning at the employee level to create the transformation they needed at the organizational level. The other questions they were struggling with are: "How can we appropriately trigger employees to learn?" "How can we ensure that employees are ready to learn?" and "How do we best support them while they engage in learning processes?"

Christine knew that it is important to engage employees in their learning goals. Telling employees what to do may cause them to push back. Employees want to make their own conclusions (Horvath, Herleman, & McKie, 2006; Rock & Schwartz, 2006). In cultures that promote self-learning, employees determine what they need to know and when they need to know it in the course of doing their jobs. This may mean that individuals are responsible for keeping up with changing technology or changes in industry standards as they engage in solving problems, improving work processes, or creating new products and services. In cultures that do not promote self-learning, employees are either informed what training they need and when or are given few opportunities, resources, or encouragement to learn. In self-learning learning environments, employees are ultimately responsible for recognizing their own developmental needs and assume responsibility for their own learning. To do this, they need to actively seek performance feedback for how they are doing currently as well as plan for future skill requirements; as part of this process they need to set development goals, investigate opportunities for development, evaluate their progress, and adjust their goals. And this needs to be an official part of their jobs, for which they are held accountable. For this to be effective, there needs to be a lot of organizational and supervisor support (Rodgers & Hunter, 1991). Employees need to know a lot about the organization—its goals, needs, directions, challenges, and future plans. They need to have resources, learning options, feedback, and rewards for both engaging in and using the new learning (see London & Smither, 1999, and Sessa & London, 2006) to name a few things. For PRSII to promote a self-learning culture, employees would have to engage in a transformation as they were expected to begin to take charge of their own learning. Employees at PRSII were beginning to be exposed to such a culture in a number of different ways. The organization was putting in place PRSII University, with an emphasis on action learning and online learning; they were encouraging the development of communities of practice. The performance management system being developed would be another link—employees would be expected to do, receive feedback on, and be rewarded for all that was listed above.

What Christine, the CEO, the VP of HR, and the rest of the top management team also decided was that, while a performance culture no longer served them well, a learning culture could also be fraught with problems. What they needed was a performance and learning culture. That is, rather than changing their strong performance culture to something else entirely, they could adjust it to include a self-learning component. This would handle the temporary need of weakening the culture (as they introduced the self-learning component) without losing the capability of quickly re-strengthening the culture when the time was right. They envisioned the following:

1. *Remaining focused on organizational goals*—but these were new goals that would help them respond locally. To do this, they were restructuring the rather rigid and top-driven hierarchy with fixed, functionally based divisions to a team-based structure in which teams were organized within countries, regions, and clients as needed. They wanted the teams to be able to expand and contract depending on what was needed, and employees could become members of multiple teams. This would more quickly allow teams to be responsive to customer needs.
2. *Increasing diversity within the company via self-learning*—and thereby changing employee mental models and knowledge.
3. *Integrating talent management systems*—recruiting and hiring, learning and development, performance management, succession planning, and leadership development.
4. *As part of the talent management integration, updating their performance management system to include a self-learning component*—focusing on identifying current and expected future gaps,

building skills and knowledge, AND the actual changes in behavior as a result of the learning. This would include putting into place learning-oriented goals, in addition to performance-oriented goals and learning performance support tools. They would continue to emphasize processes rather than outcomes, with an emphasis on innovation rather than efficiency. They expected that these changes would trigger employees to learn *adaptively*, *generatively*, and *transformatively*.

As this was quite an ambitious transformation in such a large company, Christine had tried looking for companies to bench-mark with. She wasn't surprised that she could not find a company doing the same thing as PRSII, but she had been able to glean learnings from a number of different companies.

Acxiom

One company that she had learned from was Acxiom, a data-mining company (based on Kiser, 2002). Like DPSII, Acxiom had struggled with how to be flexible enough to meet its clients' highly specialized needs. In this company, the top-driven chain of command was replaced by a decentralized, results-driven environment in which managers of individual business units now had considerable autonomy to make their own decisions and to be responsive to customers. Employees were assigned to work on teams that cut across conventional departmental lines to focus directly on major customer and business issues. While this company had also transformed as she was hoping PRSII would, what she had really gleaned the most from the company is how they "triggered" the organization, the employees, and the new teams to learn transformatively. They had gotten rid of titles and made it clear that employees could go to whomever they needed to get the job done, everyone was given the same size cubicles with an open format to maximize face-to-face communication, and the company had reorganized around teams that could expand and contract based on needs. The triggers for learning were strong, clear, and consistent across multiple channels. When the new decentralized team-based structure went into place, Christine was pretty sure that employees were quite aware that they weren't going to be able to work in the same way anymore, that they would need to transform in order to remain successful at Acxiom, and the direction that they needed to transform toward.

Seagate

Another company that she learned from was Seagate, a worldwide leader in the design, manufacture, and marketing of hard disc drives, and the 2006 *Forbes* magazine company of the year. Seagate worked hard to develop a performance-based culture to reward individual contributions and promote accountability throughout its immense employee base. They had also reorganized around market segments and had instituted a self-learning performance culture to help managers with the additional skill development needs stemming from the reorganization and other business needs. From this company Christine learned how they used a continuous, integrated, and online approach to performance and learning, which she thought really helped employees be not only ready to learn, but ready to learn what was needed by the organization. First, Seagate's entire talent management approach now breaks down into four regularly scheduled quadrants that create a continuous year-long cycle: planning, aligning, developing, and evaluating. Planning and aligning involve setting goals down to the individual job level. Next, creating development plans, succession management, and running reports also include their learning management system, which houses all the content that they have. Learning management, developed in conjunction with the Harvard Business School, again supports their overall talent management process, giving direct support and linkage. Evaluations are a big part of this: At the end of the year, all of this is rolled into performance evaluations. Managers with direct reports can always see their employees' goals, development, and measures (Warden, 2008).

The document Christine was poring over this morning outlined the new individual-level performance management system that she, the VP of HR, and several others had been designing for first- and mid-level managers. Performance management also encompasses other employees, teams, departments, and the entire organization, but those were for another day, although they would eventually all link together. Tomorrow she and the VP of HR would present the document to the top management team to discuss it, adjust it, and plan how to put it into place. She leaned forward to read the document. She had included a number of sidebars in the document with the basics and some definitions to make sure everyone was on the same page. Although most of the executives were well-versed in performance management basics, what was important here was understanding performance management from a learning perspective. She hoped that everyone would read them. The sidebars included:

What Performance Management Is and How It Is Linked to Learning

Performance management is the process whereby the organization continually assists its employees in setting performance goals, collecting information regarding performance from relevant sources, summarizing performance data to provide feedback from the organization to the employee(s) regarding their performance, and evaluating and resetting goals in light of their performance feedback. Thus from a learning perspective, performance management triggers and directs employees to learn via performance goals, raises their readiness to learn what is needed via expected future rewards, and guides them in that learning via feedback.

Why Companies Have Performance Management Systems

Companies use them for two reasons: evaluation of employees' performance and development of employees. Legally, performance management systems are necessary to provide business necessity justification for personnel decisions such as selection, compensation, promotions, demotions, layoffs, and firing (see Martin, Bartol, & Kehoe, 2000). Companies also use performance management systems for the development of their employees; the feedback gathered from managers, clients, customers, and other employees regarding employees' performance is used to facilitate awareness and learning about employees' performance and used to set goals for future learning.

The Incompatibility of Evaluation Versus Development

The two purposes of performance management can be incompatible. Knowing that they are being evaluated (and rewarded on that evaluation) can cause employees to focus on performance, as they want to be seen as competent and do not want to risk making mistakes or perhaps even failing. With this orientation, employees will learn by adaptation—change their goals—and they will find some way to reach these new goals. However, employees may be afraid to engage in either generative or transformative learning if there is a risk of failure.

On the other hand, knowing that they are expected to learn and develop within their job (and rewarded for doing so) can cause employees to seek out challenges to gain new skills and competencies, with less worry about whether they are immediately successful or not—they have a mastery goal orientation (Whinghter, Cunningham, Wang, & Burnfield, 2008). Employees with a mastery goal orientation are more open to generative and possibly transformative learning.

Therefore, it is useful to diverge and converge these separate purposes over the course of the performance management cycle.

How Performance Management Affects Learning

Christine leaned back again. She wanted to instill the idea in her peers and the CEO that, while performance management was a system that could encourage learning within individuals, it actually was also a PART of the learning occurring at the organizational level—the organization would "learn" with the new performance management system as well. Performance management triggers a "system" to learn by providing goals to meet. And it provides feedback to the system regarding whether those goals are being met. Feedback is crucial in the living systems model. Without feedback, a living system can change, but it cannot learn. Without feedback, a system cannot determine the extent to which it is moving toward its goals, or whether it needs to change in some way to achieve those goals (or even change the goals themselves).

Christine thought that two things had to be kept in mind about feedback: When and how often should feedback occur? If there is too long between a change and feedback, then the link may actually be broken. For example, if an employee is trying to change her or his behavior to be more in line with the goals of the organization, but only receives feedback once a year, the employee may react by trying something new and not repeating it, engaging in the new behavior sporadically (but not knowing if it is working or not), or doing more and more of that behavior assuming it is working. During learning, there is a detriment in performance. If feedback is given too soon, the employee may lose confidence in trying out new behaviors (Sessa & London, 2006).

Christine continued to read her presentation:

Current Performance Management System

PRSII has been using management by objectives (MBO) since the very inception of the organization when Peter Drucker himself spoke to the organization's top executives. MBO encourages the participation by all managers at all levels of the organization, which serves two functions: first, there is commitment from top executives which increases the effectiveness of the MBO system (Rodgers & Hunter, 1991), and second, this helps ensure that goals that are set at lower levels will be aligned toward the larger organizational goals (as each lower level can use the next higher level to help determine goals). Managers set goals for themselves and their subordinates to achieve over a specific time period. These goals are based on organizational strategy, departmental needs, and from all participants that the manager relates to (including customers when appropriate). Managers receive feedback throughout the year based on perceptions of how well they are meeting the goals. In addition, goals are also periodically assessed and may be altered. Finally, MBO is concerned with the outcomes or results or goals and not necessarily the pathway (that is, the behavior) to the goals.)

(Continued)

GOALS OF THE PROPOSED PERFORMANCE MANAGEMENT SYSTEM

1. Keep the traditional performance management system with some modifications: Manager and supervisor are responsible for setting goals. Supervisor is responsible for *evaluating* achievement of yearly goals. Understand that this portion of the performance management system drives performance goal orientation and adaptive learning.

   a. Anyone supervising others would be asked to include a performance goal regarding his or her behaviors, learning, and outcomes around performance appraisals on his or her own performance appraisal, encouraging adaptive learning to seriously engage in the performance management system.

   b. Support learning through access to and reward for using PRSII's online learning modules on the company strategy, goals, and objectives; how to create departmental and individual goals; how to develop MBO plans; how to assess accurately; and how to give feedback that anyone in the company could access.

   c. VP of human resources will gather MBO goals and objectives at the beginning of the cycle and the extent to which the goals and objectives were met at the end of the cycle to develop various reports at different organizational levels to determine what goals and objectives were being set and whether and how they were being met.

2. Add a new component to the performance management system: a self-learning component. Based on MBO goals set between the manager and her or his supervisor, the manager, along with her or his learning development coordinator, will develop a separate set of learning goals that will eventually fold back into the traditional MBO system. Understand that this portion of the performance management system drives a mastery orientation and generative and transformative learning.

   a. The focus is on engaging employees in self-learning by having them take control of their own learning. Employees self-identify the need for learning on the generative and transformational level that will result in personal and organizational growth. They will be held accountable for their learning to themselves and their learning development coordinators as they progress through the learning process. They may be rewarded for progress in reaching learning goals, but will not be "punished" for lack of progress.

b. Chief learning officer will gather reports from learning development coordinators to develop various reports at different organizational levels on learning processes engaged in and learning outcomes reached to track organizational learning and assess effectiveness.

c. Chief learning officer and VP of human resources would be able to determine performance, including learning, performing, and outcome effectiveness. These reports will help guide the full integration of talent management systems. These reports will also give an ongoing snapshot of how the performance management system was working and where modification might be needed.

DISCUSSION QUESTIONS

- What is the appropriate balance of performing, learning, and effectiveness in the performance management system? How do we emphasize learning without undercutting the importance of performance and effectiveness?

- How do we ensure that managers and their supervisors have the time required to properly collect performance feedback and conduct performance interviews?

- How do we help managers get the qualitative and quantitative information they need to make useful and accurate assessments?

- How do we create an environment of trust such that managers are open to revealing learning gaps and weaknesses in order to fully develop their potential and facilitate organizational development and change?

Christine recalled: Traditionally, in performance management, employees and their managers define goals and tasks to reach these goals based on what the organization is asking them to emphasize. They compare the goals and tasks with perceptions of progress—typically at the end of the yearly cycle. If a discrepancy exists between the perception and the goal, the employee attempts to reduce the discrepancy by applying resources toward the accomplishment of the goal or altering the goal (see Vancouver, 1997).

The learning occurring in this scenario is adaptive and very powerful. It is often incremental and unnoticed or unconscious. Employees and their managers alike do not recognize that learning is occurring. In performance management, feedback reinforces and controls the goals and behaviors targeted—"you get what you measure." Systems react to feedback by continuing to do what is reinforced and discontinuing doing what is not reinforced. In performance management, employees and their managers set goals based on organizational strategies, needs of the department, and so forth. But unless employees are reinforced for their performance-related behaviors via some sort of feedback, the goals, strategies, and needs will have little actual impact on the employees' actual behavior (Kerr, 1995; Luthans & Stajkovic, 1999).

The VP of HR had also reminded Christine that it is often the case that organizations and managers reinforce behaviors and outcomes that they do not want, and that they are not even aware that they are doing so. For instance, in many situations, organizations verbally indicate that they want to see team-oriented behaviors and cooperation, but their performance management system is rewarding individual performance and competition, which results in the "wrong" kind of learning.

"Okay," Christine thought, "the new part encourages *generative* learning. *Generative* learning is proactively learning and applying new skills, knowledge, and behavior to improve performance. This type of learning is purposeful. When employees have a goal or see the need, they will attend training programs, earn degrees, observe others, or do whatever it takes to keep their behaviors, knowledge, and skills up-to-date with what is needed in their jobs (or next job), their organizations, their professions, or even their lives. When this type of self-learning works well, changes and improvements in performance can be measured and tracked. A potential downside of encouraging self-learning is that individuals may engage in learning that is not linked to business needs. In addition, if reinforced improperly, individuals may begin to spend too much time on learning and not enough time on performing. However, individuals who successfully balance learning and performance are able to face an uncertain future and handle emergencies that may arise as continuous "just in time" learning becomes a habit.

And the new part of the performance management system will also hopefully add *transformative* learning (as needed). When employees engage in *transformative* learning, they undergo a dramatic and fundamental change in the way they see themselves and the organization—and even the world in which they interact (see Sessa & London, 2006). At Acxiom, employees needed to transform from working in a more rigid hierarchy with well-defined roles to a team-based structure in which employees might be called on to take multiple roles on different teams as needed. Christine thought, "Our employees will have to transform this way as well. They will also have to transform to take control of their own learning." Potential downsides of transformative learning include the potential performance deficits that occur while transformation is taking place, knowing when to stop the transformation process and concentrate on performing, and the risk that the transformation may not be successful. Transformations are not to be engaged in lightly.

Christine began to read again:

Further description of new addition to the performance management system, creating two loosely connected systems:

1. Chief learning officer with learning coordinators are responsible for assisting managers with developmental plans. Each learning coordinator will serve a number of PRSII employees.
   a. Manager creates own learning plan (for the coming year) based on MBO created with supervisor, with assistance

(Continued)

---

of a learning coordinator. This learning plan is related to but separate from the MBO plan created with supervisor. The learning plan will focus on the learning components necessary to reach current performance goals and to grow in order to meet future performance and career goals.

b. Learning coordinator helps manager identify areas of learning through the use of 360-degree feedback and other mechanisms, helps choose methods for addressing areas of learning, helps guide the manager in the learning, and helps manager decide how to evaluate self in the learning.

c. Manager develops plan, communicates plan to relevant others, is responsible for following plan and evaluating self. Meets with learning coordinator throughout year as needed to assess and alter plan and gain information necessary to reach learning goals.

d. Information is collected regarding progress toward learning goals (training attended, books read, sources sought out) at the end of the year. Learning coordinator assists in this. Together the manager and the learning coordinator create a report identifying amount and type of learning that occurred.

e. The direct supervisor is given the report to identify amount/type of learning that occurred. Supervisor uses input in performance evaluation at the end of the cycle.

DISCUSSION QUESTIONS

- Who should be the learning coordinators? The learning coordinators can be employees who work for the organization who have special training in organizational learning and development but who will remain separate from employees responsible for other personnel functions OR can be consultants with special training in organizational learning and development.
- How can we do this economically?

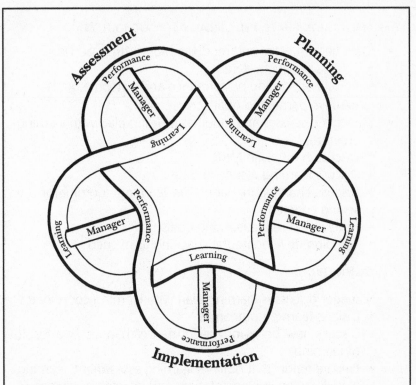

Figure 10.1 The Three-Phase Performance Management Process.

PLANNING PHASE

- Manager creates MBO with Supervisor
  - Set goals
  - Set performance objectives
  - Set performance outcomes needed to reach goals
  - Establish resources needed to meet objectives and goals
  - Identify supports and barriers to achieving goals
- Manager creates learning plan with learning coordinator
  - Discuss goals, performance, and outcomes as set in performance appraisal with supervisor
  - Identify areas of learning
  - Develop learning plan

(Continued)

Implementation Phase, Periodically Throughout Year

- Manager discusses and modifies MBO with supervisor:
  - Discuss results to date
  - Review and refine performance and outcome goals
  - Remove barriers to goal achievement
- Manager discusses and modifies learning plan with learning coordinator
  - Discuss changes in MBO
  - Discuss learning results to date
  - Discuss changes manager and learning coordinator are seeing enacted
  - Review and refine learning goals
  - Ongoing developmental coaching as needed

Assessment Phase

- Manager discusses learning plan with learning coordinator
  - Discuss learning outcomes
  - Discuss new behaviors/performance/changes as a result of learning
  - Prepare report that outlines learning assessment, learning plan, learning implementation, and learning outcomes
- Manager discusses MBO and learnings with supervisor
  - Discuss and obtain feedback on performance and outcomes, whether they met goals and objectives
  - Discuss and obtain feedback on learning outcomes and how learning outcomes impacted performance and outcomes
  - Discuss possible "environmental constraints" (for which there is documented evidence) that might be constraining performance and discuss how to deal with these constraints
  - Discuss performance and learning goals to prepare for implementation for next performance period

---

Christine sat back. Would this work? The one thing that she really took from her understanding of living systems was that an "outsider" can never direct a living system to learn. He or she can only "disturb" the system's status quo with hopes that the stimulation would trigger learning and could support the system during the learning process. The living system determines which triggers warrant a response. Teachers, consultants, facilitators, mentors, coaches, development coordinators, and other parties can impose triggers, provide needed resources, give feedback, and reinforce learning in the direction that the organization needs, but they cannot make the learning occur, predict what will be learned, or even make the system use what it learns. She and the top management team had to be open to unintended consequences of all the changes they were making. The final part of her report went into considerable detail regarding keeping the change on track and assessing their progress. She had found diagnostic tools in London and Sessa (2007) to help:

Evaluating Our Progress So Far

1. What is happening? Transform the structure and culture of the company.
   a. Our focus remains on organizational goals. But these are new goals that will help us respond locally. This includes restructuring to a responsive and fluid team-based structure at a country, regional, or client level.
   b. We are integrating talent management systems.
   c. We are incrementally updating the performance management system to incorporate generative and transformative learning by introducing a separate learning component.
2. In what directions are the forces for learning and change?
   a. The top management team is the initial force for the change.
   b. Changes are being made at the organizational level, but requiring individuals to adopt new roles and new work patterns as well as take control of their own learning. This could result in some bottom-up forces (as yet unidentified) as well.
3. Which system characteristics are affecting "readiness to learn"?
   a. Employees are being expected to be open to new ideas, roles, and goals. They need to be open to a changing

(Continued)

---

culture that is decentralizing both their roles and their learning to be more under their own control to the degree that this fits in with organizational goals.

b. At the organizational level, we are creating new reports on learning, performance, and outcomes to help guide higher level strategic initiatives.

4. What factors are barriers to learning and change?

a. A huge barrier is that, despite competition, the company is still successful and growing its markets. It has a strong performance culture that is entrenched throughout the organization. Employees who have been successful in the current culture would have to unfreeze, learn, and refreeze into the new culture.

5. Which factors are facilitators of learning?

a. The triggers are strong, clear, and consistent across multiple channels—for example, we are aligning our entire talent management system.

b. Readiness to learn is being stimulated by new goals.

c. The organization is putting resources into place to support learning.

d. The feedback channels and reinforcements are being put into place to support learning.

6. What are the external and internal forces for learning?

a. Competitors are the external forces for transforming the organization.

b. The organizational changes are forces on the individual employees.

c. Employee willingness to accept new patterns of working, new goals, new expectations, and new reinforcements are also forces that need to be addressed.

7. What types of learning are needed?

a. The organization is engaged in transformative learning as it restructures to meet changing environmental needs.

b. Employees need to engage in *adaptive* (via the performance management system), *generative* (via the new goals in the performance management system), and *transformative* learning (via the new roles they are expected to take on).

8. What is happening?

That, Christine, the organization, and the employees would see within the next year. They would need to track how well the process is working and to revise the process depending on evidence of its value. Christine thought there might be three possibilities that they would need to deal with:

1. Managers don't take the new learning system seriously. They maintain a strong performance goal orientation and adapt to the learning system by going through the motions but not actually becoming self-learners and engaging in generative and transformative learning.
2. Managers get overly involved in the learning system. They lose their performance goal orientation and concentrate solely on mastery goal orientation. Individuals engage in learning for learning's sake, they spend too much time on learning, and do not link it to business needs. Not enough time is spent on performance, and performance deficits are thus greater than expected.
3. Managers strike a good balance between learning and performance. Managers maintain both a performance goal orientation and a mastery goal orientation. There is some detriment in performance, but as the learning is directed around needs, the detriments tend to disappear.

Conclusion

We leave this fictitious case early in the story. The company is in the idea stage; nothing has yet been implemented. Would it work exactly "as planned"? Probably not, as changes of this nature calling for multiple kinds of learning at multiple levels within an organization tend to have complex and unintended consequences. People can respond to the same triggers in markedly different and unexpected ways. And learning at the individual level can be "effective" for the individuals involved but not necessarily what was expected or desirable at the organizational level. But it would "work" in some form, and with use, assessment, and modification, it could work in a way that would fit or even change the needs of the organization.

The intention behind writing this chapter was not to suggest to human resource professionals how to do performance management in their own organizations. Rather, our intention was to provide a different perspective on performance management with the goal of transforming how we view the organization, employees, and, in particular, the performance management system.

We introduced the idea that there are three kinds of learning: adaptive, generative, and transformative, and how performance management impacts that learning. Performance management systems powerfully impact adaptive learning, often in unintended ways. But with planning, they can encourage and drive generative and transformative learning as well. In this particular case, we suggested that one way of encompassing generative and transformative learning into the performance management system is to separate learning goals from performance and effectiveness goals. But that certainly isn't the only option—what would work in PRSII isn't necessarily the right path for other organizations.

We also discussed how learning at the individual level is impacted by and impacts the organization. In this case, organizational needs were driving change in organizational systems that would impact individual learning, which would in turn lead back to organizational change. This case demonstrates the complexities of how all the systems within the organization are intertwined and how changing one has a broad influence across the organization.

To help in the next step, looking at your own performance management system, we provide two lists. The first includes questions to help you assess what kind of learning is taking place using the current performance management system. The second includes questions to help guide you to change or develop a performance management system that includes the types of learning needed by the organization.

Questions to Help You Assess the Kind of Learning Taking Place in the Current System

What kind of learning does your current performance management system encourage now?

Triggers for Learning

- How closely is the current performance management system integrated into the mission, strategy, goals, and culture of the organization?

- What is emphasized in the performance management system? Do employees have goals for learning, behaviors, and/or outcomes? What is the balance between the three?
- How often do employees receive feedback? What form does the feedback take? What does the feedback emphasize? What do employees get feedback on? Who (or what) provides the feedback? Is feedback for performance or learning purposes?
- How are employees rewarded and what are they rewarded on? What are they "punished" for doing/not doing? What is not rewarded that you think should be rewarded? What is "punished" that you think should not be punished? (Remember to think about informal and often unintended reward and punishment structures. Often we provide organizational contingencies that we are not even aware of.)

Readiness to Learn

- How seriously is the performance management system taken within the organization? By top management? By managers?
- How is the performance management system currently being used? Is it being used for evaluation purposes? For development purposes? For both? (For neither?)
- Given the design and use of the performance management system, is it encouraging a performance goal orientation, a mastery goal orientation, neither, or both?
- What role do managers play in the development of their own performance management? What kind of input do they have?
- Can and under what conditions can performance goals be renegotiated?
- What resources do managers have at their discretion for learning?

Processes and Outcomes for Learning

- What type(s) of learning are called for in the performance management system?
- What is the climate for learning in the organization? Is upper management supportive of a truly learning culture?
- Are employees rewarded for trying new behaviors and risk taking? What happens if an otherwise well-regarded employee

demonstrates a detriment in performance or makes a mistake or fails at something?

- How are engagement in learning and learning outcomes evaluated in the performance management system?

Questions to Help Imbue Performance Management Systems with Learning

Triggers for Learning

- What is happening in the organization (new or changing mission, goals, strategy, and/or culture)?
- What is happening in the outside world (competitors, changing environment, new laws or policies, other)?
- What kind of change will the organization need?
- What direction must the organization go?
- In order to change the organization, what type(s) of employee learning are needed (adaptive, generative, or transformative)?
- How is the performance management system being changed to address organizational changes and type of learning called for?
- How are other systems within the organization being changed to address these changes and the type of learning called for?
- How closely are the current performance management system and other systems integrated into the changing mission, strategy, goals, or culture of the organization?
- What should be emphasized in the performance management system? Are there goals for learning, behaviors, and/or outcomes? What is the balance among the three?
- Are individual-level goals clearly linked back to the organizational needs?
- How often do you want employees to receive feedback? What form will the feedback take? What will the feedback emphasize? What will managers receive feedback on? Who (or what) will provide the feedback? Will feedback be for performance or learning purposes? If for both, how will this be handled?
- How will employees be rewarded and what will they be rewarded on? Will they be rewarded in some ways for taking the performance management system seriously?

Readiness to Learn

- How will organization goals, needs, directions, challenges, future plans, and so forth be communicated to employees? Will this communication occur in multiple formats?
- How are employees learning about how they fit into the organization, how what they do impacts the organization?
- How will employees be included in the development, assessment, and adjustment of their learning, performance, and outcome goals? What is their role? What is the extent to which they determine the kind of learning they need?
- How will employees be held responsible for determining what they need to know in the course of doing their jobs and preparing for the future?
- What support will be available to encourage employees to assess their own capabilities?
- What opportunities, resources, and encouragement are being made available to employees to help overcome a resistance to change and to encourage them to learn? What kind of guidance and support will they receive from their supervisors? From top management? From other systems within the organization?
- How will employees obtain feedback and rewards for engaging in and using new learning? How will feedback and rewards be linked to new learning?

Process and Outcomes for Learning

- How will detriments in performance, mistakes, and failures be handled?
- How will a climate be created that supports calculated risks? That includes a safe environment for expressing new ideas and trying them out?
- How will changes be documented? What role will employees have in documenting their own changes? How will they learn assessment techniques?
- How will top management be a role model for learning?

Creating a learning environment and a performance management system that rewards learning is not difficult. Many performance management systems involve teaching employees how to navigate the organizational terrain. However, creating a learning-oriented performance management system that involves employees taking control of their own performance development and that truly encourages learning *that the organization wants its members to engage in* is a much more difficult feat. The current case study by no means encompasses all or most of the situations and difficulties that organizations will encounter in attempting to create a learning culture, but gives an example of how one fictional organization might deal with some of the hurdles encountered. Using the definitions, information, and diagnostic questions provided by this article may start other organizations on a path to creating a learning culture in their own companies.

References

Beinhocker, E. (2006). The adaptable corporation. *McKinsey Quarterly, 2,* 76–87.

Bernardin, H. J., & Beatty, R. W. (1984). *Performance appraisal: Assessing human behavior at work.* Boston: Kent.

Capra, F. (1997). *The web of life: A new scientific understanding of living systems.* New York: Anchor.

Horvath, M., Herleman, H. A., & McKie, R. L. (2006). Goal orientation, task difficulty, and task interest: A multilevel analysis. *Motivation and Emotion, 30,* 171–178.

Jacques, E. (2002). *The life and behavior of living organisms: A general theory.* Westport, CT: Praeger.

Jex, S. M. (2002). *Organizational psychology: A scientist practitioner approach.* Hoboken, NJ: John Wiley & Sons.

Kerr, S. (1975). On the folly of rewarding A, while hoping for B. *Academy of Management Journal, 18*(4), 769–775, 779–783. Reprinted in R. P. Vecchio (Ed.) (1997), *Leadership: Understanding the dynamics of power and influence in organizations* (pp. 246–256). Notre Dame, IN: Notre Dame University Press.

Kiser, P. J. (2002, December). *Acxiom rebuilds from scratch.* (Workforce Management). Fromhttp://www.workforce.com/archive/feature/23/37/13/index.php.

Laszlo, E. (2002). *The systems view of the world: A holistic vision of our time.* Cresskill, NJ: Hampton Press.

Lebas, M. J. (1995). Performance measurement and performance management. *International Journal of Production Economics, 41,* 23–35.

London, M., & Sessa, V. I. (2007). How groups learn, continuously. *Human Resource Management, 46*(4), 651–659.

London, M., & Smither, J. W. (1999). Empowered self-development and continuous learning. *Human Resource Management, 38*(1), 3–15.

Luthans, F., & Stajkovic, A. D. (1999). Reinforce for performance: The need to go beyond pay and even rewards. *Academy of Management Executive, 13*(2), 49–57.

Martin, D. C., Bartol, K. M., & Kehoe, P. E. (2000). The legal ramifications of performance appraisal: The growing significance. *Public Personnel Management, 29*(3), 379–206.

Rock, D., & Schwartz, J. (2006, Summer). The neuroscience of leadership. *Strategy and Business, 43.*

Rodgers, R., & Hunter, J. E. (1991). Impact of management by objectives on organizational productivity. *Journal of Applied Psychology, 76*(2), 322–336.

Sessa, V. I., & London, M. (2006). *Continuous learning in organizations: Individual, group, and organizational perspectives.* Mahwah, NJ: Lawrence Erlbaum Associates.

Sorensen, J. B. (2002). The strength of corporate culture and the reliability of firm performance. *Administrative Science Quarterly, 47,* 70–91.

Vancouver, J. B. (1997). The application of HLM to the analysis of the dynamic interaction of environment, person, and behavior. *Journal of Management, 23*(6), 795–819.

Warden, B. (2008). Seagate uses yearlong evaluations to help integrate talent efforts [Electronic Version]. Talent Management. Received March 12, 2008, from http://www.talentmgt.com/departments/application/2008/February/536/index.php.

Whinghter, L. J., Cunningham, C. J. L., Wang, M., & Burnfield, J. L. (2008). The moderating role of goal orientation in the workload-frustration relationship. *Journal of Occupational Health Psychology, 13*(3), 283–291.

Wriston, B. (2007). Creating a high performance culture. *Organizational Development Journal, 25,* 8–16.

CHAPTER 11

DIAGNOSING, UNDERSTANDING, AND DEALING WITH COUNTERPRODUCTIVE WORK BEHAVIOR

Leanne Atwater and Teri Elkins

Introduction

Managers supervise many types of employees, most of whom perform effectively most of the time. However, inevitably, performance problems arise that must be assessed and dealt with. Although performance has historically been conceptualized as the quality and/or quantity of an employee's work product, organizations have recently begun to view performance in broader terms, including task performance as well as citizenship and counterproductive behaviors. Moreover, research indicates that managers place as much weight on counterproductive behaviors as on task performance when evaluating employees (Rotundo & Sackett, 2002). Organizations are becoming increasingly concerned about the counterproductive aspect of performance due to its prevalence and cost (Penney & Spector, 2005). Much of the cost associated with counterproductive work behaviors may be significantly reduced by implementing prompt and appropriate responses. This chapter will be devoted to discussing how to deal with a variety of counterproductive work behaviors through the diagnosis of potential causes and selection of proper non-punitive and/or punitive responses including termination.

Types of Counterproductive Work Behavior (CWB)

Counterproductive work behavior (CWB) has been defined as "volitional acts that harm or intend to harm organizations and their stakeholders (for example, clients, co-workers, customers, and supervisors)" (Spector & Fox, 2005, pp. 151–152). Accumulating evidence shows that CWBs are pervasive and expensive. Harper (1990) estimated that up to 75 percent of employees have engaged in theft, computer fraud, embezzlement, vandalism, sabotage, or fraudulent absenteeism; the cost of these CWBs may reach hundreds of billions of dollars a year. Research has identified five dimensions of CWB, including abuse against others, production deviance, sabotage, theft, and withdrawal (Spector, Fox, Penney, Bruursema, Goh, & Kessler, 2006). The nature, prevalence, and consequences of each CWB dimension will be described in the following sections.

Abuse Against Others

Behaviors classified as abuse against others are those that cause or are intended to cause physical or psychological harm to other organizational constituents, including managers, co-workers, subordinates, and customers (Spector, Fox, Penney, Bruursema, Goh, & Kessler, 2006). Abuse against others in organizations appears to be emotion-based and related to hostile aggression. Specific behaviors in this category of CWB may include mild deviance referred to as incivility, and more severe behaviors such as workplace violence and sexual harassment.

Incivility

Incivility has been defined as "low-intensity deviant behavior with ambiguous intent to harm the target, in violation of workplace norms for mutual respect" (Andersson & Pearson, 1999, p. 457). Incivility may include rude and discourteous behaviors such as "taking credit for others' efforts, spreading rumors about colleagues, leaving office equipment jammed instead of taking the time to fix it, flaming co-workers through nasty e-mail messages, neglecting to acknowledge subordinates, leaving snippy voice-mail messages, and so on" (Pearson, Andersson, & Porath, 2005, p. 178). Studies have shown that the instigators of workplace incivility are more likely to be men, and behaviors are more likely to be targeted toward subordinates or those with less power or status in the organization (Pearson & Porath, 2005). Incivility is a prevalent problem in today's organizations. Disturbingly, a survey of government employees found that 71 percent had experienced some form of incivility in the past five years (Cortina, Magley, Williams, & Langhout, 2001). Recipients of incivility have reported a number of negative outcomes including psychological distress, lower job satisfaction, worry, and turnover (Aquino, Tripp, & Bies, 2001; Cortina, Magley, Williams, & Langhout, 2001). Incivility can also have long-term organizational costs. When a work unit develops a reputation of incivility, it can spread and become an accepted norm of behavior, making it difficult to attract good employees (Anderson & Pulich, 1999).

Workplace Aggression/Violence

Unfortunately, evidence shows that, when unaddressed, incivility incidents can escalate over time to more severe and even more costly forms of abuse such as physical aggression and other types of workplace violence (Pearson & Porath, 2005). The National Institute for Occupational Safety and Health (NIOSH) estimated that up to eighteen thousand people a week are attacked by someone while they are at work (LeBlanc & Kelloway, 2002). Estimates have put the cost of workplace violence alone at near $4.2 billion annually (Bensimon, 1997). Targets of workplace violence experience a number of negative outcomes in addition to physical injuries, including harm to their psychological well-being, lower organizational commitment, and increased turnover intentions (LeBlanc & Kelloway, 2002). Outcomes such as these may be even more pronounced when violence is initiated by another organizational member compared to a member of the general public (a customer or client) because of damage to trust of co-workers and the organization (O'Leary-Kelly, Griffin, & Glew, 1996).

Sexual Harassment

Two distinct types of sexual harassment, quid pro quo and hostile work environment, are prohibited by Title VII of the 1964 Civil Rights Act as forms of sex discrimination. Quid pro quo harassment is defined as "unwelcome sexual advances, requests for sexual favors, and other verbal or physical conduct of a sexual nature . . . when (1) submission to such conduct is made either explicitly or implicitly a term or condition of an individual's employment" or "(2) submission to or rejection of such conduct by an individual is used as the basis for employment decisions affecting such individual" (29 CFR 1604.11(a)(1) and (2)). Hostile work environment is unwelcome behavior that "has the purpose or effect of unreasonably interfering with an individual's work performance or creating an intimidating, hostile, or offensive working environment" (29 CFR 1604.11(a)(3)) and is "sufficiently severe or pervasive 'to alter the conditions of the victim's employment and create an abusive working environment'" (*Meritor Savings Bank v. Vinson* (477 U.S. 57, 1986) quoting *Henson v. City of Dundee*, 682 F.2d 897 at 904).

Surveys of women indicate that 24 percent believe they have been sexually harassed, while 58 percent report experiencing potentially harassing behaviors (Ilies, Hauserman, Schwochau, & Stibal, 2003). Sexual harassment is also experienced by men; 15.4 percent of the U.S. Equal Employment Opportunity Commission's (EEOC) sexual harassment claims were filed by men in fiscal year (FY) 2006, which is an increase from 11.6 percent in FY 1997 (EEOC, 2007). Victims of sexual harassment have reported a number of negative individual and organizational outcomes, including psychological harm, reduced self-esteem, anxiety, lower job satisfaction, decreased organizational commitment, withdrawal, absenteeism, intent to turnover, and lower job performance (Bowling & Beehr, 2006; Fitzgerald, Drasgow, Hulin, Gelfand, & Magley, 1997; Glomb, Munson, Hulin, Bergman, & Drasgow, 1999; Schneider, Swan, & Fitzgerald, 1997; Willness, Steel, & Lee, 2007). Sexual harassment can also lead to costly legal action; it has been estimated that juries award sexual harassment victims an average of $250,000 in damages (Zugelder, Champagne, & Maurer, 2006).

Production Deviance

Production deviance includes poor performance, sabotage, theft, and withdrawal behaviors. Production deviance behaviors are acts of displaced aggression typically targeted at organizations rather than individuals (Neuman & Baron, 1997; Spector, Fox, Penney, Bruursema, Goh, & Kessler, 2006).

Passive Production Deviance

Production deviance involves more passive behaviors such as not performing a job effectively or correctly (Spector, Fox, Penney, Bruursema, Goh, & Kessler, 2006). Advances in technology have given rise to a more contemporary form of production deviance, cyberloafing, which occurs when employees use their employers' e-mail and Internet connections for personal reasons during work hours (Lim, 2002). It has been estimated that 84 percent of employees send/receive personal e-mails (Vault.com, 2005) and 64 percent surf the Internet (*The Straits Times*, 2002) on work time. Cyberloafing can be detrimental to companies, resulting in a 30 to 40 percent decrease in productivity (Verton, 2000).

Sabotage and Theft

Employee sabotage entails damaging or destroying an organization's property (Chen & Spector, 1992). It has been estimated that this form of deviance costs employers approximately $200 billion per year (Murphy, 1993).

Employee theft can range from minor offenses such as taking office supplies home to more serious infractions, including embezzlement. Research has indicated that theft is a widespread problem in organizations, with reports of up to 75 percent of employees taking an employer's property home on at least one occasion (Bennett & Robinson, 2000). The cost of employee theft to organizations has been estimated at $60 billion to $120 billion annually (www.corporatecombat.com/statistics). In addition to monetary losses, employee theft causes severe distractions for managers and can result in decreased morale and damage to companies' reputations (Grossman, 2003).

Withdrawal

Employee withdrawal behaviors can take many forms, including faking sick, taking excessive breaks, absenteeism, lateness, and leaving work early. Withdrawal is viewed as a form of avoidance or escape (Spector, Fox, Penney, Bruursema, Goh, & Kessler, 2006) and occurs frequently in organizations. For instance, in 1995, 29 percent of supermarket employees surveyed admitted to calling in sick when they were not (Boye & Jones, 1997). These types of actions can have ramifications beyond the obvious affecting co-workers' morale and motivation (Koslowsky, Sagie, Krausz, & Singer, 1997) as well as customer service when service positions cannot be adequately staffed.

Diagnosing the Causes of CWB

As a manager, the first challenge in dealing with CWB is to correctly diagnose the root of the problem. This is generally done by talking to the problem individual, talking to the individual's co-workers, and observing the employee's behavior and patterns. It is important not to jump to quick conclusions but rather to take time to try to clearly understand what is going on and avoid making attributional errors. One common error that can occur in diagnosing causes of employees' behaviors is the fundamental attribution error in which, "regardless of actual performance, those observing the performance of others are more likely to attribute poor performance to internal stable conditions (for example, ability). Because of their different perspective, performers are more likely to attribute their performance to external causes than are observers" (Ilgen & Davis, 2000, p. 54). Attributing negative performance or behavior to internal causes is even more likely if the employee has a history of poor work performance (Mitchell & Wood, 1980).

The purpose of diagnosing the cause(s) of CWB is to choose an appropriate course of action to take. When supervisors misattribute the cause of behaviors, the selected course of action may be inappropriate. For example, when poor performance is attributed to the person as opposed to the environment, responses are more punitive and are aimed at changing the subordinate in some way (Green & Liden, 1980). If the poor performance is actually related to an external cause, punishment is likely to be ineffective in changing the employee's behavior and may lead to negative consequences.

Counterproductive behaviors in the workplace have often been handled by creating policies and rules along with enforcement mechanisms that are primarily punitive. However, evidence suggests that these measures are not always effective at reducing CWB and promoting desirable employee behaviors (Sackett & DeVore, 2002). To properly address CWB, it is important to first develop an accurate understanding of why employees are engaging in the behaviors and then utilize the causal information to help determine appropriate responses, which may include non-punitive as well as punitive options. Managers are likely to uncover a variety of reasons for undesirable behaviors through their observations and discussions with employees. This section will explore some potential individual and organizational contributors to CWB that research has detected.

Individual Contributors

Research indicates that drug and alcohol abuse affects roughly 17 percent of the workforce, costing organizations about $150 billion a year in lost productivity and related expenses (Ivancevich, 2004; Strazewski, 2001). Substance abuse can also contribute to aggression toward co-workers and subordinates (Greenberg & Barling, 1999). Other factors that may play a role in CWB include family problems such as divorce, ill parents, ill children, and financial problems. For example, research shows that economic need can act as a trigger for employee theft (Mustaine & Tewksbury, 2002). Counterproductive work behaviors may also occur as a result of employees' personality and psychological issues. Trait anger, the tendency to respond in a hostile manner to frustrating situations (Spielberger, 1991), is related to workplace violence as well as aggression directed at the organization (Douglas & Martinko, 2001; Hershcovis et al., 2007). Fox and Spector (1999) found that anger correlated .59 with self-reported CWB.

Supervisors should be careful when diagnosing personal issues such as substance abuse, illness, and psychological problems due to legal constraints created by the Americans with Disabilities

Act (ADA), state legislation, and state common law. One method for dealing with substance abuse is to test employees. Because the ADA does not protect current illegal drug use as a disability, drug testing is permitted under the act. However, state laws may place restrictions on drug testing. For example, California's constitutional privacy protection has limited the use of drug testing by California employers (Bahis, 1998). It is important for employers to be aware of state legislative constraints. When a manager suspects that drug or alcohol use is contributing to CWB, it is important not to accuse the employee of substance abuse. Erroneous accusations regarding substance abuse, psychological problems, or physical impairments can lead to defamation claims as well as ADA violations under the "regarded as" category of protection, which prohibits discrimination based on incorrect assumptions regarding disabilities.

Rather than addressing suspicions regarding personal issues, supervisors should document and discuss the *specific undesirable behaviors* that employees are engaging in. If requested by an employee, companies must also provide reasonable accommodations for mental or physical impairments under the ADA. It is important to note, however, that accommodations need not excuse employees from performing essential job functions; someone who cannot perform essential job functions is considered unqualified and thus not protected ((29 C.F.R. 2(l)(1-3)). Additionally, the presence of a protected disability does not prevent companies from taking disciplinary action in response to employee misconduct (EEOC, 2000). Referrals to confidential Employee Assistance Programs (EAPs) can be made to provide employees with assistance they may need for non-work-related issues. These programs will be discussed in more detail later in the chapter.

Job Context Contributors

Poor Interpersonal Relationships

The presence of high-quality relationships among employees is critical to the success of organizations. Hanson (1986) found that positive interpersonal relationships between managers and staff were three times more powerful in predicting profitability in forty major companies than were the three next most powerful variables combined, which included firm size and growth rate, market share, and capital intensity. Further illustrating the importance of relationships, interpersonal conflict in the workplace is correlated with a number of CWBs, including sabotage, aggression, hostility, theft, withdrawal behaviors, production deviance, and abuse against others (Boswell & Olson-Buchanan, 2004; Chen & Spector, 1992; Hershcovis et al., 2007; Spector, Fox, Penney, Bruursema, Goh, & Kessler, 2006). The following sections will address research related to undesirable employee behaviors resulting from poor relationships with supervisors and co-workers.

Relationships with Supervisors
Research on managerial career derailment lists insensitive, abusive, or bullying supervision and micromanagement as two aspects of supervision that will derail a manager's career and keep him or her from advancing in an organization (McCall & Lombardo, 1983). This is likely because these behaviors do not promote top employee performance and can contribute to a number of undesirable employee behaviors. More recently, attention has been focused on what is termed "toxic" leadership and management. The term toxic is used because bad behaviors on the part of leaders and managers are like toxins; they negatively affect people around them (Goldman, 2006).

Toxic leaders tend to follow a certain set of rules including: (1) they must be in control of every aspect of the organization at all times, (2) when problems arise they immediately find a guilty party to blame, (3) they do not make mistakes or they cover them up, (4) their philosophy is "do as you are told," (5) they do not trust anyone, and (6) they keep up the organization's image at all costs (Appelbaum & Roy-Girard, 2007). This type of leader also sends mixed messages, frequently changes directions, and avoids making decisions until the last possible moment (Appelbaum & Roy-Girard, 2007). Because toxic leaders are often rewarded for achieving short-term goals regardless of how they treat people, they tend to cause high levels of despair, anger, low morale, poor communication, and depression among employees (Brett & Stroh, 2003). Overall, toxic leaders create a work environment that can have severe negative effects on employees (Fitzgerald, 2002; Fitzgerald & Eijnatten, 2002) and the organization, including

CWB (Duffy, Ganster, & Pagon, 2002) and reduced organizational performance (Dunlop & Lee, 2004).

Recent research examining supervisors' treatment of employees has indicated that poor leadership is related to interpersonal aggression directed toward supervisors (Hershcovis et al., 2007). Studies have found that abusive supervision, hostile (non-physical) behavior directed at subordinates (Tepper, 2000), is also related to supervisor-targeted aggression (Inness, Barling, & Turner, 2005). The relationship between abusive supervision and aggression toward supervisors is particularly strong when the employee works due to financial need more than for personal fulfillment reasons (Dupre, Inness, Connelly, Barling, & Hoption, 2006). In addition to aggression, CWB directed at individuals such as incivility and CWB targeting organizations such as theft can also result from poor supervisory treatment of employees (Andersson & Pearson, 1999; Mitchell & Ambrose, 2007). Organizations should be concerned not only about addressing CWB stemming from poor supervisor-employee relationships, but should also recognize toxic or abusive leaders and take steps to remove them or modify their behavior (Appelbaum & Roy-Girard, 2007). It should not be overlooked that toxic leaders themselves may work for another toxic leader.

Relationships with Co-Workers
Most people have worked with others who are annoying, disruptive, uncivil, or persistent bullies. Gallup (2004) estimated that roughly 17 percent of employees nationally were actively disengaged from their jobs. These are the cynical, negative individuals who constantly complain about how they are treated and try to convince others to join their cause. Additionally, studies have estimated that 30 percent of the workforce has been subjected to bullying behaviors (Rayner, Hoel, & Cooper, 2002), defined as "persistent hostile treatment in the workplace" (Rayner & Keashly, 2005). As discussed previously, incivility is also a prevalent problem in today's organizations. One of the dangers associated with counterproductive co-workers is that they can lead recipients of negative behaviors to display CWB themselves. Research has found that the experience of incivility is related to withdrawal, theft, physical aggression, faking sickness, and

decreasing work quantity and quality (Aquino, Tripp, & Bies, 2001; Cortina, Magley, Williams, & Langhout, 2001; Pearson, Andersson, & Porath, 2000; Penney & Spector, 2005).

Co-workers can also create performance problems if they have set unrealistically low standards for performance among themselves. When Glenn Tilton took over at United Airlines, he says the culture was one of indulgence (Personal Communication, April 12, 2007). Employees had convinced themselves that they deserved to be overpaid for too little work. Pilots were working nearly half the number of hours per month as other airlines and being paid more than most. This is a situation in which the norms of the group created a productivity problem that could be characterized as a form of production deviance.

Feelings of Injustice

Perceptions of fairness in the workplace can lead to a number of positive outcomes, including increased motivation, effectiveness, productivity, and performance (Colquitt, Conlon, & Wesson, 2001; Cropanzano, Bowen, & Gilliland, 2007; Rupp & Cropanzano, 2002). Organizational justice can also promote positive attitudes toward supervisors and increase the degree to which employees are willing to accept constructive criticism (Leung, Su, & Morris, 2001). On the other hand, feelings of injustice related to outcomes, procedures, and interpersonal treatment can have undesirable consequences, including CWB.

Distributive justice refers to perceptions of fairness regarding outcomes employees receive, such as promotions, pay, and other types of rewards (Adams, 1963, 1965). According to equity theory, outcomes perceived as fair, comparing one's own inputs and outcomes relative to others, can contribute to motivation and performance; if rewards are viewed as inequitable, demotivation may result (Adams, 1965). Perceptions of inequity can also lead employees to engage in CWB aimed at the organization as well as individuals, including theft, production deviance, including cyberloafing, sabotage, aggression, and withdrawal (Ambrose, Seabright, & Schminke, 2002; Fox, Spector, & Miles, 2001; Greenberg, 1990; Greenberg, 1993; Lim, 2002; Spector, Fox, Penney, Bruursema, Goh, & Kessler, 2006). These acts are typically focused on restoring what employees believe they lost or deserve as a result of the perceived inequity. It is important to note that equity is a perception and may not always be objectively accurate. Nonetheless, those perceptions are important and managers should be aware of situations that create inequity beliefs. An example:

> Susan has been working for you for three years. Susan has been a solid performer . . . not earthshaking but dependable . . . and has received above satisfactory performance evaluations. Recently, you have noticed that Susan's performance has been falling off. You are concerned about the cause of this recent change. Susan started her job at $12.00 per hour three years ago. Since that time she has received one pay increase and now makes $12.50 per hour. Her counterparts in other departments in the organization and in a similar organization across town are making $15.00 per hour. Susan feels under-compensated and therefore under-appreciated.

One of the causes of demotivation is a sense of inequity, or a perception that one is not being adequately rewarded in comparison to others. Rewards can be monetary, time off, cushy assignments, or whatever the organization has to distribute. When individuals feel they are under-rewarded compared to others, one way to restore equity is to reduce one's level of effort. Susan has been doing the bare minimum, taking longer breaks than acceptable, and leaving early. In this case, perceived inequity has resulted in CWB.

Procedural justice is the perceived fairness associated with procedures used to determine outcomes (Leventhal, 1980; Thibaut & Walker, 1975). To be viewed as fair, Leventhal (1980) asserted that procedures should be ethical, applied consistently, and free from error and bias. Additionally, fair procedures should include opportunities for employees to appeal, grieve, and voice their opinions. Research has found relationships between procedural justice and CWB aimed at the organization as well as individuals (Fox, Spector, & Miles, 2001). Studies indicate that procedural injustice is related to abuse against others, sabotage, theft, withdrawal behaviors, and production deviance including cyberloafing (Colquitt, Noe, & Jackson, 2002; Lim, 2002; Schwarzwald, Koslowsky, & Shalit, 1992; Spector, Fox, Penney, Bruursema, Goh, & Kessler, 2006). Moderators of the procedural justice-CWB relationship have also been identified. For example, absenteeism resulting from perceptions of procedural injustice is particularly likely among employees with low power distance orientations (those who see few differences among those with different levels of status or power) (Lam, Schaubroeck, & Aryee, 2002). Alcohol tends to exacerbate the effects of injustice on aggression against co-workers and subordinates (Greenberg & Barling, 1999).

Interactional justice includes perceptions of how employees feel they are treated by others. Interactional justice consists of two components: informational and interpersonal (Bies & Moag, 1986; Colquitt, 2001). Informational justice refers to the extent to which a decision-maker is truthful and provides an adequate explanation for an outcome, while interpersonal justice is concerned with treating employees with respect and dignity. Research has demonstrated that perceived interactional injustice is related to aggression toward individuals in the organization (Hershcovis et al., 2007). Feeling over-controlled by a supervisor can lead to perceptions of poor interpersonal treatment, which can result in aggression toward the supervisor (Greenberg & Barling, 1999; Inness, Barling, & Turner, 2005). Aggression toward supervisors is curtailed, however, when sanctions exist for aggressive behavior (Dupre & Barling, 2006). In addition to aggression, research has found that interactional injustice is related to theft (Colquitt & Greenberg, 2003; Greenberg, 1993; Lind, Greenberg, Scott, & Welchans, 2000), sabotage (Ambrose, Seabright, & Schminke, 2002), absenteeism (Gellatly, 1995), and cyberloafing (Lim, 2002).

Greenberg (1990) examined two plants of a company undergoing pay cuts. Managers agreed to provide different types of explanations to employees in the two plants to assess the impact of the explanation. In one plant, the reduction in pay was clearly explained, remorse and sympathy were offered, and questions were answered. In the second plant, employees were merely told of the pay cut in a short meeting. In the plant where the remorseful explanation was given, theft rates increased 1.5 percent following the reduction in pay, whereas in the plant where no remorse was provided, theft increased 5 percent. Clearly, the explanations mattered and reactions were different when employees perceived they were being treated unfairly.

Job Dissatisfaction

Job satisfaction is comprised of employees' attitudes regarding different aspects of their jobs, including pay, job tasks, promotion opportunities, supervisors, and co-workers (Locke, 1976; Spector,

1997). Research has indicated that dissatisfaction with one's job is related to theft, tardiness, absenteeism, production deviance, sabotage, and aggression (Lau, Au, & Ho, 2003; Hershcovis et al., 2007; Mustaine & Tewksbury, 2002; Spector, Fox, Penney, Bruursema, Goh, & Kessler, 2006). In properly diagnosing job dissatisfaction as a potential cause of CWB, it is important to identify specific job components that employees are unhappy with.

Situational Constraints

Situational constraints such as a lack of training may occasionally be the cause of performance problems (Grote, 2006). According to the frustration-aggression hypothesis (Dollard, Doob, Miller, Mowrer, & Sears, 1939; Spector, 1975), the inability to perform can lead to frustration when the attainment of goals is inhibited; aggression may be a response to this frustration. Results of a meta-analysis indicated that situational constraints that may exist in organizations, including unavailability of resources and training, are related to aggressive acts directed at the organization (Hershcovis et al., 2007). Other research has found that employees frustrated with organizational limitations may engage in sabotage, interpersonal aggression, hostility, theft, production deviance, and withdrawal behaviors (Chen & Spector, 1992; Spector, Fox, Penney, Bruursema, Goh, & Kessler, 2006).

Organizational Climate

Organizational climate is important for establishing behavioral norms and identifying employee conduct that is undesirable in the workplace. Climate can be reflected in tolerance for particular behaviors, the existence and implementation of policies, and expectations-focused training (Williams, Fitzgerald, & Drasgow, 1999). Climates regarding ethics and sexual harassment are influential antecedents of CWB. Research has found that employees who are at a conventional level of cognitive moral development (those who internalize rules and meet others' expectations of right and wrong behavior) engage in less theft when there is an ethics program in place than when no such program exists (Greenberg, 2002). Studies have identified organizational climate regarding sexual harassment as one of the primary contributors to the occurrence of sexual harassment in the workplace (Fitzgerald, Drasgow, Hulin, Gelfand, & Magley, 1997; Willness,

Steel, & Lee, 2007). The lack of punitive actions taken against harassers is a particularly important aspect of an organization's sexual harassment climate contributing to the occurrence of harassing behaviors (Hulin, Fitzgerald, & Drasgow, 1996). Setting clear behavioral expectations through policies can also help curtail workplace incivility. A number of companies include explicit statements regarding employee conduct in their policies. For example, Quaker Oats articulates specific expectations indicating that employees must treat one another with consideration, dignity, and respect (Pearson, Andersson, & Porath, 2000).

Dealing with Counterproductive Work Behavior

After identifying potential causes of counterproductive performance issues, managers should then determine the appropriate course of action to take. The selected action(s) should focus on changing employees' behaviors as well as addressing diagnosed contributors to those behaviors. "Discipline as defined by the behavior and policies of many U.S. organizations means punishment. . . . The employee errs and management determines the penalty that fits the crime, operating under the belief that by treating the individual progressively worse he will become progressively better" (Harvey, 1987, p. 26). However, punishment alone can create an adversarial relationship between managers and employees, rather than concentrating on common goals. There are certainly behaviors for which immediate punishment or even termination is warranted or legally required, such as theft, sexual harassment, violence, and sabotage. However, other behaviors, such as milder forms of incivility, production deviance, and withdrawal, may be more effectively addressed exclusively with non-punitive approaches or through a combination of non-punitive and punitive actions. The following sections will discuss a variety of non-punitive and punitive approaches that either alone or in combination may be used to effectively deal with CWB.

Non-Punitive Approaches

Alignment

Solutions to performance and behavior problems often emphasize confrontation and managerial control (that is, discovering a performance problem, telling the employee what he or she is doing wrong, and monitoring future performance). As part of this process, research has found that many managers first attempt to make sense of the problems, an approach referred to as alignment (Morris, Gaveras, Baker, & Coursey, 1990). Alignment serves a purpose beyond the establishment of the manager's control; it creates a new understanding between a manager and an employee about how activities are to be performed. In utilizing the alignment approach, "Managers . . . clearly express a preference for problem-solving measures that are capable of handling problems without necessitating bold and complicated confrontation" (Morris, Gaveras, Baker, & Coursey, 1990, p. 308). To handle problems without confrontation, Morris, Gaveras, Baker, and Coursey (1990) found that managers do one of the following:

1. Initially pass over the issue and do nothing but continue to monitor the employee's performance/behavior. It is possible that what happened was a fluke and will not occur again. This is only a reasonable course of action if the problem was not severe.
2. Help the employee correct the undesirable behavior without making an issue out of the performance or problem.
3. Find technical solutions or adjustments in work arrangements that might eliminate the problem. Perhaps the employee has great difficulty arriving on time given morning duties at home. The manager might change the employee's work schedule to accommodate this.
4. Hold "nice meetings" wherein a problem is addressed with the entire group rather than an individual culprit. While managers may use this technique, it is inadvisable as a routine practice. However, it may be an effective way to restate performance expectations.

Alignment may also be a useful mechanism to confirm both the existence of CWB and a manager's diagnosis of factors contributing to the employee's behavior. To this end, Morris, Gaveras, Baker, and Coursey (1990) advocated investigative moves in which the manager determines that he or she and the employee are in agreement regarding actual and expected behaviors. Seeking explanations directly from the employee is also recommended. One manager responded to a question about how to deal with an employee who has begun to show disinterest in her job by stating, "I'd try to find out the reason for the change and see if she felt unnecessary and would like to become the backup in another position or learn something new" (Morris, Gaveras, Baker, & Coursey, 1990, p. 315).

Corrective Feedback

Constructive feedback or counseling is a good first step in the performance improvement process. This may be a particularly effective approach for less severe problems for which discipline may not be necessary and may cause negative side-effects. Constructive feedback can also send a positive message by demonstrating that the supervisor is interested in helping the employee. It allows the supervisor to better understand what might be the source of the problem, and it requires little other than the manager's time and effort (Braid, 1986). Despite the potential benefits of constructive feedback, the sensitive and potentially anxiety-provoking nature of this approach (Cardno, 2001) can result in managers avoiding or delaying giving feedback to poor performers (Bond & Anderson, 1987; Larson, 1989) and distorting feedback to make performance seem less negative (Larson, 1986). In these cases the employee is not getting an accurate picture of the problem. It has been reported that negative feedback can sometimes result in reduced employee performance (Geddes & Baron, 1997). This may be caused by delay or distortion of feedback as well as the way that constructive feedback is received by the employee. For example, there is ample evidence that the degree of negative feedback is often denied by its intended recipients (Kluger & DeNisi, 1996). When feedback is denied, increased performance rarely follows. Although providing negative feedback can be risky, it is often necessary to communicate a gap in desired and actual performance (Ilgen & Davis, 2000). We will next discuss factors managers should consider in deciding whether to give corrective feedback and in conducting an actual feedback meeting.

Deciding Whether to Give Corrective Feedback

While managers may believe it is their duty and obligation to provide corrective feedback to an employee who is displaying a behavior or performance problem, Latting (1992) suggested four guidelines that managers should first consider in deciding whether to give corrective feedback. First, corrective feedback should only be given if the underlying motive is to help the employee by providing information. Feedback should not be disguised as corrective if the true intent is to control, to express aggression, or to justify a manager's actions. Too often critical feedback is given as a substitute for aggression (Bartolome, 1986–1987). Second, Latting (1992) suggested that corrective feedback is effective only if the receiver is able and willing to take appropriate action. There is little point in giving negative feedback if the likely result is a strong negative reaction and low probability that positive change will result. Third, the manager should consider whether the organizational system is likely to reward the desired behavior before giving corrective feedback. If there is no reward for improved performance and no consequence for lack of improvement, there is likely little point in providing feedback. Finally, the manager should assess his/her standing as a credible, trustworthy source before providing corrective feedback.

In assessing credibility, the notion of an "emotional bank account" may be helpful to examine. Covey (1989) suggested that every employee has an emotional bank account that his or her supervisor manages. A supervisor makes deposits into an employee's emotional bank account with such acts as being straightforward, following through, being kind and respectful, and providing supportive feedback. Corrective feedback is viewed as a withdrawal from the bank account. When deposits have been minimal, corrective feedback will not be taken well or likely acted upon. It is recommended that supervisors maintain a 3 to 1 ratio of deposits to withdrawals. Trust in a manager's motives for giving negative feedback is also important and should be evaluated. Managers tend to overestimate the amount of trust subordinates have in them and underestimate the negative effects of emotional bank withdrawals on trust and respect (Atwater, Waldman, Carey, & Cartier, 2001; Butterfield, Trevino, & Ball, 1996).

Giving Constructive Feedback
Communicating negative feedback to employees is a delicate task. Mistakes in attributions such as the fundamental attribution

error discussed earlier can occur during the feedback process and are one of the major contributors to feedback ineffectiveness. The ineffectiveness is largely due to differences in causal perceptions characteristic of the fundamental attribution error which makes disagreement between the feedback source and recipient more likely (Ilgen & Davis, 2000). In providing an employee with constructive feedback, it is important to focus on accurate internal or external factors that the employee and/or manager can control. Softening the blow of negative feedback by addressing contributors that are beyond the employee's control reduces the likelihood that performance will improve because, once the person believes he or she was not responsible, there is no need to exert further effort (Ilgen & Davis, 2000).

The tone of negative feedback is also influential in how the feedback is received by employees. Managers often avoid giving negative feedback until their annoyance level is very high, resulting in inaccurate recollections (Ilgen, Fisher, & Taylor, 1979) and feedback that is overly harsh and biting (Larson, 1989), which can decrease employees' motivation and self-efficacy (Deci & Ryan, 1985). Excessively negative feedback may also make the recipient more likely to react with verbal aggression toward the sender in an attempt to prove a point or discount the accuracy of the feedback (Rudawsky, Lundgren, & Grasha, 1999). Acknowledging positive aspects of an employee's work performance or behavior can be effective in mitigating negative reactions to constructive feedback by maintaining motivation and cooperation (Lizzio, 2003).

In attempts to improve performance, it is important for managers to set standards so employees can establish appropriate goals and to clarify expectations. In addressing standards, managers should clearly communicate gaps in current and desired behavior or performance, create a plan of action, and establish a mechanism for monitoring progress (Lizzio, 2003). The small wins strategy for motivating employees (Eden, 1990) suggests that it is important for individuals to achieve success. Providing reasonable timeframes for employees to meet standards with sensitivity to individual differences in ability and experience is advisable (Bobko & Wise, 1987). Doing so may mitigate negative reactions to feedback and provide employees with the knowledge necessary to improve their performance or behavior. Managers may also consider pairing corrective feedback with the promise of rewards for better performance. Research has indicated that punishment alone is not effective in decreasing absenteeism. Attempts to reduce absenteeism were effective, however, when both positive reinforcers and punishment were used (Nicholson, 1976).

As previously discussed, employee voice and the use of explanations are important aspects of organizational justice perceptions. Managerial behaviors that increase opportunities for employee voice lead to fewer negative reactions to negative feedback and help minimize resistance as well as decrease the likelihood of legal challenges (Gilliland & Langdon, 1998). Inviting ideas and reactions to managers' feedback can be effective in building commitment for improvement and preventing employees from becoming upset (Lizzio, 2003). However, managers need to be careful not to exhibit certain elements of fair treatment in the absence of others. For example, providing the opportunity for employees to voice their opinions but failing to consider seriously anything that was said can be more damaging than no opportunity for voice at all (Folger, 1977; Leung & Li, 1990). Managers can demonstrate that they value employees by commenting on and engaging in a discussion of employees' ideas and objections (Lizzio, 2003).

Demonstrating respect for employees and preventing embarrassment are important aspects of interactional justice, which can effect how negative feedback is received (Lizzio, 2003). When unpleasant news must be delivered, an adequate and remorseful explanation can help reduce employees' negative reactions (Bies & Shapiro, 1987). Research has found that when supervisors provided explanations for negative performance feedback (apologizing for the outcomes, explaining the event as unavoidable, or justifying it as helpful to the individual in the long run), employees reported reduced anger and less perceived unfairness (Tata, 2002). Moreover, the manager's expression of regret also resulted in employees reporting a greater intent to change future behavior.

In performance situations in which people experience repeated negative feedback or punishment, they become somewhat habituated to it and decrease attention to it. They react with "That is just the way I am, or what I can do" and reduce efforts to avoid the negative feedback because they have merely accepted it as the way it is (Mikulincer, 1994). With repeated failures, expectations are lowered (Ilgen & Hamstra, 1972) and individuals are likely to avoid trying to improve. Redundant information can also be viewed as insulting and patronizing (Ilgen, Fisher, & Taylor, 1979) and should be avoided unless it is clear the employee doesn't understand what has been said.

Self-Management Training for Improving Job Performance

Self-management has been described as a set of behavioral and cognitive strategies that help people structure their environment, including the environment at work (Manz, 1986), and involves self-motivation and understanding of the behaviors needed to meet performance standards or goals. Training in self-management as a method to improve behavior has been demonstrated in a number of contexts, including blue-collar workers and sales personnel (cf. Frayne & Geringer, 2000; Frayne & Latham, 1987). Social cognitive theory provides a pertinent backdrop for understanding how and why self-management training works (Bandura, 1986). Essentially, social cognitive theory suggests that self-efficacy or one's belief in his or her ability to do a job, anticipated outcomes, goal setting, and reinforcements operate together to help individuals reach performance goals. Self-efficacy works by influencing an individual's choices about what behaviors to undertake, how much effort should be exerted, and how long to persist when obstacles are confronted. Those with higher self-efficacy perform better because they are willing to exert more effort and will persist longer. The cycle repeats as one realizes through effort and persistence that he or she can perform, which further enhances self-efficacy. Research examining the effectiveness of self-management has found that this type of training increases performance and self-efficacy (Frayne & Geringer, 2000) and decreases absenteeism (Frayne & Latham, 1987).

To implement self-management training, Frayne and Geringer (2000) have outlined the following steps, which describe actions that should be taken by the employee:

1. Identify the behaviors to modify (for example, attendance)
2. Establish goals (short-term and long-term) for those behaviors (for example, no unplanned missed days for three months, no more than three missed days in twelve months, excluding actual sick days)

3. Maintain a record of progress toward goal attainment (for example, record attendance weekly)
4. Establish self-rewards and self-punishments for performance relative to goals (for example, purchasing a gift for oneself at month end)
5. Prepare a written contract with himself or herself that specifies expectations, plans, and contingencies for the changed behavior. This serves as a form of goal commitment. (For example, must not miss work; must retire to bed by midnight; no drinking alcohol on work nights; no missed days for three months.)
6. Identify pitfalls to applying the self-management techniques. What are the high-risk situations or temptations that may cause the individual to withdraw from his or her plans? (For example, must turn down invitations to party on weeknights or must insist that one return home by 11:30 p.m.)

Positive Discipline

Positive discipline is a performance management system that emphasizes organizational justice, commitment building, and individual employee responsibility for performance improvement (Osigweh & Hutchison, 1989). Human resource management experts assert that this type of approach is effective because: "Adult learning theory will tell you that when you treat people like adults, they will respond in kind" (Falcone, 2007, p. 107). In a positive discipline system, problems are initially addressed informally through coaching and counseling, followed by more formal steps including an oral reminder, a written reminder, and decision-making leave (Osigweh & Hutchison, 1989).

If informal coaching or counseling has not resolved an employee's performance problems, an oral reminder should be provided to the employee in a formal, documented performance improvement discussion with the supervisor. In this meeting, the employee should be reminded in a positive rather than a punitive manner about specific performance expectations and the employee's responsibility for meeting those expectations. Gaps between actual and desired performance should be clearly specified. A discussion of causes and solutions to performance deficiencies is also helpful. If performance problems persist, another meeting and a written reminder placed in the employee's personnel file are warranted (Osigweh & Hutchison, 1989). Employees can earn the right to have the reminder removed if the problem is solved and there are no recurring problems after one year.

The final stage of positive discipline includes a decision-making day in which the employee is given a paid day off to decide whether to commit to making the necessary performance changes or to resign (Falcone, 2007; Osigweh & Hutchison, 1989). In addition, some employers ask employees to prepare a written commitment letter on the decision-making day that proposes a plan for improving performance (Sunoo, 1996). If the employee has decided to correct performance deficiencies, a discussion with the supervisor regarding specific expectations occurs and a documented written reminder is administered. In both the meeting and the reminder, it should be emphasized that failure to meet the stated expectations in the future will result in termination (Osigweh & Hutchison, 1989).

It could be argued that providing employees with a paid day off is simply rewarding them for poor performance. However, proponents of positive discipline argue that an unpaid decision-making day is equivalent to an unpaid suspension and may result in anger, resentment, further performance deficiencies, and other negative organizational outcomes. Paid decision-making leave removes the stigma associated with punishment, allows the employee to self-reflect, and may reduce blame placed on others for performance deficiencies (Falcone, 2007). Additionally, paid leave may act as a demonstration of good faith, can induce guilt rather than anger, minimizes the need for employees to save face, increases defensibility of the decision if the employee is later terminated, is easier for the supervisor to implement, and is consistent with a culture that espouses the value of treating employees with dignity and respect (Grote, 2006). Complaints from other employees have led some companies to make the decision-making leave unpaid. Companies have also opted against paid leave for certain offenses such as absenteeism (Sunoo, 1996).

Union Carbide has implemented a positive discipline system throughout a number of its union and non-union facilities in the United States and Canada with a great deal of success (Osigweh & Hutchison, 1989). Results of employee attitude surveys administered before and after the implementation of positive discipline revealed a number of positive changes. After the company began using positive discipline, supervisors responded earlier to performance problems, and employees reported higher-quality relationships with their supervisors, increased morale, and better-quality communications. Additionally, the company has experienced a decline in absenteeism as well as disciplinary grievances. Properly training supervisors is critical to the success of positive discipline. Union Carbide conducts extensive training focusing on the difficulties associated with discipline, components and philosophy of positive discipline, and skill-building in handling performance problems. Their training emphasizes the goal of reminders as obtaining an employee's agreement to make desired changes in performance. It is theorized that this type of agreement is more likely to improve performance than punitive action (Osigweh & Hutchison, 1989). Other companies such as Frito Lay, the Texas Mental Health Department, Verizon, and General Electric have also reported successes using positive discipline as evidenced by reduced turnover, fewer grievances, and better attendance (Harvey, 1987).

Employee Assistance Programs

Employee Assistance Programs (EAPs) emerged in the 1950s focusing on mental health and substance abuse issues. Today, these programs are provided by an estimated 70 percent of companies and provide employees with confidential assistance for a broad range of topics, including mental health, substance abuse, marriage/family problems, financial difficulties, and legal issues (Chima, 2002; Owens, 2006). Employees' personal problems such as these can cost employers up to $200 billion per year (McShulskis, 1996). Research examining the effectiveness of EAPs in addressing personal issues has found that these programs can decrease employees' symptoms and increase their ability to function (Greenwood, DeWeese, & Inscre, 2005). EAPs can also result in a number of positive organizational consequences including increased productivity, improved work relationships, and decreased absenteeism (Selvik & Bingaman, 1998).

A recent trend in EAPs that may provide further benefits to individuals and organizations is the inclusion of employee coaching services. Coaching has been described as "a collaborative process that helps people attain their workplace objectives" and tends to focus on goal-setting, self-directed learning, personal growth, egalitarian relationships, and solution development (Triner & Turner, 2005, p. 1). Coaching services are offered to address a variety of issues including employee performance, team building, change management, skill development, career development, feedback processing, and conflict management (Morgan, Harkins, & Goldsmith, 2005). In making EAP referrals for traditional services or coaching, it is important for managers to make employee utilization voluntary rather than mandatory when substance abuse or mental/physical health are potential issues (Falcone, 2003). In these cases, requiring employees to use EAP services could create a perceived disability problem under the Americans with Disabilities Act. Research suggests that voluntary utilization may be increased by developing a written EAP policy, distributing information regarding EAP procedures to employees, and providing supervisors with EAP training (Weiss, 2003).

Punishment—Is It Necessary and Will It Solve the Problem?

Workforce management issued a report in 2003 detailing the ten biggest mistakes made by employers that lead to costly litigation (Gilmore, 2003). Two of these mistakes involve discipline: failing to take and document disciplinary action and failing to quickly enact progressive discipline in response to poor performance. Legal action can result from disciplinary avoidance when some type of punitive action for CWB is necessary under the law. For example, the EEOC and the U.S. Supreme Court have established that companies can be held legally liable if they fail to take prompt corrective action in response to sexual harassment in the workplace (29 C.F.R. § 1604.11(d); *Faragher v. City of Boca Raton, Burlington Industries v. Ellerth*). This means that, after determining that an instance of sexual harassment has occurred, companies must take appropriate action against the harasser. Depending on the nature of the harassment, appropriate action may include varying degrees of punishment, a combination of punishment and non-punitive actions, or termination.

The failure to enact discipline when warranted not only leads to costs associated with legal action, but also losses due to decreased productivity and lower employee morale. Negative organizational consequences, including legal claiming behaviors, can occur when employees perceive unfair treatment on the job (Lind, Greenberg, Scott, & Welchans, 2000). Part of fair treatment on the job involves providing employees with a just disciplinary process and appropriate sanctions. This section will discuss how the disciplinary process can be utilized by supervisors to appropriately address performance-related problems, foster feelings of fairness among punishment recipients and others, and avoid costly mistakes associated with improper discipline administration.

Punishment Research: Supervisors', Recipients', and Observers' Perspectives

Supervisors' Punishment Decisions: Determinants and Goals

When determining what sanctions to levy for employees' performance-related infractions, it is important that managers consider appropriate factors and apply decision rules consistently. Managers take a number of work-related factors into consideration when determining punishment, including work history (Butterfield, Trevino, & Ball, 1996; Fandt, Labig, & Urich, 1990), offense and outcome seriousness (Hook, Rollinson, Foot, & Handley, 1996; Liden, Wayne, Judge, Sparrowe, Kraimer, & Franz, 1999; Mitchell, Green, &Wood, 1981; Rosen & Jerdee, 1974), length of service (Rollinson, 2000), and fairness perceptions (Butterfield, Trevino, & Ball, 1996). Studies have also identified some non-work-related variables that influence punishment decisions such as effects on the recipients' families (Butterfield, Trevino, & Ball, 1996), gender (Bellizzi & Hasty, 2002), liking the recipient (Fandt, Labig, & Urich, 1990), and personal problems (Klaas & Wheeler, 1990). Causal attributions also influence decisions of managers and groups; both prefer more serious sanctions for infractions attributed to internal rather than external causes (Liden, Wayne, Judge, Sparrowe, Kraimer, & Franz, 1999). Regarding consistency, research has found that, while human resource managers rely heavily on their organizations' consistency norms in making punishment decisions, line managers place less emphasis on the past treatment of employees

(Klaas & Wheeler, 1990). Overall, it appears that managers use appropriate work-related factors in making punishment decisions, but also allow concerns related to personal issues to influence their judgments and do not always administer discipline consistently. Given the costs associated with discipline mistakes, organizations should provide managers with training focusing on the appropriate discipline decisions and consistent application of discipline decision rules.

Managers have indicated that they administer punishment to accomplish a number of different goals, including changing an employee's behavior, earning respect, and sending a message to others (Butterfield, Trevino, & Ball, 1996). Do managers actually achieve these goals? Is punishment in response to performance deficiencies effective? Research examining the effects of punishment on recipients and observers addresses these questions and provides some guidance for managers in making punishment decisions and for the punishment administration process.

Effects of Punishment on Recipients
Research has found that recipients do view discipline as effective in changing behavior and increasing awareness of expectations (Atwater, Waldman, Carey, & Cartier, 2001). Consistent with recipients' beliefs, results of other studies examining discipline effectiveness have indicated that discipline can achieve supervisors' goals and have identified some important moderators of the discipline-outcome relationship. In a study of supervisor-subordinate dyads, subordinates were more likely to perform citizenship behaviors and less likely to engage in destructive behaviors when they perceived that they had some control over the discipline procedures and sanction determination (Ball, Trevino, & Sims, 1994). In this study, subordinates' performance improved when they believed that their punishment was appropriately severe and consistent with that of others with similar infractions. Subordinates with weak "just world" beliefs (those with just world beliefs tend to believe that people get what they deserve) and high negative affectivity were particularly likely to perceive that they had less control and view the disciplinary action as overly harsh. Thus, individual differences as well as components of procedural justice such as voice and consistency influence the extent to which discipline results in desired employee behaviors.

Even when discipline effectively modifies employees' behaviors, research indicates that recipients may experience a variety of negative consequences that supervisors should be aware of. In a study examining employees' and managers' perceptions, discipline recipients reported experiencing bad feelings about their organization and job, income loss, loss of respect for the manager, unhappiness, anger, and embarrassment (Atwater, Waldman, Carey, & Cartier, 2001). Recipients also indicated that they believed managers used discipline as a demonstration of power and authority, because of personality conflicts, and for unknown reasons. In comparing perceptions of managers and recipients, this study further found that recipients were more likely to believe that the discipline was not handled properly and to believe that discipline was less justified. Punishment can also result in anger and hostility, which have been found to contribute to CWB (Judge, Scott, & Ilies, 2006). Feelings of injustice among unionized employees can result in an additional negative consequence, that is, discipline opposition in the form of a grievance (Gordon & Bowlby, 1989). It is recommended that managers become more aware of the negative consequences perceived by recipients and receive training in how to communicate clear performance-related concerns leading to the discipline (Atwater, Waldman, Carey, & Cartier, 2001). Fewer negative consequences should occur when employees know what behaviors will result in punishment and when they perceive punishment as fair.

Other research examining discipline recipients has suggested that gender may contribute to perceptions of discipline fairness. Atwater, Carey, and Waldman (2001) found that when women administered discipline, they were viewed as less effective and the punishment was perceived as less fair than when discipline was levied by men. Interestingly, men who were disciplined by women perceived the most problems with the discipline process and reported the most negative outcomes. Follow-up studies indicated that these perceptual differences may be due to gender biases as well as different behaviors exhibited by male and female supervisors in the discipline process. Managers should be aware of gender-based perceptual and behavioral differences and receive training in proper discipline administration.

When disciplining employees, managers often utilize social accounts to explain why punishment is needed (Butterfield,

Trevino, & Ball, 1996). Social accounts, which may include excuses, justifications, and apologies, can be effective tools for managing subordinates' perceptions of fairness if the explanations are viewed as adequate (Bies, 1987). Research has found that face-saving explanations that allow recipients to experience less embarrassment or maintain their self-images result in increased perceptions of interactional fairness and more positive evaluations of the supervisor (Charles & Atwater, 2008). In the study done by Charles and Atwater, apologizing for the delivery of disciplinary action and for its negative effects was particularly effective in increasing justice perceptions, while justifications were associated with the most positive behaviors, including changing future behaviors and improving performance. Refusing to provide an explanation negatively affected recipients' attitudes and behaviors. The study also found that employees in low-quality supervisor/subordinate or leader member exchange (LMX) relationships reacted to discipline more negatively than those who had high-quality relationships with their supervisors. Tata (2002) also found evidence of the effectiveness of apologies in reducing anger, increasing interpersonal justice perceptions, and intentions to change future behaviors. In this study, apologies also heightened the effectiveness of excuses (explaining why there was no other choice available) when the two types of social accounts were combined.

Effects of Punishment on Observers
Research has found that the use of punishment and termination in response to performance problems is positively related to overall unit performance (O'Reilly & Weitz, 1980). It is suggested that the relationship between sanctions and unit performance might be explained by social learning theory; observers learn from the punishment of others and change their own behaviors. Consistent with this view, a study of student temporary workers indicated that observers who witnessed a supervisor reducing the pay of another employee subsequently increased their performance more than those who witnessed a threat of a pay cut or no punishment (Schnake, 1986). Research has also found a positive relationship between the use of appropriate punishment and observers' reported motivation, productivity, and satisfaction (O'Reilly & Puffer, 1989).

Interestingly, observers in this study perceived inequity when deserved punishment was not administered. This finding suggests that justice perceptions may play a key role in the way observers react to the punishment of others in the workplace.

Trevino (1992) presented a justice-based framework for observers' perceptions of punishment in organizations that is a useful tool for examining how employees react to a co-worker's discipline. The model views punishment in a larger social context and posits that employee misconduct and subsequent managerial responses influence observers' perceptions of justice and future attitudes and behaviors. In support of Trevino's (1992) model, research has indicated that observers hold justice-based views regarding whether and how poor performers should be punished and that the consistency of punishment with co-workers' expectations affects their turnover intentions and attitudes toward their managers (Neihoff, Paul, & Bunch, 1998). Research also suggests that punishment creates expectations regarding future sanctions for unethical behaviors. Results of a study examining sexual harassment and sabotage found that when an employee was punished harshly for these forms of unethical and counterproductive work behaviors, observers expected harsh punishment for future unethical acts (Trevino & Ball, 1992). Observers in the study also viewed harsh punishment as more fair for unethical acts and reported more positive emotions than when the employee received more lenient punishment or no punishment at all. Interestingly, research has found that vicarious learning can occur even in instances when discipline is perceived as unfair by observers (Atwater, Waldman, Carey, & Cartier, 2001). However, this learning, particularly if it takes place when a discipline event occurred in public, is often accompanied by negative consequences such as negative emotions and negative feelings regarding the supervisor. So while it may be advantageous for others to know the severity of a discipline event, the discipline should not be delivered in front of observers.

Progressive Discipline

Progressive discipline originated in the 1930s as a response to the National Labor Relations Act of 1935 establishing "just cause" standards for discipline and termination (Guffey & Helms, 2001). In a progressive discipline program, managers formally, directly, and promptly communicate problems, including performance deficiencies, to employees (Falcone, 1998). The failure to meet performance standards or goals results in sanctions beginning with an oral warning then progressing to more severe actions for repeat offenses, including written warnings, suspension, and termination (Guffey & Helms, 2001). To ensure due process (a critical element for the success of progressive discipline), it is important that supervisors do the following: (1) communicate specific expectations and consequences for failing to meet expectations, (2) provide sufficient time for performance improvement, (3) make sure that discipline is administered consistently, (4) provide employees with an opportunity to respond, and (5) ensure that the selected sanction is appropriate for the infraction (Falcone, 1997; Falcone, 2000).

One of the most important factors in determining appropriate sanctions is the severity of the employee's offense (Falcone, 1998). Severity can be assessed using the following criteria (Leap & Crino, 1998):

1. The extent to which incident created disruption to the workflow
2. Damage to products or equipment
3. Whether a safety hazard was created
4. Whether a customer or employee suffered bodily injury
5. Conduct in light of training or professional norms
6. Whether the behavior was a legal violation
7. If the behavior resulted in misappropriation of resources
8. The impact on morale of co-workers
9. Whether the behavior is a danger signal for more serious problems
10. If employee's actions damaged the image of the organization
11. If problem undermined management's authority

In addition to severity, managers should consider the ease with which the behavior can be corrected, how similar issues were dealt with in the past, and the employee's past performance and tenure when determining appropriate punishment (Falcone,

1998; Leap & Crino, 1998). Mitigating circumstances and factors beyond the employee's control (for example, weather, unclear instructions, inadequate supervision, or others) are also important to examine (Leap & Crino, 1998).

Meeting with the employee to communicate performance deficiencies and resulting disciplinary action is a potentially unpleasant and difficult task. Day (1993) has suggested the following guidelines to increase the effectiveness of disciplinary meetings:

1. Be clear about what you hope the discipline will accomplish. The person should not leave wondering what the conversation was all about.
2. Meet in private.
3. Be calm. Don't attempt to deliver discipline when you are angry or upset.
4. Schedule a meeting with *little* lead time. Allowing too much time leads to greater defense building.
5. Allow enough time for the meeting and don't allow interruptions. This sends a message that the discipline meeting is important.
6. Prepare opening remarks. A minor amount of small talk is OK, but quickly get to the point.
7. Don't be evasive about the purpose.
8. Allow the person to share his or her side and be willing to take criticism.
9. Establish a follow-up plan (two to three weeks).
10. End on a positive note, letting the person know you are confident in his or her ability to change behavior in a positive way in the future.

Although progressive discipline systems offer the advantages of emphasizing the serious nature of continuing offenses and providing employees with a series of corrective opportunities before termination, a number of disadvantages have been cited (Grote, 2006; Guffey & Helms, 2001). Critics of progressive discipline argue that this type of system obligates supervisors to administer discipline for every offense, consumes too much of a supervisor's time, focuses more on past offenses than on performance improvement, leads to adversarial supervisor-subordinate relationships, takes away employee responsibility for performance improvement, and fosters supervisory resistance to discipline resulting in the tolerance of performance deficiencies (Osigweh & Hutchison, 1989). Supervisors may also delay the process until the problem is so severe that it is necessary to build a case for dismissal.

It has been asserted that many of the disadvantages associated with progressive discipline may be alleviated by implementing aspects of positive discipline programs described previously (Guffey & Helms, 2001). Companies that wish to retain some of the beneficial punitive components of a progressive disciplinary system while decreasing their negative effects might consider utilizing a hybrid model in which positive discipline reminders are incorporated into the progressive discipline process. This type of system has been implemented with some success by the Internal Revenue Service (IRS) as a response to problems with the agency's disciplinary program, including racial disparities in the administration of disciplinary actions. Some of the positive discipline actions taken by the IRS include diversity awareness training, the development of "rules of conduct" lesson plans, and policy reminders (Guffey & Helms, 2001).

Discipline Recommendations

The administration of discipline is an important and difficult task with effects reaching beyond the recipients alone. In this section, we have highlighted studies examining the effects of discipline on employees with performance or behavior issues, their co-workers, managers, and organizations. Overall, research results indicate that thorough investigation, planning, and preparation are essential to disciplinary effectiveness. Specific recommendations arising out of this research regarding making punishment decisions and holding a disciplinary meeting include the following:

1. Determine whether there are legal issues that should be taken into account.
2. Consider only work-related factors.
3. Apply policies and decision-making rules consistently.
4. Allow employees a voice in the discipline process.
5. Make the punishment consistent with the severity of the offense.

6. Provide managers with discipline-related training.
7. Provide employees with clear explanations coupled with apologies for the ill effects on the recipient.
8. Communicate clear performance expectations.
9. Communicate specific consequences for future infractions.
10. Provide employees with sufficient time to improve their performance or change their behavior.
11. Express confidence in the employee's ability to improve

When All Else Fails—Termination

Unfortunately, there are situations in which managers' efforts to diagnose performance problems, develop non-punitive performance improvement strategies, and administer disciplinary actions do not result in increased employee performance or improved behavior. At this point, employers should strongly consider termination. In fact, the failure to promptly terminate poorly performing or problem employees has been cited as one of the most costly legal mistakes that employers make. Long-term retention, in spite of continued performance deficiencies or behavior problems, can result in losses due to missed opportunities and organizational inefficiencies (Lind, 1997), can decrease the veracity of a performance-based defense, and may increase the likelihood of legal action (Gilmore, 2003). Under the doctrine of *negligent retention* (failing to terminate when it is clearly called for), the legal risk associated with failing to terminate is particularly high in situations involving known substance abuse, threats of or actual workplace violence, as well as severe forms of incivility in which an employee presents a foreseeable risk of harm to others (Zugelder, Champagne, & Maurer, 2000). In addition to legal risk, postponing termination of employees with performance problems can lead to a number of other negative organizational consequences such as resentment by co-workers who may have to bear unfair workloads (Grote, 2006).

After making the decision to terminate a poorly performing or problem employee, two issues should be reviewed in preparation for the termination discussion. First, it is important to consider legal parameters that may place restrictions on employee termination. Second, some thought should be given to the termination process and how the termination decision is communicated to the employee.

Legal Parameters: Employment At-Will and Its Exceptions

According to the doctrine of employment at-will, employment relationships formed for an indefinite period of time can be terminated at-will by either the employee or the employer (Dunford & Devine, 1998). Although this doctrine is the prevailing standard today, a number of contractual, common law, and statutory exceptions place restrictions on employee termination. For example, employment at-will status can be negated by a collective bargaining agreement or written contract establishing "just cause" termination standards or other contractual terms such as length of employment (Muhl, 2001; Rothstein, Craver, Schroeder, & VanderVelde, 1994). If there is an explicit agreement in place, the manager should identify the termination provisions and ensure that they have been properly followed.

Contractual obligations can also be enforceable under the implied contract common law exception to employment at-will recognized by many states (Muhl, 2001). Implied contracts can be created by statements made in employee handbooks establishing "just cause" termination standards and delineating procedures to be followed prior to termination (Rothstein, Craver, Schroeder, & VanderVelde, 1994). If a "just cause" standard or specific discipline and termination processes exist, the manager should ensure that the company has documentation of inadequate performance, deficiencies have been communicated to the employee, and processes have been properly followed. Some states also recognize other common law exceptions, including the covenant of good faith and fair dealing, which prohibits terminating employees for the purpose of depriving them of benefits earned during their employment, and public policy, which prohibits terminating employees for refusing to perform an illegal act, whistle-blowing, exercising legal rights, and performing a civic duty (Rothstein, Craver, Schroeder, & VanderVelde, 1994). Wrongful termination claims based on these exceptions can be minimized by ensuring that there is performance or behavior-related documentation to support the termination decision and that issues related to public policy are not present in poorly performing employees' situations. For a more comprehensive discussion of state common law exceptions to employment at-will, see Walsh and Schwartz (1996). Termination restrictions can also be found in state statutes. Employers should check with state government employment agencies in states in which their companies operate for comprehensive information regarding state statutes.

A number of federal statutes have been passed that create restrictions on employee terminations in all states. For example, it is illegal to terminate an employee for engaging in union activities (National Labor Relations Act of 1935), exercising minimum wage and overtime pay rights (Fair Labor Standards Act of 1938), reporting safety violations (Occupational Safety and Health Act), exercising vested pension rights (Employee Retirement Income Security Act), and whistle-blowing (Civil Service Reform Act, the Whistleblower Protection Act, and the Sarbanes-Oxley Act). Federal statutes also prohibit termination for a discriminatory reason. Illegal bases of discrimination include sex, pregnancy, race, national origin, color, religion (Title VII of the Civil Rights Act of 1964 and the Equal Pay Act), age (Age Discrimination in Employment Act), and disability (The Americans with Disabilities Act and the Rehabilitation Act). Discrimination laws have also made it illegal to terminate employees in retaliation for filing discrimination claims, participating in a discrimination investigation, or opposing what is reasonably believed to be a discriminatory practice. To decrease the possibility of retaliation claims being brought by terminated employees and increase the chance of winning such claims that do arise, legal experts have suggested that employers carefully document performance problems early, communicate clear performance expectations to employees, apply discipline and termination policies consistently, and provide the employee with honest, specific reasons for the termination (Archer & Lanctot, 2007).

Process Considerations

Legal experts have suggested that organizations make a number of mistakes in the termination process that contribute to wrongful discharge claims, including breaching progressive discipline rules, poor treatment of the employee during termination, failing to provide outplacement services, and failing to recognize the psychological difficulty caused by termination (Tobias, 2000).

This section will examine legal research examining specific factors in the termination process that increase the likelihood of legal action and will make recommendations for properly handling the termination process.

Academicians have theorized that perceptions of injustice may explain why mistakes made in the termination process increase the likelihood of legal action (Dunford & Devine, 1998). Research examining the relationship between treatment of employees during the termination process and subsequent legal claiming behaviors has found support for the mediating role of justice perceptions. In a study of unemployed individuals who had lost their jobs, results indicated that longer notice of termination and assistance in finding a new job positively affected perceptions of fair treatment during termination (Lind, Greenberg, Scott, & Welchans, 2000). Perceptions of fair treatment among the participants were significantly negatively related to consideration of legal claiming, which predicted actual claiming behaviors. There was also a significant positive relationship between blaming the employer and legal claiming for fired employees. Further research on blame has indicated that terminated employees are more committed to legal claiming when they make external attributions, blaming their supervisor or the organization for their termination (Groth, Goldman, Gilliland, & Bies, 2002). This finding was particularly true for employees with longer tenure. It is suggested that fair procedures may help reduce external attributions made by terminated employees, thus reducing legal claiming behaviors.

In a study examining the interactive effects of distributive, procedural, and interactional justice, Goldman (2003) found that distributive justice significantly affected legal claiming when both procedural and interactional justice were low, suggesting that legal action may be reduced by implementing fair termination procedures and by ensuring that employees are treated appropriately during the time of termination. Results of the study further indicated that state anger (a temporary emotion) and trait anger (a more permanent personality orientation) help explain the relationship between justice and legal claiming. For example, when injustice is perceived, a terminated employee feels anger about the situation and the anger affects legal claiming.

Additionally, results indicated that those high in trait anger are more likely to engage in legal claiming as a result of perceived injustice than those low in trait anger (presumably because trait anger is more likely to persist than state anger).

From an ethics perspective, employees deserve fair processes and treatment during terminations (Van Bogaert & Gross-Schaefer, 2005). As indicated by research, fair termination procedures and considerate treatment can mitigate the potential negative effects of termination, including legal claiming (Goldman, 2003; Groth, Goldman, Gilliland, & Bies, 2002; Lind, Greenberg, Scott, & Welchans, 2000). Perceptions of procedural justice can be enhanced in the termination process by providing employees with input and voice, consistently applying procedures, and providing for appeals (Goldman, 2003). Viewing termination as the final step in a progressive or positive disciplinary process and allowing employees to express their opinions, to provide and receive feedback regarding their performance, and to appeal performance evaluations and disciplinary actions throughout the process are effective ways to increase feelings of procedural fairness. These measures could provide the additional benefit of reducing attributions of employer blame for poor performance and subsequent termination (Groth, Goldman, Gilliland, & Bies, 2002). Exit interviews may also provide terminated employees with a voice and provide employers with valuable information regarding employees' opinions and concerns.

To increase perceptions of interactional justice, managers should treat employees with dignity and respect during the termination process and offer them truthful explanations regarding why they are being terminated (Goldman, 2003; Lind, Greenberg, Scott, & Welchans, 2000). Potentially humiliating practices such as conducting terminations in front of others and immediately escorting a terminated employee from the worksite should be avoided if possible (Dunford & Devine, 1998; Lyncheski, 1995). To properly prepare supervisors for the process of terminating poorly performing employees, companies should provide training focused on fair procedures, appropriate treatment, anger responses, and conflict management techniques (Goldman, 2003).

Termination Recommendations

Organizations face legal risks and other negative outcomes if terminations are not justified and handled properly. In this section, we have outlined federal and state statutory and common law as well as termination process issues identified by research that should be considered prior to terminating employees. Specific recommendations based on termination law and research are as follows:

1. Determine whether the employee is at-will or if there are contractual terms or collective bargaining agreements to be aware of.
2. Make certain that the termination does not violate federal or state statutes or common law.
3. Determine whether the company's disciplinary policies were correctly and consistently applied prior to the termination.
4. Ensure that performance- or behavior-related documentation exists that substantiates the termination.
5. Ensure that past performance or behavior deficiencies have been communicated to the employee.
6. Communicate honest, specific reasons for the termination to the employee.
7. Provide appropriate notice of termination, except in situations that warrant immediate termination such as aggression toward a co-worker, sabotage, and theft.
8. Treat terminated employees with dignity and respect.
9. Conduct terminations face-to-face in a private setting.
10. Provide employees with opportunities to voice their opinions and opposition.
11. Provide managers with termination-related training.

Summary

This chapter has addressed myriad types of CWBs, their potential causes, and suggestions for remediation. Clearly, CWB is a major problem in organizations today, and it is often ignored or addressed improperly (for example, too late, with intense emotion, without offering solutions). In the interests of employee morale, productivity, and potential legal action, CWB needs to be taken seriously. It is our hope that this chapter has provided useful insights for managers in recognizing and handling CWB in their organizations.

References

Adams, J. S. (1963). Toward an understanding of inequity. *Journal of Abnormal and Social Psychology, 67*, 422–436.

Adams, J. S. (1965). Inequity in social exchange. In L. Berkowitz (Ed.), *Advances in experimental and social psychology* (Vol. 2, pp. 267–299). New York: Academic Press.

Ambrose, M. L., Seabright, M. A., & Schminke, M. (2002). Sabotage in the workplace: The role of organizational justice. *Organizational Behavior and Human Decision Processes, 89*, 947–965.

Anderson, P., & Pulich, M. (1999). Managing the temperamental employee. *The Health Care Supervisor, 17*(4), 28–36.

Andersson, L. M., & Pearson, C. M. (1999). Tit for tat? The spiraling effect of incivility in the workplace. *Academy of Management Review, 24*, 452–471.

Appelbaum, S. H., & Roy-Girard, D. (2007). Toxins in the workplace: Affect on organizations and employees. *Corporate Governance, 7*(1), 17–28.

Aquino, K., Tripp, T. M., & Bies, R. J. (2001). How employees respond to personal offense: The effects of blame attribution, victim status, and offender status on revenge and reconciliation in the workplace. *Journal of Applied Psychology, 86*(1), 52–59.

Archer, R. M., & Lanctot, S. T. (2007). Are your hands tied? A practical look at employee claims for retaliation. *Employee Relations Law Journal, 33*, 53–64.

Atwater, L. E., Carey, J. A., & Waldman, D. A. (2001). Gender and discipline in the workplace: Wait until your father gets home. *Journal of Management, 27*, 537–561.

Atwater, L. E., Waldman, D. A., Carey, J. A., & Cartier, P. (2001). Recipient and observer reactions to discipline: Are managers experiencing wishful thinking? *Journal of Organizational Behavior, 22*, 249–270.

Ball, G. A., Trevino, L. K., & Sims, Jr., H. P. (1994). Just and unjust punishment: Influences on subordinate performance and citizenship. *Academy of Management Journal, 37*, 299–322.

Bahis, J., (March, 1998). Dealing with drugs: Keep it legal. *HR Magazine,* 104–116.

Bandura, A. (1986). *Social foundations of thought and action: A social cognitive theory.* Englewood Cliffs, NJ: Prentice-Hall.

Bartolome, F. (1986–1987). Teaching about whether to give negative feedback. *Organizational Behavior Teaching Review, 11,* 95–104.

Bellizzi, J. A., & Hasty, R. A. (2002). Supervising unethical sales force behavior: Do men and women managers discipline men and women subordinates uniformly? *Journal of Business Ethics, 40,* 155–166.

Bensimon, H. (1997). What to do about anger in the workplace. *Training and Development, 51,* 28–32.

Bennett, R. J., & Robinson, S. L. (2000). Development of a measure of workplace deviance. *Journal of Applied Psychology, 85,* 349–360.

Bies, R. (1987). The predicament of injustice: The management of moral outrage. *Research in Organizational Behavior, 9,* 289–319.

Bies, R. J., & Moag, J. F. (1986). Interactional justice: Communication criteria of fairness. In R. J. Lewicki, B. H. Shepherd, & M. H. Bazerman (Eds.), *Research on negotiations in organizations* (Vol. 1, pp. 43–55). Greenwich, CT: JAI Press.

Bies, R.J., & Shapiro, D. L. (1987). Interactional justice: The influence of causal accounts. *Justice Research, 1,* 199–218.

Bobko, P., & Wise, L. (1987, September). *Towards a methodological understanding of standard setting: Are we satisfied with our satisfaction benchmarks?* Paper presented at the Measurement Research Symposium, Bell Communications Research Corporation, Cherry Hill, New Jersey.

Bond, C. F., & Anderson, E. L. (1987). The reluctance to transmit bad news: Private discomfort or public display? *Journal of Experimental Social Psychology, 23,* 176–187.

Boswell, W. R., & Olson-Buchanan, J. B. (2004). Experiencing mistreatment at work: The role of grievance filing, nature of mistreatment and employee withdrawal. *Academy of Management Journal, 47,* 129–139.

Bowling, N. A., & Beehr, T. A. (2006). Workplace harassment from the victim's perspective: A theoretical model and meta-analysis. *Journal of Applied Psychology, 91,* 998–1012.

Boye, M. W., & Jones, W. J. (1997). Organizational culture and employee counterproductivity. In R. A. Giacalone & J. Greenberg (Eds.), *Antisocial behavior in organizations* (pp. 172–183). London: Sage.

Braid, R. W. (1986). Using counseling to end marginal performance. *Supervisory Management, 31*(1), 26.

Brett, J. M., & Stroh, L. K. (2003). Working 61 plus hours a week: Why do managers do it? *Journal of Applied Psychology, 88,* 67–78.

Burlington Industries, Inc. v. Ellerth, 118 S.Ct. 2257 (1998).

Butterfield, K. D., Trevino, L. K., & Ball, G. A. (1996). Punishment from the manager's perspective: A grounded investigation and inductive model. *Academy of Management Journal, 39,* 1479–1512.

Cardno, C. (2001). Managing dilemmas in appraising performance: An approach for school leaders. In D. Middlewood & C. Cardno (Eds.), *Managing teacher appraisal and performance* (pp. 143–159). London: Routledge Falmer.

Charles, A. C., & Atwater, L. (2008). Perceptions of interactional justice in the delivery of discipline: The importance of explanations. Working Paper.

Chen, P. Y., & Spector, P. E. (1992). Relationships of work stressors with aggression, withdrawal, theft and substance use: An exploratory study. *Journal of Occupational and Organizational Psychology, 65,* 177–184.

Chima, F. O. (2002). Employee assistance and human resource collaboration for improving employment and disabilities status. *Employee Assistance Quarterly, 17,* 79–94.

Colquitt, J. A. (2001). On the dimensionality of organizational justice: A construct validation of a measure. *Journal of Applied Psychology, 86,* 386–400.

Colquitt, J. A., Conlon, D. E., & Wesson, M. J. (2001). Justice at the millennium: A meta-analytic review of 25 years of organizational justice research. *Journal of Applied Psychology, 86,* 425–445.

Colquitt, J. A., & Greenberg, J. (2003). Organizational justice: A fair assessment of the state of the literature. In J. Greenberg (Ed.), *Organizational behavior: The state of the science* (pp. 165–210). Mahwah, NJ: Lawrence Erlbaum Associates.

Colquitt, J. A., Noe, R. A, & Jackson, C. L. (2002). Justice in teams: Antecedents and consequences of procedural justice climate. *Personnel Psychology, 55,* 83–109.

Cortina, L. M., Magley, V. J., Williams, J. H., & Langhout, R. D. (2001). Incivility in the workplace: Incidence and impact. *Journal of Occupational Health Psychology, 6,* 64–80.

Covey, S. R. (1989). *The seven habits of highly effective people: Restoring the character ethic.* New York: Simon and Schuster.

Cropanzano, R., Bowen, D. E., & Gilliland, S. W. (2007). The management of organizational justice. *Academy of Management Perspectives, 21,* 34–48.

Day, D. (1993, May). Training 101: Help for discipline dodgers. *Training & Development, 47*(5), 19.

Deci, E. L., & Ryan, R. M. (1985). *Intrinsic motivation and self-determination in human behavior.* New York: Plenum.

Dollard, J., Doob, L. W., Miller, N. E., Mowrer, O. H., & Sears, R. R. (1939). *Frustration and aggression.* New Haven, CT: Yale University Press.

Douglas, S. C., & Martinko, M. J. (2001). Exploring the role of individual differences in the prediction of workplace aggression. *Journal of Applied Psychology, 86,* 547–559.

Duffy, M. K., Ganster, D., & Pagon, M. (2002). Social undermining in the workplace. *Academy of Management Journal, 45*, 331–351.

Dunford, B. B., & Devine, D. J. (1998). Employment at-will and employee discharge: A justice perspective on legal action following termination. *Personnel Psychology, 51*, 903–934.

Dunlop, P. D., & Lee, K. (2004). Workplace deviance, organizational citizenship behavior, and business unit performance: The bad apples do spoil the whole barrel. *Journal of Organizational Behavior, 25*(1), 67–80.

Dupre, K. E., & Barling, J. (2006). Predicting and preventing supervisory workplace aggression. *Journal of Occupational Health Psychology, 11*, 13–26.

Dupre, K. E., Inness, M., Connelly, C. E., Barling, J., & Hoption, C. (2006). Workplace aggression in teenage part-time employees. *Journal of Applied Psychology, 91*, 987–997.

Eden, D. (1990). *Pygmalion in management: Productivity as a self-fulfilling prophecy.* Lexington, MA: Lexington Books

EEOC (1998). *Compliance manual, Section 8: Retaliation.* Retrieved February 15, 2008, from http://eeoc.gov/policy/docs/retal.html.

EEOC (2000). EEOC enforcement guidance on the Americans with Disabilities Act and psychiatric disabilities. Retrieved February 25, 2008, from http://eeoc.gov/policy/docs/psych.html.

EEOC (2007). Sexual harassment charges EEOC and FEPAs combined: FY 1997–FY 2006. Retrieved February 21, 2008, from http://eeoc.gov/stats/harass.html.

Falcone, P. (1997). The fundamentals of progressive discipline. *HRMagazine, 42*, 90–93.

Falcone, P. (1998). Adopt a formal approach to progressive discipline. *HRMagazine, 43*, 55–59.

Falcone, P. (2000). A blueprint for progressive discipline and terminations. *HR Focus, 77*, 3–5.

Falcone, P. (2003). Dealing with employees in crisis. *HRMagazine, 48*, 117–121.

Falcone, P. (2007). Days of contemplation. *HRMagazine, 52*, 107–112.

Fandt, P. M., Labig, C. E., & Urich, A. L. (1990). Evidence and the liking bias: Effects on managers' disciplinary actions. *Employee Responsibilities and Rights Journal, 3*, 253–265.

Faragher v. City of Boca Raton, 118 S.Ct. 2275 (1998).

Fitzgerald, L. (2002). Chaos: The lens that transcends. *Journal of Organizational Change Management, 15*(4), 339–358.

Fitzgerald, L., Drasgow, F., Hulin, C., Gelfand, M., & Magley, V. (1997). Antecedents and consequences of sexual harassment in organizations: A test of an integrated model. *Journal of Applied Psychology, 82*, 578–589.

Fitzgerald, L., & Eijnatten, F. (2002). Chaos speak: A glossary of chaotic terms and phrases. *Journal of Organizational Change Management, 15*(4), 412–423.

Folger, R. (1977). Distributive and procedural justice: Combined impact of "voice" and improvement on experienced inequity. *Journal of Personality and Social Psychology, 35,* 108–119.

Fox, S., & Spector, P. E. (1999). A model of work frustration-aggression. *Journal of Organizational Behavior, 20,* 915–931.

Fox, S., Spector, P. E., & Miles, D. (2001). Counterproductive work behavior (CWB) in response to job stressors and organizational justice: Some mediator and moderator tests for autonomy and emotions. *Journal of Vocational Behavior, 59,* 291–309.

Frayne, C. A., & Geringer, J. M. (2000). Self-management training for improving job performance: A field experiment involving salespeople. *Journal of Applied Psychology, 85*(3), 361–372.

Frayne, C. A., & Latham, G. P. (1987). Application of social learning theory to employee self-management. *Journal of Applied Psychology, 72*(3), 387.

Gallup (2004). *Getting personal in the workplace: Are negative relationships squelching productivity in your company?* Retrieved March 6, 2009, from http://gmj.gallup.com/content/11956/Getting-Personal-Workplace.aspx.

Geddes, D., & Baron, R. A. (1997). Workplace aggression as a consequence of negative performance feedback. *Management Communication Quarterly, 10*(4), 433–454.

Gellatly, I. R. (1995). Individual and group determinants of employee absenteeism: Test of a causal model. *Journal of Organizational Behavior, 16,* 469–485.

Gilliland, S., & Langdon, J. (1998). Creating performance management systems that promote perceptions of fairness. In J. Smither (Ed.), *Performance appraisal: State of the art in practice.* San Francisco: Jossey-Bass.

Gilmore, R. (2003). Employers' biggest legal mistakes: Ten things that can explode into costly lawsuits, unionization and an unhappy workforce. Retrieved January 18, 2008, from http://www.workforce.com/archive/article/23/48/94.php?ht=employer%20mistakes%20employer%20mistakes.

Glomb, T. M., Munson, L. J., Hulin, C. L., Bergman, M. E., & Drasgow, F. (1999). Structural equation models of sexual harassment: Longitudinal explorations and cross-sectional generalizations. *Journal of Applied Psychology, 84*(1), 14–28.

Goldman, A. (2006). High toxicity leadership: Borderline personality disorder and the dysfunctional organization. *Journal of Managerial Psychology, 21*, 733–746.

Goldman, B. M. (2003). The application of referent cognitions theory to legal-claiming by terminated workers: The role of organizational justice and anger. *Journal of Management, 29*, 705–728.

Gordon, M. E., & Bowlby, R. L. (1989). Reactance and intentionality attributions as determinants of the intent to file a grievance. *Personnel Psychology, 42*, 309–329.

Green, S. G., & Liden, R. C. (1980). Contextual and attributional influences on control decisions. *Journal of Applied Psychology, 65*(4), 453.

Greenberg, J. (1990). Employee theft as a reaction to underpayment inequity: The hidden cost of pay cuts. *Journal of Applied Psychology, 75*, 561–568.

Greenberg, J. (1993). Stealing in the name of justice: Informational and interpersonal moderators of theft reactions to underpayment inequity. *Organizational Behavior and Human Decision Processes, 54*, 81–103.

Greenberg, J. (2002). Who stole the money and when? Individual and situational determinants of employee theft. *Organizational Behavior and Human Decision Processes, 89*, 985–1003.

Greenberg, L., & Barling, J. (1999). Predicting employee aggression against coworkers, subordinates and supervisors: The roles of person behaviors and perceived workplace factors. *Journal of Organizational Behavior, 20*, 897–913.

Greenwood, K. L., DeWeese, P., & Inscre, P. S. (2005). Demonstrating the value of EAP services: A focus on clinical outcomes. *Journal of Workplace Behavioral Health, 21*, 1–10.

Grossman, R. J. (2003). The five-finger bonus. *HRMagazine, 48*, 38–44.

Grote, R. (2006). *Discipline without punishment.* New York: AMACOM.

Groth, M., Goldman, B. M., Gilliland, S. W., & Bies, R. J. (2002). Commitment to legal claiming: Influences of attributions, social guidance, and organizational tenure. *Journal of Applied Psychology, 87*, 781–788.

Guffey, C. J., & Helms, M. M. (2001). Effective employee discipline: A case of the Internal Revenue Service. *Public Personnel Management, 30*, 111–127.

Hanson, G. (1986). *Determinants of firm performance: An integration of economic and organizational factors.* Unpublished doctoral dissertation, University of Michigan Business School. (As cited in D. Tourish and O. Hargie, 1998, Communication between managers and staff in the NHS. *British Journal of Management, 9*, 53–71).

404 PERFORMANCE MANAGEMENT

Harper, D. (1990). Spotlight abuse—save profits. *Industrial Distribution*, *79*, 47–51.

Harvey, E. (1987). Discipline vs. punishment. *Management Review*, *76*, 3, 25–29.

Henson v. City of Dundee, 682 F.2d 897 (CA11 1982).

Hershcovis, M. S., Turner, N., Barling, J., Arnold, K. A., Dupre, K. E., Innes, M., LeBlanc, M. M., & Sivanathan, N. (2007). Predicting workplace aggression: A meta-analysis. *Journal of Applied Psychology*, *92*, 228–238.

Hook, C. M., Rollinson, D. J., Foot, M., & Handley, J. (1996). Supervisor and management styles in handling discipline and grievance: Part one comparing styles in handling discipline and grievance. *Personnel Review*, *25*, 20–34.

Hulin, C. L., Fitzgerald, L. F., & Drasgow F. (1996). Organizational influences on sexual harassment. In M. S. Stockdale (Ed.), *Sexual harassment in the workplace: Perspectives, frontiers, and response strategies. Women and work: A research and policy series* (Vol. 5, pp. 127–150). Thousand Oaks, CA: Sage.

Ilgen, D. R., & Davis, C. A. (2000). Bearing bad news: Reactions to negative feedback. *Applied Psychology: An International Review*, *49*, 550–565.

Ilgen, D., Fisher, C. D., & Taylor, M. (1979). Consequences of individual feedback on behavior in organizations. *Journal of Applied Psychology*, *64*, 349–371.

Ilgen, D. R., & Hamstra, B. W. (1972). Performance satisfaction as a function of the difference between expected and reported performance at five levels of reported performance. *Organizational Behavior and Human Performance*, *7*, 359–370.

Ilies, R., Hauserman, N., Schwochau, S., & Stibal, J. (2003). Reported incidence rates of work-related sexual harassment in the United States: Using meta-analysis to explain reported rate disparities. *Personnel Psychology*, *56*, 607–631.

Inness, M., Barling, J., & Turner, N. (2005). Understanding supervisor-targeted aggression: A within–person, between–jobs design. *Journal of Applied Psychology*, *90*, 731–739.

Ivancevich, J. (2004). *Human resource management.* New York: McGraw-Hill.

Judge, T. A., Scott, B. A., & Ilies, R. (2006). Hostility, job attitudes, and workplace deviance: Test of a multilevel model. *Journal of Applied Psychology*, *91*, 126–138.

Klaas, B. S., & Wheeler, H. N. (1990). Managerial decision making about employee discipline: A policy-capturing approach. *Personnel Psychology*, *43*, 117–134.

Kluger, A., & DeNisi, A. (1996). The effects of feedback intervention on performance: A historical review, a meta-analysis and a preliminary feedback intervention theory. *Psychological Bulletin, 119*, 254–284.

Koslowsky, M., Sagie, A., Krausz, M., & Singer, D. (1997). Correlates of employee lateness: Some theoretical considerations. *Journal of Applied Psychology, 82*, 79–88.

Lam, S. S. K., Shaubroeck, J., & Aryee, S. (2002). Relationship between organizational justice and employee work outcomes: A cross national study. *Journal of Organizational Behavior, 23*, 1–18.

Larson, J. (1986). Supervisors' performance feedback to subordinates: The role of subordinate performance valence and outcome dependence. *Organizational Behavior and Human Decision Processes, 37*, 391–408.

Larson, J. R. (1989). The dynamic interplay between employees' feedback-seeking strategies and supervisors' delivery of performance feedback. *Academy of Management Review, 14*, 21–41.

Latting, J. K. (1992). Giving corrective feedback: A decisional analysis. *Social Work, 37*, 424–430.

Lau, V. C. S., Au, W. T., & Ho, J. M. C. (2003). A qualitative and quantitative review of antecedents of counterproductive behavior in organizations. *Journal of Business & Psychology, 18*, 73–99.

Leap, T., & Crino, M. (1998). How serious is serious? *HR Magazine, 43*(6), 43–48.

LeBlanc, M. M., & Kelloway, E. K. (2002). Predictors and outcomes of workplace violence and aggression. *Journal of Applied Psychology, 87*, 444–453.

Leung, K., & Li, W. (1990). Psychological mechanisms of process control effects. *Journal of Applied Psychology, 75*, 613–620.

Leung, K., Su, S., & Morris, M. (2001). When is criticism not constructive? The roles of fairness perceptions and dispositional attributions in employee acceptance of critical supervisory feedback. *Human Relations, 54*(9), 1155–1187.

Leventhal, G. S. (1980). What should be done with equity theory? New approaches to the study of fairness in social relationships. In K. Gergen, M. Greenberg, & R. Willis (Eds.), *Social exchange: Advances in theory and research* (pp. 27–55). New York: Plenum Press.

Liden, R. C., Wayne, S. J., Judge, T. A., Sparrowe, R. T., Kraimer, M. L., & Franz, T. M. (1999). Management of poor performance: A comparison of manager, group member, and group disciplinary decisions. *Journal of Applied Psychology, 84*, 835–850.

Lim, V. K. G. (2002). The IT way of loafing on the job: Cyberloafing, neutralizing, and organizational justice. *Journal of Organizational Behavior, 23*, 675–694.

Lind, E. A. (1997). Litigation and claiming: Antisocial behavior or legitimate regulation? In R. Giacalone & J. Greenberg (Eds.), *Antisocial behavior in organizations* (pp. 150–171). Thousand Oaks, CA: Sage.

Lind, E. A., Greenberg, J., Scott, K. S., & Welchans, T. D. (2000). The winding road from employee to complainant: Situational and psychological determinants of wrongful termination claims. *Administrative Science Quarterly, 45*, 557–590.

Lizzio, A. (2003). The role of gender in the construction and evaluation of feedback effectiveness. *Management Communication Quarterly, 16*(3), 341–379.

Locke, E. A. (1976). The nature and causes of job satisfaction. In M. Dunnette (Ed.), *Handbook of industrial and organizational psychology* (pp. 1297–1350). Chicago: Rand-McNally.

Lyncheski, J. E. (1995). Employee terminations: Use fairness and compassion. *HR Focus, 72*, 19.

Manz, C. C. (1986). Self-leadership: Toward an expanded theory of self-influence processes in organizations. *Academy of Management Review, 11*(3), 585.

McCall, M., & Lombardo, M. (1983). *Off the track: Why and how successful executives get derailed.* Technical Report #21. Greensboro, NC: Center for Creative Leadership.

McShulskis, E. (1996). Employee assistance programs effective but underused? *HRMagazine, 41*, 19–20.

Meritor Savings Bank v. Vinson, 477 U.S. 57 (1986).

Mikulincer, M. (1994). *Human learned helplessness: A coping perspective.* New York: Plenum Press.

Mitchell, M. S., & Ambrose, M. L. (2007). Abusive supervision and workplace deviance and the moderating effects of negative reciprocity beliefs. *Journal of Applied Psychology, 92*, 1159–1168.

Mitchell, T. R., Green, S. G., & Wood, R. E. (1981). An attributional model of leadership and the poor performing subordinate: Development and validation. In B. M. Staw & L. L. Cummings (Eds.), *Research in organizational behavior* (pp. 187–234). Greenwich, CT: JAI Press.

Mitchell, T. R., & Wood, R. E. (1980). Supervisors' responses to subordinate poor performance: A test of an attributional model. *Organizational Behavior & Human Performance, 25*(1), 123–138.

Morgan, H., Harkins, P., & Goldsmith, M. (2005). *The art and practice of leadership coaching: 50 top executive coaches reveal their secrets.* Hoboken, NJ: John Wiley & Sons.

Morris, G. H., Gaveras, S. C., Baker, W. L., & Coursey, M. L. (1990). Aligning actions at work: How managers confront problems of employee performance. *Management Communication Quarterly, 3*, 303–333.

Muhl, C. J. (2001). The employment-at-will doctrine: Three major exceptions. *Monthly Labor Review, 124,* 3–11.

Murphy, K. R. (1993). *Honesty in the workplace.* Pacific Grove, CA: Brooks/Cole.

Mustaine, E. E., & Tewksbury, R. (2002). Workplace theft: An analysis of student-employee offenders and job attributes. *American Journal of Criminal Justice, 27,* 111–127.

Neihoff, B. P., Paul, R. J., & Bunch, J. F. S. (1998). The social effects of punishment events: The influence of violator past performance record and severity of the punishment on observers' justice perceptions and attitudes. *Journal of Organizational Behavior, 19,* 589–602.

Neuman, J. H., & Baron, R. A. (1997). Aggression in the workplace. In R. A. Giacalone & J. Greenberg (Eds.), *Antisocial behavior in organizations* (pp. 37–67). Thousand Oaks, CA: Sage.

Nicholson, N. (1976). Management sanctions and absence control. *Human Relations, 29*(2), 139–151.

O'Leary-Kelly, A. M., Griffin, R. W., & Glew, D. J. (1996). Organization-motivated aggression: A research framework. *Academy of Management Review, 21,* 225–253.

O'Reilly, C. A., & Puffer, S. M. (1989). The impact of rewards and punishments in a social context: A laboratory and field experiment. *Journal of Occupational Psychology, 62,* 41–53.

O'Reilly, C. A., & Weitz, B. A. (1980). Managing marginal employees: The use of warnings and dismissals. *Administrative Science Quarterly, 25,* 467–483.

Osigweh, C. A. B., & Hutchison, W. R. (1989). Positive discipline. *Human Resource Management, 28,* 367–383.

Owens, D. M. (2006). EAPs for a diverse world. *HRMagazine, 51,* 91–96.

Pearson, C. M., Andersson, L. M., & Porath, C. L. (2005). Workplace incivility. In S. Fox and P. E. Spector (Eds.), *Counterproductive work behavior: Investigations of actors and targets* (pp. 177–200). Washington, DC: American Psychological Association.

Pearson, C. M., & Porath, C. L. (2005). On the nature, consequences, and remedies of workplace incivility: No time for "nice"? Think again. *Academy of Management Executive, 19,* 7–18.

Penney, L. M., & Spector, P. E. (2005). Job stress, incivility, and counterproductive work behavior (CWB): The moderating role of negative affectivity. *Journal of Organizational Behavior, 26,* 777–796.

Rayner, C., Hoel, H., & Cooper, C. L. (2002). *Workplace bullying: What we know, who is to blame and what can we do?* London: Taylor Francis.

Rayner, C., & Keashly, L. (2005). Bullying at work: A perspective from Britain and North America. In S. Fox & P. E. Spector (Eds.),

Counterproductive work behavior: Investigations of actors and targets (pp. 271–296). Washington, DC: American Psychological Association.

Rollinson, D. J. (2000). Supervisor and manager approaches to handling discipline and grievance: A follow-up study. *Personnel Review, 29,* 743–768.

Rosen, B., & Jerdee, T. H. (1974). Factors influencing disciplinary judgments. *Journal of Applied Psychology, 59,* 327–331.

Rothstein, M. A., Craver, C. B., Schroeder, E. P., & VanderVelde, L. S. (1994). *Human resources and the law.* Washington, DC: BNA Books.

Rotundo, M., & Sackett, P. R. (2002). The relative importance of task, citizenship, and counterproductive performance to global ratings of job performance: A policy-capturing approach. *Journal of Applied Psychology, 87,* 66–80.

Rudawsky, D. J., Lundgren, D. C., & Grasha, A. F. (1999). Competitive and collaborative responses to negative feedback. *International Journal of Conflict Management, 10*(2), 172–190.

Rupp, D. E., & Cropanzano, R. (2002). The mediating effects of social exchange relationships in predicting workplace outcomes from multifoci organizational justice. *Organizational Behavior and Human Decision Processes, 89,* 925–946.

Sackett, P. R., & DeVore, C. J. (2002). *Counterproductive behaviors at work.* Thousand Oaks, CA: Sage.

Schnake, M. E. (1986). Vicarious punishment in work settings. *Journal of Applied Psychology, 71,* 343–345.

Schneider, K. T., Swan, S., & Fitzgerald, L. F. (1997). Job-related and psychological effects of sexual harassment in the workplace: Empirical evidence from two organizations. *Journal of Applied Psychology, 82,* 401–415.

Schwarzwald, J., Koslowsky, M., & Shalit, B. (1992). A field study of employees' attitudes and behaviors after promotion decisions. *Journal of Applied Psychology, 77,* 511–514.

Selvik, R., & Bingaman, D. (1998, September/October). EAP outcomes from the client's point of view. *EAP Digest,* pp. 21–23.

Spector, P. E. (1975). Relationships of organizational frustration with reported behavioral reactions of employees. *Journal of Applied Psychology, 60,* 635–637.

Spector, P. E. (1997). *Job satisfaction: Application, assessment, causes, and consequences.* Thousand Oaks, CA: Sage.

Spector, P. E., & Fox, S. (2005). The stressor-emotion model of counterproductive work behavior. In S. Fox & P. E. Spector (Eds.), *Counterproductive work behavior: Investigations of actors and targets* (pp. 151–174). Washington, DC: American Psychological Association.

Spector, P. E., Fox, S., Penney, L. M., Bruursema, K., Goh, A., & Kessler, S. (2006). The dimensionality of counterproductivity: Are all counterproductive behaviors created equal? *Journal of Vocational Behavior, 68*, 446–460.

Spielberger, C. (1991). State trait anger expression inventory. Odessa, FL: Psychological Assessment Resources.

Strazewski, L. (2001). Facing facts about workplace substance abuse. *Rough Notes, 144*(5), 114–118.

Sunoo, B. P. (1996). Positive discipline: Sending the right or wrong message? *Personnel Journal, 75*, 109–110.

Tata, J. (2002). The influence of managerial accounts on employees' reactions to negative feedback. *Group & Organization Management, 27*, 480–503.

Tepper, B. J. (2000). Consequences of abusive supervision. *Academy of Management Journal, 43*, 178–190.

The Straits Times. (2000, April 4). Cyberslackers at work.

Thibaut, J., & Walker, L. (1975). *Procedural justice: A psychological analysis.* Mahwah, NJ: Lawrence Erlbaum Associates.

Tobias, P. H. (2000). Ten deadly sins in handling dismissal cases. *Employee Rights Quarterly, 1*, 63–66.

Trevino, L. K. (1992). The social effects of punishment in organizations: A justice perspective. *Academy of Management Review, 17*, 647–676.

Trevino, L. K., & Ball, G. A. (1992). The social implications of punishing unethical behavior: Observers' cognitive and affective reactions. *Journal of Management, 18*, 751–768.

Triner, J., & Turner, S. (2005). Professional coaches and employee assistance practitioners: Serving corporate and individual clients. *Journal of Workplace Behavioral Health, 21*, 1–14.

Van Bogaert, D., & Gross-Schaefer, A. (2005). Terminating the employee-employer relationship: Ethical and legal challenges. *Employee Relations Law Journal, 31*, 49–66.

Vault.com. (2005). Vault internet use in the workplace survey of over 1,100 employees. Retrieved March 10, 2008, from http://www.vault.com/surveys/internetusesurvey/home.jsp.

Verton, D. (2000). Employers ok with e-surfing. *Computerworld, 34*, 16.

Wallace v. DTG Operations, 442 F.3d 1112 (8th Cir. 2006).

Walsh, D., & Schwarz, J. L. (1996). State common law wrongful discharge doctrines: Up-date, refinement, and rationales. *American Business Law Journal, 33*, 645–689.

Weiss, R. M. (2003). Effects of program characteristics on EAP utilization. *Employee Assistance Quarterly, 18*, 61–70.

Williams, J. H., Fitzgerald, L. F., & Drasgow, F. (1999). The effects of organizational practices on sexual harassment and individual outcomes in the military. *Military Psychology, 11*, 303–328.

Willness, C. R., Steel, P., & Lee, K. (2007). A meta-analysis of the antecedents and consequences of workplace sexual harassment. *Personnel Psychology, 60*, 127–162.

Zugelder, M., Champagne, P., & Maurer, S. (2006). An affirmative defense to sexual harassment by managers and supervisors: Analyzing employer liability and protecting employee rights in the United States. *Employee Responsibilities & Rights Journal, 18*, 111–122.

CHAPTER 12

FORCED RANKINGS: PROS, CONS, AND PRACTICES

Peter G. Dominick

> *"The new law of evolution in corporate America seems to be survival of the unfittest. Well, in my book you either do it right or you get eliminated. . . ."*
> GORDON GECKO IN OLIVER STONE'S FILM,
> *WALL STREET.*

> *You can't eat the orange and throw the peel away—a man is not a piece of fruit.*
> WILLY LOMAN, IN ARTHUR MILLER'S PLAY,
> *THE DEATH OF A SALESMAN*

A 2005 survey conducted by the Society for Human Resource Management (SHRM) asked, "Does your organization utilize forced ranking (for example, a system whereby a specified percentage of those being evaluated must receive the highest and lowest ratings) to evaluate employees?" Of the 330 human resource professionals who responded, 276 (almost 84 percent) reported that their companies did not use forced ranking. Another eleven respondents reported that their companies used no form of performance appraisal (about 3.3 percent of the entire sample). Among the forty-three people who indicated their companies did use forced ranking, only two (less than 1 percent of the entire sample) reported that their forced ranking process always led to employee terminations. Another seventeen indicated that no employees were ever dismissed as a result of the process.[1]

Although the popularity of forced ranking may be on the rise, as these survey results suggest, it is hardly the prevailing approach to performance evaluation.[2] Arguably however, during the past several years, no other aspect of performance management has garnered as much attention in the popular press. Since 2000, articles about forced ranking have appeared in such prominent international media outlets as *Time* (Greenwald, 2001), *The New York Times* (Abelson, 2001; Anonymous, 2003; Holland, 2006), *BusinessWeek* (McGregor, 2006), *Fortune* (Boyle, 2001), *The Economist* (Anonymous, 2000), *Financial Times* (Donkin, 2005, 2007), *The Chicago Tribune* (Osterman, 2003), and *USA Today* (Armour, 2003). This attention is due in part to the high profile of one of its major proponents, Jack Welch, but it also reflects the fact that forced ranking is a topic that elicits strong visceral reactions from laypersons, human resource (HR) professionals, and researchers alike.

On one hand, the process is used by many admired companies such as General Electric (GE), Sun-Micro Systems, and Hewlett-Packard (Grote, 2005). Its proponents laud the approach for its abilities to promote more accurate ratings, identify high-potential employees, and hold poor performers accountable. On the other hand, forced ranking has been tried and rejected by other notable companies like Xerox and PepsiCo (Olson & Davis, 2003). Still others like Goodyear and Ford have backed away from forced ranking, at least in part because of the legal land mines they found themselves confronting. The process also has the dubious distinction of being linked to Enron (Greenwald, 2001), with some characterizing it as emblematic of the cutthroat, backroom deal-making culture that led to the company's demise (Shermer, 2008).

This chapter reviews the rationale underlying the use of forced rankings in performance management and explores why it is so controversial. Drawing upon research and the experiences of organizations that have adopted the approach, it describes what we know about its effectiveness overall and in relation to other performance appraisal techniques. Is the process, for example, as demoralizing as many of its detractors assert? Can one ever say, as do some of its advocates, that forced ranking is superior to other well-designed and executed approaches to managing performance? This chapter also discusses important situational and legal considerations that must be taken into account and stresses important steps to keep in mind when trying to implement forced ranking. It concludes with some thoughts about how forced ranking should be considered in relation to several emerging trends, perspectives, and challenges shaping human resource practices today.

Defining Forced Ranking

Virtually all performance rating systems can be grouped into one of two general categories: *absolute* and *relative* (Cascio, 1991). Absolute systems such as behaviorally anchored rating scales (BARS), weighted checklists, and behavioral observation scales (BOS) involve making judgments about people in relation to descriptions of job-related behaviors and/or traits. Under such systems, all individuals are independently assessed against the same standards, and it is conceivable that multiple individuals could attain essentially the same rating in relation to either specific behaviors and traits or overall performance.

Relative rating and forced ranking are synonymous terms. Such approaches require raters to assess individuals in relation to one another. The criteria used for making those comparisons might (and typically does) include job-related behaviors and traits, but ratees' assessment results are determined by where they are positioned in relation to others in a given peer group. In other words, the main objective is not *just* to determine whether a particular person is a highly effective, adequate, or poor performer but to be able to say who is best, who is next best, right on down, in some cases, to who is worst.

The term "forced ranking" is frequently used by the popular press, employment professionals, and researchers to describe all forced ranking systems (Olson & Davis, 2003). There are, however, various forms of forced rankings. This fact should be kept in mind when considering the relevance of pros and cons espoused by supporters and critics of the systems. One should also note that different writers have used different terms to describe the same variation of forced ranking. For instance, that which management consultant Dick Grote calls "forced ranking" in his 2005 book, *Forced Ranking*, others have called "forced distribution."

At the same time, Grote uses the term forced distribution to describe another variant. For the purposes of this chapter, I will describe some common variations drawing where appropriate on the labels used by Grote.

The most basic approach is sometimes referred to as a "totem pole" approach because it involves ranking all employees in a particular work group from best to worst.

Forced or fixed distribution methods come in several sub-variants. The most controversial tends to use a normal distribution in which employees are slotted into the bell curve of a normal distribution and then described by the percentage group they represent (for example, the top 10 percent). The use of quartile distinctions (such as top 25 percent, top 50 percent, bottom 50 percent, and bottom 25 percent) is another variant. In many cases, once an individual is assigned to a quartile, he or she is typically further ranked against others in the same quartile (Olson & Davis, 2003). Still, in other cases organizations might only use the distribution method to identify those people who are among the very best or very worst (perhaps the top 10 percent of a workforce or the bottom 10 percent) performers. According to Grote (2005), another distinguishing characteristic of a forced distribution system is that an organization's performance appraisal criteria are the basis for locating people within the distribution. He also includes under this label any rating distribution scheme regardless of whether it is required (forced) or recommended (guidelines) (Grote, 2005, p. 140).

According to Grote, the term "forced ranking" applies to those systems that operate independent of and in addition to an organization's performance appraisal process. It is this variant that was made famous (or infamous, depending on your point of view) by Jack Welch and General Electric. While the assessment criteria still need to be job-related, they are usually different from those used in the formal appraisal process. The approach still requires some sort of ranking distribution scheme (for example, General Electric's top 20 percent; vital 70 percent; bottom 10 percent), but by being independent of the appraisal process it serves to further highlight comparisons between individuals (Grote, 2005, p. 140). Table 12.1 provides examples of several rating distribution schemes.

Table 12.1 Rating Distribution Examples.

Sun Micro Systems*	General Electric*	Ford* (abandoned process)	Dick Grote's Recommended Approach**
Superior: 20 percent	Top: 20 percent	A performers: 10 percent	Distinguished/Superior (20 to 30 percent)
Sun Standard: 70 percent	Vital: 70 percent	B performers: 80 percent	Fully successful (60 percent or more)
Under-performing: 5 percent	Bottom: 10 percent	C performers: 10 percent	Need improvement (10 to 15 percent) Unsatisfactory (less than 5 percent)

* Greenwald, 2001; ** Grote, 2005, p. 148

Finally, before turning to a discussion of the positions for and against forced ranking, it is important to realize that, in addition to the distinctions described above, forced ranking systems also vary based on design features and policies unique to a particular organization. Even forced ranking supporters acknowledge that their fairness and usefulness depend largely on how they are implemented and whether or not they are accompanied by other changes in the overall performance management system. For example, General Electric initially assigned employees to one of five grades but streamlined that into three grades. "We had a system where 90 percent of employees felt demoralized," says Bill Conaty, senior vice president of human relations (Grote, 2005).

It is perhaps within the details of such policies that much of the controversy regarding forced ranking ultimately resides. For instance, Blume, Baldwin, and Rubin (2007) identified four program design elements that could affect fairness perceptions and influence applicant attraction perceptions: (a) the consequences for low performers (for example, termination versus development), (b) the differentiation of rewards among high and low performers, (c) comparison group size, and (d) the frequency and consistency of feedback. Earlier, Folger and Cropenzano (1998) stressed that for any type of rating format to be viewed as fair it should provide for performance and developmental goals, be based on behaviors, and be based on detailed information. While these features are more readily associated with absolute rating systems, they can and sometimes are integrated with forced ranking systems.

The Pros and Cons of Forced Ranking Systems

Most arguments for and against the process can be grouped in relation to four general concerns that are important to people on both sides of the debate. These are concerns for fairness and accuracy; performance; morale; and legal compliance. For each of these areas, I'll first describe the general positions taken by advocates and opponents of forced ranking. Next, I'll consider what relevant research does and does not say about the positions taken.

Fairness and Accuracy

Forced choice advocates argue that the process combats the problem of artificially inflated ratings. While there is little empirical evidence to characterize the extent to which appraisal ratings are inflated, there is plenty of anecdotal support (Grote, 2005). For example, before Ford chose to implement a forced ranking process (that it later abandoned), 98 percent of its managers had been rated as "fully meeting expectations" (Olson & Davis, 2003). Many managers, they argue, are reluctant to single people out as being less than satisfactory, and this tendency is likely to be even more prevalent in environments that discourage open conflict and when managers are not regularly trained on how to rate and to deliver tough messages about performance (Olson & Davis, 2003). Specifying fixed percentages at the top and bottom of a ranking system, they assert, ensures a fairer distribution of pay, ensuring that organizations have funds to award top performers and that they don't over-reward poor performers.

Some proponents further stress that most absolute rating systems remain unfair, even if managers are already doing a good job of making judgments and at providing feedback to individuals. This is because the failure to differentiate alienates top performers and prevents them from getting the rewards and recognition they deserve (Grote, 2005).

Still others argue that ranking is also fairer to poor performers. The candid nature of the process, they assert, at least lets people know where they stand so that they might have an opportunity to do something about it. Grote, for instance, quotes one manager who advocated the process: "In non-ranking organizations, you will probably never know where you stand until you are passed over for promotion, not given a key assignment, or laid off" (Grote, 2005, p. 32). Jack Welch, in defending GE's policy to terminate the bottom 10 percent, asserts that doing so enables those individuals to move on into environments in which they *can* succeed. As he explained in an annual letter to shareholders, "Not removing that bottom 10 percent early in their careers is . . . a form of cruelty because inevitably a new leader will come along and take out that bottom 10 percent right away, leaving them, sometimes midway through their careers, stranded" (Hymowitz, 2001).

Critics of forced ranking argue that fitting employees into predetermined performance distributions can never be fair. They are most strongly opposed to the use of normal distributions. In order for normal distributions to occur, they point out, one must have randomly occurring events, but in organizations people are specifically recruited, selected, and trained for their jobs and are then expected to fulfill unique job responsibilities. While those processes may not be perfect, they are far from random.

In addition to the problem of randomness, applying the process to groups of fewer than one hundred is statistically problematic (Olson & Davis, 2004). In fact, attaining a normal distribution requires sample sizes in the hundreds or even thousands (Weatherly, 2004).

This fact presents a double-edged sword. Many organizations using forced ranking do in fact include large numbers of employees in the process. GE applies the process to its roughly five thousand managerial employees (Olson & Davis, 2004), and Sun Microsystems applies the process to all of its more than forty thousand employees (Greenwald, 2001). When Ford was attempting to use the process, they included eighteen thousand (Grote, 2005). However, initial comparisons typically occur within smaller work groups before being "rolled up" for comparisons with employees from other groups. Few organizational departments or teams have the kinds of numbers that would justify the sorts of distributions sought and, in those instances where they do, critics note, it seems implausible that raters could have sufficient knowledge of each person's performance such that they could make accurate comparisons between them. Thus, while extending comparison groups beyond the span of control of individual managers enhances the probability of a normal distribution, it also inevitably creates an evaluation context in which raters are less likely to be familiar with ratee performance. Since most managers have only five to fifteen direct reports (Davison, 2003), one must ask how far beyond the average manager's span of control it is reasonable to go to attain a large comparison group (Blume, Baldwin, & Rubin, 2007).

Other criticisms have been targeted toward the rating criterion used. Too often, say critics, rankings are based on subjective judgments tied to standards that are interpreted inconsistently. It is worth noting that some forced ranking proponents actually advocate the use of broader standards, but they don't view them as being vague. In his book, Grote quotes one HR manager who said, "Our criteria [for forced ranking comparisons] used to be 'flexible, curious, and collaborative, now it's just 'right results, right behaviors'" (Grote, 2005, p. 78). While acknowledging that it can help to give managers more specific criteria, especially the first time through a ranking process, Grote also tends to support this HR manager's position. He goes on to write: "In the final analysis all that rankers are being asked to determine is who delivers the best results and has the most potential, and who delivers the least" (Grote, 2005, p. 79).

Critics like Tom Coens and Mary Jenkins (advocates for abolishing performance appraisals in general) challenge this line of reasoning. As Coens explains, "There's an assumption that a manager can know the precise performance level of an employee, when this sort of ranking is really a very subjective judgment that depends on many factors" (Hymowitz, 2001). For instance, employees who belong to a particularly talented or productive unit may receive poorer rankings than they would if being considered in relation to those in a less talented group. Ed Lawler regards the forced distribution approach as a bureaucratic solution to a serious leadership failure. "It ignores," he says, "the reality that in some work groups there are no poor performers and in others there are no good performers. It causes managers to disown the appraisal event and to essentially say, I was just following the rules" (Lawler, 2003a). Others note that, while employees who are either outstanding or weak may stand out, trying to distinguish among the vast majority of employees in the middle can be difficult if not impossible.

Still another set of criticisms stems from the argument that forced ranking is just as susceptible to favoritism, manipulation, and organizational politics as any other process. In calling forced ranking a "bankrupt strategy," Dick Beatty has said, "it can send the wrong message and drive good people out who fear they will be judged unfairly, while mediocre workers hunker down or play political games to survive" (Bates, 2003). The same article that quoted Beatty later went on to provide examples from another critic of the ways in which the process can be manipulated. These include managers who avoid having to assign low grades to any of their people by trading them with supervisors of other groups. Others may even carry poor performers throughout the year, just so they can have someone to rank at the bottom (Bates, 2003). Additional tactics include making deals with other managers to ensure one's own employees are sufficiently supported in ranking meetings. Still others simply note that forced ranking processes typically depend too much on the willingness of managers to fight for valued employees "during what can become a brutal horse trading session" (Greenwald, 2001). In a recent essay, Shermer (2008) quotes former Enron managers who described how the process was frequently manipulated there. He writes:

> Here is one typical conversation recounted by an unnamed manager: "I was wondering if you had a few minutes to talk some PRC [performance ranking committee]." She replied, "Why—you want to cut a deal?" "Done,' I said—and just like that we cut our deal." Another manager described the PRC system as creating "an environment where employees were afraid to express their opinions or to question unethical and potentially illegal business practices. Because the Rank and Yank system was both arbitrary and subjective, it was easily used by managers to reward blind loyalty and quash brewing dissent.

It is important to stress that such manipulation need not be the case. They are certainly not built into the premise of how forced ranking systems should work and, to the extent such conversations characterize the process at Enron, they were symptomatic of broader deficiencies in its leadership and corporate culture. Nonetheless, anyone even considering the use of forced ranking should be mindful of how politics and social influence can play a role.

Research Perspectives on Forced Ranking Fairness and Accuracy

When operating free from biases, be they based in overt political manipulations or the result of more subtle cues, relative rating formats have been shown to offer psychometric advantages over absolute approaches. Two meta-analyses (Heneman, 1986; Nathan & Alexander, 1988) examining the differences between the two approaches have found that relative formats have stronger correlations with results-oriented criteria like production quantity and sales volume. They also did a better job in relation to the assessment of certain underlying skills like general cognitive ability, verbal and quantitative ability, perceptual speed, and spatial/mechanical ability. Their superiority, however, is not so clearly established when it comes to assessing leadership skills or when trying to judge individual effectiveness when outcomes are team-based.

It is also important to recognize that fairness is as much a matter of perception as it is one of fact. In one recent study, Roch, Sternburgh, and Caputo (2007) demonstrated that people perceived each of the absolute rating systems described to them in a survey as being fairer than any of the relative rating systems described in the same survey. It should be noted that theirs was a policy-capturing study and was not based on subjects actually using these systems, although they did control for whether or not people had prior experience as performance appraisal raters or ratees.

Murphy and Cleveland (1991), in particular, have argued that relative ratings produce negative reactions principally because they are not consistent with two objectives important to many people being rated: to obtain feedback and to convey information. They note, for instance, that feedback obtained from a relative process is also dependent on what others in the comparison group have done, potentially making it a less objective source of information.

Practitioners interested in using forced ranking need to at least be mindful of results like those discussed above because they help to highlight the kinds of concerns employees will have about the process. Forced ranking proponents also stress, however, that it is possible to address many of the concerns through the ways in which they design their forced ranking and integrate them with other aspects of performance management.

In addition, it further helps to consider how people form fairness perceptions based on their reactions to the way decisions are made (procedural justice) and their reactions to the outcomes of those decisions (distributive justice). Most research suggests that perceptions of procedural justice become increasingly important when the outcomes (distributive justice) are perceived to be unfair (Brockner & Wiesenfeld, 1996; Folger & Cropenzano, 1998). Moreover, the reverse also tends to be true. Distributive justice generally matters more when procedural justice is low. These relationships can be important to how forced rankings are perceived. Specifically, expect people's final rankings to influence their perceptions of the process. It may be reasonable for some organizations to take the position that the perceptions of their top-ranked performers are what matter most, and because the outcomes are positive for those individuals, they are more likely to view the process favorably. However, most organizations also need to value and rely on the larger segment of their workforce not ranked at the top. Many of these people, by virtue of their rankings, will have lower perceptions of the process's distributive justice, therefore leading them to also discount its procedural justice.

One practical implication is that forced ranking processes should be as transparent as possible in order to combat the very natural negative reactions many employees are likely to experience. This should include clarity about the criteria for ranking decisions and the people involved in making those decisions (examples of what some researchers would describe as informational justice). It should also include careful consideration of the ways in which ranking results are communicated back to employees (what some researchers would term interpersonal justice). In addition, our understanding of justice perceptions helps explain why organizations need to think carefully about the consequences associated with one's rankings, examples of which include whether or not to terminate lowest-ranked personnel, the kinds of coaching and development support provided in relation to one's ranking, opportunities to find new positions, get promoted, and so on. They also help to highlight the value of gradually introducing forced ranking systems and their consequences. For instance, many proponents advocate rolling the process out first for top managers and including a moratorium before beginning to use the process to terminate.

The point is that fairness perceptions of forced ranking are also a function of related policy and implementation practices. Operating on the premise that fairness is a key determinant of how attractive people find performance appraisal systems, Blume, Baldwin, and Rubin (2007) looked at the ways in which certain design characteristics affected the perceived attractiveness of forced distribution rating systems. They found that forced distribution rating systems with less stringent consequences (for example, where poorly ranked employees are not terminated) are viewed more favorably. The other factors that enhanced perceived favorability were using a sufficiently large comparison group and ensuring that the process provided for frequent feedback. They also found some important individual differences that tended to shape reactions. Females were less attracted than males to forced distribution systems when the consequences of poor performance were more stringent. Not surprisingly, people with higher cognitive ability tended to value systems that highly differentiated rewards in relation to ranking.

These results reinforce the fact that system design features do matter and that organizations should carefully consider the unique characteristics of their workforce and the traits they wish to attract. At the same time, keep in mind that this was a policy-capturing study using college students as subjects. While they are representative of an important recruiting target for many organizations, they are not necessarily representative of a more experienced workforce that may be taking other factors into account when making judgments related to fairness (Blume, Baldwin, & Rubin, 2007).

Another recent set of studies by Schleicher, Bull, and Green (2007) looked at rater reactions to using a forced distribution rating system. They examined how fairness and perceived difficulty with the ranking task were influenced by (1) the consequences associated with having to rank others and (2) whether or not there was a high degree of variability in the performance of those being rated. Results for the two studies were quite similar. Subjects were less likely to perceive the procedure to be fair and more likely to describe it as difficult when it had administrative consequences for those being rated (grades in Study 1 and termination, promotions, and pay in Study 2) and when there was little variability in the performance of those being rated/ranked. In addition, the researchers found in both studies that having a high need for affiliation led people to perceive the task as being more difficult.

The studies demonstrate that manager reactions and personal characteristics need to be taken into account when deciding whether or how to introduce forced ranking. The researchers also suggest that their results argue for moving slowly, allowing managers and employees time to get used to a forced ranking approach before attaching administrative consequences (such as terminations, promotions, pay). Not doing so could have significant implications for morale and other outcomes. They further note that their findings would support the view that forced ranking approaches should not be used unless there is good reason to believe that there is considerable performance variability among those to be ranked (Schleicher, Bull, & Green, 2007).

In closing, there still remain many open questions regarding how forced ranking affects accuracy and fairness perceptions. One such set of questions may pertain to the ways in which assimilation and contrast effects influence subsequent rankings of ratees. Open research questions notwithstanding, clearly, fairness matters to people on both sides of the forced ranking debate. While the above discussion does not provide definitive answers, it does highlight key fairness considerations that organizations need to be thinking about when exploring the use of forced ranking systems. Some of those considerations are summarized in the exhibit below.

Exhibit 12.1 Forced Ranking Fairness and Accuracy: Strategic Considerations.

- Carefully assess the accuracy of existing appraisal processes. Determine whether rater inflation or other inaccuracies are pervasive problems. Also assess why other efforts to correct them may have failed.
- Take stock of employee and manager perceptions.
  - Know what they value about existing performance management processes and employee development programs.
  - Also understand what they find to be most troubling.
  - Carefully consider fairness perceptions with regard to existing practices.
- Consider the corporate culture and what might need to change for it to better support candid feedback and constructive conflict.
- Make sure the workforce to be ranked is large enough and that there is sufficient variability in performance to justify using forced ranking.

- Make sure your management team can agree on the criteria for ranking employee performance.
- Develop plans for training people and monitoring the use of forced ranking.
- Consider how forced ranking will likely be perceived by the kinds of people you want to attract to your organization.

Performance Improvement

According to its proponents, forced ranking processes contribute to improved performance in several important ways. At its heart the process is about differentiating between talent levels (between individuals, but also between groups and departments) in ways that absolute performance appraisals cannot. When done correctly, this differentiation ensures that company resources are directed toward those who contribute the most and/or have the potential to make a positive difference. These resources include compensation and other rewards like promotions, leadership development, and training support in general. They might also include support in the form of resources to get a job done. Overall, they argue the process better ensures that a company can get an optimal return on its investments in human capital. As Jack Welch has explained, "A company that bets its future on its people must remove the lower 10 percent, and keep moving it every year—always raising the bar of performance and increasing the quality of its leadership" (General Electric Company, 2000).

In making the business case for forced ranking, proponents go further by elaborating on other important contributions. The process, they argue, requires a company to clarify what it really values and the criteria for defining success for individuals and the organization overall. In other words, forced ranking systems offer clarity that helps people focus their efforts. Along the way, it reinforces the values of a merit-based culture and is likely to attract individuals who themselves value achievement and performance. In making the case for forced ranking, Dick Grote goes even further by arguing that another important business outcome includes the process's potential to provide valuable information about managers' abilities to identify and champion talent, a critical aspect of their leadership ability (Grote, 2005).

Not surprisingly, those opposing the process challenge many of the performance assertions made by proponents. For one thing, they question the sustainability of policies that call for replacing the bottom 10 percent (or any percent) every year. At some point, they stress, organizations begin terminating people who are quite capable. The financial and emotional costs of replacing them will exceed any performance gains one might attain (Weatherly, 2004). Even Dick Grote agrees that few companies can tolerate the kind of regular turnover that occurs at companies like GE and that using the process to terminate employees should be a short-term measure until other processes are in place (Grote, 2005).

They also take issue with claims regarding employee development. They agree that the systems will influence how development is pursued, but not always in ways that are in the interests of the organization or its employees. As Ed Lawler has observed, the process can make it difficult to devote attention toward developing future talent. "It hardly makes sense for managers to invest in developing individuals who are marginal performers when they believe that in a very short time they will have to eliminate the employees whom they develop" (Lawler, 2003a). Other critics note that under such systems, those in the middle ranks (the bulk of an organization's workforce) frequently receive the least development attention. In many cases, those at the bottom may receive coaching or the benefit of other interventions to help them redeem their performance (Weatherly, 2004). Likewise, those at the top are also supported, while those in the middle are left to contemplate the fact that they are just considered to be average (Greenwald, 2001).

At the same time, others point out that the process diverts attention away from the kinds of behavior and performance that really contribute to success in today's organizations (Kluger & Nir, 2007). Some suggest that forced ranking can discourage risk taking and is likely to encourage people to cover up mistakes at the expense of organizational learning. Moreover, they say the process penalizes those managers and departments that already set high performance standards, with the result being an eventual downturn in the standards and expectations they establish.

Some of the biggest criticisms are reserved for the ways in which forced ranking can undermine collaboration and other contextual behaviors known to contribute to performance. Instead, they assert that forced ranking systems pit employees against each other, undermining teams, which are often intentionally put together with varying talents in mind. As one former Enron manager noted about using the process within his team, "It was agonizing because everyone played a unique role . . . all the relationships instantly became strained" (Greenwald, 2001). There are also numerous reports of employees who, believing they have been graded unfairly, feel angry and unappreciated and as a result don't want to collaborate with colleagues who received higher rankings (Hymowitz, 2001).

To be fair, many of the arguments regarding the misdirection of behavior have been applied to performance appraisal in general. In their book, *Abolishing Performance Appraisal*, Coens and Jenkins quote Peter Scholtes, who said, "We live our lives in webs of interdependence and yet we keep telling ourselves the story that we are independent" (Coens & Jenkins, 2003, p. 33; Kluger & Nir, 2008). Their point is, in part, that performance appraisal systems put a focus on evaluating individuals rather than on teams. In their view, this fact demonstrates the deeply embedded and erroneous assumption that individuals' behavior, and not team performance, principally determines organizational success (Kluger & Nir, 2008). Even still, there are also many performance appraisal proponents (such as Ed Lawler and Richard Beatty) who agree that forced ranking systems go too far and make it difficult, if not impossible, to sustain a collaborative culture.

Many of the critiques pertaining to how forced ranking systems affect performance also relate to broader arguments suggesting that Corporate America has at its peril overemphasized individual talent and achievement as keys to success. For instance, in discussing potential risks from the use of forced ranking systems, Dick Grote acknowledges prescient points from Malcolm Gladwell's 2002 *New Yorker* essay entitled "The Talent Myth." Gladwell (2002) writes, "Groups don't write great novels and a committee didn't come up with the theory of relativity. But companies work by different rules. They don't just create, they execute and compete and coordinate the efforts of many different people, and the organizations that are most successful at that task are the ones where the system (not individuals) is the star."

Forced ranking proponents do not dismiss such criticisms as irrelevant. Grote (2005), for instance, acknowledges that forced ranking systems can lead to cultures that over-emphasize individual accomplishment. But he argues that such a risk can be mitigated by the ways in which ranking criteria are defined and the ways in which other aspects of performance management also support and reward collaboration.

Research Perspectives on Forced Ranking and Performance

When it comes to performance improvement, proponents and critics of forced ranking have both found support for their positions within the limited research that does exist. One study demonstrating the efficacy of forced ranking approaches was conducted by Scullen, Bergey, and Aiman-Smith (2005). Using a well-crafted simulation that took into account reasonable estimates for factors like selection validity, selection ratios, and voluntary turnover, these researchers were able to demonstrate that by repeatedly removing those ranked in the bottom percentage of a given workforce, organizations could potentially attain significant gains in overall performance and productivity. The researchers demonstrated continual (albeit at decreasing rates) improvements over a ten-year period, with most of the gains occurring within the first 3.5 to 4.5 years.

The study's authors, however, note several important limitations. These include not being able to model how existence of the process influences abilities to attract talent in the first place. The authors also point out that, in their simulation, correlations between turnover and performance were zero, while in practice the nature of that relationship is more variable. In addition, they did not factor in hiring and training costs, compensation policies or morale factors, and other affective outcomes. Nor could their simulation fully model implications for teamwork and collaboration or the potential for adverse impact.

In terms of field research, at least one survey suggests that forced ranking is favored by top-performing firms. A 2004 Sibson

Consulting Group study found that among those firms in the top 40 percent with respect to total return to shareholders, 20 percent used forced ranking. Only 14 percent of those in the bottom 40 percent for return to shareholders used the approach (Grote, 2005; Kochanski, Alderson, & Sorenson, 2004). These results, while intriguing, could hardly be considered confirmation of causality.

Moreover, at least one other field study suggests that the improvements reported in Scullen, Bergey, and Aiman-Smith's simulation do not always occur. Lawler (2003b) surveyed senior-level HR professionals from fifty-five Fortune 500 companies and reported on respondents' judgments of the effectiveness of their firms' performance management systems. Sixteen of the fifty-five organizations used forced distribution systems as part of their performance management process. He found that, when it came to their system's ability to differentiate between levels of performance (identify and reward top talent, identify and manage out poor performers), the average response from those firms using forced distribution systems was higher than the average derived from those firms that did not use it. However, when it came to impressions of their system's overall effectiveness (its capacity to help the business be successful, support business strategy, develop talent, and link individual performance to unit performance), the average responses from those firms that did not use forced distributions were higher. In particular, the biggest differences were obtained for perceptions of their systems' capacity to develop individuals' skills and ability.

Lawler also looked specifically at those firms that tied terminations to their performance management systems. Of those, twelve used forced distributions and twenty-one did not. In these cases he found that the averages with respect to a system's capacity to differentiate were virtually the same for those using forced distribution and those not using it. When it came to overall effectiveness of their appraisal systems, those not using forced distributions had a higher average overall, and for twelve of the fourteen items comprising this dimension of the survey.

Lawler suggests reasons for his findings may include the fact that using forced distributions makes managers uncomfortable, leading them to make bad judgments. They may also feel less committed to the process, which then sends mixed messages to employees. He also noted the ways in which forced distributions can promote competition among employees. His explanations, while plausible and consistent with the views of other critics, cannot be substantiated by the data he presented. In addition, while there were clear trends in the data he summarized, none of the differences was statistically significant. One might also wonder whether or not line managers and senior management share the same impressions as the HR professionals surveyed.

However, studies regarding the effects of social comparison processes do add credence to Lawler's (and others') contention that forced ranking systems can have a negative effect on teamwork and collaboration. This line of research has consistently shown that competitive behavior is likely to result from any comparison process when the dimension that is the basis for comparison is one that relates to an individual's self-identity (Tesser, 1988). Further, the intensity of that competitive response is likely to increase when the person or persons against whom one is being compared are considered commensurate (that is, part of one's peer group) (Goethals, 1986) and to the extent that individuals are more familiar with each other (friends or co-workers versus strangers) (Jones & Rachlin, 2006). All of these factors easily characterize the context in which most forced ranking comparisons are typically made.

Another contributing factor is a person's perception of his or her current ranking in relation to others' rankings. Some studies have shown that people are less inclined to cooperate with another person when that person is closely ranked to them and when cooperating has the potential to advance the other person's standing (Garcia & Tor, 2007; Garcia, Tor, & Gonzalez, 2006). This effect intensifies when both individuals are more highly ranked. Moreover, the reluctance to cooperate persists even when doing so would improve an individual's performance in an absolute sense. These conclusions, however, are largely based on experimental studies and do not take into account other factors that might shape actual workplace behaviors such as the way jobs are designed, leadership, and organizational values and norms.

There is clearly room for additional research exploring relationships between forced ranking and performance. It would help, for instance, to know more about how forced ranking systems' influence on performance is related to contextual considerations like organizational culture and individuals' values. It would also help to better understand whether forced ranking has a more positive effect on the performance of some jobs as opposed to others. One might also explore whether other organizational policies and practices can offset any negative effect forced ranking has on cooperative behavior. Ultimately, there are good performance-related arguments to be found among both those who oppose and those who support the forced ranking processes. While these arguments and related research are not definitive, they do help to highlight the issues that any organization needs to consider when making choices about whether or how to use forced ranking. Several of those issues are summarized in Exhibit 12.2.

Exhibit 12.2 Forced Ranking and Performance: Strategic Considerations.

- Make sure you understand the kinds of behaviors (for example, individual effort and achievement versus teamwork) that drive performance and how they might be affected by forced ranking.
- Not all company cultures can easily absorb forced ranking. It seems best suited to aggressive, competitive, and fast-paced cultures. Collaborative or bureaucratic cultures will have to make more adjustments.
- Develop plans that clarify how you'll devote resources to employee development based on ranking results. Establish separate plans for top performers, mid-level performers, and poor performers.
- Take current turnover rates into consideration, especially if you plan to use rankings to terminate.
  - Understand the costs associated with turnover in your organization.
  - Carefully consider whether your organization can tolerate more turnover and if suitable replacements are available.

Employee Morale

As has been the case regarding fairness, accuracy, and performance, forced ranking supporters and critics both have reasonable points to make when it comes to the ways in which the systems can influence employee attitudes and morale. On one hand, proponents often focus on the perspectives of top performers who, they assert, are finally able to get the rewards and recognition they deserve.

Grote (2005) cites several different surveys demonstrating that many employees are less than satisfied with their company's abilities to differentiate between talent. He cites a 2002 Hay Group employee attitude survey reporting that 32 percent of the employees surveyed from 335 companies agreed that poor performance was tolerated. He also notes a Watson-Wyatt Worldwide Study reporting that fewer than 40 percent of the organizations in their study felt the existing performance management system failed to establish clear goals or provide candid feedback (p. 14). He further notes that, according to Hewlett-Packard's former CEO Carly Fiorina (p. 15), prior to implementing their forced ranking process, more than 80 percent of employees felt the company dealt poorly with poor performers (no data, however, is available to describe their feelings about their current forced ranking system). A similar trend was stressed by Woolen (2003), who reported that 96 percent of the managers they polled want their companies to move more aggressively against poor performers.

Forced ranking critics focus some of their concerns on the ways in which the process affects the morale and attitudes of those not rated among the top. They stress that too often the process leaves lower-ranked personnel angry and bewildered, unable to reconcile the forced ranking outcome with the fact that they had been receiving good to effective performance ratings throughout their careers. In many cases an employee can wind up being ranked at the bottom, even though he or she has performed well and met his or her objectives over a given period of time (Guralnik & Weatherly, 2003).

Some go further by pointing out that putting people into buckets frequently becomes a self-fulfilling prophecy by shaping self-efficacy perceptions (Kluger & Nir, 2008) and in accordance with cognitive resource perspectives may direct a person's attention away from the tasks at hand by putting him or her on the defensive, encouraging the person instead to focus on preserving self-esteem and identity. Still others stress that too often choosing to use the process undermines the role of effective leadership in shaping morale and driving performance (Bates, 2003; Lawler, 2003a). The process, they argue, creates a culture that downplays managers' responsibilities for developing their talent and being accountable for how their personnel perform.

Forced ranking supporters do acknowledge the need to treat people with dignity, regardless of where they are ranked. They stress that most companies do not immediately fire those ranked at the bottom and that many well-designed forced ranking systems incorporate coaching and development into the ways in which low-ranked employees are handled. They are also, however, quick to point out that keeping poor performers around for too long (for example, more than one cycle of rankings) can lower standards and drive good people away (Bates, 2003).

As noted previously, critics also express concerns for the ways in which the processes shape attitudes toward cooperation and other helping behaviors. They further suggest that using the process can seriously undermine trust between managers and their workforce, as well as the sense of overall organizational commitment (Guralnik & Wardi, 2003). At the same time, it seems overreaching to say that forced ranking systems definitively reduce or increase levels of trust between workers and managers. Among other things, the effects will likely depend on the nature of trust relationships when the system is implemented, the quality of existing appraisal practices, and the ways in which the system aligns with company values and actions.

As a result, forced ranking proponents stress the need to be flexible when implementing the process. This includes fully engaging managers in discussions about design criteria and consequences from using the system. It also includes being willing to adopt an incremental approach to implementation.

Along the same lines, both sides agree that existing cultural norms and values play an important role in how people react to forced ranking. While there are no hard and fast statistics regarding which companies have succeeded with the process and which have not, most observers agree that forced ranking is more favorably received in companies with a high-pressure, results-oriented culture (Bates, 2003). Others have also noted that forced ranking systems seem to be more acceptable at high-tech, manufacturing, and financial service organizations, rather than in the public sector and retail sector (Todd & Ramachandran, 2007). In fact, poor cultural fit is frequently given as the reason for why some companies have tried the process and subsequently abandoned it. These were the ostensible positions taken by both Ford and Goodyear when they dropped the process after trying it, although both were also being challenged in court over their use of the process when they chose to abandon it.

Research Perspectives on Forced Ranking and Morale

Although the debate over how forced ranking shapes morale is impassioned, research on the relationships between them is limited. Nonetheless, that which does exist can help inform practitioner choices and approaches to forced ranking. Certainly the previously discussed research regarding fairness perceptions is relevant, as is research pertaining to social comparison processes. For example, to the extent that such processes discourage collaboration and promote self-interest, we might also expect that they have implications for other contextual dimensions of performance such as organizational commitment and citizenship behaviors.

In their study of how a performance appraisal process affects trust, Mayer and Davis (1999) demonstrated that trust perceptions of top management improved for those employees who had the opportunity to participate in a new appraisal process designed to enhance perceived accuracy and instrumentality (recognizing and rewarding employee contributions). Although their study did not involve the use of forced ranking, its results reinforce the importance of taking ratee reactions into account (Murphy & Cleveland, 1991). To the extent that trust perceptions can influence employee satisfaction, behavior, and performance, those contemplating the use of forced ranking need to understand employees' perceptions of any existing appraisal processes on one hand and, on the other, should work to ensure that any new system is perceived to be accurate and instrumental. Management must be able to convey how the forced ranking process and/or aspects of the performance management system will ensure that judgments are based on detailed information, allow for constructive feedback, and offer developmental opportunities (Blume, Baldwin, & Rubin, 2007; Folger & Cropenzano, 1998).

Going forward there remain many opportunities to further examine how forced ranking processes affect morale and related affective outcomes. One important question will center on the differences between how the process influences the attitudes of highly rated versus lower rated performers. Based on the arguments put forth by supporters, we might expect that morale for top performers can be enhanced. Other investigations might help us to better understand the extent to which having support systems (such as coaching or development planning) can mitigate negative reactions that might otherwise occur. Still others might want to consider longitudinal effects on morale or the ways in which organizational culture determines reactions to the use of forced ranking. In addition, it would help to know more about how the use of forced ranking affects leader-member relationships via trust perceptions or perceptions of a leader's personal power.

Although the existing research is indeed scant, when taken together with the arguments put forth by forced ranking advocates and critics, it is still possible to highlight morale-related strategic considerations and questions that practitioners will want to keep in mind. They are summarized in Exhibit 12.3.

Legal Considerations

Like all employment practices, forced ranking processes are subject to laws protecting employees against discrimination (for example, Title VII, Civil Rights Act of 1991, Age Discrimination in Employment Act, and The Americans with Disabilities Act). Moreover, it is important to keep in mind that, in addition to federal laws, state laws also apply, which in some cases give greater latitude when it comes to both bringing and proving claims of discrimination.

Among the various kinds of discrimination that occur in the workplace, forced ranking has been most susceptible to claims of age discrimination under the federal government's Age Discrimination in Employment Act (ADEA) and similar state laws. Virtually all of these cases have centered on claims of adverse impact (scenarios in

**Exhibit 12.3 Forced Ranking and Morale:
Strategic Considerations.**

- Develop plans to communicate:
  - How the process was designed
  - How the forced ranking process will work
  - What employees can expect of the managers rating them
  - What will be expected of them in the process
- Don't let forced ranking become an excuse that reinforces bad development practices.
- Again, consider organizational culture, especially in terms of trust and openness.
- Understand what your organization currently does to recognize and nurture contextual behaviors and teamwork. Be mindful of how forced ranking might affect those efforts.
- Understand what morale is currently like for top performers and also other employees.
- Look for opportunities to provide employees with a voice in the process:
  - Appeal processes
  - Self-assessments
- Develop plans to integrate forced ranking with development initiatives and other programs that support employee efforts to improve.
- If forced ranking is not being used for development, make sure employees understand how development is supported by other performance management systems.

which an employment practice, while not designed to intentionally discriminate, nonetheless has a discriminatory effect on members of a protected group, which in the case of the ADEA are employees over age forty).

Generally speaking, adverse impact claims under the federal ADEA have met with limited success. Although plaintiffs may be able to demonstrate a discriminatory effect for a given practice, employers have still been able to defend themselves by demonstrating that the practice in question is based on reasonable factors other than age (RFOA). Some state courts, however, have been more receptive to adverse impact claims based on age (Anonymous, 2005).

In recent years many prominent organizations have been involved in adverse impact cases over their use of forced ranking (for example, Ford, Goodyear, Microsoft, and Sprint). In most instances the AARP has assisted the aggrieved employees in bringing their cases to court, and all have centered on the fact that a disproportionate number of older workers receive lower rankings. To date, almost all of these cases have been settled out of court. Exxon, though, has won two cases regarding the use of its forced ranking system (Grote, 2005, p. 215).

Taken together, the results of these cases suggest that forced ranking is a clearly defensible practice when implemented with care. At the same time, those considering forced ranking should recognize that the process may expose them to the potential costs and bad press that accompanies discrimination lawsuits. Exhibit 12.4 highlights some key steps organizations should take to better ensure the defensibility of any forced ranking process they implement. These summary points are derived from more elaborate discussions provided by Grote (2005), Woolen (2003), and Bates (2003).

Key Implementation Steps

An important theme in this chapter has been that part of the controversy surrounding forced ranking is also a function of how it is implemented. For a detailed discussion of how to implement a forced ranking process, I would direct readers to Grote's book on the topic. Nonetheless, the following paragraphs briefly high-light some important design and implementation steps.

System Design

1. Decide how you are going to use ranking. Keep in mind that some organizations have chosen to use forced distributions as a tool to regulate ratings within their existing performance appraisal process. Others (for example, GE) use forced ranking as a process that is independent of but complementary to the

Exhibit 12.4 Forced Ranking and Legal Defensibility: Strategic Considerations.

- Keep legal counsel apprised of your plans.
- Conduct a thorough review of existing appraisal processes:
  - Try to identify any marginal employees with a history of good appraisals.
  - Look for any biases in relation to membership in a protected class.
- Introduce the ranking process gradually, starting at the top.
- To reduce suspicions, openly communicate the system's objectives and how it operates.
- Establish clear guidelines for ranking sessions:
  - Guard against inappropriate comments.
  - Ensure ranking criteria are used consistently and objectively.
- Try to incorporate multiple sources of information when possible:
  - Peer assessments
  - 360-degree feedback results
- Make sure that titles and positions of those to be ranked are comparable (for example, don't put first-line supervisors, administrative assistants, and vice presidents in the same ranking pool).
- Ranking decisions are best made by managers who have direct experience with those being ranked.
- Provide extensive training for raters.
- Establish formal systems for reviewing ranking results.
- If the process is being used to terminate, offer reasonable, if not generous, severance packages.

---

appraisal process. Grote (2005), for instance, stresses that if you plan to use forced ranking, you should first make sure you have improved the content and mechanics of your appraisal process.

2. Determine the consequences you'll want to associate with ranking results (terminations, promotions, development planning, or others) and when those consequences will start to take

effect. Many organizations have elected to implement the process gradually, either by using it first for senior personnel or by incrementally introducing consequences. You'll also want to think about how frequently you'll conduct rankings. Most organizations do it on an annual basis. Other decisions will include defining the ranking pool. Comparability is important, with some organizations using titles or salary grades as the basis for making that decision. Those doing the ranking should include managers who have direct responsibility for the people being ranked.

3. Ensuring that the criteria used for ranking decisions are clearly job related is critical. Some organizations rank employees in relation to discreet competencies that may be weighted in order to obtain an overall rank. As mentioned earlier, others rely on relatively few broader criteria that reflect important organizational values and standards. One common approach is similar to that used by Amgen, a financial services organization (Pyles, 2008). They use a nine-box behavior/results matrix. Employees are placed into a grid based on how they are ranked in relation to (a) whether their behavior exceeds, meets, or fails to meet standards and (b) whether their results exceed, meet, or fail to meet standards. Others also factor in potential for development as an important ranking criterion.

4. As previously discussed, decisions about communication have important implications for how the system will be accepted and can have legal implications. It will be important to let people know why and how the system was designed, who will be affected, and what the consequences are.

System Implementation

1. Raters should be trained on how to interpret rating criteria, on how to make accurate behavioral observations, and on the mechanics of participating in ranking discussions. This training is especially important when part of the rationale for introducing the process is to reduce rating inflation and other biases.

2. The ranking sessions themselves need to be well designed. Using a facilitator is highly recommended, and the sessions should be constructed to ensure that the discussions about each employee are highly specific and descriptive in relation to

ranking criteria. Some organizations provide rankers with briefing books to be used as starting points. Expect ranking sessions to be lengthy and impassioned discussions.

3. Organizations need to have clear and somewhat standardized procedures that define the discussions they will have with employees after they have been ranked. Depending on the consequences associated with ranking outcomes, the discussions will have to be clear about implications for termination, future development, and ongoing responsibilities.

Concluding Comments

The purpose of this chapter has not been to argue definitively for or against using forced ranking. Instead, by describing challenges and opportunities, the goal has been to help interested parties understand the forced ranking debate before settling on a course of action for their own organizations. Clearly, there are many successful companies using the process and also many successful companies that do not. There remains much more to learn. We know little, for instance, about how cultural differences influence the effectiveness of forced ranking. Given the global nature of today's economy, practitioners and researchers would benefit from a deeper appreciation for how the process aligns with cultural values and legal frameworks that exist outside of the United States (Blume, Baldwin, & Rubin, 2007).

Ultimately, for any given enterprise, decisions about whether or how to use forced ranking will likely come down to one of cultural fit and/or commitment to change. To that end, it can help to consider the kinds of issues and questions posed in Exhibit 12.4. It can also help to reflect again on the two quotes that opened this chapter. Surely there is middle ground somewhere between the demands of Gordon Gecko and the laments of Willy Loman. That is to say, the forced ranking debate exemplifies how the practice of performance management challenges us to balance organizational performance requirements with concerns for personal dignity and development. Even as they pertain to forced ranking, these two issues need not be at odds, but maintaining that balance certainly requires forethought and hard work.

References

Abelson, R. (2001, March 19). Companies turn to grades, and employees go to court. *New York Times*, p. A1.

Anonymous. (2000, January 8). Face value: Fast and unafraid. *The Economist*, 354(8152), 68.

Anonymous. (2003, March 17). AARP joins in age discrimination lawsuit. *New York Times*, p. C2.

Anonymous. (2005, Winter). The U.S. Supreme Court's 2004 term: Disparate impact claims under the Age Discrimination in Employment Act. *Labor Law Journal*, 56(4), 271–279.

Armour, S. (2003, July 23). Job reviews take on added significance in down times; More companies use them to rank workers for cutbacks. *USA Today*, p. B4.

Bates, S. (2003, June). Forced ranking. *HR Magazine*, pp. 62–68.

Blume, B. D., Baldwin, T. T., & Rubin, R. S. (2007, April). *All forced distribution systems are not created equal.* Paper presented at the 22nd Annual Conference of the Society for Industrial and Organizational Psychology. New York City.

Boyle, M. (2001, May 28). Performance reviews: Perilous curves ahead. *Fortune*, 143(11), 187.

Brockner, J., & Wiesenfeld, B. M. (1996). An integrative framework for explaining reactions to decisions: Interactive effects of outcomes and procedures. *Psychological Bulletin, 120*, 189–208.

Cascio, W. (1991). *Applied psychology in personnel management* (4th ed.). Englewood Cliffs, NJ: Prentice Hall.

Coens, T., & Jenkins, M. (2000). *Abolishing performance appraisals: Why they backfire and what to do instead.* San Francisco: Berrett-Koehler.

Davison, B. (2003). Management span of control: How wide is too wide? *Journal of Business Strategy, 24*(4), 22–29.

Donkin, R. (2005, October 13). Survival of the fittest or corporate eugenics? *Financial Times*, p. 9.

Donkin, R. (2007, June 14). An opportunity to make talent more visible. *Financial Times*, 7.

Folger, R., & Cropenzano, R. (1998). *Organizational justice and human resource management.* Thousand Oaks, CA: Sage.

Garcia, S. M., & Tor, A. (2007). Rankings, standards and competition: Task vs. scale comparisons. *Organizational Behavior and Human Decision Processes, 102*.

Garcia, S. M., Tor, A., & Gonzalez, R. D. (2006). Ranks and rivals: A theory of competition. *Personality & Social Psychology Bulletin, 32*, 970–982.

General Electric Company (2000). *Annual report.*

Gladwell, M. (2002, July 22). The talent myth: Are smart people over-rated? *The New Yorker.*

Goethals, G. R. (1986). Social comparison theory: Psychology from the lost and found. *Personality and Social Psychology Bulletin, 12,* 261–278.

Greenwald, J. (2001, June 18). Rank and fire. *Time, 157*(24), 38.

Grote, D. (2005). *Forced ranking: Making performance management work.* Boston: Harvard Business School.

Guralnik, O., & Wardi, L. A. (2003). *Forced distribution: A controversy.* SHRM White Paper, Alexandria, VA.

Hay Group. (2002). Achieving outstanding performance through a "culture of dialogue." Working paper. New York: Hay Group.

Heneman, R. L. (1986). The relationships between supervisory ratings and results oriented measures of performance: A meta-analysis. *Personnel Psychology, 39,* 811–826.

Holland, K. (2006, September 10). Performance reviews: Many need improvement. *New York Times,* http://www.nytimes.com/2006/09/10/business/yourmoney/10mgmt.html?scp=3&sq=&st=nyt.

Hymowitz, C. (2001, May 15). In the lead: Ranking systems gain popularity but have many staffers riled. *Wall Street Journal,* p. B1.

Jones, B., & Rachlin, H. (2006). Social discounting. *Psychological Science, 17,* 283–286.

Kluger, A., & Nir, D. (2007). Feedforward first—feedback later. Working paper.

Kochanski, J., Alderson, C., & Sorenson, A. (2004, October 6). The state of performance management study. *Perspectives, 12.*

Lawler, E. E. (2003a). The folly of forced ranking. *Strategy & Business,* 3rd Quarter.

Lawler, E. E. (2003b). Reward practices and performance management effectiveness. *Organizational Dynamics, 32,* 396–404.

Mayer, R. C., & Davis, J. H. (1999). The effect of the performance appraisal system on trust for management: A quasi-experimental field study. *Journal of Applied Psychology, 84*(1), 123–136.

McGregor, J. (2006, January 9). The struggle to measure performance. *Business Week,* p. 26.

Murphy, K. R., & Cleveland, J. N. (1991). *Performance appraisal: An organizational perspective.* Boston: Allyn and Bacon.

Nathan, B. R., & Alexander, R. A. (1988). A comparison of criteria for test validation: A meta-analytic investigation. *Personnel Psychology, 41,* 517–535.

Olson, C. A., & Davis, G. M. (2003, March). Pros and cons of forced ranking and other relative performance ranking systems. *Society for Human Resource Management legal report.* Alexandria, VA: SHRM.

Osterman, R. (2003, September 7). Is it really fair to grade workers on a curve? *Chicago Tribune,* p. 5.

Pyles, S. (2008). *AmTrust Bank on forced ranking.* CorpU TV. http://tv.corpu.com/default.aspx?id=7&nav1=1% 20&nav2=0.

Roch, S. G., Sternburg, A. M., & Caputo, P. M. (2007). Absolute vs. relative performance rating formats: Implications for fairness and organizational justice. *International Journal of Selection and Assessment, 15*(3), 302–316.

Ramachadran, R., & Todd, S. (2007, July 31). *The debate over forced ranking,* Webinar. Corporate University Xchange. http://www.corpu.com/research/document/313/the-debate-over-forced-ranking/.

Schleicher, D. J., Bull, R. A., & Green, S. G. (2007). *Rater reactions to forced distribution rating systems.* Paper presented at the 22nd Annual Conference of the Society for Industrial and Organizational Psychology, New York City.

Scullen, S. E., Bergey, P. K., & Aiman-Smith, L. (2005). Forced distribution rating systems and the improvement of workforce potential: A baseline simulation. *Personnel Psychology, 58,* 1–32.

Shermer, M. (2008, February). Do all companies have to be evil? *Scientific American.* http://www.sciam.com/article.cfm?id=do-all-companies-have-to-be-evil.

Society for Human Resources Management. (2003, September 16). Weekly online poll: Does your organization use forced ranking? http://moss07.shrm.org/Research/SurveyFindings/Articles/Pages/utilizeforcedrankingsytems.aspx.

Society for Human Resources Management. (2005, April 19). Weekly online poll: Does your organization use forced ranking? http://moss07.shrm.org/Research/SurveyFindings/Documents/Does_20your_20organization_20utilize_20forced_20ranking_2.

Tesser, A. (1988). Toward a self-evaluation maintenance model of social behavior. In L. Berkowitz (Ed.), *Advances in experimental social psychology, 21,* 193–355. St. Louis, MO: Elsevier Academic Press.

Weatherly, L. A. (2004). *Comparative performance appraisal methods: Forced ranking.* SHRM white paper. Alexandria, VA: SHRM.

Woolen, B. (2003). *Forced ranking: The controversy continues.* White paper. New York: Work Lab Consulting.

Notes

1. These results were virtually identical to a similar survey SHRM conducted in 2003.
2. In his book *Forced Ranking* (2005, p. 23), Dick Grote estimates, based on his experience, that 25 percent of all companies use forced ranking. Others have estimated about 20 percent.

CHAPTER 13

TECHNOLOGY AND PERFORMANCE MANAGEMENT

What Role Does Technology Play in Performance Management?

Autumn D. Krauss and
Lori Anderson Snyder

Whereas other chapters in this book are focused on the *content* of performance management (for example, use of goals or competencies in performance management) or how performance management operates under specific organizational situations (for example, in a team-based work structure), this chapter is concerned more with the *process* of performance management and what role technology can play when developing and using a performance management system.

In particular, the chapter touches on the following issues: how technology can be used for performance management, how technology enables a performance management system to serve its central purposes and complete its primary activities, what challenges are associated with using a technology-based performance management system, and what practical issues must be considered when implementing an automated performance management system. The chapter concludes with some best practices for how to optimally use technology to facilitate the performance management process.

As defined, performance management is "a continuous process of identifying, measuring, and developing the performance of individuals and teams and aligning performance with the strategic goals of the organization" (Aguinis, 2007, p. 2). Correspondingly, a performance management *system* is the structure and procedures that are implemented in an organization to accomplish these performance management objectives. This chapter focuses on the empirical literature and practitioner resources that discuss how technology is used to automate some of the components of a performance management system (for example, performance assessment) or the system in its entirety. As an overview of what is to come, Exhibit 13.1 summarizes the top ways that technology can be used to assist in accomplishing each performance management activity that is outlined in Aguinis (2007). These and other recommendations will be discussed in more detail within later sections of this chapter.

By definition, a performance management system does not need to incorporate technology; however, recent surveys have suggested a growing interest in using technology for performance management purposes. Specifically, a survey in 2006 confirmed that performance management software functionality was ranked as the highest priority over other automated human resource systems (such as training), although approximately 66 percent of respondents also indicated that they did not currently use any technology solutions for performance management purposes (Lawson, 2006). Although these numbers suggest that interest in using technology for performance management is relatively high, this is a recent trend and adoption rates are still low. Also, the design of technology solutions for performance management has been driven by organizational challenges and practitioner needs, not based on a foundation of academic research. In reality, limited research has been conducted to examine the concept of performance management as a system and the implications of technology for performance management. The scant research related to this topic over the past decade has focused on two subjects, namely electronic performance monitoring and

Exhibit 13.1 Best Practice Recommendations for How Technology Can Be Used for Each Stage of the Performance Management Process.

Prerequisites

- Provide mapping tools so business units can visually articulate how their strategy aligns with the broader organization's priorities.
- Complete job analysis activities to identify the position's critical job tasks and KSAs.
- Collect quantitative or qualitative data on performance dimensions and rating formats before they are finalized.
- Offer access to performance management standards and processes as they are established and/or revised.

Performance Planning

- Use a shared electronic workspace to collaboratively create a performance plan.
- Incorporate automated messages to alert stakeholders when the performance plan is modified.
- Link the plan and associated performance competencies to an online database of organizational training and development opportunities.

Performance Execution

- Use EPM to report current performance status and performance status changes to managers for coaching and feedback opportunities.
- Track achievement of performance goals and revise prioritization of goals and projects over time.
- Submit electronic requests for performance feedback from stakeholders upon project completion.
- Store performance rater profiles in the form of connections within a professional networking structure.

Performance Assessment

- Track objective performance indicators (such as profitability) over the performance period.

(Continued)

Exhibit 13.1 (*Continued*)

- Collect subjective performance data using technology-enabled methodologies such as computerized adaptive rating scales.
- Create a managerial dashboard to aggregate performance data and provide a window into performance results.
- Provide analytics and reporting tools for managers to summarize performance and identify performance trends.

Performance Review

- Use data from an integrated performance portal to identify the appropriate time for a performance review, rather than basing it on the calendar year.
- Offer online managerial training of performance review and feedback best practices.
- Utilize technology services to conduct the performance review in the case of virtual manager-subordinate relationships.

Performance Renewal and Recontracting

- Use performance reports to revise the previous performance plan.
- Update performance goals at the individual and business unit level to reflect new performance initiatives and to align with new organizational strategic goals.
- Aggregate performance data over the employee lifecycle to create a graphical timeline of performance.

Succession Planning

- Use data from the performance management system to identify and track high-potential employees.
- Create a networking portal for employees to post professional profiles and review developmental and mentoring opportunities.
- Administer online developmental and promotional assessments to identify employee strengths and weaknesses.
- Offer tools for employees to map their anticipated career paths.

telework. These two areas of research and practice are briefly reviewed below to provide a historical context related to technology's role in performance management.

Technology of the Past: What Role Has Technology Previously Played in Performance Management?

Technology played a role in the performance management process well before the term "performance management" was popular and when performance management activities were conceptualized as separate human resource functions (for example, performance appraisal, succession planning, coaching). Historically, two major research streams relevant to technology and performance management existed in the industrial psychology literature: electronic performance monitoring (EPM) and performance management of telecommuting workers.

Electronic Performance Monitoring

EPM includes the surveillance, measurement, recording, and compilation of work-related activities of employees using electronic means (Bates & Holton, 1995; Stanton, 2000). Thus, EPM primarily contributes to the effort to measure performance, via indicators such as productivity, accuracy, speed, and errors. The ability to collect information continuously and in real time provides several benefits: objective measurement, continuous observational opportunity, immediate reporting, and assessment of physically distant employees. While EPM generally addresses the need to measure employee behavior and outputs, it may also contribute to other goals of performance management, such as the provision of feedback, by allowing managers to achieve the conditions of specificity, accuracy, and timeliness needed to provide effective feedback to subordinates (Stanton, 2000). EPM may also contribute to the development of performance standards by requiring managers to contemplate the content and frequency of assessment measures prior to requesting monitoring data.

The use of EPM has been questioned by some for invading employee privacy, and has been connected to increased stress and health complaints, lower-quality work relationships, and lower employee control perceptions (Bates & Holton, 1995; Hawk, 1994). As a result, a stream of research has provided guidance on best practices for the development of EPM systems to yield the most positive employee response. The scope of tasks monitored has been related to employee reactions, such that EPM focused only on job-relevant activities is related to greater acceptance of EPM, reduced perceptions of invasion of privacy, and increased procedural justice perceptions (Alge, 2001; Grant & Higgins, 1991; McNall & Roch, 2007). Employee control also impacts reactions to EPM systems (Aiello & Svec, 1993; Amick & Smith, 1992), with individuals reporting more positive responses when given discretion as to when they are monitored or what types of tasks are monitored. Employees who are offered an opportunity to participate in the development of the EPM system or to voice their opinions about the system generally possess more positive attitudes and perceptions as well (Alge, 2001; Westin, 1992).

The purpose of the monitoring is also related to employee response. EPMs designed for employee development rather than prevention of undesirable behavior are viewed more positively, and those connected with feedback and appraisal systems are also favored (Amick & Smith, 1992; Chalykoff & Kochan, 1989; Wells, Moorman, & Werner, 2007). Monitoring at the group rather than individual level also has promise in terms of fostering positive employee reaction. This approach may mitigate the increased stress related to EPM and improve acceptance (Aiello & Kolb, 1995; Aiello & Svec, 1993). Use of a combination of individual and group monitoring may also lead to greater acceptance (Grant & Higgins, 1991). Other factors that warrant consideration include frequency of monitoring and the roles and number of people who receive monitoring results (Grant & Higgins, 1991; Hawk, 1994). Additional research suggesting current levels of performance and difficulty of standards affect reactions to EPM should be noted. Individuals or groups who are already performing well or who strive to meet easy standards may perform better and be more satisfied when monitored, while performance and satisfaction among those still learning the task or given difficult standards may decrease (Aiello & Kolb, 1995; Stanton, 2000).

These research findings and best practices regarding EPM have implications for using an automated system for broader performance management purposes. The incorporation of technology is likely to affect a variety of aspects of employee life, including job attitudes, social interactions, and work behavior. Thus, short- and long-term effects of technology across a spectrum of outcomes should be considered and assessed. Additionally, the inclusion of user input into the design of the technology system and procedures for its use, as well as the solicitation of user reactions to the technology system once implemented, have the potential to increase acceptance rates and justice perceptions. Finally, if an EPM system is already in place, the structure and processes should be leveraged and the data should be integrated when building out additional automated performance management tools.

Telecommuting and Performance Management

Insight into the performance management challenges and best practices for telecommuting workers should also be incorporated into the design and use of automated performance management systems, specifically systems that are meant to serve employees working in virtual, distributed, or global environments. For instance, researchers have noted the challenges of managing the performance of teleworkers (Cascio, 2000) and have primarily suggested a renewed focus on traditional performance management principles, with modifications for enhanced clarity in a virtual work environment. Cascio (2003) proposed that the essential components of defining, facilitating, and encouraging performance are even more critical in a virtual work environment than in a traditional one. The importance of developing clear, objective goals is promoted in the absence of frequent face-to-face communication between the subordinate and supervisor (Ellison, 1999; Illegems & Verbeke, 2004; Manoochehri & Pinkerton, 2003). Work agreements or contracts may be established to determine allocation of assignments, preferred communication methods, and specification of performance expectations and standards.

The need to monitor employee achievement of goals in an objective manner is also stressed. Managers should move from assessing time or activities to measuring projects or results (Cascio, 2003; Grensing-Pophal, 1999). Such assessments may focus on quality, quantity, timeliness, and cost-effectiveness, among other dimensions, using electronic monitoring or more subjective assessments (USOPM, 2003). Managers must feel comfortable relinquishing control over details and may need to utilize more active project management techniques, including providing not only project deadlines but also timelines for completion of milestones, and requesting frequent updates on project status. Ongoing assessment of performance in relation to specified goals is likely to keep the focus of workers and managers on primary tasks, as well as reduce the delay in providing feedback to employees.

While frequent electronic performance feedback may assist in coaching and developing teleworkers, more direct methods are helpful but challenging to use. A study of managers experienced at supervising teleworkers indicated that regular face-to-face meetings or scheduled electronic visual communications via videoconferencing may be a useful addition to coaching efforts (McGraw & Kelly, 1995). Introducing new tasks or assignments and offering the same training opportunities available to in-office workers may also assist in building new skill sets among telecommuting workers.

These challenges associated with monitoring and supporting the performance of teleworkers are consistent with the issues that will arise when implementing a technology-based performance management system for employees working in virtual, distributed, or global environments. The suggestions offered for managing teleworkers from Cascio and others point to the importance placed on using sound research-based performance management principles, not to using a technology solution as a panacea when managing employees virtually. That being said, a technology solution that enables the use of proven performance management techniques offers many benefits when managing virtual employees, including easy access to consistent information across the employee base. This benefit, along with others associated with using technology to support various performance management purposes and processes, is elucidated further in the next two sections.

Technology As an Enabler: How Does Technology Support the Goals and Purposes of Performance Management?

When used appropriately, technology can facilitate the accomplishment of several performance management system goals and purposes. Aguinis (2007) identified the following six purposes of a performance management system: strategic, administrative, informational, developmental, organizational maintenance, and documentational. Below, examples are provided as to how technology can support a performance management system to serve each of these purposes.

Strategic Purposes

For a performance management system to serve a strategic purpose, the critical characteristic is for an individual employee's goals to be aligned with those of the overall organization (Aguinis, 2007). In the goal-setting literature, allowing employees insight into the broader goals of their departments, business lines, and companies and where their individual goals fit into these strategic objectives has been identified as an important source of motivation for employees (Locke & Latham, 1990). Regardless of whether goals are "cascaded down" from the organization's overall business initiatives to those of individual contributors or "rolled up" from teams to departments to business lines, a technology-based performance management system offers the opportunity to set these goals in a systematic way and allow the resulting goals to be accessible to all employees.

For instance, capabilities are available in automated systems to enter goals and alert the owners of relevant business units when goals have been entered. Managers should be using the goals of other business units that are closely aligned to inform their own unit's goal development. Mapping tools are also available to indicate how the goals across individuals or business units relate to each other (for example, how each goal of an individual team member relates to one or more goals of his or her overall team). After goals have been input and accepted by the goal owners and their supervisors through the system, it is critical that they be available for public consumption across the organization, at least in a summarized form if not in their entirety. In the case of a distributed workforce where the goals of the corporate executive team or even regional management are not visibly present or readily communicated to line employees, knowledge of and access to these goals are imperative for a strong organizational culture across the enterprise (McAleese & Hargie, 2004). A technology-based performance management system can serve this need by allowing employees continual access to this information, not just when the executive team discusses it at an annual company meeting.

Administrative Purposes

For a performance management system to effectively serve an administrative purpose, data in the system must be available to inform administrative decisions made about employees (for example, salary adjustments, recognition of exemplary performance). There are two primary ways that automation of a performance management system can support this purpose. First, an automated system allows for easier data entry, data extraction, and summarization than a paper-based system does. For example, the employee can easily store commendations and favorable comments in the system; often, these data points are not stored with personnel files and annual performance reviews that are generally accessed when making decisions such as for merit increases and "performer of the year." Those responsible for the administrative decisions can easily access the data. These data could be available to responsible parties across the company without accessing a physical employee file. Finally, at least in the case of standard performance assessment forms and associated data, an automated system can offer reporting and metric tools that summarize and compare performance across employees for the purposes of making larger administrative decisions (such as layoffs). As an aside, if an automated system was implemented and employees were informed of their responsibility to enter performance-related information and correspondingly the process whereby the data would be used to make important administrative decisions, employees would be more motivated to input performance information in the system, and a more accurate picture of performance over time and from different perspectives would be available.

Second, automation allows the opportunity to integrate the performance management system with other human resource applications, most notably the payroll and compensation system for administrative purposes, which is likely automated as well. Integration of these automated solutions allows for the efficient sharing of information between the systems, which is important given that performance management data should be informing administrative decisions (for example, during annual performance reviews, compensation adjustments are entered into the performance management system and they are automatically reflected in the payroll system). The integration of a performance management system with other systems within the talent management suite is discussed in more detail later in this chapter.

Informational Purposes

The use of technology for a performance management system arguably supports the informational purpose the best. By nature, a technology-based performance management system allows for the continuous process of performance management and also the continuous communication of information collected through the performance management process. The motivation literature indicates that goals should be adjusted over time to remain relevant and shared with appropriate stakeholders to increase accountability (Donovan & Williams, 2003). Additionally, performance feedback should be provided in a timely fashion for it to effectively stimulate behavioral alterations (Locke & Latham, 1990). Technology can support these principles by creating an opportunity for employees to readily update performance goals over time, managers to provide just-in-time performance feedback to their reports, and employees to make performance goals as widely accessible as appropriate.

Finally, if the performance management system is used on a regular basis similar to the frequency of use for automated time and attendance systems that are prevalent across organizations, it can serve as a vehicle for performance-focused communication blasts. These could be as basic as managers being notified when employees update their performance goals or as comprehensive as a notification to all those in a position across the entire enterprise when an update has been made to the performance competency model. These real-time updates are critical for the performance management process to remain relevant for each employee over time.

Although entering performance information into an automated system should not replace more direct forms of communicating about performance, it can offer a method for performance information to be communicated in an ongoing and consistent fashion. How many times do supervisors lose the opportunity to share performance feedback because they cannot immediately connect with the employee or do not want to send an email that will get buried in an inbox? How often would subordinates seek direction for a prioritization of performance goals if the request could be made efficiently and couched in the context of performance improvement instead of just another question in the midst of many? Assuming a user-friendly interface that allows for these communications to occur quickly and painlessly, an automated performance management system can serve the role of facilitating these communications—with the added benefit of documenting this dialogue for later performance conversations.

Those who are more technologically savvy might think that instant messaging (IM) meets the criterion of quick and painless, and note that this type of technology is surely being used to communicate performance information today. While appropriate for some conversations (such as clarification on an email, follow-up questions on a specific task, or requests for a status update), IM does not give the weight and priority to these communications that substantive performance conversations warrant and does not offer the opportunity for easy documentation and aggregation. By both differentiating these performance communications from other communications via IM and email and storing them in a specific location that houses other important performance data, these communications have been elevated in their importance and documented for future conversations.

Developmental Purposes

Another purpose of a performance management system is to provide developmental feedback to employees for both immediate short-term use as well as long-term career planning. In addition to an automated system supporting the provision of general performance feedback on an ongoing basis, it can also serve as a way to collect performance feedback on a project basis. Employees can specify their current projects and assignments along with the project stakeholders in the performance management system. When the employee updates the system when a project has been completed, the system solicits performance feedback from the project stakeholders. This feedback can be readily available to the employee and/or can be provided to the employee's manager to serve as the basis for a future coaching session.

As part of an annual performance review, a select number of competencies can be identified by a supervisor and his or her subordinate as the focus of development efforts for the next year. On a regular basis, managers can input performance feedback, even with a numerical rating on these specific competencies as the employee works over the course of the year to strengthen his or her behavior in these targeted areas. At year's end, system data can display changes in performance on these competencies over time, eliminating common errors that occur at review time (recency effect) (Lowe, 1986). Finally, a career path and a long-term developmental plan are critical for an employee to remain motivated in his or her role and committed to the organization (Arnold, 2002). Some examples of career paths that are relevant for an individual's specific position can be available in the system, the critical behavioral competencies for other positions within the organization can be accessed by the individual for review, and career pathing tools can be used by an individual to construct his or her own career path, insert a projected timeline, share the path with mentors, and adjust the path over time.

Organizational Maintenance Purposes

Organizational maintenance as a purpose of a performance management system refers to workforce planning activities that require insight into the current status and future needs of an organization's human capital. Undoubtedly, an automated performance management solution offers the benefit of having performance data across the enterprise in an aggregated form and available for interpretation. For instance, a common workforce planning activity that leverages performance management information is a talent audit, whereby current stock is taken of the workforce's skills, abilities, and experiences for the purposes of forecasting future needs (such as recruitment or training) and making strategic business decisions (for example, adequate talent to move into a new vertical market, appropriateness of organizational restructuring) (Aguinis, 2007). Conducting a talent audit with an integrated electronic performance data repository is much easier than with performance data stored in paper form or in varying electronic sources (spreadsheets, databases, payroll systems), assuming that sufficient reporting and analytic tools are available through the system to summarize and analyze the data so that accurate conclusions can be drawn. More details with respect to performance management reporting and analytics tools are offered later in the chapter.

Documentation Purposes

Of all the purposes of a performance management system, the purpose of documentation is probably the primary use—or at least one of the central foci of many performance management systems (Aguinis, 2007). Surely, paper-based performance management systems serve this purpose through carefully maintained employee files. Can a technology-based system offer an advantage over a paper-based system to meeting this need? The benefit of automation here is consistent with the themes described above, namely the ease to access, enter, organize, and summarize information. A supplementary advantage is that, assuming integration with other systems, all performance-oriented data (such as goals, reviews, compensation, feedback, and objective metrics such as sales) can be stored in one location. At times when documentation is needed, it is often needed with some urgency. Access to aggregated information in one portal is an advantage of an automated system during these times.

As outlined above, technology can serve a role in accomplishing each of the purposes of a performance management system. Beyond these general purposes, there are several components that, taken together, encompass a performance management system. Guidelines and specific ideas for how technology can be used to support these components are discussed below.

Technology's Role in the Process: How Does Technology Facilitate the Different Components of the Performance Management Process?

Aguinis (2007) proposed that the process of performance management involves six steps: prerequisites, performance planning, performance execution, performance assessment, performance review, and performance renewal and recontracting. In general, technology offers opportunities to execute these steps in an efficient and effective manner. Existing human resource information technology (HRIT) systems may currently provide some of the options discussed below, although few would offer all. In general, it appears that managerial self-service programs, which allow managers access to databases of employee records and performance information as well as tools to analyze the data, are less common than portals allowing employees access to personal human resource information (Stone, Stone-Romero, & Lukaszewski, 2003). As is evident from the examples below, to be maximally effective when completing the six steps of the performance management process, managers and employees need to collaborate regularly and be shared owners of the process; because of this, a portal for both managers and employees to enter, access, and revise performance information is imperative.

Prerequisites

The prerequisites step includes the identification of a company's strategic goals and the completion of job analysis activities for the targeted positions. Technology may assist in developing and communicating the organization's mission and priorities as well as ensuring that unit-level missions and priorities are in alignment with the organization as a whole. Electronic integration of performance management data with other human resource functions via an HRIT system can also assist in ensuring that performance goals created for an individual employee contribute to an organization's strategy.

A variety of technological means exist to identify a position's tasks and required knowledge, skills, and abilities (KSAs), to collect ratings on the frequency and criticality of tasks and KSAs, and to compile these data for the development of job descriptions. This topic is not the focus of this chapter, however. Readers may find useful information on this topic in Peterson, Mumford, Borman, Jeanneret, and Fleishman (1999) and McEntire, Dailey, Osburn, and Mumford (2006). During the prerequisites stage, consideration may also be given to issues regarding the implementation of new or revised performance management systems. Because user involvement in planning the system is related to subsequent support and acceptance of the system (Cawley, Keeping, & Levy, 1999; Roberts, 2003), technology can be used to invite employee participation in providing input about performance dimensions and rating formats and testing trial versions of an automated solution. Information such as comprehensiveness of performance dimensions, ease of use and interpretation of rating formats, and perceived system fairness and usefulness may be collected in an effort to maximize ratee positive reactions to the appraisal system (Ilgen, Fisher, & Taylor, 1979; Keeping & Levy, 2000). In addition, the input of supervisors, potential raters, and other stakeholders may be solicited. Communication about the standards and process of the performance management system, which is essential for a due-process approach to performance appraisal (Folger, Konovsky, & Cropanzano, 1992), can also be accomplished through online messages and resources posted on the company intranet.

Performance Planning

After identifying the organizational strategy and job requirements, performance planning entails developing a shared understanding of expected behaviors and results, which are then specified in a performance plan (Aguinis, 2007). Technology may be used to assist an employee and manager in virtually creating and storing a performance plan. By using shared electronic workspaces such as those available through Google Apps and Microsoft Office Live Workspace, the plan may be created, modified, and updated by either party while the other person at a different location actually watches in real time as the changes are made. See Figures 13.1 and 13.2 for standard examples of what shared electronic workspaces look like from Google Apps and Microsoft Office Live Workspace. Video demonstrations of these offerings are also available from these vendors online. This approach may promote employee commitment to goals through participatory goal setting processes (Roberts, 2003), as well as continuous awareness of goals, with both the manager and employee having constant access to the plan for review. These technological tools can be particularly helpful to complete the performance planning process when manager and employee do not work out of the same location, as is the case for many supervisor-subordinate dyads these days (MCIWorldCom, 2001).

The performance plan may include courses of action for improvement, suggestions for continued development and enrichment, and a timeline for completion. Versions of the plan could be stored in HRIT systems, with any changes over time digitally tracked. Automated messages could be sent to both the

Figure 13.1 Example of Shared Workspace with Google Apps.

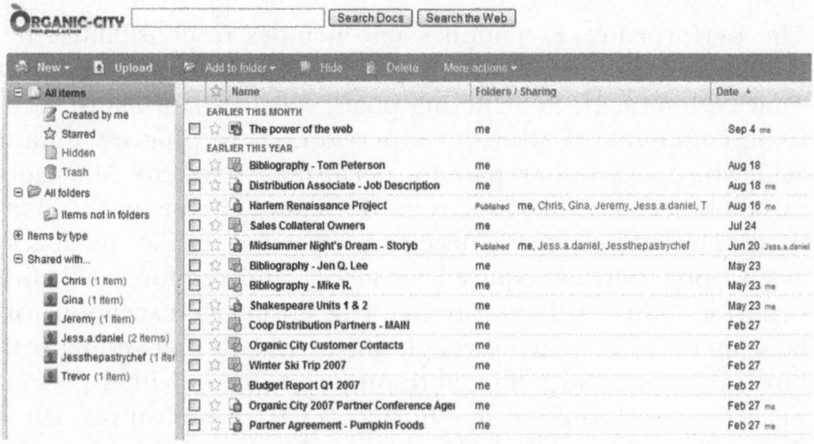

Figure 13.2   Example of Shared Workspace with Microsoft Office Live Workspace.

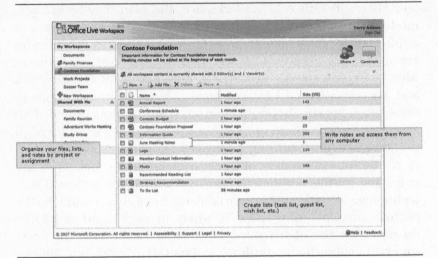

manager and employee when changes are made, such as recording the completion of a task. In addition, an online database of organizational training and development opportunities may be linked to the plan, providing suggestions for current and future development.

Performance Execution

The performance execution stage includes responsibilities for both managers and employees (Aguinis, 2007). Employees must show commitment to achieving goals, solicit performance feedback, communicate with the supervisor, share progress toward achieving goals, and prepare for performance reviews. Managers must observe and document performance, revise initial standards and objectives as necessary, provide regular feedback, ensure provision of required resources, and reinforce effective behavior. Many of these aspects of performance execution can be seamlessly integrated through the use of HRIT, providing real-time information with limited resource burden on either person. Electronic performance monitoring (EPM) based on objectives determined cooperatively by the employee and manager can report current performance status to both employee and manager portals. In addition, the prioritization of goals and projects can be frequently reviewed and updated if this information is available via an automated platform. These pieces of data can assist the employee in consistently tracking performance and achievement of goals, allowing regular review of performance, rather than waiting until performance review time to self-appraise, and maximizing opportunity to alter behavior (Latham, Mitchell, & Dossett, 1978). EPM tools can also be used to send automatic notification to the manager when performance status changes, offering the manager an opportunity to provide immediate coaching and feedback.

During performance execution, automated tools can provide employees with means to solicit feedback from sources other than their supervisors. On an ongoing basis and at the end of each performance deliverable, the employee can submit an electronic request to associated co-workers and customers for performance feedback using a standardized multi-source feedback tool incorporating relevant performance dimensions, which results in data for immediate feedback and future performance reviews (Stone, Stone-Romero, & Lukaszewski, 2003). Given research indicating the usefulness of peer and other feedback for development (Bettenhausen & Fedor, 1997; Farh, Cannella, & Bedeian, 1991), this functionality presents an opportunity to add richness to performance data with limited requirements from peer raters. Information relevant to the invited raters (for example, rater profile, connection to employee) could be stored in the system in a way similar to a connection in LinkedIn, a professional networking site. The compilation of a web of feedback providers for the employee offers both a simple means of reviewing possible raters and their relationships to the target employee and advantages in soliciting feedback by making requests to raters with maximal knowledge of the employee's performance in relevant areas.

Performance Assessment

Performance assessment as an ongoing technology-driven process eliminates the requirement of collecting performance information once or twice a year before the scheduled performance review. EPM and goal-tracking software can collect a variety of metrics across time, avoiding the error of weighing recent performance more heavily on appraisals (Stone, Stone-Romero, & Lukaszewski, 2003). Essential personnel records, including absenteeism, disciplinary actions, and grievances against an employee, can be tracked and considered with other performance data. For positions with objectively measurable outcomes, indicators such as productivity, accuracy, speed, sales, and errors may be assessed, while for more subjective outcomes, quality of deliverables, use of available resources, and timeliness of meeting objectives may be of concern. The presence of situational constraints that impact performance outcomes should be considered and measured as well (Cardy & Miller, 2003).

Managerial self-service programs provide access to various types of integrated performance information, as well as tools for analyzing data and generating reports (Gueutal, 2003). Such programs may offer not only a view into historical information, but also mechanisms to collect current subjective performance evaluation data. Computerized adaptive rating scales, which use adaptive testing principles to estimate performance using an item response theory algorithm, assist managers in providing ratings with less error (Schneider, Goff, Anderson, & Borman, 2003). In this process, raters complete a paired-comparison of statements scaled to performance effectiveness levels (such as one statement reflecting above-average performance and one reflecting below-average performance), and the iterative process of choosing the statement most representative of the ratee's behavior leads to more precise, interval scale ratings of performance. Multi-source feedback ratings from supervisors, peers, subordinates, and customers may be solicited following important project milestones or at regular intervals. Databases of ratings arranged by ratee and rater provide opportunities to analyze the rating process, such as identifying common errors and providing feedback to raters about their performance during the rating process (Kavanagh, Gueutal, & Tannenbaum, 1990; Stone, Stone-Romero & Lukaszewski, 2003). For instance, the system may monitor ratings for severe leniency, such as a rater who provides the highest available rating for several ratees across multiple dimensions. This rater could be prompted with an automated message regarding the importance of providing accurate feedback that differentiates among ratees, without requiring a personal intervention from a supervisor that makes the rater uncomfortable. Alternately, identification of common biases across a group of raters may indicate the need for expanded rater training. An additional type of performance information, portfolios, may also be incorporated into performance databases (Johnson & Isenhour, 2003). In these databases, employees can house supporting documentation of their performance based on project management schedules and activity reports as timelines are met.

HRIT systems may assist not only in analyzing a variety of performance indicators, but also in generating the narrative that is included in individual feedback reports (Cardy & Miller, 2003). This option provides assistance, particularly for managers with little experience in providing feedback or who are lacking in writing skills, but should really only be used to establish a base draft of the feedback report. Software programs also provide review services to examine the potential for discriminatory language or legally problematic statements (Cardy & Miller, 2003).

Ideally for the performance assessment stage, technology is used to support the collection of both objective performance metrics and subjective performance ratings in a consistent and frequent manner from multiple sources throughout the performance period. These data are integrated and available to the supervisor via a performance dashboard with analytics and reporting tools that can be used to identify performance trends, which is the basis of the conversation come performance review time.

Performance Review

The process of conducting the performance review meeting is often considered the most difficult and unpleasant aspect of performance management (Aguinis, 2007; Geddes & Baron, 1997). In addition, evidence exists that feedback does not always result in performance improvement (Kluger & DeNisi, 1996). Thus, technology has ample opportunity to enhance the performance review meeting by fostering more positive attitudes and increasing the effectiveness of performance feedback. Performance data linked with workflow systems can alert managers to the optimal time for reviewing performance, rather than relying on a standard schedule (Gueutal, 2003). Supervisors and others providing performance feedback should be trained via online technology in performance review best practices, such as focusing feedback on tasks, presenting solutions to problems, and offering an opportunity for employees to express their feelings (Kluger & DeNisi, 1996).

Technology, such as videoconferencing or web conferencing, may be used to conduct the actual appraisal review meeting in the case of telecommuters who are physically distant or for supervisors who are geographically separate from their subordinates. In addition, this format could allow for multiple stakeholders at different locations to be present at the meeting. Data from EPM or other performance assessment solutions should be available to support the performance review conversation, and technological support tools may be provided to assist supervisors in following the most effective steps to providing feedback. For instance, interactive online guides may be available in managerial self-service programs to assist managers in following a series of steps through a flow diagram, offering advice about interpreting numerical performance information and integrating subjective information, identifying areas of strength and weakness, and consolidating performance information into a structured and focused performance review.

Performance Renewal and Recontracting

Activities in the performance renewal and recontracting phase refer back to those in the performance planning stage (Aguinis, 2007). The manager collaborates with the employee to consider revision of the performance plan from the previous cycle, taking into account all available information collected in the intervening timeframe. Broader system data are used to identify necessary changes in individual performance goals based on the cascading of new organizational and departmental strategic priorities. Performance data should be stored in such a way that a graphical view of an employee's performance trends over time could be created. This view would represent performance over the employee's lifecycle and could be used to evaluate improvement over time, much better than independent reviews stored separately in a database. Assuming quantitative data are available from performance ratings every year (for example, numerical ratings on different competencies or an overall rating), the graph could not only show changes in an individual's performance ratings over time but also how the individual performed that year in relation to the average ratings for others in his or her workgroup or position in the company. These reference points would be particularly helpful during the performance renewal and recontracting stage when performance plans and goals are adjusted for the next performance cycle.

Succession Planning

In addition to the six steps of performance management proposed by Aguinis (2007), technology also has the potential to contribute to organizational succession planning. Data generated through the six performance management stages and stored in a performance management system can be used to identify and track high-potential employees, determine and offer developmental opportunities, and establish potential mentoring relationships (Stone, Stone-Romero, & Lukaszewski, 2003). Systems data could facilitate turnover analyses to identify areas of concern for the retention of promising employees. Portals may be developed for employees to post internal WebPages similar to social networking sites (for example, Facebook; Bersin, 2007) with their experiences and interests so that matches can be made across the enterprise with any developmental or mentoring opportunities (for example, short-term job assignments or permanent position openings). Interested employees could subscribe to notifications of new postings based on matches with keywords. Succession planning may also be facilitated through the use of technology solutions for the actual delivery of developmental and promotional assessments, simplifying the process of identifying and matching high performers to appropriate positions. Such technologies include online media-rich assessments, such as virtual reality simulation or video-based simulation, and computerized adaptive testing (Jones & Dages, 2003). Integrated personnel assessment platforms can assist in capturing and compiling all essential personnel information and support other stages of assessment, such as scoring the assessment and generating the assessment results report.

Exhibit 13.2 expands on the discussion of technology's role in the process by describing a case study of the implementation of an enterprise-wide performance management system using a variety of technological tools. This case articulates specific examples of the integration of technology into each step in the process of performance management.

Exhibit 13.2 Case Study of Enterprise-Wide Performance Management System.

Prerequisites

A team of managers from various levels of the organization used groupware to review and revise the organization's mission and develop organizational goals and objectives relevant for the current strategic direction. This new mission and a model of core organizational competencies were shared with all employees to maximize employee involvement and support. Using mapping software, units generated specific unit-level performance goals and ensured continuity across units by maintaining focus on the organizational mission as well as incorporating the core organizational competencies across all jobs. Job descriptions were revised by managers and employees using shared electronic workspaces to ensure the descriptions were relevant for the updated organizational mission. An automated HRIT platform was configured to collect, store, analyze, and report performance-related information and to support integration with other HR functions. Employees were encouraged to view a beta version of the platform, and feedback on the new system was solicited from employees and management prior to official launch. Raters were required to complete online rater training before their first use of the performance management system.

Performance Planning

Employees and managers used online job-description-based templates to establish and revise individualized performance plans, which were stored on a shared platform in the HRIT system. Technology-based methods of measuring behaviors (online project-based multi-source feedback) and objective results (EPM related to quality, quantity, cost and/or time) were established. Specific goals for development were set and linked to organizational training and development opportunities when appropriate. Reminders of developmental goals and dates of milestones in the performance management process were automated.

Performance Execution

Subjective and objective performance data were collected regularly across the performance cycle and housed in the HRIT system. Minimum frequencies of EPM and multi-source feedback for observation and documentation of performance were established and users were prompted if standards were not met. EPM data were available in real time through manager and employee portals. Employees requested project-based behavioral assessment ratings from stakeholders and completed self-ratings.

Performance Assessment

Managers and employees were provided with automated monthly goal tracking reports in addition to the opportunity to view EPM data in real time. The HRIT system allowed managers or employees to leave messages for one another regarding the results of the monthly report. In addition to established subjective and objective metrics, employees compiled additional information in performance portfolios available on the platform for managers to view. Managers used automated reporting tools to integrate all available measures of performance and goal attainment.

Performance Review

The review meeting was framed around a competency-based feedback report used across the enterprise, as well as performance and goal-attainment analyses specific to the job and employee. An interactive best-practices strategy tool assisted managers in preparing for the meeting, while successful performance feedback provision and coaching were demonstrated by example via online role-play videos. Employees were permitted to make electronic notations on the final performance review report in order to provide an additional opportunity for voice.

(Continued)

Exhibit 13.2 (*Continued*)

Performance Renewal and Recontracting

A shared HRIT workspace was used to document changes in the performance plan agreed on in the review meeting. Any changes in the organizational or unit-level mission and objectives were incorporated into individual performance plans to ensure continuous relevance of all goals and performance metrics. Over the interim until the next appraisal, manager and employee viewed past and present performance and future goals on the platform in real time and via monthly reports, ensuring continual attention to relevant behaviors and results.

Succession Planning

Performance data and trends were mined to identify candidates for developmental opportunities and potential promotion. Employees were also given tools to pursue professional development. Online assessment activities provided an opportunity to identify weaknesses in core skills and suggested methods of development. Employees had access to information on career paths and associated requirements for promotion on the HRIT system.

These past two sections spoke largely to the myriad uses that technology can serve when working to accomplish the goals and carry out the primary components of performance management. It is worth discussing, however, the challenges that can arise when trying to utilize technology for performance management purposes. Some of these are described below.

Technology As a Challenge: What Complications Does Technology Create in the Performance Management Process?

As outlined above, automating a performance management system offers several benefits, most notably those related to the centralization of data, integration of performance data with information from other systems, and ease of data input and retrieval. Unfortunately, the same characteristics of technology that make these benefits possible can also create challenges if the technology does not function properly, is used inappropriately, or is relied on too heavily. Below, several challenges associated with using technology for performance management purposes are outlined. These challenges should be considered fully during the development of specifications for an automated solution and a model of the performance management process.

Information Overload

Technology allows for voluminous amounts of performance data to be continuously collected and instantaneously accessed, making information overload a real concern for both managers and employees. Although the concept has been discussed for some time (Schneider, 1987), it has been studied with increased focus within the past decade across disciplines such as organizational science, marketing, and education (Eppler & Mengis, 2004). In general, research has shown that information technologies exacerbate information overload and that information overload can have detrimental effects on the fulfillment of job responsibilities, experience of stress, and likelihood of working overtime and taking work home (Klausegger, Sinkovics, & Zou, 2007).

Across disciplines, strategies have been proposed to mitigate information overload. The following recommendations are of particular relevance for a technology-based performance management system: create a graphical display of how the system components are organized and where the user currently is located in reference to the system's broader structure (Chen, Kinshuk, Wei, & Chen, 2008); use branching logic to organize data around performance competencies instead of in a linear fashion based on time; offer searching functions based on key words; and incorporate a personal "clippings" area for particularly useful or frequently accessed performance information (Kear & Heap, 2007). Finally, provide tools for managers to organize, summarize, and analyze performance data, offering them assistance in turning the information into "intelligence" (Klausegger, Sinkovics, & Zou, 2007).

Overexposure

Making the collection and sharing of performance-related information through an automated system a frequent work behavior runs the risk of diluting the importance and value of the information due to overexposure. This challenge has been tackled in the area of surveys, where the phenomenon has been labeled "survey fatigue" and "over-surveying" (Porter, Whitcomb, & Weitzer, 2004; Saari, 1998). Recommendations on ways to avoid overexposure and more specifically develop effective electronic performance surveys can be leveraged from the employee survey literature (Thompson, Surface, Martin, & Sanders, 2003). For example, organizational owners of the performance management system should challenge themselves to develop novel ways to keep interaction with the system engaging and make sure that every request for data (for example, a request for performance feedback on a co-worker) is necessary and includes an explanation as to the reason for the request, whether anonymity is possible, and how the data will be used.

Time Requirements

Although automation of paperwork alleviates some time commitments on individuals responsible for the performance management process, particularly those in human resources, if the system is clunky or slow, it could require more time from others, particularly employees inputting information into the system or trying to access data through integrated portals. Couple the increased time commitment with a negative experience from user-interface inadequacies, and those utilizing the system will likely experience substantial computer frustration, resulting in decreased productivity and negative affective reactions (Lazar, Jones, & Schneiderman, 2006). Also, as indicated above, technology should facilitate the collection of performance data, the re-visitation of performance goals, and the provision of performance feedback on a more ongoing basis than what is feasible with a paper-based system. If these practices are adopted, an automated system could actually be more time-intensive, particularly for managers who were previously only approached annually for performance reviews.

This challenge underscores the importance of implementing a solution that is streamlined and offers efficient ways to work with the data. With respect to methods of data collection that minimize time commitments, similar to the challenge of overexposure, best practices can be gleaned from research and practice in surveys, where the "pulse survey" has been created to collect employee feedback often and with minimal intervention (Wells, 2006). A pulse survey includes a short set of questions that is administered more frequently than traditional annual employee surveys, often in an attempt to measure the "pulse" of an organization over time and with less intrusion on employees. Finally, as with all technological implementations, additional time will be needed until users are familiar with and feel comfortable with the solution. This expectation must be set across the organization to ensure that commitment to the system does not weaken shortly after implementation because of the additional time requirements.

Over-Reliance on Automation

Given the money and time required to develop and implement an automated performance management system, organizational leaders may be inclined to assume that the technology will now do the work of performance management, but this is not the case. Technology facilitates the process of performance management, but performance management is still largely a people process, meaning that every employee, in varying ways, must be accountable for performance management, and select individuals must be champions and owners of the performance management process.

Lessons can be learned from on-boarding, another important human resource function for which automated systems have been developed. Currently, the trend is for companies to automate their new-hire paperwork such that employees read and complete the paperwork online, even using an electronic signature to sign the forms (Tarquinio, 2006). Clearly, this is not a comprehensive on-boarding system, given that on-boarding also consists of orienting new employees to their specific job tasks and associated work expectations as well as socializing them into the company's norms, culture, and team dynamics (Bauer, 2007). In the same way, companies may fall victim to thinking they have a comprehensive performance management system because they automate administrative/paperwork processes (for example, if on an annual basis, an employee uploads his self-evaluation and approves his review). The key here is to fully understand what performance management includes, as defined in the other chapters of this book, and then set the expectations of organizational members that the role of technology is to support these performance management components, not replace them.

Miscommunication

Technology can greatly support the communication of information during performance management; however, the use of technology to communicate information related to an important and emotionally charged topic such as job performance can also create opportunities for confusion and frustration. Two points are worth mentioning here with respect to communication challenges when using technology for performance management. First, this issue has been cited as a challenge for some time in the broader context of sharing any type of information via tools such as email and instant messaging. The ease of using these tools has resulted in information being shared without thorough consideration of the content by the sender, which also enhances the opportunity for misinterpretation by the receiver. While this issue may be relevant in the case of a performance management system, the use of a separate performance-specific system to enter and access this information will likely mitigate this problem. The act of entering a specific portal to provide performance feedback and the knowledge that the feedback will be available for future review and use should result in the sender providing more carefully considered feedback.

Second, similar to any system that offers individuals the opportunity to write reviews of some sort (think about writing reviews of submissions for the annual SIOP conference), capabilities can be built into the system to give the reviewee voice and protect the integrity of the system. For instance, feedback can be solicited from select individuals who possess adequate knowledge of the employee's performance, or exact timeframes can be specified for when performance feedback will be accepted. The target employee can add comments as a supplement to the feedback so that his or her perspective is documented, which is an opportunity for voice and may result in more favorable fairness perceptions (Erdogan, Kraimer, & Liden, 2001). Finally, similar to how some listserves and message boards function, a member of human resources could monitor the performance feedback and "approve" it for posting. Admittedly, the practicality of this last recommendation must be evaluated in light of internal resources and the likelihood of inappropriate postings.

Technology Literacy

By definition, an automated performance management system requires system users to possess certain knowledge and skill to use the technology. The extent to which this poses a challenge is dependent upon several factors, including who will be interacting with the system (for example, all employees or only human resource personnel), the nature of these interactions (for example, clicking a button to approve a performance review once a year or revising performance goals on an ongoing basis), and the current jobs and associated requirements for those who will be interacting with the system (for example, software engineers or retail clerks). In general, if the system is being used to the fullest extent possible and its capabilities are being maximized to meet the six purposes described above, all employees should be interacting with the system on a frequent basis, which will require a level of technology literacy.

Assuming the use of sound change management principles and the provision of adequate training when the system is implemented, using the automated system will not likely present a hindrance for most employees. For those workers who have little interaction with technology, such as in the case of many hourly employees, a larger-scale initiative that occurs well before the implementation of the system is needed to provide training with hands-on practice and an opportunity for workers to fully understand how the system will directly benefit them, which result in greater comfort with technology and better system adoption rates (Marler, Liang, & Dulebohn, 2006; Venkatesh, Morris, Davis, &

Davis, 2003). These types of workers might also not use or have access to a computer as part of their jobs. Obviously, this must be considered when determining what level of interaction will be required with the automated system. Novel ideas may also be considered, such as loading software onto technologies that these workers do use as part of their job, for instance, a point-of-sale system for a retail or food service worker.

Overall, the challenges outlined above can be largely mitigated both through careful planning of the technology requirements of the solution and through development of sound performance management practices, which are necessary for an effective system whether it uses technology or not. During this planning process, several practical decisions are made centering on the creation, implementation, and support of the system. It is these practical issues that we turn to next.

Taking Technology System-Wide: How Do You Implement a Technology-Based Performance Management System?

Although technology can be used to support the individual components of the performance management process such as in those ways described above, the trend is to use a technology solution to automate and incorporate all of the performance management activities that comprise the system. This section highlights some of the important practical points to consider when using this latter approach.

Decide Whether to Buy or Build

When planning to implement an automated performance management system, due diligence must occur early to decide whether building or buying a system is more appropriate, given organizational priorities, needs, and resources. The largest factors that will dictate whether building or buying a solution is the right choice are whether organizational resources are available internally to build the solution and how customized and complex the solution needs to be to meet organizational requirements.

While the price tag for buying a solution may seem large, a comprehensive analysis to estimate the costs to build the solution must be undertaken. These costs for building the solution are not solely financial for purchases of technology software and hardware but also include the expertise and time of internal technology resources (Halogen, 2006). Many organizations might not have this type of talent internally and will need to contract some of the work to technology vendors anyway.

The second factor when considering whether to buy or build a solution is the complexity and uniqueness of the organization's performance management requirements. As system requirements increase, the likelihood of an "out-of-the-box" solution meeting these needs decreases. An intermediary option is to buy a standard technology solution that includes access to configuration tools, which offers the opportunity to further customize the solution to support the organization's specific needs. Regardless of whether an organization is initially leaning toward building or buying the solution, the first step is to develop an internal product requirements document (PRD) that specifies the required functionality for the solution and then engage with technology vendors to preview their capabilities. To identify vendors of performance management software and learn about their product offerings, readers are referred to the 2007 Gartner report *MarketScope for Employee Performance Management Software* (Holincheck, 2007), which includes a comprehensive evaluation of twenty-eight performance management software vendors by impartial industry analysts. By first developing system requirements and then reviewing what functionality is available in the marketplace, buyers can make an educated decision as to whether a current product offering can meet the organization's needs or whether a custom solution must be developed.

Use Change Management Strategies

The implementation of a technology-based performance management system should be viewed like any other large-scale organizational change. It has been acknowledged in the literature that enterprise-wide implementations of technology solutions do fail on a regular basis and that the failure is often attributed to employee resistance (Kwahk & Kim, 2008). To reduce the likelihood of failure for this reason, change management techniques should be used to foster readiness for change (Armenakis, Harris, & Mossholder, 1993) by educating the organization about the rationale behind the change; gaining support for the solution from key stakeholders who are widely respected and can serve as internal change agents; offering sufficient training well in advance of implementation so that users feel competent in their ability to navigate the system; and providing substantial resources and support when the system goes live should users experience any challenges (Marler, Liang, & Dulebohn, 2006). Additionally, when developing the PRD, a committee should be formed that includes representatives from all business lines and organizational levels (both managers and individual contributors). This committee can provide input as to which feature functionalities are general requirements across business lines and levels and which should be open for variation across these vectors. This ensures that the system requirements and processes developed acknowledge the unique needs of different business units and constituencies, while still creating a level of consistency across the enterprise.

If both new performance management processes and new technology to support these processes are implemented at the same time, users run the risk of being overwhelmed and confused, and the technology may be blamed for challenges that are actually due to insufficient vetting of new processes (Sinangil & Avallone, 2001). For this reason, it is recommended that new performance management practices be introduced first, allowing for employees to work with these new processes, employee feedback to be solicited, and changes to be made to ensure optimal functioning prior to introducing the technological components. In essence, this represents a phased implementation approach whereby the content, process, and tools are introduced before the technological infrastructure is rolled out.

Remember That Content Is King

As was alluded to earlier when describing the challenges of relying too heavily on technology, it is imperative that, coinciding with the effort to create a viable technology solution, significant focus be placed on developing the content that will be housed within the solution and tools that will maximize the effectiveness of the content. This means applying research findings to create content such as relevant behavioral competencies and rating scales for performance assessment and tools such as training for supervisors on how to deliver effective performance feedback and provide effective coaching to subordinates (Latham, Almost, Mann, & Moore, 2005).

An easy analogy can be drawn to another area of human resources in which technology solutions are plenty but content is still king, namely, hiring employees using applicant tracking systems (ATS). An ATS enables applicants to apply online and hiring managers or recruiters to use an online portal to review their applications, administer selection assessments, initiate background checks, and move the applicants through the hiring workflow (ERE, 2007). While this solution ensures that the staffing process is efficient, it certainly does not ensure that the staffing process is effective. All the appropriate content (for example, job-relevant and valid assessments) and tools (for example, interview training for hiring managers) must still be in place, or the solution is only enabling the company to hire the wrong people faster. Also in the case of performance management, what is so great about more efficiently evaluating people against standards that are not relevant for their jobs or important for overall organizational strategy and success? The right content needs to be in place before performance management technology can offer any real advantages to an organization.

Keep Integration in Mind

It is fitting that the topic of integration is the last major area that is addressed in this chapter, given that it represents the long-term goal for virtually all efforts to automate a performance management system. Moreover, many of the benefits cited above with respect to using technology for performance management purposes can only be fully experienced if integration of the solution with other human resource applications is achieved. These other human resource applications generally refer to other talent management solutions such as an ATS for recruitment and selection, a learning management system (LMS) for training, and solutions available for workforce planning and compensation (Levensaler, 2007). Depending on an organization's industry and priorities, it might also make sense to integrate the performance management solution with software used for operational purposes such as time and attendance, scheduling, and sales.

Practically speaking, integration of technology solutions can mean different things. In reality, there is a continuum of integration capabilities, and an organization must determine which level of integration is a "must have" as compared to a "nice to have." This integration continuum can run from completely separate systems that are housed in different places and do not share information to solutions that share data behind the scenes but still function as separate systems to systems that are integrated such that an employee can use a single sign-on to access all the systems and reporting tools can pull data across systems for analysis. For instance, integration may allow human resource personnel to search by employee and have access to all relevant data across multiple systems (for example, application and assessment data from the ATS, training classes taken from the LMS, performance reviews and developmental plans from the performance management system, time and attendance from the scheduling software, and compensation history pulled from a separate system). With any type of integration along this continuum, it is important to plan for ongoing support needs from the vendor(s) of the system(s). This ongoing support includes initial design, implementation, training, and integration as well as regular system maintenance and upgrades. Planning for this support means both having the expectation that there will be a reliance on a third party to service the system needs and earmarking dollars in the system budget for this ongoing support.

The importance of solution integration and the frequency of integrating performance management solutions with other human resource applications can be observed from reports and surveys completed by industry analysts. Research by Bersin and associates showed that buyers of talent management suites (for example, a system that includes more than one human resource application, including performance management) are looking to achieve benefits such as consolidating systems, standardizing on one vendor, and minimizing manual data transfer (Levensaler, 2007). Additionally, survey results showed that human resource managers will sacrifice depth of feature functionality in any specific talent management application to have breadth and integration of multiple solutions including performance management. Finally, the top two integration priorities indicated by survey respondents both involved performance management (performance management with learning management and performance management with succession planning), and the most common current integrations were performance management with succession planning and compensation management.

The 2007 Gartner MarketScope report expanded its focus beyond performance management to include compensation management and succession planning solutions because there was significant industry focus on the integration amongst these three applications (Holincheck, 2007). The report showed that, while integration is recognized as important, vendors have not currently integrated solutions for many clients and no vendor is strong across all of these applications, reflecting that the use of integrated performance management solutions is still in its infancy. Whatever a company's objectives for an automated performance management system, some level of integration should be one of them, and efforts should be made early on in the planning and implementation phases to ensure infrastructure is built that will support integration in the future.

Technology Best Practices: What Are the Best Practice Recommendations for Using Technology for Performance Management Purposes?

This purpose of this chapter was to address the role that technology can play in performance management, the benefits that are offered and the challenges experienced if technology is used to support performance management processes, and the practical issues that should be considered when implementing an automated performance management solution. The last section offered some best practice recommendations for using technology for performance management purposes.

Substantial information was provided about the potential benefits and challenges related to the incorporation of technology into a performance management process. Based on this information, recommendations are put forth in Exhibit 13.3 with respect to how to ensure that the use of technology will make a positive contribution to a performance management system.

Exhibit 13.3 Best Practice Recommendations Associated with Using Technology for Performance Management.

Capitalizing on the Benefits

- Use technology capabilities to allow ready access to performance management information across the enterprise.
- Use technological capabilities to disseminate performance management information to a wide group of stakeholders and alert those stakeholders when the information is updated.
- Use technology capabilities to aggregate performance data and integrate performance information with data housed in other human resource applications.
- Use technology capabilities to facilitate the continuous process of performance management whereby performance data are consistently entered, accessed, updated, and used for performance management purposes (for example, providing performance feedback).
- Use technology capabilities to document performance-related conversations and actions.
- Use technology capabilities to automate requests for performance feedback on a project basis.
- Use technology capabilities to support the summarization, analysis, and interpretation of performance data.
- Use technology capabilities to offer access to positions' competencies and provide career pathing tools that allow employees to specify career paths in alignment with development plans and targeted positions' competencies.

Avoiding the Complications

- Consider system requirements (hardware and software) to ensure system performance is optimal and not characterized by slow response times.
- Create a user-friendly interface that offers employees an opportunity for efficient and effective interaction with the performance management system.
- Incorporate feature functionality that will rely on visual display as much as possible to show performance data, use branching logic that is consistent with business processes, allow for user customization to support common actions in the system (for example, a favorite reports tab), and offer intuitive searching capabilities.
- Consider the resource burden on individuals when requesting performance information by providing a context for the request and using a short form to structure the request.
- Set appropriate expectations about the increased time requirements to use the system until sufficient expertise is developed and the important role that people will still play in the performance management process after the technological solution is introduced.
- Ensure the appropriateness and integrity of performance data entered into the system by offering the employees an opportunity to respond to performance feedback and creating a role in human resources that will monitor the information as it is entered.
- Provide adequate training on the system, including technical training, especially if computer literacy is not a central job requirement for the people who will be interacting with the system.
- Execute a communication campaign to ensure that all those who will utilize the system are familiar and comfortable with the technology prior to its implementation.

Additionally, in the optimal situation, technology is not solely used to automate individual performance management components but instead to automate the entire performance management system in an integrated fashion. Exhibit 13.4 provides a list of the important practical points for consideration when implementing a system-wide technology solution.

Exhibit 13.4 Best Practice Recommendations for How to Implement an Automated Performance Management System.

- Ensure a clear performance management process has been established and quality performance management content (for example, performance competencies) has been created prior to implementing a technology solution.
- Form a committee of stakeholders across business units and organizational levels that will manage the internal effort.
- Prepare a comprehensive estimate of the internal costs of building a solution, including people resources if this option is being considered.
- Determine the complexity of the solution needed based on the organization's performance management process and the extent to which the process differs across business units and organizational levels.
- Prepare a PRD that outlines required functionality prior to engaging with technology vendors.
- Consider the solution implementation as a large-scale change management initiative and utilize change management strategies to increase user readiness for change.
- Provide users with a user acceptance testing (UAT) environment prior to the system going live so that users can experiment with the solution and notify the project team of any deficiencies they identified.
- Establish a comprehensive internal (and external, if applicable) support system for users after the system goes live.
- Ensure that technology specifications allow for integration with other human resource applications.
- Create a long-term implementation plan for integration across human resource and operational applications so that the maximum benefits of an automated performance management solution can be achieved.

References

Aguinis, H. (2007). *Performance management.* Upper Saddle River, NJ: Pearson.

Aiello, J. R., & Kolb, K. J. (1995). Electronic performance monitoring and social context: Impact on productivity and stress. *Journal of Applied Psychology, 80,* 339–353.

Aiello, J. R., & Svec, C. M. (1993). Computer monitoring of work performance: Extending the social facilitation framework to electronic presence. *Journal of Applied Social Psychology, 53,* 537–548.

Alge, B. J. (2001). Effects of computer surveillance on perceptions of privacy and procedural justice. *Journal of Applied Psychology, 86,* 797–804.

Amick, B. C., & Smith, M. J. (1992). Stress, computer-based work monitoring and measurement systems: A conceptual overview. *Applied Ergonomics, 23,* 6–16.

Armenakis A. A., Harris S. G., & Mossholder K. W. (1993). Creating readiness for organizational change. *Human Relations, 46,* 681–703.

Arnold, J. (2002). Careers and career management. In N. Anderson, D. S. Ones, H. K. Sinangil, & C. Viswesvaran (Eds.), *Handbook of industrial, work, & organizational psychology* (Vol. 2, pp. 115–132). Thousand Oaks, CA: Sage.

Bates, R. A., & Holton, B. F. III. (1995). Computerized performance monitoring: A review of human resource issues. *Human Resource Management Review, 5,* 267–288.

Bauer, T. N. (2007). From new employee socialization to new employee on-boarding: Applying theory to practice. In K. S. Zimberg & C. P. Intuit (Chairs), *Advances in newcomer socialization: Ensuring new employee success through on-boarding.* Symposium conducted at the annual convention of the Society for Industrial and Organizational Psychology, New York, New York.

Bersin, J. (2007). Social networking: Meet corporate America. Retrieved April 1, 2008, from http://www.bersin.com/tips_techniques/07_nov_socialnetwork.asp.

Bettenhausen, K. L., & Fedor, D. B. (1997). Peer and upward appraisals: A comparison of their benefits and problems. *Group & Organization Management, 22,* 236–263.

Cardy, R. L., & Miller, J. S. (2003). Technology: Implications for HRM. In E. Salas & D. Stone (Eds.), *Advances in human performance and cognitive engineering research* (Vol. 3, pp. 99–118). Oxford, UK: Elsevier Science.

Cascio, W. F. (2000). Managing a virtual workplace. *Academy of Management Executive, 14,* 81–90.

Cascio, W. F. (2003). How technology facilitates virtual work arrangements. In E. Salas & D. Stone (Eds.), *Advances in human performance and cognitive engineering research* (Vol. 3, pp. 1–12). Oxford, UK: Elsevier Science.

Cawley, B. D., Keeping, L. M., & Levy, P. E. (1998). Participation in the performance appraisal process and employee reactions: A meta-analytic review of field investigations. *Journal of Applied Psychology, 83*, 615–633.

Chalykoff, J., & Kochan, T. A. (1989). Computer-aided monitoring: Its influence on employee job satisfaction and turnover. *Personnel Psychology, 42*, 807–834.

Chen, N. S., Kinshuk, Wei, C. W., & Chen, H. J. (2008). Mining e-learning domain concept map from academic articles. *Computers & Education, 50*, 1009–1021.

Donovan, J. J., & Williams, K. J. (2003). Missing the mark: Effects of time and causal attributions on goal revision in response to goal-performance discrepancies. *Journal of Applied Psychology, 88*, 379–390.

Ellison, N. B. (1999). Social impacts: New perspectives on telework. *Social Science Computer Review, 17*, 338–356.

Eppler, M., & Mengis, J. (2004). The concept of information overload: A review of literature from organization science, accounting, marketing, MIS, and related disciplines. *The Information Society, 20*, 325–344.

Erdogan, B., Kraimer, M. L., & Liden, R. C. (2001). Procedural justice as a two-dimensional construct: An examination in the performance appraisal account. *Journal of Applied Behavioral Science, 37*, 205–222.

ERE. (2007, September). *Applicant tracking systems: Industry analysis and buyer's guide.* New York: Author.

Farh, J. L., Cannella, A. A., & Bedeian, A. G. (1991). Peer ratings: The impact of purpose on rating quality and user acceptance. *Group & Organization Studies, 16*, 367–386.

Folger, R., Konovsky, M. A., & Cropanzano, R. (1992). A due process metaphor for performance appraisal. In B. M. Staw & L. L. Cummings (Eds.), *Research in organizational behavior* (Vol. 13, pp. 129–177). Oxford, UK: Elsevier Science.

Geddes, D., & Baron, R. A. (1997). Workplace aggression as a consequence of negative performance feedback. *Management Communication Quarterly, 10*, 433–454.

Grant, R. A., & Higgins, C. A. (1991). The impact of computerized performance monitoring on service work: Testing a causal model. *Information Systems Research, 2*, 116–142.

Grensing-Pophal, L. (1999, January). Training supervisors to manage teleworkers. *HR Magazine*, pp. 67–72.

Gueutal, H. G. (2003). The brave new world of eHR. In E. Salas & D. Stone (Eds.), *Advances in human performance and cognitive engineering research* (Vol. 3, pp. 13–36). Oxford, UK: Elsevier Science.

Halogen. (2006). *Performance appraisal software: Build vs. buy?* Ottawa, ON: Author.

Hawk, S. R. (1994). The effects of computerized performance monitoring: An ethical perspective. *Journal of Business Ethics, 13,* 949–957.

Holincheck, J. (2007). *Marketscope for employee performance management software.* Stamford, CT: Gartner, Inc.

Ilgen, D. R., Fisher, C. D., & Taylor, M. S. (1979). Consequences of individual feedback on behavior in organizations. *Journal of Applied Psychology, 64,* 349–371.

Illegems, V., & Verbeke, A. (2004). Telework: What does it mean for management? *Long Range Planning, 37,* 319–334.

Johnson, R. D., & Isenhour, L. C. (2003). Changing the rules? Human resources in the 21st century virtual organization. In E. Salas & D. Stone (Eds.), *Advances in human performance and cognitive engineering research* (Vol. 3, pp. 119–152). Oxford, UK: Elsevier Science.

Jones, J. W., & Dages, K. D. (2003). Technology trends in staffing and assessment. *International Journal of Selection and Assessment, 11,* 247–252.

Kavanagh, M., Gueutal, H. G., & Tannenbaum, S. (1990). *Human resource information systems: Development and application.* Boston: Kent.

Kear, K. L., & Heap, N. W. (2007). Sorting the wheat from the chaff: Investigating overload in educational discussion systems. *Journal of Computer Assisted Learning, 23,* 235–247.

Keeping, L. M., & Levy, P. E. (2000). Performance appraisal reactions: Measurement, modeling, and method bias. *Journal of Applied Psychology, 85,* 708–723.

Klausegger, C., Sinkovics, R. R., & Zou, H. (2007). Information overload: A cross-national investigation of influence factors and effects. *Marketing Intelligence & Planning, 25,* 691–718.

Kluger, A. N., & DeNisi, A. (1996). The effects of feedback interventions on performance: A historical review, a meta-analysis, and a preliminary feedback intervention theory. *Psychological Bulletin, 119,* 254–284.

Kwahk, K. Y., & Kim, H. W. (2008). Managing readiness in enterprise systems-driven organizational change. *Behaviour & Information Technology, 27,* 79–87.

Latham, G. P., Almost, J., Mann, S., & Moore, C. (2005). New developments in performance management. *Organizational Dynamics, 34,* 77–87.

Latham, G. P., Mitchell, T. R., & Dossett, D. L. (1978). The importance of participative goal setting and anticipated rewards on goal difficulty and job performance. *Journal of Applied Psychology, 63,* 163–171.

Lawson. (2006). Survey: Performance management tops priority list for HR systems. Retrieved April 1, 2008, from http://www.lawson.com/wcw.nsf/pub/new_079E01.

Lazar, J., Jones, A., & Schneiderman, B. (2006). Workplace user frustration with computers: An exploratory investigation of the causes and severity. *Behaviour & Information Technology, 25,* 239–251.

Levensaler, L. (2007). *What is the talent management suite? And what are vendors actually delivering?* Paper presented at the 11th annual HR Technology Conference and Exposition, Chicago, Illinois.

Locke, E. A., & Latham, G. P. (1990). *A theory of goal setting and task performance.* Englewood Cliffs, NJ: Prentice-Hall.

Lowe, T. R. (1986). Eight ways to ruin a performance review. *Personnel Journal, 65,* 60–62.

Manoochehri, G., & Pinkerton, T. (2003). Managing telecommuters: Opportunities and challenges. *American Business Review, 21,* 9–16.

Marler, J. H., Liang, X., & Dulebohn, J. H. (2006). Training and effective employee information technology use. *Journal of Management, 32,* 721–743.

McAleese, D., & Hargie, O. (2004). Five guiding principles of culture management: A synthesis of best practice. *Journal of Communication Management, 9,* 155–170.

McEntire, L. E., Dailey, L. R., Osburn, H. K., & Mumford, M. D. (2006). Innovations in job analysis: Development and application of metrics to analyze job data. *Human Resource Management Review, 16,* 310–323.

McGraw, B., & Kelly, B. (1995). Successful management in the virtual office. Retrieved April 1, 2008, from http://bamcgraw.home.mindspring.com/guide/telgd1.htm#toc.

MCIWorldCom. (2001). Meetings in America III: A study of the virtual workforce in 2001. Retrieved April 1, 2008, from http://emeetings.wcom.com/meetingsinamerica/articles/pressrelease1.php3.

McNall, L. A., & Roch, S. G. (2007). Effects of electronic monitoring types on perceptions of procedural justice, interpersonal justice, and privacy. *Journal of Applied Social Psychology, 37,* 658–682.

Mero, N. P., & Motowidlo, S. J. (1995). Effects of rater accountability on the accuracy and the favorability of performance ratings. *Journal of Applied Psychology, 80,* 517–524.

Mero, N. P., Motowidlo, S. J., & Anna, A. L. (2003). Effects of accountability on rating behavior and rater accuracy. *Journal of Applied Social Psychology, 33,* 2493–2514.

Peterson, N. G., Mumford, M. D., Borman, W. C., Jeanneret, P. R., & Fleishman, E. A. (1999). *An occupational information system for the 21st century: The development of O*NET.* Washington, DC: American Psychological Association.

Porter, S. R., Whitcomb, M. E., & Weitzer, W. H. (2004). Multiple surveys of students and survey fatigue. *New Directions for Institutional Research, 121,* 63–73.

Roberts, G. E. (2003). Employee performance appraisal system participation: A technique that works. *Public Personnel Management, 32,* 89–98.

Rogelberg, S. C., Spitzmueller, C., Little, I., & Reeve, C. L. (2006). Understanding response behavior to an online special topics organizational satisfaction survey. *Personnel Psychology, 59,* 903–923.

Saari, L. M. (1998, April). Surveys in a global corporation: Managing oversurveying and quality. In S. G. Rogelberg (Chair), *Surveys and more surveys: Addressing and dealing with oversurveying.* Symposium conducted at the annual convention of the Society for Industrial and Organizational Psychology, Dallas, Texas.

Schneider, S. C. (1987). Information overload: Causes and consequences. *Human Systems Management, 7,* 143–153.

Schneider, R. J., Goff, M., Anderson, S., & Borman, W. C. (2003). Computerized adaptive rating scales for measuring managerial performance. *International Journal of Selection and Assessment, 11,* 237–246.

Sinangil, H. K., & Avallone, F. (2002). *Organizational development and change.* In N. Anderson, D. S. Ones, H. K. Sinangil, & C. Viswesvaran (Eds.), *Handbook of industrial, work, & organizational psychology* (Vol. 2, pp. 332–345). Thousand Oaks, CA: Sage.

Stanton, J. M. (2000). Reactions to employee performance monitoring: Framework, review, and research directions. *Human Performance, 13,* 85–113.

Stone, D. L., Stone-Romero, E. F., & Lukaszewski, K. (2003). The functional and dysfunctional consequences of human resource information technology for organizations and their employees. In E. Salas & D. Stone (Eds.), *Advances in human performance and cognitive engineering research* (Vol. 3, pp. 37–68). Oxford, UK: Elsevier Science.

Tarquinio, M. (2006). *Onboarding benchmark report: Technology drivers help improve the new hire experience.* Boston: Aberdeen Group.

Thompson, L. F., Surface, E. A., Martin, D. L., & Sanders, M. G. (2003). From paper to pixels: Moving personnel surveys to the web. *Personnel Psychology, 56,* 197–227.

United States Office of Personnel Management. (2003). Telework: A management priority. Retrieved April 1, 2008, from http://www.telework.gov/documents/tw_man03/prnt/manual.asp.

Venkatesh, V., Morris, M. G., Davis, G. D., & Davis, F. D. (2003). User acceptance of information technology. *MIS Quarterly, 27,* 425–478.

Wells, L. (2006, April). Measuring dramatic culture change through pulse survey results. In L. A. Bousman & L. S. Carr (Chairs), *Extending the knowledge: Corporate-wide actions from employee research.* Symposium conducted at the annual convention of the Society for Industrial and Organizational Psychology, Dallas, Texas.

Wells, D. L., Moorman, R. H., & Werner, J. M. (2007). The impact of the perceived purpose of electronic performance monitoring on an array of attitudinal variables. *Human Resource Development Quarterly, 18,* 121–138.

Westin, A. F. (1992). Two key factors that belong in a macroeconomic analysis of electronic monitoring: Employee perceptions of fairness and the climate of organizational trust or distrust. *Applied Ergonomics, 23,* 35–42.

CHAPTER 14

AUTHENTIC PERFORMANCE

The Valuation of Behavior as a Negotiated Business Outcome

Thomas Diamante

"The greatest deception men suffer is from their own opinions."
LEONARDO DA VINCI

The Valuation of Work Behavior: An Overview

The act of "valuing" performance is complex, interactive, and, to the extent the organization allows, it is negotiated (or created) by an exchange between the observer and the object being observed. In the work context, the observer (supervising manager) and the observed (the employee) interact to arrive at the "valuation" of job behavior. I suggest that *performance negotiation is the on-going process by which a supervisor and employee arrive at an agreement about the value of an employee's contribution to business.* The end result is the delivery of a performance review that yields value to both the recipient and the employing organization.

Employee value is created, not found. Value is sculpted in organizations and the tools used are imperfect (Landy & Farr, 1980; Latham & Latham, 2000). Many variables contribute to the difficulties of "measuring" or "placing value" on performance. Unwanted influence (that is, mistakes) on performance ratings emanates from many sources. These are known as errors of leniency, contrast, and central tendency—all indicating a failure to accurately rate, measure, or value performance. In addition, unwanted variance leaks into assessments based on personality dimensions unrelated to performance, such as those linked to group affiliations and/or visible human differences (Latham & Wexley, 1981).

Research indicates that managers can be aware of evaluative errors, yet they are still willing to make them, typically for political reasons (inside the organization) (Longenecker, Gioia, & Sims, 1987). Efforts to overcome these obstacles are not achieved simply. For example, training does not appear to solve the problem of error inherent to the performance rating process (Latham & Latham, 2000).

Complicating the matter further is the fact that performance unfolds over time. It is not a static event. The time period typically selected to "label" performance (and place a metric on it) is usually one year. During this time period it is reasonable to expect that every day brings differing levels of performance or value. Performance "looks" different on different days. The observer too may "look at it" differently on different days, depending on business, political, or personal circumstances (Longenecker, Gioia, & Sims, 1987).

The observer and the employee bring human characteristics known to influence evaluations—personal history, past learning experiences, personality, implicit assumptions about trait clustering, cognitive complexity, and other less flattering "biases" such as social stereotypes, organizational/political motives, gender stereotypes, racial/ethnic prejudices, and preconceived notions about age and work abilities. Furthermore, as the two parties bring these elements to the table, there is the potential for them to *interact*. The intensity and consequences of the sparks generated continue to ignite applied psychological empirical research (Reb & Cropanzano, 2007).

The complexity of measuring reality is not limited to social or applied psychological sciences. Hard sciences speak of the "observer effect," explaining that the very act of measurement is, in itself, an imposition on that which is being measured. As a result, it is impossible to measure or know "reality" without simultaneously influencing it. Hence, for instance, in physical terms it is impossible to know both the position of a particle and its speed—since "touching" or measuring the particle alters the path and velocity of that which is being measured. Measurement, it seems, is by definition an elusive construct.

People take performance conversations personally. The conversation affects employees on an emotional level. The conversation affects salary and future possibilities and is a direct attempt to discuss an individual's value-add to the employer.

The term "performance negotiation" implies that performance requires a "give and take" or that it is an interactive process between two or more individuals in order to reach a mutually agreed-on outcome (Lax & Sebenius, 1986). The current trend focusing on multi-source feedback is an example of a tactic intended to reduce conflict by adding "more" perspectives to the picture (Goodstone & Diamante, 1998). Arguably, however, input from several wrong perspectives is not necessarily more valuable than input from one correct perspective. Additionally, there appears to be a trend to assume that agreement among many is more likely indicative of reality than the "outlier" data point. This may or may not be the case, depending, of course, on whether the views of the many are in themselves biased for one reason or another, intentionally or not (Longenecker, Gioia, & Sims, 1987).

This chapter proposes a systemic model for planning performance negotiation (see Figure 14.1). I suggest that organizational, individual, and interpersonal issues be engineered into the process of managing/negotiating performance to yield desired outcomes. Figure 14.1 proposes that learning and business outcomes are optimized when organizational antecedents are in place, when individuals bring stated personal characteristics, and that the interaction between organizational antecedents and personal characteristics is enhanced by focused social exchanges. High-quality social exchanges are evident based on the interaction between leaders and members of the organization being evaluated, which in turn produces "authentic" learning and business outcomes. It is proposed that when socio-psychological conditions are "ripe," they enhance social exchange through three key mechanisms:

Figure 14.1 Systemic Model for Performance Negotiation.

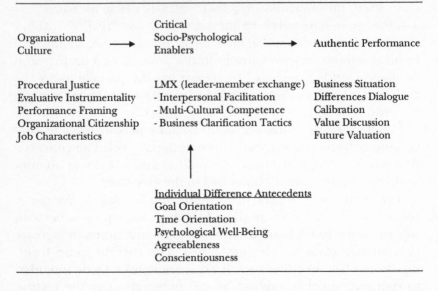

Organizational Culture	Critical Socio-Psychological Enablers	Authentic Performance
Procedural Justice	LMX (leader-member exchange)	Business Situation
Evaluative Instrumentality	- Interpersonal Facilitation	Differences Dialogue
Performance Framing	- Multi-Cultural Competence	Calibration
Organizational Citizenship	- Business Clarification Tactics	Value Discussion
Job Characteristics		Future Valuation

Individual Difference Antecedents
Goal Orientation
Time Orientation
Psychological Well-Being
Agreeableness
Conscientiousness

(1) interpersonal facilitation, (2) multi-cultural competence, and (3) business clarification tactics. Guidelines for enabling "authentic engagements" are provided later in this chapter.

Components of Performance Negotiation

Employees reciprocate fair treatment. It's that simple. You get what you give (Organ, 1990). The processes by which employees "evaluate" their sense of being treated fairly is known as the process of social exchange (Organ & Moorman, 1993). Interpersonal exchange is pivotal in all negotiation strategies (Prien, 1987). Engineering healthy social exchange improves the efficacy of performance management processes, including how the review is negotiated.

Setting the Stage: Organizational Culture

There is nothing more regrettable than a bad hire or, for that matter, a good hire that turns bad. And there is nothing more regrettable than an inaccurate (bad) performance review. Such inadequate human resource processes place business at unnecessary risk. Talent walks out the door or, on the other hand, needed talent is rejected or squandered.

Bad job performance speaks for itself, but who speaks for good performance that is reviewed poorly? The industrial and organizational psychological profession offers human resource professionals significant direction in terms of "how" to design (validate) personnel decision-making practices to satisfy legal/professional standards (see, for example, Diamante, 1993). Technical, empirical validation studies typically do not address, however, how information collection (the assessment) is viewed from the perspective of the party being assessed. There is a human component to the process of being "measured." The object being measured is always "affected." Performance negotiation is open to this reality.

The identification (and agreement) of what constitutes "solid performance" is changing within most organizations. Clear-cut business outcomes produced by a single individual are rare in most organizations. Requirements are high for work group learning, constant feedback, and adaptive learning systems, so that adjustments to desired team goals can be made (Silberstang & Diamante, 2008).

The fact that role responsibilities (and work team accountabilities) are in a constant state of change complicates "normal" problems of human perception, evaluation of others, and interpersonal communication (Heslin, Latham, & VandeWalle, 2005; Landy & Farr, 1980; London, 2001). Product offerings are in motion, business models experience new forms, and leadership requirements bring challenges all their own. Performance under conditions of change is a discovery process. Leadership characteristics for digital business models, for instance, have been proposed (Diamante & London, 2002), and future trends where web-based business applications replace operations and mandate "old" competencies into obsolescence are explored on a regular basis, both theoretically and practically (Friedman, 2006). On a practical level, calibration of performance, as a *negotiated business outcome,* is a reality.

Procedural Justice and Evaluative Instrumentality

What workers actually "do" remains a critical issue for productivity and morale (Oldham & Hackman, 1980). How organizations actually "work" (the presence of procedural justice) affects employee views of the evaluation process that in turn is linked to organizational citizenship behavior, or the desire to help others and/or take on additional responsibilities/take charge for making organizational improvements (OCB) (Kamdar, McAllister, & Turban, 2006; Penner, 2002). Research demonstrates that OCB affects supervisory judgments of overall job performance. Whiting, Podsakoff, and Pierce (2008) recently evidenced the effect of helping behaviors on overall performance ratings. There is an interplay between what employees "do" and what organizations "do"—and this affects how people evaluate each other in that context.

Procedural justice or the institutionalization of "due process" is linked to a variety of positive business outcomes (Kamdar, McAllister, & Turban, 2006). Specifically, OCB appears to be a direct correlate (Konovsky & Pugh, 1994; Tepper, Lockhart, & Hoobler, 2001; Tepper & Taylor, 2003). To the extent that employees perceive their employer as just and good, that "due process" is institutionalized, evaluative instrumentality is hypothesized to be higher than if "due process" or procedural justice is viewed to be low. I suggest that procedural justice can enhance the efficacy of performance reviews and its negotiation. This is done through "evaluative instrumentality" and organizational "performance framing."

Performance Framing

The terms "performance framing" and "evaluative instrumentality" are being introduced here to address the critical nature of the employee's (recipient's) "cognitive schema" for understanding performance feedback. Performance framing is the organizational communication of business conditions that lead to inferences about good/bad (valuable/worthless) work behavior. The judgment that the utility of the review, from the perspective of the party receiving the feedback, is "useful" is "evaluative instrumentality." Evaluative instrumentality is then the subjective interpretation of performance feedback as being unbiased—be this for developmental purposes, merit-based pay qualification, or any other outcome.

It is suggested that evaluative instrumentality of the feedback is a subjective determination that leads to an internalized "level of acceptance" and that this brings commensurate impact on employee work attitudes and behavior.

Organizational Citizenship

Organizational citizenship behavior (OCB) appears to be moderated by the job characteristic autonomy and its consequent effect on psychological states. The role discretion effect (McAllister, Wolfe Morrison, Kamdar, & Turban, 2007; Zellars, Tepper, & Duffy, 2002) is the term used to describe the relationship between OCB and the psychological state of "control" (a sense of personal responsibility) (Oldham & Hackman, 1980). OCB is expected when role discretion is high.

McAllister, Wolfe Morrison, Kamdar, and Turban (2007) reviewed research linking OCB and procedural justice. Citing the work of Tepper, Uhl-Bien, Kohut, Rogelberg, Lockhart, and Ensley (2001), Tepper and Taylor (2003) and Zellars, Tepper, and Duffy (2002), these reviewers explained that high levels of procedural justice and autonomy (role discretion) were a powerful, motivating combination leading to high levels of OCB. Interactions between procedural justice and the job characteristic of autonomy were also noted by McAllister, Wolfe Morrison, Kamdar, and Turban (2007). For example, when procedural justice was low and role discretion was high, OCB appears to be withheld. When procedural justice was high and role discretion was high, OCB was not found to be stronger than when procedural justice was high and role discretion was low. Clearly, the institutionalization of fair evaluative processes is critical for all aspects of performance management, likely also offering a level of litigious protection as well.

Attention should be given to creating work environments that breed healthy OCB expectations. Employees who view their jobs more broadly are OCB-prone (Parker, Williams, & Turnover, 2006, cited in McAllister, Wolfe Morrison, Kamdar, & Turban, 2007). Socialization processes, newcomer orientations, competency models, job enrichment/characteristics design, and leadership behaviors are all ways to encourage or promote a healthier OCB environment (Parker, Wall, & Jackson, 1997, cited in McAllister, Wolfe Morrison, Kamdar, & Turban, 2007).

Job Characteristics

OCB is optimized under conditions whereby the work itself leads to high intrinsic work motivation. It is suggested here that employees with higher levels of autonomy, a psychological state derived from the work itself, will enter performance discussions more positively than employees with lower levels of autonomy. Performance negotiation is more effective when the work itself leads to the psychological state of autonomy (Oldham & Hackman, 1980).

In addition, intrinsically motivated employees will enter performance discussions more positively than employees who are extrinsically motivated. As a result, job characteristics are an important aspect of performance and the ensuing, inevitable "negotiation" or delivery of the performance evaluation. Finally, work environments high in OCB are more likely to benefit from performance negotiations than work environments low in OCB.

Critical Socio-Psychological Enablers: Individual Differences Make a Difference

The challenge of performance review and its negotiation lies within. Individual differences interact with various features of the performance review process. Fundamentally, the empirical evidence demonstrates that bias bleeds into the evaluative process through various means (Hulin, Henry, & Noon, 1990; Landy & Farr, 1980; Levy & Williams, 2004; London, 2001; Quinones, Ford, & Teachout, 1995; Sturman & Trevor, 2001). In general, bias is introduced from (1) the evaluator's notion of what behaviors or traits are implicitly linked (Heslin, Latham, & VandeWalle, 2005), (2) the political motives of the evaluator (Longenecker, Gioia, & Sims, 1987), (3) the relationship between the person being evaluated and the evaluator (Tepper, Uhl-Bien, Kohut, Rogelberg, Lockhart, & Ensley, 2006), and (4) the "way" performance unfolds in the workplace (that is, trends and variance) (Reb & Cropanzano, 2007). Psychological characteristics of the employee (and the evaluator) include cognitive ability, personality, time orientation, goal orientation, and overall psychological well-being. These constructs (and their interactions) bring implications for how performance needs to be planned for and discussed (Bell & Kozlowski, 2002; Frederickson & Joiner, 2002; Kamdar & Van Dyne, 2007).

Leader-Member Exchange (LMX): The Shortest Distance to an Agreement on Valuation

To reiterate, everyone is fallible and the performance appraisal process merely reflects this reality. None sees the world as it is; we impose meaning on the world based on who we are.

The employee, the supervisor, leadership—bring human qualities that co-mingle with the tools and processes and personalities present when performance review time comes around. These complex interactions influence our perception of what we observe, how it is viewed, and why it is important or meaningful to the organization (valued). It is important to realize that both the supervising manager and the employee being reviewed bring personality traits. The dynamic that develops, however, I suggest, is the responsibility of the manager.

The following therefore emphasizes the need to understand the personality of the employee so the supervising manager can factor his or her own personality and "control" the dynamic to realize a favorable negotiated performance review. To reiterate, an object that is mundane to one person can trigger intense emotional reactions from someone else harboring thoughts (based on experiences) about that object that others do not share. In short, how we think, feel, and behave is a phenomenological event that, at work, is applied to how we view, measure, and value the behaviors of others. These principles of personality psychology and social-psychological research have been applied to executive coaching (Diamante & Primavera, 2004), 360-degree performance feedback analytics (Goodstone & Diamante, 1998), and in general this social systems orientation provides the foundation for much of the groundwork in the field of organization development (Beer & Walton, 1990; Katz & Kahn, 1966).

Moderators in the proposed Systemic Model of Performance Negotiation (Figure 14.1) encapsulate key organizational elements and individual differences that lead to positive, negotiating responses to performance feedback. While the model and its moderators require empirical investigation, it is built for applied psychologists and managers as a practical framework for understanding how to pave a road toward performance negotiation.

The significance of considering personality variables in planning for a performance discussion and possible "negotiation" lies in its critical contribution to the "exchange" that will inevitably ensue. The interaction between the supervisor and the employee will generate creativity, new insights, and potential developmental actions or it can lead to higher levels of disagreement, conflict, and ongoing performance problems. Personality of both the supervisor and the employee will feed into this dynamic.

Mature managers will likely have a read on their personal strengths and weaknesses based on feedback from others over the years (for example, assessment center feedback, 360-degree feedback participation, succession planning sessions). Undoubtedly, the performance negotiation plan should take into account the maturity (or self-awareness) of supervisory management. More conscientious, agreeable managers are likely more self-aware, offer higher levels of self-efficacy upon entering a performance discussion, and are therefore "more capable" of handling the discussion regardless of the nature of the employee being addressed (London, 1995).

Kamdar and Van Dyne (2007) suggested that high-quality social exchanges between leaders and employees (LMX) can compensate for "problematic personality traits" (low conscientiousness and/or low agreeableness). Personality is enhanced by a strong, supportive work context. This brings implications for the planning of performance review processes (the negotiation), as "troublesome" situations demand the orchestration of more frequent, more strategic communications. The better the quality of relationships, the more positive is the expectation that a performance review can go well, regardless of personalities involved. Kamdar and Van Dyne (2007) astutely point out that, whereas managers often inherit (and do not select) employees, the key to producing positive outcomes lies in the ongoing social exchange, whether among team members (TMX) or between leaders and employees (LMX).

Close, supportive supervising relationships are beneficial, especially when the "natural" character of the employees requires an extra helping hand. Kamdar and Van Dyne (2007) provided evidence that suggests high-quality social exchange relationships, that is, leader-member social exchange (LMX), are a key variable in defining work outcomes. High-quality work relationships can "neutralize" task conflicts or override misperceptions, miscommunications, or incongruous employee-supervisor personalities.

Interpersonal Facilitation

Interpersonal exchanges can be enhanced. There are two principal ways to do it. Based on the literature in social psychology, two orthogonal dimensions appear to be applicable to the workplace (Berman, 1969). These dimensions are active (expressiveness versus passive restrictiveness) and receptive (acceptance versus rejection). Essentially, the literature indicates, with a good degree of clarity, that interpersonal exchanges are optimized under conditions of positive regard when there is active engagement.

Interpersonal actions that are openly warm, empathetic, accepting, and "objectively" evident in nature enhance relationships (not requiring interpretation of subtle messages). The positive outcomes of such social interactions cross psychological disciplines (Dalton, 1996; Goodstone & Diamante, 1998; Matarazzo, 1965; Smith & Glass, 1977).

In management, supervisory ratings of performance have been strongly affected by interpersonal facilitative behavior (Van Scotter & Motowidlo, 1996). Linkages between job satisfaction and job performance appear to be moderated by the psychological well-being of the employee (Wright, Copranzano, & Bonett, 2007). It was suggested that the mixed history of performance-satisfaction empirical results requires consideration of psychological well-being (PWB). PWB, we suggest here, is a critical yet often overlooked variable in business literature focused on interpersonal work dynamics. Potential incremental explanatory power may reside in PWB in linking performance and attitudinal measures to organizational climate and management control tactics (that is, efficacy of 360-degree processes; correlates of job characteristics; affect of culture). High-quality interpersonal facilitation (or LMX, leader-member exchange) is key to readiness for performance feedback.

Multi-Cultural Competence

Supervisory competence to engage in healthy, positive dialogue with employees requires solid interpersonal skills, the capability to engage in a non-threatening conversation, self-confidence, and solid understanding of the role requirements and overall business objectives. More than this, globalization, diverse workforces, and more consequent complex idiosyncratic differences bring additional demands on the supervisor (Burkard, Johnson, Madson, Pruitt, Contreras-Tadych, & Kozlowski, 2006). In particular, cultural responsiveness and unresponsiveness in cross-cultural supervision are noteworthy.

For example, Burkard, Johnson, Madson, Pruitt, Contreras-Tadych, & Kozlowski (2006) studied supervisees of color and European American supervisees of culturally responsive and unresponsive cross-cultural supervision. In unresponsive situations, that is, cultural issues were ignored or discounted (if not dismissed by supervisors), negative impact on supervisor-supervisee relations was revealed, negative affect on the supervisee was measured, and work outcomes suffered.

Performance negotiation is enhanced to the extent that interpersonal relations are genuine. LMX, as an indicator of authenticity in an interpersonal engagement, is an evolving construct. Cross-cultural and a multitude of tangible (visible) and intangible (invisible) differences continue to complicate management relationships. Multi-cultural competence in supervision is required to equip a manager to deliver performance feedback. Multi-cultural competencies will include the capability to address (and not be dismissive of or disinterested in) cross-cultural issues. The global economy, web-based business applications, and emerging technologies enable differences to collide at unprecedented speed and frequency.

These collisions bring new-found opportunity as global and cultural differences add colors to the management palate. For instance, how time is measured and managed, how work and leisure time are valued, the pace of work/life itself, and time orientation in general are valid avenues for exploration. As organizations learn how to prepare managers to get better at understanding and delivering feedback to employees, bringing intense differences, emanating from global/cultural/ethnic/individual/other differences, a focus on negotiating performance will become more and more critical.

For example, Brislin and Kim (2003) explored cross-cultural issues and offered practical managerial guidelines reflecting diverse views/values on issues such as the use of time, the role of time as status symbol (Asian CEOs have fewer but longer meetings than American CEOs, maintained less structure in a daily schedule to remain open to the unexpected event), and the importance of time orientation on how an individual approaches problem definition and solution (for example, factoring the past can be viewed as a waste of time by a manager who is present-oriented).

Performance negotiation demands parameters be set by supervision. Operating objectives that are directive should be driven by the competencies and/or business results or outcomes for which the employee is accountable. All of this demands that the supervisor be capable of beginning a performance negotiation by framing the conversation relative to the organization's mission and consequent role requirements. It is only with an agreed sense of business parameters that relevant individual and interpersonal characteristics can be identified and discussed. Management must clarify objectives of the business, of business units, and of individual roles in each unit.

Business Clarification Tactics

Business clarification tactics require fundamental social/group dynamics (Schein, 1969) integrated with concise messages about the competitive business situation. The linkage between the business situation and the roles, competencies, and expected performance outcomes should be delineated. Conveying the results of a competitive business analysis (SWOT: strengths, weaknesses, opportunities, threats) can effectively tie human competencies to performance demands. The rationale driving necessary performance expectations, the means of measurement, and the consequences of evaluation require clarity.

I suggest that the higher the stakes for the employee (in terms of psychological/effort investment), then the greater the need for consequential clarity. For instance, in highly entrepreneurial environments (where success is positioned upon intellectual capital/professional delivery), the linkage between professional accomplishments and equity (or business growth) requires connectivity. These messages lead to business and performance clarity. Everyone knows what is needed, why it is needed, and, if success comes, how the whale will be split. Fairness in splitting the

3

spoils will make or break organizational loyalty and/or the effort to build the business.

Process dynamics that bring a dual focus on task and process are proposed when preparing for a profitable performance negotiation. Tactical mechanisms that lead to desired outcomes are to ensure (1) that direction is evident (what we will discuss, why it is important, and how it will lead to desired benefits), (2) that the manager assumes the initiative to drive the conversation toward a value-add outcome, and (3) that accountabilities along the way are itemized. Mutually beneficial business outcomes are then more likely to be realized. A task-focused discussion on business objectives using a process consultation model will establish the "texture" of the performance dialogue as non-threatening and productive.

Schein (1969) also indicates the importance of keeping the conversation on-track using tactics such as harmonizing, clarifying, and restating and/or discussing how and whether decisions will be made along the way. Managed dialogue reduces interpersonal strain, levels the playing field so that supervisor and supervisee feel equally advantaged, and eliminates unnecessary posturing or positioning to influence the dynamics since the ground rules are discussed up-front.

Optimally negotiated business outcomes result from organizational antecedents that lead to valuable social exchanges moderated by a host of individual difference variables. Managed well, this model enables the supervisor and the employee to assess "value" in an *authentic fashion*, leading to a concrete, genuine, joint business outcome. Figure 14.1 expresses this notion.

Individual Difference Antecedents

Goal Orientation: To Improve Myself or Be the Envy of Others

Predictors of learning and performance remain of interest (Bell & Kozlowski, 2002). To the extent that conversations between the supervising manager and the employee incorporate a desire to assess past behavior (performance) while also addressing the opportunity to enhance learning, motivational elements appear ripe for consideration in the planning of the performance negotiation (Campbell, Faley, & Fehr, 1986).

The literature discusses goal orientation (GO) as a dichotomous variable. Individuals are motivated to achieve because (1) they are driven to learn or master subject matter/craft or (2) they are driven by a desire to be positively evaluated by others (Farr, Hofmann, & Ringenbach, 1993). The former is referred to as an "adaptive response pattern" relative to the effect such motivation brings for organizations. Specifically, GO that is "learning-oriented" is correlated with positive business benefits when such an individual faces work challenges and/or failure (VandeWalle, 1997). The "adaptive" aspect of this orientation appears as resilience and/or the capability to identify opportunities for personal growth when confronting failure.

This concept is very similar to the work of Seligman (1986) in his identification and consequent research on explanatory thinking styles. In Seligman's taxonomy, he identified interpretive internal thoughts as having positive (optimistic) or negative (pessimistic) elements (Seligman, Rashid, & Parks, 2006). More positive orientations or interpretations of "failure" were specific, temporary, and externalized (situational) in focus. Contrarily, explanatory thinking styles that were global, permanent, and internal (for example, "I can't learn") lead to a downward performance spiral negating the possibility to grow from the experience. The latter "pessimistic" or "maladaptive response pattern" is similar to the "performance orientation" of the GO construct.

Importantly, the research on explanatory thinking style and GO share the insight that motivational elements are important in predicting the behavioral and attitudinal outcomes of the experience of failure. A performance orientation or a pessimistic explanatory style leads to the avoidance of difficult situations or withdrawal from challenges relative to those with a learning orientation or an optimistic explanatory style (Seligman, 2007). It has been suggested that learning orientations protect positive behavioral outcomes by securing the individual's self-efficacy for the task at hand (Bell & Kozlowski, 2002; Kozlowski, Gully, Brown, Salas, Smith, & Nason, 2001), where self-efficacy is an internal belief that one can perform a specific task successfully.

The practical managerial implications of this research are simple. Managers are well-advised to learn the GO or explanatory styles of their employees and plan performance feedback accordingly. This means that communications should touch not only the "behaviorally objective" realities of business outcomes but also the supervising manager should explore thoughts/interpretations (and predilections) of the employee *in advance* of the proverbial shoe-dropping. Certainly, managers could benefit from training programs on exactly how to do this, perhaps incorporating the rubrics of GO or explanatory style into their management development programs or perhaps *as part of* their preparation to provide performance feedback to others. Where GO is challenging for management, it is advised that communications regarding the performance review process itself be delivered strategically (and often) to overcome potential "self-explanatory" blockades to growth.

Time Orientation: The Psychology of Experience

A very exciting area of research is the study of time orientation (Zimbardo & Boyd, 1999). Whereas Eastern philosophies readily incorporate "time" as amorphous, non-linear, and malleable (Surya Das, 1997), Western sciences are only beginning to "scratch the surface" of the concept from an applied perspective. To the extent that the psychological orientation of an individual, that is, the *experience* of "a moment in time" (in the linear sense), manifests as "understanding" or *the making of sense* out of experience, time orientation brings practical managerial implications to the planning and execution of a performance review.

One's sense or attention to "time" can influence perception and consequent judgments. The individual's experience at any given moment in time is contingent upon past experiences, present capabilities to understand or impose meaning, and/or the desire or motivation (or predilection) to apply the experience onto future or expected situations. Phenomenology is the study of human understanding or psychology from the perspective of the person experiencing it. All other "sources" of reality are irrelevant or are only as relevant as the individual makes them. Managers must come to know how employees view, interpret, see, and impose meaning on their work experiences. Better tools and tactics can find clever ways to collect information, but inevitably, *what is done* with this information depends on employee phenomenology. Time orientation is more than philosophy. It is practical.

Time perspective unfolds behaviorally in the extent to which individuals calibrate or consider consequences of their behavior. Psychologically, time perspective affects how an individual interprets events or circumstances. For instance, an individual with a history of learning that performance at work is rarely rewarded or measured accurately brings a negative history from which to interpret next week's scheduled performance review. Consequently, the manager faces not only the challenge of delivering the performance appraisal today but harbors all the pain and anxiety of yesterday.

On the other hand, a future-oriented manager is focused on the achievement of future goals and enters the performance conversation seeking opportunities to be conscientious and action-oriented, as that one (small) moment in time is merely something that can be used to affect one's destiny (Zimbardo & Boyd, 1999). Past-oriented, present-oriented, and future-oriented managers all focus, select, and "value" different snapshots of the linear sequence of work behaviors differently. All are right. All are wrong.

Job performance itself is time-sensitive. That is, work behavior is an ongoing event that expresses itself over time. To the extent that a performance review is a "measure" of that behavior (or set of behaviors/competencies), the metric is challenged by the fact that that which is being measured is in constant motion. Hence, measuring "it" at any one single point in time leads to potential inaccuracies. In a sense, performance is a dynamic concept bringing magnitude (strength) and direction (trend).

Performance can vary over time due to a variety of factors. Reb and Cropanzano (2007) reviewed this literature and signaled a call for research and practice to pay more attention to "salient" characteristics. One salient element in the Reb and Cropanzano (2007) study was directional trend over time (relative to constant means). As was expected, positive trend performance metrics led to more positive overall evaluations than negative trend performance metrics, even when mean behavior was held constant (more complex performance expressions were also examined). The researchers offered the burden of the evaluative cognitive task as the mechanism by which a *gestalt* was instituted to ease the burden and bring "coherence" or closure to the performance evaluation picture. That is, supervising managers "simplify" information based on what they "attend to"—clustered dots are quickly connected to view the performance as a "circle."

To the extent that evaluator and employee share "psychological time," judgments/agreements about what is taking place will likely vary, and this has an implication for the planning for negotiation. An employee disposed to a past time orientation where performance in the first quarter was exceptional will likely recall less (or value less) the downward trend during the fourth quarter. The supervising evaluator may be focused on the present, emphasizing the last point on the chart, in this case falling well below the employee's average performance for the entire performance cycle. And so, time introduces a further wrinkle in the performance measurement process that requires attention.

Psychological Well-Being: Internal States Influence Performance

The psychological well-being of the employee moderates responses to performance feedback. The more "robust" the psychological make-up of the individual, the more likely constructive criticism will be beneficial toward growth. Psychological well-being (PWB) is measured and understood in the literature as an affective dimension; it is a construct focused on affective states (Frederickson & Losada, 2005; Wright & Cropanzano, 2004). Affective state of the employee can influence performance (Beal, Weiss, Barros, & MacDermid, 2003) just as changes in skills/knowledge can affect performance (Sturman, 2003).

Problem solving and decision making correlate with PWB (Isen, 2002) and such competencies enhance job performance (Wright & Cropanzano, 2000). Recently, field data from management of a large capital customer services organization identified psychological well-being as a moderator of job satisfaction and job performance (Wright, Cropanzano, & Bonett, 2007).

The inclusion of non-financial components (PWB) to the traditional management (financial) way to enhance "business" was recently put forward as an "organizational wellness" initiative (Diamante, Natale, & London, 2006). These reviewers offered practical scorecards and diagnostic instrumentation to assist with implementation of practices that potentially benefit both people and profit.

In summary, there appear to be organizational components that contribute to overall psychological and behavioral outcomes in the workplace. These outcomes include organizational citizenship behavior, job satisfaction and commitment, and various measures of productivity. The production of positive work outcomes may be moderated by individual characteristics. This review proposed that the goal orientation (GO) of the individual, the level of agreeableness and conscientiousness, the time orientation (TO) of the individual, the valence of evaluative instrumentality, and the overall psychological well-being of the individual all catalyze the breeding of healthy work cultures. The following addresses the implications of these relationships for preparing the individual for a performance negotiation, a process wherein the goal is to optimize outcomes for the manager, the employee, and the organization.

Agreeableness: Seeking Common Ground

To the extent that performance measurement calls for a desire for "agreement," personality characteristics that lend themselves to this dynamic are advantageous. The agreeable personality is such a trait. Agreeable individuals will be more receptive toward, less resistant to—and perhaps more curious about—the observations of the supervising manager. Intuitively, this makes sense, but agreeableness, while beneficial for performance negotiation, has not fared well empirically as a correlate of business outcomes (Hogan, Hogan, & Roberts, 1996; Mount & Barrick, 1995).

It is likely that the reason for this lies in the outcome measures themselves, where agreeableness is not predictive when task performance is not necessarily highly dependent upon being flexible, caring, or tolerant of differences (Mount & Barrick, 1995). Despite the inability to empirically link agreeableness to task performance (Johnson, 2003), as an interpersonal dynamic, agreeable personalities will be more receptive to contrary or divisive information than a disagreeable personality will be (Hogan, Hogan, & Roberts, 1996). Consequently, where the potential for disagreement is reasonably high, interaction with an agreeable personality will most certainly be preferred over interaction with a disagreeable individual. Performance negotiation is such an instance.

Conscientiousness: Diligence and Destiny

Conscientiousness, unlike agreeableness, benefits from empirical backbone when it comes to work outcome predictions. Conscientious individuals are dependable, diligent, and achievement-oriented. Kamdar and Van Dyne (2007) studied the effects of personality and workplace social exchange relationships in the context of the predictive power on task performance and citizenship performance. In their review they remarked that conscientiousness was one of the most significant correlates of job performance. Citing the works of Barrick, Mount, and Judge (2001), Hough, Eaton, Dunnette, Kamp, and McCloy (1996), Hurtz and Donovan (2000), and Salgado (1997), conscientiousness and outcome measures of job performance seem to work hand-in-hand. In addition, conscientious individuals are more altruistic and are more likely to volunteer (OCB) than those low on the conscientiousness dimension (Konovsky & Organ, 1996; Motowidlo & Van Scooter, 1994).

Supervising managers therefore benefit from agreeable, conscientious employees. The benefits are directly realized in terms of work outcomes and, on an emotional level, where difficult conversations lie, it is proposed that employees higher on these characteristics will be more receptive to (or tolerant of) information that runs counter to their viewpoints, understandings, or perceptions than employees who are lower on the dimensions of conscientiousness and agreeableness. As a result, it is advised that supervising managers consider these employee characteristics when planning for performance feedback to optimize the benefits of such a conversation and/or to plan an effective negotiating strategy.

Performance Negotiation: The High Quality Social Exchange

This section provides research-based guidelines for the conduct of and preparation for a performance review. The goal is to deliver a performance review so that the "negotiation" or conversation between giver and receiver of information leads to positive business and individual outcomes.

Performance negotiation requires engagement between supervisor and employee. Genuine engagement requires a "fit" or "congruity" between the supervising manager and the employee or a mechanism to adapt. Where congruity exists, engagement prospers. Where incongruity resides, a "compensatory approach" is advised. This adaptive mechanism will serve to enhance the quality of social exchange between parties. The underlying assumption of this compensatory dialogue is that to enhance LMX is to come closer to "truth"—yielding the valuation of "authentic performance."

High-quality social exchange is enhanced through compensatory dialogue that brings congruity to incongruous interpersonal dynamics. It is recommended that the compensatory dialogue be structured to reduce the risk of a performance negotiation impasse (Frederickson, 2001; Kamdar & Van Dyne, 2007; Takeshi & Heine, 2008).

The compensatory dialogue is best executed in a non-threatening manner with a self-critical focus (Chang, 2008). The mutual sharing of values, styles, and psychological feeling states can make the conversation genuine (Frederickson, 2001; Okun, 2002; Takeshi & Heine, 2008). In addition, there is reason to consider that higher-quality social exchange transforms work motivation toward intrinsic sources and improves self-efficacy (Tsai, Chen, & Liu, 2007). These spontaneous behaviors advance the development of a performance negotiation culture (George & Jones, 1997).

Where agreeableness/conscientiousness is indicated, the manager is advised to enhance LMX through a dialogue that is reciprocity focused. Social exchange addressing reciprocity legitimizes the value, utility, and personal meaningfulness of the performance evaluation process. This legitimization, it is suggested, enhances evaluative instrumentality and compensates for an otherwise disagreeable recipient or incongruous dynamic.

Research suggests that OCB is optimized when there is a perception of fairness and reciprocity in the workplace. Therefore, conversations focused on reciprocity promise to improve LMX even if upon entry to the conversation there is resistance (Kamdar, McAllister, & Turban, 2006). Where GO is misaligned due to a focus on "performance" rather than "learning," for instance, this compensatory model advises social exchange on the issue of the need for achievement (n/ach) to reorient the recipient.

Where TO appears asynchronous, managerial exchanges with the supervised employee(s) can benefit from a focus on what matters, when, and how best to measure it. Sharing differences on time dimensions will enhance an understanding of each other's values. Finally, where PWB appears challenging, it is advised that the manager support or encourage the employee to improve on specific tasks or challenges that bring the advantage of enhanced self-efficacy, this construct being a powerful dynamic linked to business performance (Bandura, 2007; De Rue & Morgeson, 2007; Tsai, Chen, & Liu, 2007).

These suggested social exchanges exemplify a work environment that is fair and equitable, provides a sense of role discretion (autonomy/personal control), and frames performance so that business needs and interpersonal dynamics are factored into the structuring of a compensatory dialogue. In addition, such exchanges enhance person-role fit, a dynamic construct that appears malleable and useful in the retention and development of human capital (DeRue & Morgeson, 2007). High-quality social exchange indicates a culture that supports performance negotiation practices.

Authentic Performance: A Step-Wise Approach to Valuation

Phase I: Business Situation Analysis

Management and employee meetings are conducted to review business results and discuss a competitive analysis of the situation. Emphasis is placed on the strengths, weaknesses, opportunities, and threats facing the enterprise. On a business unit level, supervising managers apply this analysis to work teams and individual role responsibilities. The latter communications can be done on a group basis or strategically. Where "mediating factors" threaten or bring friction to the performance management process, one-on-one discussions are advised.

Phase II: Differences Dialogue

Senior management assumes responsibility for developing leadership competencies. These competencies are addressed and enhanced through professionally sound assessments and suitable feedback channels (Diamante & Primavera, 2004). Leadership development is optimized for business execution and incorporates targeted mediating factors to accelerate growth of a performance culture. This requires attention to TO, GO, PWB, and the personality characteristics of agreeableness/conscientiousness. These variables should be discussed to not only increase self-awareness (of leadership), but also to view their implications vis-à-vis the workforce and immediate direct reports. Where feasible, assessments can be incorporated to enable sharing of such information with direct reports to optimize the potential for engaging in a "differences dialogue." This dialogue is to be performance-focused, where differences receive attention relative to performance management/measurement in the context of sustaining a competitive business advantage.

Phase III: Calibration

The calibration of performance measurement is to be led by senior management, but buy-in from those affected should be gained. Focused on advancing competitive stance, the performance metrics should incorporate hard, business outcomes (direct contributions), soft business outcomes (indirect contributions), and contextual manifestations (that is, competencies providing guidelines for behavior in the business situation).

Phase IV: Value Discussion

All relevant parties to performance management engage in a value discussion. This discussion can alter calibration and/or serve to solidify understanding. The key to an effective value-based metric conversation is agreement about the definition of the business problem(s) being faced and/or overall competitive situation. Performance is only "discussable" in the context of a larger "performance framing" so that everyone can understand the instrumentality of its measurement, personally, financially, and organizationally.

Phase V: Future Valuation: Immediate Next Steps

Clarity is the goal as the organization understands what is at stake, how it can achieve specified business goals, and what this means for everyone in the organization (performance). The performance metrics are shared, applied regularly (monthly, quarterly), and discussed often. Everyone should be aware of the "score" at the business level (are we beating our competitors, making progress against them) and everyone should be aware of their individual business contributions toward that end.

Performance Negotiation Applied: A Venture Capital Case Study

A targeted investment is not realizing the level of growth expected. Private investors aren't sitting still. After several attempts at "motivating" the CEO, no progress is realized. In this case, progress is being measured by various measures of preparedness for product commercialization. The firm is a technology-based venture that customizes educational programs for a specialized industry in which regulatory compliance makes such programs mandatory. Competition that is equally technically savvy (in terms of design and delivery) is slight. Investors bring strong connections to that industry, but they know that this venture is not the only show in town. Timing into the market is key, but quality and building a culture that can sustain product development and delivery can't be overlooked. It is concluded that business execution is too slow. Impatience grows. The consultant is called in.

A twenty-member start-up, the venture is now three years old. The consultant interviews the CEO and senior managers, and eventually focus groups are run as well to include everyone. These assessments are focused on simple questions: (1) Are you managed well? (2) Are you happy with your pace of project acceleration? and (3) What do you need more of/less of in order for you to be more effective in your role? Deliberately "open" in nature, these questions bring overlapping content and direction to the consultant from various organizational levels. The employees feel un-managed, there is no sense of timing below the CEO level (product commercialization) and, for the most part, "managers" are really just highly paid programmers—"most of them avoid interacting with people."

"Performance, in this context, is ephemeral. Standards being neither known or shared and interpersonal relations being centered on daily programming needs, this is start-up acting like it wants to be a start-down," the consultant informs the venture capitalist (VC).

"I suppose we are all focused on the technology, it is truly differentiating and promises to eventually be disruptive," explains the VC. "As we grew, we left it up to our CEO to manage the place, but he's a Ph.D. physicist, out of another technology firm—I didn't think he could build a company, but he can build product." The VC is direct: "How do we get everybody focused and project-driven? How do we get performance synchronized in there?"

"For starters, we need to establish policy and procedures that secure a sense of due process and fairness. We need someone accountable for that too. Right now, everyone thinks it's the Wild West—you get what you can and hope that nothing sneaks up on you." "That's not good if you want them to feel like they can have genuine conversations," adds the consultant. "Instead, they take justice into their own hands."

"In addition, there seems to be a disagreeable nature to many of the programmers and perhaps even among your senior people. Your technical staff is constantly combative, argumentative, and perhaps even intentionally disagreeing just to see what happens—to shake up senior management," observed the consultant. "How do I fix that?" asked the VC.

"Problem is that senior management really does not have the right to engage these folks on important issues requiring dialogue. Plus, they aren't all that concerned about their interpersonal styles and their effect on those around them. Senior managers have been too aloof, distant, and many times even cold or dismissive of the employees. This appears true for many, but especially it seems to be a problem where cultures collide. For instance, a programmer informed me that he is always three jumps ahead of his management team—that he sees problems for the future of the business but he gets pushed to only fix for today. 'Worry about tomorrow, tomorrow,'" his project

(Continued)

manager says to him, in a condescending tone. "This leads to unhealthy strain, a lack of collaborative problem solving, and a waste of talent," advises the consultant.

This scenario likely resonates with human capital professionals. The fix in this case requires a combination of interventions to address antecedents that are lacking in the culture (that is, procedural justice, operating objectives, competency models, performance framing). In addition, group and individual obstacles exist. Time orientations are implicated, as are other personal characteristics. Systemically, there is a need to address all of this and, until this is done, progress toward a performance-based culture will not occur. All stakeholders are not on the same page. Investors view the business situation as threatening and hold the perspective that this investment is performing too slowly. Project managers view the situation as a technical challenge that requires more focused attention and information from emerging technologies that are not yet available. Leadership is busy calculating profitability forecasts based on numerous assumptions shared with no one. Here are some suggestions we made, based on our Systemic Model for Performance Negotiation.

PHASE I: BUSINESS SITUATION REVIEW

- Consultant facilitates meeting between VC team, CEO, and senior management.
- Senior manager "waterfalls" this review into the organization.
- Parallel financial interests are clarified for all "giving" their professional collateral (and capabilities) to this growth proposition (value is market-driven, alignment means everyone generates wealth or benefits from a wealth-generation vehicle/stock options).
- Performance management is identified as the lever for growth.

PHASE II: DIFFERENCES DIALOGUE

- Leadership (CEO, senior management) assessed by team of industrial psychologists.
- Feedback on leadership team offered to VC equity partners.

- Equity breakdown scenarios are discussed and shared organization-wide.
- Project managers are assessed using independent consultants, standardized personality instruments, and a qualitative 360 process.
- Multi-source feedback implemented for leadership.
- Coaching provided for CEO and senior management team.

PHASE III: CALIBRATION

- VC equity partners review progress of coaching/assessments.
- Consultants map key differences/interpersonal challenges.
- CEO, senior managers articulate business outcomes (direct/ indirect contributions) and a competency model is constructed (leadership, project manager, and technical staff).
- Time, trends, and mean performance are openly discussed and incorporated into the process of negotiating reviews.
- Performance is a dual process; built however, on a properly framed, mutually advantageous playing field.

PHASE IV: VALUE DISCUSSION

- VC equity partners and senior management review performance metrics vis-à-vis competitive activity and market alignment.
- Adjustments are made in focus/shared throughout the organization (including the rationale).
- The need to make key contributors to business value (intellectual capital) "true partners" is realized; all employees eventually receive a level of ownership.

PHASE V: IMMEDIATE NEXT STEPS

- Performance is measured regularly (some do it monthly, others quarterly).
- Supervising managers held accountable for the review being a dialogue.
- Performance dialogues lead (unexpectedly) to business unit meetings capitalizing on the identification of shared business obstacles/individual development needs.

(Continued)

- Project rotational/matrix management opportunities are implemented.
- CEO focuses on project management monitoring, shifting orientation to a present "stance."
- VC equity partners meet with CEO to align CEO focus with investor plan to "flip" the venture in the next three years, circumstances allowing.

In time, the consultants are "weaned" and it is noted that communications are easier, more frequent, and genuine. Attention to the five phases of the negotiation process is enabling authentic conversations among diverse stakeholders.

Finally, where resistance remains, managers are coached to improve LMX via the appropriate tactic. For instance, agreeableness (or lack thereof) is identified and the manager is informed/given the skills to engage in dialogues with the employee that center on reciprocity. As the "antidote" for being disagreeable, the manager is now focused on discussing any point of conflict with a conversation about what the employee wants/needs relative to what the business wants/needs. The goal is to find "reciprocity"—a place in which there is little or no room for disagreement. Such exchanges require a level of frequency commensurate with the level of disagreeableness faced.

Multiple stakeholders understand that there are multiple perspectives. Value is ultimately measured by the profits everyone shares when the venture goes public or is sold. Interpersonal friction stemming from individual performance measurement is mitigated as parallel financial interests bond organizational members. Everyone stands to win (or lose) together so getting the means to the end right becomes the principal driving force behind performance negotiation.

It became mandatory that each manager break down performance into trends, some sense of variance, and an overall average. This leads to added focus on the valuation process itself, to interesting conversations among managers, and unexpectedly revealed operational problems when senior managers noticed similar trends among employees. This operational side-effect was soon to become one of the critical advantages for imposing the dual trend dialogue performance negotiation process. Three years subsequent to the implementation of a systemic approach to performance negotiation, the venture was sold. Investors realized a 17x multiple, and employees chose to either exercise their stock options or become shareholders in another promising venture.

References

Bandura, A. (2007). Much ado over a faulty conception of perceived self-efficacy. *Journal of Social and Clinical Psychology, 26,* 641–658.

Barrick, M. R., Mount, M. K., & Judge, T. A. (2001). Personality and job performance at the beginning of the new millennium: What do we know and where do we go next? *International Journal of Assessment & Selection, 9,* 9–30.

Beal, D. J., Weiss, H. M., Barros, E., & MacDermid, S. M. (2005). An episodic process model of affective influences on performance. *Journal of Applied Psychology, 90,* 1054–1068.

Beer, M., & Walton, E. (1990). Developing the competitive organization: Intervention and strategies. *American Psychologist, 45,* 154–161.

Bell, B. S., & Kozlowski, S. W. (2002). Goal orientation and ability: Interactive effects on self-efficacy, performance and knowledge. *Journal of Applied Psychology, 87,* 497–505.

Berman, R. (1969). Dimensions of interpersonal facilitation in psychotherapy and child development. *Psychological Bulletin, 72,* 338–352.

Brislin, R. W., & Kim, E. S. (2003). Cultural diversity in people's understanding and uses of time. *Applied Psychology: An International Review, 52,* 363–382.

Burkard, A. W., Johnson, A. J., Madson, M. B., Pruitt, N. T., Contreras-Tadych, D. A., & Kozlowski, J. M. (2006). Supervisor cultural responsiveness and unresponsiveness in cross-cultural supervision. *Journal of Counseling Psychology, 53,* 288–301.

Campbell, J. D., Faley, P. J., & Fehr, B. (1986). Better than me or better than thee? Reactions to interpersonal and intrapersonal performance feedback. *Journal of Personality, 54,* 479–493.

Chang, E. C. (2008). *Self-criticism and self-enhancement.* Washington, DC: APA.

Dalton, M. (1996). Multi-rater feedback and conditions for change. *Consulting Psychology Journal, 48,* 12–16.

De Rue, D. S., & Morgeson, F. P. (2007). Stability and change in person-team and person-role fit over time: The effects of growth satisfaction, performance and general self-efficacy. *Journal of Applied Psychology, 92,* 1242–1253.

Diamante, T. (1993). Unitarian validation of a mathematical problem solving exercise. *Journal of Business and Psychology: Special Issues— The Test Validity Yearbook, 7,* 383–401.

Diamante, T., & London, M. (2002). Leadership in the age of digital technology. *Journal of Management Development, 21,* 404–416.

Diamante, T., Natale, S., & London, M. (2006). Organizational wellness. In S. Sheinfeld-Gorin & J. Arnold (Eds.), *Health promotion in practice.* San Francisco: Jossey-Bass.

Diamante, T., & Primavera, L. (2004). The professional practice of executive coaching: Principles, practices and decisions. *International Journal of Decision Ethics, 1,* 148–178.

Farr, J. L., Hofmann, D. A., & Rigenbach, K. L. (1993). Goal orientation and action control theory: Implications for industrial and organizational psychology. In C. L. Cooper & I. T. Robertson (Eds.), *International review of industrial & organizational psychology* (pp. 193–232). Hoboken, NJ: John Wiley & Sons.

Frederickson, B. L. (2001). The role of positive emotions in positive psychology: The broaden-and-build theory of positive emotions. *American Psychologist, 56,* 218–226.

Frederickson, B. L., & Joiner, T. (2002). Positive emotions trigger upward spirals toward emotional well-being. *Psychological Science, 13,* 172–175.

Frederickson, B. L., & Losada, M. F. (2005). Positive affect and the complex dynamics of human flourishing. *American Psychologist, 60,* 678–686.

Friedman, T. L. (2006). *The world is flat: Updated and expanded.* New York: Farrar, Straus and Giroux.

George, J. M., & Brief, A. P. (1996). Motivational agendas in the workplace: The effects of feelings on focus of attention and work motivation. *Research in Organizational Behavior, 18,* 75–109.

George, J. M., & Jones, G. R. (1997). Organizational spontaneity in context. *Human Performance, 10,* 153–170.

Goodstone, M., & Diamante, T. (1998). Organizational use of therapeutic change: Strengthening multi-source feedback systems through interdisciplinary coaching. *Consulting Psychology Journal, 50,* 152–163.

Heslin, P. A., Latham, G. P., & VandeWalle, D. (2005). The effects of implicit person theory on performance appraisal. *Journal of Applied Psychology, 90,* 842–856.

Hogan, R., Hogan, J., & Roberts, B. W. (1996). Personality measurement and employment decisions. *American Psychologist, 51,* 469–477.

Hough, L. M., Eaton, N. K., Dunnette, M. D., Kamp, J. D., & McCloy, R. A. (1996). Criterion related validities of personality constructs and the effects of response distortion on those validities. *Journal of Applied Psychology, 75,* 581–595.

Hulin, C. L., Henry, R., & Noon, S. (1990). Adding a dimension: Time as a factor in the generalizability of predictive relations. *Psychological Bulletin, 107,* 328–340.

Hurtz, G. M., & Donovan, J. J. (2000). Personality and job performance: The big five revisited. *Journal of Applied Psychology, 85,* 869–879.

Isen, A. M. (2002). A role for neuropsychology in understanding the facilitating influence of positive affect on social behavior and cognitive processes. In C. R. Snyder & S. J. Lopez (Eds.), *Handbook of positive psychology.* New York: Oxford University Press.

Johnson, J. W. (2003). Toward a better understanding of the relationship between personality and individual job performance. In M. R. Barrick & A. M. Ryan (Eds.), *Personality at work: Reconsidering the role of personality in organizations* (pp. 60–82). San Francisco: Jossey-Bass.

Judge, T. A., & Ilies, R. (2002). Relationships of personality to performance motivation: A meta-analytic review. *Journal of Applied Psychology, 87,* 797–807.

Kamdar, D., McAllister, D. J., & Turban, D. B. (2006). All in a day's work: How follower individual differences and justice perceptions predict organizational citizenship behavior, role perceptions and behavior. *Journal of Applied Psychology, 91,* 841–855.

Kamdar, D., & Van Dyne, L. (2007). The joint effects of personality and workplace social exchange relationships in predicting task performance and citizenship behavior. *Journal of Applied Psychology, 92,* 1286–1298.

Katz, D., & Kahn, R. L. (1966). *The social psychology of organizations.* Hoboken, NJ: John Wiley & Sons.

Konovsky, M. A., & Organ, D. W. (1996). Dispositional and contextual determinants of organizational citizenship behavior. *Journal of Organizational Behavior, 17,* 253–266.

Konovsky, M. A., & Pugh, S. D. (1994). Citizenship behavior and social exchange. *Academy of Management Journal, 37,* 656–669.

Kozlowski, S. W. J., Gully, S. M., Brown, K. G., Salas, E., Smith, E. A., & Nason, E. R. (2001). Effects of training goals and goal orientation traits on multi-dimensional training outcomes and performance adaptability. *Organizational Behavior & Human Decision Processes, 85,* 1–31.

Landy, F. J., & Farr, J. L. (1980). Performance ratings. *Psychological Bulletin, 87,* 72–107.

Latham, G. P., & Latham, S. D. (2000). Overlooking theory and research in performance appraisal at one's peril: Much done, more to do. In C. L. Cooper & E. A. Locke (Eds.), *Industrial and organizational psychology: Linking theory with practice.* Oxford: Blackwell.

Latham, G. P., & Wexley, K. (1981). *Increasing productivity through performance appraisal.* Boston: Addison Wesley.

Lax, D. A., & Sebenius, J. K. (1986). *The manager as negotiator.* New York: Free Press.

Levy, P. E., & Williams, J. R. (2004). The social context of performance appraisals: A review and framework for the future. *Journal of Management, 30,* 881–905.

London, M. (1995). *Self and interpersonal insight.* Oxford: Oxford University Press.

London, M. (2001). *How people evaluate others in organizations.* Mahwah, NJ: Lawrence Erlbaum Associates.

Longenecker, C. O., Gioia, D. A., & Sims, H. P. (1987). Behind the mask: The politics of employee appraisal. *Academy of Management Executive, 1,* 183–193.

Matarazzo, J. D. (1965). Psychotherapeutic processes. *Annual Review of Psychology, 16,* 181–224.

McAllister, D. J., Wolfe Morrison, E., Kamdar, D., & Turban, D. (2007). Disentangling role perceptions: How perceived role breadth, discretion, instrumentality and efficacy relate to helping and taking charge. *Journal of Applied Psychology, 92,* 1200–1211.

Motowidlo, S. J., & Van Scotter, J. R. (1994). Evidence that task performance should be distinguished from contextual performance. *Journal of Applied Psychology, 79,* 475–480.

Mount, M. K., & Barrick, M. R. (1995). The big five personality dimensions: Implications for research and practice in human resources management. In G. R. Ferris (Ed.), *Research in personnel and human resources management* (Vol. 13, pp. 153–200). Greenwich, CT: JAI Press.

Oldham, G., & Hackman, J. R. (1980). *Work redesign.* Boston: Addison-Wesley.

Okun, B. F. (2002). *Effective helping: Interviewing and counseling techniques* (6th ed.). Pacific Grove, CA: Brooks Cole.

Organ, D. W. (1990). The motivational basis of organizational citizenship behavior. In B. M. Staw & L. L. Cummings (Eds.), *Research in organizational behavior* (pp. 43–47). Greenwich, CT: JAI Pres.

Organ, D. W., & Moorman, R. H. (1993). Fairness and organizational citizenship behavior: What are the connections? *Social Justice Research, 6*, 5–18.

Parker, S. K., Wall, T. D., & Jackson, P. R. (1997). "That's not my job": Developing flexible employee work orientations. *Academy of Management Journal, 40*, 899–929.

Parker, S. K., Williams, H. M., & Turnover, N. (2006). Modeling the antecedents of proactive behavior at work. *Journal of Applied Psychology, 91*, 636–652.

Penner, L. A. (2002). Dispositional and organizational influences on sustained volunteerism: An interactionist perspective. *Journal of Social Issues, 58*, 447–467.

Prien, H. (1987). Strategies for third-party intervention. *Human Relations, 40*, 699–720.

Quinones, M. A., Ford, J. K., & Teachout, M. S. (1995). The relationship between experience and job performance: A conceptual and meta-analytic review. *Personnel Psychology, 48*, 887–910.

Reb, J., & Cropanzano, R. (2007). Evaluating dynamic performance: The influence of salient gestalt characteristics on performance ratings. *Journal of Applied Psychology, 92*, 490–492.

Salgado, J. F. (1997). The five factor model of personality and job performance in the European community. *Journal of Applied Psychology, 82*, 30–43.

Schein, E. H. (1969). *Process consultation.* Boston: Addison-Wesley.

Seligman, M. E. P. (1986). Explanatory style as a predictor of productivity and quitting among life insurance sales agents. *Journal of Personality and Social Psychology, 50*, 832–838.

Seligman, M. E. P., Rashid, T., & Parks, A. C. (2006). Positive psychotherapy. *American Psychologist, 61*, 774–788.

Seligman, M. E. P. (2007). Coaching and positive psychology. *Australian Psychologist, 42*, 266–267.

Silberstang, J., & Diamante, T. (2008). Phased and targeted work group learning interventions. In V. Sessa & M. London (Eds.), *Work group learning.* Mahwah, NJ: Lawrence Erlbaum Associates.

Smith, M. L., & Glass, G. V. (1977). Meta-analysis of psychotherapeutic outcome studies. *American Psychologist, 32*, 752–760.

Sturman, M. C. (2003). Searching for the inverted U-shaped relationship between time and performance: Meta-analyses of the experience/performance relationship. *Journal of Management, 29*, 609–640.

Sturman, M. C., & Trevor, C. O. (2001). The implications of linking the dynamic performance and turnover literatures. *Journal of Applied Psychology, 86,* 684–696.

Surya Das, L. (1997). *Awakening the Buddha within.* New York: Bantam Doubleday.

Takeshi, H., & Heine, S. J. (2008). The role of self-criticism in self-improvement and face maintenance among Japanese. In E. C. Chang (Ed.), *Self-criticism and self-enhancement: Theory, research and clinical implications* (pp. 105–122). Washington, DC: APA.

Tepper, B. J., Lockhart, D., & Hoobler, J. (2001). Justice citizenship and role definitions. *Journal of Applied Psychology, 86,* 789–796.

Tepper, B. J., & Taylor, E. C. (2003). Relationships among supervisors and subordinates' justice perceptions and organizational citizenship behavior. *Academy of Management Journal, 46,* 97–105.

Tepper, B. J., Uhl-Bien, M., Kohut, G. F., Rogelberg, S. G., Lockhart, D. E., & Ensley, M. D. (2006). Subordinates' resistance and managers' evaluations of subordinates' performance. *Journal of Management, 32,* 185–209.

Tsai, W. C., Chen, C. C., & Liu, H. L. (2007). Test of a model linking employee positive moods and task performance. *Journal of Applied Psychology, 92,* 1570–1583.

VandeWalle, D. (1997). Development and validation of a work domain goal orientation instrument. *Educational and Psychological Measurement, 57,* 995–10105.

Van Scotter, J. R., & Motowidlo, S. J. (1996). Interpersonal facilitation and job dedication as separate facets of contextual performance. *Journal of Applied Psychology, 81,* 525–531.

Whiting, S. W., Podsakoff, P. M., & Pierce, J. R. (2008). Effects of task performance, helping, voice, and organizational loyalty on performance appraisal ratings. *Journal of Applied Psychology, 93,* 125–131.

Wright, T. A., & Cropanzano, R. (2000). Psychological well-being and job satisfaction as predictors of job performance. *Journal of Occupational Health Psychology, 5,* 84–94.

Wright, T. A., & Cropanzano, R. (2004). The role of psychological well-being in job performance: A fresh look at an age-old quest. *Organizational Dynamics, 33,* 338–331.

Wright, T. A., Cropanzano, R., & Bonett, D. G. (2007). The moderating role of employee positive well-being on the relation between job satisfaction and job performance. *Journal of Occupational Health Psychology, 12,* 93–104.

Zellars, K. L., Tepper, B. J., & Duffy, M. K. (2002). Abusive supervision and superordinates' organizational citizenship behavior. *Journal of Applied Psychology, 87*, 1068–1076.

Zimbardo, P. G., & Boyd, J. W. (1999). Putting time in perspective: A valid, reliable individual difference metric. *Journal of Personality and Social Psychology, 77*, 127–128.

CHAPTER 15

ASSESSING PERFORMANCE MANAGEMENT PROGRAMS AND POLICIES

Stanley B. Silverman and
Wendy M. Muller

Assessing Performance Management Programs and Policies

A recent study reports that only 45 percent of HR professionals think that their performance management system currently in use is valuable to the organization (OnPoint Consulting, 2007). Why is this so? The problem likely lies in the bare-bones approach to performance management that many organizations utilize. Often, the performance management system consists of only an annual performance evaluation that is used for administrative purposes. In addition, while these evaluations may be useful, researchers and practitioners alike have observed a phenomenon referred to as the "vanishing performance appraisal" (Cropanzano, Bowen, & Gilliland, 2007). Organizations report that performance reviews are required and managers often report that they conducted them, yet many employees in these same organizations report that they never received a review. *What if we took assessment seriously?* This chapter will go beyond the customary annual performance evaluation by using six assessment points that are embedded in a comprehensive model of performance management.

Model Overview

In order to clearly illustrate the performance management system we propose, Figure 15.1 depicts our performance management model. In addition, to help clarify the model and the six assessment points, we will use a hypothetical manufacturing company, Palisades Inc., which employs one thousand salaried employees. The average span of control for each manager is approximately eight subordinates. Figure 15.2 is the timeline for Palisades Inc.'s performance management process, along with each assessment point. For the sake of clarity, the 2010 calendar year will serve as the cycle for implementation of the performance management process. Exhibit 15.1 is a glossary of the assessment points of the performance management system. Figure 15.3 shows the sequence of the six assessment points. Tables 15.1 & 15.2 display the organizational and individual precursors, respectively. In addition, we will follow two Palisades employees, Michael and Anna, at various points throughout the process. While we are using 2010 as the implementation year, in order to clarify the six assessment points, whenever we use examples of Palisades or its employees, it will be as though the assessment data has already been collected.

Assessment Point 1: Organizational Precursors

The purpose of evaluating organizational precursors and administering the organizational precursor scale (OPS) is to first gather a baseline measure of current performance management behaviors and, second, to determine what should be emphasized during the training phase of the performance management system (Silverman, Pogson, & Cober, 2005). Organizations that support individual change will be better able to facilitate change in the organization (Mauer, Mitchell, & Barbeite, 2002). The OPS (Silverman, Pogson, & Cober, 2005) will measure the extent to which effective performance management behaviors are currently being exhibited (see Table 15.1). The OPS assessment takes place twice during the performance management cycle. Assessment Point 1 will take place in June 2009 and Assessment Point 5 will take place in January 2011. Ideally, data will be

Figure 15.1 Performance Management Model.

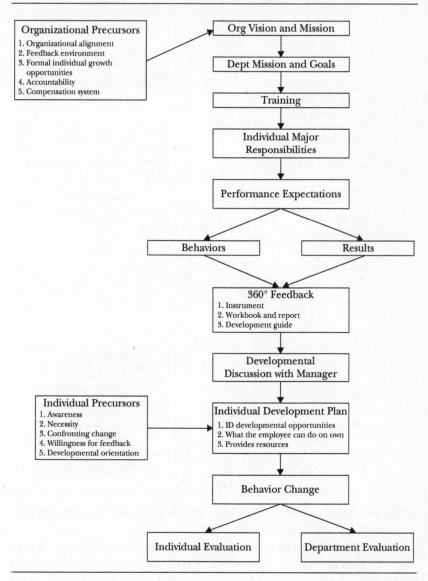

Figure 15.2 Timeline for Palisades Inc.

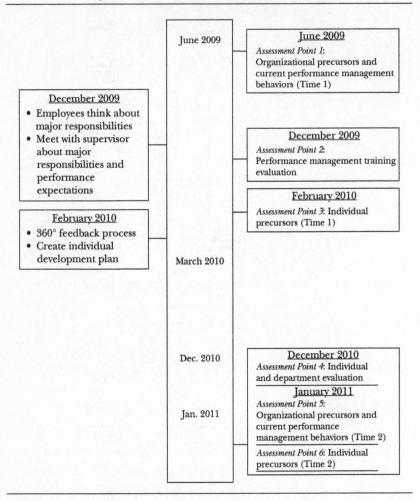

collected from all managers and employees affected by the performance management system.

The OPS will derive a 1 to 5 score on each organizational precursor. Managers and subordinates will rate each organizational precursor. Precursors will be assessed by both managers and employees, and data from this questionnaire will not only help determine what training needs to be done, but scores on the organizational precursors will also show how ready and supportive an organization is for change.

Exhibit 15.1 Glossary of the Assessment Points.

Assessment Point 1: Organizational precursors and current performance management behaviors measured by the Organizational Precursor Scale (OPS) (Time 1)	The OPS will assess how much support organizations give to individual change and development and the extent to which current effective performance management behaviors are present. The data will determine training emphasis.
Assessment Point 2: Performance management training evaluation	Following the performance management training, training evaluation will take place at the reaction and learning level.
Assessment Point 3: Individual precursors (Time 1)	The individual precursors assess how ready employees are to grow and develop. Based on scores on these precursors, it will be determined how much individual guidance is needed during development.
Assessment Point 4: Individual and department evaluation	These evaluations take place at the end of the year and serve as a formal performance appraisal to make administrative decisions. Both the individual and department will be assessed to see whether major goals and responsibilities have been met for the year.
Assessment Point 5: Organizational precursors and current performance management behaviors measured by the Organizational Precursor Scale (OPS) (Time 2)	This assessment of organizational precursors and performance management behaviors will be compared to *Assessment Point 1*. The goal is to have increases on the organizational precursors and performance management behaviors after implementation of the performance management system.
Assessment Point 6: Individual precursors (Time 2)	This assessment of individual precursors will be compared to *Assessment Point 3*. The goal is for employees to have higher scores on individual precursors after implementation of the performance management system.

Figure 15.3 Sequence of Assessment Points.

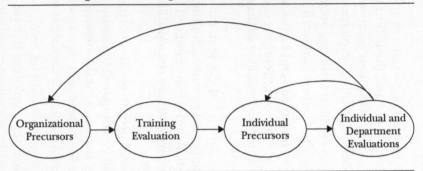

Organizational Alignment

The first organizational precursor, organizational alignment, describes how well the organization's vision, mission, and values are aligned throughout the departments and employees in the organization.

A rating of "1" indicates that there is little to no integration of organizational and individual expectations. This can be problematic because individuals in organizations that have low organizational alignment may not identify with the direction of the organization. This may lead to problems down the line, such as turnover. A rating of "3" on the precursor of organizational alignment signals that the organization has a clearly defined vision, mission, and values and has some connections to the individual level, but needs to enhance these connections. Finally, a rating of "5" on the organizational precursor of organizational alignment indicates that the organization has a clearly defined mission, vision, and values, and that these are completely connected with the individuals in the organization. This is the ideal rating for organizational alignment. An effective performance management system will be the driver that connects the organizational vision, mission, and values to the individual level.

Feedback Environment

The second organizational precursor is the organizational feedback environment. This describes how strongly feedback is

Table 15.1 Organizational Precursors Items.

	1	2	3	4	5
Organizational Alignment	[Little integration of organizational and individual expectations]	—	[Clear vision, mission, and values and some connection to individual level]	—	[Well-defined organizational vision, mission, and values that are aligned down through the individual level]
Organizational Feedback Environment	[Inconsistent performance related practices throughout the organization]	—	[Job-related systems that reinforce valued behaviors and results in parts of the organization]	—	[Clear job-related systems that reinforce valued behaviors and results throughout the entire organization]
Formal Development and Learning Opportunities	[Provides few development and learning opportunities for employees]	—	[Provides adequate development and learning opportunities for employees]	—	[Organizational priority is one of creating a culture of continual development and learning opportunities]
Accountability	[Organization has little accountability for organizationally valued changes]	—	[Organization has inconsistent accountability for organizationally valued changes, that is, depends on the manager]	—	[Organization has clear accountability for organizationally valued changes]
Compensation System	[A lack of variable pay systems]	—	[Moderate pay for performance systems where pay is associated with organizational change]	—	[Clear pay for performance systems where pay is a positive force for organizational change]

From Silverman, Pogson, and Cober, 2005

Table 15.2 Individual Precursors.

	1	2	3	4	5
Awareness	[Little awareness of areas that may need to be changed]	—	[Moderate awareness of areas that may need to be changed]	—	[Highly aware of areas that may need to be changed]
Sense of Necessity	[Shows a little desire to change]	—	[Shows a moderate desire to change]	—	[Shows a strong desire to change and understands the importance of change]
Confronting Change	[Low understanding of the steps needed for change]	—	[Moderate understanding of the steps needed for change]	—	[Strong understanding of the steps needed for change]
Willingness for Feedback	[Little openness and emotional readiness for feedback from others]	—	[Moderate openness and emotional readiness for feedback from others]	—	[Strong desire and emotional readiness for feedback and open to candid opinions from others]
Development Orientation	[Seldom seeks out opportunities for growth and development]	—	[Occasionally seeks out opportunities for growth and development]	—	[Continually seeks out opportunities for growth and development]

From Silverman, Pogson, and Cober, 2005

engendered into the organization's culture. This includes informal as well as formal feedback. Furthermore, feedback systems should be in place that provide for specific feedback directed at the task level (Kluger & DeNisi, 1996). Vague feedback about overall performance is clearly not as helpful to employees as a comment about the specific task being performed. Tying the feedback into the daily operation of the organization also shows the employee that they make an impact on the organization and what they do is important to the functioning of the organization.

Like the precursor described previously, a score on the organizational feedback environment is on a 1 to 5 scale. A "1" on the precursor of organizational feedback environment indicates that the organization does not have a consistent feedback process in place. Feedback may or may not be given informally or even in a formal setting besides the annual performance review. Some managers may give feedback while others do not. Clearly there are not systems in place that provide for adequate and necessary feedback.

A rating of a "3" on organizational feedback environment indicates that some type of system for delivering feedback does exist, but it may not be consistent throughout the organization. The feedback given is job-related and centers on the behavior and results valued by the organization. This feedback most likely is given in formal settings, such as with a meeting with a supervisor. However, these practices may not be consistent across the organization; they may differ between departments or even managers.

A rating of a "5" on organizational feedback environment indicates that the organization has a defined feedback system that is implemented across the entire organization. This system includes both a developmental component and an evaluation component. High scores on this organizational precursor are especially important because organizational feedback environment is critical to the success of a performance management system.

Formal Individual Growth Opportunities

The third organizational precursor is formal individual growth opportunities. Ratings on this organizational precursor indicate how focused an organization is on providing learning and developmental opportunities for their employees. These opportunities should also be clearly communicated to the employees. Employees should know that these opportunities exist for all, not just a select few.

A rating of a "1" on the precursor of formal individual growth opportunities indicates that employee perceptions are that there are few or no opportunities for individual growth in terms of development and learning that the organization offers. Employees generally do not get the sense that the organization supports learning and growth. A rating of a "3" on formal individual growth opportunities indicates that there are some opportunities that are available to employees. These programs are generally considered adequate by the employees, but the connection between these opportunities and the culture of the organization is unclear. Last, a rating of a "5" on the organizational precursor of formal individual growth opportunities signifies that not only are there formal programs for individual development and growth, but these opportunities are highly encouraged and considered part of the culture of the organization. The performance management system should require that an individual development plan be created for each employee as a formal part of the process.

Accountability

The fourth organizational precursor is accountability. Accountability reflects whether the appropriate managers and employees are held responsible for the consequences of not making needed change. This includes both changes in behaviors and results that will improve the organization and those that will be a detriment to the organization.

A rating of a "1" on the organizational precursor of accountability indicates that there is little accountability across the organization for the necessary individual change needed for the organizational alignment discussed earlier. Without accountability, there is a lot of blaming of others, and it is likely that no or minimal change will occur, and these changes may not be valued highly by the organization. A senior-level executive commented to one of the authors recently, "I have been immensely successful throughout my career. Why would I change the set of behaviors we are discussing?" If there are no consequences and no accountability for the needed change, why would the individual change? A rating of a "3" on the precursor indicates that there is some accountability for change, but it is inconsistent. A rating of a "5" on accountability indicates that those who create organizationally valued changes are appreciated, and those in the organization who do not make necessary change are consistently held accountable. This can be reinforced by the performance management system through the individual major responsibilities and corresponding performance expectations and by holding individuals accountable for the change inherent in the individual performance plans.

Compensation System

The fifth organizational precursor is the compensation system. If behaviors that lead to effective results for the organization are rewarded, employees should be more likely to continue to strive for these achievements. Moreover, the compensation system is a way to link the behaviors of the individual to the values and success of the organization. By doing this, the organization demonstrates to the employees how important their behaviors are to the success of the organization.

A rating of a "1" on the organizational precursor of compensation system indicates that there is no or little connection from individual behaviors and results to the pay of employees. This means that employees do not see a connection from their behaviors and achievements to the values of the organization. This may give employees little reason to behave in ways that benefit the organization, as they see no direct reward for doing so. It is our experience that, when asked, most human resource professionals believe they have a pay-for-performance system in place. Yet managers and employees alike do not see that same connection. A rating of a "3" on the precursor of the compensation system indicates that there is some pay-for-performance going on, but that it may not be well defined by the organization. A rating of a "5" on the organizational precursor of the compensation system indicates that there are clear guidelines imposed and communicated to employees on when and how achievements and individual change are rewarded by pay. This connection should be created and/or strengthened through the performance management system.

Example of Assessment Point 1 at Palisades Inc.

Palisades Inc. has just completed the OPS. Because they are planning to implement a new performance management process, they chose to administer the OPS online to all managers and employees who would use the new process. In addition, two open-ended questions were used that asked about the strengths of the current performance management process and the areas that required improvement. Scores on each individual precursor varied from a score of "2" to a score of "4." Therefore, some areas require more training and change than others. Hence, each organizational precursor will be briefly discussed below.

Palisades Inc. had an overall organizational alignment score of "3." Upon reviewing the individual items, the organizational vision and mission are clearly well defined, but there are not good connections with the individual level in most areas. It is clear that some work needs to be done to align the organizational mission and vision with individual expectations. The importance of role clarity, along with the clarifying of major responsibilities and corresponding performance expectations, will need to be emphasized in the training.

In the organizational feedback environment area, Palisades had a rating of "2." This showed that Palisades did not have a very strong feedback culture. Feedback that was given was not seen as particularly job-related, and the behaviors and results that are valued by the organization were not perceived as being reinforced by individual managers. In addition, the open-ended questions showed a perception by a large number of employees regarding concerns with favoritism and that ratings were inconsistent across managers. Rater error training will need to be a component of the training as well.

While Palisades Inc. did not have particularly good scores on the precursors of organizational alignment and organizational feedback environment, scores on formal individual growth opportunities were better. A score of "4" was obtained. This showed that there were many ways that employees could learn and develop skills within Palisades Inc. However, the one area that showed a need, based on responses from employees, was that little effort was spent on creating development plans. Thus, this is an area that only needs a little improvement.

On the organizational precursor of accountability, Palisades Inc. received a score of "3." This means that there is some accountability for organizational change, but it is inconsistent. In order to improve scores in this area, Palisades needs to make sure that managers are held responsible for organizationally relevant changes, or the lack thereof.

On the last organizational precursor, the compensation system, Palisades Inc. earned a score of "3." Palisades does increase pay for positive individual change, but inconsistently. Palisades Inc. needs to work on creating a stronger tie for pay-for-performance, and make this an incentive for organizationally valued change.

As can be seen from the OPS data that Palisades collected, implementing a new performance management process and emphasizing the needed training to go along with it will be critical to its success.

Training

Training will be conducted based on data collected from Assessment Point 1. The data will serve as a needs assessment, which will indicate what aspects of training should be emphasized. To ensure successful implementation of the performance management system, both employee and managerial training will be conducted. The training will include administrative as well as process training (Silverman, 1991).

The administrative aspect of the training session will include information about how the new system differs from the previous one, how to fill out forms, and other tasks that will facilitate the implementation of the performance management system. Both the manager and the employee will have the same training about the performance management system, including the timeline for implementation of the process (see Figure 15.1).

Process training will include clarifying job responsibilities and expectations, diagnosing and coaching employee performance problems, and giving direction as to how to give effective feedback (Gregory, Levy, & Jeffers, 2008; London & Smither, 2002). The skill development aspect of the training gets at how to clarify one's major responsibilities and performance expectations (Silverman & Wexley, 1986). Role clarity is especially important to ensure that employees have a clear understanding of what their jobs entail, which could lead to improved job performance (Whitaker, Dahling, & Levy, 2007). Both employees and managers can benefit from skill development training. Skill development will be based on current needs of the organization and individuals. These needs will be based on the organizational and individual precursor data. In addition, managerial training will be given to demonstrate how to conduct a developmental discussion and how to complete an overall performance review for their employees.

Rater error training will be conducted to reduce errors in the 360-degree process and in the performance review (Silverman & Wexley, 1986). Rater error training involves informing raters of the types of errors commonly made and using DVD scenarios that allow participants to make the errors themselves. The goal of rater error training is for raters to provide greater accuracy in their ratings. Ideally, subordinates would receive error training as well as managers, but often this is not feasible in organizations and only managers receive the training. Using performance dimension training along with practice ratings can increase rating accuracy (Hauenstein, 1998).

Assessment Point 2: Training Evaluation at the Reaction and Learning Levels

While data from Assessment Point 1 was used to help design the training process, the purpose of Assessment Point 2 is to evaluate the *reactions* of the managers and employees to the training program content with regard to its usefulness on the job. Evaluation of training at the *learning* level is also necessary to ensure the trainees have developed the necessary skills to effectively implement the performance management process. The learning level is assessed by evaluating the quality of the major responsibilities and performance expectations that are created by the managers and employees during the training process.

Implementation of Performance Management System at the Individual Level

Individual major responsibilities are critical aspects of the job that must be done by the employee for departments to meet their goals and expectations (Silverman, 1991). The responsibilities are decided upon by both manager and subordinate. Some of the major responsibilities are inherent to the job and remain static; others, such as key projects, may change over time. The major responsibilities should be ranked from most important to least important.

There are two types of performance expectations in the performance management system that define effectiveness on each major responsibility. First, behavior-oriented performance expectations are created for each major responsibility. These behaviors must be observable and controllable. Meeting these expectations is critical for successful performance and aligns with those organizationally valued behaviors.

The second type of expectation, results-oriented performance expectations, should also be developed for each major responsibility. These standards are dependent upon employee actions and under employee control. Furthermore, standards need to be quantifiable and define effective performance for each major responsibility. These results-oriented expectations or standards help to align the individual with the mission and goals at the departmental as well as the organizational level. Every manager in the organization should be required to have a major responsibility, Managing Employee Performance and Development, along with a set of behavior and results-oriented performance expectations. The managers should be rated on the major responsibility (along with all others) to assure that, in this case, the performance management program and policies are effectively implemented as they were designed.

To illustrate the performance management system at the individual level, two fictional employees, Michael and Anna, will be followed at various points throughout the process.

Michael

Michael has been a manager at Palisades for three years. He is a production manager and several of his major responsibilities include ensuring product quality, overseeing production, hiring and managing departmental employees, and budgeting. These major responsibilities are fairly static and will not change much from year to year. Michael also has some major responsibilities specific for the current year. One of these major responsibilities is to work with the research and development team to develop a new product.

Anna

Anna has been a marketing manager at Palisades for five years. Some of her major responsibilities include conducting market research, hiring and managing marketing staff, and developing successful marketing strategies. This year, Anna was asked to conduct surveys to identify new markets for Palisades Inc. The first three major responsibilities listed are static; they are essential tasks for her position. The survey project is a dynamic major responsibility; it is specific to that calendar year.

Michael and Anna would meet with their manager in December to clarify these major responsibilities as well as performance expectations.

360-Degree Feedback

Once the manager and employee have met to clarify the employee's role through major responsibilities and performance expectations, the employee participates in the 360-degree feedback process. The 360-degree instrument assesses areas for development from multiple rating sources including managers, direct reports, self, peers, and sometimes customers. It is important that employees know that this will be used only for developmental purposes and not for administrative purposes (London, 2001).

After employees are rated on these dimensions and data is compiled, a feedback report and a workbook will be given to each employee. The 360-degree feedback report will contain the results of ratings of each of the items on the 360 assessment from all sources, as well as a summary of overall ratings on each dimension. The 360 developmental workbook will give individuals a series of activities that will help them understand the feedback report and create a developmental action plan.

In addition to the workbook, a development guide will be provided with resources for developing skill dimensions. These resources are composed of activities and readings that individuals can do on their own to further their career goals.

Assessment Point 3: Individual Precursors, Time 1

Individual precursors will be measured twice during the performance management cycle: February 2010 (Assessment Point 3) and January 2011 (Assessment Point 6). Evaluation of individual precursors is important because it gives a manager an idea of a particular employee's receptiveness for feedback and change at a given point in time (Linderbaum & Levy, 2007). Each dimension will be assessed by several items rated on a 1 to 5 scale (see Table 15.2).

While the previous assessment points have been directed at the organization, at Assessment Point 3 the individual precursors are directed at the employee. These precursors include awareness, a sense of necessity, confronting change, willingness for feedback, and developmental orientation (Silverman, Pogson, & Cober, 2005). Manager ratings of these precursors indicate how ready an individual is to implement change in his or her actions and behaviors. Employees with higher ratings on these precursors are more likely to change and develop than those with lower scores on these precursors. Ratings of the individual precursors will be discussed with the employee during a developmental discussion with the manager.

Awareness

A score of a "1" on awareness indicates that the employee has little or no idea that his or her behaviors and actions need to change, while a score of "3" indicates that the individual is aware that some change is needed in certain areas. A score of "5" indicates that the individual is highly aware of the areas that he or she needs to improve.

Michael

In preparation for this discussion, Michael's manager completed the Individual Precursor Scale to help guide the developmental discussion. The score on Awareness, the first individual precursor, is very important, as it is the first step toward successful development and change. Without awareness, individuals cannot change because they don't know what to change, don't believe they need to change, and do not know how to change. Michael, unfortunately, is perceived by his manager as not very aware of the need for change. He was rated a "2" by his manager on the individual precursor of awareness. As a result of this rating, Michael's manager knows that he must clearly emphasize those areas that need development and why they are important.

Anna

Anna, on the other hand, was rated a "4" on awareness. This indicates that she has a good idea of what behavior she needs to improve. This is very helpful because if an individual is aware of the need for changing his or her behavior, he or she is more motivated to change and develop.

Necessity

The second individual precursor, sense of necessity, indicates what sense of urgency the individual has regarding change in his or her behavior and confronting the problems head-on. A rating of a "1" on this dimension indicates that the individual has no desire to change his or her behavior. A rating of "3" on this precursor indicates that the individual does show some desire to change his or her behavior. Finally, a rating of "5" on the precursor of necessity indicates that the individual understands the importance of change in behavior and has a strong desire to do so.

On necessity, the second individual precursor, Michael scored a "1." This score is heavily influenced by his score on awareness. Because he is not aware of the changes to be made, he cannot really feel the need for change. As well as being aware of the need for behavior change, Anna also sees the importance of this change and what an impact it will make on Palisades Inc., as well as for her own personal growth. Anna was rated as a "4" on the individual precursor of necessity.

Confronting Change

The third individual precursor, confronting change, involves knowing what to do to change his or her behavior, as well as knowing what problem prompts this change. A score of a "1" on this precursor shows that the individual has demonstrated little understanding of the steps needed in order to change his or her behavior. A score of a "3" indicates that the individual shows some understanding of what steps to take to change his or her behavior. Finally, a score of a "5" on confronting change shows that the individual has a clear understanding of how to change his or her behavior.

On the precursor of confronting change, Michael scored a "1." He does not exhibit understanding of how to change. Again, this is not especially surprising, given Michael's low score on awareness. While Anna is aware of the importance of changing her behavior, she is not as adept at confronting change. On the third organizational precursor of confronting change, Anna rated a "2." She has the desire to change, but she's not quite sure how to do so.

Willingness for Feedback

The fourth individual precursor, willingness for feedback, indicates how receptive an individual is to receiving both negative and positive feedback on his or her behavior and performance. A score of a "1" on this individual precursor indicates that the individual does not seem to be open or seems defensive when feedback is given. A score of a "3" on this dimension indicates that the individual appears to be open and emotionally prepared to receive feedback. A score of a "5" on willingness for feedback indicates that the individual has a strong desire for and is emotionally ready to receive candid feedback from others.

On the individual precursor, willingness for feedback, Michael scored a "2." He is receptive to feedback from others at times, but only if it is positive feedback. He becomes defensive whenever negative feedback is given, especially about an area in which he feels he is an expert. On willingness for feedback, Anna scored a "3." She welcomes feedback most of the time, but is more receptive from some people than others. Improvement in this area would be important for Anna's development as a manager.

Development Orientation

The fifth individual precursor, development orientation, indicates how much an individual wants to learn new things to further develop skills. A rating of a "1" on the precursor indicates that the individual does not seek out opportunities for individual growth. A rating of a "3" indicates that the individual will seek out opportunities for individual growth and development on occasion. Last, a rating of a "5" on development orientation shows that the individual has shown a strong desire for developmental activities and seeks these opportunities regularly.

For both Michael and Anna, it is important to remember that the organizational environment is an important contributor to the individual's ratings on the individual precursors. For

Michael received a "2" on this precursor. Because he is not very aware of his need to change, he does not seek opportunities for learning and development very often. On the other hand, Anna was rated a "3" on the individual precursor of development orientation. She has a strong drive to improve, but does not always seek out available opportunities. Furthermore, she tends to take advantage of these opportunities only if it is clear that engaging in them will lead to advancement in the company. She is not as concerned about her personal growth.

Looking at the example of Michael, you can see how important awareness is in evaluating readiness to change. In sum, Michael obtained below-average scores on all individual precursors, and one can see how the other four individual precursors are related to the low rating on awareness. Due to the unfavorable scores on these individual precursors, Michael will need a great deal of guidance to overcome his limitations and change his behavior.

In sum, Anna is aware of the need for behavior change and how important it is for her personally as well as the organization. However, she could have a better idea of how to actually change, that is, what she needs to do. She is fairly receptive to feedback and reaches out for some developmental opportunities, but she could improve on both of these dimensions. Thus, the focus of her development plan should be on the steps she needs to take to change.

example, if the organization does not have a culture conducive to feedback seeking, this could affect an employee's rating on the individual precursor of willingness for feedback. Organizational precursors can limit scores on individual precursors.

It is important to note that improvement on individual precursors can be affected by the state of the organization's organizational precursors. For example, few individuals will be likely to seek feedback if they are not encouraged to do so. Also, if regular feedback is not given, individuals will be less likely to seek it. Thus, it is imperative to look at the performance management system as a whole, not just its parts. All of the parts of the performance management system are related, and a poor component of one part of the system can be detrimental to other areas.

Developmental Discussion and Creation of Individual Development Plans (IDPs)

The manager and employee should then conduct a development discussion to create an individual development plan based on the 360-degree feedback process. During the meeting with the manager, it is time to discuss the feedback report from the process and to consider both future career goals and enhancing performance on the responsibilities for the employee's current position.

The individual development plan involves identifying developmental opportunities for current major responsibilities and future career growth. These opportunities can go beyond the employee's current position in the organization. Rather, this plan can also further the employee's personal career path, the protean career.

In the protean career perspective, the emphasis is on obtaining skills that would be useful for the life of one's career as well as for self-fulfillment (Hall & Moss, 1998). The protean career contract (adapted from Hall & Moss, 1998, p. 26) is as follows:

1. Career is managed more by the employee.
2. A career is a lifelong series of experiences, skills, learning, and transitions.
3. Development is continuous learning, self-directed, relational, and found in work challenges.
4. Development is not (necessarily) formal training, retraining, or upward mobility.
5. The organization provides challenging assignments, developmental relationships, information, and other developmental resources.
6. The goal is psychological success and increased job performance.

Assessment Point 4: Evaluation at Individual and Department Levels

The purpose of Assessment Point 4 is to conduct individual reviews that serve as formal performance reviews and evaluate departmental performance. These reviews will be used for administrative purposes, such as for promotions and merit raises.

Individual performance reviews will be conducted once a year. Palisades Inc. will conduct individual and departmental evaluations in December 2010. For the individual evaluations, each major responsibility will be rated on a 1 to 5 scale, with "3" being "meets expectations." Recall that behavioral and results-oriented performance expectations were agreed on for each major responsibility at the beginning of the year. This review will assess whether an employee has exceeded, met, or not met expectations on each of his or her major responsibilities.

The departmental evaluation will also take place in December 2010. The review will be conducted by the department manager, who will examine and document attainment of departmental goals that were set at the beginning of the year. If the goals and benchmarks from the previous year have not been met, the ratings on the departmental evaluation will be low. Numerous data sources could give some insight into why benchmarks were not being met. For example, if the performance goal that Palisades set earlier in the year is not met, precursor data and 360-degree evaluations could provide some information explaining why the goal was not met. Are individuals improving? If so, departmental performance should increase in the following year. In sum, the many sources of information collected will make it easier to target the specific problem and fine-tune that element of the performance management system, instead of overhauling the entire system.

Assessment Point 5: Organizational Precursors, Time 2

As you recall, organizational precursor data was collected before implementing the current performance management system. Now that the performance management system is in place, organizational precursors are measured again, to identify changes that have occurred along with the new system.

Palisades Case

The organizational precursors of organizational alignment and feedback environment went from "2" and "3," respectively, to a score of "4." Thus, along with the implementation of the performance management system, Palisades employees saw more alignment between the organizational level and the individual level. Thus, these two precursors showed marked improvement.

Great improvement was made in the area of formal individual growth opportunities. While the organization was initially rated as a "2," it is now rated as a "4." Palisades has made great strides in making developmental opportunities available to employees. Since the feedback environment was enhanced by requiring all employees to have individual development plans, it facilitated growth and development by emphasizing these developmental opportunities based on feedback from Assessment Point 1. Thus, Palisades Inc. developed programs to help improve employee performance and encourage personal and career growth.

Another improvement made was to accountability. Managers were trained to be consistent in implementing the performance management system and making sure that consequences exist for employee behaviors, whether their behaviors were beneficial to the organization or detrimental. Making accountability a critical major responsibility of all managers helped to increase the rating from a "3" to a "4."

A pay-for-performance system was implemented and linked to valued behaviors and results of employees. On the first evaluation, there was some evidence that behaviors that led to positive outcomes were rewarded financially, but these rewards were inconsistent. Thus, many employees felt that their efforts did not lead to financial gain. To remedy this, Palisades Inc. implemented a new pay system, one in which behaviors and results leading to positive outcomes are financially rewarded. As there is now a detailed pay-for-performance system in place, Palisades' score on the organizational precursor of compensation system increased to a "4."

Assessment Point 6: Individual Precursors, Time 2

At Assessment Point 6, ratings will be made on the same five individual precursors collected at Time 1. After these ratings are made, both sets of ratings will be compared. The results of these comparisons will be used to determine how much an employee has improved or changed in that year.

Michael's Individual Precursor Ratings at Time 2

After his manager completed the individual precursor questionnaire for the second time, Michael's awareness score improved from a "2" to a "4." This is a very important improvement, as now the focus of Michael's development can be on actual changes instead of being merely aware of the necessary changes.

Along with awareness, Michael's score on necessity improved from a "2" to a "4." Not only is Michael now aware of the needed changes, but he feels that they are necessary for his progress. Similarly, on confronting change, Michael scored a "3," which is an improvement from the "1" he received on the first assessment of individual precursors. He still does not know exactly what he needs to do at all times to change his behavior, but he now recognizes what these steps are in some areas.

Willingness for feedback improved to a "3." Because of his continual focus on the individual development plan, Michael takes feedback much better than before. Receiving negative feedback is still a little difficult for him, but he has been able to use it constructively at times. This area needs continued work, but Michael has made the first steps in personal development. On the final precursor, development orientation, Michael was rated a "3." Due to greater awareness of his weaknesses, he has been able begin to take part in some developmental activities to further personal growth.

(Continued)

Overall, Michael showed a great deal of improvement between Time 1 and Time 2 when the individual precursors were assessed. This is likely due to the new performance management system that has a strong focus on development. Ultimately, Michael and his manager must look for the connection between his development plan and his job performance. Because Palisades has had improvement in its organizational precursors, it is more likely that individuals will learn and develop.

Anna's Individual Precursor Ratings at Time 2

Anna's awareness score remained a "4." Because her score on this individual precursor was good to begin with, developing this skill was not the focus of her development. Likewise, her score on necessity remained a "4."

Great improvement was made on the precursor of confronting change. Initially, Anna was rated a "2" in this area. She was aware of the changes she needed to make, but did not know the steps she needed to take to do so. Anna's rating has improved to a "4." Because of her individual development plan, she now has some action steps in place for her to make these changes.

On the willingness for feedback dimension, Anna was rated a "4." This is an improvement from the "3" she was rated last time. While she had been fairly good about receiving feedback before, Anna was more willing to receive and accept negative feedback.

On the individual precursor of development orientation, Anna has improved greatly, from a "3" to a "5." Specifically, she has learned that her personal growth is just as important as her advancement at Palisades. Working with the protean career contract helped her gain a learning-oriented focus, as opposed to only a performance-oriented focus.

Determine Changes to Be Made in 2011 Performance Management Process

The performance management system is not going to be exactly the same from year to year. The format will remain the same, but some of the goals of the organization and individual major responsibilities will change.

These changes are essential for development of both the organization as well as the individual. As the organization plans for what needs to be accomplished in the next year, similarly, employees meet with their managers to determine their job responsibilities and performance expectations for 2011. And so the process begins again.

Conclusion

In order to maximize the successful implementation of the performance management system described in this chapter, there needs to be support at the very top of the organization. The most effective means to maximize buy-in at the top is when senior management effectively models the process. In addition, successful implementation is enhanced when the following occurs:

- Managers and employees are held accountable for their aspects of the implementation process.
- The assessment points are seen as a critical part of building an organization with a learning and development culture.
- Role clarity is taken very seriously in order to align each individual's role and performance expectations with the organizational and team mission, values, and strategy.

References

Cropanzano, R., Bowen, D. E., & Gilliland, S. W. (2007). The management of organizational justice. *Academy of Management Perspectives*, *21*, 34–48.

Gregory, J. B., Levy, P. E., & Jeffers, M. (2008). Development of a model of the feedback process within executive coaching. *Consulting Psychology Journal*, *60*, 42–56.

Hall, D. T., & Moss, J. E. (1998). The new protean career contract: Helping organizations and employees adapt. *Organizational Dynamics, 26,* 22–38.

Hauenstein, N. M. A. (1998). Training raters to increase the accuracy of appraisals and the usefulness of feedback. In J. W. Smither (Ed.), *Performance appraisal: State of the art in practice* (pp. 404–442). San Francisco: Jossey-Bass.

Kluger, A. N., & DeNisi, A. (1996). The effects of feedback interventions on performance: A historical review, a meta-analysis, and a preliminary feedback intervention theory. *Psychological Bulletin, 119,* 254–284.

Linderbaum, B. G., & Levy, P. E. (2007). The development and validation of the feedback orientation scale. Paper presented at the 22nd Annual Meetings of the Society for Industrial and Organizational Psychology, New York, New York.

London, M. (2001). The great debate: Should multi-source feedback be used for administration or development only? In D. W. Bracken, C. W. Timmreck, & A. H. Church (Eds.), *The handbook of multi-source feedback: The comprehensive resource for designing and implementing MSF processes* (pp. 368–385). San Francisco: Jossey-Bass.

London, M., & Smither, J. W. (2002). Feedback orientation, feedback culture, and the longitudinal performance management process. *Human Resource Management Review, 12,* 81–100.

Mauer, T. J., Mitchell, D. R. D., & Barbeite, F. G. (2002). Predictors of attitudes toward a 360-degree feedback system and involvement in post-feedback management development activity. *Journal of Occupational and Organizational Psychology, 75,* 87–107.

OnPoint Consulting. (2007, April). Performance management: Moving from scorecard to strategic tool, ensuring your performance management system supports the achievement of business results. New York: OnPoint Consulting.

Silverman, S. B. (1991). Individual development through performance appraisal. In K. N. Wexley (Ed.), *Developing human resources.* Washington, DC: BNA Books.

Silverman, S. B., Pogson, C. E., & Cober, A. B. (2005). When employees at work don't get it: A model for enhancing individual employee change in response to performance feedback. *Academy of Management Executive, 19,* 135–147.

Silverman, S. B., & Wexley, K. N. (1986). Avoiding rater error training. Akron, OH: Human Resource Decisions, Inc.

Whitaker, B. G., Dahling, J. J., & Levy, P. E. (2007). The development of a feedback environment and role clarity model of job performance. *Journal of Management, 33,* 570–591.

CHAPTER 16

PERFORMANCE MANAGEMENT OF THE FUTURE

Nancy T. Tippins and Susan H. Coverdale

Successful performance management programs in the workplace of the future will depend on a number of components. Minimally, the characteristics of jobs, the contextual demands of the organization, and the attributes of the people who fill the jobs will define what performance management processes are required and which are effective. However, many factors shape jobs, people, and the workplace. For example, global competition, natural resources, historical precedents, labor supplies, and economic forces determine what jobs exist in what locations. Education, family, and the culture in which workers live can influence their values and shape their job choices.

The purpose of this chapter is to review the current trends that are likely to affect performance management programs of the future. We begin by first reviewing these general trends from a broad perspective. We will then discuss the effects these trends may have on performance management programs and the ways performance management programs will need to be adapted to remain effective. In Table 16.1, we have summarized the notable changes in worker attitudes and workplace requirements, the main effects these changes have on the performance of work, and the primary implications they have for performance management systems.

Table 16.1 Impetus for Changes to Performance Management Systems.

Change	Effect in Workplace	Changes to Performance Management Systems
Changes in Workplace		
Work teams	• Less opportunity to observe work behavior	• Reliance on sources of information/feedback from individuals other than first-line supervisor, including peers and customers • Need to develop methods for evaluating individual contribution to overall job performance
Geographically dispersed teams	• Lack of face-to-face contact with supervisor and peers • Less opportunity to observe work behavior of others • More remote supervision • Greater diversity of cultures, values, beliefs, political systems, education, experience, and other factors	• Use of technology to convey performance management information about jobs, feedback on performance, development opportunities • Reliance on sources of information/feedback from individuals other than first-line supervisor, including peers and customers • Emphasis on cultural diversity in performance management systems

Flexible definition of a job	• Different performance standards for different aspects of an assignment • Broad skill sets required • Increased importance placed on employee flexibility and adaptability	• Customization of performance management systems for broad conceptualization of jobs • Emphasis on and evaluation of adaptability
Outsourcing	• Members of team not employees of the same company • Legal problems with managing performance of outsourced employees	• Feedback from others who are not formal members of team • Influence on performance in ways other than formal performance management systems
Remote work arrangements (e.g., hotelling and telecommuting)	• Distance from peers, supervisor, and direct reports • Less face-to-face interaction; more electronic communication • Less opportunity to observe work behavior • More remote supervision	• Use of technology for communications among peers, supervisors, direct reports, and customers

(Continued)

Table 16.1 (*Continued*)

Change	Effect in Workplace	Changes to Performance Management Systems
Flexible work schedules	• Less face-to-face time with peers, supervisor, and direct reports • More remote supervision	• Use of technology for communications among peers, supervisors, direct reports, and customers
Job sharing	• Less opportunity to observe work behavior • Lack of clarity about who is responsible for what • Confusion over whether job performance or person being rated	• Reliance on sources of information/feedback from individuals other than first-line supervisor, including peers and customers • Adaptation of performance evaluation systems to job sharing situations (e.g., supervisory training on rating performance) • Need to develop methods for evaluating individual contribution to overall job performance
Flat organizational structure	• Large spans of controls for supervisors; less time for each employee • Fewer promotional opportunities	• Greater reliance of sources of information other than the first-line supervisor • Use of other forms of development (e.g., cross-functional assignments, mentoring)

Matrix management	• Confusion of responsibility for performance management • Potentially inconsistent messages	• Multiple sources of responsibility for performance management • Adaptation of performance evaluation systems to matrix management situations (e.g., supervisory training)
Multi-media communication modes	• Lack of visual cues in some modes • Lack of consistency in performance in some modes • Lack of privacy in some modes	• Multiple sources of communications including time for face-to-face interactions
Global business	• Differences in performance standards • Greater cultural diversity of teams	• Customization of performance management systems to reflect differences based on location and culture
Technology	• Technology pervading all areas of work • Employees expect access to technology	• Use of technology for performance management
Change	• Rapid change in work requirements • High likelihood of employees changing jobs and careers	• Ability to adapt performance management systems to continual influx of new employees

(Continued)

Table 16.1 (*Continued*)

Change	Effect in Workplace	Changes to Performance Management Systems
Changes in Worker Characteristics		
Number of qualified workers	• Fewer qualified workers • Growing number of workers lacking basic skills	• Emphasis on development of existing employees • Emphasis on development of basic skills • Customization of communication for employees of lower literacy
Employee expectations of job	• Continuing expectations for personal growth and development for some • Desires for rapid career progression for some • Desires for valued rewards and recognition commensurate with performance • Work-family balance	• Emphasis on employee development • Emphasis on alternatives to promotions • Customization of rewards and recognition programs • Communications on trade-offs between work and family time

Loyalty of employers and employees	• Employers are more willing to let employees who lack needed skills go and less likely to provide re-training • Employees are less likely to remain with employers if their needs are not met	• Emphasis on immediate benefits of employment • Communications on applicability of skills to multiple careers
Changing supervisory relationships	• Supervisors not available to assist in decision making for direct reports • Less command and control supervision • More collegial relationships with supervisors	• Need to evaluate and reward employees for taking responsibility and acting independently • Participative goal setting and problem solving relative to performance management

Some would rightly say the future is unknowable. Certainly, we are unable to anticipate cataclysmic events and predict how these events will affect the way work is performed or how workers' attitudes toward work might be changed. However, one could also argue that the future is predictable in broad terms based on what we know today. Many of the trends that are emerging and apparent in the workplace today are likely to continue and have an even stronger effect tomorrow.

A study of all the factors that might influence the nature of work performed in the future and the workers who perform it is beyond the scope of this chapter. However, we have provided a brief review of major workplace changes that are evident today and are likely to strengthen in the future. In the interest of space, we have not documented all of the sources that have allowed us to identify these as legitimate trends. These trends come from a broad review of popular periodicals and business literature. The interested reader is directed to summary books such as one produced by the Rand Corporation for the U.S. Department of Labor, *The 21st Century at Work* (Karoly & Panis, 2004), and the American Management Association's *The New Workforce* (Hankin, 2005), as well as newspapers and other periodicals. The website for the Society for Human Resource Management (www.shrm.org) contains a great deal of information on workplace trends as well. The U.S. Department of Labor (www.bls.gov) is an excellent source of information regarding workforce statistics for the United States.

Rather than convince the reader that changes in the workforce are taking place or that all these changes will soon be embedded into every employee's work life, we hope, instead, to stimulate the reader to consider how these changes may affect performance management programs. It is also important to note that these changes do not reflect all workplace conditions or the attributes of all workers in the workforce; rather, we have selected these trends because they seem to be affecting significant numbers of employers and employees and appear likely to continue shaping the requirements of performance management programs in the foreseeable future.

Worker and Workplace Trends

Changes in the Workplace

Work teams. Organizations are increasingly turning to the use of teams for task accomplishment and emphasizing team performance. These often autonomous employees work together toward a common goal for which they are jointly held responsible and plan and organize their own work in the absence of supervisory oversight. Shared responsibilities among team members present challenges as the supervisor is charged with evaluating an employee's contribution to the team effort as well as the overall success of the team's performance without having been directly involved him- or herself.

Geographically dispersed teams. Increasingly, work teams are composed of members who work in geographically different locations. Team members may work in different buildings on the same campus, different cities, and even different countries. Sometimes, team members live in different time zones and vastly different cultures. Because of the physical or temporal distances between supervisor and employee, direct methods of supervision no longer work. Often corporations construct these teams composed of employees from different locations due to the need for a particular expertise or because of the high cost, both in terms of dollars and employee satisfaction, of moving employees. In many global businesses, members representing all geographic areas are required to ensure the universal applicability of decisions made. These teams can be highly cohesive groups of people who interact extensively or a number of individuals who are assigned tasks that are part of a greater whole and work independently. Supervisors and team members may need to build relationships with people of diverse backgrounds without face-to-face contact or the benefit of informal opportunities for socializing. In some cases, team members will be vitally aware of each other's performance; in others, team members will have no idea.

Flexible definition of a job. In the past, jobs were clearly defined as a set of related tasks that were performed to achieve a particular goal. Recent trends suggest that jobs are becoming broader in the scope of tasks to be performed and that workers are being asked to shift tasks more frequently. Whether or not the concept of a job has changed *or* the belief that jobs as they once were performed simply do not exist anymore is arguable. What remains apparent, though, is that more workers are being asked to develop broad skill sets and bring high levels of adaptability to meet changing work requirements.

Outsourcing. Many organizations are focusing on their core capabilities and outsourcing work that is not part of their main mission. Ongoing outsourcing can add another dimension to geographical dispersion within teams. Not only can team members be geographically dispersed, but they can literally work for another company. Concern regarding co-employment laws often results in strict limitations on who supervises whom, preventing supervisors of one company from managing performance of employees in the outsourced firm. Yet, in many cases, these are the very employees who are vital to the success of the team.

Remote work arrangements (such as hotelling and telecommuting). Another growing trend is the use of alternate work arrangements that allow some workers to work away from their "office" location some, if not all, of their work time. In "hotelling" arrangements, workers who travel extensively may not have a fixed office; instead, their company provides temporary offices from which they work when they have a need to be in a company location. "Telecommuting" arrangements allow workers to perform their jobs some place other than a company office, typically from their homes. These alternate work arrangements have multiple purposes, ranging from reducing expenditures for office space to enhancing the worker's quality of life. All result in profound alterations to how and when employees and supervisors interact with one another.

Flexible work schedules. Another alternate work arrangements is flexible work schedules that may include undefined work schedules, schedules that require attendance only during core hours, and flex-time in terms of specific working days and/or starting and ending times. Similar to remote work arrangements, flexible schedules are often intended primarily to enhance the worker's quality of life. The benefits to the employer may be less clear but probably include the ability to attract and retain capable workers.

Regardless of the benefits, flexible work schedules can decrease the amount of time supervisor and direct report (as well as team members) spend with each other, changing how performance is managed and evaluated.

Job sharing. Job sharing allows two or more people to hold the same job. Typically, one person is available during normal work hours for part of the week and the other for the remaining time. For example, one person may work mornings and the other afternoons. Often, each person's schedule allows some overlap time to share information and transfer responsibilities. Although a worker may be physically present, the supervisor has new challenges in evaluating each individual's performance of the job. The amount of observation time for each individual may be cut in half, and there may be some lack of clarity as to which employee is responsible for what work outcome. In addition, the organization may need to redefine commitment to the job and reassess the importance of full-time work for career progression.

Flat organizational structure. A growing trend in many American corporations is the removal of layers of management, which usually results in increased numbers of direct reports for the remaining supervisors. The rationale behind the flattening of the organization varies. One reason is to move upper-level managers closer to their customers by eliminating middle managers. Another is that, by eliminating superfluous layers of management, the flatter hierarchy results in significant cost savings and efficiencies. Implementing performance management processes can be challenging when a manager supervises large numbers of people who perform diverse functions. In addition, flatter organizations may provide fewer promotional opportunities. Those who are promoted may find that the reduction in the layers of management results in a substantial increase in the scope of the job and the commensurate skill requirements.

Matrix management. Matrix management, in which individual workers have multiple reporting relationships, has been used by organizations for many years. However, recent focus on cost efficiencies in many businesses may have increased the number of such relationships. One person often has multiple responsibilities and reports to multiple supervisors, each of whom must evaluate the individual on a subset of all the work performed. Therefore, no one supervisor has a complete picture of an individual's performance. Often, there is no one supervisor totally responsible for helping the individual with all the aspects of performance management and career development. The diffused responsibility can lead to conflicting developmental advice or no direction whatsoever. From the supervisor's perspective, matrix management can often confuse the responsibilities of performance management and lead to inconsistent messages being communicated to the employee.

Multi-media communication modes. Many of the alternative work arrangements discussed above are successful because communications are facilitated by different kinds of technologically enhanced media. Although some of these modes of communication (such as telephone service) have high fidelity, the face-to-face aspect is lost completely. Other modes (such as videoconferencing) are almost as good as being physically present but may involve technical problems that inhibit clear communications. Supervisors who communicate through these tools have to consider carefully the effect of the communication mode on the quality of the performance management discussions and decide whether anything is an acceptable substitute for a face-to-face performance discussion.

Global business. Another significant trend of recent years is the growth of international business in which an organization conducts its business around the globe and has employees from many different countries and cultures working together. Although cultural differences may be more difficult to recognize than language differences, the cultural differences may significantly shape what is considered acceptable performance and what is not. Supervisors and employees must attend to the effect cultural differences have on how work is accomplished and the implications for how individuals interact with one another. In addition, job requirements must be carefully differentiated from local customs that are followed despite actual job needs. For example, developing a relationship with a customer may be a requirement of the job; taking the customer to lunch may be a cultural expectation.

Technology. It is difficult to write anything concerning business in the 21st century without acknowledging the role of technology. Technology has significantly changed how many jobs are performed. Workers entering the workforce since the mid-1980s when the Internet became widely available have grown up with technology and are comfortable using it not only to perform their work but also to communicate with their colleagues, supervisors, and customers.

Change. Similarly, the workforce today has experienced radical changes in the workplace. These changes include what work is performed, how it is performed, and who (or what) performs it. Although employees may not be entirely comfortable with the nature and pace of change, most have adapted to it. In many cases, these workers have come to expect change in their work as a natural course of events.

The likelihood of change in the worker's career is also very high. It seems rare today for someone to retire from a company with forty years of service. Although workers today may not expect to make a great many personal career changes, the reality is that many will have large numbers of jobs and several careers in their lifetimes. In some cases, these changes will be forced upon them; in others, they may be seeking different kinds of work and rewards or attempting to develop new skills.

Changes in Worker Characteristics

Much has been made of the career expectations and attitudes toward work of recent generations of workers entering the workforce. Some groups are described as being self-centered and focused on the financial benefits of work; others are portrayed as more altruistic, seeking a sense of purpose in life. Characterizing an entire age cohort by a single set of values is foolhardy, as significant individual differences within virtually any group exist. It is also important to note that the characteristics of these populations minimally refer to those who possess basic skills including speaking English. In many cases, these groups are limited to those with high school education or more. Nevertheless, notable trends in worker attitudes are emerging. In many cases, these changes in worker attitudes and expectations are not limited to a particular age group. In other cases, the trends are associated with the particular experiences a group has had (or has not had).

Number of qualified workers. In the United States, there has long been a concern that the number of qualified workers is shrinking and that there will be an insufficient number of employees to fill critical positions in the future. Documents such as *Workforce 2000* (Johnston & Packer, 1987) predicted dire shortages of educated workers capable of meeting the needs of business and industry and a plethora of the undereducated, as well as recent immigrants who lacked facility in the English language. Although many of the predictions failed to materialize, a significant number of American workers remain unskilled or undereducated, and immigration patterns suggest the stream of workers who lack basic literacy and numeracy skills will continue. If these predictions are true, competition for qualified workers will be fierce. Moreover, employers will be forced to modify the way they manage low-skill employees as traditional ways of communicating information about current and future jobs may no longer be successful.

If the number of qualified candidates for positions does shrink, the competition for those who are qualified will be inversely proportional to their availability. To attract and keep these scarce resources, employers will be forced to conform to the needs and expectations of these workers. Thus, performance management programs will need to be modified in many ways.

Not all countries are contemplating a shortage of qualified workers. Many countries, particularly those in Eastern Europe and Asia, have expanding economies and large numbers of educated workers. For example, a white paper from the Society for Human Resource Management (SHRM) (Gross & Minot, 2008) reports a large population of educated workers in India, which has over ten thousand colleges and universities that produce 2.5 million graduates per year. Shrinking pools of capable labor in the United States and growing pools in other countries, coupled with differential labor costs, may well harbinger continuing shifts where work is performed.

Employee expectations of the job. Current evaluations of workforce trends suggest that employees, particularly the qualified ones, have expectations about what a job should provide. A significant segment of the workforce expects opportunities for personal growth and development and is apt to seek other employment if these opportunities are not forthcoming. Closely related to personal development is the opportunity for rapid career progression, which may be all the more difficult in a flattening organization in which promotions will be fewer for most employees. Many workers today also anticipate rewards and recognition commensurate with their efforts and the company's performance and expect reward systems to take into account their own values. Another common expectation of today's workforce is work-family balance. Although the concept has many different meanings, across virtually all, the term connotes the employer's acknowledgement of the importance of personal pursuits as well as the importance of work.

Loyalty of employer and employees. A notable change in the American workforce in the last twenty years is the loyalty that employers show toward employees and that employees show to employers. Often, employers regard workers' value as temporary or replaceable. An employee is valued only as long as his or her skills are current or cannot be replaced more economically through outsourcing. At the same time, employees are likely to perceive an employer as beneficial to them only as long as the job is interesting, promising for the future in terms of skill-building, accommodating to their personal situations, and/or well-paying. Many changes in employment trends are at least part of the cause of this changing relationship between employee and employer. For example, global competition has forced many employers to cut extraneous expenses, including excess payroll and those expenses devoted to employee development or re-training. Changes in employee pension plans, either terminations or switches to defined contribution plans, have lessened the financial sting of frequent job changes for employees. For many reasons, some employers cannot expect employees to remain with them long term. A future challenge for many businesses will be determining whom to keep and how to keep them.

Changing supervisory relationships. The physical distance of many employees from their supervisors has resulted in new styles of "hands off" supervision. Often employees must act independently and direct their own work because there is no supervisor physically present, or the supervisor who is close by supervises too many employees to assist in making work decisions for all of his or her direct reports. In addition, in place of traditional command-and-control supervisory styles, more collegial styles are emerging. Many employees in today's workplace expect to participate in important decisions regarding their work.

Keeping Performance Management Effective in the 21st Century

Those of us who are responsible for designing and implementing performance management systems should attend to the changes in the workplace and the worker population discussed above, along with other changes that alter work and the context in which it is performed. In some cases, we should continue and expand the use of current best practices; in others, we must develop new processes that will help ensure effective job performance. In many cases, the goal of the performance management system remains constant. What is new is the way in which that goal should be accomplished. Importantly, those of us who design performance management systems must remember that all members of the workforce are not equally skilled or may not possess the same values and interests. What is best practice for one group of employees may not be effective for another. The next section of this chapter highlights the impact that many workplace and worker changes will have on performance management systems and recommends possible approaches that can be taken to deal with them in an effective manner.

Performance management programs must guide the behavior of employees. Since the inception of formal performance management programs, a fundamental criterion of effective systems has been an explanation of what good performance looks like. Unless the employer can communicate expectations clearly, workers are unlikely to achieve the goals set for them. Although such programs are currently in place in many organizations, these programs may need to be adapted in the future to ensure these expectations continue to be effectively communicated to the target worker.

The workforce trends mentioned above have numerous implications for how employee behavior is directed. For example, programs that explain work requirements and standards of performance using written English may need to be adapted for the non-English-speaking worker or even the worker who is illiterate.

Technology may be a more efficient way to communicate the requirements of jobs that are constantly changing. Programs that once concentrated solely on how work is performed may need to be expanded to include information concerning when work is to be performed and what the boundaries of appropriate behavior are. Some capable employees who lack strong role models will also need assistance understanding what acceptable work behaviors are. Some workers with differing values must learn that their employer has a different set of values that require different forms of work behavior. Similarly, feedback mechanisms must be designed to convey information back to employees in a manner that employees understand.

In teams composed of widely dispersed members, the team manager may be challenged to find a medium and a time to communicate with each employee. Time for interactive discussion of work issues among all team members may be even more difficult to find. Face-to-face meetings may be difficult if not impossible. Technologically enhanced communications such as conference calls and web-based presentations may lack key features for team building, such as time for informal interactions that allow team members to get know one another. Although there are no easy solutions, employers might consider combining several of these options. For example, a team might have a face-to-face meeting once a year that is supplemented by monthly conference calls at the most reasonable time and weekly emails.

The employer must also take into consideration the motivating effects of such communications, particularly when work is not the primary focus of the employee or when the labor market is competitive and employees can easily find other employment. Obviously, the employer must avoid offending employees. At the same time, there must be a motivating component to these communications that encourages employees to stay with the job and to improve and develop skills. For example, an employer might describe what the employee is expected to do and what the rewards for competent performance are. In addition, the employer might describe what career paths are available and what the benefits to those jobs are.

Performance management processes must motivate employees to set and achieve work goals that are beneficial to the company and may not be congruent with the employee's values. Performance management programs have long been used to shape employee behavior; however, in the past, employer and employee often shared similar values and goals. Employers assumed that many of their workers aspired to jobs of greater responsibility and were motivated by the compensation that career progress brought, and the remainder were committed to performing well consistently. Today, many workers place a great deal of value on things other than their jobs and financial remuneration. Placing a high value on family or personal time may inhibit employees from committing the time required to develop the complex knowledge and skills that are requisite for higher-level jobs. In some cases, achieving competence in an area may not be valued as much as personal time or pursuit of other outside interests. When jobs are plentiful, the allure of another, less demanding job may be strong. When the traditional bonds to a company such as pensions and public expectations of loyalty fray, the desire to stay put can become particularly tenuous. At times, some organizations will choose whether they deal with the problems of motivating their workforce, adapting their work to the values of their employees, or the problems of constantly dealing with turnover and replacing the workforce. One approach, when workers are marginally invested in their jobs and the supply of competent workers is low, is to incorporate both educational and motivational components in the performance management system to explain the costs and benefits of different jobs and career paths. Employers may also explain how various aspects of performance further the pursuit of personal interests. For example, an employer might stress how good work on an employee's part leads to high levels of corporate performance, which in turn assures job security. Job security presumably is a benefit to those whose primary interest is providing for their families.

As always, the supervisor who provides performance feedback will need the skills to accurately assess his or her employees' current abilities as well as provide accurate information about the possibilities for the future. In addition, the manager must understand the requirements of other jobs so that his or her coaching directs the employee in appropriate ways. The process of developing the skill sets of a worker who is doubtful about the rewards of doing so will not be a simple one or one guaranteed to succeed. Another significant component of the manager's responsibilities will be to assist the individual employee in setting goals related to skill development and continuously pursuing them.

Tools within the performance management system to motivate employees can take many forms. Perhaps the most fundamental is to train managers extensively in the requirements of an array of jobs, the evaluation of competencies, provision of constructive feedback, effective means of developing competency, and so forth. Because of the increasing demands on supervisors, relying solely on supervisors to inform and motivate subordinates may not be sufficient, and the coaching relationship will need to be supplemented with other tools such as web-based career planning sites that contain information about job requirements and development opportunities.

Some employers find that their motivational efforts are not sufficient to counteract the effects of differing value systems. Consequently, they try to align work requirements with employee needs. For example, they lower their expectations regarding how many hours should be devoted to work and when and where those hours should be worked.

Performance management processes need to incorporate the technological tools with which workers and supervisors are comfortable. Technology is the most notable recent workplace change. It has changed the nature of how work is performed as well as *what* work is performed. At this point, an entire generation has been raised using sophisticated technological tools and the Internet. More recent entrants into the workforce are comfortable with an array of digital devices and expect the immediacy of communications they offer. Many aspects of performance management systems have already incorporated technology; however, to remain effective and to foster user buy-in, performance management processes will need to incorporate technology and its many tools.

In many organizations, performance evaluations are administered electronically, which eases the administrative burden and allows for tracking of objective performance data. Communications about the way in which the work should be performed, the criteria against which performance will be evaluated, and the actual performance results can be accessed by the employee electronically and on demand. Goal-setting and follow-up activities can be electronically recorded, and tracking documentation can be easily accessed and maintained. Record-keeping for administrative performance assessments and evaluations of those data, such as adverse impact analyses, between-person evaluations, and identification of organizational strengths and weaknesses can be aided through technology. To be effective, performance management must continue to use technology to enhance the performance management processes. Moreover, performance management programs must adapt to the continual stream of new technology available. For example, text messaging and podcasts might be used to instruct employees or remind managers of their supervisory responsibilities.

The potential of using technology in performance management systems has not been fully explored, and the ways in which technology can aid both the employee and the supervisor in fostering development and sustaining high levels of performance is not completely defined. However, it seems reasonable to speculate that technology can facilitate more than simple data storage and reporting. One promising area is accurate evaluations. For example, future performance evaluation processes might be "computer adaptive." A supervisor might rate employees on a series of behavioral descriptors representing each dimension until an accurate evaluation of ability is established.

Despite the vast potential of technology for improving performance management systems, it is important to remember that a segment of the American workforce remains functionally or technologically illiterate. Some lack the basic skills to use technology-enhanced tools effectively; others lack the familiarity with technology or the access to use such tools effectively. Consequently, organizations that use components of their performance management system based on technology must take into account that such tools may be inaccessible to a portion of the workforce and seek more appropriate alternatives.

While technology appears to be a panacea for many of the problems created by new work arrangements, it is also important to note that technology is not always a cost-effective option for all organizations. Smaller organizations may not be able to afford the initial investment. Larger organizations may not be able to afford the continual updates and maintenance of the system. Good systems will not be effective if they are not populated with information relevant to the organization and its jobs.

Performance management processes must respond to workers' expectations of timely performance feedback. Many workers are used to timely access to web-based, job-related information such as training modules, job aids, and performance data (for example, production figures, sales volumes). Consequently, many expect continuous capturing and reporting of performance information and timely performance feedback. The days of a once-a-year review of an employee's performance based on the supervisor's memory of events that happened months prior to the feedback session may be gone. Employees can legitimately expect that supervisors document performance via technology regularly and provide feedback at frequent intervals.

Timely performance feedback is closely tied to the use of technology. Examples of technology-enabled feedback might include electronic capturing of production data that is continuously updated and accessible to the employee and the supervisor or automatic reporting that provides performance data regularly. Technology may also enable regular discussion sessions between supervisor and employee as well as with remote team members. Some organizations use weekly telephone calls to provide feedback and direction for the future.

The availability of almost continuous performance feedback may have a downside, particularly for employees with low skills or low levels of commitment. Instead of providing information that serves to guide future performance, frequent performance data may be perceived as overly intrusive—"Big Brother" monitoring every action an employee takes. Others may be overwhelmed by the amount of information available and lack the ability to process all of it and identify the important trends.

Performance management processes must take into account the difficulties posed by the lack of opportunity to observe performance. Because many employees will not work in the same place as their supervisors or on the same schedule, direct observation of performance will become more difficult. This lack of contact is more problematic in service work than in production work. Although products can be inspected after they are produced, services are harder to evaluate unless directly observed. When the supervisor cannot monitor work directly, collection of different forms of performance data than have been used in the past (for example, customer surveys or self-report data) may be useful in evaluating and managing performance. In some cases, the monitoring process itself may be outsourced to firms that provide "secret shoppers" or professional monitors who can listen to customer interactions on the telephone and rate the employee.

Multi-rater feedback may supplement a single supervisor's evaluation because it can solicit information from those who have actually interacted with the employee. Because there are still open questions about the use of multi-rater feedback for performance evaluation, research needs to focus on how to gather accurate performance information from peers and direct reports.

Performance management processes must communicate work standards and performance feedback to employees who are widely dispersed. Another challenge to face in the design of performance management systems in the future is the effective communication of performance-related information to employees who work in different locations from their supervisors or who work on different schedules. Therefore, in addition to retooling the design of performance management systems themselves, the designers of performance management programs must also determine the medium for effective communication to support those systems.

To date, little research has explored the effects of alternatives to face-to-face feedback on performance. Although technology-based forms of communication have the important feature of immediacy, many alternatives have their drawbacks. Telephone communications lack the visual cues that face-to-face conversations have. Video teleconferencing does not always produce high-quality images, can lack privacy, and is subject to technological glitches that affect the continuity of the discussion. Emails often cannot convey the tone implied. Feedback-givers have to examine the pros and cons of using alternatives to face-to-face communication.

Distributing information on work standards and expectations via technology also has pros and cons. On the positive side, such information is readily available and can be easily updated.

Less positively, many workers are not comfortable accessing and searching informational databases. The lack of opportunity to discuss performance issues interactively is often a negative feature. Many sites allow the user to pose questions, but answers may take some time and may be a particular drawback for those who lack the time to return to a site repeatedly. The information on most sites lacks the depth and richness of information that might come from a supervisor's personal experiences.

Workers in different time zones often have no time during "normal business hours" when they can discuss work plans together in "real time." Alternatives to rotating the time of meetings to minimize the effect on some employees' personal time include a sequence of meetings on the same topic or taping the original meeting so that it can be shown at more convenient times.

Performance management processes need to take into account varying standards of performance across locations. Employers, particularly global employers, may find that performance standards for jobs of similar or identical titles differ by work location. In some cases, this is because the job requirements are actually different. In other cases, cultural norms may affect performance standards. Regardless of the cause of varying standards, effective performance management requires a clear statement of job requirements and the standards against which performance will be measured.

Therefore, as employers expand operations, whether within a country or around the globe, they must define the fundamental requirements of the job—regardless of where the job is performed. A supplemental task is to identify any differences in job requirements based on a particular work location. For example, a regional office in the United States may require its salespeople only to sell, while another regional office in the United States expects them to participate in customer training as well as sell. A regional office outside the United States may require its sales force to participate in the installation of the equipment they sell. Another regional office may expect a salesperson to visit each client every month to ensure the equipment is properly functioning. In the United States, sales representatives may be expected to entertain clients. In Eastern Europe, meals and entertainment may be ethically unacceptable. Sales, training, installation of equipment, and even client visits and entertainment are all requirements of a sales job, but not of all sales jobs in all locations. Thus, performance management systems may need to be malleable enough to incorporate the common elements of a job as well as the elements that are specific to a particular area or location.

Performance management processes need to take into account varying standards of performance across types of work arrangements for employees. In addition to the more traditional full-time or part-time worker, an employee may also work for an organization under a number of other arrangements, ranging from a "permalancer" (a long-term, contract employee) to "temp-to-perm" (a worker who is hired as a temporary worker in anticipation of a permanent, full-time position becoming available) to a consultant or contractor (a worker who performs a defined set of tasks and who is usually an employee of another firm or self-employed). Successful organizations will make clear their expectations for performance for each type of employee. Contracts will often specify performance expectations and deadlines, but feedback, development, and coaching are rarely provided. It merits noting that setting standards for workers performing under some types of work arrangements raises significant co-employment issues and legal liability. Nevertheless, the organization hiring the subcontracting firm must carefully set standards and clearly communicate them.

Performance management programs must incorporate employee preferences and be sensitive to cultural differences among employees. Another outcome of global expansion is the increase in differing expectations employees may have concerning performance management. Although cultural differences in this respect are not as great as once thought, differences in preferences for how goals are set, comfort in planning and organizing work, and styles for giving feedback and setting expectations about receiving it do exist. For example, in some cultures giving direct critical feedback may not be commonly acceptable. In others, giving feedback to supervisors or peers may not be considered acceptable.

As companies develop an international workforce, future performance management systems must be flexible enough to adapt to cultural differences while maintaining some common features and standards across the corporation. Cross-cultural research on performance management programs that could be used to guide these changes is not plentiful, so the developers must consider local customs and emphasize cultural sensitivity to the managers who provide performance feedback. Similarly, the performance management system may need to place special emphasis on aspects of the system that are unfamiliar or uncommon in the cultures in which it is being implemented. To eliminate bias and unfair treatment, training in cross-cultural expectations will be necessary in many settings, and evaluation of managers on their cultural sensitivity may be warranted.

Performance management programs must allow for the provision of critical or negative feedback in a positive, motivating way to retain and develop employees. The difficulty of finding and training good employees in the future heightens the importance that must be placed on retaining them. Employees who feel devalued by performance feedback have always been at risk to leave to find an employer who demonstrates a higher level of respect for the individual. When the labor supply was plentiful, many of these employees were replaceable. As the labor supply tightens, retaining skilled employees becomes more important.

As in the past, performance management programs of the future must be sensitive to the needs of employees and clear in communicating their value to the organization. We are not advocating avoiding negative feedback; rather we suggest that it be provided in a way that will be understood and accepted by the employee and used constructively. The ultimate goal is to motivate the employee to do a better job. In addition to ensuring the performance management program emphasizes employee value, supervisors may need special training to provide feedback effectively.

Performance management programs must be aligned with the ways in which jobs are defined. Many workers today are expected to have broad skill sets and perform an array of tasks in one job that may once have been associated with several different jobs. Thus, these workers must possess a high degree of flexibility and quickly shift from one task to another. Consequently, performance management systems must also adapt to the changing ways in which jobs are constituted and the characteristics of the workers who must perform them.

Performance management systems might be adjusted in multiple ways to deal with broadly defined, shifting jobs. One obvious way to do this is to ensure that the content of measured performance dimensions accurately reflects the array of responsibilities inherent in the position. Other important components of successful performance to evaluate include the ability to acquire new skills and learn various tasks quickly and the ways in which employees adjusts to new assignments. This will require performance evaluation at intervals consistent with the changes in the job. For example, rather than waiting twelve months, evaluation and feedback would be provided as the employee completes a significant work assignment and moves to another.

Performance management programs must be aligned with corporate goals and strategies. Ideally, an individual's goals support those of the individual's group, which in turn support the goals of broader groups—and ultimately those of the entire organization. Measurement tools such as balanced scorecards and dashboards may be used to show the extent to which the individual has met his or her own goals and contributed to those of the broader organization. Such tools may also motivate employees by showing the results of their individual contributions.

Performance management programs need to address the performance of individuals and teams of individuals who share jobs or work cooperatively to achieve their goals. As more organizations incorporate teamwork, they must find ways to evaluate each employee's individual work accomplishments and contribution to the team as well as assess overall team performance.

In the past, performance management systems have tended to address the performance of the individual. Some systems have tried to evaluate the individual's contribution to the team, but often this involved only the supervisor's perspective rather than that of other team members. Multi-rater feedback can also be used to evaluate an individual's contribution to a team. As noted above, however, there are important concerns about collecting performance information about an individual from his or her peers, and more research is required to define the conditions under which such data are best collected and used.

It is common to assess the productivity of a team; however, evaluation of how the team functioned in producing results is more rare. For example, a team is more likely to be evaluated on how much it produced or how many customer inquiries it handled than on the extent to which team members shared information or helped those who had an excessive workload. As teams become a more integral unit of the organizational structure, performance management systems must address how to evaluate an employee's contribution as an individual and as a team member.

A special case of teamwork is the job-sharing arrangement described above. Performance management systems must be sensitive enough to determine who is responsible for what; adapted to evaluate the job sharers and their respective contributions; and broad enough to develop both people in the job-sharing arrangement.

Performance management plans must recognize employee contributions with rewards that are valued by the employee. All workers expect to be rewarded and recognized for their efforts. But, compared with their counterparts today, designers of performance management systems of yesterday were more likely to share the same value systems as employees being evaluated. As today's workforce diversifies, the values individuals place on traditional rewards such as money and promotions are likely to vary considerably. The rewards must conform to the employees' values. Unfortunately, this is not simply a matter of determining what the new value system is. Each employee has a different set of values, and these may change over time. How this difference could be accommodated is not clear. One possibility is a cafeteria-style reward plan similar to those that are offered in many benefits packages. An employee might choose a monetary bonus or time off as a reward. Those employees who value their status as subject-matter experts may have the option of choosing management or expert tracks for career progression.

Performance management programs must continue to emphasize the importance of corporate values and ethical behavior. Many organizations now see benefits in emphasizing corporate values to focus employees on the mission of the organization and define what is acceptable behavior and what is not. Ethical behavior in U.S. corporations has received more scrutiny in the aftermath of a number of corporate scandals and subsequent litigation (for example, Enron and WorldCom) as well as passage of the Sarbanes-Oxley Act. Difficult to observe, the requirement for ethical behavior must be regularly communicated and the results evaluated.

For corporate values and ethical behavior to be meaningful to each employee, performance management programs must define how they have been incorporated into the workplace and what the implications are in terms of the employees' work behavior. It will not be enough to say what the values are; supervisors must help to interpret how corporate values are displayed in the context of employees' work and, certainly, must serve as role models themselves.

Performance management programs must incorporate non-task expectations and develop standards of success for them. Many jobs have responsibilities and expectations that go beyond actual job requirements. In recent years, the value of contextual performance or organizational citizenship behaviors (OCBs) to overall organizational functioning has been highlighted. In addition, some organizations have expectations about employee behavior outside of work, and performance management systems must serve to communicate what they are and set standards of success so that such behavior can be evaluated.

Although, by definition, OCBs are not always required, they add significantly to the functioning and harmony of a work group. Often performance evaluation focuses only on job requirements and ignores the OCBs. But if an organization wants employees to display them, they must communicate them to the employees, evaluate them, and reinforce them. Similarly, some organizations require employees to engage in community service or continuous learning. Again, if the organization wants employees to engage in this kind of behavior, the performance management systems must emphasize and, as appropriate, reward it.

Conclusion

In summary, three clear trends that affect performance management systems have emerged. First, individual values and needs are diverse and changing, and the heterogeneity of the workforce is increasing. Second, technology is embedded into almost every aspect of work, including performance management. Third, global expansion is increasing the diversity of employees and the cultural contexts in which they work. For performance management systems to be aligned with organizational goals and individual needs, they must consider all three trends.

Table 16.1 provides a summary of prevalent changes in worker attitudes and workplace requirements, the effects these changes have on how work is performed, and the implications they have for performance management systems. It is important to note the contradictions. For example, we are saying that employers will work to retain qualified employees and will, at the same time, be quick to release employees who are no longer needed. Both are true some of the time for some employers. The professionals who design performance management systems can no longer assume that employees are willing to follow the employer's rules and must assume that performance management programs will be tailored to the particular approach that employers take for managing their human resources.

Performance management programs must be adaptable to meet the changing requirements of the workplace and the characteristics of the employees who work there. In many cases, this means continuing best practices in performance management or extending them. In other cases, changes in the workforce and workplace require more radical changes in performance management programs. The professionals responsible for developing these programs must stay abreast of the changes in workplace trends and the attitudes and skills of the workforce. In addition, they must incorporate psychological research such as that described in this book. Perhaps most importantly, industrial and organizational psychologists who work in this area must recognize that continuing change is a given and that the pace of work-related changes will continue to escalate.

References

Gross, A., & Minot, J. (2008). Workforce issues in India: HR needs to understand. http://www2.shrm.org/India/07_understand.asp accessed 8/10/08.

Hankin, H. (2005). *The new workforce: Five sweeping trends that will shape your company's future.* New York: AMACOM.

Johnston, W. B., & Packer, A. E. (1987). *Workforce 2000: Work and workers for the twenty-first century.* Indianapolis: Hudson Institute.

Karoly, L. A., & Panis, C. W. A. (2004). *The 21st century at work: Forces shaping the future workforce and workplace in the United States.* Santa Monica, CA: Rand.

CHAPTER 17

BEST PRACTICES IN PERFORMANCE MANAGEMENT

James W. Smither and Manuel London

Over the past few years, practitioners talk less of "performance appraisal" and more of "performance management." In some instances, this appears to be a change in name only. But in many instances, it reflects a paradigm shift from thinking of performance appraisal as a discrete event to a continuous process of performance management (Latham & Mann, 2006; Latham, Almost, Mann, & Moore, 2005). Most definitions of performance management (for example, Aguinis, 2009; Aguinis & Pierce, 2008; Cascio, 2006; den Hartog, Boselie, & Paauwe, 2004; Hedge & Borman, 2008) include a common set of core elements: goal setting, feedback, employee development (and coaching), performance evaluation, and rewarding performance. In this chapter, we draw on the insights and recommendations of the authors who contributed chapters to this book, as well as other research, to develop a sketch of best practices in performance management.

What Is Job Performance?

Before discussing best practices, it is useful to first clarify what we mean by "performance." Campbell, McCloy, Oppler, and Sager (1993, pp. 40–41) stated that performance is

"something that people actually do and can be observed. . . .
Performance is what the organization hires one to do, and do well.
Performance is not the consequence or result of action, it is the
action itself."

In applied settings, performance management encompasses task
performance, contextual performance (Borman & Motowidlo, 1993)
and organizational citizenship behaviors (Podsakoff, Ahearne,
& MacKenzie, 1997), adaptive performance (that is, adapting to
complex, novel, turbulent, or unpredictable work environments),
and dealing with counterproductive behaviors (such as antisocial
behavior, incivility, sabotaging equipment, stealing from the company, blaming or gossiping about co-workers, deviant behaviors,
withholding effort), and changes in performance over time (that
is, performance trends; Reb & Cropanzano, 2007; Schmitt, Cortina,
Ingerick, & Wiechmann, 2003).

Goals

A central premise of performance management systems is that
individual (and team) goals need to be closely aligned with higher-
level organizational goals. For example, Schiemann (Chapter 2 in
this book) describes how Continental Airlines selected on-time performance to be an organization-wide goal in part because so many
different roles (for example, logistics, pilots, flight attendants, gate
agents, maintenance, baggage handlers) can affect on-time performance. On-time performance thereby served as a unifying goal
for different functional groups across the organization.

One trend related to organizational goal setting is the use of
balanced scorecards. Kaplan and Norton's (1992, 1996) balanced
scorecard framework is based on the premise that focusing only
on financial goals and measures is insufficient because such measures are lag indicators (that is, they describe merely the outcomes
of leaders' past actions) and can promote behavior that sacrifices
long-term value for short-term performance. Balanced scorecards select a limited number of critical measures within each of
four perspectives (financial, customer, internal processes, learning
and innovation). Recently, the balanced scorecard concept has
been extended to include strategy maps (Kaplan & Norton, 2004),

which show the cause-and-effect relationships among the multiple measures on a balanced scorecard including leads, lags, and feedback loops. Effective balanced scorecards are closely linked to the organization's strategy so that people can understand the strategy by looking only at the scorecard and its strategy map (Kaplan & Norton, 2001, 2004). Balanced scorecards heighten awareness of the potential tradeoffs among various goals and thereby help ensure that the organization does not optimize one goal (for example, profit) at the expense of another (for example, customer satisfaction; Schiemann, Chapter 2 in this book). In sum, balanced scorecards can provide an overarching framework that drives and aligns organizational, department, team, and individual goal setting. For example, in some organizations, each employee and each team explicitly links goals to specific elements in the organization's balanced scorecard.

Goal setting at the individual and team levels is a central element of effective performance management (Latham & Mann, 2006; Heslin, Carson, & VandeWalle, Chapter 3 in this book). Perhaps the most central principle of goal-setting theory, illustrated in hundreds of studies, is that specific, difficult goals lead to higher performance than "do your best" goals (Locke & Latham, 1990). Moreover, specific, difficult goals have positive effects not only for individuals and teams but also for organizations (Baum, Locke, & Smith, 2001; Rodgers & Hunter, 1991). The benefits of goals occur because goals focus employees' attention on a specific objective (rather than other activities), lead to higher levels of effort to attain those objectives, enhance persistence in the face of setbacks and obstacles, and stimulate employees to develop new approaches and strategies when faced with complex tasks (Latham, 2004; Locke & Latham, 2002, Heslin, Carson, & VandeWalle, Chapter 3 in this book).

Self-efficacy (that is, the employee's belief that he or she can attain the goal) also plays a central role in goal setting and attainment (Bandura, 1986). Self-efficacy can be enhanced by providing the employee with mastery experiences (for example, by breaking down complex tasks into smaller, easier steps that gradually become more challenging), enabling the employee to observe a role model (who is perceived as similar to the employee on a number of attributes) successfully perform the task, and providing verbal encouragement that the employee has the ability to learn and perform the task successfully (Heslin, Carson, & VandeWalle, Chapter 3 in this book). Goal commitment can be strengthened in several ways (Locke & Latham, 2002; Heslin, Carson, & VandeWalle, Chapter 3 in this book), including having people make a public commitment to the goal (Cialdini, 2001), increasing self-efficacy, and increasing the attractiveness of outcomes associated with goal attainment (for example, by communicating a compelling vision, providing monetary incentives, or changing employees' perceptions concerning the consequences of attaining or not attaining the goal; Latham, 2001).

The benefits of difficult goals on performance are diminished when task complexity is high (for example, when the task involves many acts and information cues that are interrelated and change over time) (Wood, Mento, & Locke, 1987). Assigning challenging distal goals during the early stages of skill acquisition on a complex task can lead to decrements in performance (Kanfer & Ackerman, 1989). However, proximal (that is, short-term, intermediate) goals can be helpful (when coupled with distal goals) during the early stages of skills acquisition on complex tasks (Latham & Seijts, 1999). Feedback related to proximal goals can provide (a) markers of progress (thereby increasing self-efficacy) and (b) information that can help people change strategies when it appears that their current task strategies are suboptimal (Latham & Seijts, 1999). Providing learning goals during the early stages of skills acquisition on complex tasks can also be helpful because such goals direct attention to learning the task rather than worrying about a distal performance outcome (Noel & Latham, 2006; Winters & Latham, 1996).

A meta-analysis by Rodgers and Hunter (1991) found that the widely used performance management approach called management by objectives (MBO), which combines goal setting, participation in decision making, and objective feedback, was associated with productivity gains in sixty-eight out of seventy studies. Also, when top management's commitment to MBO was high, the average gain in productivity was 56 percent, versus only 6 percent when commitment from top management was low.

Feedback

Feedback plays a vital role in performance management in that, without feedback, the effect of goals on performance is diminished (Erez, 1977; Locke & Latham, 1990; Neubert, 1998). Feedback can serve both an informational purpose and a motivational purpose (Ilgen, Fisher, & Taylor, 1979).

Yet feedback does not always enhance performance. In their review of performance feedback in organizational settings, Alvero, Bucklin, and Austin (2001) found that feedback yielded desired and consistent effects in 58 percent of the sixty-four applications they reviewed, mixed effects (that is, desired effects in some, but not all, of the participants, settings, and/or behaviors analyzed) in 41 percent of the applications, and no effects in only 1 percent of the applications. In a widely cited meta-analysis, Kluger and DeNisi (1996) found that feedback interventions, on average, improved performance ($d = .41$); however, in about one-third of the studies examined, feedback had a negative effect on performance. There was also large variability among effect sizes, and this variability could not be explained by feedback sign (that is, positive versus negative feedback), thereby suggesting that positive feedback leads to performance improvement for some people (or in some situations), whereas negative feedback leads to performance improvement for other people (or in other situations).

Delivering Feedback

Kluger and DeNisi (1996) found that feedback that directs the recipient's attention to the task is more effective than feedback that directs the recipient's attention to the self and away from the task. Viswesvaran (2001) summarized the conditions for appraisal feedback to have a positive effect as including a balanced review (both positive and negative) of the employee's performance, discussing no more than two limitations in one meeting, a participative style that allows the employee to state his or her views, and good ongoing communication between the supervisor and employee outside of the appraisal meeting. Ilgen and Davis (2000) have argued that the most important issue when providing negative feedback is to strike a balance so that it becomes possible for the recipient to accept responsibility for performance that did not meet expectations, while at the same time not lowering the recipient's self-concept.

Multi-Source Feedback

Multi-source feedback refers to collecting performance evaluations from more than one source. A variant of multi-source feedback, called 360-degree feedback, collects feedback from key constituents who represent the full circle of relevant viewpoints: supervisor(s), peers, direct reports, and in some cases customers. A meta-analysis (Smither, London, & Reilly, 2005) of twenty-four longitudinal studies found that improvement in direct report ($d = .15$), peer ($d = .05$), and supervisor ratings ($d = .15$) over time is generally small. Moderator analyses found that improvement was greater when feedback was used only for developmental purposes (rather than for administrative purposes). This review also presented a theoretical framework and reviewed empirical evidence suggesting that performance improvement is more likely for some feedback recipients than others. Specifically, improvement is most likely to occur when feedback indicates that change is necessary, recipients have a positive feedback orientation, perceive a need to change their behavior, react positively to the feedback, believe change is feasible, set appropriate goals to regulate their behavior, and take actions that lead to skill and performance improvement.

Not surprisingly, performance improvement is likely only for feedback recipients who take appropriate action. For example, Smither, London, Flautt, Vargas, and Kucine (2003) found that managers who worked with an executive coach were more likely than other managers to set specific (rather than vague) goals, to solicit ideas for improvement from their supervisors, and to improve in terms of subsequent direct report and supervisor ratings. However, the differences between managers who worked with a coach and those who did not were small in magnitude (albeit statistically significant). In a five-year study of upward feedback, Walker and Smither (1999) found that (a) managers who met with direct reports to discuss their upward feedback improved more than other managers and (b) managers improved more in years when they discussed the previous year's feedback with direct reports than in years when they did not discuss the previous year's feedback with direct reports. Hazucha, Hezlett, and Schneider (1993) found that managers who participated in training programs and other development activities (for example, receiving coaching and feedback, reviewing progress quarterly) after receiving multi-source feedback were more likely to improve than other managers.

Employee Development

Although employee development can occur through formal training and education, in the context of performance management more emphasis is usually placed on development through ongoing coaching (usually from supervisors) and other less formal approaches to development such as mentoring, task force assignments, and learning from challenging work (Zaleska & de Menezes, 2007).

The value of formal organizational training has been widely documented. A comprehensive meta-analysis of the impact of organizational training (Arthur, Bennett, Edens, & Bell, 2003) found medium to large effect sizes for reaction ($d = .60$), learning ($d = .63$), behavior ($d = .62$), and results ($d = .62$) criteria, as well as positive effects for enhancing cognitive, psychomotor, and interpersonal skills. The economic utility (positive return on investment) of corporate training has also been demonstrated (Morrow, Jarrett, & Rupinski, 1997). Despite the widespread positive effects usually associated with formal training, some confidence intervals from meta-analyses include zero indicating that not all training is effective.

A meta-analysis by Keith and Frese (2008) found that error management training (EMT), which encourages learners to make errors during training and to view errors as opportunities to learn what does not work, was more effective ($d = 0.44$) for post-training transfer performance (but not for within-training performance) than error avoidant training or exploratory training without error encouragement. EMT was especially effective for performance on adaptive tasks (that is, novel problems that require the development of new solutions) relative to analogical tasks (that are similar or analogous to the training task).

Self-management training has also been shown to increase performance as well as self-efficacy (Frayne & Geringer, 2000) and decrease absenteeism (Frayne & Latham, 1987; Latham & Frayne, 1989). It involves (1) identifying the behaviors to modify, (2) establishing goals for those behaviors, (3) maintaining a record of progress toward goal attainment, (4) establishing self-rewards and self-punishments for performance relative to goals, (5) identifying high-risk situations that might frustrate goal attainment, and (6) preparing a written contract with oneself that lists goals, plans, contingencies, and so on.

Coaching

The shift in emphasis from performance appraisal (a discrete event) to performance management (a continuous process) has focused attention on the important role of coaching in employee performance and development (Latham, Almost, Mann, & Moore, 2005). Over sixty years ago, Lewis referred to coaching as "really just good supervision" (1947, p. 316). And being an effective coach continues to be viewed as an essential feature of effective management (Hamlin, Ellinger, & Beattie, 2006).

Peterson (Chapter 4 in this book) argues that organizations should use coaching in an organized, systematic manner to address specific business needs (for example, accelerating the development of high-potential managers, on-boarding new leaders, driving a change in culture). Organizations can also specify criteria for who delivers coaching, for who receives coaching, and for the coaching process itself. Ideally, coaching is integrated into the organization's overall talent management strategy, and investments in coaching are aligned with business strategy.

Peterson emphasizes that effective coaching involves (1) a working relationship between the coach and person that is characterized by trust, acceptance, and understanding; (2) helping the recipient develop insight about critical success factors and how others perceive the recipient relative to those factors; (3) building the recipient's motivation to change by clarifying personal and organizational reasons for change and focusing on small, easy steps to initiate the process; (4) enhancing the recipient's capabilities by sharing new ideas and best practices, pointing to useful learning resources and opportunities, and exploring alternative ways to handle difficult situations; (5) facilitating application of new skills to specific situations in which change is appropriate (that is, real-world practice); (6) encouraging the recipient to make specific commitments for action, following up on the person's commitments, and encouraging the person to seek feedback from others; and (7) helping the recipient to anticipate and address barriers while working with senior leaders to create a supportive climate for development.

There is some evidence that coaching skills can be developed. For example, a program designed to enhance managers' coaching skills had a positive effect on five of eight target behaviors (Graham, Wedman, & Garvin-Kester, 1993). Heslin and colleagues (Heslin, Latham, & VandeWalle, 2005) found that managers who held incremental beliefs (that is, ability is malleable and can therefore be developed with effort) were more likely than managers who held entity beliefs (that is, ability is fixed, innate, and unalterable) to recognize both improvements and declines in employee performance. In a separate study, these authors used a ninety-minute workshop based on self-persuasion techniques (Aronson, 1999) to help participants who initially held entity beliefs to acquire incremental beliefs and to sustain those beliefs over a six-week period. This change led to greater acknowledgement of improvement in employee performance than was exhibited by entity theorists in a placebo control group. They also found that inducing incremental beliefs increased entity theorist managers' willingness to coach an employee who was performing poorly, as well as the quantity and quality of their performance improvement suggestions (Heslin & VandeWalle, 2008; Heslin, VandeWalle, & Latham, 2006).

A number of studies have found evidence supporting the value of coaching. For example, a survey by Ellinger, Ellinger, and Keller (2003) found that supervisory coaching behaviors (such as providing and asking for feedback, helping employees think through issues by asking questions rather than providing solutions, setting expectations, providing resources) were positively related to employee job satisfaction and performance (also see Acosta-Amad & Brethower, 1992; Bennett, 1987; Cannon & Edmondson, 2001; Edmondson, 1999; Gyllensten & Palmer, 2005; Konczak, Stelly, & Trusty, 2000; Rappe & Zwick, 2007; Scandura, 1992).

More recent theoretical and empirical work suggests that coaching is likely to be effective in some settings but not in others. For example, Hackman and Wageman's (2005) theory of team coaching proposes that coaching interventions that focus on team effort, strategy, and knowledge and skill will facilitate team effectiveness more than interventions that focus on members' interpersonal relationships. Also, they suggest that timing is important in determining the optimal type of coaching such that motivational coaching will be most helpful at the beginning of a performance period, consultative coaching will be most helpful at the midpoint of a performance period, and educational coaching (that is, helping the team capture what can be learned from the collective work just completed) will be most helpful after performance activities have been completed. In a study of external leadership of self-managing teams, Morgeson (2005) found that supportive coaching (reinforcing the team for its self-management behaviors and thereby fostering a sense of competence and independence in the team without becoming directly involved in the team's task work) was positively related to perceptions of leader effectiveness, however active coaching (that is, becoming directly involved in helping the team perform its work) and leader sense making (that is, the leader interpreting events for the team) were negatively related to satisfaction with leadership (but positively related to perceptions of leader effectiveness when disruptive events occur).

Executive Coaching

Executive coaching has been defined as a short- to medium-term relationship between an executive and a consultant with the purpose of improving the executive's work effectiveness (Feldman & Lankau, 2005). Executive coaching can take a number of different forms. Some executives use coaching to learn specific skills, others to improve performance on the job or to prepare for advancement in business or professional life, and still others to support broader purposes, such as an executive's agenda for major organizational change (Witherspoon & White, 1996). Generally, executive coaching includes several stages, such as establishing the coaching relationship, data gathering (about the executive and the organization), feedback (presenting the executive with the results of the data gathered from interviews, psychological assessments, multi-source feedback, and so forth), goal setting, periodic coaching sessions, and evaluation (to determine progress toward the goals of coaching) (Feldman & Lankau, 2005; Smither & Reilly, 2001). Although human resource professionals who sponsor executive coaching have positive perceptions of its benefits (Dagley, 2006), the vast majority of articles about executive coaching have relied on case studies or vignettes as illustrations or sources of evidence, and only a small number of empirical studies have examined the impact of executive coaching (Feldman & Lankau, 2005). Of these, many have relied on self-reports and surveys of coaching recipients to evaluate the impact of coaching. These studies have found that coaching recipients perceive coaching as valuable and believe they benefited from it (for example, progress toward goals, sustained behavior change) (Evers, Brouwers, & Tomic, 2006; Feggetter, 2007; Hall, Otazo, & Hollenbeck, 1999; Hollenbeck & McCall, 1999; Kombarakaran, Yang, Baker, & Fernandes, 2008; McGovern, Lindemann, Vergara, Murphy, Barker, & Warrenfeltz, 2001; Wasylyshyn, 2003; Wasylyshyn, Gronsky, & Haas, 2006). A small number of studies have relied on somewhat more objective indicators (relative to self-reports). Olivero, Bane, and Kopelman (1997) found that a management development program and coaching increased productivity, with coaching resulting in a greater gain compared to a management development program alone. Luthans and Peterson (2003) found that a combination of 360-degree feedback and coaching was associated with improvements in co-workers' ratings of the feedback recipients (managers) and improvements in job satisfaction, organizational commitment, and turnover intentions for the managers and their employees. However, there was no control group and the design of the study also did not allow the authors to disentangle the effects of coaching from those of the 360-deree feedback. Smither, London, Flautt, Vargas, and Kucine (2003) used a quasi-experimental design to examine 1,361 managers who received multi-source feedback; 404 of those managers worked with an executive coach to review their feedback and set goals. One year later, managers who worked with an executive coach were more likely than other managers to have set specific (rather than vague) goals, solicited ideas for improvement from their supervisors, and improved more in terms of direct report and supervisor ratings. Although executive coaching had a statistically significant and positive effect, the effects sizes were quite small. Bowles, Cunningham, De La Rosa, and Picano (2007) found that middle (but not executive-level) managers who volunteered to receive eight hours of formal training followed by, on average, six to seven hours of coaching outperformed (for example, on achievement of quotas) managers who had not received the training and coaching. However, because the participants were volunteers and the coaching was combined with formal training, the impact of coaching on performance remains uncertain. Support from an external (to the team) coach was related to the emergence of shared leadership in teams, whereby leadership is distributed among team members rather than focused on a single designated leader (Carson, Tesluk, & Marrone, 2007). In sum, the limited research indicates that sponsors and recipients have favorable reactions to coaching, and some positive benefits have been found. However, due to limitations in the design of most studies, practitioners must await more research before firm conclusions about the impact of executive coaching can be drawn.

Performance Evaluation

Because objective measures of performance are not available for many jobs, subjective (for example, supervisor) ratings play a central role in evaluating employee performance. Even when objective measures are available, research has repeatedly shown that ratings of performance are only modestly related to objective measures of performance (Bommer, Johnson, Rich, Podsakoff, & Mackenzie, 1995; Cascio & Valenzi, 1978; Heneman, 1986; Kirchner, 1960; Seashore, Indik, & Georgopoulos, 1960). Although this likely reflects limitations associated with ratings, it also likely reflects problems with objective measures such as criterion deficiency and contamination. Wexley and Klimoski (1984) suggested that there is no "true" job performance. Instead, ratings and objective measures (for example, productivity) are different indicators that tap different aspects of performance.

For many decades, effort was focused on creating rating formats that might reduce rating errors. Examples include forced choice (Sisson, 1948), critical incidents (Flanagan, 1954), behaviorally anchored rating scales (Smith & Kendall, 1963), mixed standard scales (Blanz & Ghiselli, 1972), behavioral observation scales (Latham, Fay, & Saari, 1979; Latham & Wexley, 1977), and performance distribution assessment (Kane, 1986). At the same time, rater training programs focused on reducing rater errors such as halo and first impressions (Latham, Wexley, & Pursell, 1975). But a review by Landy and Farr (1980) noted that rating formats or scales had little if any effect on reducing rating errors or increasing agreement among raters. (However, rating format can have other effects. For example, raters generally prefer behavioral observation scales relative to behavioral expectation scales or trait scales; and behavioral observation scales, relative to graphic rating scales, yield higher levels of goal clarity, acceptance, and commitment (Tziner & Kopelman, 1988; Wiersma, van den Berg, & Latham, 1995).

This led to cognitive approaches to (or models of) performance appraisal (see DeNisi, 1996, for a summary) that looked at how raters recognize, attend to, and observe employee behavior (or other information related to employee performance); represent, organize, and store this information in memory; retrieve the information from memory and integrate the information to form a judgment about or evaluation of the employee. More recently, conceptual models have emphasized the important role of context and goals in appraisals (Murphy & Cleveland, 1991, 1995). For example, a meta-analysis by Jawahar and Williams (1997) found that the purpose of the appraisal influences leniency in ratings such that appraisals obtained for administrative purposes (for example, to influence pay raises or promotions) were about one-third of a standard deviation higher than those obtained for employee development or research purposes, especially when the ratings were made by practicing managers in real-world settings. Trust in the appraisal process (whether a rater believes that others in the organization will provide fair and accurate appraisals) also affects leniency in ratings (Bernardin & Orban, 1990). Raters high in agreeableness provide more lenient ratings when they expect to have a face-to-face meeting with the employee, but this effect is attenuated when using a behavior checklist rather than a graphic rating scale (Yun, Donahue, Dudley, & McFarland, 2005). Similarly, raters accountable to others with authority or higher status provide more accurate ratings compared with raters who are accountable to a lower-status audience and raters who do not have to justify their ratings (Mero, Guidice, & Brownlee, 2007).

Problems with the concept of rater errors (although long noted by some) have become more widely acknowledged. For example, in some instances, employees might perform effectively (or ineffectively) across several dimensions (or a group of employees might all be especially effective performers). In such instances, rater "errors" might actually be associated with more accurate ratings (Cooper, 1981a, 1981b). This led to a shift in rater training to increase accuracy rather than reduce errors (Bernardin & Buckley, 1981; Bernardin & Pence, 1980; Hauenstein, 1998). Such training (often referred to as "frame of reference training") generally involves familiarizing raters with the definitions and behavioral indicators of each performance dimension, providing opportunities to complete practice ratings (using either written vignettes or videos to present the performance examples), and delivering feedback concerning the accuracy of the practice ratings (by comparing them with target ratings that represent the organization's estimate of the effectiveness levels demonstrated in the performance examples). A cumulative research review by Woehr and Huffcutt (1994) showed that frame of reference training is an effective approach to increase rating accuracy.

There is no easy, practical solution to the problems associated with ratings. One approach used by many organizations is to require supervisors to share, discuss, and justify their ratings of employees with others (for example, the supervisor's manager or a panel of peers). This approach might help calibrate ratings made by different supervisors and lessen unjustifiable leniency in ratings, but as Murphy (2008) notes, it also makes raters more vulnerable to social influence effects (such as norms about rating distributions) that might actually reduce the accuracy of ratings in some instances.

Forced Distributions

During the past several years, perhaps no other aspect of performance management has garnered as much attention in the popular press as the use of forced distributions or rankings (Dominick, Chapter 12 in this book). In absolute rating systems (such as behaviorally anchored rating scales and behavioral observation scales), raters make judgments about the extent to which each employee displays specific job-related behaviors. Because all employees are evaluated relative to the same behaviors (standards), it is possible that all employees could receive the same rating. In contrast, relative rating systems, which include forced ranking or distribution systems, require raters to evaluate employees relative to one another, determining which employees are best, next best, and so on. Often, most employees are placed into one of the top three categories of a five-point rating scale (10 percent in the top category, 20 percent in the next category, 60 percent in the middle category, and the remaining 10 percent in the bottom two categories).

Advocates argue that forced distribution systems reduce or eliminate artificially inflated ratings (Taylor & Wherry, 1951), thereby enabling organizations to identify and adequately reward top performers while also holding poor performers accountable. They also argue that forced distributions are fair to poor performers because the system lets such employees know where they stand so they have an opportunity to do something about it (perhaps by moving to other organizations or jobs where they can succeed). Critics argue that forced distributions are as susceptible to favoritism, manipulation, and organizational politics as any other rating process and that they are unreasonable when the number of employees in the rating group is small. Concerns have also been raised about the effects of forced distribution systems on perceived fairness and employee morale (McBriarty, 1988) as well as legal compliance (Dominick, Chapter 12 in this book).

Emerging research suggests that more favorable reactions to forced distribution rating systems are likely to occur when (a) there are not severe consequences for poorly ranked employees, (b) the group to be ranked is reasonably large, (c) there is variability in performance among those being ranked, (d) there is a process to ensure that employees receive frequent feedback, and (e) the culture is results-oriented where success does not depend heavily on teamwork (Blume, Baldwin, & Rubin, 2007; Guralnik, Rozmarin, & So, 2004; Schleicher, Bull, & Green, 2007). In a survey of human resource professionals, Lawler (2003) found that, compared to those not using forced distributions, those using forced distributions judged their systems as better able to differentiate between levels of performance (to identify and reward top talent, identify and manage out poor performers), but also judged their systems as less effective at developing talent and less effective overall.

Rewarding Performance

Performance management systems generally seek to link rewards (for example, money or recognition) to performance. Heneman and Gresham (1998) note that pay for performance plans can focus on individual performance (merit pay, skill-based pay, piece rates, sales commissions, employee suggestion systems), team performance (team incentives, team recognition), or organizational performance (gainsharing, profit sharing, stock ownership).

One potential downside of individual-level pay for performance is that employees might see little value in cooperating with co-workers (which can create problems when cooperation would benefit the group or organization as a whole). At the team level, team incentives can be used in situations in which (a) the team produces an identifiable output and (b) it is difficult or impossible to measure the contribution of individual team members. Usually, the incentive is divided equally among team members. One downside to pay for performance at the team level is what has been referred to as "social loafing" or "free riding," where some employees limit their efforts when they believe that their individual contributions cannot or will not be assessed and others on the team will work very hard to ensure the team's success (Albanese & Van Fleet, 1985; Cooper, Dyck, & Frohlich, 1992; Heneman & von Hippel, 1995; Kidwell & Bennett, 1993; Shepperd, 1993). When individual contributions to team success can be assessed, then team rewards can be distributed proportional to those contributions. Consistent with what would be expected based on social loafing or free rider research, the size of the group moderates the effectiveness of group pay plans, with a larger impact occurring in smaller firms (Rynes, Gerhart, & Parks, 2005).

At the facility or organization level, gainsharing plans provide rewards for cost (or time) savings or revenue enhancement. Heneman and Gresham (1998) note that an attractive feature of gainsharing plans is that they pay for themselves because rewards are not distributed until costs are reduced or revenue is enhanced. Gainsharing plans generally use joint committees of employees and managers who solicit, screen, and help implement suggestions from employees. The cost savings or increased revenues are split between employees (with each employee receiving an equal amount) and management (who can reinvest the money).

Profit-sharing plans are based on the financial performance of the entire organization (as measured by a predetermined metric such as net income, return on assets, economic value added, earnings per share, or other measures) and can provide employees with the associated reward soon after the amount of profit has been determined or can defer payment until the employee retires (or a combination of both). Stock ownership and stock options can also link pay to organizational performance. One issue associated with all organization-level pay for performance plans has been referred to as the "line of sight' problem where employees see little connection between their performance and the performance of the organization as a whole (Heneman & Gresham, 1998). This is especially likely to be a problem when poor organizational performance and hence low plan payouts are perceived as being due to factors beyond employees' control such as poor decisions of executives (Rynes, Gerhart, & Parks, 2005).

Heneman and Gresham also argue that pay for performance plans should be matched to business objectives. For example, skill-based pay plans would be a good fit for employee development objectives; individual plans (for example, piece rate) and gainsharing plans would be a good fit for productivity (for example, revenue enhancement or cost reduction) objectives; team recognition and team incentives would be a good fit for teamwork objectives; and profit sharing would be a good fit for profit objectives.

Many organizations link pay to performance at multiple levels (merit pay, team incentives or recognition, and profit sharing) in an attempt retain the advantages of each approach while minimizing its potential negative consequences (Rynes, Gerhart, & Parks, 2005). Unfortunately, little research exists concerning the consequences of combining several approaches (for exceptions, see Crown & Rosse, 1995, and Wageman, 1995).

Research on Pay for Performance

In a survey of Fortune 500 companies, Lawler (2003) found that respondents thought that performance management systems are more effective when there is a strong connection between appraisals and rewards (salary increases, bonuses, stock awards). Research generally supports this belief. However, exempt employees tend to be more supportive of performance based pay than nonexempt employees, who are more supportive of pay based on seniority and cost of living (Heneman, 1992).

Generally, individual-level plans (piece rate, sales commissions) have larger effects on productivity than unit-level plans (such as gainsharing), which in turn have a greater impact than corporate-wide plans such as profit sharing (Heneman & Gresham, 1998; Rynes, Gerhart, & Parks, 2005). A meta-analysis by Judiesch (1995) concluded that the increase in output due to individual incentive compensation systems is on average 33 percent. A meta-analysis by Guzzo, Jette, and Katzell (1985) also found that financial incentives had a positive effect on performance ($d = .57$). Finally, a meta-analysis by Jenkins, Mitra, Gupta, and Shaw (1998) found the correlation between financial incentives and performance quantity was .34, with field experiments (.48) yielding effects twice as large as those found in lab experiments (.24), however financial incentives were not related to performance quality.

Unfortunately, very little research exists concerning the impact of merit pay (the most popular method of linking pay to performance) on subsequent behavior and performance, although there is a good deal of research on attitudinal reactions to merit pay (Heneman & Gresham, 1998; Heneman & Werner, 2005; Rynes, Gerhart, & Parks, 2005). A detailed research review by Heneman and Werner (2005) found that merit pay was usually but not always associated with positive employee attitudes (satisfaction with pay, the job, or the employer), but its relationship to improved performance has been inconsistent and sometimes disappointing (sometimes a positive but sometimes no effect on performance). There is little evidence about the effects of skill-based pay on productivity. Rochat (1998) studied gainsharing in thirty-seven organizations and concluded that such plans were markedly successful.

Recently, there has been debate about the consequences of stock options, in part driven by examples where executives have manipulated stock prices for personal gain (Rynes, Gerhart, & Parks, 2005) and in part driven by recent research that has shown stock options sometimes have negative consequences. For example, Sanders and Hambrick (2007) found that the more a CEO is paid in stock options, the more extreme the subsequent performance of the CEO's firm and the more likely that the extreme performance will be a big loss rather than a big gain. Prior to June 2005, there was no requirement that stock options granted to employees had to be recognized as an expense on the firm's income statement, although their cost was disclosed in footnotes to financial statements. Stock options are likely to be less attractive to many firms since 2005 when the Financial Accounting Standards Board began to require that companies treat employee stock option compensation as an expense on corporate income statements (thereby making the cost of such options more transparent).

In sum, research indicates that pay for performance can have very positive effects on performance, although problems can occur when such programs are poorly implemented (see reviews by Heneman & Gresham, 1998; Rynes, Gerhart, & Parks, 2005). However, much of the research about pay for performance is based on studies for which an objective performance measure was available. This raises the question of whether pay for performance is useful in the many settings where no objective measure of performance is available and hence performance is assessed via ratings (which suffer from poor inter-rater reliability).

In addition to their effects on performance, Rynes, Gerhart, and Parks (1995) note that pay for performance plans can potentially create sorting effects that lead different types of people to apply to and stay with the organization. For example, individuals with high ability (Trank, Rynes, & Bretz, 2002; Trevor, Gerhart, & Boudreau, 1997), self-efficacy (Cable & Judge, 1994), and need for achievement (Bretz, Ash, & Dreher, 1989) appear to be more attracted to organizations where pay is closely linked to individual performance.

Special Issues in Performance Management

Dealing with Counterproductive Work Behavior

Atwater and Elkins (Chapter 11 in this book) review research and offer recommendations about dealing with counterproductive work behavior (CWB). CWB can include abuse against others (for example, incivility, workplace violence, sexual harassment), production deviance such as poor performance, sabotage (damaging or destroying the organization's property), theft (potentially ranging from minor offenses such as taking office supplies home to embezzlement), and withdrawal behaviors such as absenteeism and lateness. Dealing effectively with CWB requires accurately diagnosing the cause of the problem. These causes include drug and alcohol abuse, family problems, financial problems, the employee's personality (trait anger), interpersonal conflict in the workplace, abusive supervision or toxic leadership, co-workers who are disruptive, uncivil, or bullies, feelings of injustice, job dissatisfaction, inadequate resources or training, and organizational climate (for example, concerning ethics or sexual harassment).

Managers generally prefer to handle performance problems in a way that does not require bold and/or complicated confrontation. Examples include helping the employee correct the undesirable behavior without making an issue out of the problem, identifying adjustments in work arrangements that might reduce or eliminate the problem (for example, changing an employee's work schedule who has difficulty arriving on time due to problems at home), or restating performance expectations in a group setting. Unfortunately, it is not uncommon to delay (or entirely avoid) giving feedback to poor performers or to distort such feedback to make it appear less negative. When considering punishment, managers typically consider the employees' work history, the severity of the offense, the effect on the employee's family, and the extent to which the manager likes the employee. Punishment can have negative effects on recipients, such as embarrassment, anger, loss of respect for the manager, and bad feelings about the organization. When punishment is perceived as appropriate, it can have positive consequences on observers, such as enhanced motivation, satisfaction, and performance (and the absence of punishment when it is deserved can increase observers' feelings of inequity).

Managing Team Performance

According to Kozlowski and Ilgen (2006), effective teams perform well (as judged by relevant others), have satisfied members, and are viable (that is, members are willing to remain in the team). Team effectiveness is shaped by cognitive, interpersonal, motivational, affective, and behavioral processes (Kozlowski & Ilgen, 2006). Important team cognitive processes include team climate, team mental models (shared knowledge structures or information), transactive memory (members' understanding of the unique knowledge held by individual team members or "who knows what"), and team learning (team members acquiring knowledge and skills through experience and interaction). Interpersonal, motivational, and affective processes include team cohesion, team efficacy (a shared belief in the team's ability to attain a given level of performance on a specific task) and potency (a shared belief in the team's ability to be effective across multiple tasks and contexts), team affect (the mean and dispersion of affect across team members), and team conflict. Behavioral processes include coordination of effort and actions (while reducing social loafing), team member competencies, and team regulation (the ability of the team to self-regulate and adapt to shifting circumstances and demands).

Salas, Weaver, Rosen, and Smith-Jentsch (Chapter 6 in this book) describe four important team capacities and how each can be developed: adaptive capacity, leadership capacity, management capacity, and technical capacity. With regard to *adaptive capacity*, simulation-based training can allow teams to practice different task strategies in environments that replicate the real world but without the risks associated with failure. Teams can develop awareness of their external environment as well as the internal workings of the team via team cue recognition training and perceptual contrast training. Training in team communication skills can also help ensure that important changes detected by one team member are quickly and accurately communicated to the rest of the team. Guided error training can help teams learn when the routine response is not the correct response and how to deal with novel situations. Team learning orientation and psychological safety can help teams learn from their past performance.

With regard to *leadership capacity*, the team's leader or its members need to create a shared vision that is aligned with the vision of the broader organization, manage external expectations (for example, by seeking feedback and ambassadorship), and have malleable individual and team goals that can be revised to reflect unforeseen changes in the team's external environment. Because of the interdependent nature of work in teams, organizations should be cautious about using individual incentives that might undermine cooperation.

To build *management capacity*, organizations need to (a) develop measures that are diagnostic of performance (to understand "why" outcomes occurred), (b) gather performance data from multiple sources, (c) measure typical (rather than maximal) team performance continuously (so that real-time feedback can be provided), and (d) include teamwork (collaboration) as well as task-work competencies in performance evaluations.

Technical capacity requires that team members must be competent at their individual tasks (task work) and at managing the interdependencies between their own work and that of other team members (teamwork). Teams must be able to leverage all of the expertise and experience on the team by ensuring that all members feel comfortable contributing, the team has accurate transactive memory (members know who knows what on the team), and each team member's input is weighted by the person's expertise rather than the person's formal status. Shared mental models can be developed via cross-training or inter-positional knowledge training. And after-event reviews, not only of team failures but also of team successes, can enhance team performance and yield richer mental models.

Technology in Performance Management

Krauss and Snyder (Chapter 13 in this book) describe a variety of ways by which technology can facilitate the effectiveness of performance management. For example, goals can be made accessible to all employees, and employees can easily update their goals over time. Employees can enter information about current projects into the system (along with the contact information for the project's stakeholders) and, when a project is completed, the system can automatically solicit feedback from those stakeholders (and make the feedback available to the employee, the manager, and designated stakeholders). Technology can help the employee and manager to create, store, and revise a performance plan in a shared electronic workspace (especially when the employee and manager are not co-located). An online database of training and development opportunities can be linked to the plan. Sample career paths (and associated competencies) can be available in the system and used by employees to construct their own potential career paths and share the information with mentors or coaches. Performance data stored in the system can be used to identify and track high-potential employees, determine appropriate developmental opportunities, and help create mentoring relationships. Technology can also help managers complete formal appraisals, for example, by generating an initial draft narrative to be included in an employee's feedback report and reviewing final appraisal narratives for discriminatory language or other statements that might raise legal concerns.

Despite the potential advantages of technology-supported performance management, there are a number of challenges, such as information overload, time required to input data, frustration associated with inadequate user interfaces, and the requirement that users have a reasonable level of technology literacy.

Performance Management Across Cultures

Day and Greguras (Chapter 8 in this book) note that a major obstacle to effective performance management in multinational companies is understanding and coping with the role of national culture. Culture shapes expectations about what is appropriate behavior.

Cross-cultural implementation of a performance management system is often accompanied by challenges, such as subtle differences in interpreting the competencies used to evaluate performance and the extent to which managers are willing to communicate negative feedback to employees in a direct manner (as well as the willingness of employees to provide feedback to their managers and the receptivity of managers to such feedback).

Using the eight cultural dimensions identified in Project GLOBE (House, Hanges, Javidan, Dorfman, & Gupta, 2004), Day and Greguras (Chapter 8 in this book) describe how culture can affect performance management practices. In high *individualism* cultures, individual goals and achievement are important and employees are likely to change companies often, whereas in low individualism cultures (that is, high collectivism cultures), group goals, harmony, and achievement are likely to be valued and long-term employment with the same company is more common. Easterners (generally high collectivism cultures) are more likely to take context into consideration (leading to more external attributions for performance), whereas Westerners (generally high individualism cultures) tend to focus primarily on the person or object (rather than its context) and hence fail to acknowledge the role of contextual factors. Employees from high collectivism cultures are also likely to rate themselves more modestly than employees from high individualism cultures rate themselves.

In high *power distance* cultures, people accept unequal distribution of power in organizations and hence show considerable deference to those in authority, whereas in low power distance cultures, power and information are more widely shared across organization levels and hence employees would be expected to be more comfortable with involvement in goal setting and providing upward feedback.

In high *humane orientation* cultures, fairness, generosity, support, and the well-being of others are especially important, whereas in low humane orientation cultures, greater emphasis is placed on self-interest, self-enjoyment, and material possessions. When interacting with their employees, managers from high humane orientation cultures might be expected to display more support, concern, and tolerance for errors (and contextual performance in general is likely to be more valued in high humane orientation cultures).

In high *uncertainty avoidance* cultures, employees tend to prefer order and formal procedures (for example, clear documentation as part of the performance management process) and are likely to show less tolerance for rule violations and more resistance to change, whereas in low uncertainty avoidance cultures, employees tend to prefer more informal interactions (and perhaps less formal feedback), trust verbal agreements made with others, and display more tolerance for rule violations and less resistance to change.

High *performance orientation* cultures value initiative and results and reward high performance, whereas low performance orientation cultures are more likely to value and reward seniority and loyalty.

High *future orientation* cultures tend to delay gratification, have longer strategic horizons, and value intrinsic motivation and long-term success (and are therefore likely to set long-term goals and emphasize employee development and succession planning), whereas low future orientation cultures place a greater emphasis on immediate rewards and extrinsic motivation (and are therefore likely to emphasize short-term goals).

Cultures with high *gender egalitarianism* place little or no emphasis on an employee's gender in determining roles (and hence will likely provide equal opportunities for men and women in career development), whereas cultures with low gender egalitarianism are more likely to place males in powerful roles. Where gender egalitarianism is low, female managers might face resentment (especially when conveying negative feedback); where gender egalitarianism is high, male managers who condescend to female employees are likely to be viewed unfavorably.

Finally, high *assertiveness* cultures value direct and blunt communication, whereas low assertiveness cultures value modesty and face-saving (and hence view assertive communication as inappropriate). Thus, negative feedback is likely to be communicated more directly and clearly in high assertiveness cultures.

Of course, within any country, there can be wide variations in cultural practices; hence Day and Greguras emphasize that there is a risk in taking the generalizations associated with these cultural dimensions too far. Moreover, the strength of the organization's culture relative to national culture is an important consideration. In a strong organizational culture with broad acceptance concerning its core values, norms, and desired behaviors, organizational culture can trump national culture.

Performance Management in the Future

Tippins and Coverdale (Chapter 16 in this book) have described workplace trends and their implications for performance management in the future. Each of these trends points to a challenge for practitioners (as well as to a direction for future research). For example, the increase in geographically dispersed teams (sometimes in different countries and time zones) raises questions such as how to address the fact that the opportunity to directly observe performance is no longer feasible (which is likely to pose a greater problem in service work than production work) and how to address changes in how and when managers interact with employees. The increasing use of outsourcing can further exacerbate such challenges in that "team members" who are vital to organizational success can literally work for another company. Although technology (videoconferencing, instant messaging, email) offers some potential solutions to communication in geographically dispersed teams, we need to know more about the consequences of using these technologies in place of face-to-face interactions (for example, how does the absence of nonverbal cues affect the effectiveness of feedback delivered electronically?). Changes in worker characteristics, including predicted declines in the number of qualified workers and changing employee expectations, also have potential implications for performance management. How should performance management processes be designed to deal with unskilled or under-educated workers who often lack basic literacy and numeracy skills? How can performance management processes be modified to deal effectively with employees who are predicted to increasingly expect opportunities for personal growth and development, rapid career progression (which will be especially difficult as organizations tend to become flatter), and work-family balance, and how can rewards be tailored to match the values of such employees?

Table 17.1 Best Practices in Performance Management.

Definition	Performance encompasses task performance, contextual performance, and organizational citizenship behaviors, adaptive performance, and changes in performance over time. Performance management involves systems and processes to monitor and improve these elements of performance.
Goal Setting	Balanced scorecards heighten awareness of the potential tradeoffs among various goals. They provide an overarching framework that drives and aligns organizational, department, team, and individual goal setting. For individuals, teams, and organizations, specific, difficult goals lead to higher performance than "do your best" goals because goals focus employees' attention on a specific objective (rather than other activities), lead to higher levels of effort to attain those objectives, enhance persistence in the face of setbacks and obstacles, and stimulate employees to develop new approaches and strategies when faced with complex tasks. Self-efficacy can be enhanced by providing the employee with mastery experiences, enabling the employee to observe a role model successfully perform the task, and providing verbal encouragement that the employee has the ability to learn and perform the task successfully. Goal commitment can be strengthened by having people make a public commitment to the goal, increasing self-efficacy, and increasing the attractiveness of outcomes associated with goal attainment. Providing learning goals during the early stages of skills acquisition on complex tasks directs attention to learning the task rather than worrying about future performance outcomes.
Feedback	Feedback that directs the recipient's attention to the task is more effective than feedback that directs the recipient's attention to the self and away from the task.

(*Continued*)

Table 17.1 (*Continued*)

Training and Development	The value of formal organizational training has been widely documented for learning, behavior, and results criteria. Organizational training also generally has a positive return on investment. Self-management training increases performance and decreases absenteeism. People are taught to identify behaviors to develop, establish goals, maintain a record of progress, establish self-rewards and self-punishments, recognize high-risk situations, and prepare a written contract for themselves.
Coaching	Coaching should be integrated into the organization's overall talent management strategy and aligned with business strategy. Organizations should target coaching to specific needs, such as accelerating the development of high-potential managers, on-boarding new leaders, and driving a change in culture. Effective coaching includes (a) a working relationship between the coach and recipient characterized by trust, acceptance, and understanding; (b) helping the recipient develop insight about critical success factors and how others perceive the recipient relative to those factors; (c) building the recipient's motivation to change by clarifying personal and organizational reasons for change and focusing on small, easy steps to initiate the process; (d) enhancing the recipient's capabilities by sharing new ideas and best practices, pointing to useful learning resources and opportunities, and exploring alternative ways to handle difficult situations; (e) facilitating application of new skills to specific situations in which change is appropriate (that is, real-world practice); (f) encouraging the recipient to make specific commitments for action, following up on the person's commitments, and encouraging the person to seek feedback from others; and (g) helping the recipient to anticipate and address barriers while working with senior leaders to create a supportive climate for development.
Performance Evaluation	One way to improve performance evaluation is to ask managers to share, discuss, and justify their ratings of employees with others. This approach calibrates ratings made by different supervisors and lessens unjustifiable leniency (although raters may become more vulnerable to social influences). Forced distribution systems are more accepted when there are not severe consequences for poorly ranked employees, the group to be ranked is reasonably large, there is variability in performance, employees receive

Rewarding Performance

Organizations' reward systems link pay to performance at the individual level (e.g., individual merit pay), team level (team incentives, team recognition), unit level (gainsharing), and organizational level (profit sharing).

Team Performance

Team effectiveness is shaped by cognitive, interpersonal, motivational, affective, and behavioral processes. Organizations systematically develop four important team capacities: adaptive capacity, leadership capacity, management capacity, and technical capacity.

Technology

Technology can make goals accessible to all employees, track project accomplishments and roadblocks, solicit feedback, share performance plans, communicate and deliver development opportunities, provide information about career path options, store and review performance data, track high-performance employees, and facilitate the completion of performance appraisals.

Cultural Factors

Culture can affect many aspects of performance management, including the relative importance of individual versus group goals, the extent to which long-term employment with the same company is valued, the willingness to acknowledge the role of contextual factors in shaping performance, the favorableness of self-evaluations, the extent of deference shown to those in authority, whether information is widely shared across organization levels, willingness to provide upward feedback, a manager's tolerance for errors, the amount of resistance to change, preference for informal versus formal interactions and feedback, the value attached to performance versus seniority and loyalty, the focus on short-term versus long-term success and rewards, the likelihood of women being accepted in powerful roles, and whether interpersonal communication is direct and blunt (versus face-saving). When there is a strong organizational culture with broad acceptance concerning its core values, norms, and desired behaviors, organizational culture can trump national culture.

Conclusion

Our aim in this book has been to provide a comprehensive overview of the field of performance management. Although the chapters segment different components, performance management is truly an integrated field. The components go hand-in-glove in continuous interaction. In applying the constructs, research findings, and examples of best practices discussed throughout this book and summarized in this chapter (see highlights in Table 17.1), an organization can establish a *performance management culture*—one in which discussing individual, team, and organizational performance is acceptable and encouraged; feedback is formative and aimed at continuous improvement; and there is mutual support between supervisor and subordinate, peers at the same organizational level, and teams within and between organizational sub-units. The findings presented throughout this book provide clear guidance for best HR practice that should be useful to line managers and HR practitioners.

References

Acosta-Amad, S., & Brethower, D. M. (1992). Training for impact: Improving the quality of staff's performance. *Performance Improvement Quarterly, 5,* 2–12.

Aguinis, H. (2009). *Performance management* (2nd ed.). Upper Saddle River, NJ: Pearson Prentice Hall.

Aguinis, H., & Pierce, C. A. (2008). Enhancing the relevance of organizational behavior by embracing performance management research. *Journal of Organizational Behavior, 29,* 139–145.

Albanese, R., & Van Fleet, D. D. (1985). Rational behavior in groups: The free-riding tendency. *Academy of Management Review, 10,* 244–255.

Alvero, A. M., Bucklin, B. R., & Austin, J. (2001). An objective review of the effectiveness and essential characteristics of performance feedback in organizational settings. *Journal of Organizational Behavior Management, 21,* 3–29.

Aronson, E. (1999). The power of self-persuasion. *American Psychologist, 54,* 873–890.

Arthur, W., Jr., Bennett, W., Jr., Edens, P. S., & Bell, S. T. (2003). Effectiveness of training in organizations: A meta-analysis of design and evaluation features. *Journal of Applied Psychology, 88,* 234–245.

Atwater, L., & Elkins, T. (2009). Diagnosing, understanding, and dealing with counterproductive work behavior. In J. W. Smither & M. London (Eds.), *Performance management: Putting research into practice*. San Francisco: Jossey-Bass.

Bandura, A. (1986). *Social foundations of thought and action*. Englewood Cliffs, NJ: Prentice Hall.

Baum, J. R., Locke, E., & Smith, K. (2001). A multi-dimensional model of venture growth. *Academy of Management Journal, 44*, 292–303.

Bennett, B. B. (1987). *The effectiveness of staff development training practices: A meta-analysis (coaching)*. Ph.D. dissertation, University of Oregon. Retrieved September 11, 2008, from Dissertations & Theses: A&I database. (Publication No. AAT 8721226).

Bernardin, H. J., & Buckley, M. R. (1981). Strategies in rater training. *Academy of Management Review, 6*, 205–212.

Bernardin, H. J., & Orban, J. A. (1990). Leniency effect as a function of rating format, purpose for appraisal, and rater individual differences. *Journal of Business and Psychology, 5*, 197–211.

Bernardin, H. J., & Pence, E. C. (1980). Effects of rater error training: creating new response sets and decreasing accuracy. *Journal of Applied Psychology, 65*, 60–66.

Blanz, F., & Ghiselli, E. E. (1972). The mixed standard scale: A new rating system. *Personnel Psychology, 25*, 185–199.

Blume, B. D., Baldwin, T. T., & Rubin, R. S. (2007, April). All forced distribution systems are not created equal. Paper presented at the 22nd Annual Conference of the Society for Industrial and Organizational Psychology. New York, New York.

Bommer, W. H., Johnson, J., Rich, G. A., Podsakoff, P. M., & Mackenzie, S. B. (1995). On the interchangeability of objective and subjective measures of employee performance: A meta-analysis. *Personnel Psychology, 48*, 587–605.

Borman, W. C., & Motowidlo, S. J. (1993). Expanding the criterion domain to include elements of contextual performance. In N. Schmitt & W. C. Borman (Eds.), *Personnel selections in organizations*. San Francisco: Jossey-Bass.

Bowles, S., Cunningham, C. J. L., De La Rosa, G. M., & Picano, J. (2007). Coaching leaders in middle and executive management: Goals, performance, buy-in. *Leadership & Organization Development Journal, 28*, 388–408.

Bretz, R. D., Ash, R. A., & Dreher, G. F. (1989). Do people make the place? An examination of the attraction-selection-attrition hypothesis. *Personnel Psychology, 42*, 561–581.

616 PERFORMANCE MANAGEMENT

Cable, D. M., & Judge, T. A. (1994). Pay preferences and job search decisions: A person-organization fit perspective. *Personnel Psychology, 47,* 317–348.

Campbell, J. P., McCloy, R. A., Oppler, S. H., & Sager, C. E. (1993). A theory of performance. In N. Schmitt & W. C. Borman (Eds.), *Personnel selection in organizations* (pp. 35–70). San Francisco: Jossey-Bass.

Cannon, M. D., & Edmondson, A. C. (2001). Confronting failure: Antecedents and consequences of shared beliefs about failure in organizational work groups. *Journal of Organizational Behavior, 22,* 161–177.

Carson, J. B., Tesluk, P. E., & Marrone, J. A. (2007). Shared leadership in teams: An investigation of antecedent conditions and performance. *Academy of Management Journal, 50,* 1217–1234.

Cascio, W. F. (2006). Global performance management systems. In G. K. Stahl & I. Björkman (Eds.), *Handbook of research in international human resource management* (pp. 176–196). Northampton, MA: Edward Elgar.

Cascio, W. F., & Valenzi, E. R. (1978). Relations among criteria of police performance. *Journal of Applied Psychology, 63,* 22–28.

Cialdini, R. B. (2001). *Influence: Science and practice.* Needham Heights, MA: Allyn & Bacon.

Cooper, C. L., Dyck, B., & Frohlich, N. (1992). Improving the effectiveness of gainsharing: The role of fairness and participation. *Administrative Science Quarterly, 37,* 471–490.

Cooper, W. H. (1981a). Ubiquitous halo. *Psychological Bulletin, 90,* 218–244.

Cooper, W. H. (1981b). Conceptual similarity as a source of illusory halo in job performance ratings. *Journal of Applied Psychology, 66,* 302–307.

Crown, D. F., & Rosse, J. G. (1995). Yours, mine, and ours: Facilitating group productivity through the integration of individual and group goals. *Organizational Behavior and Human Decision Processes, 64,* 138–150.

Dagley, G. (2006). Human resources professionals' perceptions of executive coaching: Efficacy, benefits and return on investment. *International Coaching Psychology Review, 1*(2), 34–44.

Day, D. V., & Greguras, G. J. (2009). Performance management in multinational companies. In J. W. Smither & M. London (Eds.), *Performance management: Putting research into practice.* San Francisco: Jossey-Bass.

den Hartog, D. N., Boselie, P., & Paauwe, J. (2004). Performance management: A model and research agenda. *Applied Psychology: An International Review, 53,* 556–569.

DeNisi, A. S. (1996). *Cognitive approach to performance appraisal: A program of research.* New York: Routledge.

Dominick, P. G. (2009). Forced rankings: Pros, cons, and practices. In J. W. Smither & M. London (Eds.), *Performance management: Putting research into practice.* San Francisco: Jossey-Bass.

Edmondson, A. (1999). Psychological safety and learning behavior in work teams. *Administrative Science Quarterly, 44,* 350–383.

Ellinger, A. D., Ellinger, A. E., & Keller, S. B. (2003). Supervisory coaching behavior, employee satisfaction, and warehouse employee performance: A dyadic perspective in the distribution industry. *Human Resource Development Quarterly, 14,* 435–458.

Erez, M. (1977). Feedback: A necessary condition for the goal setting-performance relationship. *Journal of Applied Psychology, 62,* 624–627.

Evers, W. J. G., Brouwers, A., & Tomic, W. (2006). A quasi-experimental study on management coaching effectiveness. *Consulting Psychology Journal: Practice and Research, 58,* 174–182.

Feggetter, A. J. W. (2007). A preliminary evaluation of executive coaching: Does executive coaching work for candidates on a high potential development scheme? *International Coaching Psychology Review, 2,* 129–142.

Feldman, D. C., & Lankau, M. J. (2005). Executive coaching: A review and agenda for future research. *Journal of Management, 31,* 829–848.

Flanagan, J. C. (1954). The critical incident technique. *Psychological Bulletin, 51,* 327–358.

Frayne, C. A., & Geringer, J. M. (2000). Self-management training for improving job performance: A field experiment involving salespeople. *Journal of Applied Psychology, 85,* 361–372.

Frayne, C. A., & Latham, G. P. (1987). Application of social learning theory to employee self-management of attendance. *Journal of Applied Psychology, 72,* 387–392.

Graham, S., Wedman, J. F., & Garvin-Kester, B. (1993). Manager coaching skills: Development and application. *Performance Improvement Quarterly, 6,* 2–13.

Guralnik, O., Rozmarin, E., & So, A. (2004). Forced distribution: Is it right for you? *Human Resource Development Quarterly, 15*(3), 339–345.

Guzzo, R. A., Jette, R. D., & Katzell, R. A. (1985). The effects of psychologically based intervention programs on worker productivity: A meta-analysis. *Personnel Psychology, 38,* 275–291.

Gyllensten, K., & Palmer, S. (2005). Can coaching reduce workplace stress? A quasi-experimental study. *International Journal of Evidence Based Coaching and Mentoring, 3,* 75–85.

Hackman, J. R., & Wageman, R. (2005). A theory of team coaching. *Academy of Management Review, 30,* 269–287.

Hall, D. T., Otazo, K. L., & Hollenbeck, G. P. (1999). Behind closed doors: What really happens in executive coaching. *Organizational Dynamics*, 39–52.

Hamlin, R. G., Ellinger, A. D., & Beattie, R. S. (2006). Coaching at the heart of managerial effectiveness: A cross-cultural study of managerial behaviours. *Human Resource Development International, 9*, 305–331.

Hauenstein, N. M. A. (1998). Training raters to increase the accuracy of appraisals and the usefulness of feedback. In J. W. Smither (Ed.), *Performance appraisal: State of the art in practice* (pp. 404–442). San Francisco: Jossey-Bass.

Hazucha, J. F., Hezlett, S. A., & Schneider, R. J. (1993). The impact of multi-source feedback on management skills development. *Human Resource Management, 32*, 325–351.

Hedge, J. W., & Borman, W. C. (2008). Career and performance management with consultants. In J. W. Hedge & W. C. Borman (Eds.), *The I/O consultant: Advice and insights for building a successful career.* Washington, DC: American Psychological Association.

Heneman, R. L. (1986). The relationship between supervisory ratings and results-oriented measures of performance: A meta-analysis. *Personnel Psychology, 39*, 811–826.

Heneman, R. L., & Gresham, M. T. (1998). Performance-based pay plans. In J. W. Smither (Ed.), *Performance appraisal: State-of-the-art in practice.* San Francisco: Jossey-Bass.

Heneman, R. L., & von Hippel, C. (1995). Balancing group and individual rewards: Rewarding individual contributions to the team. *Compensation and Benefits Review, 27*(4), 63–68.

Heneman, R. L., & Werner, J. M. (2005). *Merit pay: Linking pay to performance in a changing world.* Greenwich, CT: Information Age Publishing.

Heslin, P., Carson, J. B., & VandeWalle, D. (2009). Practical applications of goal setting theory to performance management. In J. W. Smither & M. London (Eds.), *Performance management: Putting research into practice.* San Francisco: Jossey-Bass.

Heslin, P. A., Latham, G. P., & VandeWalle, D. M. (2005). The effect of implicit person theory on performance appraisals. *Journal of Applied Psychology, 90*, 842–856.

Heslin, P. A., & VandeWalle, D. (2008). Managers' implicit assumptions about personnel. *Current Directions in Psychological Science, 17*, 219–223.

Heslin, P. A., VandeWalle, D., & Latham, G. P. (2006). Keen to help? Managers' implicit person theories and their subsequent employee coaching. *Personnel Psychology, 59*, 871–902.

Hollenbeck, G. P., & McCall, M. W. (1999). Leadership development: Contemporary practices. In A. I. Kraut and A. K. Korman (Eds.), *Evolving practices in human resource management.* San Francisco: Jossey-Bass.

House, R. J., Hanges, P. J., Javidan, M., Dorfman, P. W., & Gupta, V. (Eds.). (2004). *Culture, leadership, and organizations: The GLOBE study of 62 societies.* Thousand Oaks, CA: Sage.

Ilgen, D. R., & Davis, C. A. (2000). Bearing bad news: Reactions to negative performance feedback. *Applied Psychology: An International Review, 49,* 550–565.

Ilgen, D. R., Fisher, C. D., & Taylor, M. S. (1979). Consequences of individual feedback on behavior in organizations. *Journal of Applied Psychology, 64,* 349–371.

Jawahar, I. M., & Williams, C. R. (1997). Where all the children are above average: The performance appraisal purpose effect. *Personnel Psychology, 50,* 905–925.

Jenkins, D. G., Mitra, A., Gupta, N., & Shaw J. D. (1998). Are financial incentives related to performance? A meta-analytic review of empirical research. *Journal of Applied Psychology, 83,* 777–787.

Judiesch, M. K. (1995). The effects of incentive compensation systems on productivity, individual differences in output variability and selection utility. *Dissertation Abstracts International Section A: Humanities and Social Sciences. 55*(12-A), 3914.

Kane, J. S. (1986). Performance distribution assessment. In R. Berk (Ed.), *Performance assessment: Methods and applications* (pp. 237–274). Baltimore: The Johns Hopkins University Press.

Kanfer, R., & Ackerman, P. L. (1989) Motivation and cognitive abilities: An integrative/aptitude-treatment interaction approach to skill acquisition. *Journal of Applied Psychology, 74,* 657–690.

Kaplan, R. S., & Norton, D. P. (1992). The balanced scorecard: Measures that drive performance. *Harvard Business Review, 70,* 71–80.

Kaplan, R. S., & Norton, D. P (1996). *The balanced scorecard: Translating strategy into action.* Boston: Harvard Business School Press.

Kaplan, R. S., & Norton, D. P. (2001). Transforming the balanced scorecard from performance measurement to strategic management: Part I. *Accounting Horizons, 15,* 87–104.

Kaplan, R. S., & Norton, D. P. (2004). Strategy maps. *Strategic Finance, 85,* 26–35.

Keith, N., & Frese, M. (2008). Effectiveness of error management training: A meta-analysis. *Journal of Applied Psychology, 93,* 59–69.

Kidwell, R. E., & Bennett, N. (1993). Employee propensity to withhold effort: A conceptual model to intersect three avenues of research. *Academy of Management Review, 18*, 429–456.

Kirchner, W. K. (1960). Predicting ratings of sales success with objective performance information. *Journal of Applied Psychology, 44*, 398–403.

Kluger, A. N., & DeNisi, A. (1996). Effects of feedback intervention on performance: A historical review, a meta-analysis, and a preliminary feedback intervention theory. *Psychological Bulletin, 119*, 254–284.

Kombarakaran, F. A., Yang, J. A., Baker, M. N., & Fernandes, P. B. (2008). Executive coaching: It works! *Consulting Psychology Journal: Practice and Research, 60*, 78–90.

Konczak, L. J., Stelly, D. J., & Trusty, M. L. (2000). Defining and measuring empowering leader behaviors: Development of an upward feedback instrument. *Educational and Psychological Measurement, 60*, 301–313.

Kozlowski, S. W. J., & Ilgen, D. R. (2006). Enhancing the effectiveness of work groups and teams. *Psychological Science in the Public Interest, 7*, 77–124.

Krauss, A. D., & Snyder, L. A. (2009). Technology and performance management. In J. W. Smither & M. London (Eds.), *Performance management: Putting research into practice*. San Francisco: Jossey-Bass.

Landy, F. J., & Farr, J. L. (1980). Performance rating. *Psychological Bulletin, 87*, 72–107.

Latham, G. P. (2001). The importance of understanding and changing employee outcome expectancies for gaining commitment to an organizational goal. *Personnel Psychology, 54*, 707–716.

Latham, G. P. (2004). The motivation benefits of goal setting. *Academy of Management Executive, 18*, 126–129.

Latham, G. P., Almost, J., Mann, S., & Moore, C. (2005). New developments in performance management. *Organizational Dynamics, 34*, 77–87.

Latham, G. P., Fay, C. H., & Saari, L. M. (1979). The development of behavioral observation scales for appraising the performance of foremen. *Personnel Psychology, 32*, 299–311.

Latham, G. P., & Frayne, C. A. (1989). Self-management training for increasing job attendance: A follow-up and a replication. *Journal of Applied Psychology, 74*, 411–416.

Latham, G. P, & Mann, S. (2006). Advances in the science of performance appraisal: Implications for practice. In G. P Hodgkinson & J. K. Ford (Eds.), *International review of industrial and organizational psychology* (Vol. 21). Hoboken, NJ: John Wiley & Sons.

Latham, G. P., & Seijts, G. H. (1999). The effects of proximal and distal goals on performance on a moderately complex task. *Journal of Organizational Behavior, 20*, 421–429.

Latham, G. P., & Wexley, K. N. (1977). Behavioral observation scales for performance appraisal purposes. *Personnel Psychology, 30*, 255–268.

Latham, G. P., Wexley, K. N., & Pursell, E. D. (1975). Training managers to minimize rating errors in the observation of behavior. *Journal of Applied Psychology, 60*, 550–555.

Lawler, E. E. (2003). Reward practices and performance management system effectiveness. *Organizational Dynamics, 32*, 396–404.

Lewis, P. B. (1947). Supervisory training methods. *Personnel Journal, 25*, 316–322.

Locke, E. A., & Latham, G. P. (1990). *A theory of goal setting and task performance.* Englewood Cliffs, NJ: Prentice Hall.

Locke, E. A., & Latham, G. P. (2002). Building a practically useful theory of goal setting and task motivation: A 35-year odyssey. *American Psychologist, 57*, 705–717.

Luthans, F., & Peterson, S. J. (2003). 360-degree feedback with systematic coaching: Empirical analysis suggests a winning combination. *Human Resource Management, 42*, 243–256.

McBriarty, M. A. (1988). Performance appraisal: Some unintended consequences. *Public Personnel Management, 17*, 421–434.

McGovern J., Lindemann, M., Vergara, M., Murphy, S., Barker, L., & Warrenfeltz, R. (2001). Maximizing the impact of executive coaching: Behavioral change, organizational outcomes, and return on investment. *The Manchester Review, 6*, 1–9.

Mero, N. P., Guidice, R. M., & Brownlee, A. L. (2007). Accountability in a performance appraisal context: The effect of audience and form of accounting on rater response and behavior. *Journal of Management, 33*, 223–252.

Morgeson, F. P. (2005). The external leadership of self-managing teams: Intervening in the context of novel and disruptive events. *Journal of Applied Psychology, 90*, 497–508.

Morrow, C. C., Jarrett, M. Q., & Rupinski, M. T. (1997). An investigation of the effect and economic utility of corporate-wide training. *Personnel Psychology, 50*, 91–119.

Murphy, K. R. (2008). Explaining the weak relationship between job performance and ratings of job performance. *Industrial and Organizational Psychology: Perspectives on Science and Practice, 1*, 148–160.

Murphy, K. R., & Cleveland, J. N. (1991). *Performance appraisal: An organizational perspective.* Boston, MA: Allyn & Bacon.

Murphy, K. R., & Cleveland, J. N. (1995). *Understanding performance appraisal: Social, organizational, and goal-based perspectives.* Thousand Oaks, CA: Sage.

Neubert, M. J. (1998). The value of feedback and goal setting over goal setting alone and potential moderators of this effect: A meta-analysis. *Human Performance, 11,* 321–335.

Noel, T., & Latham, G. P. (2006). The importance of learning goals versus outcome goals for entrepreneurs. *International Journal of Entrepreneurship and Innovation, 7,* 213–220.

Olivero, G., Bane, K. D., & Kopelman, R. E. (1997). Executive coaching as a transfer of training tool: Effects on productivity in a public agency. *Public Personnel Management, 26,* 461–469.

Peterson, D. B. (2009). Coaching and performance management: How can organizations get the greatest value? In J. W. Smither & M. London (Eds.), *Performance management: Putting research into practice.* San Francisco: Jossey-Bass.

Podsakoff, P. M., Ahearne, M., & MacKenzie, S. B. (1997). Organizational citizenship behavior and the quantity and quality of work group performance. *Journal of Applied Psychology, 82,* 262–270.

Rappe, C., & Zwick, T. (2007). Developing leadership competence of production unit managers. *Journal of Management Development, 26,* 312–330.

Reb, J., & Cropanzano, R. (2007). Evaluating dynamic performance: The influence of salient gestalt characteristics on performance ratings. *Journal of Applied Psychology, 92,* 490–492.

Rochat, K. D. (1998). Gainsharing plan effectiveness and its correlates. *Dissertation Abstracts International: Section B: The Sciences and Engineering. 59*(6-B), 3106.

Rodgers, R., & Hunter, J. E. (1991). Impact of management by objectives on organizational productivity. *Journal of Applied Psychology, 76,* 322–336.

Rynes, S. L., Gerhart, B., & Parks, L. (2005). Performance evaluation and pay for performance. *Annual Review of Psychology, 56,* 571–600.

Salas, E., Weaver, S. J., Rosen, M. A., & Smith-Jentsch, K. A. (2009). Managing team performance in complex settings: Research-based best practices. In J. W. Smither & M. London (Eds.), *Performance management: Putting research into practice.* San Francisco: Jossey-Bass.

Sanders, W. M. G., & Hambrick, D. C. (2007). Swinging for the fences: The effects of CEO stock options on company risk taking and performance. *Academy of Management Journal, 50,* 1055–1078.

Scandura, T. A. (1992). Mentorship and career mobility: An empirical investigation. *Journal of Organizational Behavior, 13,* 169–174.

Schiemann, W. A. (2009). Aligning performance management with organizational strategy, values, and goals. In J. W. Smither & M. London (Eds.), *Performance management: Putting research into practice.* San Francisco: Jossey-Bass.

Schleicher, D. J., Bull, R. A., & Green, S. G. (2007, April). *Rater reactions to forced distribution rating systems.* Paper presented at the 22nd Annual Conference of the Society for Industrial and Organizational Psychology. New York, New York.

Schmitt, N., Cortina, J. M., Ingerick, M. J., & Wiechmann, D. (2003). Personnel selection and employee performance. In W. C. Borman, D. R. Ilgen, & R. J. Klimoski (Eds.), *Handbook of psychology, Volume 12, Industrial and organizational psychology.* Hoboken, NJ: John Wiley & Sons.

Seashore, S. E., Indik, B. P., & Georgopoulos, B. S. (1960). Relationships among criteria of job performance. *Journal of Applied Psychology, 44,* 195–202.

Shepperd, J. A. (1993). Productivity loss in performance groups: A motivation analysis. *Psychological Bulletin, 113,* 67–81.

Sisson, E. D. (1948). Forced choice: The new army rating. *Personnel Psychology, 1,* 365–381.

Smith, P. C., & Kendall, L. M. (1963). Retranslation of expectations: An approach to the construction of unambiguous anchors for rating scales. *Journal of Applied Psychology, 47,* 149–155.

Smither, J. W., London, M., Flautt, R., Vargas, Y., & Kucine, I. (2003). Can working with an executive coach improve multi-source feedback ratings over time? A quasi-experimental field study. *Personnel Psychology, 56,* 23–44.

Smither, J. W., London, M., & Reilly, R. R. (2005). Does performance improve following multi-source feedback? A theoretical model, meta-analysis, and review of empirical findings. *Personnel Psychology, 58,* 33–66.

Smither, J. W., & Reilly, S. P. (2001). Coaching in organizations: A social psychological perspective. In M. London (Ed.), *How people evaluate others in organizations: Person perception and interpersonal judgment in I/O psychology.* Mahwah, NJ: Lawrence Erlbaum Associates.

Taylor, E. K., & Wherry, R. J. (1951). A study of leniency in two rating systems. *Personnel Psychology. 4,* 39–47.

Tippins, N. T., & Coverdale, S. H. (2009). Performance management of the future. In J. W. Smither & M. London (Eds.), *Performance management: Putting research into practice.* San Francisco: Jossey-Bass.

Trank, C. Q., Rynes, S. L., & Bretz, R. D., Jr. (2002). Attracting applicants in the war for talent: Differences in work preferences among
high achievers. *Journal of Business and Psychology, 16,* 331–345.

Trevor, C. O., Gerhart, B., & Boudreau, J. W. (1997). Voluntary turnover and job performance: Curvilinearity and the moderating
influences of salary growth and promotions. *Journal of Applied
Psychology, 82,* 44–61.

Tziner, A., & Kopelman, R. (1988). Effects of rating format on goal-
setting dimensions: A field experiment. *Journal of Applied Psychology,
73,* 323–326.

Viswesvaran, C. (2001). Assessment of individual job performance: A
review of the past century and a look ahead. In N. Anderson, D.
Ones, H. K. Sinangil, & C. Viswesvaran (Eds.), *Handbook of industrial, work, and organizational psychology: Volume 1: Personnel psychology.* Thousand Oaks, CA: Sage.

Wageman, R. (1995). Interdependence and group effectiveness.
Administrative Science Quarterly, 40, 145–180.

Walker, A. G., & Smither, J. W. (1999). A five-year study of upward
feedback: What managers do with their results matters. *Personnel
Psychology, 52,* 393–423.

Wasylyshyn, K. M. (2003). Executive coaching: An outcome study.
Consulting Psychology Journal: Practice and Research, 55, 94–106.

Wasylyshyn, K. M., Gronsky, B., & Haas, J. W. (2006). Tigers, stripes, and
behavior change: Survey results of a commissioned coaching program. *Consulting Psychology Journal: Practice and Research, 58,* 65–81.

Wexley, K. N., & Klimoski, R. (1984). Performance appraisal: An update.
In K. Rowland & G. Ferris (Eds.), *Research in personnel and human
resources* (Vol. 2). Greenwich, CT: JAI Press.

Wiersma, U. J., van den Berg, P. T., & Latham, G. P. (1995). Dutch reactions to behavioral observation, behavioral expectation, and trait
scales. *Group & Organization Management, 20,* 297–309.

Winters, D., & Latham, G. (1996). The effect of learning versus outcome
goals on a simple versus a complex task. *Group and Organization
Management, 21,* 236–250.

Witherspoon, R., & White, R. P. (1996). Executive coaching: A continuum of roles. *Consulting Psychology Journal: Practice & Research, 48,*
124–133.

Woehr, D. J., & Huffcutt, A. I. (1994). Rater training for performance
appraisal: A quantitative review. *Journal of Occupational and
Organizational Psychology, 67,* 189–205.

Wood, R. E., Mento, A. J., & Locke, E. A. (1987). Task complexity as
a moderator of goal effects: A meta-analysis. *Journal of Applied
Psychology, 72,* 416–425.

Yun, G. J., Donahue, L. M., Dudley, N. M., & McFarland, L. A. (2005). Rater personality, rating format, and social context: Implications for performance appraisal ratings. *International Journal of Selection and Assessment, 13*, 97–107.

Zaleska, K. J., & de Menezes, L. M. (2007). Human resources development practices and their association with employee attitudes: Between traditional and new careers. *Human Relations, 60*, 987–1017.

Name Index

A

Abelson, R., 412
Ackerman, P. L., 99, 100, 164, 588
Acosta-Amad, S., 593
Acton, B., 203, 211, 212
Adams, J. S., 22, 369
Addams, H. L., 14
Aguinis, H., 1, 2, 3, 4–5, 10, 12, 14, 15, 22, 30, 36, 38, 446, 453, 458, 459, 460, 465, 466, 467, 585
Ahearne, M., 307, 586
Aiello, J. R., 450
Aiman-Smith, L., 428, 429
Albanese, R., 600
Alderson, C., 429
Alexander, G., 122
Alexander, R. A., 420
Alge, B. J., 91, 450
Allan, C., 157, 174
Almost, J., 479, 585, 592
Alvero, A. M., 589
Ambrose, M. L., 368, 369, 371
Amick, B. C., 450
Ancona, D. G., 209, 214, 224
Anderson, E. L., 375
Anderson, N., 207, 221
Anderson, P., 361
Anderson, S., 464
Andersson, L. M., 360, 368, 369, 373
Appelbaum, S. H., 367, 368
Aquino, K., 361, 369
Arad, S., 174
Archer, R. M., 394
Ariss, S. S., 123
Armenakis, A. A., 478
Armour, S., 412
Armstrong, M., 200

Arnaud, A., 236
Arnold, J., 457
Aronson, E., 97, 593
Aronson, Z. H., 309
Arthur, W., Jr., 591
Aryee, S., 371
Ash, R. A., 604
Ashwood, E. L., 204, 216, 221
Atwater, L. E., 106, 376, 385, 386, 387, 388, 604
Au, W. T., 372
Aubé, C., 28
Austin, J. R., 213, 223, 589
Avallone, F., 478
Aycan, Z., 273, 282

B

Bachrach, D. G., 307
Bahis, J., 366
Bainbridge, S. M., 236, 243, 244
Baird, L. S., 66
Baker, D. P., 198
Baker, W. L., 375
Baldwin, T. T., 119, 120, 169, 172, 173, 416, 418, 422, 423, 435, 440, 600
Ball, G. A., 376, 384, 385, 387, 388
Bancroft, E., 250
Bandow, D., 209, 225
Bandura, A., 90, 95, 96, 97, 98, 166, 174, 176, 379, 512, 587
Bane, K. D., 595
Barach, P., 198
Baranowski, L., 34
Barbeite, F. G., 528
Barker, L., 595
Barling, J., 365, 368, 371

627

Subject Index

Page references followed by *fig* indicate an illustrated figure; followed by *t* indicate a table; followed by *e* indicate an exhibit.

A

Abilities: description of, 127; GAPS Grid framework for conversations about, 127, 128*t*. *See also* KSAs (knowledge, skills, and attitudes)

Abolishing Performance Appraisal (Coens and Jenkins), 427

Accountability: best coaching practices for, 133*t*; best practices for building culture of coaching, 150*t*; on coaching business need, 137; comparing performance management and development coaching on, 130–131*t*; Development Pipeline framework component of, 119–120, 122; "horizontal," 76; increasing CEO performance, 250; organizational cultures that evoke, 80; as organizational precursor, 533*t*, 536–537; performance management systems need for, 75–76

Accountability coaches, 138

Ad hoc coaching: description of, 116; manager's role in, 120–121

Adaptive capacity: description of team, 200; team performance best practices for, 202*t*–203*t*, 210–213

Adult learning theory, 380

Age Discrimination in Employment Act (ADEA), 435–437

Air traffic controller (ATC) tasks, 99

Airlines case study: cascading the goals, 70; clear and agreed-on strategy, 66–67; competencies supporting the strategy, 71, 73; Competency Evaluation Worksheet, 72*t*; linking strategic scorecard to accountabilities, 71*fig*; rewards used in, 73–74; strategic value map, 69*fig*; strategy pillars of, 66*fig*; translating strategy to measures, 67–70

Alignment: business impact of low, 50–52; definition and concepts related to, 46–48*fig*; drivers of, 52–64; importance of, 48–50; as organizational precursor assessment point, 532, 533*t*

Alignment drivers: acceptance/passion for vision, strategy, and goals, 57–58; clear and agreed-on vision and strategy, 55–56; incentives encouraging capabilities to achieve goals, 62–64; overview of, 52–54; timely feedback on goal attainment/drivers, 61–62; translation of vision and strategy into goals, 56–57

Allied Signal, 75

American Express, 46

American Management Association, 562

American Society of Quality, 50

Americana Association of Retired Persons (AARP), 437

Job dissatisfaction, 371–372
Job performance. *See* Performance
Job sharing, 565
Job tasks: Air traffic controller
(ATC), 99; changing definitions
of, 563–564; changing employee
expectations related to, 568–569;
connecting feedback to specific,
589–590; goal-setting theory on
complexity of, 98–100
Journal of Applied Psychology (JAP), 3
J.P. Morgan, 319
"Just cause" standard, 393
Justice: distributive, 369–370,
395–396, 421–422; interactional,
371, 378, 395–396; procedural,
370–371, 395–396, 421, 495–496,
497; termination and related issues
of, 395–396

K
Key Bank of Utah, 13*e*
KFC, 92
KLA-Tencor Corporation, 18
Kmart Corp., 7
Kraft Foods Inc., 244
KSAs (knowledge, skills, and
attitudes): contextual performance
and required, 300; front-line
worker, 188*t*–191; identifying team
performance, 28; performance
planning consideration of, 16;
performance renewal and
recontracting for, 25–26;
technological means to identify,
460. *See also* Abilities

L
Leader member exchange (LMX):
high quality social exchange
during, 510–514; performance
negotiation and, 499–501;
response to discipline related
to, 387; theory of, 304. *See also*
Managers; Supervisors

Leadership: as contextual
performance antecedent, 303–305;
performance management role
modeling by, 79; servant, 305;
toxic, 367–368
Leadership capacity: description of
team, 201; team performance best
practices, 203*t*–205*t*, 213–218
Learning: definition of, 330;
evaluating training at levels of
reaction and, 540–543; how
performance management
affects, 340–341, 344–346, 348;
how performance management
is linked to, 339; metacognition
role in, 175–176; moderately
structured, 164–165*t*, 166; self-
efficacy role in, 174, 176–177,
587; structured, 164, 165*t*;
transformative, 345; unstructured,
164, 165*t*. *See also* Informal
learning; Training; Transfer
of learning
Learning culture: adaptive,
generative, and transformational
nature of, 334–336; focus of,
336–337; how performance
management affects, 340; "living
systems" metaphor for, 333–334;
processes and outcomes for
learning, 353–354, 355–356;
readiness for learning in, 335, 355;
triggers for learning in, 352–353,
354. *See also* PRSII (PayRoll
Services International, Inc.) case
study
Learning management system
(LMS), 480
Learning partners, 138
Learning theory, 380
Legal cases: *Burlington Industries
v. Ellerth*, 383; *Faragher v. City of
Boca Raton*, 383; *Henson v. City of
Dundee*, 362; *Meritor Savings Bank v.
Vinson*, 362

The Editors

James W. Smither is Lindback professor of human resource management at La Salle University. He teaches undergraduate and graduate courses in human resources management, training and development, and leadership skills. Previously, Dr. Smither was a senior manager/group leader in corporate human resources for AT&T, where he was responsible for developing and validating employee selection programs for management-level positions. He received his B.A. (in psychology) from La Salle and has an M.A. from Seton Hall University, an M.A. from Montclair State University, and a Ph.D. in industrial/organizational psychology from Stevens Institute of Technology. Dr. Smither has written over fifty scholarly articles and chapters; his research has been published in top-tier journals such as *Personnel Psychology, Journal of Applied Psychology,* and *Organizational Behavior and Human Decision Processes.* He is currently a consulting editor at the *Journal of Applied Psychology.* From 1997 to 2003, he served as associate editor of *Personnel Psychology.* He is a Fellow of the Association for Psychological Science and the Society for Industrial and Organizational Psychology. He has consulted with over fifty firms in human resources and leadership development. He's worked with companies in a variety of industries such as telecommunications, semiconductor, accounting, airline, consumer products, aerospace, financial, packaging, casino, health care, pharmaceutical, education, and government.

Manuel London is the associate dean of the College of Business at the State University of New York at Stony Brook. Dr. London is director of the Center for Human Resource Management. He holds a joint appointment in the Department of Psychology. He is also Stony Brook's faculty director of the Undergraduate College of Leadership and Service. Dr. London's career spans his professorship at major research universities—in particular, the University of Illinois at Champaign/Urbana from 1974 to 1977 and Stony Brook University from 1989 to the present. For the twelve intervening years, he was a researcher and human resource practitioner at AT&T. Dr. London is a pioneer in the now popular field of multisource (360-degree) feedback. As a practitioner and consultant, Dr. London has worked on program development and publications in the areas of performance management, feedback, managing marginal performers, and the manager as coach and developer. Dr. London received the Book Award from the Society for Human Resource Management for *Change Agents: New Roles and Innovation Strategies for Human Resource Professionals.*